# Interactive Behaviour at Work

# Interactive Behaviour at Work

3rd edition

MAUREEN GUIRDHAM

An imprint of Pearson Education
Harlow, England • London • New York • Boston • San Francisco • Toronto • Sydney • Singapore • Hong Kong
Tokyo • Seoul • Taipei • New Delhi • Cape Town • Madrid • Mexico City • Amsterdam • Munich • Paris • Milan

**Pearson Education Limited**
Edinburgh Gate
Harlow
Essex CM20 2JE
England

and Associated Companies throughout the world

*Visit us on the World Wide Web at:*
www.pearsoned.co.uk

First published under the Prentice Hall imprint 1990
Second edition 1995
**Third edition 2002**



ISBN 978-0-273-65590-9

**British Library Cataloguing-in-Publication Data**
A catalogue record for this book is available from the British Library

**Library of Congress Cataloging-in-Publication Data**
Guirdham, Maureen.
Interactive behaviour at work / Maureen Guirdham.—3rd ed.
p. cm.
Rev. ed. of: Interpersonal skills at work / Guirdham Maureen, 2nd ed. 1995.
ISBN 0-273-65590-6 (pbk. : alk. paper)
1. Organizational behavior. 2. Psychology, Industrial. 3. Interpersonal relations. I. Guirdham, Maureen. Interpersonal skills at work. II. Title.

HD58.7+
158.2′6—dc21 2001055460

13 12 11 10 9 8 7
12 11 10 09 08

Typeset in 10/13pt Palatino by 35
Printed and bound in Malaysia, VVP

In memory of Quentin

# Contents

## Part 3 Process extensions

# Preface

The new title of this third edition of *Interpersonal Skills at Work* reflects the way in which the field has matured. Over the past ten years, the subject has developed from a marginal option available on only a few business and management courses to a mainstream module on numerous courses. From consisting usually of a set of useful but unstructured exercises without research underpinning, modules have become carefully constructed courses combining theory, research and practice. At the same time, the term 'interpersonal' is coming to have a particular meaning – that of 'maximising the presence of the personal'. As this emphasis is not a major focus of this book, it seemed appropriate to adopt the more general *Interactive Behaviour at Work* for the title, although in places within the text the word 'interpersonal' is used with its extant meaning of 'between persons'. The text has been updated to take account of the considerable volume of new relevant research, especially in the fields of social psychology and communication.

Other trends reflected in this new edition include the exponential increase in trans-national working (and studying!) within Europe – thus there is increased emphasis on a European focus and intercultural work interaction. There is a new chapter on 'Working across cultures', which covers both working in diverse organisations and internationally, including sojourning. There is also expanded coverage of cultural and intercultural aspects of all topics, and European and global examples are given throughout. National differences within Europe in attitudes and behaviour are highlighted. More use has been made of European research and theorising.

The focus of the book continues to be on face-to-face interaction but the changing context of that interaction includes computer-mediated communication. The behavioural implications of this development are drawn out and provide a comparison with face-to-face interaction. Like its predecessor editions, *Interactive Behaviour at Work* covers most relevant theory and research on a comprehensive range of topics and applications. (According to all reviewers, it is the only text in the field to do so.) These features allow an in-depth understanding that the student can apply widely. At the same time, it provides a practical guide: most areas of theory and research are ultimately resolved into 'how to', bullet-pointed guidance. Skill development is supported with work-related exercises. A web-based Instructor's Manual is downloadable from www.booksites.net/guirdham to those teachers and facilitators who have adopted this textbook.

# Acknowledgements


## AUTHOR'S ACKNOWLEDGMENTS

I would like to thank all those interviewees who helped with my research, the reviewers whose comments on the 2nd edition and the proposal for this one were invaluable and my friend E. D. Berman MBE, for the time he generously gave to edit portions of the book.

## PUBLISHER'S ACKNOWLEDGMENTS

We are grateful to the following for permission to reproduce copyright material:

Guardian Newspapers Limited for an extract adapted from "Delhi Calling" by L. Harding published in *The Guardian*, 9th March 2001 © The Guardian 2001; and the International Association of Business Communicators for an extract adapted from their published material; Figure 2.4 from *Culture's Consequences* (2nd edition) by Hofstede, G. (2001), Thousand Oaks, Calif.: Sage, reproduced with permission of the author and copyright holder; Table 4.1 from 'Self-efficacy theory: toward a unifying theory of behavioural change' by Bandura, A., in *Psychological Review*, vol. 84, no. 3, p. 195, © American Psychological Association, reproduced with permission; Table 5.1 from 'The impact of induced affect on the perception of variability in social groups' by Stroesner, S. J. and D. M. Mackie, in *Personality and Social Psychology Bulletin*, vol. 18, pp. 546–554 © Corwin Press Inc. 1992, reprinted by permission of Sage Publications Inc., and also from 'Mood and stereotyping: affective states and the use of general knowledge structures' by Bless, H., N. Schwartz and M. Kemmelmeier, in *European Review of Social Psychology*, (Stroebe, W. and M. Hewitson (eds)), vol. 7, pp. 63–94 © John Wiley and Sons Ltd. 1996, reproduced with permission; Figure 10.1 adapted from 'Conflict and conflict management' by Thomas, K. W. (1976) in *Handbook of Industrial and Organizational Psychology*, (Dunnette, M. D. (ed.)), Chicago, Ill.: Rand McNally, with permission from Houghton Mifflin Co.; Figure 10.3 from *The Anatomy of Relationships*, with the permission of The Peters Fraser & Dunlop Group Limited Employment Agents, (Argyle, M.); Table 10.4 from a paper given by Khoo, G. P. S. at the *Pacific Region Forum on Business and Management* © David See-Chai Lam Centre for International Communication 1994, website URL: http://www.cic.sfu.ca/forum; Figure 11.9 from 'Conflict Management, efficacy and performance in organizational teams' by Alper, S., Tjosovold, D., and K. S. Law, in *Personnel Psychology*, vol. 53, no. 3, pp. 625–642, © Personnel Psychology 2000, reproduced with permission.

# Part 1

# CORE CONCEPTS

# 1 Work and interactive behaviour

## CHAPTER INTRODUCTION

The term interactive behaviour, as used in the title of this book, refers to the reciprocal communication conduct of two or more persons. It covers both their overt behaviour and the factors and processes underlying it. It also extends to the use of communication for purposes such as self-presentation, co-operation, influencing others, working in groups and leadership. The main emphasis in the book is on face-to-face interactive behaviour, which is the most complex and demanding of all forms of communication. It uses more channels of communication than any other type and requires immediate responses. As the book's title suggests, the focus is on work interactions, rather than those occurring in private life. The work context strongly affects the nature of interactive behaviour. Similarly, interactions underpin and even constitute modern work.

The aim of this chapter is to help readers increase their understanding of:

- the significance of interactive behaviour at work;
- sources of complexity in work interactions, including business ethics, diversity and cross-cultural working;
- interpersonal skills at work;
- work activities that depend on skill in dealing with people.

The last section provides explanatory chapter summaries for the rest of the book and guidance on using the material.

## THE SIGNIFICANCE OF INTERACTIVE BEHAVIOUR AT WORK

In the late twentieth and early twenty-first century, a number of factors increased the significance of how we interact with one another at work.

The *nature of most work changed*. Chapter 2 describes how the arrival of the 'knowledge society', technological change, globalised competition and, in the older industrialised countries, the growth of the service sector and shrinking of manufacturing revolutionised work and work organisations. In turn, new approaches to work and organisation changed the way we need to deal with and relate to others at work.

A major theme of this book is the *impact on work interactions* of European integration through the European Union (EU). In this context the conclusions of the European Managerial Decision-making Project (a six-country study of over 900 managers in 70 companies) on the benefits of trans-European corporate integration are especially interesting. The findings show that one benefit is consistently given as number one by respondents from all six countries: 'It aids interpersonal co-operation/skill transfer.' Second, in five out of six countries, is that 'It creates motivation to improve individual performance.' The remaining reasons differ widely by country and culture. These findings shows the importance that managers across Europe attach to interpersonal co-operation.[1]

**Box 1.1**

A European Round Table publication (1990) listed the main issues regarding management education in northern countries as communication skills, holistic thinking, business initiative and broad education; in Latin countries as flexibility and management science and in English-speaking countries as communication skills and strategic thinking.

A study of graduates, 91 per cent from EU countries, average age 25, found the following. Most were seeking to work abroad for three years and more than half intended to spend a major part of their career working internationally. Their major career values were management, dedication, lifestyle and challenge. The qualities they perceived as needed for success as managers were interpersonal skills and conceptual effectiveness.

*Source*: Van Dijk, J. J. (1995) 'Transnational management in an evolving European context' in T. Jackson (ed.) *Cross-cultural Management*. Oxford: Butterworth-Heinemann.

*Globalisation* hugely increased the economic impact of international communication. John Naisbitt, author of the book called *The Global Paradox*, wrote 'The idea of countries and borders is important symbolically and culturally, but not too relevant in a single world economy dominated by person-to-person communications.'[2] However, one reaction to globalisation is tribalism, exemplified, for instance, in French resistance to cultural imperialism in the form of American film imports and legal bans on 'franglais'. Tribalism places obstacles in the way of people understanding one another and truly communicating. These barriers can only be overcome by high levels of skill in interactors' behaviour. It has become vital to understand cultural variations in behaviour at work.

*Workforces changed*. In Europe a far higher proportion of all jobs are now part-time, and in the UK there are more women in work than men. Despite the painfully slow pace of progress against racial discrimination, the workforce is increasingly multi-ethnic at all levels. Equal opportunities, valuing diversity and ensuring that everyone at work has the appropriate interpersonal attitudes, are more important than ever.

**Box 1.2**

'If you want to book a flight with British Airways after 8 p.m., you're talking to Texas; and if you want your Internet provider's technical assistance at any time you're probably talking to California or Bangalore. This can lead to misunderstandings; recently, I wanted to book a flight to Athens from London at short notice. The young Texan quoted £800 plus; I made a joke about the kinds of services I'd expect if I paid that much. "Yes, Ma'am", he said. He had no sense of humour.'

[Or was he just being polite?]

*Source*: Interview with a British woman entrepreneur; author's research.

The triumph of the market, privatisation and internal markets meant that *everyone became a 'customer'* and everyone's work became a service for other 'customers'. Customers have to be treated with care. An important part of customer care depends on skilled interactive behaviour.

In the field of business, technological change and globalised competition led to *small and medium-sized enterprises* growing in importance. America's Fortune 500 companies accounted for only 10 per cent of the US economy in 1995, down from 20 per cent in 1970. It was small and medium-sized businesses that eventually pulled America and the UK out of recession in the late 1980s, while the big companies were still busy downsizing.

As the capacity to produce quality products spreads around the world, the competitive edge goes to innovation and swiftness to market, where small companies have an advantage in agility, flexibility and the enthusiasm that comes from belonging to a small team playing in the major leagues. As a result, big companies try to act like small companies in order to survive. Jack Welch, Chief Executive of General Electric was quoted as saying, 'What we are trying relentlessly to do is get that small-company soul – and small company speed – inside our big company body.' Percy Barnevik of Asea Brown Boveri, which generates $3 billion of turnover from 1,200 businesses scattered over the globe, each of which is three-quarters autonomous, says 'We are not a global business. We are a collection of local businesses with intense global co-ordination.'

Small company competitive advantage depends on not being bureaucratic, not so much because of the overhead, though that is part of it, but because bureaucracy slows companies down. However, bureaucracy performs an important function to do with organising and co-ordinating different people's work into a larger whole. If bureaucracy is abandoned or reduced, it has to be replaced. In successful small and large companies it is replaced by a combination of technology and more use of interpersonal communication, networking, influencing – in other words, interactive behaviour.

It is often argued that the *impact of information and communication technology* makes face-to-face interactions at work less important. Computer networks, personal computers, electronic mail and so on may indeed reduce the amount of face-to-face interaction that takes place at work. However, what matters is not the quantity of interactions but their crucial importance – their impact on the effectiveness and efficiency with which work gets done. It is possible, even likely, that technological change which reduces the number of interactions increases rather than reduces their significance, as they have to compensate for the deficiencies of impersonal communication. It seems unlikely that exchanges of messages in the form of words, graphs and figures on visual display units can support high levels of motivation or greatly promote job satisfaction. In fact, such communication technology may be seen as a threat to work relationships. Newer forms, such as video instant messaging, reduce the negative 'hard data' effect, but still do not provide the communication level of face-to-face interaction.

An article in May–June 2000 in the *Harvard Business Review* drew attention to the importance of interpersonal interaction for business success in the new economy. The article refers to companies that are regularly successful innovators. They are 'knowledge brokers'. These companies bring together otherwise disconnected pools of ideas, often recycling old ones in new forms. The process involves capturing good ideas, keeping ideas alive, imagining new uses for old ideas and putting promising ideas to the test. An example is the 3M corporation, where engineers developed a way to create tiny prisms on the surfaces of lenses for overhead projectors. A centre called OTC (Optics Technology Center) was formed to discover ways to spread the technology, known as microreplication, throughout 3M. It is now used in traffic lights, industrial grinders, mouse pads and dozens of other 3M products. The article attributes successes such as this to high levels of interpersonal interaction within the organisation: 'An effective broker develops creative answers to hard problems because people within the organisation talk a lot about their work and about who might help them do it better. Company-wide gatherings, formal brainstorming sessions, and informal hallway conversations are just some of the venues where people share their problems and solutions.'[3]

From another angle, Charles Handy, in an April 2001 article, described the need for face-to-face communication in a high-tech environment:

> The reality is that high-tech needs a bit of high-touch to work well, because it is hard to know how far you can rely on someone whom you never meet. There is also the research that showed that 80 per cent of any communication is to do with the verbal expression, the body language and the eye contact. Leave all those out and you are down to 20 per cent effectiveness. No wonder those e-mails get misunderstood. No wonder, either, that a firm's travel expenditure tends to rise in line with their expenditure on ICT (Information and Communications Technology). We need to know what sort of person hides behind that cryptic e-mail address.[4]

Hallowell[5], writing in 1999, gave two examples of emotional issues getting out of control because all communication was by e-mail or voice mail. One concerned a Chief Finance Officer worrying about valued employees asking for a transfer: 'Will they complain that the CFO is a lousy boss? What if? What if?' The second example concerned a brand manager, whose phone call to his boss had not been returned and who had not been invited to a strategy meeting. His response was 'What's wrong with my performance?' Hallowell argues that to raise matters such as these and put probable misunderstanding right, face-to-face conversation is needed. Colleagues need to experience 'the human moment', authentic psychological encounters that can happen only when two people share the same physical space. Without them, the mental health of employees suffers. They are plagued by worry and start to feel worn out by all the non-human interactions that fill their days. Human moments require both physical presence and attention. Talking by telephone or 'travelling six hours together by plane working separately' is no substitute. Lack of human moments can undermine cohesiveness. The organisational culture turns unfriendly and unforgiving, as the following example shows. Ray, a senior systems manager with a large investment company, said,

> I don't talk to people as much as I used to. And sometimes the results are very damaging. A guy sends me an e-mail 'We were not able to access the following application and we need to know why' and he'd c.c.'d [copied] it to his supervisor just to show him he was doing something. 'We need to know why' – peremptory tone, c.c.'d it; I responded in kind. We became adversaries, instead of trying to solve the problem.

## SUMMARY – THE SIGNIFICANCE OF INTERACTIVE BEHAVIOUR AT WORK

Changes in the nature of work and organisational forms, European integration, globalisation and its counterpart of tribalism, increasing workforce diversity, the triumph of the market and the growing economic importance of small firms are increasing the significance of interactive work behaviour. Information technology and communication, even if they reduce the quantity of work-based interactions, increase the importance of their quality. Figure 1.1 shows the factors bearing on the increased importance of interactive behaviour at work.

## SOURCES OF COMPLEXITY IN WORK INTERACTIONS

Studying work-based interactions is necessary, not only because they are important, but also because they are complex.

- Although on the surface they deal mainly with substantive items, such as budgets, contracts or pack designs, underneath they often involve a hotbed of attitudes, feelings and relationships.

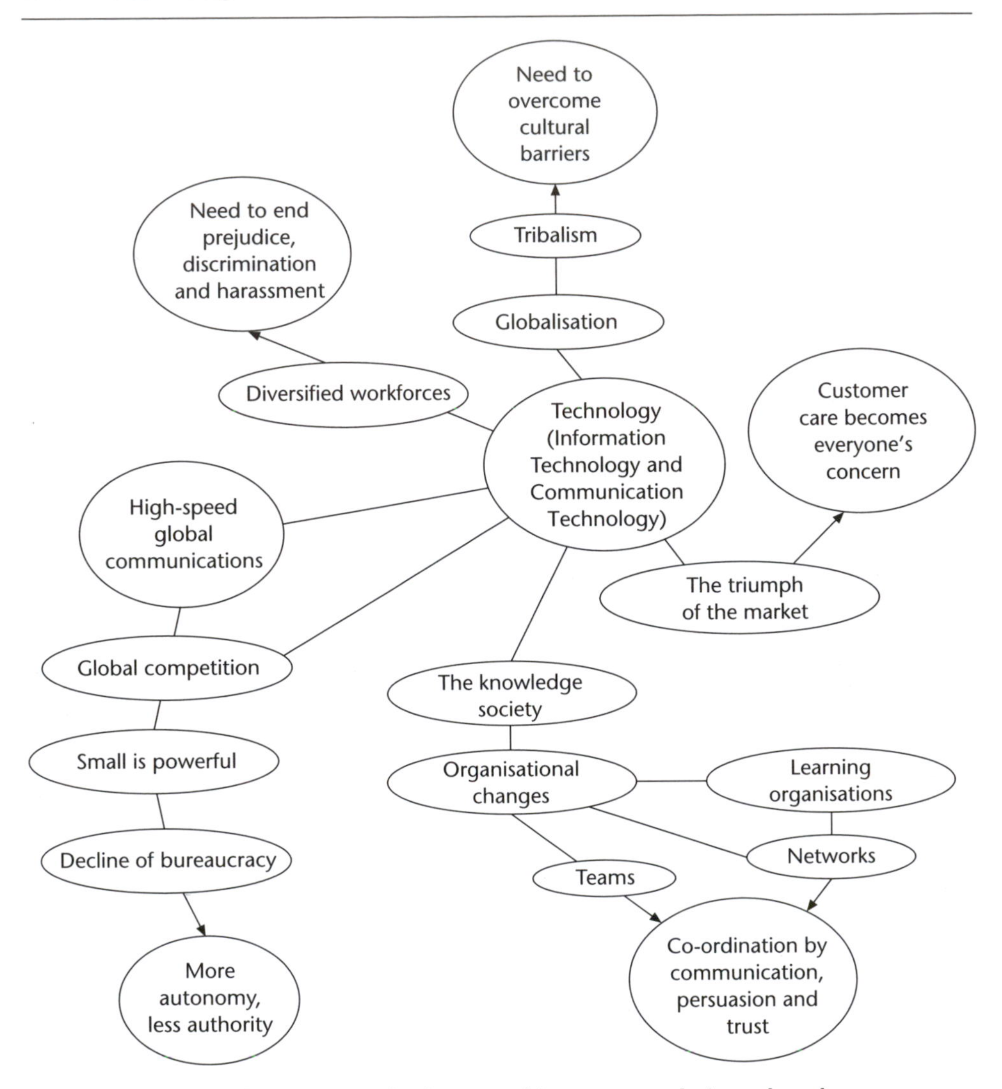


**Figure 1.1 Factors bearing on the increased importance being placed on interpersonal skills at work.**

- Many work-related interactions involve 'mixed motives'. These are a mixture of co-operative, competitive and conflictual drives and urges. For instance, the sales staff may be keen to co-operate with the credit department to work out a better system of identifying bad payers. At the same time, however, they may want to make the credit department take the blame for losing customers who are wrongly refused credit because they are erroneously recorded as bad payers. Mixed-motive situations require 'high behavioural flexibility to manage optimally. A person with a narrower range of behavioural skills is less likely to exploit the integrative potential fully. He [sic] may either engage in bargaining to the exclusion of collaborative problem-solving or withdraw or become passive.'[6]

- When representatives speak or negotiate for a department or organisation, they in effect have a constituency of people to whom they are answerable. These constituents exert pressure on the representatives, who have continually to bear in mind the attitudes of their absent colleagues.
- Separate meetings or discussions at work are usually episodes in continuing relationships. Many are affected by past events that the interactors remember. In all cases, the participants try to predict the future effect of what is being said, agreed or done and are influenced by what they anticipate.
- Often interactions at work are not one-to-one but happen in groups or are team-to-team or multi-party. This means that people who are addressing remarks to one individual have constantly to keep in mind how the others are reacting to what they say.
- Like all interactions, work meetings take place in a 'behavioural context'. In part, what this expression implies is that appropriate behaviour at work is different from appropriate behaviour with friends or family, while what is suitable in public places such as cinemas or trains is different again. The behavioural context acts as a constraint, prohibiting some ways of behaving, enforcing others, and having an effect on how appropriate different styles and manners are. For instance, in many families kissing is practically an enforced form of greeting, whereas the work-related activities shown in Table 1.1 share a behavioural context in which kissing is an unacceptable form of greeting. At work, the behavioural context includes the location and the occasion. The staff dining room is usually the setting for more informal manners than a committee room, and the office party for less distance between boss and subordinate than an appraisal interview. Also included in the context are the structural features of the working relationships among the participants – boss/subordinate relationships are different from those between lateral colleagues. A more detailed analysis of this aspect of the behavioural context is given in Chapter 2.

In addition to these intrinsic sources of complexity in work interactions there are some that have grown in importance in recent years. These include business ethics, workforce diversity and trans-national working. Business morality has always been important but ethical issues now attract growing attention. In part this may be due to a widespread perception that the power of business in many cases now exceeds that of governments. There is also a view that a framework for business ethics cannot be reached by simply applying personal ethics. A 1997 study 'seems to challenge a traditional assumption that in ethical dilemmas [individuals] are autonomous moral agents, acting on the basis of their own values alone.'[7] The study found that the influence of an individual's personal

**Table 1.1 Application activities for interpersonal skills at work**

| |
|---|
| Fact-finding and diagnostic interviewing |
| Selection interviewing |
| Giving performance feedback |
| Reprimanding |
| Firing |
| Coaching and instructing |
| Training |
| Counselling |
| Reporting back |
| Obtaining agreement to a planned course of action |
| Asking for resources |
| Negotiating |
| Mediating between disputing parties |
| Selling |
| Representing a section, department or organisation 'ceremonially' or in other ways |
| Presenting for new business |
| Liaising with clients and customers |
| Handling customer and client requests and complaints |
| Dealing with agents and distributors |
| Obtaining good service from suppliers and advisers |
| Planning and problem-solving in groups |
| Interorganisational group work |
| Committee work |
| Chairing meetings |

values was the weakest of seven researched, despite its prominence in the literature. Organisational and small-group influences were much stronger. Work interactions are complicated by the need to accommodate to other people's moral attitudes while sustaining one's own. As Chapter 2 substantiates, workforce diversity and trans-national working in Europe are increasing exponentially. Diversity and trans-national working have profound implications for the basis of interactions. It is no longer enough to rely on modes of interacting based on a homogeneous culture, a moral consensus and traditional hierarchical relations. Instead 'it is necessary to locate and articulate diverse philosophies and their practical applications to daily work issues.'[8] The complexity of work-related interactions means that people at work need to be perceptive about others and to have a broad repertoire of self-presentation, communication and influencing skills, plus the ability to recognise what skills are likely to be relevant in a given situation.

## SUMMARY – SOURCES OF COMPLEXITY IN WORK INTERACTIONS

Suppressed emotional and attitudinal influences, mixed motives, pressure from constituents, the history and anticipated future of relationships, the presence of multiple parties and the constraints of the work context all add complexity to work-based interactions. Increasing emphasis on ethics, diversity and transnational working have added to this. The effect is make heavy demands on the skills of the participants. They have to learn to adjust their approach to the context and to the changing situation as well as to differences among the people with whom they deal.

## INTERPERSONAL SKILLS AT WORK

This section first discusses the reasons for the increasing concern with interpersonal skills at work and then gives an outline of what these skills consist of. An increase in the importance of interactive behaviour at work necessarily increases the importance of individuals' interpersonal skills, but there are other reasons too.

- While skilled interpersonal interaction can be thought of as 'the cornerstone of organisational functioning', and 'face-to-face relationships . . . as the glue that holds organisations together',[9] unskilled interaction can lead to lack of internal co-operation and co-ordination, inability to take decisions, undermining of strategies, internecine conflict and even the break-up of companies. The history of mergers and acquisitions is full of examples of these costly failures.
- To take decisions, people at work need information, and they get much of it from contact with other people. There are important types of information which are not available from computerised systems. For example, it may be only a manager who knows about an overall plan that will provide the framework for a project, only a colleague who remembers the past history behind a current problem – a history that rules out certain apparent solutions – and only the sales force who can predict how retailers would be likely to react to a change in pack design. Interpersonal communication serves to provide information and facilitate decision-making. In decentralised organisations these are becoming more widespread responsibilities.
- Among the greatest challenges to contemporary organisations, however, are not the problems of setting objectives or making decisions, but those of implementation. Widespread and better planning, vastly increased information, and sophisticated, computerised decision-making techniques are reducing the uncertainties of goal-setting and choice-making. In contrast, implementing decisions successfully has not become any easier and organisations are under increased pressure to take initiatives and respond swiftly to competitors. Implementation depends largely on interpersonal relationships and skills:

  > We have learned something about implementation in the last forty years or so, and what we have learned takes us back to one fundamental principle: societies, organisations and families are human groups, and the face-to-face relationships among the

members of these groups are a basic element of any social action. Whatever else we need in the way of systems, procedures and mechanisms, the process of social action always starts with face-to-face relationships among people. Such relationships are the links in the implementation chain.[10]

**Box 1.3**

A 1997 survey found that communication skills are valued highly in public accounting firms, where professionals at all levels communicate as part of their jobs. They also found that partners and managers want their entry level professionals to have effective communication skills at the onset. Further, these skills increase in importance as accounting professionals progress from entry-level to manager to partner (Stowers and White, 1999).

Goby and Lewis (1999) investigated how important auditors perceive interpersonal, oral and written skills to be to them at different stages of their professional careers and the degree to which they think that they need to improve in these skills. As expected, newly graduated audit assistants perceived the greatest need for improvement in all three skills. However, they also perceived that written skills were of lesser importance to them than interpersonal and oral skills.

*Sources*: Goby, V. P. and J. H. Lewis (1999) 'Auditors' communication requirements: a study of five MNCs [multi-national companies] in Singapore', *Business Communication Quarterly*, vol. 62, no. 4.
Stowers, R. H. and G. T. White (1999) 'Connecting accounting and communication: A survey of public accounting firms', *Business Communication Quarterly*, vol. 62, no. 2.

- Among other trends that have led to the increased interest in interface skills at work is the growth of teamwork. More and more the tasks of contemporary organisations, particularly those in high technology and service businesses, require teamwork. Task forces, project teams and committees are key elements in the modern workplace. Teamwork depends not just on the technical competence of the individuals composing the team, but on their ability to 'gel'. To work well together, the team members must have more than just team spirit. They also need collaborative skills – they must be able to support one another and to handle conflict in such a way that it becomes constructive rather than destructive. If conflict is handled so that it is constructive, then better decision-making and problem-solving can result from people advocating different solutions and discussing them with each other. Destructive conflict, on the other hand, means that discussion is turned into bitter contest, resulting in worse, not better, solutions (or no solution at all) and can cause lasting damage to working relationships. Avoiding destructive conflict while obtaining the benefits of constructive conflict depend on the people involved behaving in ways that can only be achieved if they are adept in collaborative skills.

**Box 1.4**

> Words like 'self-management' and 'employee empowerment' are quickly becoming the contemporary battle cry of . . . industry. The emphasis has shifted from a focus on management control of employees, to a decentralisation of power and the provision of opportunity for workers, at all levels, to exercise increasing influence over themselves . . . workers become to a large degree their own managers . . . (this) involves an increasing reliance on workers' creative and intellectual capabilities, not just their physical labour. Procter and Gamble, General Motors, Ford, Digital Equipment, IDS, Honeywell, Cummins Engines, Boeing and Caterpillar have all applied a team approach with teams empowered to assign tasks, solve quality problems, select team members and train and counsel them. W. L. Gore and Associates (makers of GoreTex) electronic, medical, fabrics, etc. with a $1 billion turnover and approaching 5,000 employees, has gone further – they have no titles, hierarchy or structures except those required by law; no plant is allowed to get too big for everyone to know one another, which means 150 to 200 people in 44 plants; employees are called 'associates' and have sponsors, not managers; and there is a lattice structure in which teams form themselves as a leader finds associates to work with.
>
> *Source*: Shipper, F. and C. C. Manz (1992) 'Employee self-management without formally designated teams: an alternative road to empowerment', *Organizational Dynamics*, vol. 21, no. 2, pp. 48–60.

- Finally, people feel happier when they are getting on well with others; their quality of life is enhanced. This means that, to some degree, relationships may be substitutes for career progress and ever-growing pay packets. If economic growth slows so that increasing material rewards is not a general option, the contribution of interpersonal skills to improving work relationships and hence job satisfaction could be increasingly important.

Thus, it appears, interpersonal skills at work are important and getting more important. They can make an important contribution to profits through, for instance, increasing sales from repeat business and cutting costs through greater internal co-operation, sharing of information and learning. 'So what?' may be asked. After all, interpersonal skills are not a subject like accounting or public administration, engineering or medicine, law or architecture where there is clearly a good deal to know and learn. Dealing with other people is something we all do all the time, and have since babyhood. Why do we need to study it? To some extent this is a powerful argument, and probably explains why interpersonal skills was a latecomer to management courses and even later to other vocational courses. However, though we do all have plenty of experience of dealing with others, and, in some ways, remarkable levels of skills, we nearly all have important deficiencies which significantly affect how we and our organisations perform. Second, there are work-based activities, such as giving performance feedback or making business presentations, in which day-to-day life gives us little practice. These activities are best understood and developed as applications of generic interpersonal skills, but all the same they repay special study, just as applied economics requires something to be added to pure economics. Table 1.1 lists some of the work-based activities mainly depending on skill in dealing with people. They range from simple reporting back to a colleague on a completed task to full-scale, formal, multi-party negotiations. Interpersonal skills are important not just for managers or those who aspire to be managers; they are needed by engineers, accountants, lecturers and teachers, nurses, bankers, clerics, secretaries, architects, shop assistants, lawyers, air hostesses, doctors and anyone else who needs to take a serious interest in how to deal effectively with the other people in their working lives.

**Box 1.5**

A study of 457 managers found that management activities consisted mainly of communication, networking, human resource management and traditional management tasks.

*Source*: Luthans, F., R. M. Hodgetts and S. A. Rosenkrantz (1988) *Real Managers*. Cambridge: Ballinger.

Although they are various, as Table 1.1 shows, the entire range of interactive work activities in all categories of relationship depends on a small set of interpersonal skills. These are the core interpersonal skills – 'core' because they are the basis of all human interaction, private as well as work-based. The core skills are: understanding other people's behaviour, self-presentation, communicating and influencing by persuading or using power. These core skills are not separate and independent. Influencing, for instance, depends on understanding others, self-presenting and communicating effectively.

- Understanding others refers to interpreting others' speech and actions. Naturally, this includes speaking the same language as they do and grasping what it is that they are saying. However, in all but the most superficial meetings we also need to look beyond the surface content of what others say to consider their values, motives, emotions, beliefs, attitudes and intentions. Mostly, we do this without thinking about it, although the process is highly skilled. Unfortunately, though, we do tend to select, distort, over-interpret and judge too rapidly.
- Self-presentation means managing the impression we give to other people. Giving an impression is unavoidable but it is easy to give a false or undesirable one. Because other people are not perfectly accurate in interpreting behaviour, they can often receive a false impression of our attitudes, emotions and motives. On top of this, many of us sometimes express ourselves in ways that are misleading to others, especially in gestures, bodily movements and

voice. By understanding how these non-verbal behaviours are usually interpreted, and by increasing our control over them, we can reduce how often we convey an impression that is different from the one we intend. Self-presentation involves understanding the mindset of the perceiver.

- Communicating means getting messages across and understood. As well as reducing environmental noise that stops messages from being received, good communication involves taking steps to ensure they are understood. It usually also involves trying to get them believed and accepted. This means trying to create a climate that helps the other person listen well, not a defensive climate in which they reject or ignore our message because of the way we express it. Communication also implies being receptive to what others are saying, both verbally and in body language.
- Much communication at work is designed to influence others' behaviour, attitudes, opinions or beliefs. There are two main influencing skills – persuading and using power. Though they have the same objective, the two skills depend on understanding different concepts and acting in different ways.

Like those in private life, work-based interactions can occur repeatedly with the same individuals; in this way they acquire the characteristics of relationships. They can also take place between several or many participants, so that they are affected by group dynamics. Thus special knowledge and skills are needed in relationships and groups. Working with people from a different culture or social background also calls for particular knowledge and skills. Finally, leading other people calls for skills that combine all the others as well as adding some more.

- Working in relationships requires using the five core skills but also adapting for the history and memories of past interactions and the expectation of future meetings. In work relationships, interactions are governed by norms and role expectations, while conflict and competition, over time, can have powerful effects.
- Working in groups requires the skill of handling multiple interpersonal interactions simultaneously, while applying an understanding of group processes to problem-solving or carrying out a project.
- Working interculturally requires openness to others' culturally influenced values and ways of behaving. We also need to make appropriate adaptations to our own behaviour, manage anxiety and uncertainty caused by the intercultural situation and, in the case of sojourning, overcome culture shock. A large number of subsidiary traits and processes are needed to achieve these.
- Leaders have special responsibility for structuring group discussion, progressing tasks and managing work relationships.

Interpersonal skills at work do not exist in isolation and cannot be developed without reference to their context. They depend on an understanding of work

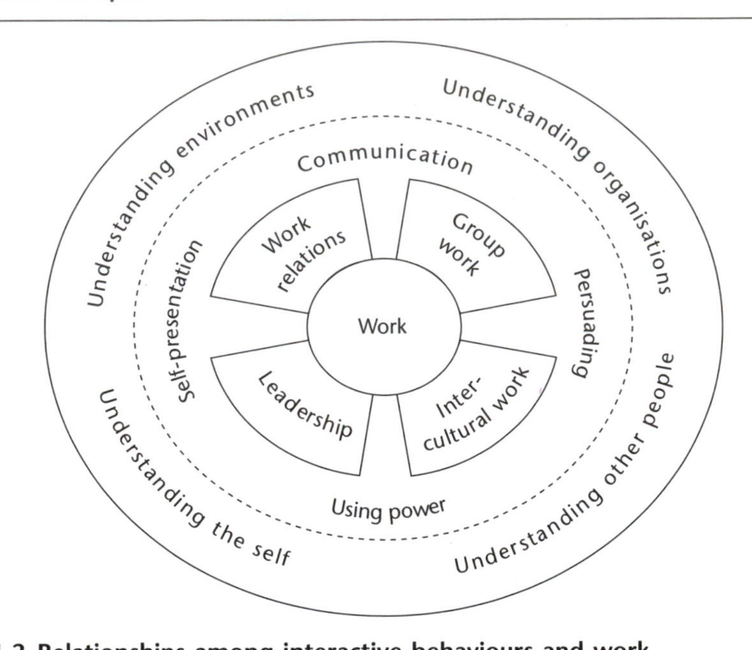


**Figure 1.2 Relationships among interactive behaviours and work.**

and the organisational context in which it takes place and on a knowledge of human behaviour and the factors underlying it. They are also part of our whole selves; our development of interpersonal skills should be integrated with our personal development more generally. Figure 1.2 shows the relationship of the skills to each other and to their context.

Despite the importance and demanding nature of interpersonal skills, some may doubt the need for related theories and knowledge on the grounds that, like other skills, interpersonal skills are an ability to do some things, rather than to know some things. After all, acquiring the skill of riding a bicycle is not a matter of reading books on gravity and the human sense of balance, but of learning by trial, error and practice. Learning to ride a bicycle is a good analogy for how we normally learn interpersonal skills and how most of us have acquired the very considerable level we already possess; however, it is not necessarily a skill whose components are explicit and transferable. There is another kind of skill that few of us would recommend should be learned in the same way as riding a bicycle – surgery is a good example. We expect, for our own protection, that surgeons will have a good deal of knowledge, not just about the usual location and appearance of the organs they are cutting into, but about anatomy, physiology, disease and medicine generally. No doubt they rarely use most of their knowledge but it is there, may be needed in an emergency, and subtly informs and controls the actions of their hands. Surgeons' knowledge and understanding are needed because of the complexity of our bodies. It is the same with interpersonal skills.

People, relationships and the situations surrounding interactions create such complexity that relying exclusively on learning by doing is limiting and slow. It can also be very painful. Even if it is not, unlike surgery, usually a matter of life and death, it can damage and even terminate relationships.

## SUMMARY – INTERPERSONAL SKILLS AT WORK

Increasing awareness of the costs to organisations of ineffective interactive behaviour, the continuing need for information only available from interpersonal sources, the demands of implementation, increasing use of teamwork and concern with the quality of working life all contribute to a growing understanding of the importance of interpersonal skills. Because the skills we have acquired by socialisation need understanding, adapting and honing to meet the demands of the (changing) work environment, the subject is one that repays study and practice.

Effective interactive behaviour at work depends on a set of core skills, their extensions and applications. The core skills are understanding others, self-presentation, communicating, and influencing by persuading or using power. Their extensions are to work relationships, groupwork, intercultural working and leadership. Their applications are to a wide range of work activities, some of which are listed in Table 1.1. Figure 1.3 illustrates the symbiotic relationship between work-related activities and core interpersonal skills.

## ABOUT THIS BOOK

This book describes and analyses the concepts and ways of behaving that are needed to deal with and relate to other people at work. The three chapters following this one, Chapters 2 to 4, explain the impact on work interactions of

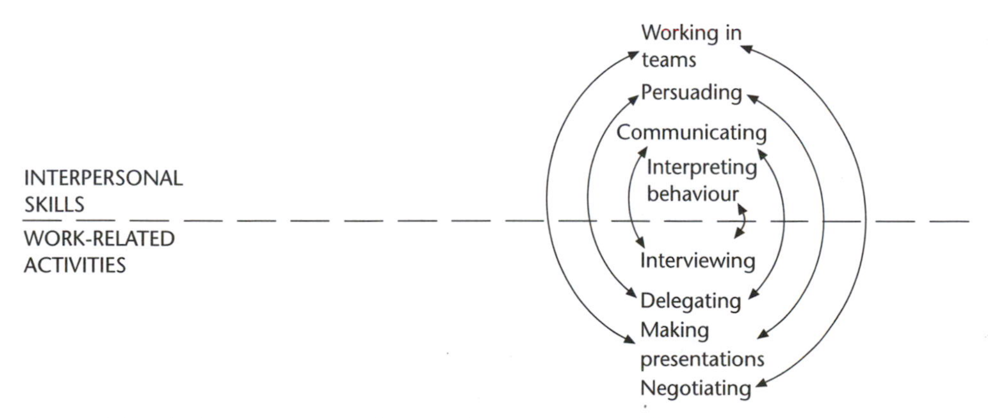


**Figure 1.3 Work-related activities and interpersonal skills.**

work environments and organisational contexts and how they are changing, introduce the key concepts for understanding interpersonal behaviour, and discuss the 'self' and its development as key factors in our interactive behaviour. Chapters 5 to 13 analyse interactive behaviour, using a framework of the core interpersonal processes and their extensions. In this section I introduce the rest of the book chapter by chapter and make some comments on how to use the material.

## Chapter 2 Work environments and interactions

Because how we and others behave interactively at work is affected by our environment and by what kind of organisation we work in, this chapter provides the conceptual tools for understanding these effects. The nature of work and work-based interactions changes as the environments impinging on organisations and their personnel change. Recent economic and political changes in Europe have directly altered work-based interactions by diversifying workforces. Cultural differences must now be understood and taken into account. Indirectly, work interactions have been altered through the responses of organisations to the increased competitive pressures brought about by global changes in communications and technology. Roles, power and the patterns of communication are different in organisations that have adopted new forms and cultures than in traditional hierarchies and bureaucracies. Interactive work behaviour is affected by these differences in roles, power and who communicates with whom. Organisational, professional and computer-mediated communication also affect how we interact. At the same time, constraints on work-based communication have increased due to the raised profiles of issues concerning ethical behaviour and equal opportunities.

## Chapter 3 People at work

Attempts have been made recently to model interaction itself, using a framework called social exchange theory. The models contribute some insight, but for fuller understanding it is still necessary to look at the psychological factors affecting behaviour at work. These include values, motivations, emotions, beliefs, attitudes, intentions, abilities and traits. Social influence and the effects of differences in background on behaviour at work are also discussed in this chapter.

## Chapter 4 The self at work

In all interactions, what we ourselves do and what happens to us have a special personal significance. Therefore, a better understanding of the self is needed to understand interactive behaviour, especially as research has shown that our untutored self-knowledge is both limited and often erroneous. This chapter discusses the self-concept and how it is formed, plus aspects such as self-esteem, self-delusion and cultural variations in the sense of self. Effective interactive behaviour, at work as elsewhere, also requires that we can cope with problems such as stress and plan our interactions to gain our objectives. We also have to develop our selves (our qualities and our skills), to deal effectively with others in the environment of a working life that is currently being changed radically by external and organisational forces. This chapter covers personal development through efficacy (gaining confidence in our ability to master skills), a capacity for independent learning and an ethical framework.

### Chapter 5 Understanding others

This chapter deals with the foundation for the other interpersonal processes. The foundation comprises how we interpret other people's overt behaviour to try to understand its meaning and the underlying factors and processes influencing it. Thus the chapter analyses perceiving in general and perceiving people, including groups, and shows how errors arise in these processes. It discusses how to perceive more accurately and with more differentiation. The methods include knowing what can and cannot be inferred validly from verbal and non-verbal behavioural cues, reducing biases through being aware of them, active listening and practising empathy. Work applications include interviewing and selection interviewing.

### Chapter 6 Self-presentation at work

The theme of this chapter is how to give the impression that we intend to rather than advocating any particular impression to aim at. There are ethical concerns about impression management, which are discussed. A basis for understanding and improving self-presentation is provided by a discussion of facework, E. Goffman's 'performance' approach and impression management models which treat self-presentation as goal-directed and influenced by their context, especially at work. The next section covers how impressions are affected by verbal self-presentation through messages, communicator style and framing; and how non-verbal self-presentation affects them. The point is made that there is a difference between what cues really signify, covered in Chapter 5, and what most people take them to signify, which affects impressions. Assertiveness is a way of interacting that enables people to achieve impression control in difficult situations. It provides a way to deal with anxiety and aggressive behaviour. Self-introductions to new colleagues, team impression management, expressing opinions and making or handling complaints are work applications of self-presentation.

## Chapter 7 Communicating at work

Skilled communication builds on interpreting other people's behaviour accurately and on impression control. Communicating means transmitting, receiving, interpreting and responding to messages, whether verbal or non-verbal. The chapter opens by discussing different forms of interactive communication and the many factors affecting it. Competent communication both achieves the communicator's goals and is appropriate. Appropriate communication matches others' expectations and practices, which vary cross-culturally. Process, individual and inter-group barriers must be overcome. Facework, 'politeness', communication accommodation, grounding and adjusting for cultural variations are among the ways to achieve competent communication. The work activities linked to communicating are coaching, mentoring, consultancy and employee communications.

## Chapter 8 Persuading

This chapter opens by showing how exerting influence through persuading is different from using power and has different consequences. Then the meaning and methods of gaining compliance are explained. Persuading, as opposed to exerting power, is linked to attitude change, which is discussed next. Social judgement theory, dissonance theory, reward theory, balance theory, reinforcement theory, repetition, fear appeals, two-sided appeals, need satisfaction, and the adoption of innovation are all discussed as ways of bringing about attitude change. Skilled persuasion involves adjusting techniques, messages and styles for the target's likely attitudes, motivations, method of information processing and culture as well as the situation. Personal selling, networking, making presentations, introducing change and subordinate–manager influence are work activities drawing heavily on persuasive skills.

## Chapter 9 Using power

For exerting power during interactions, it is perceived power that matters. However, the 'objective' power balance will bear on those perceptions, and for this reason this chapter explains two structural theories of power, deterrence and network exchange theory, and their cognitive versions which include power/dependence theory. The influence people can wield, though, depends on how much power they and the targets believe them to have, however well- or ill-founded those beliefs. This analysis provides a framework for understanding how to exert power and how to handle other people's power attempts. The framework is based round the target's beliefs and attitudes on the one hand and the influencer's relative power sources, credibility and skill in mobilising power on the other. Discussions of legitimacy, authority, power sources, reward and punishment, power needs, promises, threats and their comparative risks and consequences fit into this framework. A final section touches on gaining and retaining power. The sample work activities here are business meetings – i.e. inter-organisational meetings, in which relative power is always an issue – and explicit negotiations.

## Chapter 10 Work relationships

The history and anticipated future of work relationships introduce new variables into work interactions. Interdependence and social orientations, roles, norms and conformity as well as co-operative, competitive and conflict behaviour are all concepts that help us understand and be more effective in work relationships. Other important material in Chapter 10 covers conflict resolution, cultural differences in work relationships and coping with prejudice, discrimination and harassment. Giving performance feedback, reprimand interviewing, customer relations and mediating are work activities with strong links to this chapter.

## Chapter 11 Working in groups and teams

This chapter opens with material on the processes of group development that must precede effective group performance. Then the chapter shows how different aspects of group structure impact group members' behaviour. These structural influences are communication patterns, power and status relations, norms and group roles. (These roles differ somewhat from the positional roles discussed in Chapter 10.) Conformity pressures and their consequences in groupthink and risky/cautious shifts come next. The section which follows covers inter-group relations, particularly inter-group conflict and conflict resolution. Improving decision-making in problem-solving groups and working effectively in teams are the work applications.

## Chapter 12 Working across cultures

Working in diverse organisations or internationally imposes new and different demands on interactors. Intrinsic inter-group biases, actual and perceived cultural differences, anxiety and other factors can lead to barriers such as exclusion of out-group members, divergent communication, suppression of differences, misunderstanding and negative evaluations. Contact, communication and co-operative interdependence have been suggested as forces promoting intercultural co-operation. In addition, however, individuals need to develop a set of traits and skills for intercultural work. These are mainly based around knowledge of, and respect for, others' cultures, unbiased social perception, adapting communication and emotional intelligence. Living and working abroad lead to culture shock. This can be overcome by understanding and through methods that overcome stress and lead to adaptation and growth. Working in culturally diverse groups and international negotiating are work activities calling for the skills described in this chapter.

### Chapter 13 Leadership

This chapter deals with achieving and sustaining leadership in face-to-face interactions. It opens with a discussion of trait, style and contingency leadership theories. This is followed by how transformational leadership is enacted. There is material on gaining acceptance as a leader, which explains what people expect from their leaders and how this varies across Europe. There is a section on how to communicate, self-present and frame leadership effectively. Following this there is a section on participative leadership and building teams through co-operative goal setting, managing differences and dealing with inter-team competitiveness and conflict. The chapter continues with sections on diversity issues in leadership and distributed leadership. Two work-based activities are presented: chairing meetings and delegating.

## USING THIS BOOK

Wherever possible, the text is based on research, much of it from the social psychology and communications literatures. Guidance on how to behave effectively in interactions at work is based on an interpretation of the theories and research in the text. It is given in boxes entitled 'How to . . .'. Because of the wide scope of the book, subjects cannot always be treated in depth and readers are recommended to use the Further Reading at the end of each chapter.

Each chapter has an Introduction. This includes a listing of the main chapter topics in the form of objectives for helping readers to increase their understanding and skill. The main chapter topics are each provided with a summary. The chapters conclude with an Overview.

The boxes are of three kinds: those giving practical guidance, referred to above, those covering aspects of the subject which the author wishes to highlight, such as critiques and European variations, and those providing extra illustrative materials. These last are often based on the author's own interviews; unlike the other tables and the figures, they are not given headings, to allow readers to interpret them for themselves. Most boxes are not referred to in the main text.

The exercises offer a range of opportunities, from simple knowledge testing to private problem analysis, group discussions and role plays. Most chapters contain questionnaires and scales for performance rating of various skills. Where needed, how to score and analyse these is given in the Appendix. Although they are generally presented in a 'self-completion' format, most can easily be adapted for use either by other class members, or by the other participant(s) or observers in an interaction, in order to give feedback.

## CHAPTER OVERVIEW

Economic and political developments in Europe and worldwide have increased the significance of interactive behaviour at work for both organisational and personal success. Technological developments, while decreasing the amount of face-to-face interactive behaviour, have made its quality even more important. These factors, together with the substantial and growing complexity of work interactions, make the study of interactive work behaviour important for anyone whose work brings them into contact with other people.

When people at work increase their interpersonal skills level, both they and their organisations benefit. Individuals gain through better and less stressful working relations and better personal adjustment. Increased confidence leads to more willingness to interact and therefore more experience of a wider range of encounters. Organisations benefit internally from more and better internal communication, fewer interpersonal conflicts and better management of human resources. Externally, they gain improved relations with customers or clients, suppliers and advisers and better agreements. These gains can feed through into profits.

A wide range of work-related activities depends mainly on the interpersonal skills of those taking part, but these skills can be grouped under a small number of headings: understanding others' behaviour, self-presentation, communicating, influencing by persuading or using power, work relationships, working in groups, or cross-culturally, and leadership.

## EXERCISES

1. What are collaborative skills? What sorts of things do you think people who are using collaborative skills might do or say? How would people who lack collaborative skills be likely to behave if they have different opinions from other people in a meeting?

2. 'The quality of one's work relationships depends largely on one's interpersonal competence.' Discuss.

3. Table 1.2 is a Difficult Situations questionnaire which invites you to score the degree of difficulty you would anticipate in each of the 25 situations listed. When you have completed your questionnaire, you can analyse it, following the instructions given in the Appendix. Do this to show which of five common types of situation are more or less stressful for you personally – according, that is, to the 'self-report' you have made in the questionnaire.

### Table 1.2 Difficult Situations questionnaire

This questionnaire is designed to help you analyse which of several different types of social situation that arise at work you find most awkward to handle or most inclined to sap your self-confidence. Like the other questionnaires in this book, it contains only a small number of items; this is because they are not intended to reveal facets of your personality or psychology of which you are unaware, but to help you think systematically about aspects of your feelings and behaviour which are already familiar to you. To use the questionnaire, rate each of the following situations according to the degree of discomfort or awkwardness you would expect to experience in it. Try to visualise each situation as clearly as possible before rating it, then circle the appropriate number: 1 for an extremely low level of difficulty, 5 for a very high level of difficulty, 2, 3 or 4 for levels in between.

| | *Circle the appropriate number* | | | | |
|---|---|---|---|---|---|
| | *Low Difficulty* | | | *High Difficulty* | |
| 1 Dealing with cross or aggressive customers | 1 | 2 | 3 | 4 | 5 |
| 2 Sharing an office with your boss | 1 | 2 | 3 | 4 | 5 |
| 3 Asking for a pay rise | 1 | 2 | 3 | 4 | 5 |
| 4 Mixing socially at work | 1 | 2 | 3 | 4 | 5 |
| 5 Asking 'seniors' from other departments for information which will take them time to get | 1 | 2 | 3 | 4 | 5 |
| 6 Dealing with awkward porters/cleaners/ administrators | 1 | 2 | 3 | 4 | 5 |
| 7 Making decisions in a group | 1 | 2 | 3 | 4 | 5 |
| 8 Correcting a subordinate for an error | 1 | 2 | 3 | 4 | 5 |
| 9 Business lunches | 1 | 2 | 3 | 4 | 5 |
| 10 Going late into an important meeting | 1 | 2 | 3 | 4 | 5 |
| 11 Telephoning a busy manager (stranger) for a research interview | 1 | 2 | 3 | 4 | 5 |
| 12 Chairing a meeting | 1 | 2 | 3 | 4 | 5 |
| 13 Telling your boss he or she has made a mistake | 1 | 2 | 3 | 4 | 5 |
| 14 Reprimanding a subordinate (e.g. for being late) | 1 | 2 | 3 | 4 | 5 |
| 15 Complaining to a colleague about noisy disturbance | 1 | 2 | 3 | 4 | 5 |
| 16 Going for a job interview | 1 | 2 | 3 | 4 | 5 |
| 17 Speaking up from the floor in a large meeting | 1 | 2 | 3 | 4 | 5 |
| 18 Giving a formal speech to 50 strangers | 1 | 2 | 3 | 4 | 5 |
| 19 Approaching a group who are talking to join in their conversation | 1 | 2 | 3 | 4 | 5 |
| 20 Firing a subordinate | 1 | 2 | 3 | 4 | 5 |
| 21 Firing a supplier | 1 | 2 | 3 | 4 | 5 |
| 22 Cold calling as a representative | 1 | 2 | 3 | 4 | 5 |
| 23 Asking your boss for a favour | 1 | 2 | 3 | 4 | 5 |
| 24 Explaining a personal problem to your boss | 1 | 2 | 3 | 4 | 5 |

Adapted from Michael Argyle (1983) *The Psychology of Interpersonal Behaviour*, 4th edn. Harmondsworth, Middlesex: Penguin Books, p. 78.

4. Identify the sources of complexity in the meeting described below:

   At the weekly departmental meeting four section leaders and their Head of Department are discussing the next year's allocation of staff development and training time to the four sections. The main thrust of staff training in the organisation in the next year will be directed at improving information technology (IT) skills and the application of IT to the company's activities. For this reason the discussion focuses on which sections have most need for staff with IT skills, which are most likely to be able to spare staff time for training and which contain individuals most amenable to retraining.

However, one section leader, Mary Russell, is particularly concerned to obtain a share of the allocation at least proportional to the number of staff in her section. Last year they got less than their 'share' and this was resented by her staff who felt she had let them down. Another section leader, Peter White, who personally dislikes and feels threatened by IT, is trying to steer away from getting a large share of the allocation for his section. A third, Steven Browne, does not care how much he gets, so long as it is more than his rival, Sarah Land. He also suspects the Head of Department of favouring Sarah, who, admittedly, has an excellent performance record, but 'Who wouldn't', Steven argues to himself, 'when she regularly gets more than her fair share of resources?'

5. Give non-work (private-life) examples of occasions when you would need to exercise each of the following 'first-order' interpersonal skills: interpreting other people's behaviour; presenting yourself; communicating; influencing by persuasion; using power; working in groups and meetings; leading and facilitating groups and meetings.

6. Although in the text each interactive work activity is linked to a particular primary interpersonal skill, the point is made that others are also needed. Which do you think are the second and third most important for the following work-related activities and why?

   (a) Selling
   (b) Selection interviewing
   (c) Mentoring
   (d) Negotiating
   (e) Chairing meetings

7. Working in groups of four, compare your own work-related interpersonal problems with those of other course members. Produce a summary list of these problems for your group. The descriptions should not reveal the details which will identify the individual or the organisation. Keep the list to provide material for discussions later in the course.

8. It is not easy to assess realistically how good your interpersonal skills really are, and where your strengths and weaknesses lie. Getting feedback, in the way suggested for personal development in Chapter 4, is extremely valuable. Here is another exercise you can do, which can be quite revealing.

   Interpersonal skills audit. Collect a sample of about 20 well-remembered interactions at work. They should be with a range of people and representative of your normal range of work activity – for instance, if you go to many interdepartmental meetings, a fair number should be included in your sample. Trivial interactions, such as fixing an appointment, should also be included.

You may prefer to collect them all in one or two days, or to spread them out. It is vital, though, not to bias your sample. For example, avoid bias towards those that you felt satisfied with, or, alternatively, those that upset you. Record as much as you can remember of the dialogue and body language as soon after the interaction as possible. Then, for each interaction, answer the following questions: (Questions a to k are posed in terms of a one-to-one interaction, but for multi-person meetings those dealing with 'the other person' should be expanded to cover everyone present).

(a) How much of the dialogue and body language can you remember? (Are you aware of large blanks in your memory?)
(b) What was the other person trying to achieve in this interaction? Why?
(c) What were their feelings at different points? What are their attitudes to the topics you discussed? How do you know or think you know?
(d) What sort of person are they? What makes them tick? What excites them, interests them, bores them or depresses them? How good are their interpersonal skills? Can they relate effectively to people from cultural backgrounds different from their own? Can you? Are they prejudiced sexually, racially or towards people with disabilities? Are you?
(e) What sort of person do you imagine they think you are? Why do you think that?
(f) What do they think you think about the topic discussed in the interaction? Why? How can you tell?
(g) How equal was the distribution of listening/talking in the interaction? How appropriate was that distribution? Did you prevent the other person talking when they wanted to? Were you prevented from talking when you wanted to? Never, sometimes or often? If often, why?
(h) What were your goals in this interaction? How far were they met? Did they conflict with the goals of the other person present?
(i) Did you need to influence the other person in any way? Did you succeed? If so, how? If not, why?
(j) What was the power balance between you and the other person? How far did it bear on the process or the outcome?
(k) What ground rules for behaviour (norms) affected this interaction?

The next two questions apply only to meetings:

(l) Think about the other people present two at a time. How did they each behave to the other? Did they compete, fight, support, lead, follow, ignore? How do they feel about one another?
(m) What was going on under the surface? Was there political activity? Sexual activity? Tacit oppression of women, people of colour or people with disabilities? Are you sure?

There are no right or wrong answers to these questions. The acid test is how fully you are able to answer them. If you found them difficult to answer fully, you have some work to do on your interpersonal skills. Look more carefully at which ones gave you most trouble as a guide to areas of particular difficulty. Complete the Difficult Situations questionnaire. If you found it easy to answer them all fully, you may be highly skilled or you may be complacent. Are you sure you are defining 'fully' fairly?

## FURTHER READING

Huczynski, A. and D. Buchanan (1991) *Organizational Behaviour*, 2nd edn. Hemel Hempstead: Prentice Hall.

Mole, J. (1992) *Mind Your Manners: Managing the Culture Clash in the Single European Market*. London: Nicholas Brealey.

Robbins, S. and P. Hunsaker (1989) *Training in Interpersonal Skills – Tips for Managing People at Work*. Hemel Hempstead: Prentice Hall.

Schoonover, S. C. (1988) *Managing to Relate: Interpersonal Skills at Work*. Reading, Mass.: Addison Wesley.

This book divides basic skills into four groups – interaction, inquiry, directive influence and strategic influence.

## REFERENCES

1. Segalla, M., L. Fischer and K. Sandner (2000) 'Making cross-cultural research relevant to European corporate integration: Old problem, new approach', *European Management Journal*, vol. 18, no. 1, pp. 38–51.
2. Naisbitt, J. (1994) *The Global Paradox: The Bigger the World Economy, the Smaller its Most Powerful Players*. London: Nicholas Brealey.
3. Hargadon, A. and R. I. Sutton (2000) 'Building an innovation factory', *Harvard Business Review*, May–June, pp. 157–166.
4. Handy, C. (2001) 'The Workers' Revolution', *The Times Magazine*, 28th April, p. 15.
5. Hallowell, E. M. (1999) 'The Human moment at work', *Harvard Business Review*, Jan./Feb., pp. 58–66.
6. Walton, R. E. and R. B. Mckersie (1966) *A Behavioural Theory of Labour Negotiations: An Analysis of a Social Interaction System*. New York: McGraw-Hill.
7. Voakes, P. S. (1997) 'Social influences on journalists' decision making in ethical situations', *Journal of Mass Media Ethics*, vol. 12, no. 1, pp. 18–35.
8. Brislin, T. and N. Williams (1996) 'Beyond diversity: expanding the canon in journalism ethics', *Journal of Mass Media Ethics*, vol. 11, no. 1, pp. 16–27.
9. Leavitt, H. J. and J. Lipman-Blumen (1980) 'A case for the relational manager', *Organizational Dynamics*, vol. 8, no. 4, pp. 27–41.
10. Schein, E. H. (1983) 'SMR Forum: Improving face-to-face relationships', *Sloan Management Review*, Winter, pp. 43–52.

# 2 Work environments and interactions

## CHAPTER INTRODUCTION

This chapter shows how differences in the conditions and arrangements under which work is done affect the interactions among the people doing the work and the interpersonal skills they need to do it effectively. Work interactions are affected by differences in the broader environment in which the business or other organisation operates. They are also affected by how work is organised, communication practices, the 'climate' with regard to prejudice, discrimination and harassment and the organisation's policies. However, work environments are not static 'givens' which affect how work is done and how people at work interact. They are also dynamic products of that work and those interactions. They can, and sometimes should, be changed by them. These relationships are shown in Figure 2.1.

The focus in this chapter is on how contexts affect interactions. The coverage of the contexts themselves is necessarily brief. For more in-depth material, other books are listed in 'Further Reading'.

Interacting effectively at work involves understanding how such interactions are affected by:

- economic, cultural, ethical and other environments;
- the fact of organisation and the structure of work relationships;

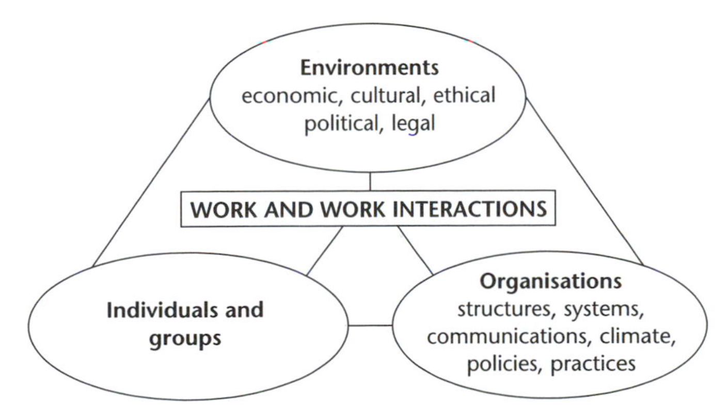


**Figure 2.1 Relationships among environments, organisations, individuals/groups and work.**

- organisations' forms and cultures;
- organisational, professional and mediated communication;
- prejudice, discrimination and harassment in organisations and societies;
- organisations' diversity policies and practices.

## ECONOMIC, CULTURAL, ETHICAL AND OTHER ENVIRONMENTS

A wide range of factors external to the organisation affect how people interact on the job. These include the legal and political systems, which need to be analysed country by country, as well as the broader economic, cultural and ethical environments covered here.

### Economic environments

European businesses and organisations of all kinds are being affected by the following changes:

- To survive increased competition from newly industrialised nations, European companies have had to become flexible and innovative. These qualities demand making better use of human resources by, among other things, better co-operation through improved communication.
- The growth of the service sector requires more service-oriented work forces[1] (i.e. staff who relate to customers and clients and try to understand and solve their problems).
- Pooling knowledge may now be a primary function for individuals and for organisations as a whole. 'In the knowledge society, the purpose and function of every organisation, business and non-business alike, are the integration of specialised knowledge into a common task.'[2]
- Globalisation and European 'trans-nationalisation' have resulted in more cross-border competition and operations as well as international mobility of personnel. These changes require managers to make different national styles work together, achieve reciprocal learning and solve intercultural communication problems.[3]
- Technological change imposes needs for teamwork, decentralisation of decision-making and workers learning continuously and fast.[4] Charles Handy, interviewed for the *Harvard Business Review* in 1995, suggested more far-reaching changes. Enterprises would exist as activities, not as buildings, their only visible sign an e-mail address. 'Hot desking' would increase. In international business, video-conferencing would become the norm. Mobile phones and laptop computers would lead to people working almost continuously, even while travelling. An office would be like a club: a place for eating, meeting

**Box 2.1**

India is well on the way to becoming the call centre capital of the world, with a turnover doubling in size every two months. Western companies sub-contracting their call centre operations to Delhi or Bangalore include British Airways, Harrods, Debenhams, Top Shop, Dorothy Perkins, Burton, Monsoon and American Express.

Most callers are 'spectacularly unaware' that their call has been re-routed thousands of miles away, to an Indian call centre, which takes calls about credit card bills or insurance claims from all over the UK. Callers are greeted with 'Good afternoon', when it is already evening in India and dark. 'Should the caller lob in a reference to David Beckham or the Queen Mother, Indian staff are able to give a suitable off-the-cuff reply. . . . Screens in the call centre show the current weather in the caller's country. Staff are taught to minimise their Indian accents, speak more slowly and watch the BBC news.'

*Source*: Harding, L. (2001) 'Delhi Calling', *The Guardian*, 9 March.

and greeting, with rooms reserved for activities, not people. He commented, 'The more virtual the organisation, the more its people need to meet in person because of the loss of the "security blanket" of "belonging" to a place; however, membership can replace a sense of belonging to a place with a sense of belonging to a community.'[5]

All these trends demand skilled interaction from those affected. Figure 2.2 is a diagram showing the major economic factors that impact on interaction at work.

## Cultural environments

Companies operating in the global market are increasingly faced with 'cultural' problems. . . . Today, especially in the European market, this means integrating many national value systems into a competitive organisational culture. When a German, for example, believes his [sic] opinion is best, who is to say that the French or Spanish managers' are better?[6]

Research indicates that the dominant values in a national culture have a profound effect on organisations and organisational behaviour. For instance, French and Italian firms have strong centralised hierarchical structures in which patriarchal influence is strong; in contrast, Northern European firms, such as Dutch and German firms, are more decentralised.[7]

The workforces of many European organisations will be more diverse in the twenty-first century than ever before. They will be made up of women to the same degree as men, people from many different national and ethnic backgrounds and more people with disabilities. More openness about differing sexual orientations and family structures and more acceptance of varying religious groups' rights will increase the apparent diversity. The organisations' customers, clients

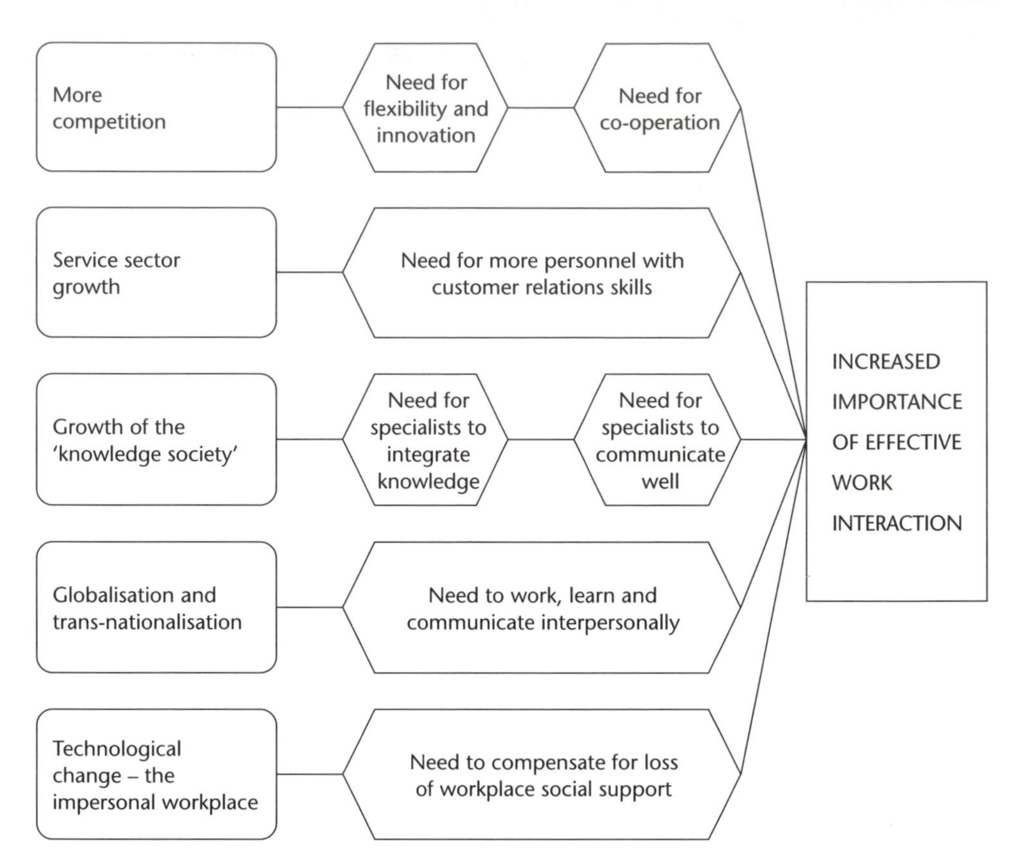


**Figure 2.2 Major economic factors and their impact on work interaction.**

**Box 2.2**

## European variations in attitudes to work

In France, intellectualism is accepted, logic expected, but pragmatism may be distrusted, whereas in the United Kingdom, common sense and precedent have more credibility than logical analysis: 'cleverness' and intellectualism are suspect. Germans place most emphasis on technical competence – engineers are more respected than marketing or financial specialists.

Germany is conservative in terms of geographical and career mobility. Deference is shown to competent authority figures, age has a strong influence on seniority. Germans value material success and stigmatise failure. They are ambitious but also co-operative towards colleagues, who, because of the seniority principle, do not represent a threat.

Italians, collectivist by European standards, show loyalty and honesty towards their in-group, but out-groups, especially institutions, are seen as fair game. In Spain, success is seen as more a matter of luck or influence than ability or performance, whereas in the United Kingdom it is seen as closely related to performance.

The Dutch have high efficacy beliefs, leading to innovativeness, joined to a strong preference for orderliness. They are egalitarian. Work and leisure overlap. Sweden, too, is strongly egalitarian, seeking compromise and consensus, avoiding conflict, using arbitration rather than adversarial litigation or negotiation. However, unlike the Dutch, Swedes keep private and business life mainly apart, as do the Germans and Italians.

and other external individuals and bodies will be equally or more diverse, both in their domestic markets and, of course, internationally.

**Box 2.3**

- 'Nowhere do cultures differ so much as inside Europe. The founder of the European community, Jean Monnet, once declared: "If I were again facing the challenge to integrate Europe, I would probably start with culture".'
- 'When Marks and Spencer, a British retailer, abruptly announced the closure of its stores on the European continent . . . [it] was not simply flouting French [and Belgian] law, as a court . . . vigorously told it, it was challenging a continental way of thought . . . a notion of the worker as partner. [Works councils or worker seats on supervisory boards, reflecting this concept, prevail in Germany, Austria, France, Belgium, the Netherlands, Sweden, Denmark and Norway.] To . . . Britons, the issues were and are those of market efficiency. But . . . to most continentals, the argument was not about corporate efficiency but about society: not by chance do "social" and its like mean "to do with labour" in several European languages.'

*Sources*: Trompenaars, F. (1993) *Riding The Waves of Culture*. London: Nicholas Brealey.
*The Economist*, 14 April 2001, p. 39.

One way to analyse the effects on work behaviour brought about by diversity is in terms of culture. One definition of culture gives it as

> A pattern of basic assumptions – invented, discovered or developed by a given group as it learns to cope with its problems of external adaptation and internal integration – that has worked well enough to be considered valid and therefore to be taught to new members as the correct way to perceive, think and feel in relation to these problems.[8]

This definition is broad enough to include different types of groups, not just nations.

Cultural differences, it is suggested, among other matters affect how far we get involved in work, how we accord status and manage time, our feelings and relationships and how we relate to nature. Such differences often lead to culture clashes, with effects on organisations' performance. For instance, *The Economist* of 22 July 2000 reported that in the first quarter of 2000, sales in America for SAP, Europe's biggest software firm, actually fell year-on-year. The story continued:

> SAP's founding co-chairman has always viewed America ambivalently, distrusting the 'froth' in the technology sector. Although North America is SAP's biggest market by far, SAP America has never been included in the highest councils at SAP's HQ, a fact that may account for an exodus of 200 senior staff since last year. Although the lack of American-style stock options undoubtedly contributed to the defections, the biggest cause cited by leavers was poor leadership.[9]

Geert Hofstede, whose studies of culture are amongst the most recognised in the field, has identified four cultural values which together help to define and differentiate cultures.[10] These values are power distance, uncertainty avoidance, collectivism versus individualism and femininity versus masculinity.

1. Power distance (PD) is closely related to inequality. An unequal distribution of power exists in every society, but to differing degrees. In low-PD cultures, work interactions are affected by the high value placed on egalitarianism. Relations are open and informal, information flows are functional and unrestricted. Organisations tend to have 'flat' hierarchies or matrix structures. In high-PD cultures, in contrast, rigid vertical hierarchies, formal relations and restricted information flows strongly influence work interactions.

In Hofstede's sample, most European countries clustered at the bottom (equal) end of the power distance scales, with only Yugoslavia (12), France (15/16) and Belgium (20) in the top 20 out of 57.

2. Uncertainty avoidance, like power distance, exists to some degree in all cultures, because the future is inherently uncertain. Again, however, cultures vary in the levels of uncertainty that people expect and are expected to tolerate. Some societies have a norm of low uncertainty avoidance. In these societies, interactions at work are influenced by the following values. The uncertainty inherent in life is accepted. Each day is taken as it comes, stress is low and people are more at ease with themselves. Time is 'free'. Hard work is not seen as a virtue in itself. People's self-control tends to be less rigid. Aggressive behaviour is frowned on and emotional display is less. Conflict and competition are seen as containable and potentially constructive. Dissent is accepted and there is more tolerance for deviance and for the young. Nationalism and conservatism are lower. Achievement is measured in terms of recognition. Relativism and empiricism are important bases for beliefs, attitudes to rules are flexible and include the idea that if the rules are being consistently broken, they should be changed. Attitudes to authority figures are that they are there to serve the citizen. Common sense and generalists are valued. In high uncertainty avoidance cultures, the inverse set of values governs interactions at work.

European countries varied widely in their scores on the uncertainty avoidance scales, with 6 in the top 20 (including Greece and Portugal at numbers 1 and 2), 7 in the middle 20 and 4, including the United Kingdom, in the lowest quartile.

3. Individualism versus collectivism are terms that refer to 'a cluster of attitudes, beliefs and behaviours toward a wide variety of people'.[11] While individualist cultures draw upon the 'I' as primary focus, collectivist cultures draw upon the 'we' identity. Individualist cultures value autonomy, choice and the right not to be imposed on by others, while collectivist cultures value interdependence, reciprocal obligation and the right to give and receive support in interactions with others. However, the distinction between individualism and collectivism

masks many differences within each category. For instance, Costa Rica and Japan are both collectivist but bear little resemblance to each other.[12]

**Box 2.4**

- Schwartz interpreted the individualism–collectivism construct in terms of autonomy versus embeddedness of the person in relations with the group.
- Triandis: Western samples are approximately 17 per cent of mankind.

*Sources*: Schwartz, S. (1994) 'Cultural dimensions of values: Toward an understanding of national differences', in Kim, U., H. C. Triandis, C. Kagitcibasi, S-C. Choi and G. Yoon (eds) *Individualism and Collectivism* (pp. 85–119). Thousand Oaks, Calif.: Sage.
Triandis, H. C. (1994) *Culture and Social Behavior.* New York: McGraw Hill.

The point that in collectivist cultures relationship prevails over task and vice versa in individualist cultures is very significant for interaction at work. In a collectivist society people may strongly identify with and be emotionally attached to their work colleagues. They form an 'in-group' and regard others as an 'out-group'. This is more the case in some collectivist countries than in others but the feeling that it should be this way is nearly always present. This explains why naive Western businessmen who try to force quick business in a collectivist culture condemn themselves to being treated as outsiders whose overtures are usually rejected.

Most European cultures scored highly on individualism, with 14 inside the top 20 and only 3 outside on this scale.

4. Masculinity/femininity has a meaning as a cultural variable that is rather different from its usual meaning. Masculinity means that the society's dominant values are material success and progress, while concern for people takes second place and is relegated to women; femininity means the 'opposite' set of values. At work, masculine societies stress decisiveness and assertiveness, place emphasis on competition among colleagues and on performance. They look to resolve conflicts by fighting them out. In feminine societies, where people 'work to live, rather than living to work', stress is laid on consensus, solidarity and quality of work life. Compromise and negotiation are seen as the best ways to resolve conflicts.

On masculinity European cultures are polarised, with 7 countries ranking in the top 20, 3 in the middle 20 and 7 Scandinavian countries clustering at the bottom of the scale.

Figure 2.3 shows the distribution of the European countries included in Hofstede's research by their ranking on the four dimensions. Figure 2.4 gives Hofstede's account of the causal factors and the societal consequences of cultural influence.

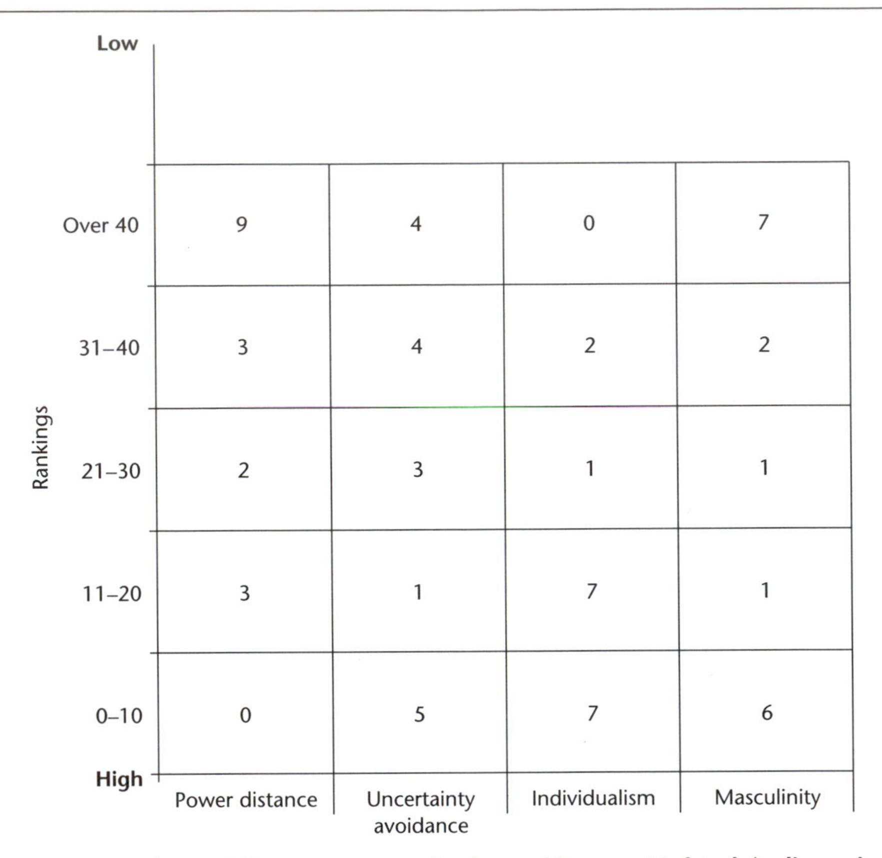


| Rankings | Power distance | Uncertainty avoidance | Individualism | Masculinity |
|---|---|---|---|---|
| Over 40 | 9 | 4 | 0 | 7 |
| 31–40 | 3 | 4 | 2 | 2 |
| 21–30 | 2 | 3 | 1 | 1 |
| 11–20 | 3 | 1 | 7 | 1 |
| 0–10 | 0 | 5 | 7 | 6 |

**Figure 2.3 Numbers of European countries by rankings on Hofstede's dimensions of culture.**

*Note*: the countries highest on a dimension have the lowest numerical ranking.

Hofstede suggests that culture patterns remain stable across many generations. This makes culture a relatively permanent influence on behaviour, so that it is more useful than transitory influences in understanding and predicting the behaviour of others. (A longitudinal analysis by James Tsao[13] of magazine advertising in Taiwan and the United States aimed to assess trends in the two populations' time orientation and communication styles. Despite the increasing industrialisation of Taiwan, this paper published in 1997 shows that any expected convergence of advertising styles had not occurred. The conclusion drawn was that Western values had not been fully adopted in Taiwanese advertising, while US advertising strategy was adapting in a different direction.) All the same, cultures do evolve, however slowly. On surface dimensions, such as dress and leisure activities, some collectivist cultures are clearly changing towards individualism. The changes may go deeper. On the basis of unexpected findings that Japanese people showed less concern for in-group members than Americans and scored higher on self-

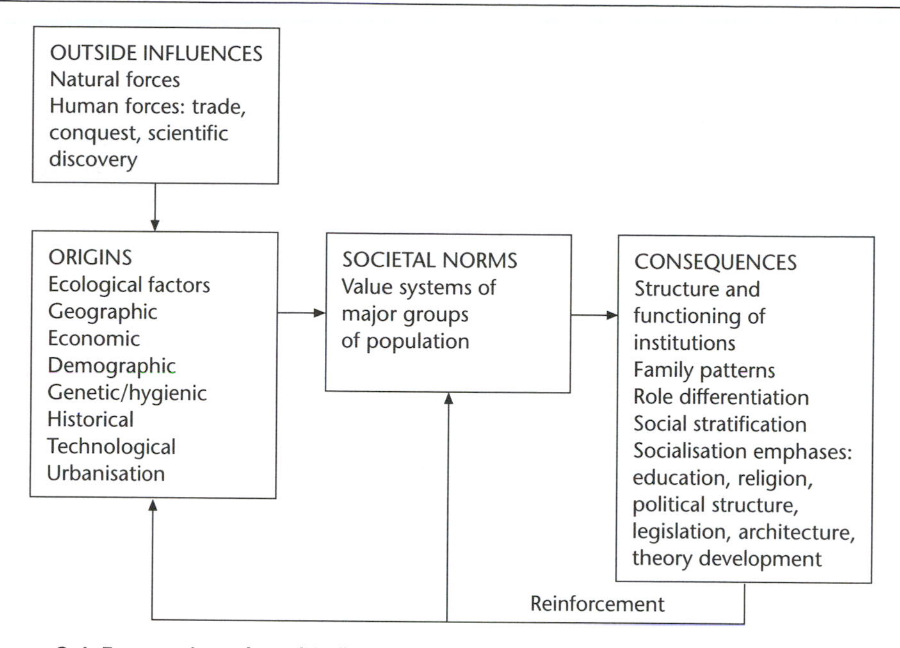


**Figure 2.4 Factors in cultural influence.**

*Source*: Hofstede, G. (2001) *Culture's Consequences* (2nd edition). Thousand Oaks, Calif.: Sage Publications. Reproduced with permission.

reliance/competitiveness measures, Stephan *et al.*[14] argued in 1998 that it cannot be assumed that classifications based on decades-old data are valid today. However, studies suggest that emotional dimensions change much more slowly, possibly because they are embedded during early socialisation.[15]

There have been attempts to speed up cultural convergence. For instance, from the early 1980s, the European Commission and Parliament made a series of attempts to use television as a tool to foster a European identity in audiences and to strengthen popular support for European integration. However, in the judgement of Theiler,[16] they failed. He wrote:

> They stumbled over the resistance mounted by some national governments and/or were frustrated by continued audience preferences for national as opposed to foreign or non-national television programs. All this, I contend, points to the underlying difficulties of trying to promote among mass publics a cultural form that stands divorced from their respective national contexts.

What effect has the Internet had on culture? A 1998 study of the development of an Internet culture in Kuwait found that local cultural practices limit adaptations to globalisation.[17] Hongladarom[18] found that, instead of erasing local cultural boundaries, creating a worldwide monolithic culture, the Internet both reduplicates the existing cultural boundaries and creates an umbrella cosmopolitan culture which is needed if people from disparate cultures are to communicate.

Box 2.5

## Critique of concepts and studies of culture

- Hofstede (1991) himself criticised the questions asked in surveys such as his own, saying that 'instruments (ie questionnaires) cover only issues considered relevant in the society in which they were developed.' One question used to assess power distance is an example: 'How frequently are employees afraid to express disagreement with their managers?' The question assumes that high frequency means a tendency to accept orders unquestioningly. However, expressing disagreement may 'mean' something different in different cultures. In Germany it 'means' putting forward a different position in a task-based discussion, in France, questioning the superior's personal leadership (Segalla *et al.*, 2000).
- Hofstede has also been criticised because the dimensions of national culture that are tested are psychological dimensions and so are distanced from issues of language, non-verbal behaviour, decision-making, communicator style and other organisational communication factors. However, although there have been many criticisms of Hofstede's work, including his own given above, and especially of the exhaustiveness of the dimensions and of the nations not included in his sample, there is general agreement that the dimensions he proposed have validity. For instance, a 1994 review of 61 replications of Hofstede's research concluded that the cultural differences predicted by Hofstede were generally confirmed (Sondergard, 1994).
- Since 1994, there has been a kind of consensus that the dimension of individualism–collectivism is the primary dimension that differentiates clusters of cultures from an international perspective. However, this seems to be mainly following Triandis (1994, p. 4), who said only that he suspected that it is the most important: 'One of the cultural differences that I have investigated more than others, because I suspect it is the most important kind of difference, is the difference between cultures that are individualistic and cultures that are collectivist.'
- Pepitone (2000) suggested that the study of culture should be broadened to include mass cultures, such as

  > puritan, consumer, corporate, bourgeois, working class, Southern, macho and the most diffuse of all – popular culture. If our eyes and ears are to be believed, such mass cultures are becoming the most powerful behavior–attitude–belief-shaping forces in the world. It is not hyperbole to suppose that we are entering the age of mass cultures and leaving the age of group cultures.

  Mass cultures, he suggested, are 'owned' by people who are not part of enduring communities. They are transmitted by media, imitation and contagion, rather than tradition. Often there is little transmission of mass culture across generations. They are commodities promoted by economic interests and consumed by those exposed to the promotion, based in the need to create or modify identity. Nevertheless they are distinct patterns of values, beliefs, world views, conduct and interests that people share, identify with, express and act on.
- Another view of modern cultures is that there are issue cultures, defined as unstable interpretive packages, of which the progay and antigay or pro- and anti-abortion 'camps' are examples. These affect collective identity, the nature of conflict, the relationship between adversaries and appropriate rhetorical strategies (Smith and Windes, 1997).
- In fact, Fourboul and Bournois (1999) suggested that

  > Because of its [culture's] many meanings, wouldn't it be better to use the word in the plural? Companies contend with a patchwork of cultures: national culture, social culture or status (skilled

**Box 2.5** ***continued***

worker, technician, clerical worker, manager, etc.), historical culture (by company unit) and professional culture. These different subgroups overlap and are brought together within the corporate culture.

*Sources*: Fourboul, C. V. and F. Bournois (1999) 'Strategic communication with employees in large European companies: a typology', *European Management Journal*, vol. 17, no. 2, pp. 204–217.
Hofstede G. (1993) *Cultures and Organizations*. Maidenhead: McGraw-Hill.
Pepitone, A. (2000) 'A social psychology perspective on the study of culture: An eye on the road to interdisciplinarianism', *Cross-Cultural Research*, vol. 34, pp. 233–249.
Segalla, M., L. Fischer and K. Sandner (2000) 'Making cross-cultural research relevant to European corporate integration: old problem, new approach', *European Management Journal*, vol. 18, no. 1, pp. 38–51.
Smith, R. R. and R. R. Windes (1997) 'The progay and antigay issue culture: interpretation, influence and dissent', *Quarterly Journal of Speech*, vol. 83, no. 1, 28–48.
Sondergard, M. (1994) 'Research note: Hofstede's consequences: a study of reviews, citations and replications', *Organization Studies*, vol. 15, pp. 447–456.
Triandis H. (1994) *Culture and Social Behavior*. New York: McGraw Hill.

## Ethical environments

Business ethics have important implications for all work interactions. For instance, the whole setting for discussions of advertising campaigns, employee relations or international negotiations will be radically different in a company whose ethical position is 'Anything legal is acceptable if it serves the bottom line' from one adopting the stakeholder approach described below. Interest in business ethics is increasing exponentially, in part because concerns are growing about the power of corporations – for instance, to over-ride governments. According to one view of ethics, moral questions are essentially questions of the distribution and use of power.[19] This view holds that, although neither good nor evil in essence, power in practice is always corrupted by self-interest. This applies even to groups with beneficent intentions. The quest for power comes from anxiety and insecurity resulting from the human ability to discern hazards, particularly social hazards. As a result, social problems are interpreted through the lens of self-interest. Justice can be attained only through a balancing of power. A balancing of power is at the root of two of the most influential ethical approaches for business over the last few years, the stakeholder and social capital approaches, which I discuss next.

1. A stakeholder approach means that an organisation's objectives expressly take account of the wishes and demands of all the internal and external parties affected. Stakeholder theory includes the idea that an organisation has relationships with many constituent groups (such as customers, employees and the local population near its factories) that affect and are affected by its decisions. The interests of all legitimate stakeholders have intrinsic value and no set of

interests should dominate the others.[20] Relationships characterised by mutual trust and co-operation are morally desirable. Thus, stakeholder theory clashes head on with the 'bottom line is all' approach to business. However, despite its ethical core, stakeholder theory in most versions includes a supporting instrumental theory. Firms whose managers establish and maintain mutually trusting and co-operative relationships with their stakeholders will achieve competitive advantage over those whose managers do not.[21] Sveiby[22] describes relationships with stakeholders as an intangible asset which should be entered in a business's balance sheet. McEvily *et al.*[23] make the business case for a stakeholder approach with the argument that one of only a few durable sources of competitive advantage is having resources that are well protected from imitation and substitution. Barriers to substitution include raising the level of performance that competition believes necessary for substitution to be profitable, through continuous improvement, lock-in and market deterrence. Each of these strategies requires the co-operation of certain stakeholders, whose payoffs from co-operation depend on the firm's future behaviour. A firm can persuade its stakeholders to co-operate by credible commitment to carry out specific promises or threats. Increasing credible commitment is a function of sharing specific knowledge.

2. Social capital is broadly defined as an asset that inheres in social relations and networks. It is jointly owned, not controlled by any one individual or entity, not marketable, and not knowledge itself. It is an asset that must be managed appropriately if its value is to be realised. It changes as relationships and rewards change over time and disappears when the relations cease to exist. It is a moral resource, the supply of which increases with use. More is better than less.[24]

The concept of social capital originated in criticisms of economic theories that assume fragile, dyadic exchanges. These provide an 'under-socialised model of human action that does not take into account how actors are embedded in social systems'.[25] Systems with strong social capital are characterised by generalised trust, which rests on norms and behaviours that are shared with others in the social unit as a whole. 'Ironically . . . strong interpersonal ties (like kinship and intimate friendship) are less important than weak ties (like acquaintanceship and shared membership in secondary associations) in sustaining community cohesion and collective action.' Social capital theories state that societies that have established patterns of trust, co-operation and social interaction (generally known as civil society) will enjoy a more vigorous economy, more democratic and effective government and fewer social problems. Organisations strong in social capital will exhibit resilient trust, even among individuals connected generally rather than personally.[26] An atmosphere of trust is often a boon to organisational efficiency but such an atmosphere is easily jeopardised by poor institutional design. In the modern workplace, for example, close monitoring of workers can be counterproductive. If workers feel they are not trusted, they may have no qualms about shirking whenever the supervisor's back is turned. On the other hand, workers who are trusted to do their jobs with minimal supervision may be more likely to repay that trust by working conscientiously.

The points argued above derive from Western culture. Clearly, ethical beliefs are affected by culture so that to impose the beliefs of one culture in dealing with people from another could itself be considered morally questionable, as well as likely to be unproductive. Donaldson[27] argued that there are six ethical 'vocabularies', or aspects of ethics, some of which are more cross-culturally valid than others. They are the social contract, self-perfection through self-control, maximisation of human welfare, avoidance of human harm, rights and duties and virtue and vice. The last two concepts (rights/duties, virtue/vice) seem to cross national and cultural boundaries better than the others, such as 'self-perfection through self-control', which assumes a Western view of individualism and human perfectibility.

### Other environments

It is widely agreed that there have been other changes in the European environment that influence work interactions: a decreasing emphasis on religion, a commitment to the democratic process, work as an important value in itself and the drive towards the quality of life. These pan-European changes contrast with the social and cultural diversity of Europe, particularly on the organisational 'surface' of economic and social life.[28]

## SUMMARY – ECONOMIC, CULTURAL, ETHICAL AND OTHER ENVIRONMENTS

Changes in the European economic environment have led to increased needs for employees to be skilled in interaction. The needs arise from competitive pressures for better utilisation of human resources, more staff in service businesses dealing with customers and clients face-to-face, the need for the knowledge of different specialist workers to be integrated, the challenges of cross-cultural management, learning and communication, the technological developments which increase the need for teamwork and decentralised decision-making and, in virtual organisations, the need to provide substitutes for the social rewards previously supplied to employees by the workplace.

The growing diversity of European workforces and markets means that cultural differences increasingly influence interactions at work. Despite criticism, cultural difference is still usually analysed in terms of power distance, uncertainty avoidance, masculinity/femininity and individualism/collectivism. European countries are quite similar on power distance (where they are low) and individualism (where they are high). Low power distance makes interactions at work relatively informal and egalitarian, while high individualism makes them competitive, unemotional and little affected by group memberships. European countries differ far more on uncertainty avoidance and masculinity/femininity. Interactions at work in the high uncertainty avoidance countries tend to be higher in stress, governed by rules and the work ethic, intolerant of dissent and deviance; in the low uncertainty avoidance countries the reverse tends to be true. In masculine cultures, interactions at work are affected by acceptance of overt conflict and the higher valuation placed on success and achievement than relationships. In feminine cultures the reverse tends to be true.

A belief in the importance of ethical business behaviour is growing, though still tending to be justified in terms of business advantage. Power and benefit sharing through the stakeholder approach and the elevation of trust-based relations in the form of social capital are two ethical approaches that have gained prominence in recent years. It is important to remember, however, that ethical approaches such as these are culture-specific.

## THE STRUCTURE OF WORK RELATIONSHIPS AND THE FACT OF ORGANISATION

The majority of work is done with other people. Where work is done by two or more people who interact, there is organisation. It may be implicit but it must exist. For instance, if two flat-mates are cooking a meal together in one kitchen, they must agree, even if tacitly, on the menu, the timing of the meal, who will do what and who will occupy which spaces and use which surfaces and equipment at what times. Many of the features of most work are absent from this situation. There is no employment relationship, no power structure and no monetary consideration, but there is and must be organisation, even if it only consists in one person telling the other, 'For heaven's sake get out of the kitchen and leave me to it.' Otherwise the meal will not be produced.

Collective, organised activity not only gets things done and gives rise to material benefits well beyond those available to people acting alone, it also provides psychological satisfactions. It is fundamental to all known human societies, and in most is institutionalised in formal organisations such as schools and universities, military and civil services, churches, hospitals, charities and businesses. When work is done in formal organisations it is affected by that fact: people's behaviour and the nature of their interactions are different. For instance, if the two people who were preparing a meal were working, not in the privacy of a flat, but as employees in a hotel kitchen, we would expect that one person would have greater authority than the other, and hence more 'say-so', while laid-down

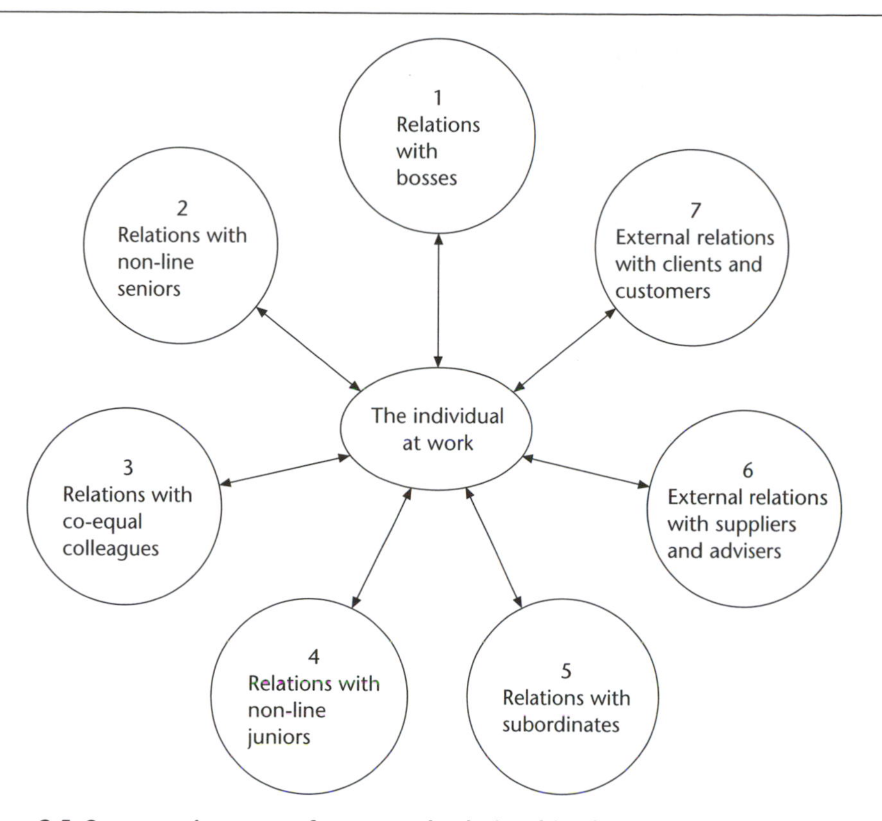


**Figure 2.5 Seven main types of structural relationship that an individual can have at work.**

procedures might make the cooking arrangements much less negotiable. A major factor influencing the tone of interactions at work is who the participants are, in terms of their relationships within an organisational framework – whether they are boss–subordinate, lateral co-equals, customer-suppliers, or what.

Figure 2.5 sets out the seven main kinds of structural relationship that an individual can have at work. These include relations with five categories of colleagues in the same organisation – bosses, subordinates, co-equals, non-line seniors in another section or department and non-line juniors. There are also two categories of relationship with people from outside organisations – customers and clients, to whom a service is provided by the organisation, and suppliers and advisers, who supply a service to the organisation. Many individuals have work relationships in most, but not all, of these categories – for instance, they may have no subordinates or no contact with outside suppliers. The number and importance of the different types of relationship will also change with the job. The different kinds of relationship shown in Figure 2.5 vary in at least the following ways:

- In some there is a formal authority structure, in others there is not. A formal authority structure means that both, or all, parties to a relationship are members of an organisation in which they are required to work together. Obviously, in relations between members of different organisations, no formal authority structure governs the relationships between the parties.
- In those relationships where there is a formal authority structure, the parties may be equals or superior–subordinate, with differences in their relative status and power.
- The goals and aims of the parties may be shared, similar, divergent or conflicting.
- Interactions in some relationships are based on economic exchange.

All these differences affect the seven types of relationship identified in Figure 2.5.

1. Managers function within a formal authority structure and have higher status and power than their subordinates. When interacting with them, subordinates usually acknowledge these facts by, for instance, listening more, deferring and asking the manager's opinion more. What degree of 'subordination' is appropriate will vary. One factor affecting it is what is the norm in the organisation or culture. In France and Germany, for instance, owing to different educational systems – elitist in France, egalitarian in Germany – managers occupy different positions. In France there is a wide gulf, 'distance' from subordinates is very important, challenging it is a 'little revolution'; in Germany, distance is less, the model is co-operative and managers see themselves as coaches. Criticism in Germany serves to reinforce the appearance of being an active member of the team fighting for better results. Leaders unable to integrate the ideas of their subordinates and to support their commitment to the organisation are considered weak.[29]

Another major influence will be the manager's chosen style, which may be participative, democratic or autocratic. If a boss is participative, subordinates are likely to talk more and defer less than if the boss is autocratic. Significantly, however, the boss's preference has more influence than the preference of the subordinate. In most activities, bosses' and subordinates' goals are shared or similar, with any divergent or conflicting ones tending to be personal rather than to do with the organisation's objectives. Disagreements between them are therefore more likely to concern means – strategies, tactics or ways of behaving – more than ultimate ends. Neither person is directly paying the other, except when the manager is the owner of the enterprise, nor is any good or service being bought or sold. Therefore interactions are not based on economic exchange, and bargaining, though it may occur, is more often implicit than explicit.

2. The authority of non-line seniors is limited and often ill-defined; this can create uncertainty for the junior participants in interactions. It can be difficult

for them to decide whether to assert their position as the representative of their own department or to defer to the other's seniority. In these relationships, too, there is often quite a high ratio of divergent or conflicting to convergent goals, because of inter-departmental rivalries. Apart from these two differences, these relationships are structurally similar to those with bosses.

3. Although in relations with lateral colleagues neither person is higher or lower in the formal authority structure, such a structure does exist. This means that disputes can be resolved by appealing to a higher authority, which is not generally possible in relations with 'outsiders' such as customers or suppliers. Status and power are roughly equal, and there is no economic basis for interaction and thus no formal bargaining. If the lateral colleagues work in different departments or sections the parties will probably have some divergent goals as well as shared and similar ones; if not, shared goals may predominate. Informal groups most often arise among lateral colleagues, based on shared work, common interests and frequent interaction. Such informal groups have a powerful influence on all types of work behaviour of their members, including their interactions with each other. Research by Kramer[30] showed that employees who change jobs within an organisation adjust better if they have frequent, high-quality communication with their peers. Kramer argues that there should be more focus on peer communication rather than superior–subordinate communication at such times.

4. In relations with non-line juniors, authority and status positions are the reverse of those for relations with non-line seniors, while that for goals is the same.

5. In relations with subordinates, authority, status and power positions are the reverse of that in relations with a boss, but goals and the basis of interaction are similar.

6 and 7. External relations, with suppliers or advisers and with customers or clients, are similar to each other except for the relative power position. A buyer usually has more power than a seller.[31] However, many factors can alter this. For instance, a monopolistic supplier or a major bank is scarcely in a low-power position relative to minor customers or clients.

Except for power, the behavioural context of interactions between suppliers and customers or advisers and clients is similar. In both cases a formal linking structure is absent and so there can be no appeal to an overarching authority. Status differences are important and should be considered carefully when deciding who should represent the organisation in various external relationships. Junior buyers should not be sent to meetings with the sales director of an important supplier. Often in external relations there are more conflicting and divergent than convergent goals because the basis of interactions is economic. There is an intrinsic conflict between buyers and sellers over price.

These contextual differences make behaviour that is appropriate in one relationship quite inappropriate in another. In addition, there are these other structure-related influences on how people need to behave at work:

- The fact that they are enacting roles, such as sales manager or secretary.
- The fact that they are subject to direct and indirect pressure from other members of the organisation. For instance, during an appraisal interview with a young but high-performing subordinate, a manager might wish to encourage by hinting at early promotion, but be prevented from doing so by the need not to upset older subordinates who expect their seniority to be rewarded first.
- The fact that what they are free to say or do is constrained by policies and influenced by overall organisational cultures and climates. For instance, in academic institutions, managers are rarely free to commit their staff to activities without first consulting the staff affected. In other types of organisation, on the other hand, managers are often constrained from revealing plans to subordinates who may be affected by them.

## SUMMARY – THE STRUCTURE OF WORK RELATIONSHIPS AND THE FACT OF ORGANISATION

Formal organisation imposes constraints and structures on work relationships. Interactions within seven different types of work relationship are affected by differences in authority, relative power, similarity or difference of goals, whether or not economic exchange and implicit bargaining are involved and role, constituency and organisational policy pressures.

## ORGANISATIONAL FORMS AND CULTURES

Formal organisations usually differ from the arrangements in a shared kitchen in being designed. Activities and functions are grouped, responsibilities allocated and patterns of relationships specified to achieve some set of aims. Historically, most organisational designs have been hierarchical, designed to permit a few members to direct, co-ordinate and control the activities of the majority. Over recent years, however, dissatisfaction has grown with some aspects of the way hierarchies function, and in particular with how well they are adapted to their changing environments. This has led to greater experimentation in organisational forms – in some Western countries, matrixes, federations, networks and adhocracies are becoming common.

Organisations have cultures. These can be understood as

> beliefs about the way work should be organized, the way authority should be exercised, people rewarded, people controlled. What are the degrees of formalization required? How much planning and how far ahead? What combination of obedience

> and initiative is looked for in subordinates? Do work hours matter, or dress, or personal eccentricities? What about expense accounts, and secretaries, stock options and incentives? Do committees control or individuals? Are there rules and procedures or only results? These are all parts of the culture of an organisation.[32]

It has been argued that organisational culture is the 'prime mover' instead of structure, strategy or politics.[33]

Power, role and task cultures are different types of organisational culture. They are closely linked to the type of structure of the organisation. In power cultures, everything depends on a central power source (who is often the founder of the organisation), with rays of control spreading outwards. They work on precedent. Decisions are based on the wishes of the central power source. Control is exercised by selection of key individuals, occasional forays from the centre or summonses to the centre. 'Who you know' matters more than what you know. In a role culture, the role, or job description, is more important than the person who fills it. In a task culture, concern with the task predominates. People are given considerable discretion, and management concentrates on getting the right people lined up with the right task. Influence depends more on expertise than position power, though not exclusively; influence is therefore widely dispersed, while groups or teams are more influential than individual position-holders. More recently, other concepts of organisational culture have developed corresponding to the newer forms of organisation.

The purpose of this section is to identify key features of both traditional and newer organisational forms and cultures and to look at their implications for interactions at work.

1. Hierarchies with power cultures are usually depicted as a pyramid in which power and control flow down from the narrow top to the wide base, while accountability flows upwards. The early business hierarchies were mostly set up by entrepreneurs and their cultures were power cultures. In a strictly hierarchical organisation, most of the important interactions are between bosses and subordinates. There is often an overlay of conforming to the second-guessed wishes of the 'big chief' and there may be an undermining of the established order if a subordinate is actually or potentially a protégé of the central power-holder. Trust is likely to be minimal.

2. Bureaucracies with role cultures result when hierarchical organisations introduce control through rules and procedures. Designed to use resources efficiently and rationally, in bureaucracies structure, technology and job design are governed by a set of principles. These include that each person should be exclusively accountable to his or her immediate supervisor (chain of command), the number of subordinates reporting to a supervisor or manager should be limited (span of control), there should be clear, written responsibilities for every job (job description), jobs should consist of closely related activities so that the

workers can gain proficiency through practice (division of labour) and promotion should be on the basis of technical competence (meritocracy).[34] These principles lead to a role culture. They also strongly affect the character of work interactions, which are often formal and conformist. There is a tendency to 'put things in writing'. In a bureaucracy, the manager's power is limited to what s/he has authority for and by the accepted policies and rules of the organisation. Bureaucratic organisations sometimes ignore people's social needs and needs for personal growth, leading to alienation and anomie, low motivation, high absenteeism and deliberate output restriction. An 'informal organisation', complete with its own tacit but well-understood rules and procedures, may grow up alongside the formal one, often undermining it.

**Box 2.6**

An entrepreneur who was seconded to the UK Ministry of the Environment found it irksome that people he worked with daily and knew well continued to call him 'Mr X' at all times. So he went to them and asked 'Can't you call me Ed?' 'No', they said, 'We can't.'

*Source*: interview, author's research. (Note: the entrepreneur was an American, so I have used the anecdote elsewhere to illustrate cultural differences.)

There have been many attempts to overcome the limitations of bureaucracies. For instance, businesses in turbulent environments, such as the telecommunications industry, sometimes cut across the boundaries of the formal organisation by inter-departmental meetings at which relatively junior scientists and technologists might have as much or more influence than senior managers in production departments. In more extreme circumstances, where markets as well as products have to be created, as in the early dot.com and biotechnology industries, the formal organisation is often all but abandoned in practice. People are given substantial scope to define their own jobs and contributions. In large organisations, instead of one pyramid, there may be divisionalisation, with several hierarchies, each corresponding to a different market, geographic region or technology. The centre acts as banker and supplier of certain services, such as Human Resource Management, to the separate divisions.

Hierarchies vary in how steep they are. During the 1990s, many large companies in Europe shifted from steep to flatter pyramids. In IBM UK, for instance, the number of management tiers was reduced from seven to four. Modifications such as these increase the proportion of interactions between lateral equals and reduce the proportion of manager–subordinate interactions.

The basic principles and problems of bureaucracies are left unaltered by the developments just described, while they each bring their own problems. For instance, flatter pyramids reduce career opportunities, which can demotivate personnel. Ultimately, many businesses and other organisations have concluded that a more fundamental set of changes is needed to meet the effects of globalised competition, the growth of the service sector, the arrival of the knowledge economy, technological change and European integration. As a result, 'new' organisational forms have been emerging. The most significant seem to be matrix organisations, federal organisations, network organisations, adhocracies and organisations built around knowledge workers.

3. Matrix organisations operate like a grid, in which functional specialisms form the rows while project teams, trouble-shooting teams or business units form the columns. The rows are marked by continuity; the columns may be either temporary, as with project teams, or semi-permanent, as with business units. Matrix organisations usually have task cultures. They can be responsive to changing conditions and can provide satisfying work environments with multiple opportunities. People are used flexibly. Communication between managers is greater, because the system requires it. On the other hand, people have two (or more) bosses, which can produce role conflict.

4. Companies that have adopted versions of the federalist model include General Electric, Johnson and Johnson, Coca-Cola, BP, Royal Dutch Shell and Unilever. Federal organisations are based on a set of beliefs; autonomy releases energy; people have the right to do things in their own way so long as it is in the common interest; they need to be well informed, well intentioned and well educated to interpret the common interest; they respond better to being led than to being managed.[35] In federal organisations power and resources are widely distributed. Different interest groups contend with other interest groups for the control of resources and territory. A federal organisation relies as much on influence, trust and empathy as on formal power and explicit controls. Authority must be earned from those over whom it is exercised, by respect or agreement. People have both the right and the duty to 'sign their work'. Each person has an inner ring of baseline responsibility and an outer ring of limits of authority. In between there lies an area of discretion. Twin hierarchies, one of status and one linked to the task, are necessary and useful.

Careers are opportunities to work on a succession of interesting and challenging projects, rather than climbing a ladder of power. Personal and people 'consultancy' skill is recognised as much as technical and professional expertise. Teams are prominent features of federal organisations. The section on 'teamworking' in Chapter 11 gives more detail on the implications of federal organisations for work interactions.

5. Network organisations consist of flexible units and teams. Their structure is intended to support organisational learning. Learning organisations aim to 'continuously transform themselves' by developing the skills of all their people.[36] There is a danger that, in traditional organisations, while individuals learn, the

organisation does not. Many companies are still operating in this mode, but some, such as BP, Eastman Kodak, Arthur Andersen, Gruppo GFT and Raco Bell, have started to develop mechanisms that transfer learning from individuals to a group. They aim to provide for organisational renewal, keep an openness to the outside world and support a commitment to knowledge.

The key structural element for learning organisations is the use of organisational networks, clusters, projects, teams and taskforces. BP, for instance, starting in 1988, changed its engineering centre organisation from a typical functional structure to a business unit system. This consists of groups of many small units working in teams, and specialist service clusters, which facilitate both external co-ordination and internal selection and training.[37] Technological advances, faster-changing environments and cynical publics require 'tremendous learning – how to collaborate, how to become more trusting and open in communications, how to deal with dependency in the new kinds of fluid hierarchical relationships, how to wield personal vs. positional power without losing the commitment of subordinates, how to design organisations with fluid boundaries, and so on.'[38] The emphasis on interaction skills in this list speaks for itself.

A key factor in implementing a 'learning organisation' approach successfully is recognising, encouraging and rewarding those managers whose behaviour reflects openness, systemic thinking, creativity, a sense of personal efficacy and empathy. This leads to new forms of appraisal, including upward appraisal of managers by subordinates. As part of the learning organisation concept, interaction skills issues are for the first time reflected in structure, instead of structure being independently determined and people left to adapt. Successful project forms are decided according to how good the project leader is as a leader and how cohesive the project team is as well as the requirements of the task, such as complexity, diversity and speed requirements.[39]

Crossan *et al.*[40] identified integrating as a key stage in transferring learning from individuals to the organisation. Integrating requires the members of a work group to develop shared understanding and to take co-ordinated action. Obviously, these processes rely on language, so that for an organisation to learn and renew, its language must evolve. Not all conversational styles are equally effective, however, for developing shared meaning, which points to the need for skill. The most effective is dialogue – collective thinking and inquiry. Dialogue can transform the quality of conversation and, in particular, the thinking that lies beneath it.[41]

6. Adhocracies are now common in innovative firms in the aerospace and electronics industries, and in client-based industries such as consulting, advertising and investment banking. In these fields work is coming to consist of a series of different opportunities to apply knowledge and skills, rather than a set of repeated tasks. Work increasingly requires establishing and maintaining relationships based on external or internal clients' needs and problems. In

adhocracies, employees perform a series of different roles, as they are members of different project teams, either successively or simultaneously. An executive may be a catalyst in one team, a progress monitor in another and responsible for implementation in another. The project teams themselves are set up to perform a task and disappear when the task is done. In adhocracies, instead of formally reporting to and being reported to in accordance with line responsibilities, employees are required to nurture and sustain a wide variety of professional relationships.

7. Organisations built round knowledge workers reflect the fact that they are different from and must be treated differently from other workers. They possess the key factor of production and possess it exclusively. They may be in a near-monopoly position and they are in a permanent sellers' market owing to a lack of capacity of the population at large to acquire their expertise. They already number between one-third and two-fifths of all workers, and the demand for their services is still growing. Organisations have to market to obtain their services as much as they market products and services. Knowledge workers cannot be supervised effectively, because unless they know more than anyone else in the organisation about their specialism they are basically superfluous. They have to be seen as human resources, not labour, reflecting the fact that they decide in large measure what they will contribute to the organisation and how great the yield from their knowledge will be.[42]

Because no form of knowledge is intrinsically higher than any other, these organisations consist of equals who cannot be organised along boss–subordinate lines, but as a team. Management is still needed, but its role is not to command, but to inspire. The teams in these organisations will be of a new kind, developed

**Box 2.7**

### Critique of the concepts of new organisational forms

'Ironically, the language that many futurists use to describe new organizational forms – for example, decentralization, flexibility, flat span of control – draws from and reacts to the key elements of bureaucracy.

'These scholars continue to cast structure as a static feature of organizing. . . . Moreover the processes and types of control that typify these organizations do not always parallel descriptors of new organizational forms' (Putnam, 1997).

Some authors have encouraged an attempt by top management to design and manage the organisational culture. This may be an attempt to re-assert the kind of control that is relinquished with the new forms. However, this process may be neither feasible nor desirable (Barker, 1993).

*Sources*: Barker, J. (1993) 'Tightening the iron cage: concertive control in self-managing teams', *Administrative Science Quarterly*, vol. 38, pp. 408–437.
Putnam, L. L. (1997) 'Organisational communication in the 21st Century'. Informal discussion with M. Scott Poole, L. L. Putnam, and D. R. Seibold, *Management Communication Quarterly*, vol. 11, pp. 127–138.

by the Japanese. It works like a soccer team, with all the players simultaneously moving with the ball, instead of like a baseball team where each function performs sequentially. Toyota, Nissan and Honda, using these kinds of teams, now bring out a model of a car in 18 months, against the five years it takes by traditional methods.

Figure 2.6 summarises the effects of different organisational forms and cultures on the ethos of work interactions. Leaders of all the new forms of organisation need strong communication skills and a capacity for 'emotional expressiveness' to replace traditional hierarchical and control methods of motivation.[43]

National cultures have a strong influence on the structures and cultures of organisations in different countries. Saee[44] asserted that management practices are always culturally bonded. A study of nine European countries, the United States and three Asian countries found that cultures that value hierarchical structuring for social cohesion impose severe restrictions on information flow in

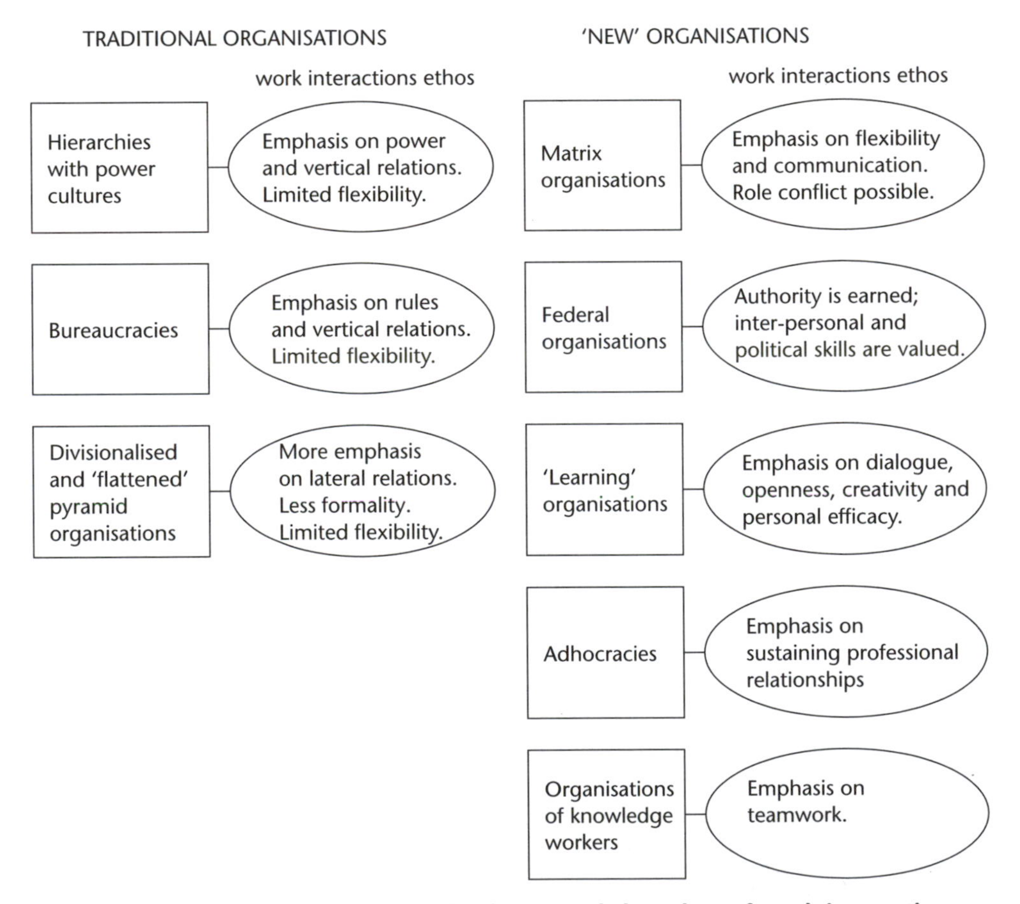


**Figure 2.6 Organisational forms and cultures and the ethos of work interactions.**

organisations.[45] For example, in cultures high on measures of uncertainty avoidance, formalisation and centralisation are prominent features of organisational structure. Decision-making, authority, responsibility and communication are distributed according to a hierarchical pattern and the climate is reserved. In fact, such organisations are characterised by the obvious features of a Weberian bureaucracy. In low uncertainty avoidance cultures, on the other hand, structures are informal and decentralised, decision-making authority and all that goes with it are widely distributed and an open climate of discussion and bargaining prevails. The business culture in France, for instance, emphasises vertical authority, defined and exclusive areas of responsibility, visibly confident and powerful hierarchies and centralised planning. This is so especially in manufacturing, although service sector growth and an increase in small to medium-sized businesses reduce this for the overall picture. Formality prevails, in order to minimise ambiguities and because close personal relationships could be manipulated to distort clear demarcation lines of responsibility / accountability.[46] In Germany, 'the technology-oriented culture is still prevalent even at the most internationally oriented firms in the German-speaking countries.' However, organisation culture may be a more important co-ordination mechanism where the management is more geocentric, less important where it is ethnocentric.[47]

Ethics can also influence organisational cultures. The ethical concept of social capital has been extended to embrace organisational social capital (OSC) as a resource reflecting the character of social relations within the firm.

- OSC is realised through members' collective goal orientation and shared trust, which create value by facilitating collective action.
- Members are those who have an employment relationship with the firm. It may be temporary, contingent or core, but excludes other stakeholders.
- It is a by-product of other organisational activities[48] that is nevertheless integral to the success of collective action.[49]

OSC arises from trust and from the willingness and ability of members to subordinate their individual goals and associated actions to collective goals and actions. This need not rise to a relational level nor be generalised throughout the organisation but 'without some level of trust, goals are unlikely to be either agreed on or attained'.[50]

## SUMMARY – ORGANISATIONAL FORMS AND CULTURES

To facilitate their work, organisations are structured. They also have cultures that usually correspond to and reinforce the structure. Technological, social and market forces impose the need for change on organisations' structures and cultures and lead to modifications and the emergence of new forms. Traditional organisational forms gave rise to a high number of boss–subordinate interactions and gave them special importance. The newer forms have reduced the number and significance of these, while increasing the importance of co-equal relations and service provider–client relations both within and outside the organisation. In addition, the need for group skills has expanded. Previously, the role of groups was largely a decision-making one, in committees or boards, but teams and project units are performance groups, and where once they were largely confined to, for instance, advertising agencies, they are now widespread. Political skills and concepts have been legitimated, while learning becomes a major objective of interaction.

Some old myths and hypocrisies have been blown away with the bureaucracies that embedded them. These include the pretence that the only legitimate concern of anybody was the organisational goal and task, which has been replaced by an acceptance that people at work have their own goals and agendas. The myth that only rational considerations affect work decisions is also replaced by more openness about the fact that people at work are whole people, with emotions and social needs that they are trying to satisfy. Power is now understood to be not the prerogative of one sector, senior management, but diffused throughout the organisation. Recognising these realities gives increased importance to all interactions and their associated interpersonal skills, despite the shift to new communication channels such as e-mail. National culture and ethical environments strongly influence which types of organisational forms and cultures predominate in different societies. The overall dependence of the organisation on the interpersonal skills of its employees is now widely understood.

## ORGANISATIONAL, PROFESSIONAL AND MEDIATED COMMUNICATION

Changes in organisational environments, forms and cultures have brought a new emphasis on work-based communication. Three aspects are discussed – organisational, professional and mediated – and their implications for interpersonal interactions at work are considered.

### Organisational communication

This term refers to both formal corporate communications and the predominant pattern of work-related communication within organisations.

Organisations and their managements use communication to manage impressions. The objectives of *corporate communications* are to establish a favourable corporate identity and reputation, to enhance performance and to ensure consistency in all internal and external communications.[51] Public relations and employee relations are forms of corporate communications directed at impression management on behalf of the organisation or its managers. Another way of looking at this is to see organisational communication as constructing and maintaining a system of shared meaning. Public relations attempts to create and maintain a positive corporate image, by participating in symbolic activities to generate support from the larger social system. Employee relations aims to develop a definition of the organisation's activities that is meaningful to the organisation's members. Communication is used to maintain cohesion, mobilise people to take action, foster organisational identification, increase commitment to organisational goals and resolve past conflicts.[52] A scenario-based experiment by Tata and Rhodes[53] showed how effective impression management messages can be. They significantly enhanced employee perceptions of fairness in the way rewards were distributed.

The predominant pattern of *work-related communication* within an organisation is strongly influenced by its structure and culture. The types of messages and how they are transmitted vary according to the positions, and especially the relative power, of the senders and receivers. National culture also has an effect. American managers 'typically use assertive, sanction-oriented, coercive messages',[54] in contrast with British managers who often disguise orders as requests. Organisational communication systems and networks can leave some categories of employees isolated. In 1997, Sias *et al.*[55] found that temporary employees, whose numbers have been increasing, suffer from communication isolation and respond by engaging in less impression management and by seeking and giving information less often. The same probably applies to the growing numbers of part-time employees.

Some scholars argue that organisational communication practices are constructed to create hegemony, which is domination through consent. Use of accepted organisational communication practices is seen as reaffirming the status quo, while those resistant to the status quo oppose through divergent communication practices.[56] Institutional discourses are concerned with establishing a hierarchy of institutional implicitness into which workers are socialised.[57]

To Judi Marshall,[58] for women organisational communication is preprogrammed with male values. Women have to 'read' the dominant culture if they are to survive as members of the subordinate group.[59] She argues that 'covert dialogues of power' constantly undermine women at work. For instance, it is widely accepted that emotions are out of place at work, although anger and its covert expressions are part of everyday functioning. Sexual innuendo and noting of physical characteristics are used to undermine women's perceived competence. There is covert exclusion of women from being allowed to change the subject. Women's contributions are trivialised: 'My goodness, you're taking this all so seriously'. Women may resist, but resistance seems largely futile as it is the form as much as the content of the communication that conveys the dominance. She claims that women are continuously working on other people's ground, translating their thoughts into male form and screening out potentially unacceptable material, defensively using muting, hesitancy and the orthodox form of expression. 'It is at the level of form that conformity tends to be demanded of those who seek membership of a cultural community.' But the medium is the message, so any feminist or women's voice content is continually contradicted and subverted.

Figure 2.7 summarises some intended and unintended consequences of organisational communication.

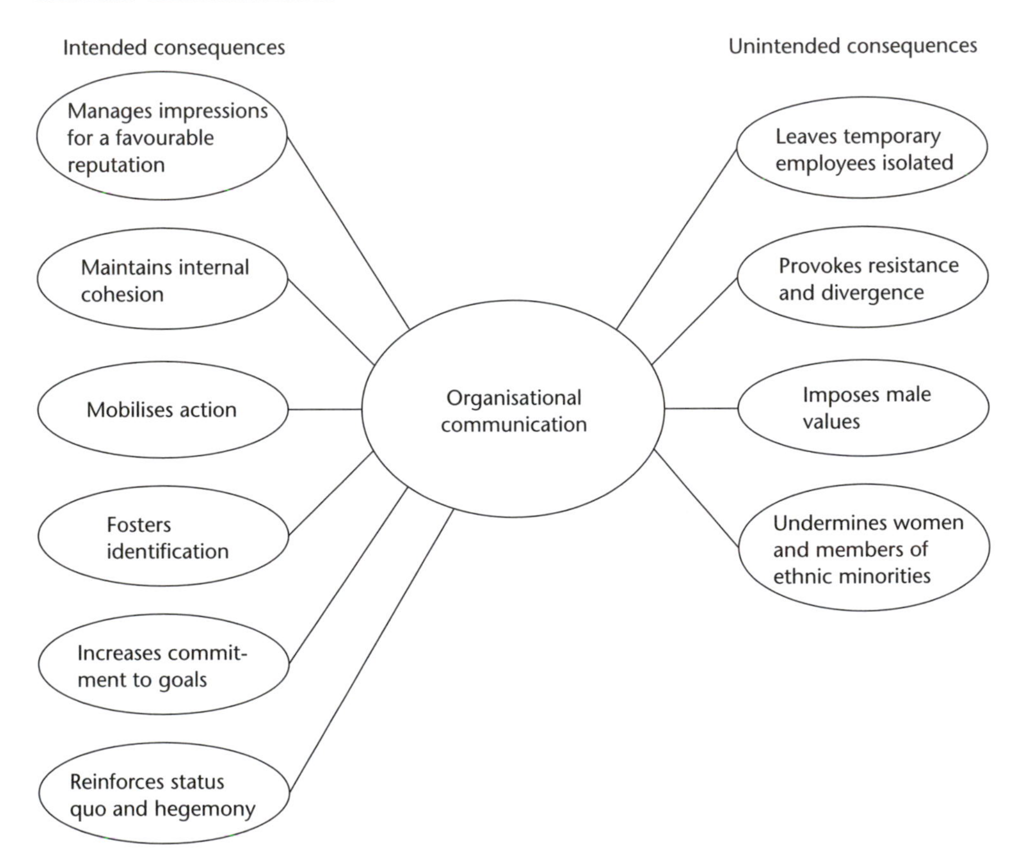


**Figure 2.7 Intended and unintended consequences of organisational communication.**

**Box 2.8**

### Critique of organisational communication concepts

Mumby and Stohl (1996) argue that a 'vast array of communicative and cultural practices . . . constitute organisational life', rather than the linear transmission of information along relatively stable organisational channels. Organisational communication is not simple and miscommunication is not necessarily the exception.

*Source*: Mumby, D. K. and C. Stohl (1996) 'Disciplining organizational communication studies', *Management Communication Quarterly*, vol. 10, no. 1, pp. 50–72.

## Professional communication

Members of different professions generally share a common language, impenetrable to outsiders, which serves several purposes, including creating and maintaining their status and power. Doctors, lawyers, engineers and even teachers use a specialised vocabulary and syntax among themselves. This excludes outsiders. In dealings with patients, clients and students they may adjust their language in the interests of being understood. However, in the area of communication style, which is a carrier of power and status, clear evidence is emerging that professionals use styles that preserve their authority in relations with outsiders. For instance, Bryna Bogoch[60] analysed 19 lawyer–client conversations in an Israeli legal aid office, aiming to reveal whether the participatory model of professional–client relationships prevails in Israel because of ideological commitments to egalitarianism, solidary and informal relationships even between strangers. Results showed that lawyer–client behaviour resembles the authoritarian model – the national ethos could not overcome the professional attitude.

## Mediated communication

Mediated interpersonal communication refers to any situation where a technological medium is introduced into interpersonal interaction. It includes telephone conversations, letters, CB radio and electronic mail. Computer-mediated communication (CMC), which includes e-mail, instant messaging, computer conferencing and voice mail, involves an interactive relationship directly among individuals or groups of individuals. Although this book is about face-to-face interaction, and mediated communication of any kind largely differs by having a reduced number of open channels (e.g. telephone conversations eliminate the channels for sight, smell and touch), it is worth considering one form of mediated communication for the contrast, in behavioural terms, with face-to-face encounters. I have chosen CMC because of the current high levels of interest in and usage of it.

**Box 2.9**

Because we send e-mails round the office all the time, you can use them to say things that would be too difficult face to face. For instance, yesterday I sent Chris, who sits at the opposite desk in our open-plan office, an e-mail asking him to stop doing what he was doing and get on with what I wanted him to do. I wouldn't have wanted that to be overheard and by using e-mail I could think through how to put it without upsetting him – jokily. The day before, I sent the 'teccies', working ten paces away, an e-mail asking them to stop uploading when we're downloading (because our work has more urgency and is slowed up when they are uploading). They sent me one back telling me to get lost, but they're doing it.

*Source*: interview with a Web editor, author's research.

By comparison with face-to-face communication, CMC has these characteristics:

- Constraints are fewer. There is no need to know the target receiver. The sender can select the target. There is no need for participants to be using the medium at the same time or to be in the same location. The participants can more easily store, retrieve or process the contents of the discussion.
- There is reduced ability to communicate by physical presence, non-verbal behaviour or paralinguistic cues. (However, of course, this 'inability' can be turned into an advantage.)
- Response time and even reception time are decided by the receiver.
- Either party can terminate the interaction simply by not responding, instead of having to turn their back or make some other obvious gesture of refusal.[61]

The parabolic growth of CMC has led to an increase in studies of its effects on work, work relationships and interpersonal interactions at work. Using electronic media leads to more open and equal communication, because observable status barriers and social context cues are lower. Often this open communication is accompanied by inappropriate (for task groups) socio-emotional behaviour, such as swearing and self-absorption. However, this may not apply where subjects are members of intact work groups. In these, authority, experience, tenure, occupation, organisational role and gender are relevant. A five month field study of computer conferencing found that established occupational status differentials affected participants' task-related communication behaviours.[62]

**Box 2.10**

In a speech, Michael Eisner, chairman of Walt Disney, argued that e-mail had served to increase the intensity of emotion within his company and become the principal cause of workplace warfare. 'With e-mail', he noted, 'our impulse is not to file and save, but to click and send. Our errors are often compounded by adding other recipients to the "cc list" and, even worse, the "bcc (blind carbon copy) list". I have come to believe that, if anything will bring about the downfall of a company or maybe a country, it is blind copies of e-mails that should never have been sent.'

*Source*: *The Economist*, 'E-Management Survey', 18 November 2000, p. 15

Fulk *et al.*[63] investigated how users of communication technology in organisations create shared meaning. They found support for the idea that individuals' technology-related attitudes and behaviours converge with those of important communication partners. What they thought about their combined network partners' attitudes and behaviours in using electronic mail predicted their own attitudes and behaviour. They also found that the effects of this social influence were stronger for co-workers than for supervisors.

Scott[64] investigated the behavioural effects of computer-based group decision support systems (GDSS) and found that identification was lower in GDSS meetings than it was in general. People who could not be seen by other members of a group expressed fewer comments indicating identification with their group. The same applied to people who were contributing anonymously, especially if hidden from view, but they also contributed more total comments.

Walther[65] found that expecting interactions with another person to continue into the future had more effect in CMC than it had face to face. As a result, Walther[66] concluded that group members working together internationally via CMC can, over the longer term, develop affection, group identity and a social orientation.

CMC allows social boundaries to be blurred but may nevertheless increase a communicator's susceptibility to the power of group influence, stereotyping and discrimination.[67] Rice[68] argued that human information-processing limits lead individuals to more instrumental use of CMCs and that their correspondents reciprocate. Adkins and Brashers[69] found that the user of a powerful language style in a CMC group was perceived as more credible, attractive and persuasive than the user of a powerless language style. Mabrito[70] found that people who suffer from fear of communicating, contribute more, initiate more topics of discussion, and feel more comfortable participating in electronic discussions with unknown audiences than they do when communicating with face-to-face audiences.

**Box 2.11**

*Computing* magazine of 20 July 2000 had an article (pp. 49–50) entitled 'If you want to get on – it's time to get personal. Interpersonal skills are the key to success in the future.'

Figure 2.8 summarises these findings.

Culturally based differences in communication style can affect how and whether members of certain cultures use CMC. Hall[71] identified Japanese culture as a high-context culture – a culture in which much of the communication is in the non-verbal realm. High-context cultures such as the Japanese would seem to have a 'handicap' in the low-context, non-verbal deficient world of CMC (specifically, text-based e-mail). However, if there is a handicap, it is probable that Japanese people will learn to communicate within the restrictions of the medium. Drummond and Hopper[72] showed that telephone users learn to overcome the loss of non-verbal cues in other ways. For example, instead of shaking their heads to show agreement, they might say, 'I agree'. There may be a similar 'development of skills' to combat the lack of non-verbal cues in computer-mediated communication.[73]

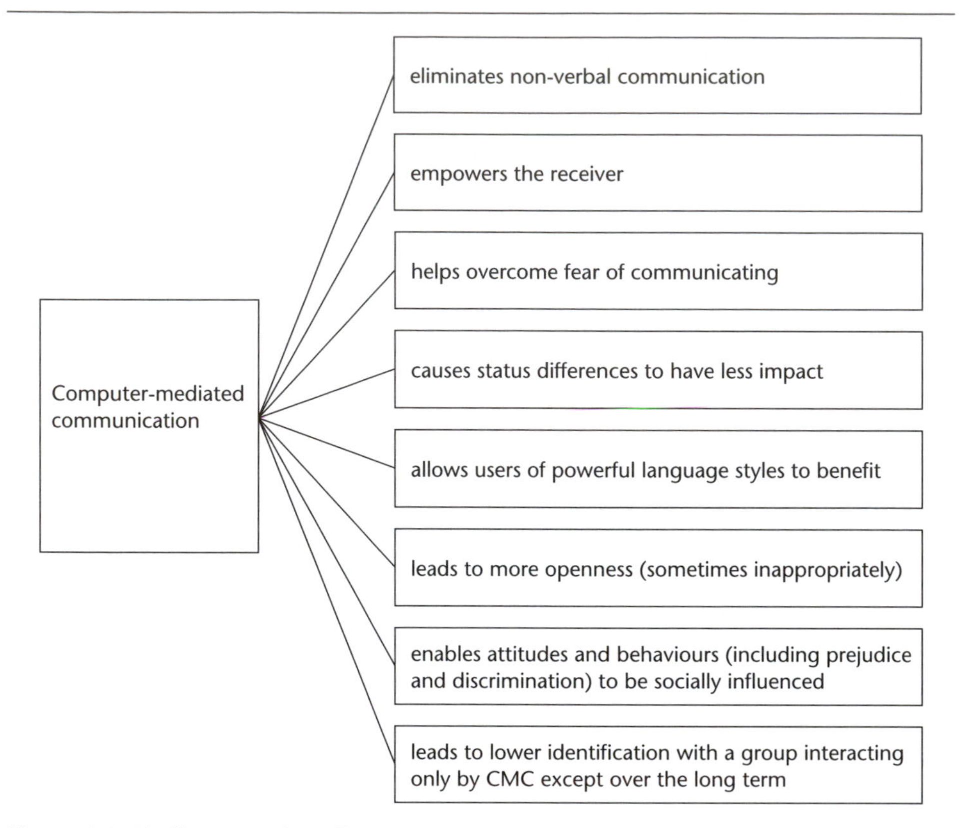


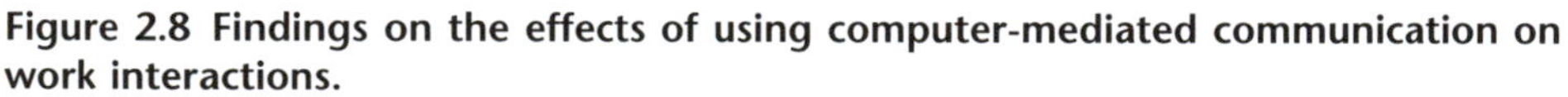

**Figure 2.8 Findings on the effects of using computer-mediated communication on work interactions.**

**Box 2.12**

The rapid increase in the Internet user population may lead to intercultural misunderstanding. Web designers need to know their audience and on the Web their audience is worldwide. A website for a communication department in the United States uses the 'OK' gesture, but this gesture has other meanings (some derogatory) in other cultures.

Meetings held through video conferencing have features consistent with shifts one might expect when time constraints apply. Awareness of deadlines increases and there is a shift at the midpoint of team projects when individuals recognise the limited time left. These challenges are directly or indirectly addressed by greater use of co-ordination mechanisms for regulating talk, such as the agenda, control by the Chair, prior preparation and protocols which vary from group to group but are used repeatedly by the same group. There is more task-focused discussion, more decisions are made and the Minutes are treated as more important.[74]

## SUMMARY – ORGANISATIONAL, PROFESSIONAL AND MEDIATED COMMUNICATION

Viewed positively, organisational communication is used to manage impressions, both internally and externally to the organisation, to create a system of shared meaning and to maintain cohesion, mobilise people to take action, foster organisational identification, increase commitment to organisational goals and resolve past conflicts. Viewed negatively, it acts to underpin the existing power relations and to oppress women and other minorities. The esoteric forms of communication used by professionals are similarly seen as supporting their power and authority vis-à-vis non-professionals. By comparison, computer-mediated communication is widely regarded as democratic, even subversive.

Other effects of CMCs on interpersonal interactions at work are beginning to be investigated by researchers. These include their effects on group identification (and hence on inter-group relations), on the primacy of instrumental versus relationship-oriented attitudes among users, on conflict and on high-context versus low-context communication. Time pressures during video conferencing are also affecting work interactions.

## PREJUDICE, DISCRIMINATION AND HARASSMENT IN ORGANISATIONS AND SOCIETIES

Sex and race have been described as the two 'dominant statuses' that determine other statuses that someone is likely to acquire. 'If we are to understand the individuals with whom we work, we must understand how these two dominant statuses have both supported and limited them in their search for fuller, richer lives.'[75] It seems to many people that other forms of status should be added to this list: those of having disabilities, being from a certain religious group, having certain sexual preferences, and so on. Prejudice, discrimination and harassment are part of the daily reality for more than half of the people at work in many European countries. Here the consequences of these behaviours for interactions at work are considered. (Ways of handling them are looked at in Chapter 10.)

### Prejudice and discrimination

Prejudice refers to attitudes to members of social groups that are differentiated by ethnicity, gender, religion and so on. In principle, prejudice can be positive; in modern usage, it usually means an irrationally hostile attitude. Discrimination means any situation in which a group or individual is treated unfavourably on the basis of arbitrary grounds, usually prejudice.

Ethnic (or race) prejudice consists of the belief that one's own cultural or 'racial' heritage is inherently superior to those of others. This is usually accompanied by negative stereotypes of particular other ethnic groups, such as Africans. Prejudice can be found in all ethnic groups, but does not imply a power base to enforce it. Racism consists of ethnic prejudice plus the use of power, either overt or covert, either intentionally or unintentionally, to enforce these prejudices and preferences. (A similar distinction could perhaps be drawn between sex prejudice and sexism.) Research suggests that in Western societies there is a powerful and widespread consensus by which ethnic groups and other social categories are ranked in a hierarchy of 'social distance'. This hierarchy can be measured by preferences for contact. Groups are seen in terms of their attractiveness as spouses, neighbours, colleagues and friends. Subordinate groups show the same pattern of out-group preferences about other groups (but not their own in-group) as dominant groups and non-ethnocentric and non-racist respondents show the same patterns as ethnocentric and racist respondents. This hierarchy means that when people are prejudiced against an out-group they will also be prejudiced against all less preferred out-groups.[76]

Prejudice against women persists worldwide. Research evidence for this continuing sex prejudice came from a 1999 study. This showed a high correlation between participants' beliefs that occupations required masculine personality or cognitive attributes for success and the extent to which those occupations had higher prestige and attracted higher earnings.[77] Gender discrimination also persists in most European countries and in most sectors and occupations, though it is more evident in those that attract high pay and status or where traditionally 'male' attributes are required. From investment banks to the police, broadcasting to computer software design, women are under-represented. In virtually all industries they still face a 'glass ceiling' that keeps them out of top management. Token highly publicised appointments do not change this overall picture. In many EU states, women account for 40 per cent or more of the workforce, and the vast majority of women between the ages of 25 and 49 are part of the workforce even when they have young children. However, a quarter of Spanish, Belgian, Danish and French women work part-time, a third of German and 42 per cent of British women do the same. These part-time jobs tend to be in the lowest-paid non-manual and manual occupations, for instance, selling, catering or cleaning. They also tend not to carry holiday or sick pay entitlements, pension rights or job security. The precariousness of women's employment positions is reflected in their much higher rate of unemployment compared with men: twice as high, in most member states of the EU. Finally, equal pay for equal work is not fully applied, although in some countries the gaps have been narrowing. In France it has been reduced from 40 per cent to 23 per cent, but in the United Kingdom men workers earn about 30 per cent more than full-time women workers, making the earnings gap 10 per cent greater than in the rest of the EU.

At a more subtle level, it can be argued that organisations 'gender' people. They make them conform to roles, norms and behaviours conventionally considered

Box 2.13

**European variations in gender prejudice and discrimination**

In Sweden the status and roles of women, like those in the other Scandinavian countries, are the highest in Europe, and probably the world. In the United Kingdom there are more women managers than in most EU countries, especially in the professions and public sector but the glass ceiling still persists. In France, bias against women persists in industry and outside Paris, but less so in the professions and services. In Spain, career women are rare, even in the professions. The Germans and Dutch have a highly conservative view of the role of women which tends to exclude women from senior management positions. In Italy there is little feminism and few women in managerial roles except in family businesses where their connections outweigh their gender. However, overt discrimination is low – Italy provides good maternity leave and childcare.

appropriate to their sex, which roles and behaviours justify excluding women from positions of power. Gendering refers to the social construction of femaleness and masculinity in organisations through power and discourse. Wendt[78] demonstrated how some women service industry workers are made powerless, how the environment and rules create women as political bodies and rob them of personal and social identity. However, Dennis Mumby[79] has pointed out that men as well as women are gendered in the workplace and that masculinity can take on various forms.

Disability can be understood as the product of the interaction between individuals and their environment, reflecting the point that many people who are disabled in one environment would not be in another, more supportive, one. Very importantly, the environment includes the way people with disabilities are perceived by others. Recent research has shown the persistence across all social groups of highly superficial bases for prejudice against people with disabilities. More negative attitudes toward mentally handicapped persons in general were expressed after exposure to deviant faces than after exposure to non-deviant faces or in the absence of exposure.[80] Other social groups, whether defined by religion, age, sexual preference, household composition (for instance 'single parent' families), social class or education, also face prejudice. There is, though, some evidence that in all cases, including ethnic, gender and disability prejudice, it has become less overt. In the case of ethnic prejudice, for example, there is now more tendency to note (and implicitly disparage) cultural differences rather than physical differences.

Members of subordinate or devalued social groups consistently report lower levels of discrimination for themselves personally than for their group as a whole. This may be because for personal ratings of discrimination they use interpersonal comparisons that are susceptible to self-serving biases and needs to maintain a positive self-image. In contrast, group ratings are primarily based on inter-group comparisons and so invoke the participants' social identity.[81]

## Harassment

The term 'harassment' means 'vexing by repeated attacks'. It is not confined to sexual harassment, though this is the most common. Schneider *et al.*[82] defined ethnic harassment as threatening verbal conduct or exclusionary behaviour that has an ethnic component and is directed at a target because of his or her ethnicity. It consists of slurs or derogatory comments and exclusion from work-related or social interaction. Irvine[83] pointed out that harassment of individuals regardless of their social group (calling people a jerk, retard, giving them the award for 'biggest screw-up of the year') is commonplace in American firms. In some it is used as a management tool. In these businesses a non-harassing person would not reach manager, because they would not be considered tough enough.

One definition of sexual harassment is

> repeated and unwanted verbal or sexual advances or sexually explicit remarks made by someone in the workplace, which are offensive to the workers involved, which cause the worker to feel threatened, humiliated, patronised or harassed, or which interfere with the worker's job performance, undermine job security or create a threatening or intimidating work environment.

Davidson and Cooper[84] state that sexual harassment is widespread. For example, they quote a study which showed that 59 per cent of women reported sexual harassment at work. A specific case is of a young female personnel officer who said the following:

> Sexual suggestions were made to me in my last job by my male boss. I was shocked as I had never put over that image, and it's distressing when you are treated like that, as a sex object. You wonder whether you have failed, or whether that person treats all women like that. I coped quite well in the end, and afterwards I just ignored it.

There is a view that sexual harassment at work is primarily about power and fear and that men (including men who strongly disapprove of harassment) and women experience these two variables under different aspects and so do not understand one another's views. In particular, men's power over standpoint and associated fear of marginalisation clashes with women's power fear of physical harm.[85]

## Impact of prejudice, discrimination and harassment on work interactions

People subjected to prejudice, discrimination or harassment experience a loss of status. The behaviour of people with and without status is predictable: high-status people behave to maintain dominance, low-status people speak and act deferentially. Kanter[86] found that when men were placed in low-status positions and were denied access to advancement and sources of power, they behaved in

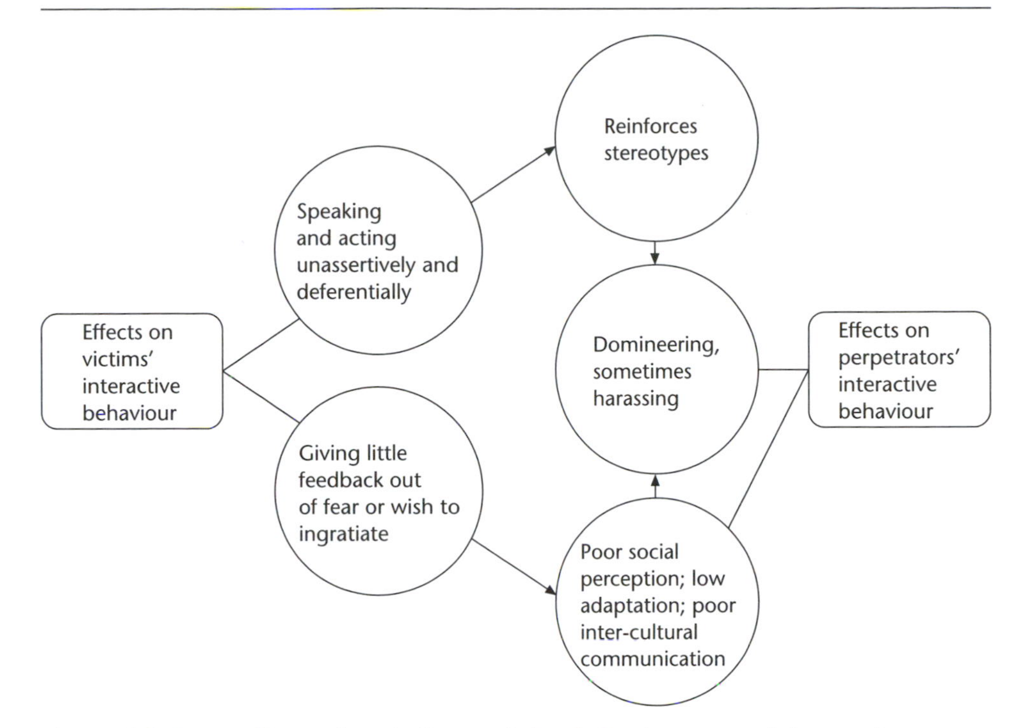


**Figure 2.9 Some effects of prejudice and discrimination on work interactions.**

unassertive, deferential ways stereotypically defined as 'feminine'. The findings of this research strongly suggested that status is linked to 'expressive' non-powerful behaviours and attitudes.

Members of dominant subcultures are often poor communicators with members of other subcultures, especially when they are in positions of power or authority within an organisation. Not only do they sometimes behave in over-assertive, domineering ways but they often have an implicit belief that the way they communicate is 'natural' or 'normal' and that people who communicate differently are therefore 'abnormal'. In addition, members of minority groups may give them little feedback on their poor communication performances, out of fear or a wish to ingratiate.

Figure 2.9 shows some effects of prejudice and discrimination on work interactions.

## SUMMARY – PREJUDICE, DISCRIMINATION AND HARASSMENT IN ORGANISATIONS AND SOCIETIES

Despite improvements in the position of minorities in recent years, members of many groups are still significantly affected by overt and covert discrimination.

Many organisations and their managers and executives are guilty of ignoring, tolerating or sustaining prejudice, discrimination and harassment. The majority of victims are members of minorities. Prejudice, discrimination and harassment create unfair and often illegal barriers to careers and satisfying jobs for people in these groups. The low status of members of discriminated-against groups contributes to their sometimes adopting an unassertive, even deferential, communication style, which can lead to their being perceived as lacking in leadership qualities. The domineering and unperceptive style of some members of dominant subcultures in authority positions leads to poor communication.

## ORGANISATIONS' DIVERSITY POLICIES AND PRACTICES

Where organisations have fully embraced diversity, have trained their staff accordingly and inculcated its principles in every way, the barriers to good work communication between subgroups are lower. Equal opportunities policies and training, on the other hand, though important, are not enough for this purpose. Their narrow focus means that the positive value of individual contributions from people of diverse backgrounds can still be ignored.

**Box 2.14**

An interview with the Personnel Director (PD) and the Assistant Personnel Director (APD) of a major UK car manufacturer began with the point that for the past three-and-a-half years partially, for 18 months intensively, the Assistant Personnel Director's role had been to upgrade the company's equal opportunities effort.

PD: 'Equal Opportunities training has happened across the company, covering Head Office, Aftersales . . . ; not much at the "X" factory, which is mainly staffed by white males. At the "Y" plant, the introduction of a new vehicle has got in the way of getting the training done, but a course for executives is due very shortly.'

APD: '14 per cent of the graduate recruitment applicants were ethnic minorities this time round.'

PD: 'Yes, so that shows some progress.'

Q: 'How many did you take?'

PD: 'Well, that's it. None.'

APD: 'Yes, but we only took nine people altogether. We got 10 per cent at the assessment centre stage, but none made it through. But that's representative. If the ethnic minorities are 6 per cent of the population, 6 per cent of 9 is less than one person.'

PD: 'Still, I'm worried that it shows a hidden bias – probably unconscious – at the assessment centre stage. You know, line managers have a strong influence on the selection at that stage.'

*Source*: interview, author's research.

Historically, diversity in organisations has had a bad image. It was thought that having a non-homogeneous workforce could lead to performance losses, through communication problems, higher conflict and lower attractiveness of employment leading to higher staff turnover. These negatives resulted partly from prejudice among members of the dominant culture of the organisation (mainly ethnic majority male) and partly from inevitable differences in the way people from different cultures perceive, think and behave.

More recently, some organisations have embodied a different set of attitudes in their policies. Their reasons vary but include obeying laws outlawing discrimination or requiring equal opportunities, pursuing ethical conduct, using the pool of talent to the full, meeting the needs of diverse user populations and markets and attaining global competitive advantage. A common attitude among business leaders is captured in the following quotation:

> While it may sound like the right and good thing to do, diversity is not a moral imperative. It is a business strategy. . . . Visionary business leaders believe . . . in the concept of dynamic tension. They do not expect all people to like each other, only to work well together. They do not want all people to agree with each other, or with them. They do expect all people to celebrate their differences – and to co-operate for a common goal. They want synergy. (p. 24)[87]

**Box 2.15**

> Joanna Foster, former Head of the Equal Opportunities Commission, said, 'It is all about the culture. You can have the policies but if the culture is such that people are afraid to take advantage of them, they are useless.'
>
> *Source*: interview, BBC1 6 o'clock News on 8 February 2001.

## SUMMARY – ORGANISATIONS' DIVERSITY POLICIES AND PRACTICES

Some organisations 'champion' diversity, valuing the positive contribution that diverse individuals can bring, others tolerate it, merely following equal opportunities' precepts, and others again treat it as a problem. These different policies and practices significantly affect the climate within which men and women, people of different ethnicities and so on conduct their work-based interactions.

## CHAPTER OVERVIEW

Work interactions are similar in many ways to those in life more generally, despite the essential focus on the task. However, the expected, appropriate and effective ways to interact at work vary according to the many environments that impinge on the organisation and its personnel. Recently, economic and political factors in Europe have increased the diversity of many people's work-based interactions. In turn, increased diversity has required cultural differences to be understood and adapted to. At the same time, the raised profile of ethical issues has increased constraints. Changes in organisational forms and cultures have produced shifts in who interacts with whom and in the power balance. Organisational and professional communication tend to reinforce the status quo and support the power bases of existing power holders; computer-mediated communication, however, may be a countervailing influence. Persisting tendencies for many organisations to have prejudice, discrimination and harassment embedded in their cultures continue to disempower members of minority groups but to what extent depends on the positive or negative diversity policies of the organisation. Overall, the main effects of recent environmental changes in Europe are a vastly increased frequency of some types of work interaction in terms of the diversity of people involved, their role relationships and their relative structural power sources.

## EXERCISES

1. Topics for assignments, private study or group debate:

   (a) Competition is more important than co-operation for economic welfare.
   (b) 'In the knowledge society, the purpose and function of every organisation, business and non-business alike, are the integration of specialised knowledge into a common task' (Drucker).
   (c) Workforce diversity is more of a problem than an opportunity.
   (d) Stakeholder theory is unrealistic.

2. Topics for group discussion and pooling of private knowledge:

   (a) How far have Charles Handy's predictions written in 1995 (see p. 30) been realised in an organisation well known to you and/or by organisations generally in your country?
   (b) How diverse is your organisation or country?
   (c) How well does Hofstede's cultural values model fit your country?
   (d) How far is stakeholder theory practised by your organisation or in your country?
   (e) How high is the 'social capital' of your organisation or country?
   (f) Learning organisations aim to 'continuously transform themselves'. Is this a good idea? Why?
   (g) Discuss three ways in which discrimination affects members of ethnic minorities.

(h) Discuss the issues raised by the material on prejudice, discrimination and harassment in this chapter, with your ideas for solutions. You may wish to refer particularly to the points made below:

- Research has shown that the men who are most likely to hold prejudiced views about women as managers are either those members of the 'old school' who hold traditional views about women generally or younger men who feel threatened by the 'infiltration' of very competent professional women. There is a fear of tokenism leading to incompetent people getting ahead 'unfairly'.
- Some women who were surveyed about gender relations at work complained that they were treated differently by their male superiors, and as a result were deprived of those good working relationships that can provide informal 'training' opportunities that are often just as important as formal training. One said her boss found it difficult having a woman executive on his staff – 'some situations like travelling together are so uncomfortable that I have had to talk to him about them, especially when we sign in at a hotel'.

3. Group discussions for video recording and future use:
   Discuss any of the topics listed in Exercise 1.

   (a) The class divides into groups of 5 or 6, mixed as far as possible in terms of nationality, culture, gender, disability, religion, sexual orientation, etc.
   (b) Each group member records his or her 'rating' ('strongly agree' to 'strongly disagree' on a 5-point scale) before the discussion and hands it in with their name on it.
   (c) The discussion is 'observed' using the following pro forma:

| Names | Pro arguments | Con arguments |
|---|---|---|
| | | |
| | | |

   (d) Video record as many of the group discussions as possible.
   (e) After an interval, (e.g. the following week) repeat (b).
   (f) The first paper is returned and compared with the new rating. Note any shifts in ratings.
   (g) The class watches a selection of the video recordings. The instructor points out any behaviours that may have been influenced by the individual's background in the terms described in a. above. The video recordings can be shown at different points during the course to observe relevant behaviours.

4. How much do you know about a culture from which a colleague, friend or contact comes? Complete the following questionnaire, then get them to check your answers.

(a) In face-to-face communication, people from Culture X stand closer together than people from your own culture do. True or False
(b) People from Culture X value an individual's initiative and achievement within the group. True or False
(c) Citizens of Culture X value obedience to authority and typically will not disagree with someone in a higher position of power. True or False
(d) When people from Culture X communicate, they use words that are clear and direct, allowing for few ambiguities. True or False
(e) People from Culture X need formal rules, absolute truths, and conformity. They also tend to avoid conflict and competition and seek consensus. Therefore, they are under less stress than their counterparts from your own culture. True or False
(f) In Culture X sex roles are highly differentiated. This means that the men from Culture X have one set of values while women from Culture X have another. True or False
(g) When people from Culture X approach a task, they tend to do one thing at a time. They take time commitments very seriously and adhere to plans inflexibly. True or False
(h) Because of the high (low) number of people per square kilometre, the people from Culture X have become a high- (low-) touch culture. True or False
(i) In Culture X, intimacy between companions of the same sex tends to be greater and more valued than male–female intimacy. True or False
(j) To the people from Culture X, failure is no big deal. They commonly sympathise with the weak and believe that nurturing individuals is more important than material success. True or False

5. Draw up a list of the ten people with whom you have most work interactions. Allocate each to one of the seven types of work relationship listed in the section called 'The structure of work relationships'. Use the concepts of formal authority structure, goals and economic exchange to describe each relationship. How far do the interactions you experience within each relationship correspond to those that would be predicted from the 'model' in this section?

6. Analyse an organisation that is well known to you and is from your own country, using the following framework:

   (a) Tallness of hierarchy (number of levels in relation to total employees).
   (b) Functional differentiation (number of functions in relation to total employees).
   (c) Share of white-collar employees (as percentage of total).
   (d) Supervisory span of control (number of employees per supervisor at the lowest level).
   (e) Administrative and commercial personnel (as percentage of total workers).

(f) Authority positions (as percentage of total workers).
(g) Authority positions (as percentage of total white-collar workers).

Working with a multi-country group, each write up your findings on a board and compare them. Discuss how far any differences may reflect cultural differences between the countries represented. Bear in mind the possibility of technological differences in the organisations' activities, other environmental factors and idiosyncratic factors in the structuring of the separate organisations.

7. Analyse any work organisation you know reasonably well to decide:

   (a) How much do its members need to be able to work in a 'boundaryless' organisation?
   (b) How far are its members allowed and expected to self-organise?
   (c) In what directions and channels do the main flows of communication and information exchange happen?
   (d) Is decision-making decentralised?
   (e) What proportion of members are 'knowledge workers'?
   (f) How well is learning transferred from individuals to groups?
   (g) How well is learning transferred from individuals to the wider organisation?
   (h) How important are vertical reporting relationships?
   (i) How much can leaders or managers depend on 'authority' to achieve their objectives?
   (j) How much must leaders or managers use interpersonal skill to achieve their objectives?

8. Use the results of your analysis in Exercise 7 to decide, for the work organisation you have chosen:

   (a) What type of structure does it have?
   (b) Is this changing? If so, how?
   (c) What type of culture does it have?
   (d) Is this changing? If so, how?
   (e) How do its structure and culture affect interpersonal relationships between its members?

9. Does your work organisation have a policy and set of procedures on discrimination and harassment? If not, why not? If so, do you know what they are? If not, find out.

## FURTHER READING

Alvesson, M. and J. D. Billing (1997) *Understanding Gender and Organizations*. London: Sage. As well as the material relevant to this chapter, chapters 6 and 7 are relevant to Chapter 13 (Leadership) of this book.

Barnett, G. A. (ed.) (1998) *Organization Communication: Emerging Perspectives VI: Power, Gender and Technology*. Especially Chapters 1, 2 and 6. Westport, Conn.: Greenwood Publishing.

Cannon, T. (1994) *Corporate Responsibility*. London: Pitman.

Davidson, M. J. and C. L. Cooper (1992) *Shattering the Glass Ceiling: The Woman Manager*. London: Paul Chapman.

Davidson, M. J. and C. L. Cooper (eds) (1993) *European Women in Business and Management*. London: Paul Chapman.

Easterby-Smith, M., L. Araujo and J. Burgoyne (1999) *Organizational Learning and the Learning Organization: Developments in Theory and Practice*. London: Sage. Especially Chapters 1, 4, 11 and 12.

Gabriel, Y., S. Fineman and D. Sims (2000) *Organizing and Organizations: An Introduction*, 2nd edn. London: Sage.

Gordon, C. (1996) *The Business Culture in France*. Oxford: Butterworth-Heinemann.

Handy, C. (1993) *Understanding Organizations*. Harmondsworth, Middlesex: Penguin.

*Harvard Business Review* (1994) *Organizational Learning*. Cambridge, Mass.: Harvard Business Review Press.

Hofstede, G. (2001) *Culture's Consequences: Comparing Values, Behaviors, Institutions and Organizations*, 2nd edition. Thousand Oaks, Calif.: Sage.

Jackson, T. (ed.) (1995) *Cross-cultural Management*. Oxford: Butterworth-Heinemann.

Legge, K. (1995) *Human Resource Management: Rhetoric and Realities*. Basingstoke: Macmillan.

Parker, M. (ed.) (1998) *Ethics & Organizations*. London: Sage.

Stohl, C. (1995) *Organizational Communication: Connectedness in Action*. Thousand Oaks, Calif.: Sage. Also relevant to Chapter 7 of this book.

Sveiby, K. E. (1997) *The New Organizational Wealth*. San Francisco: Berrett-Koehler.

Trompenaars, F. (1993) *Riding the Waves of Culture: Understanding Cultural Diversity in Business*. London: Nicholas Brealey.

Wilson, E. (2001) *Organizational Behavior Re-assessed: The Impact of Gender*. Thousand Oaks, Calif.: Sage.

## REFERENCES

1. Paauwe, J. and P. Dewe (1995) 'Human resource management in multinational corporations: theories and models', in A-W. Harzing and J. V. Ruysseveldt (eds) *International Human Resource Management*. London: Sage.
2. Drucker, P. (1992) 'The new society of organizations', *Harvard Business Review*, Sep./Oct., pp. 95–104.
3. Van Dijk, J. J. J. (1995) 'Transnational management in an evolving European context' in T. Jackson (ed.) *Cross-cultural Management*. Oxford: Butterworth-Heinemann.
4. Calori, R., M. Steele and E. Yoneyama (1995) 'Management in Europe: learning from different perspectives', *European Management Journal*, vol. 13, no. 1, pp. 58–65.
5. Handy, C. (1995) 'Trust and the virtual organization', *Harvard Business Review*, May/June, pp. 40–50.
6. Segalla, M., L. Fischer and K. Sandner (2000) 'Making cross-cultural research relevant to European corporate integration: old problem, new approach', *European Management Journal*, vol. 18, no. 1, pp. 38–51.
7. Olie, R. (1990) 'Culture and integration problems in international mergers and acquisitions', *European Management Journal*, vol. 8, no. 2, pp. 206–215.
8. Schein, E. H. (1986) *Organizational Culture and Leadership*. San Francisco, Calif.: Jossey Bass.

9. *The Economist*, 22 July 2000.
10. Hofstede, G. (2001) *Culture's Consequences: Comparing Values, Behaviors, Institutions and Organizations*, 2nd edition. Thousand Oaks, Calif.: Sage.
11. Triandis, H. C., R. Brislin and C. Hui (1988) 'Cross-cultural training across the individualism–collectivism divide', *International Journal of Intercultural Relations*, vol. 12, pp. 269–289.
12. Schwartz, S. (1994) 'Cultural dimensions of values: toward an understanding of national differences', in U. Kim, H. C. Triandis, C. Kagitcibasi, S.-C. Choi and G. Yoon (eds) *Individualism and Collectivism*. Thousand Oaks, Calif.: Sage, pp. 85–119.
13. Tsao, J. C. (1997) 'Comparisons of cultural values between Taiwanese and American advertising', *Asian Journal of Communication*, vol. 7, no. 1, pp. 58–84.
14. Stephan, C. W., W. G. Stephan, I. Saito and S. M. Barnett (1998) 'Emotional expression in Japan and the United States: the non-monolithic nature of individualism and collectivism', *Journal of Cross-Cultural Psychology*, vol. 29, no. 6, pp. 728–748.
15. Kozan, M. K. and C. Ergin (1998) 'Preference for third party help in conflict management in the United States and Turkey: an experimental study', *Journal of Cross-Cultural Psychology*, vol. 29, no. 4, pp. 525–539.
16. Theiler, T. (1999) 'Viewers into Europeans? How the European Union tried to Europeanize the audiovisual sector, and why it failed', *Canadian Journal of Communication*, vol. 24, no. 4, pp. 557–587.
17. Wheeler, D. L. (1998) 'Global culture or culture clash: new information technologies in the Islamic world – a view from Kuwait', *Communication Research*, vol. 25, no. 4, pp. 359–376.
18. Hongladarom, S. (1998) 'Global culture, local cultures and the Internet: the Thai example', *Electronic Journal of Communication*, vol. 8, no. 3/4.
19. Niebuhr, R. (1932) *Moral Man and Immoral Society*. New York: Charles Scribner's Sons. Quoted in Ferre, John P. (1990) 'Communication ethics and the political realism of Reinhold Niebuhr', *Communication Quarterly*, vol. 38, no. 3, pp. 218–225.
20. Donaldson, T. (1992) 'The language of international corporate ethics', *Business Ethics Quarterly*, vol. 2, pp. 271–281.
21. Jones, T. M. and A. C. Wicks (1999) 'Convergent stakeholder theory', *Academy of Management Review*, vol. 24, no. 2, pp. 206–221.
22. Sveiby, K. E. (1997) *The New Organizational Wealth*. San Francisco: Berrett-Koehler.
23. McEvily, S., S. Das and K. McCabe (2000) 'Avoiding competence substitution through knowledge sharing', *Academy of Management Review*, vol. 25, no. 2, pp. 294–311.
24. Leana, C. R. and H. J. Van Buren (1999) 'Organizational social capital and employment practices', *Academy of Management Review*, vol. 24, no. 3, pp. 538–555.
25. Granovetter, M. (1985) 'Economic action and social structure: the problem of embeddedness', *American Journal of Sociology*, vol. 78, pp. 1360–1380.
26. Putnam, L. L. (1997) 'Organizational communication in the 21st century; informal discussion with M. Scott Poole, L. L. Putnam, and D. R. Seibold', *Management Communication Quarterly*, vol. 11, pp. 127–138.
27. Donaldson, op. cit.
28. Van Dijk, op. cit.
29. Segalla, Fischer and Sandner, op. cit.
30. Kramer, M. W. (1996) 'A longitudinal study of peer communication during job transfers: the impact of frequency, quality, and network multiplexity on adjustment', *Human Communication Research*, vol. 23, pp. 59–86.

31. Pruden, H. O. (1969) 'The outside salesman: interorganizational link', *California Management Review*, vol. 12, no. 2, pp. 57–64.
32. Handy, C. (1976) *Understanding Organizations*. Harmondsworth, Middlesex: Penguin.
33. Deal, T. E. and A. A. Kennedy (1982) *Corporate Cultures: The Rites and Rituals of Corporate Life*. Reading, Mass.: Addison-Wesley.
34. Weber, M. (1947) *The Theory of Social and Economic Organization*, translated by T. Parsons and A. M. Henderson. Chicago, Ill.: Free Press.
35. Handy, op. cit.
36. Argyris, C. (1990) *Overcoming Organizational Defences*. New York: Prentice Hall.
37. Pedler, M., J. Burgoyne and T. Boydell (1991) *The Learning Company*. London: McGraw-Hill.
38. Schein, op. cit.
39. Huysman, M. (2000) 'An organizational learning approach to the learning organization', *European Journal of Work and Organizational Psychology*, vol. 9, no. 2, pp. 133–145.
40. Crossan, M. M., H. W. Lane and R. E. White (1999) 'An organizational learning framework: From intuition to institution', *Academy of Management Review*, vol. 24, no. 3, pp. 522–537.
41. Isaacs, W. H. (1993) 'Dialogue, collective thinking and organizational learning', *Organizational Dynamics*, vol. 22, no. 2, pp. 24–39.
42. Drucker, op. cit.
43. Conger, J. A. (1993) 'The brave new world of leadership training', *Organization Dynamics*, vol. 22, no. 2, pp. 46–58.
44. Saee, J. (1999) 'Managing across cultural frontiers: an Australian perspective', *Journal of European Business Education*, vol. 8, no. 2, pp. 35–59.
45. Laurent, A. (1983) 'The cultural diversity of Western conceptions of management', *International Studies of Management and Organization*, vol. 13, nos. 1–2, pp. 75–96.
46. Gordon, C. (1996) *The Business Culture in France*. Oxford: Butterworth-Heinemann.
47. Ruigrok, W. and L. Achtenhagen (1999) 'Organizational culture and the transformation towards new forms of organizing', *European Journal of Work and Organizational Psychology*, vol. 8, no. 4, pp. 521–536.
48. Coleman, J. (1990) *Foundations of Social Theory*. Cambridge, Mass.: Harvard University Press.
49. Nahapiet, J. and S. Ghoshal (1998) 'Social capital, intellectual capital and the organizational advantage', *Academy of Management Review*, vol. 23, pp. 242–266.
50. Leana and Van Buren, op. cit.
51. Van Riel, C. B. M. (1997) 'Research in corporate communication: an overview of an emerging field', *Management Communication Quarterly*, vol. 11, no. 2, pp. 288–309.
52. Vaughn, M. A. (1995) 'Organization symbols: An analysis of their types and functions in a reborn organization', *Management Community Quarterly*, vol. 9, no. 2, pp. 219–250.
53. Tata, J. and S. R. Rhodes (1996) 'Impression management messages and reactions to organizational reward allocations: the mediating influence of fairness and responsibility', *Communication Quarterly*, vol. 44, no. 3, pp. 379–393.
54. Stohl, C. (1995) *Organizational Communication: Connectedness in Action*. Thousand Oaks, Calif.: Sage, pp. 69–71.
55. Sias, P. M., M. W. Kramer and E. Jenkins (1997) 'A comparison of the communication behaviors of temporary employees and new hires', *Communication Research*, vol. 24, no. 6, pp. 731–754.
56. Mumby, D. K. (1997) 'The problem of hegemony: Rereading Gramsci for organizational communication studies', *Western Journal of Communication*, vol. 61, no. 4, pp. 343–375.

57. Iedema, R. A. M. (1998) 'Institutional responsibility and hidden meanings', *Discourse & Society*, vol. 9, no. 4, pp. 481–500.
58. Marshall, J. (1993) 'Viewing organizational communication from a feminist perspective: A critique and some offerings', *Communication Yearbook*, vol. 16, pp. 122–143.
59. Miller, J. B. (1976) *Toward a New Psychology of Women*. Boston: Beacon.
60. Bogoch, B. (1994) 'Power, distance and solidarity: Models of professional–client interaction in an Israeli legal aid setting', *Discourse and Society*, vol. 5, no. 1, pp. 65–88.
61. Rice, R. E. (1989) 'Issues and concepts in research on computer-mediated communication systems', *Communication Yearbook*, vol. 12, pp. 436–476.
62. Saunders, C. S., D. Robey and K. A. Vaverek (1994) 'The persistence of status differentials in computer conferencing', *Human Communication Research*, vol. 20, pp. 443–472.
63. Fulk, J., J. Schmitz and D. Ryu (1995) 'Cognitive elements in the social construction of communication technology', *Management Communication Quarterly*, vol. 8, pp. 259–288.
64. Scott, C. R. (1999) 'The impact of physical and discursive anonymity on group members' multiple identifications during computer-supported decision making', *Western Journal of Communication*, vol. 63, no. 4, pp. 456–487.
65. Walther, J. B. (1994) 'Anticipated ongoing interaction versus channel effects on relational communication in computer-mediated interaction', *Human Communication Research*, vol. 20, pp. 473–501.
66. Walther, J. B. (1996) 'Group and interpersonal effects in international computer-mediated collaboration', *Human Communication Research*, vol. 23, no. 3, pp. 342–369.
67. Postmes, T., R. Spears and M. Lea (1998) 'Breaching or building social boundaries? SIDE-Effects of computer-mediated communication', *Communication Research*, vol. 25, no. 6, pp. 689–715.
68. Rice, R. E. (1982) 'Communication networking in computer conferencing systems: A longitudinal study of group roles and system structure' in M. Burgoon (ed.) *Communication Yearbook*, vol. 6. Beverly Hills, Calif.: Sage, pp. 925–944.
69. Adkins, M. and D. E. Brashers (1995) 'The power of language in computer-mediated groups', *Management Communication Quarterly*, vol. 8, pp. 289–322.
70. Mabrito, M. (2000) 'Computer conversations and writing apprehension', *Business Communication Quarterly*, vol. 63, no. 1, pp. 39–49.
71. Hall, E. T. (1976) *Beyond Culture*. Garden City, New York: Anchor.
72. Drummond, K. and R. Hopper (1991) 'Misunderstanding and its remedies: Telephone miscommunication', in N. Coupland, H. Giles and J. M. Wiemann (eds) *'Miscommunication' and Problematic Talk*. Newbury Park, Calif.: Sage, pp. 301–314.
73. Hiltz, S. R. and M. Turoff (1985) 'Structuring computer-mediated communication systems to avoid information overload', *Communications of the Association for Computing Machinery*, vol. 28, no. 7, pp. 680–689.
74. Hart, P., L. Svenning and J. Ruchinskas (1995) 'From face-to-face meeting to video teleconferencing: potential shifts in the meeting genre', *Management Communication Quarterly*, vol. 8, pp. 395–423.
75. Epstein, D. F. (1973) 'Positive effects of the multiple negative: Explaining the success of the black professional woman', in J. Huber (ed.) *Changing Women in a Changing Society*. Chicago: University of Chicago Press, (pp. 150–173), quoted in D. S. Davenport and J. M. Yurich (1991) 'Multicultural gender issues', *Journal of Counseling and Development*, Sept./Oct., vol. 70, pp. 64–71.

76. Hagendoorn, L. (1995) 'Inter-group biases in multiple group systems: the perception of ethnic hierarchies', in W. Stroebe and M. Hewstone (eds) *European Review of Social Psychology*, vol. 6, Chichester: John Wiley, pp. 199–228.
77. Cejka, M. A. and A. H. Eagly (1999) 'Gender-stereotypic images of occupations correspond to the sex segregation of employment', *Personality and Social Psychology Bulletin*, vol. 25, pp. 413–423.
78. Wendt, R. F. (1995) 'Women in positions of service: The politicized body', *Communication Studies*, vol. 46, nos. 3 & 4, pp. 276–296.
79. Mumby, D. K. (1998) 'On masculinity. Organizing men: Power, discourse, and the social construction of masculinity(s) in the workplace', *Communication Theory*, vol. 8, no. 2, pp. 164–183.
80. Dijker, A. J., M. A. Tacken and B. van den Borne (2000) 'Context effects of facial appearance on attitudes toward mentally handicapped persons', *British Journal of Social Psychology*, vol. 39, pp. 413–427.
81. Postmes, T., N. R. Branscome, R. Spears and H. Young (1999) 'Comparative processes in personal and group judgments: Resolving the discrepancy', *Journal of Personality and Social Psychology*, vol. 76, no. 2, pp. 320–338.
82. Schneider, K. T., R. T. Hitlan and P. Radhakrishnan (2000) 'An examination of the nature and correlates of ethnic harassment experiences in multiple contexts', *Journal of Applied Psychology*, vol. 85, no. 1, pp. 3–12.
83. Irvine, W. B. (2000) 'Beyond sexual harassment', *Journal of Business Ethics*, vol. 28, pp. 353–360.
84. Davidson, M. J. and C. L. Cooper (1992) *Shattering the Glass Ceiling: The Woman Manager*. London, Paul Chapman.
85. Dougherty, D. S. (1999) 'Dialogue through standpoint: Understanding women's and men's standpoints of sexual harassment', *Management Communication Quarterly*, vol. 12, no. 3, pp. 436–468.
86. Kanter, R. M. (1977) *Men and Women of the Corporation*. New York: Basic Books.
87. Brune, B. (2000) *The Business Case for Diversity*, www.diversityinc.com/

# 3 People at work

## CHAPTER INTRODUCTION

To interact effectively at work requires a grasp of the underlying reasons why people act as they do when dealing with one another in a work context. To help us here, there are two sets of 'universal' theories and research, dealing with processes and factors that are considered to affect everyone. One set focuses directly on interaction and the other is concerned with the general psychology of behaviour. Further understanding comes from a study of the influences on how people interact that come from their various group memberships.

This chapter aims to provide underpinning knowledge of work behaviour for dealing successfully with others at work through discussions of:

- theories of social exchange, equity, attribution and interaction;
- psychological constructs which help explain behaviour, especially values, motives, goals, emotions, beliefs (including assumptions, expectations and cognitive schemas), attitudes, intentions, abilities and personality traits;
- influences on interpersonal behaviour at work which are considered to stem from differences in people's backgrounds – their ethnicity, gender or age, for instance.

In reading all this material, readers should keep in mind that it applies just as much to themselves as to others. After all, they have as much reason to want to have insight into their own behaviour as to understand other people's.

## THEORIES OF WHY AND HOW PEOPLE INTERACT

It may be surprising that anyone has troubled to ask, let alone provide theories, about why and how people interact. To most people human nature appears inherently social. Recluses are rare. At work, in addition to human nature, there are pressures such as the requirements of the task and organisational norms to make people work interactively with others.

However, in our private lives, at least, we generally have a choice. We could avoid or postpone most of the encounters we in fact go ahead with. Even at work, there is often the alternative of sending a memo or an e-mail, or the larger choice of either working from home or in a job involving minimal human contact. More than this, though, there is evidence that one of the attractions of work for many people is precisely its social side. Theories that try to explain why, such as social exchange, equity, attribution and interaction theory, carry implications for how they do it and how to do it effectively, so they are briefly outlined below.

## Social exchange theory

As its name implies, social exchange theory treats all types of meeting between people as exchanges – in effect, as quasi-economic transactions.[1] When people meet others, it says, they hope and expect to gain some benefit and are prepared to give something in return. The others are doing the same. More than this, the theory assumes that individuals who interact are self-interested. They are trying to maximise their benefits while minimising their inputs to ensure a net positive balance for themselves from the exchange. (These benefits, inputs and outcomes are sometimes material but also 'social' resources. For instance, outcomes could include feeling that their social identity as a manager has been endorsed.) Other things being equal, people with more power will do better out of their dealings with others than those with less. For example, if Person A, who is a casually employed worker and needs time off for family matters, interacts with Person B, a senior manager who wants someone to do some overtime work in anti-social hours, the theory predicts that Person B, having more power, will gain more from the 'deal' than Person A, though both may gain something.

## Equity theory

Equity theory argues that individuals in any exchange evaluate their own and others' relative contributions and outcomes.[2,3] People consider social relationships to be fair if they think those involved are getting roughly equivalent outcomes in relation to their inputs. Positive inputs can include natural gifts such as beauty or intelligence as well as more deserving ones such as effort. Negative inputs like loss of temper are deducted.

## Attribution theories

Individuals try to make sense of situations by attributing what they see others do to a cause. They are active and constructive perceivers.[4] Heider, the originator of attribution theory, suggested that people tend to divide others' actions into two categories: those due mainly to their situation and those where personality has more effect. In particular, in the case of interactions, people try to make sense out of what happens between them and the other person. They try to do this even though they may have no hard data on which to base an attribution. One common way is to try to answer three questions. These questions apply a co-variation principle to provide common-sense tests of consensus, consistency and distinctiveness:[5]

1. Do other people behave in the same way as the person we are trying to understand?
2. Has this person behaved in this way in the past?
3. Does this person behave in this way in different situations?

If the answer to question 1 (consensus) is 'No', and to questions 2 (consistency) and 3 (distinctiveness) are 'Yes', perceivers attribute the behaviour to the personality. If question 1 gets a 'Yes', they are more likely to attribute the behaviour to the situation, especially if questions 2 and 3 get a 'No'. So, for instance, if John knows that something Jane has just said to him is untrue, his attribution, according to the co-variation principle, would depend on the following. If he found that other people in Jane's department were saying the same untruth and he had clear evidence that on other occasions Jane had been truthful, he would be likely to attribute her present untruth to the situational variables. For example, he might think she had been misinformed by her manager. The reverse evidence would probably lead him to regard it as a deliberate lie.

More recent work on attribution has focused on the effects. To do this, however, it has refined the original external/internal division of attributions. Instead, people are considered to distinguish among controllable/uncontrollable and stable/unstable causes as well as Heider's situational/personality ones. In judging others, controllable behaviours are evaluated more harshly than those deemed uncontrollable. Stable attributions impact more on future expectations than unstable ones do. People's internal attributions of their own behaviours, especially of successes or failures, affect their self-esteem more than external ones do.

## Interaction theory

These three theories about behaviour (self-interested social exchange, equity and attribution) form the basis a theory of interaction.[6] Such a theory demonstrates how elements of a social exchange context affect how individuals perceive their own positions relative to others and how these perceptions in turn influence the attributions they make for others' behaviour. Figure 3.1 shows the relationships between such concepts. Thus a theory of interaction states that people's attributions are influenced by their perception of the relative power and net contribution position. In turn, their perception is influenced by the real relative power and net contribution position. Suppose, for example, a manager, Mrs Smith, wanted to talk to a junior clerk, Vikram, she might say, 'Would you come in to my office for a minute, please, Vikram?' In a different context, one where Vikram and Mrs Smith were co-workers, he might attribute Mrs Smith's demand to her

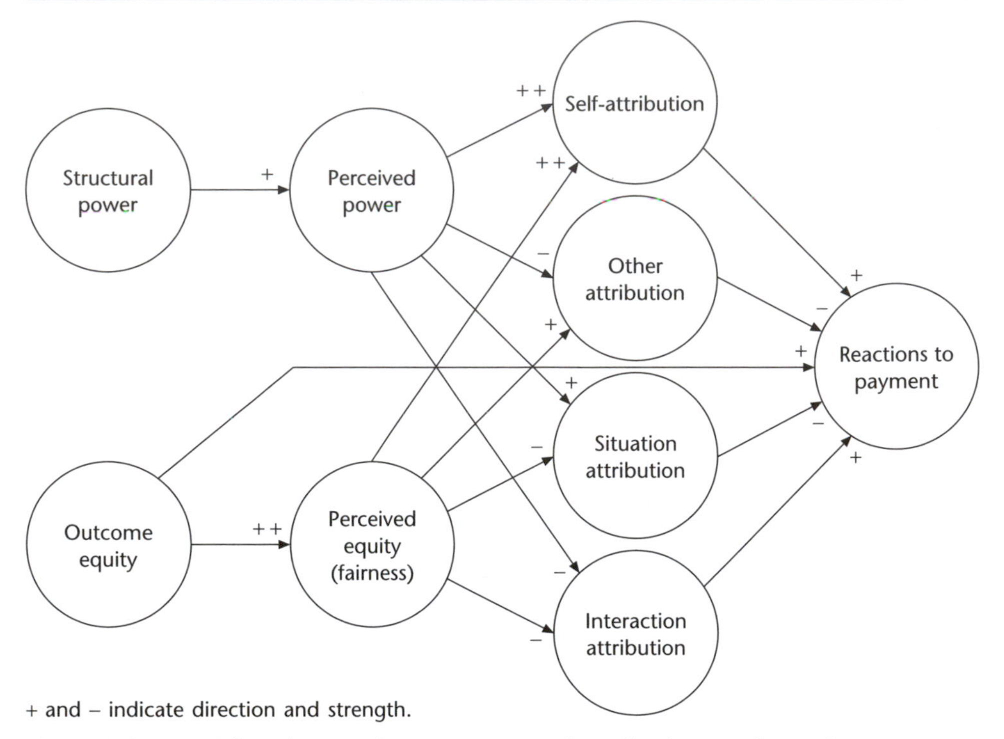


**Figure 3.1 A social exchange theory account of attributions and reactions to interaction outcomes.**

*Source*: Reprinted from Hegtvedt, K. A., E. A. Thompson and K. S. Cook (1993) 'Power and equity: What counts in attributions for exchange outcomes?', *Social Psychology Quarterly*, vol. 56, no. 2, pp. 100–119.

situation ('I wonder what's happened?'). However, in this case, because he perceives the power balance as favouring her, he might make an internal attribution ('What does she want this time?').

## SUMMARY – THEORIES OF WHY AND HOW PEOPLE INTERACT

Some aspects of interactive behaviour can be accounted for by combining theories that state the following. People treat interactions as exchanges whose outcomes are affected by the power balance. They are also concerned with the fairness of the balance between what individuals bring to a social exchange and what they take from it. They try to make sense of social situations by asking questions to decide the cause of others' behaviour. These attributions are influenced by their perceptions of the relative power position and contributions of the persons who are interacting. These perceptions are based on the actual situation. In turn their attributions affect their responses.

**Box 3.1**

### Critique of theories of how and why people interact

The theories outlined can help explain at least some instances of interactive behaviour, and may also have predictive power. Empirical research has often found good support for a number of hypotheses based on the theories (Molm, 1985). All the same, they all have certain weaknesses. First, their motivation theory is an impoverished one. Pursuit of self-interest scarcely captures the richness of the motivation theories described in the next section. Second, the role of power is exaggerated. We know that people often set the power balance aside in their face-to-face dealings. Third, the cognitive aspects of the theories are weak. Attribution theory, for instance, covers only a small part of the perception-, belief- and attitude-formation processes that we have reason to think occur.

The co-variation theory of how people decide their attributions requires people to be more objective information processors than other evidence would suggest. For instance, it has been demonstrated that people often attribute causes of their own and others' behaviour in a way that enhances or protects their own self-esteem (Zuckerman, 1979). Nevertheless, there is substantial evidence that people's inferences do in fact correspond to those that would be predicted by the theory. It is limited, though, to cases where the perceiver has multiple examples to compare.

The original distinction between situational and dispositional (external and internal) attributions has been criticised as 'so broad as to be meaningless', but it has received research support and the dichotomy is still widely used. The more elaborate set of attributions and their links to the perceiver's behaviour has been welcomed, though it is now considered probable that other attributions also occur.

*Sources*: Molm, L. D. (1985) 'Gender and power use: an experiential analysis of behaviour and perceptions', *Social Psychology Quarterly*, vol. 48, pp. 285–300.
Zuckerman, M. (1979) 'Attribution of success and failure revisited: the motivational bias is alive and well in attributional theory', *Journal of Personality*, vol. 47, pp. 245–287.

## PSYCHOLOGICAL CONSTRUCTS

The limitations of interaction theories mean we need to consider the more complex, but fuller, contributions of organisational psychology. Understanding more about why people do and say the things that they do to each other is essential to improving how we act in our own work encounters. All the skills described in this book depend on this understanding. Figure 3.2 shows the main psychological factors associated with individuals' behaviour. These constructs provide explanations for the behaviours we can directly observe but they cannot themselves be observed directly, only inferred. For this reason, we can only ever have theories about them, never certain knowledge. In spite of this, enough study and research have now been completed to satisfy many psychologists that these inferred constructs 'work'. They do provide consistent explanations for a wide range of behaviours and they do allow predictions of behaviour to be made successfully. Figure 3.2 also suggests how these psychological factors affect one another and how they affect behaviour. Attitudes, for instance, are thought to be

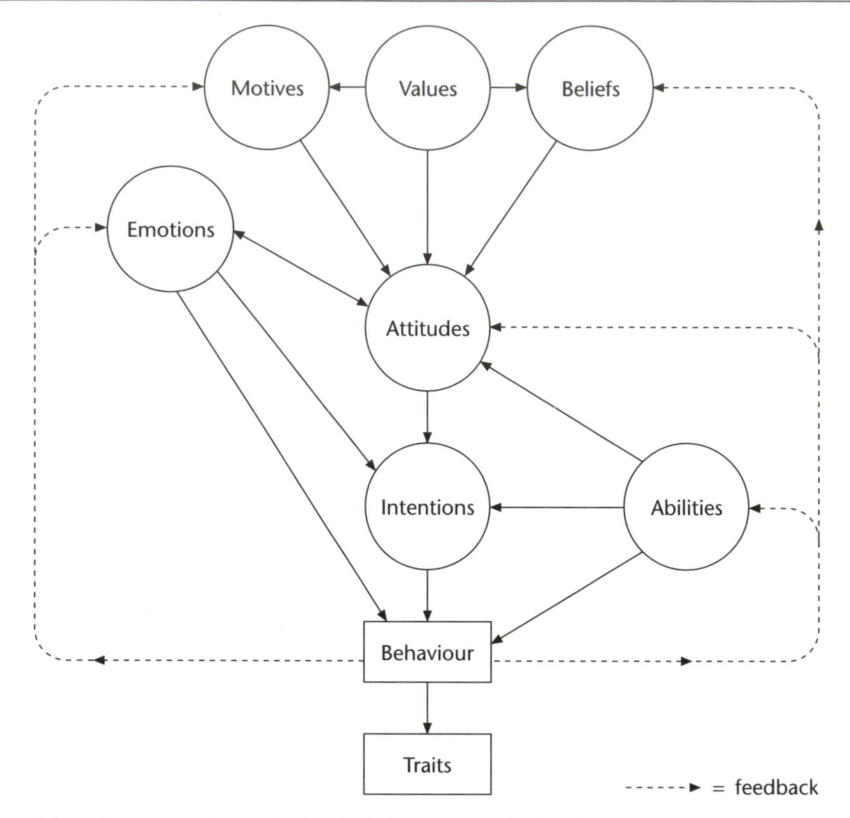


**Figure 3.2 Influence of psychological factors on behaviour.**

influenced by motives, values, emotions, and beliefs and they in turn influence intentions. Or, to take another example, our behaviour is related to what we intend to do, but we do not always carry out our intentions, because our abilities may prove inadequate, or because our emotions may intervene. Figure 3.2 is by no means complete and not everyone would agree with it even as a simplified version of the truth. But it does show why we need to try to understand values, motives, goals, emotions, beliefs, attitudes, intentions, abilities and traits if we are to understand and predict our own and other people's behaviour and to improve our own interpersonal skills. I will now discuss each in turn together with the closely related topics of the relationships among behaviour, intentions and attitudes and the causes of prejudice, discrimination and harassment.

## Values

Values are broad tendencies to prefer certain states of affairs over others. They are usually expressed by using terms such as evil or good, dirty or clean, ugly or beautiful, unnatural or natural, abnormal or normal, paradoxical or logical, irrational or rational. Values reflect our beliefs and morals as well as what we want for ourselves and want to do with our lives. Some values are religious, some humanist, some ecological. Some are cultural, some national, some familial. They have to do with our sense of good and bad. What we understand by and the importance we attach to questions of honesty, truthfulness, kindness, justice, cruelty to animals, conserving the planet, democracy, social equality, liberty and many other issues reflect our values. Accepted ways of thinking and knowing also reflect values. Fundamental values are considered to be at the core of cultural difference. Values are among the first things children learn, though not always consciously; many development psychologists believe that by the age of 10 most children have their basic value system firmly in place, and after that age, values are hard to change. Because they are acquired so early in life, many values remain unconscious. Therefore they cannot easily be discussed or revealed to outsiders.

## Motives

Motives are internal responses to needs. They result from inherited drives acting on felt needs. Needs are states of physical or psychological disturbance or discomfort. Needs, then, are conceived as being experienced by the individuals who have them as discomfort or pain, and, with drives, as motivating them to change their condition. Some needs are biological: for food, sex, rest. Others are learned: for esteem, power, self-fulfilment. Others – for security and affection – are intermediate between the learned and the biological needs. Recognising the needs that we and other people are attempting to satisfy helps in understanding our and their actions better.

Figure 3.3 shows a model of the motivation/behaviour process. Unfulfilled needs create a state of tension, felt as wanting, desiring, hoping, longing, fearing, irritation or anger. Inherited drives lead a person who feels a need to take action

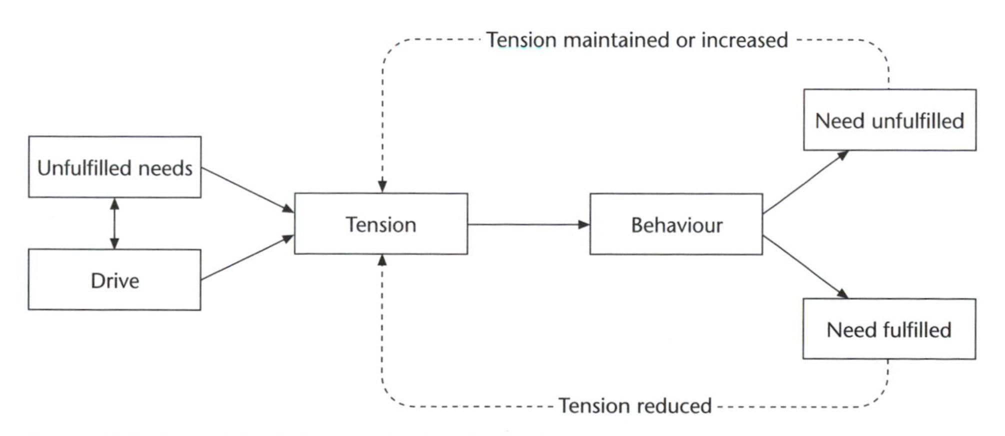


**Figure 3.3 A model of the motivation/behaviour process.**

to reduce the tension. The drives are generalised, that is to say they do not determine precisely what action will be taken. In one case, for instance, the response to the tension produced by the need for security might be to work harder at a current job, in another it might be to look around for a better-paid one. Factors other than drives help determine what the behavioural response to a need will be. These factors include beliefs and ideas, which are known technically as cognitions. If the behaviour in whole or in part satisfies the need, the tension is reduced and with it the activation of the drive. If it leaves the need unfulfilled or increases it, the tension is maintained or increased and the drive is re-activated.

The most influential analyst of people's motives for behaviour is Maslow[7] who proposed a five-fold classification of motives and needs into biological, security, affiliation, power/esteem and achievement. He also argued that these motives are arranged in a hierarchy of prepotency, whereby 'lower-order' needs are satisfied first and 'higher-order' ones only come into play when the lower-order ones are chronically gratified. Because Maslow's theory is now so widely known, I will not discuss it or the criticisms made of it in detail here. The reader is referred to the Further Reading section. However, Table 5.3 gives some cues that may reveal when people at work are being influenced by the various motives.

Another useful motive typology has been devised by McGuire.[8] This set is, perhaps, particularly relevant to this book, because it refers to motives that are closely related to communication. McGuire divides motives along four dimensions that are combined to yield 16 categories of motive. From a literature search, McGuire found that each of these motive categories could be related to a theory of behaviour put forward by one group or other of psychologists or psychoanalysts. Thus each of his 16 categories has received professional or academic support as relevant to the analysis of behaviour. Box 3.2 lists McGuire's motive categories, and briefly describes each one. For simplicity, however, it limits their classification to only two dimensions: those of internal–external focus and cognitive–affective orientation. The internal–external focus dimension distinguishes motives whose goals are internal to the person, i.e. non-social, from those whose goals are external, i.e. primarily social. The cognitive–affective dimension distinguishes the motives that orient versus those that energise the individual.

**Box 3.2**

## McGuire's motive categories and a critique

### The cognitive internal motives

1. The need for consistency. A basic desire is to have all facets of oneself consistent with each other – to attain an internal equilibrium. These facets include attitudes, beliefs, opinions and self-images.
2. The need to categorise – to make sense of the world in terms of our internal categories.

3. The need for autonomy. Self-esteem is related to a sense of having some control over what happens to us.
4. The teleological motives. People carry within their heads patterns of end states to which they strive to match their current perceptions of the world.

**The affective internal motives**

1. The need to reduce tension. The person can be viewed as a tension system such that any reduction of tension is gratifying and any increase aversive. Examples of tension theorists would include Freud.
2. The need for ego defence. Any perceived threat to someone's identity or self-image activates this need, and leads, generally, to defensive behaviour.
3. The need for assertion. As well as protecting their sense of self-worth, people need to increase both their self-esteem and the esteem they perceive others to hold them in.
4. The need for identification. People seek ego enhancement through the addition of satisfying roles to their self-concepts.

**The cognitive social motives**

1. The need to attribute causes. This is a set of motives that deals with people's need to determine what or who causes the things that happen to them.
2. The objectification needs. People use externals such as their own overt behaviour, that of other people, or various situational factors, to infer their own attitudes, feelings, satisfactions, etc.
3. The need for stimulation. The individual seeks novelty and is characteristically inquisitive, seeking after knowledge.
4. The utilitarian motives. People can be seen as striving problem-solvers, using external situations as opportunities to acquire new information or new skills for coping with life's challenges.

**The affective social motives**

1. The need for self-expression. People can gain gratification from letting others know by their actions who and what they are. It is externally focused, because the need is to express identity to other people.
2. The need for reinforcement. People need rewards and engage in behaviours that seem likely to produce rewards. When a certain behaviour has been rewarded in the past, they are motivated to repeat it.
3. The need for affiliation. There is a need to develop helpful and satisfying relationships with others, in order to be a member of certain groups.
4. The need for modelling. Basing behaviour on that of others is a common way of learning: part of the expression of this need is the tendency to like other people who are seen as similar to the self.

It seems clear that McGuire's set of motives are not all based on fundamental human needs. Some, such as the 'need' for novelty, appear simply to reflect behavioural tendencies which may or may not be based on needs. Others, such as the need to attribute causes, are learned, not innate. Still others of McGuire's set of motives can be derived from Maslow's set – the reinforcement need, for instance, from Maslow's affiliation and esteem needs. In addition, McGuire has no theory equivalent to Maslow's prepotency hierarchy to explain the inter-relations of his motive categories. Thus, McGuire's contribution to the psychology of motivation is necessarily a limited one. His expanded list of motives that may underlie people's behaviour is, however, a useful one for understanding or interpreting behaviour, and it is for that reason that it is given here.

## Goals

In psychological theory, goals (or objectives) are often subsumed under motives, but in practical work terms they are worth distinguishing. From selection interviewers to marketers, people at work need to know what those with whom they interact are consciously trying to achieve for themselves. Two types of personal goals are generally distinguished: extrinsic (such as fame, wealth or positive image) and intrinsic (such as personal growth, relatedness and community). Recent research on samples from two cultures (the United States and Russia) found that intrinsic values were rated as more important than extrinsic in both of these very different cultures.[9] This finding is consistent with the argument that intrinsic goals are better at fulfilling basic psychological needs. They are probably universal.[10]

## Emotions

Emotions are feelings. They are linked to needs and motives. For example, a person who is experiencing the emotion of hate may be motivated to seek relief by acts intended to harm another. It has been shown that six basic kinds of emotion are perceived by most people: love, happiness, surprise, anger, sadness and fear. This finding has been replicated across diverse cultures and age groups. For example, subjects from 14 countries judged the same facial expressions as showing fear, surprise, anger, disgust, contempt and sadness.

It can be hard to identify emotions – our own as well as other people's – partly because 'any emotion . . . is a complex and multifaceted phenomenon',[11] and for

**Box 3.3**

### How to identify emotions that others are experiencing

- Emotional states can be linked to physical reactions such as changes in blood pressure, heart beat rate, sweating and trembling. Some of these can be observed and give a clue to a person's emotional state. It can be useful merely to realise that someone is affected by emotion, even without knowing precisely what emotion they are feeling.
- Emotions are linked to motives: the better you understand someone's motivational pattern, the more likely you are to perceive accurately what emotion they are feeling.
- Emotions are triggered by something a person experiences. To identify their emotion, it helps to be observant about what is happening to them and sensitive to how they are likely to perceive it.
- There is evidence that when people experience emotional arousal they quite often identify which particular emotion it is they are experiencing by observing how other people react (Schacter and Singer, 1962). Our bodies do not distinguish among emotions very well. Both euphoria and extreme anger, for instance, are associated with rapid heart beat, trembling and sweating. Therefore, whether a particular piece of news at work, say about planned redundancies, leads someone to feel fear or, on the other hand, to be angry, is likely to be influenced by how those around seem to respond to it. Even when a person

**Box 3.3** ***continued***

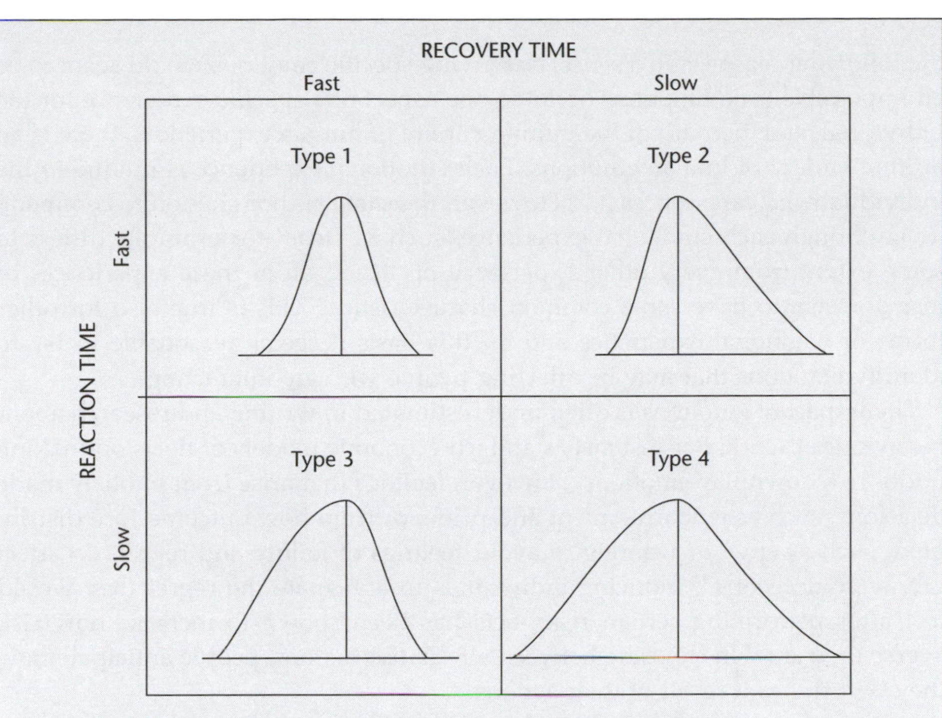


**Figure 3.4 Comparative emotional reaction/recovery times.**

*Source*: Reprinted with permission of the publisher from Boshear, W. C. (1981) 'Thinking about feelings' in J. W. Pfeiffer and J. E. Jones (eds) *The 1981 Annual Handbook for Group Facilitators*. San Diego, Calif.: University Associates.

has no way of knowing the reasons for others' reactions, they are still likely to base their own on them. Thus in groups or meetings people in similar situations may well be experiencing similar emotions.

- Emotions mount and pass at variable rates. The more intense emotions usually pass quickly, though they are powerful influences on behaviour while they last. Fear, for instance, often turns to anger quite soon and most people's anger (or euphoria) quickly stops being an active state. There is also variability from individual to individual in the rates at which emotions build up and die away. Emotional reaction and recovery times for different individuals can usefully be plotted on the kind of diagram shown in Figure 3.4. A Type 1 individual is volatile. Their emotion builds up quickly, but fades equally fast. For the Type 2 individual, emotional build-up is rapid, but the feeling is persistent. This person is potentially in the grip of emotion for long periods of time. Type 3 is relatively unemotional: slow to react, but getting over his/her emotion fast. Type 4 takes a long time to reach an emotional peak, but then takes a long time getting over it (Boshear, 1981). Naturally, also, the peak level of emotion varies from one person to another and from situation to situation.
- Non-verbal behaviour often gives the best clue to emotions, even those that people are trying to control or conceal.

*Sources*: Boshear, W. C. (1981) 'Thinking about feelings' in J. W. Pfeiffer and J. E. Jones (eds) *The 1981 Annual Handbook for Group Facilitators*, San Diego, Calif.: University Associates.
Schacter, S. and J. E. Singer (1962) 'Cognitive, social and physiological determinants of emotional state', *Psychological Review*, vol. 69, pp. 379–399.

the following reasons: 'In a sense, classifying specific emotions would seem to be an impossible task. Emotions occur as one aspect of a specific experience for the individual, and, because of the infinite variety of human experiences, there is an infinite variety of human emotions. Each emotional experience is unique to the individual who experiences it.'[12] However, the same author goes on to comment, 'Even though each emotional experience, such as "fear" for example, differs to some extent from every other experience of "fear", all of these experiences of fear do seem to have some common characteristics.' This is true also for other forms of emotional experience and on this basis it seems reasonable to try to identify emotions that may be affecting people who are interacting.

The impact of emotions is often underestimated in writing and research about behaviour at work. For instance, standard economic models of decision-making under risk downplay emotions. However, feelings that arise from publicly made decisions, such as embarrassment and pride, or from how outcomes are distributed, such as envy or wanting to avoid feelings of failure and regret, do affect economic decisions.[13] Inducing individuals to anticipate the regret they would feel after performing certain risky acts has been shown to increase how risk averse they are.[14] In choosing between alternative actions, people anticipate how they will feel as a result of their actions.

In more general psychology and in sociology, the study of the emotions is a burgeoning field. Emotions are recognised as critically involved in social control, role performance and interpersonal interaction. Recent studies have expanded our understanding of emotions by developing and testing models of how emotions are stimulated and displayed and by researching cultural variations in emotional stimulation and display. One model of emotion episodes has four elements: instigators, cognitive concomitants, physiological reaction and behavioural manifestations. So an example of an anger episode would tend to have the following elements: being treated unfairly (instigator), obsessive thinking about the event (cognitive concomitant), increased heart rate (physiological reaction) and yelling (behavioural manifestation).[15] Another model of how emotions are stimulated and displayed includes the following seven components:

1. Emotions are provoked by antecedent events. Individuals and cultures vary in what events they are emotionally sensitive to.
2. Events are coded by categorising them in terms that are recognised by the culture as relevant to particular emotions, e.g. as humiliation, insult, revenge or bereavement. Emotions are generally not elicited by events as such but by events as coded in terms of a particular event type.
3. Coded events are appraised for their implications for the subject's well-being and capability of coping with the event; so, for instance, as harmful, uncertain, someone else's fault, uncontrollable.

4. There may be a physiological reaction. This may correspond to stereotyped expectations, e.g. trembling with fear.
5. Emotional states involve changes, both of kind and degree, in people's readiness to act. For instance, getting ready to run goes with fear, the impulse to shout joyously goes with euphoria at sudden good news.
6. Action tendencies may result in directly expressive overt behaviour.
7. Individuals can regulate – either inhibit or enhance – their emotional responses.

This model corresponds quite well to how most people mentally represent emotions, as a set of antecedent events, plus physiological, cognitive, expressive and behavioural responses. This applies to people from all cultures. On the other hand, the content of the components varies. For example, Europeans and Americans are more likely to cite bodily pain or pleasure as antecedents to emotions than Japanese people are.[16]

## Beliefs

Beliefs are thoughts (cognitions) to which some degree of credence is attached. (Other kinds of cognitions, such as ideas or daydreams, may lack this element of being believed.) Beliefs affect behaviour, though not as much as common-sense would suggest. Three kinds of beliefs are of special interest for understanding interactive behaviour: assumptions, expectations and cognitive schemas.

### *Assumptions*

Assumptions are taken-for-granted beliefs that people rarely think or speak about.[17] This makes them harder to detect and may increase their behavioural effect. We all normally operate on the basis of a large set of assumptions about the objective existence and nature of the physical world, although these assumptions are disputed by many philosophers and physicists. Most people also operate with a large number of assumptions about their social world. For instance, they assume that people will behave differently at the office from in a nightclub, that people carrying briefcases are office workers, that being made redundant causes others grief, getting a large bonus joy, and so on. Personal experience may lead us to question these social beliefs, and so become conscious of them, and certainly they lack the universality of beliefs about the physical world, but nevertheless everyone operates with a large number of assumptions about human behaviour. Otherwise, they could not operate in the social world at all. The following are four sets of assumptions that have been studied for their effect on behaviour at work:

1. The best-known set concerns managers' views of their subordinates. Early research by McGregor[18] and his followers suggested that managers either assume

that people are naturally lazy and unwilling to work, which is known as a Theory X view, or that work is as natural as play, called a Theory Y view. Theory Y is the assumption that most people have the capacity to take responsibility for directing their own efforts. If people are passive, indolent and irresponsible on the job it is because of their experience in organisations and not because of some inherent weakness. Managers with Theory X assumptions believe people must be bribed, frightened or manipulated if they are to put forth any effort at all. Managers with Theory Y assumptions believe in providing intrinsic rewards such as responsibility or interesting work. Clearly, whether a manager holds a Theory X or Theory Y view is likely to strongly affect his or her interactive behaviour with subordinates.

**Box 3.4**

An estate agent commented on a purchaser's insistence on having a second timber damp survey after the first had reported no problems: 'I think it's because he's a doctor; he believes in getting a second opinion.'

*Source*: Interview, author's research.

2. Negotiators make assumptions about their opponents.[19,20] Some negotiators – hard-liners – assume their opponents to be deliberately 'trying it on' rather than defending central values. Soft-liners assume that their opponents are pursuing limited and to some degree legitimate goals. Hard-liners believe their opponents will extract any concessions they can get and that conciliation is only likely to lead to further demands but that they will back down if confronted with firm resolve. Soft-liners believe that their opponents will be willing to compromise and seek agreement. Conciliation, for them, represents a viable way forward.

3. A third set of assumptions is about interpersonal behaviour itself. People have different beliefs about how other people are likely to respond to different ways of being treated, different perceptions of others' motives and different beliefs about how to handle relationships and situations most effectively.

4. Probably the most pervasive, but least openly recognised, set of assumptions is that personality can be sex-typed. Femininity includes such gender characteristics as emotionality, sensitivity, nurturance and interdependence, and is generally attributed to women. Masculinity connotes emotional inhibitedness, assertiveness, independence, dominance and goal directedness. Most people assume masculinity to be the prerogative of men. However, equating gender characteristics with sex is increasingly recognised as a false assumption. They are now believed to be learned characteristics. It is both possible and common

for women and men to vary in the degree to which they adopt and are affected by gender roles.[21] It is not sex that matters, but those life conditions that are systematically related to it by cultural prescription, regulation or arrangement. The sexes face on a daily basis different messages, expectations, resources and opportunities.[22] People who hold the false assumptions that gender characteristics are determined by biological sex are likely to be prejudiced in their interactive work behaviour.

In addition to these four sets of assumptions, there are undoubtedly many others that influence how people act at work. Because people are often unaware of their own assumptions, and because any evidence that is obtained in the course of everyday life can usually be interpreted to fit in with quite contrary assumptions, these are slow to change.

### *Expectations*

Expectations are another kind of belief that colour interpretations of behaviour and so affect responses to other people during interactions. For example, suppose someone expects young, fair-haired women to be submissive. Then if such a woman responds to a request to work late with, 'I'll think about it', they might interpret it as unthinking acceptance, and act accordingly, when she actually said exactly what she meant.

### *Cognitive schemas*

Cognitive schemas are mental structures representing information about a topic. They vary in strength and accessibility. Take selection interviewing: a head hunter or personnel manager would have a strong and accessible cognitive schema about it, a production manager would have one of middle strength and accessibility, while a plumber might have only a weak and rather inaccessible one. Cognitive schemas relevant to interacting with others include those about other cultures and episode representations. These are thoughts about, or images of, interactions. Forgas, the originator of episode representation theory, argues that most people think of interactions mainly in terms of a small number of dimensions such as self-confidence, intimacy, involvement and formality rather than, for instance, the details of what happens. For example, one person may think of a particular encounter mainly in terms of intimacy, while another represents it to himself or herself mainly in terms of formality. How effectively two or more people interact is seen as directly related to how similar their episode representations are – to what degree they have 'matching and shared episode representations'.[23–25] The theory draws on the widely accepted statement that 'For interactions to succeed, participants must essentially agree in their social situation definition.'[26]

Research findings based on Forgas's theory have shown the following:

- socially skilled individuals see episodes more in terms of evaluation and intensity, while people who are low in social skills see them mainly in terms of anxiety;
- members of more cohesive teams have more complex episode representations of their team interactions (based on three dimensions: friendliness, intimacy and activity) than fragmented groups (with two dimensions: evaluation and friendliness);
- knowing the rules and norms governing recurring everyday interactions or social episodes is essential for good communication.

Figure 3.5 charts the different kinds of beliefs described above.

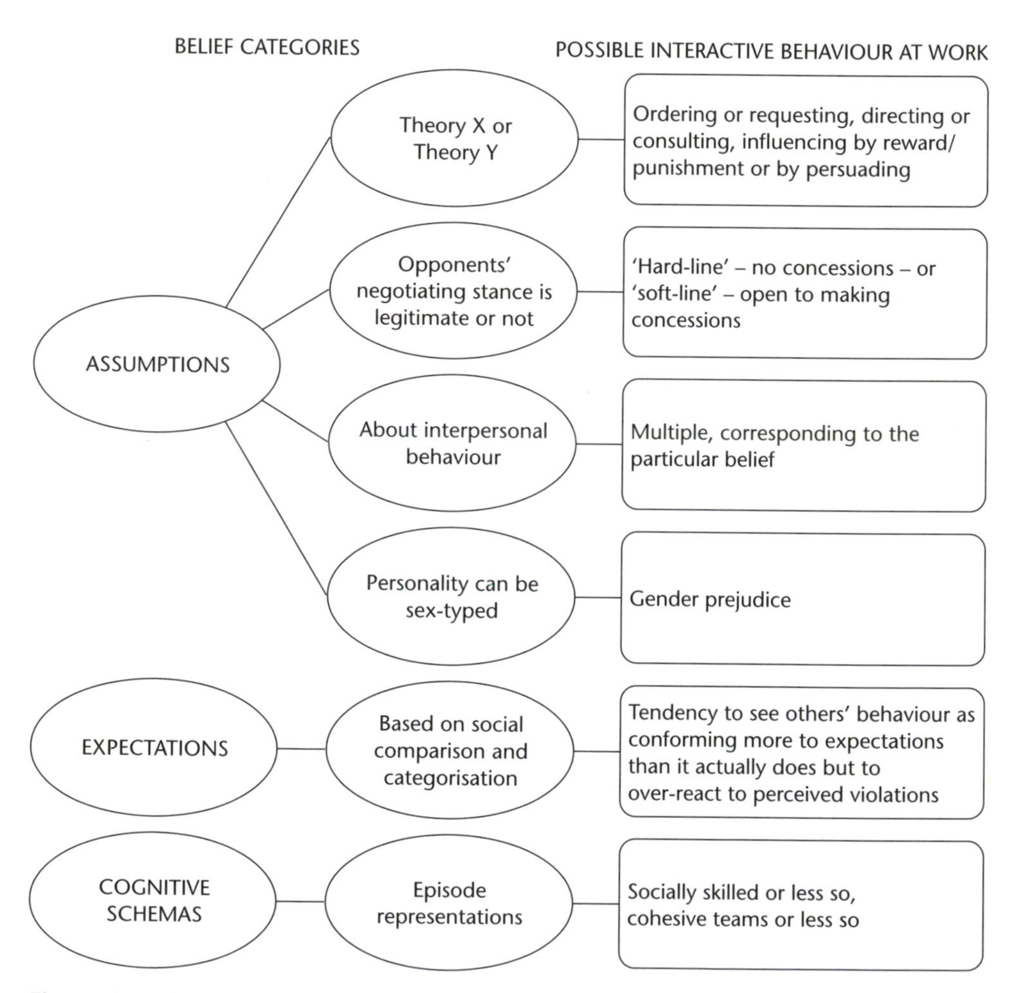


**Figure 3.5 Kinds of beliefs and how they may affect interactive behaviour at work.**

## Attitudes

Attitudes are favourable or unfavourable dispositions towards objects, people and events or towards attributes of any of these. 'I like apples' expresses an attitude; so do 'doing business with you is a pleasure', 'school dinners are disgusting' and 'doing accounts is boring'. 'John is well-meaning' or 'Brand X is cheaper' on the other hand, may or may not be attitudes, depending on whether or not the speaker has any view on well-meaningness or cheapness in that context. They could be neutral statements of beliefs without any evaluative content. One classic description of attitudes is that they are 'enduring organisations of motivational, emotional, perceptual and cognitive processes with respect to some aspect of our environment'.[27] This description emphasises the relationship between attitudes and the factors already discussed in this chapter. It stresses the point that attitudes are influenced by people's needs, feelings and beliefs.

A way of conceptualising an attitude that is related to this classic description is the so-called tri-component concept of what attitudes are. According to this theory, attitudes are composed of beliefs, feelings, known as affect, and action tendencies. Figure 3.6 shows the relationships among these factors; they overlap but are not identical. Each of these components is now looked at in more detail.

1. As attitude components, beliefs are of two kinds: what the person believes about the facts of a situation, which are labelled the informational beliefs, and evaluative beliefs. These consist of what the person believes about the merits, demerits, rights, wrongs, benefits or costs of different situations. For example, Manager A might have an informational belief that only half the members of his/her department were trained to a sufficient standard in computing skills and an evaluative belief that it was important for the efficiency of the operation that all members of the department were so trained. The combination of these beliefs would influence Manager A's attitude to how any staff development budget for the department should be spent. Manager B might have a different

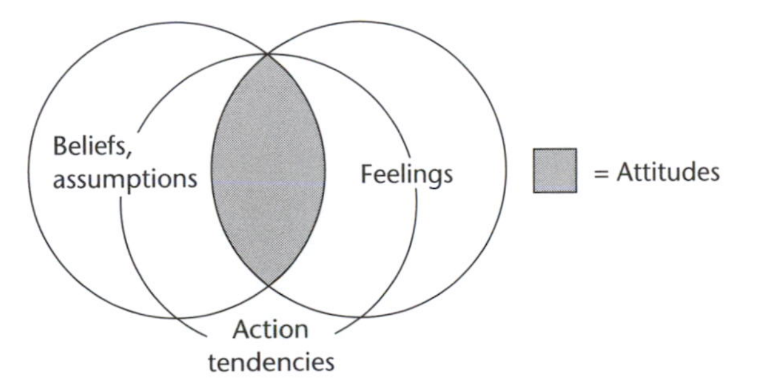


**Figure 3.6 The tri-component theory of attitudes.**

attitude from Manager A. This attitude could result from a different informational belief, for instance that all members of the department were sufficiently trained in computing skills. Or it could result from a different evaluative belief such as that, apart from certain specialists, for the members of the department to have computing skills would not add to its efficiency. The belief components of many attitudes are in the form of the kind of unquestioned assumptions described earlier. This is especially the case for the evaluative beliefs, which cannot be verified or refuted in the same way as informational beliefs.

2. The term 'affect' refers to someone's overall feeling or evaluation about a situation. The technical term is worth grasping to help prevent confusion with the kinds of feelings that are synonymous with emotions. Unlike the belief components, which usually relate to all the different aspects of the situation that an individual perceives, the affect component relates to how s/he feels about the situation as a whole. The affect element of an attitude can be measured on a scale from extremely poor to excellent or from strong dislike to strong liking. For instance, Manager A, in the staff computer-training example, might feel that the situation is unsatisfactory, while Manager B feels that it is acceptable. The main thing that distinguishes an attitude from a belief or opinion, then, is the positive or negative affect that a person has about something. A few attitudes consist almost entirely of the affect element. Simple statements such as 'I like apples' usually express attitudes that are composed almost entirely of affect. However, beliefs or opinions are part of nearly all attitudes. This is fortunate from the point of view of anyone who is trying to change others' attitudes, because research shows that the belief element of an attitude is easier to change than the affect element,[28] especially if a state of uncertainty about the facts of the matter can be aroused.

3. Holders of attitudes, according to tri-component theory, tend to act in a way that is consistent with the attitude. To continue our example, Manager A would be more likely than Manager B to spend any staff development budget on computer training for the half of the department s/he perceives to be less than sufficiently trained. However, as I shall discuss below, there are many question marks hanging over this matter of how far attitudes are normally carried through to behaviour.

Attitudes are learned or acquired, not inborn, but in many adults some attitudes, such as those to money, health and work, are central to their sense of what sort of person they are and to their personal values. In addition to centrality, attitudes can be seen as having two other dimensions, consistency and intensity. Consistency refers to the degree to which the three components of the attitude are similar or consistent with each other. For instance, a manager who persists in writing detailed memoranda to explain planned changes to staff despite believing that it would be more effective to hold meetings for the purpose and feeling anxious about the matter, has an attitude to the issue which is low in consistency. Intensity refers to the strength of the feeling involved in an attitude. Two people may both feel that the secretarial provision in a department should be reorganised, but one may feel strongly about it and the other only mildly.

**Box 3.5**

**European variations in attitudes to time**

For Germans and Swedes, punctuality is vital. In the Netherlands, poor punctuality is seen as indicating untrustworthiness.

In France, up to 15 minutes slippage is accepted and schedules can be changed at short notice for something 'more important'. In Britain, a similar amount of slippage is accepted for the start of an appointment but meetings frequently over-run by hours.

Italian attitudes to time are flexible. In Spain, delay and poor punctuality is widespread. In both these countries there is a tendency to try to cram in more than can be done in the time.

Attitudes can be ambivalent – that is, both positive and negative at the same time. Ambivalent attitudes are based on conflicting evaluations. Ambivalence is important because it results in unstable attitudes and extreme responses toward the attitude object. For example, at work competent members of ethnic minorities may be evaluated in an especially favourable way, whereas incompetent members of ethnic minorities may be evaluated in an especially unfavourable way. That is to say, ambivalent attitudes can lead to response amplification.[29]

Since the work of Moscovici[30] in the 1960s, many European social psychologists have recognised the existence of what we might call group attitudes, though they are known as social representations. When a group of individuals is confronted with something complex or unknown that has genuine social implications, they jointly construct a representation or view about it. Examples might include getting an education or making a profit. Members of a group who use these representations, either in thought or speech, will not just be making an observation but be including a positive or negative evaluation based on the group consensus.[31] Attitudes are most likely to predict behaviour when they are supported by these in-group norms.

## Intentions

Intentions are mental plans of action. Behaviour may be predicted from intention, provided that the target, action, time frame and context of the behaviour in the intention and the behaviour are equally specific and the time interval between

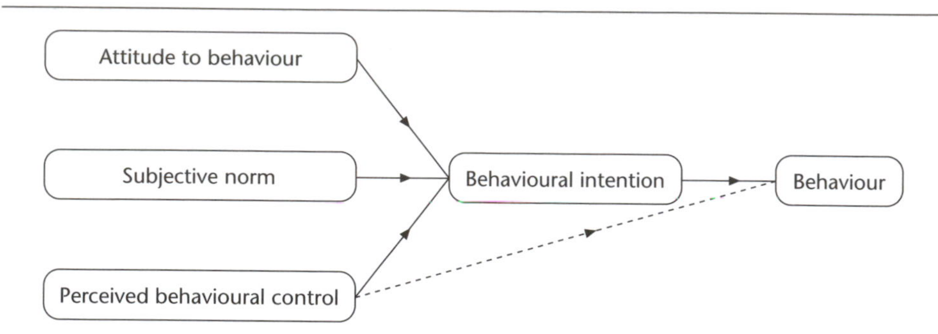


**Figure 3.7 Antecedents of behavioural intention found by Babrow *et al.***

the two measures is minimal. Thus, when they can be measured accurately, intentions usually predict what someone will do quite well – better than attitudes.[32] Even so, there are generally plenty of opportunities for things to intervene to prevent people carrying out their intentions. For instance, a person may fully intend to keep calm during a difficult meeting, but in the event be provoked into a display of temper, or may sincerely intend to arrive in good time for an interview but get delayed by a transport breakdown.

People's awareness of their own intentions is high in comparison, for instance, with their awareness of their own motives or even attitudes. This means that they can more readily reveal them but also more readily conceal or disguise them if they choose to. Working out people's intentions may not only help predict what they will do but also provide a route to understanding their attitudes or traits. Conversely, when a person's intentions cannot be assessed directly, it is useful to be able to infer them from antecedent variables, such as attitudes. Some research has been done into what antecedents are most closely linked to intentions. For instance, a 1990 study[33] found that people's intention to take part in a programme to give up smoking was predicted by their attitudes about participating, what they thought other people thought they should do, and how much control they believed themselves to have in the matter (in that order). (See Figure 3.7.) A 1996 study found that people's intentions to change their jobs could be linked to their perceptions of their interactions with top administrators, co-workers and superiors.[34]

## Relations among behaviour, intentions and attitudes

There has been research into the relationship between attitudes and behaviour for more than half a century. At first, it was expected that a strong influence of attitudes on behaviour would be found, but not the reverse. However unlikely it may seem, though, it has become clear that behaviour affects attitudes at least as much as attitudes affect behaviour. If people can be made to change what they do, they will bring their attitudes into line.[35] For example, if sales representatives regard filling out certain reports as a waste of time, it may well work better simply to insist that they do it, like it or not, than to try to get them to do it by persuading them of the reports' usefulness. Once they are filing the reports regularly they will usually be more easily convinced of their value, because then the pressure to preserve consistency is working in that direction. It can readily be seen how useful this aspect of the attitude–behaviour relationship can be in dealing with people at work. Unfortunately, though, this comparatively simple set of links is now seen as only a part of a highly complex phenomenon.

The most widely accepted model of the attitude–behaviour relationship is known as the theory of reasoned action (TRA). Its main difference from other models, and the feature that seems to give it more predictive power than them, is that it deals, not with attitudes to people, objects or institutions, but only with attitudes to actions. Thus the model suggests that instead of trying to predict how people will vote from their attitudes to parties, policies and political personalities, we should try to predict whether they will vote in a particular way from their attitude to voting in that way. The model was put forward in 1967 by Fishbein and Ajzen,[36] and was later modified by them with the addition of a new main variable.

In its later, modified, form, the theory states that behaviour is determined directly by an intention to perform it. Intention, in turn, is influenced by attitude (i.e. a person's positive or negative evaluation of performing the behaviour) and by subjective norm (i.e. the perceived social pressure to perform or not to perform the behaviour). Finally, the anticipated consequences of performing or not performing the behaviour affect both attitude and subjective norm. For attitude, a belief that performing the behaviour will lead to specific outcomes combines with evaluations of the outcomes. For subjective norm, a belief that specific individuals expect one to perform or not to perform the behaviour combines with one's motivation to comply with these specific individuals. So, the theory suggests, if Julie works through her lunch break, it is because she intends to do so. In turn, her intentions are influenced by her positive attitude towards working hard (or her negative attitude towards eating lunch) and by her awareness of social pressure to work through lunch. Her attitudes are affected by her belief about the outcome for her of working through lunch, for instance, a belief that a promotion will depend on quickly finishing the report she is working on, and her evaluation of those beliefs – perhaps she places a high value on being promoted. Her susceptibility to social pressure is also affected by her beliefs. She will be more likely to continue working through her lunch breaks if she believes that people she wants to be accepted by, such as her boss, expect her to skip lunch. TRA has been assessed as 'intuitive, insightful, explanatory and

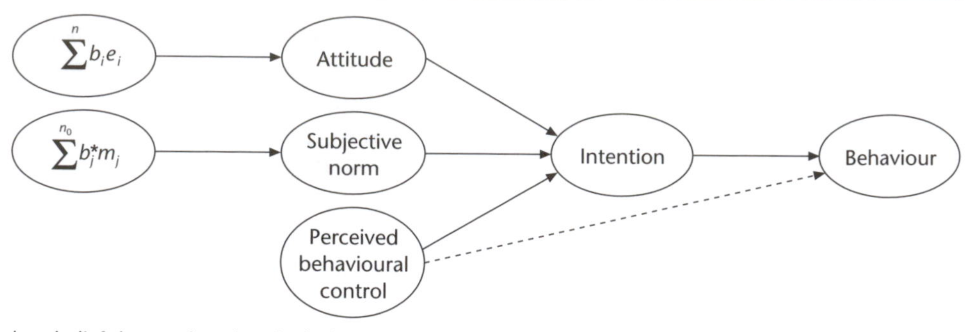


$b_i$ = belief that performing the behaviour will lead to specific outcomes;
$e_i$ = evaluations of the outcomes;
$n$ = number of instances;
$b_j^*$ = belief that specific individuals expect one to perform or not perform the behaviour;
$m_j$ = motivation to comply with these specific individuals.

**Figure 3.8 Fishbein and Ajzen's theory of planned behavior.**

parsimonious';[37] it has been applied successfully in predicting consumer, health, voting, recreational and organisational behaviour.

TRA applies only to volitional behaviour, where the person acting has full control. Much behaviour falls into another category where we have only partial control of what we do – we intend to catch the train, but it is cancelled, we intend to keep the appointment but we forget. Because we know these things can happen, our intentions take them into account. Fishbein and Ajzen therefore elaborated their theory, to extend it to behaviours not completely under volitional control, where actions are subject to interference by internal and external forces. They called this new version the theory of planned behaviour (TPB) and again it involves the addition of a variable, perceived behavioural control or PBC. PBC is defined as 'the person's belief as to how easy or difficult the performance of the behaviour is likely to be'. PBC normally affects intention along with attitude and subjective norm. It can also directly affect behaviour (bypassing intention) when PBC can be considered to 'correspond reasonably well' to actual control. However, research suggests this is a rare case. We generally have less or more behavioural control than we think we have. TPB has been found to work, that is to allow behaviour to be predicted, in studies of class attendance by college students, weight loss and voting, job seeking, giving gifts, exercising, using condoms, and so on. In 1991, Ajzen[38] reviewed 16 TPB studies which included measures of attitudes, subjective norms, perceived behavioural control and intentions and found that the multiple correlations with intentions ranged from 0.43 in the case of intention to participate in an election to 0.94 in the case of intentions to play video games.[39,40] The average multiple correlation was 0.71 (see Figure 3.8).

**Box 3.6**

## Critique of TRA and TPB theories

It has been suggested by Bagozzi (1992) that the key links in the theories need refinement by the introduction of 'self-regulatory' processes consisting of appraisal, emotional reactions and coping responses. For example, it is argued, a person will appraise the outcome of a behaviour in terms of whether it will conflict with, fulfil or otherwise interact with his or her desires. This appraisal will lead to specific emotions, such as fear or hope, and the emotions in turn will lead the person to modify his or her intentions in order to cope with the emotion aroused. So, according to this view, although Julie's intentions about working through lunch are influenced by her positive attitude towards her work (or her negative attitude towards eating lunch) and by her awareness of social pressure not to take a lunch break, and in turn, her attitudes are affected by her beliefs about the outcome for her of working through her lunch time and her evaluation of those beliefs, she may not form an intention to work through her lunch time. This might happen because she appraises that, for instance, not eating lunch would leave her without enough energy to work effectively in the afternoon. She has the emotional reaction of fearing the feeling of tiredness.

Another criticism of TPB is based on a literature review and primary research (Manstead and Parker, 1995). It contends that, although the addition of the construct 'perceived control' to the original theory of reasoned action is valuable, there are difficulties in measuring it. Only weak correlations have been found between direct and belief-based measures of the constructs. Furthermore, measures of moral norm and anticipated regret should be added to the model because they produce worthwhile increases in predictive accuracy. More attention is needed to the role played by affective beliefs in shaping behavioural intentions and behaviours themselves.

*Sources*: Bagozzi, R. P. (1992) 'The self-regulation of attitudes, intentions and behaviour', *Social Psychology Quarterly*, vol. 55, no. 2, pp. 178–204.
Manstead, A. S. R. and D. Parker (1995) 'Evaluating and extending the theory of planned behaviour' in W. Stroebe and M. Hewstone (eds) *European Review of Social Psychology*, vol. 6. Chichester: John Wiley, pp. 69–96.

## Abilities

Abilities are capacities for doing things. They are a function of aptitudes, which are inherited dispositions, and environment (including learning or training). At work a wide range of abilities can be required, depending on the job. They include manual dexterity and strength, perceptual and clerical ability, numerical, reasoning and verbal ability, interpersonal skill and organising capabilities. Managers need to be able to assess others' abilities in order to be successful in employee selection, promotion and deployment, in deciding on training needs, adjusting the style of briefing or on-the-job instruction and assessing subordinates' performance. Some abilities can be measured by standardised tests, when circumstances allow.

Perhaps the ability that is most widely valued at work is intelligence, yet after decades of debate and study there is still controversy over what intelligence is and doubt as to whether we can measure it. A 1993 review article condensed a vast literature to propose that there are basically three concepts of intelligence:

1. Spearman's '*g*'. The main idea here is of a biological difference between people which correlates with performance on virtually all mental tasks. Thus it is a property that human brains have in varying degrees, possibly neural efficiency, possibly mental speed, possibly the number of information-processing components plus results that emerge from a given table of intercorrelations of performance on various mental tasks.
2. An adjective that applies, not to people, but to specific behaviour. It is often judged by how adaptive the behaviour is, but the information needed to determine that is extremely complex.
3. A set of abilities. A. R. Jensen[41] called intelligence 'the sum total of all mental abilities', and 'the entire repertoire of a person's knowledge and skill'. This concept of intelligence differs from Spearman's '*g*' in being produced by nurture as well as nature.[42]

In the 1990s much interest was aroused by a concept called emotional intelligence, which its originators, John Mayer and Peter Salovey, called an ability.[43] They defined the concept as 'an ability to recognize the meanings of emotions and to reason and problem solve on the basis of them' 'Emotional intelligence involves the ability to perceive accurately, appraise, and express emotion; the ability to access and/or generate feelings when they facilitate thought; the ability to understand emotion and emotional knowledge; and the ability to regulate emotions to promote emotional and intellectual growth.'[44] The significance of this new concept is perhaps made clearer in this comment by two other scholars: 'Traditionally it has been assumed that cognition and emotion are separate and competing forces, with cognition representing rationality and emotion representing irrationality. However, recent theoretical and empirical work has demonstrated the symbiotic nature of the relationship between these complementary ways of apprehending and understanding the world.'[45] Research results suggest that some forms of emotional problem solving require emotional openness as well as general intelligence.

Emotional intelligence is, clearly, a construct particularly relevant to interaction skill. As Mayer and Geher[46] comment, '[There are] individual differences in the ability to connect thoughts to emotions. People who are good at connecting thoughts to feelings may better "hear" the emotional implications of their own thoughts, as well as understand the feelings of others from what they say.' In work contexts, the concept of emotional intelligence has been applied in the field of service encounters, and will be considered further under that heading in Chapter 7.

In work contexts, the traditional emphasis on abilities has been somewhat displaced by the much broader concept of competencies.[47] Job competencies are

**Box 3.7**

In an article on emotional intelligence (EI), Jill Dann, Course Tutor of the Chartered Institute of Personnel and Development course on EI, was quoted as saying: 'Results from over 500 competency based studies have shown that 80 per cent of leadership effectiveness involves EI,' and 'There was concern measured over two decades that the EI displayed by teenagers had diminished. There are a large number of political, socio-economic and technological reasons which may explain this decline in interpersonal and social skills. A discontented and emotionally illiterate youth does not bode well for the future of any nation.'

*Source*: Davies, G. (2001) 'Make use of your emotions', *Ambassador*, April, p. 22.

underlying characteristics of persons that result in effective job performance. Clearly, to be able to assess and understand characteristics that affect people's effectiveness on the job is of great concern to all at work, and particularly to managers; so what are competencies? They include motives, skills, traits, aspects of self-image or social role or a body of knowledge that is used on the job. What this set of characteristics amounts to is a model of the sources of individual behaviour – a model that is particularly related to job performance. The model is operationalisable in the sense that techniques exist for measuring the characteristics and thus predicting how an individual will perform at a particular job. Some aspects of this competencies model are particularly valuable:

- It recognises the inter-connectedness of factors such as motives, skills and self-image. Competence in a job, for instance, or any behaviour at work or elsewhere, results not just from aptitudes or acquired abilities but from the interaction of multiple factors.
- Among competency elements are some that are not underlying characteristics of an individual, but to do with job demands and organisational environments. 'Actions, their results and the characteristics being expressed, do not necessarily have a one-to-one correspondence. The action, or specific behaviour, is the manifestation of a competency in the context of the demands and requirements of a specific job and particular organisational environment. Given a different job or different organisation environment, the competence may be evident through other specific actions.'[48] This cautions us, rightly, against the dangers of over-interpreting single or small numbers of actions, and against over-confident prediction of how someone will act from our beliefs about their underlying characteristics.

## Traits and personality

Traits are enduring predispositions to act in a certain way, or habitual responses to situations. A number of behavioural propensities show a moderate degree of stability across different situations and over time. These are labelled traits. They include honesty, competitiveness and co-operativeness, self-control and industriousness. The term personality has been defined as 'the interactive aggregate of personal characteristics that influence the individual's response to the environment'.[49] It is often used to refer to a bundle of traits. Typical trait statements include: 'He is extraverted/greedy/honest' or 'She is bad-tempered/kind/conscientious'.

**Box 3.8**

One trait that has been widely discussed is that of locus of control. People with an external locus of control see themselves as relatively passive agents and believe that the events in their lives are due to uncontrollable forces. They tend to feel that the things they want to achieve are dependent on luck, chance and powerful persons or institutions. They believe that the probability of being able to control their lives by their own actions and effort is low. Conversely, people with an internal locus of control see themselves as active agents, feel that they are masters of their fates and trust in their capacities to influence the environment. They tend to assume that they can control the events in their lives by effort and skill. People with an internal locus of control are more resistant to influence attempts, less influenced by the status of an influence source, more active participants in exerting influence, more likely to attribute high intelligence to resistant targets, more trusting (because of having a greater belief in a just world) and more assertive.

Locus of control has received particular attention in the management literature because it has been considered to be highly relevant for success in managerial jobs and therefore as a selection criterion. However, this idea is clearly culture-specific. People from some collectivist cultures have, by Western standards, external loci of control without losing their ability to manage and lead successfully.

*Sources*: Brenders, D. A. (1987) 'Perceived control: Foundations and directions for communication research', *Communication Yearbook*, vol. 10, pp. 86–116.
De Brabander, J. and C. B. Hellemans (1999) 'Selection pressure induces a shift towards more internal scores on Rotter's 1-E Locus of control scale', *Current Research in Social Psychology*, vol. 4, no. 1, pp. 103–112.

Most trait statements are really judgements summarising previous behaviour and predicting future behaviour. Traits have attracted more interest from work psychologists than, for instance, moods or emotions, which pass quickly, because the qualities traits ascribe are enduring ones, and the behaviours they imply are recurring. This feature of trait judgements has led several psychologists to develop trait or personality measures.

One widely known trait-based personality theory simply distinguishes two personality types – Type A and Type B. Type A individuals tend to be impatient and competitive, to feel constantly under time pressure, to suppress feelings and to have few interests outside work. Type B people are the obverse of Type A. Interest in this theory is based mainly on research showing correlations with

**Box 3.9**

## Critique of trait concepts

Because they are judgements and predictions, trait inferences may not be very secure or reliable. For instance, whereas people would normally be accepted as authoritative about their own attitudes and emotions, they would often be regarded as poor judges of their own personality or traits. Another problem with trait statements is that because they are summary they can be imprecise. Some traits, such as sensitive or kind-hearted, are difficult to identify because they do not entail any particular set of behaviour. In fact there are many subtle problems when it comes to identifying traits: for instance, although a single act of theft will disprove the assessment 'honest', a whole day of good temper will not necessarily disprove a trait judgement of 'bad-tempered'. With these kinds of difficulties in the way of identifying traits accurately, it is not surprising that correlations have been weak when researchers have tested trait variables against observed behaviour.

*Source*: Sanford, N. (1970) *Issues in Personality Theory*. San Francisco: Jossey-Bass.

stress. Men with Type A personalities have been found to be twice as prone to heart disease and fatal heart attacks as Type B men.[50] Another set of personality measures, which is tailored more closely than some to behaviour at work, is the Myers–Briggs Type Indicator.[51] Myers' and Briggs' approach is based on the theory that traits are produced by people's preferences for certain ways of doing things, which they develop as a result of experience. In effect, Myers and Briggs see traits as the outcome of a natural process of specialisation. People try doing things one way, it works for them, so they continue using that method which has been positively reinforced. If they switch methods, they are likely to meet with comparatively less success, because they are less practised in the new ways. This experience, too, reinforces their preference for their original method. The traits Myers and Briggs identify are related to four work activities: generating information, making decisions, deciding and setting priorities, and meeting and relating to, other people. (The last of these is, of course, of particular interest here.) Each trait is treated as a continuum with contrasting preferences at each end, as, for example, a preference for generating information from external sources to a preference for generating it by internal search. Thus the traits their indicator measures are as follows:

- In the work-related activity of generating information, people's preferences can be ranged on a continuum from using data from their environment, referred to as sensing, to generating ideas and information from insight, memory and imagination, labelled intuition.
- In making decisions, the trait continuum extends from thinking, defined as using logic and analysis, to feeling, which means depending more on personal values and experience.

- To set priorities, at the extremes people prefer to act perceptively, that is, they prefer to try to understand the situation more fully, or they prefer to get issues resolved, which in Myers–Briggs' terms is to act judgementally.
- Finally, the continuum of preferences to do with managing relationships with other people, ranges from extraversion, that is preferring the company of and interaction with others, to introversion, or a preference for doing things by themselves.

This set of work-related traits and its application to the assessment of people at work may not escape the criticism of trait theories given in Box 3.9. However, in its favour it should be recorded that it has been found of value by a large number of organisations, especially for training managers.

There is a growing body of research that points to a set of personality dimensions that are implicit in most people's perceptions of others. This is the five-factor model. In addition to extraversion, the factors are neuroticism, openness to experience, agreeableness and conscientiousness. One piece of research that found considerable support for the usefulness of these variables also highlighted what people generally mean by these terms:[52]

- Extraversion means being sociable, fun-loving, affectionate, friendly, talkative. People do not use the term in its Jungian sense.
- Openness to experience means being original, imaginative, having broad interests and daring. It is seen as quite different from intelligence.
- Agreeableness is most easily understood in terms of its obverse, antagonism, which means mistrustful, sceptical, callous, unsympathetic, unco-operative, stubborn and rude, but is not related to dominance.
- Conscientiousness means being hardworking, ambitious, energetic, persevering. Its other pole is undirectedness.
- Neuroticism is opposed to emotional stability. The research found that people have a relative lack of words to convey their sense of neuroticism – only worrier, insecure, self-conscious, temperamental – but many scales. Negative affect is a strong element. High neurotics are seen as more distressed, for example by abstinence from smoking, and as more often using inappropriate coping responses such as hostile reactions and wishful thinking because they must deal more often with disruptive emotions. They may adopt irrational beliefs such as self-blame because these beliefs are cognitively consistent with the negative feelings they experience.

None of these trait-based approaches to personality explains how it develops or why it is what it is, but, according to Digman, 'While deeper causal analysis may seem to account for the structure of personality, the structure that must be explained is, for now, best represented by the five-factor model.'[53]

## Causes of prejudice, discrimination and harassment

In Chapter 2, the contextual phenomena of prejudice, discrimination and harassment and their impact on work interactions were introduced. Here, in the context of work behaviour, some explanations of their causes are examined. Early explanations were in terms of authoritarian personalities and frustration–aggression hypotheses.[54] These have been extensively criticised or refuted by research results. The authoritarian personality theory lost credibility once it was shown that anti-Semitism and authoritarianism were not significantly correlated with anti-black prejudice. The frustration–aggression hypothesis (that aggression is natural, stimulated by frustration and gets displaced onto out-groups) was discounted following questions such as why any particular group (e.g. Jewish people) should be a more obvious target for displaced aggression than any other. In addition, Bandura and Walters[55] showed that aggression could easily arise independently of frustration.

Two other theories, relative deprivation and realistic conflict of interests, are still seen as at least partial explanations. Relative deprivation is the theory that when people compare their group's situation with others, they turn against those who are better off. Realistic conflict of interests, as the name implies, suggests that inter-group hostility is caused by competition for material resources. However, signs of 'us' and 'them' have been found between groups even before competition was introduced and between groups whose members were randomly assigned, so had no cultural, physical or personality differences to account for the behaviour. Research using the minimal group paradigm (in which individuals are randomly assigned to groups) has yielded a consistent pattern of results: subjects allocate more to in-group than to out-group members. They try to maximise in-group profit. They are also competitive. This applies even when the group is explicitly random (known to subjects to be based on the toss of a coin). One way to explain these findings is in terms of the accentuation of differences being biased in favour of the in-group because individuals are deriving their social identity (even in the transient context of the experiment) from the social category that includes themselves.

**Box 3.10**

### Critique of psychological accounts of behaviour

The main strengths of these accounts is probably the way their key concepts reflect common-sense views of how the causes of individual behaviour should be analysed and the substantial support that many psychological theories have received from research. Their main weaknesses appear to be their lack of attention to the factors and processes that are the focus of sociology and social psychology. In particular, it is hard to explain interactive behaviour without fully incorporating an account of the reciprocal influence of the individual and his or her environment.

## SUMMARY – PSYCHOLOGICAL CONSTRUCTS

People's behaviour in work interactions can be explained partly in terms of their values, needs and wants, goals, feelings, beliefs or assumptions about people and relationships, expectations of others' behaviour, prior knowledge of relevant issues, cognitive schemas, attitudes, abilities, especially in terms of intelligence and emotional intelligence, their traits (whether they are reliable, honest, resilient and so forth) and possibly what their personality is. These explanations apply to our own as well as other people's behaviour.

## EFFECTS OF DIFFERENCES OF BACKGROUND

Thus far, I have dealt only with universal constructs to explain behaviour at work. However, although there are undoubtedly important universals in human behaviour and so in work behaviour (some examples are given in Box 3.11), we know that individual behaviour is also strongly influenced by a person's environment, especially the social groups to which they belong or aspire. Two motives lead to people accepting social influence: to reduce uncertainty by believing what others believe and to maintain membership in a group. There are three processes: compliance, which is agreeing in order to gain rewards and avoid punishment; identification, which is adopting opinions based on a relationship with another person; and internalisation, which is accepting influence because it is congruent with one's value system.[56] These three are in order of increasing strength and durability of the social influence effects. One mechanism by which social influence is transmitted to individuals is the expectation of accountability, which is an 'explicit or implicit constraint on virtually everything people do'.[57] People ask themselves, 'If I do this, how will others react?' This is one mechanism by which norms and roles, which will be covered in Chapter 10, affect individual behaviour. Accountability itself is probably universal, although the specific norms and values vary from one culture or time to another.

**Box 3.11**

All humans have examples of associative social behaviours (e.g. being supportive, admiring, giving resources) as similar to each other and different from behaviours that are dissociative (e.g. avoiding, being aggressive).

All humans distinguish superordinating behaviours (e.g. criticising, giving orders) from subordinating behaviours (e.g. obeying, conforming).

*Source*: Triandis, H. (1994) *Culture and Social Behavior.* New York: McGraw Hill, p. 5.

Although social influence is exercised on individuals at work by a wide range of groups, most evidence is available for cultural and gender groups. Numerous studies have shown that cultural influences affect work behaviour. One study compared conceptions of employee responsibilities and rights in the United States and the People's Republic of China. It found that on most major dimensions there are different practices and/or assumptions. These dimensions include work ethics, reward systems, interpersonal relations, policies and rules, work skills and inter-organisational relations. These differences shape the nature of management and leadership and are fundamental to approaches to management education.[58]

**Box 3.12**

An investment banker, speaking of a Russian colleague who had been working for an American bank in London for the past five years said: 'He's all right, very thorough, intelligent, smart, but he still doesn't get the point of what we're trying to do. That is, he can't or doesn't assess how commercial or marketable the ideas he has are.'

*Source*: interview, author's research.

Another study, by Iyengar and Lepper,[59] showed that Asian Americans, unlike white Americans, proved more intrinsically motivated when choices were made for them by trusted authority figures or peers. The authors commented, 'Conventional wisdom and decades of psychological research have linked the provision of choice to increased levels of intrinsic motivation, greater persistence, better performance and higher satisfaction, so theories where choice plays a central role, such as . . . attribution theory . . . motivation – might need reconceptualising to fit other cultures.' A third study pointed out that the cultural values of African-Americans can lead to particular forms of work behaviour, such as:

- drawing attention to their own positive qualities or sense of personal power – doing this sets a standard for themselves which must be met;
- confronting individuals in conflict – a co-worker is likely to go to a manager to discuss concerns about another co-worker;
- a strong belief that if they work hard and stay out of trouble they will be properly rewarded;
- interpersonal responsiveness – African-Americans vary their proxemics more, and use confirming expressions like 'Tell it', 'You're right'; however, they use lower eye contact when listening;
- group orientation;
- verbal inventiveness – talking is not just a method of exchanging information but is also used to look for expedient ways to solve problems, to take advantage of opportunities and to focus on what will and will not work;
- gaining information indirectly (for instance, asking 'What does your wife think of that?' instead of 'Are you married?').

All these behaviours, it is argued, differ from those of the majority American culture.[60]

**Box 3.13**

### National culture in aviation

The view has been widespread in aviation that the cockpit is a culture-free zone, one in which pilots of all nationalities accomplish their common task of flying safely from one point to another.

Against this view, a study found that pilots from countries such as Morocco, the Philippines and Brazil (high in power distance) accept a more autocratic type of leadership and that co-pilots may be unwilling to comment on their captains' actions or decisions. It was also found that pilots from Taiwan, Brazil and the Philippines (high in uncertainty avoidance) are likely to believe that written procedures are needed for all situations and that an organisation's rules should never be broken, even when it might be in the organisation's best interest. Pilots from cultures such as the United Kingdom, Ireland and the United States are less likely to agree.

*Source*: Helmreich, R. L., J. A. Wilhelm, J. R. Klinect and A. C. Merritt (1999) 'Culture, error and crew resource management', The University of Texas at Austin.

Aspects of cultural differences in work practices and relations that depend on or impact on interactions include work roles and norms, groupwork, manager/subordinate relations, management style and organisational cultures. These effects are discussed in the chapters covering these topics.

Sex and gender are not strong predictors of work behaviour. Even when gender differences are found, they typically account for only 1–5 per cent of the variance for any given outcome. Recent research suggests that femininity and masculinity are independent dimensions and that each dimension has multiple domains within it, including appearance, behaviour, personality and interests. There is evidence that gender stereotypes are not very accurate, because they are more extensive than actual sex differences and they contain information based on exaggerations of minor differences between the sexes.[61]

However, women do often adopt linguistic practices such as using tag questions (for instance, 'That's a good idea, don't you think?'), qualifiers (like 'perhaps', or 'might' instead of 'should') and fillers to soften their messages. Some would argue that women use qualifiers and tag questions more than men do because they have been socialised to appear and feel tentative and powerless. From a stream of research into women's professional communication, Baker[62] concluded that, although the situation modifies it, usage of qualifiers (hedges) and tags may well be related to gender. Women's communication motivations were found to be more affiliative and less power-oriented than men's. Studies also show that women's self-evaluations are more responsive to the feedback they receive than are men's. This finding has been interpreted in terms of Western women having more interdependent self-concepts (that is closer to those of someone from a collectivist culture) than Western men's.[63] There is also a view that women communicate their morality and ethics 'in a different voice' from men, though the distinctions are not exclusive or neat.[64] (Early research exclusively with men led to assumptions that justice is at the top of the ethical hierarchy. This led to women, whose ethics clustered around caring and responsibility in the middle of the resulting hierarchy, being seen as cases of arrested development![65])

**Box 3.14**

In the early 1990s, EuroDisney (now Disneyland Paris) was built outside Paris as an American-style theme park for Europe. It ran into severe financial trouble, largely because the number of visitors it attracted and their average spend were well below estimates. Many of the problems originated in the corporation's failure to adapt their formula to allow for cultural differences between Europeans and Americans. Examples are not serving alcohol in expensive restaurants within the park, and expecting that the French, like the Americans, would 'take in three or four attractions, have lunch, hang out, shop and feel good.' They didn't. Instead they wanted to go on every single (free) ride on the first day, with the result that EuroDisney earned a bad reputation for its queues. There was also high staff turnover; young French employees could not be persuaded to conform to EuroDisney's rigorous standards of appearance and behaviour. Eventually, women staff were allowed to wear non-approved shades of lipstick, nail varnish and hosiery.

Groups and social categories differ in size, status and power. This has consequences for the way members of minority groups see themselves, the way they are seen by others and their interactions.

- Members of minority groups are more likely than majority group members to see themselves in terms of their group, because the mere fact of being a member of a minority makes their group membership more conspicuous.[66] They also identify more strongly with their in-group than members of non-minorities do.[67] They are even more willing to accentuate their group membership when their in-group has high status. By comparison, for members of numerical majorities the status of their in-group is less critical.
- Relative group size and status are significant factors in the thinking and motivational processes underlying how members of groups perceive members of other groups and behave towards them. However, when reliable data are lacking, 70 per cent of people tend to overestimate the size of their in-group relative to an out-group and 40 per cent do the same with regard to status.[68,69] Since members of larger groups are less loyal,[70] these tendencies mean that in the absence of clear information, people's identification with their groups will

be lower. People also seem to conflate size and status in regard to their group. For instance, when they learn that their group is a small one, they interpret this as meaning it is low in status and when told that their group is a high-status one, they conclude that it must be a large one.

- Members of minority groups may express their identity needs differently in the presence of an audience. Members of low-status groups have been shown to be more likely to acknowledge in-group inferiority in public than in private situations.[71] The relative importance to individuals of different audiences is affected by how strongly they identify with their group. Low identifiers mainly adapt their public behaviour to what the audience is likely to appreciate. They refrain from responding in a way that might be criticised by others. Towards other members of the in-group they indicate that the in-group is as worthy as other groups but they do not seem to be prepared to defend this view in front of an out-group audience. Conversely, high identifiers admit to the in-group's problematic standing only with other members of the group. With outsiders, they defend their group, if necessary incurring the social penalties that might follow from standing up for their group in public. These findings show that lower-status group members respond strategically to the social situation in which they find themselves, while privately believing that their group is just as good or better than the other. Failure of members of low-status groups to defend their group is not, as is sometimes suggested, because they have internalised the low evaluation of their group.

## SUMMARY – EFFECTS OF DIFFERENCES OF BACKGROUND

Interactions, at work as elsewhere, are regulated and governed according to practices and values inculcated by social influence. These practices and values differ from group to group. For members of minority groups their group membership is more salient than for members of majority groups. Members of low-status groups adapt their interactive behaviour towards members of other groups according to the demands of the situation as they see it.

## CHAPTER OVERVIEW

A knowledge of what lies beneath our behaviour to one another is fundamental to developing work interaction skills. Interaction theory, which is constructed on a base of social exchange theory, equity theory and attribution theory, accounts for interaction behaviours in terms of power and desired outcomes. The chapter describes concepts from organisational psychology that deal with values, motives, emotions, beliefs, attitudes, intentions, abilities, traits and personality, and those that help in analysing the influence of social groups, to give a fuller insight into how individuals' interaction behaviour comes about.

## EXERCISES

1. Interview someone from outside your course about their work, using a previously prepared interview schedule. Record the interview as fully as possible, ideally by video recording, or by tape recording. Then ask them questions, again using an interview schedule, designed to find out how far they saw the elements of interaction theories as applying to the interaction. Focus especially on exchange, equity and attributions. Record their answers. Watch or listen to the recording with members of your group to decide how far the perceptions of the interviewee about exchange, equity and attributions could have been detected from their verbal and non-verbal expression.

   Note: a reading of the section in Chapter 5 on 'Interviewing skills' may be useful preparation for this exercise.
2. Working with another member of the course, identify four of each of the following which you can categorise as shared (similar) or dissimilar: values, needs and wants, goals, feelings, beliefs or assumptions about people and relationships, expectations of others' behaviour, cognitive schemas and attitudes.
3. Find ways to test the theory that members of minority groups identify more strongly with their groups than members of majority groups do.
4. In a mixed culture group, find five examples of how work-related perceptions vary in different cultures.
5. In a mixed culture group, work through the following list of different work-related practices and/or assumptions that people in different cultures take for granted, finding contrasting examples for each: work ethics, reward systems, interpersonal relations, policies and rules, work skills and interorganisational relations.
6. In a mixed culture group, individual members of the group complete the rating scale given Table 3.1 for the attitudes of a manager who is well known to them. Then they compare their 'findings' and discuss them.

**Table 3.1 Rating scale for managers' attitudes**

| Rate your manager on the following items: | *Strongly favourable* | | | *Strongly unfavourable* | | |
|---|---|---|---|---|---|---|
| ■ participation | X | X | X | X | X | X |
| ■ formal structure | X | X | X | X | X | X |
| ■ internal competition | X | X | X | X | X | X |
| ■ risk | X | X | X | X | X | X |
| ■ experimentation and innovation | X | X | X | X | X | X |
| ■ ascribed status | X | X | X | X | X | X |
| ■ intuition | X | X | X | X | X | X |
| ■ loyalty to the organisation | X | X | X | X | X | X |

*Since this scale is transparent, no scoring guide is needed.*

7. Discussion topics:
   (a) Does the Fishbein and Ajzen theory of reasoned action model of the attitude–behaviour link suggest any reasons why opinion polls have sometimes been poor predictors of election results?
   (b) If trait-based accounts of personality tell us nothing about how personality develops or why personalities differ, are they worth the trouble?
   (c) Montesquieu argued that residents of warmer climates are more emotionally expressive than those living in cooler ones. Do you agree?
   (d) Do you agree that with Tetlock that 'the expectation of accountability is an explicit or implicit constraint on practically everything people do'? If you agree, give examples. If you disagree, explain why and clarify how, if at all, you believe the expectation of accountability affects behaviour.
   (e) Discuss how cultural differences should be handled by organisations doing business internationally. You may wish to refer particularly to the EuroDisney case in Box 3.14.

## FURTHER READING

Argyle, M. (1989) *The Social Psychology of Work*, 2nd edn. Harmondsworth, Middlesex: Penguin. Also relevant to Chapters 4, 10 and 11 of this book.

Eagly, A. H. and S. Chaiken (1993) *The Psychology of Attitudes*. San Diego, Calif.: Harcourt, Brace, Jovanovich.

Fineman, S. (ed.) (1993) *Emotion in Organizations*, 1st edn. London: Sage. Especially the Introduction and Chapter 5. 2nd edn. London: Sage, 2000. Especially Waldron, V. R., 'Relational experiences and emotion at work'.

Haslam, S. A. (2001) *Psychology in Organizations: The Social Identity Approach*. London: Sage. Chapter 3 for Chapter 13 of this book, Chapter 5 for Chapter 7, Chapters 6, 7 and 9 for Chapter 11 and Chapter 8 for Chapter 9.

Hogg, M. A. and D. Abrams (eds) (2001) *Intergroup Relations: Essential Readings*. Hove: Taylor and Francis. Some articles are also relevant to Chapter 11.

Manstead, A. S. R., M. Hewstone, S. T. Fiske, M. A. Hogg and G. R. Semin (eds) (1996) *The Blackwell Encyclopaedia of Social Psychology*. Oxford: Blackwell.

Singh, D. (2001) *Emotional Intelligence at Work: A Professional Guide*. New Delhi: Response Books.

## REFERENCES

1. Homans, G. C. (1958) 'Social behaviour as exchange', *American Journal of Sociology*, vol. 63, pp. 597–606.
2. Lawler, E. E. (1971) *Pay and Organizational Effectiveness: A Psychological View*. New York: McGraw-Hill.
3. Walster, E., G. W. Walster and E. Berscheid (1978) *Equity: Theory and Research*. Boston: Allyn and Bacon.
4. Heider, F. (1958) *The Psychology of Interpersonal Relations*. New York: John Wiley.
5. Kelley, H. H. and J. W. Thibaut (1978) *Interpersonal Relations: A Theory of Interdependence*. New York: John Wiley & Sons.

6. Hegtvedt, K. A., E. A. Thompson and K. S. Cook (1993) 'Power and equity: What counts in attributions for exchange outcomes?', *Social Psychology Quarterly*, vol. 56, pp. 100–119.
7. Maslow, A. H. (1970) *Motivation and Personality*, 2nd edn. New York: Harper and Row.
8. McGuire, W. J. (1974) 'Psychological motives and communication gratification' in J. G. Blumler and C. Katz (eds) *The Uses of Mass Communication*. Beverley Hills, Calif.: Sage Publications.
9. Ryan, R. M., T. D. Little, K. M. Sheldon, E. Timoshina and E. L. Deci (1999) 'The American dream in Russia: Extrinsic aspirations and well-being in two cultures', *Personality and Social Psychology Bulletin*, vol. 25, no. 12, pp. 1509–1524.
10. Schwartz, S. H. (1992) 'Universals in the content and structure of values: Theory and empirical tests in 20 countries' in M. Zanna (ed.) *Advances in Experimental Social Psychology*, vol. 25. New York: Academic Press, pp. 1–65.
11. Abelson, R. P. (1981) 'The psychological status of the script concept', *American Psychologist*, vol. 36, pp. 715–729.
12. Bullmer, K. (1975) *The Art of Empathy*. New York: Human Sciences Press.
13. Larrick, R. P. (1993) 'Motivational factors in decision theories: the role of self-protection', *Psychological Bulletin*, vol. 113, no. 3, pp. 440–450.
14. Van der Pligt, J., M. Zeelenberg, W. W. van Dijk, N. K. de Vries and R. Richard (1997) 'Affect, attitudes and decisions: Let's be more specific' in W. Stroebe and M. Hewstone (eds) *European Review of Social Psychology*, vol. 8, pp. 33–66.
15. Fehr, B. and M. Baldwin (1996) 'Prototype and script analyses of laypeople's knowledge of anger' in G. J. O. Fletcher and J. Fitness (eds) *Knowledge Structures in Close Relationships: A Social Psychological Approach*. Mahwah, NJ: Lawrence Erlbaum, pp. 219–245.
16. Mesquita, B. and N. H. Frijda (1992) 'Cultural variations in emotions: A review', *Psychological Bulletin*, vol. 112, no. 2, pp. 179–204.
17. Scott, C. S. (1980) 'Interpersonal trust: A comparison of attitudinal and situational factors', *Human Relations*, vol. 33, no. 11, pp. 805–812.
18. McGregor, D. M. (1960) *The Human Side of Enterprise*. New York: McGraw-Hill.
19. Snyder, C. H. and P. Diesing (1977) *Conflict Among Nations: Bargaining, Decision-Making and System Structure in International Crises*. Princeton, New Jersey: Princeton University Press.
20. Morley, I. (1981) 'Negotiation and bargaining' in M. Argyle (ed.) *Social Skills and Work*. New York: Methuen.
21. Roberts, T.-A. (1991) 'Gender and the influence of evaluations on self-assessments in achievement settings', *Psychological Bulletin*, vol. 109, no. 2, pp. 297–308.
22. Alagana, S. W. (1982) 'Sex role identity, peer evaluation of competition, and the responses of women and men in a competitive situation', *Journal of Personality and Social Psychology*, vol. 43, pp. 546–554.
23. Forgas, J. P. (1976) 'The perception of social episodes: Categorical and dimensional representations in two different social milieus', *Journal of Personality and Social Psychology*, vol. 33, pp. 199–209.
24. Forgas, J. P. (1978) 'Social episodes and social structure in an academic setting: The social environment of an intact group', *Journal of Experimental Social Psychology*, vol. 4, pp. 434–448.
25. Forgas, J. P. (1983) 'Social skills and episode perception', *British Journal of Clinical Psychology*, vol. 22, pp. 26–41.
26. Leodolter, R. and M. Leodolter (1976) 'Sociolinguistic considerations on psychosocial socialisation' in W. McCormack and S. Wurm (eds) *Language and Man*. The Hague: Mouton, p. 327.

27. Krech, D. and R. S. Crutchfield (1948) *Theory and Problems in Social Psychology*. New York: McGraw-Hill.
28. Nystrom, P. C. and W. H. Starbuck (1984) 'Managing beliefs in organizations', *Journal of Applied Behavioural Science*, vol. 20, no. 3, pp. 277–287.
29. Eagly, A. H. and S. Chaiken (1993) *The Psychology of Attitudes*. San Diego, Calif.: Harcourt, Brace, Jovanovich
30. Moscovici, S. (1961) *La Psychanalyse, Son Image, Son Public*, 2nd edn. Paris: PUF.
31. Moliner, P. and E. Tafani (1997) 'Attitudes and social representations; a theoretical and experimental approach', *European Journal of Social Psychology*, vol. 27, pp. 687–702.
32. Manstead, A. S. R. and D. Parker (1995) 'Evaluating and extending the theory of planned behaviour' in W. Stroebe and M. Hewstone (eds) *European Review of Social Psychology*, vol. 6. Chichester: John Wiley, pp. 69–96.
33. Babrow, A. S., D. R. Black and S. T. Tiffany (1990) 'Beliefs, attitudes, intentions, and a smoking-cessation program: A planned behavior analysis of communication campaign development', *Health Communication*, vol. 2, no. 3, pp. 145–163.
34. Allen, M. W. (1996) 'The relationship between communication, affect, job alternatives, and voluntary turnover intentions', *Southern Communication Journal*, vol. 61, no. 3, pp. 198–209.
35. Festinger, L. (1957) *A Theory of Cognitive Dissonance*. Evanston, Ill.: Ron Peterson.
36. Fishbein, M. and I. Ajzen (1975) *Belief, Attitude, Intention and Behaviour*. Reading, Mass.: Addison-Wesley.
37. Bagozzi, R. P. (1992) 'The self-regulation of attitudes, intentions and behaviour', *Social Psychology Quarterly*, vol. 55, no. 2, pp. 178–204.
38. Ajzen, I. (1991) 'The theory of planned behavior – some unresolved issues', *Organizational Behavior and Human Decision Processes*, vol. 50, pp. 179–211.
39. Watters, A. E. (1989) 'Reasoned/intuitive action: An individual difference moderator of the attitude–behaviour relationship in the 1988 Presidential election', Unpublished master's thesis, Dept of Psychology, University of Massachusetts at Amherst.
40. Doll, J. and I. Ajzen (1992) 'Accessibility and stability of predictors in the theory of planned behaviour', *Journal of Personality and Social Psychology*, vol. 73, pp. 754–765.
41. Howard, R. W. (1993) 'On what intelligence is', *British Journal of Psychology*, vol. 84, pp. 27–37.
42. Jensen, A. R. (1987) 'Psychometric g as a focus of concerted research effort', *Intelligence*, vol. 11, pp. 193–198.
43. Salovey, P. and J. D. Mayer (1990) 'Emotional intelligence', *Imagination, Cognition, and Personality*, vol. 9, pp. 185–211.
44. Mayer, J. D., M. T. Di Paolo and P. Salovey (1990) 'Perceiving affective content in ambiguous visual stimuli: A component of emotional intelligence', *Journal of Personality Assessment*, vol. 54, pp. 772–781.
45. Planalp, S. and J. Fitness (1999) 'Thinking/feeling about social and personal relationships', *Journal of Social and Personal Relationships*, vol. 16, no. 6, pp. 731–750.
46. Mayer, J. and G. Geher (1996) 'Emotional intelligence and the identification of emotion', *Intelligence*, vol. 22, no. 2, 89–114.
47. Boyatzis, R. E. (1982) *The Competent Manager: A Model for Effective Performance*. New York: Wiley.
48. Ibid.
49. Guilford, R. R. (1959) *Personality*. New York: McGraw-Hill.
50. Friedman, M. and R. Rosenbaum (1974) *Type A Behaviour and Your Heart*. New York: Knopf.

51. Myers, I. B. and P. B. Briggs (1995) *Gifts Differing: Understanding Personality Type*. Palo Alto, Calif.: Consulting Psychologists Press.
52. McCrae, R. R. and P. T. Costa Jr (1987) 'Validation of the five factor model of personality across instruments and observers', *Journal of Personality and Social Psychology*, vol. 52, pp. 81–90.
53. Digman, J. M. (1990) 'Personality structure: Emergence of the five-factor model', *Annual Review of Psychology*, vol. 41, pp. 417–440.
54. Allport, G. W. (1954) *The Nature of Prejudice*. Reading, Mass.: Addison-Wesley.
55. Bandura, A. and R. H. Walters (1969) *Social Learning and Personality Development*. London: Holt, Rinehart, Winston.
56. Kelman, H. (1961) 'Processes of opinion change', *Public Opinion Quarterly*, vol. 35, pp. 57–78.
57. Tetlock, P. E. (1996) 'Accountability', in A. S. R. Manstead and M. Hewstone (eds) *Blackwell Encyclopaedia of Social Psychology*. Oxford: Blackwell.
58. Osigweh, C., A. B. Huo and Y. P. Yg (1993) 'Conceptions of employee responsibilities and rights in the United States and the People's Republic of China', *The International Journal of Human Resource Management*, vol. 4, no. 1, pp. 113–128.
59. Iyengar, S. S. and M. R. Lepper (1999) 'Rethinking the value of choice: a cultural perspective on intrinsic motivation', *Journal of Personality and Social Psychology*, vol. 76, no. 3, pp. 349–366.
60. Foeman, A. K. and G. Pressley (1987) 'Ethnic culture and corporate culture: Using black styles in organizations', *Communication Quarterly*, vol. 35, no. 4, pp. 293–307.
61. Martin, C. L. (1996) 'Gender' in A. S. R. Manstead and M. Hewstone (eds) *Blackwell Encyclopaedia of Social Psychology*. Oxford: Blackwell.
62. Baker, M. A. (1991) 'Gender and verbal communication in professional settings: A review of research', *Management Communication Quarterly*, vol. 5, no. 1, pp. 36–63.
63. Cross, S. E. and L. Madison (1997) 'Models of the self: Self-construals and gender', *Psychological Bulletin*, vol. 122, no. 1, pp. 5–37.
64. Gilligan, C. (1982) *In a Different Voice: Psychological Theory and Women's Development*, Cambridge Mass.: Harvard University Press.
65. Bloom, M. M. (1990) 'Sex differences in ethical systems: A useful framework for interpreting communication research', *Communication Quarterly*, vol. 38, pp. 244–254.
66. Fiske, S. T. and S. E. Taylor (1991) *Social Cognition*. New York: McGraw Hill.
67. Simon, B. and R. Brown (1987) 'Perceived intragroup homogeneity in minority–majority contexts', *Journal of Personality and Social Psychology*, vol. 53, no. 4, pp. 703–711.
68. Simon, B. and A. Mummendey (1990) 'Perceptions of relative group size and group homogeneity: We are the majority and they are all the same', *European Journal of Social Psychology*, vol. 20, pp. 269–286.
69. Mummendey, A., M. Blanz and S. Otten (1992) 'Positive–negative asymmetry in social discrimination – Study I – The impact of quality of resource (positive, negative) on intergroup evaluations and allocations', Berichte aus dem Psychologischen Institut IV der Universität Munster.
70. Simon, B. and T. F. Pettigrew (1990) 'Social identity and perceived group homogeneity: Evidence for the ingroup homogeneity effect', *European Journal of Social Psychology*, vol. 20, pp. 269–286.
71. Ellemers, N., C. van Dyck, S. Hinkle and A. Jacobs (2000) 'Inter-group differentiation in social context: Identity needs versus audience constraints', *Social Psychology Quarterly*, vol. 63, no. 1, pp. 60–74.

# 4 The self at work

## CHAPTER INTRODUCTION

In any and every interaction, a person's 'self' will always have a special significance for them and a special impact on what they experience. Personal identity is universally salient (although, as we shall see, the nature of the self varies across cultures). Research shows that whether their beliefs about themselves are positive or negative, people spend more time considering remarks of a partner they suspect will confirm rather than disconfirm their beliefs.[1] They also rate information about themselves as more accurate if it is consistent with their beliefs.[2] This evidence endorses the centrality (salience) of the self and the importance to individuals of maintaining their self-concept.

Therefore, this chapter aims to help readers understand how the self impacts on interaction at work by describing:

- the self-concept, self-categorisation, social identities and cultural differences in self-concepts;
- self-esteem, perceived control and self-delusion;
- coping abilities, including dealing with negative emotions, stress and gender issues and developing efficacy;
- personal development through independent learning, developing interpersonal skills and an ethical framework;
- interaction planning.

## UNDERSTANDING THE SELF

The concept of the self is a fiction (or construct) but it serves as a useful tool for thinking and speaking about ourselves and our psychological functioning. The self is a focus of knowledge (what sort of person I think I am), motivations (I try to obtain what I want for myself, especially favourable, but plausible, evaluations of myself) and regulation (I try to control myself). Self-knowledge consists of a large number of particular beliefs, only a few of which can be present in awareness at any moment. These beliefs concern our physical body, socially defined identity (including roles and relationships), personality, decisions and actions. Despite this, one central belief is that the self has a fundamental unity, so that the unitary term 'self-concept', though disputed, is still widely used and will be used here.

How we see this self is not objective. There are three sources of self-concepts. We compare ourselves with 'significant others', interpret how others respond to us and interpret our own thoughts, feelings and actions. In making social comparisons and in interpreting others' responses, protective mechanisms bias our self-concepts towards the positive. Inaccuracy in interpreting others' responses also arises because others often avoid showing us how they see us. Thus, although our self-concepts are strongly correlated with how we believe that others perceive us, they are only weakly correlated with how others actually do perceive us. In interpreting their own thoughts, feelings and actions, people 'seriously over-estimate their powers of introspection' and 'have little or no access to their own mental processes'. For all these reasons, 'self-knowledge is systematically distorted'.[3]

Our self-concept changes, sometimes from minute to minute, as we focus on different aspects of our lives. For example, if an executive remembers how s/he made a convincing presentation to the sales force the previous day, his or her self-concept at that time could include 'good presenter'. However, if the next minute s/he finds that s/he has failed to prepare the agenda for a meeting s/he is about to chair, his or her self-concept might refocus as 'forgetful'. As a result of the changing views we have of ourselves, the way we see and experience people and events also changes and so does how we behave. This section briefly outlines some points about how we come to have the self-concepts that we do.

## Self-categorisation

In Chapter 3, the importance of our social category and group memberships was pointed out. As Chapter 5 will explain, categorisation is a natural process for understanding the world. It is applied to things, events and people, including ourselves. Social categorisation means classifying the people we meet. We do it overwhelmingly with reference to ourselves, on the basis of similarities to and differences from the way we see ourselves. For example, if I see myself as hard-working, I will tend to categorise other people as more, less or equally hard-working. This is because our self is so important to us. We also self-categorise and self-stereotype. Our self-concept is partly influenced by the stereotypes of the groups to which we accept that we belong. Thus self-categorisation at once brings about two things. It causes us to perceive ourselves as having the same social identity as other members of the category. It places us in the relevant social category, or 'places the group in our head'.[4] Secondly, it leads us to behave in ways that are consistent with our stereotypes of the categories to which we accept we belong. Self-categorisation is the process that transforms a number of individuals into a group.

Figure 4.1 shows the processes of social and self-categorisation.

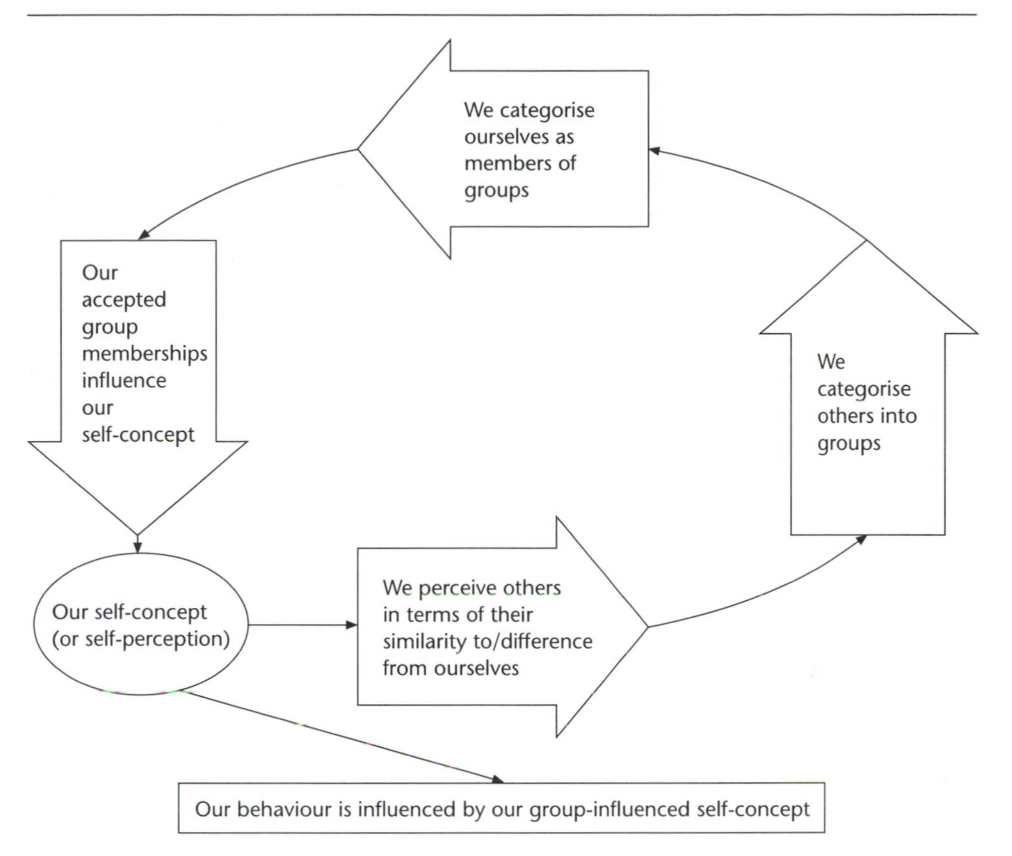


**Figure 4.1 Processes of social and self-categorisation.**

## Social identities

The social identity approach argues that 'the groups to which people belong, whether by assignment or by choice, will be massively significant in determining their life experiences.'[5] Therefore, groups have a profound impact on individuals' self-concept (or, in the language of the social identity approach, their identity). For this purpose, the term 'group' may apply either to a small face-to-face group or to an entire social category, such as a gender, ethnic or national group. A group in this sense is any collection of individuals who categorise themselves similarly. At times, people see themselves mainly as a member of a group (or social category), at other times mainly as an individual. For instance, Janet, who works as a hospital administrator and who normally thinks of herself as a complex individual, may think of herself simply as a hospital administrator when she is dealing with doctors. Or if Mark is negotiating for his company with representatives of other companies, he will tend to see himself mainly as his company's representative. In these examples, Janet's and Mark's 'collective' selves predominate; in other words, they are seeing themselves primarily as members of a group. This collective self places in the foreground those aspects of an individual that are interchangeable with others, for instance, the fact that Mark works for 'Company X' and is negotiating on its behalf. At other times, when interacting with people from a similar group or social category, the individual self predominates: in team meetings to decide on a negotiating strategy, for instance. This individual self is based on a larger set of different self-aspects. It puts an individual's uniqueness into the foreground.

There may be a cultural difference in which aspect of the self is most often activated. In Western societies, although the social context can lead to self-interpretation as the collective self, there is a tendency for the individual self to predominate. In collectivist societies, the reverse may be true. Another factor influencing the relative 'presence' of the collective or the individual self is whether the person is a member of a minority or majority group in the relevant social context. When they are in a minority, people are more likely to see themselves in terms of their collective self than are members of the majority group.[6] Thus, for example, women employees in many financial services firms, where they are in a minority, are more likely to be often conscious of being women than men in such firms are of being men.

When they are thinking of themselves as a member of a group, rather than as an individual, people identify more strongly with their group. When this happens, their behaviour is regulated more by group standards than by personal standards. This applies to perception and thinking as well, so that over-use of stereotypes, favouring of the in-group and discrimination against members of other groups all become more common. People also co-operate more when they are stimulated to think of themselves as group members rather than individuals. Tests of why they do so seem to show it is not that they feel any more strongly that their fellow group members are trustworthy, so much as that they feel more sense of self-efficacy – of being able to make a difference.[7]

Because people's self-concepts are implicated in the social groups to which they belong,[8,9] members of groups that have inferior social standing are often faced with threats to a positive self-concept. When confronted with such threats, people employ coping strategies. For instance, they may challenge the current state of affairs by systematically assigning more positive evaluations or more favourable outcomes to their in-group than to relevant out-groups. However, research has not found a consistent relationship, possibly because other strategies are used. There is other evidence, however, that people try hard to manage their social identities to preserve or maintain self-esteem. For example, a survey of white Americans found that they tend to ignore questions asking them to label themselves. That is, they resist self-labelling themselves as 'white Americans'. This may be in order to avoid the pejorative connotation of racism associated with the term 'white American'.[10]

## Different cultures' views of the self

Culture has a strong influence on our self-concepts.[11] In fact, the self is now seen as the psychological link between culture and behaviour. Individualist cultures foster an independent view of the self whereas collectivist cultures develop an interdependent self-concept. An independent self-concept involves viewing our self as separate from others, with a focus on expressing our own unique internal attributes. Behaviour is organised and made meaningful according to our own internal thoughts, feelings and actions, rather than by reference to the thoughts, feelings and actions of others. In contrast, an interdependent construal of self emphasises the connectedness of human beings to each other. A person's autonomy takes second place to fitting in with the social context. Both these views of the self involve a set of internal attributes such as abilities, opinions and personality characteristics, but in collectivist cultures these attributes are controlled in relation to the specific situation. In Japanese culture, for instance, a sense of belonging, occupying one's proper place, promoting others' goals, engaging in socially appropriate action, reliability, dependability, empathy, reciprocity and humility are all important. The concern with others involves favouring members of the in-group, such as the family or the work-group. Out-group members are likely to be treated quite differently and to experience neither the advantages nor the disadvantages of interdependence.

People with interdependent selves will typically not claim that they are better than others, will not express pleasure in the state of feeling superior to others and indeed will be likely not to enjoy it. Self-enhancement through taking personal credit for success, denying personal responsibility for failure and believing oneself to be better than average may be primarily a Western phenomenon. On the other side of the coin, people with interdependent selves are less likely to suffer from low self-esteem. Markus and Kitayama[12] argued that in Asia, critical attitudes to the self and seemingly self-effacing psychological tendencies are likely to be part and parcel of positive self-regard or self-attachment. This contrasts with the Western (and especially American) view that self-criticism and modesty often imply low self-esteem.

**Box 4.1**

### Critique of theories of cultural differences in self-concepts

- Evidence is emerging that independent and interdependent views of the self may co-exist within the same individual and the same culture, though to different degrees.
- The nature of the influence process by which culture affects an individual's self-concept has been little researched (Singelis and Brown, 1995).
- In some parts of Europe, especially those formerly under Communist control, self-criticism and modesty are highly valued.

*Source*: Singelis, T. M. and W. J. Brown (1995) 'Culture, self, and collectivist communication: Linking culture to individual behavior', *Human Communication Research*, vol. 21, no. 3, pp. 354–389.

## SUMMARY – UNDERSTANDING THE SELF

The way we relate to other people, both at work and elsewhere, is strongly influenced by the views we have of ourselves – our self-concepts. We construct our self-concepts on the basis of comparisons with others, how others respond to us and how we interpret our own thoughts, feelings and actions. We 'foreground' different aspects of our self at different times, especially whether we view ourselves as members of a group or as individuals. When our group membership predominates in our thinking, our behaviour tends to be regulated more by group standards than personal standards. Because, as Chapter 5 will show, categorisation is fundamental to the way we perceive, we categorise other people in relation to ourselves and ourselves in relation to the groups of which we accept that we are members. All these factors limit the extent to which we are the free agents that we often like to think we are. There is evidence that people try to manage their self-concepts (or social identities). There may be significant cultural differences in self-concepts, especially between cultures that inculcate independent and interdependent self-concepts. These differences can have profound effects on individuals' motivations and interactive work behaviour.

## SELF-ESTEEM, PERCEIVED CONTROL AND SELF-DELUSION

Some components of our self-concepts are neutral and non-judgemental: 'town-dweller', 'filing clerk', 'father of two', 'keen gardener' and so on. Many more, usually, are judgemental. These evaluate our abilities, our attractiveness to others and our personality. These half-conscious self-assessments of strengths and weaknesses influence what we try to do, whether we hope for success or fear failure in our dealings with others, and what our expectations are about how other people will or should behave towards us and respond to us. They are very important influences. If our assessment of our self is too negative – if we are low in self-esteem – there are enormous barriers to attaining what we need, want and are entitled to from our dealings with others. We will be afraid to ask for what we want and may avoid a whole range of different types of interactions. Other people may well take us at our own low estimate and treat us badly. People with low self-esteem choose to interact with people who give unfavourable (rather than favourable) evaluations of them as long as those unfavourable evaluations are consistent with their self-beliefs.[13] Sources of self-evaluations, similar to sources of self-concepts, include reflected appraisals (using others as a mirror in which we see ourselves), social comparisons with similar or significant others and self-perception, which means observing and interpreting our own behaviour.[14]

Three different types or levels of self-worth can be distinguished. Research by Brewer and Gardner[15] showed that these three types of self-esteem are correlated, but only moderately so. The first type is how we rate ourselves as individuals – for instance, how intelligent or motivated we think ourselves. This level is derived from comparing ourselves to relevant others, such as fellow workers.[16] The second type is interpersonal self-worth, for example, how good we think we are at getting on with other people at work. This type of self-worth evaluation derives from behaving appropriately or inappropriately for our role(s).[17] Finally, collective self-worth refers to how we value ourselves as a member of those groups or categories to which we belong – for instance, as a member of the working class or as a woman. In theory, this type of self-worth depends on the status of our in-groups in comparison with other groups.[18] However, empirical studies have shown that members of stigmatised or oppressed groups generally do not suffer from low self-esteem. For instance, the self-esteem of African-Americans is often higher than that of white Americans. One study found that individuals who compared themselves unfavourably with out-group members, regardless of who the members of the comparison group were, reported levels of self-esteem as high and depression as low as those who compared themselves favourably with out-groups. Their self-esteem was higher and depression lower than the levels of individuals who compared themselves unfavourably with in-group members.[19] It seems as if people who feel that their group does worse than others see the performance of out-group members as in some way irrelevant to their self-esteem.

Mummendey *et al.*[20] proposed that people have strategic responses to cope with and overcome an unsatisfactory group status position (or to defend a satisfactory one). They identified six possible strategies:

1. individual mobility (rising up the social or occupational ladder);
2. self-recategorisation at a higher level, e.g. 'I am a German' not 'I am an East German';
3. social competition – trying to gain a higher social status for their group;
4. realistic competition – aiming at their group receiving more material resources;
5. preference for temporal comparison rather than comparison with other groups ('We East Germans have improved our situation compared with the past');
6. re-evaluation of the material dimension ('We East Germans are more spiritual; those from the West are materialistic').

The first two strategies imply a degree of separation of the individual's self-concept from the group. The last four all imply high group identification, feelings of anger on behalf of the group, which is perceived to be (relatively) deprived, and expectations of being able to change the group's relative position.

More generally, people with high self-esteem have a relatively small gap between the way they see their actual and ideal selves. They also devalue the negative attributes they possess and the positive attributes they do not possess and have high expectations for the future. They take credit for successes and deny responsibility for failures. They self-present positively. They rate positive traits as true of themself and negative traits as untrue of themself, although apart from a small difference in academic achievement, there is little evidence that high self-esteem people perform better or have more positive characteristics than do low self-esteem people. While high self-esteem is usually advantageous, leading to greater persistence and more success, when problems are actually unsolvable, more persistence can be a waste of effort.

**Box 4.2**

### How to boost or restore your self-esteem

1. Remember that because of the way self-concepts are formed, they are not 'right' – not objective. Many components of your self-concept could be false. If in childhood you compared your performance with an older sibling, not allowing for age differences, an unrealistic and negative self-image may have resulted. The more negative your self-concept, the more likely it is to be mistaken.
2. Try to manage the impression you have of yourself. Remember that the way that you behave is not only affected by the way you feel about yourself, it also affects the self-same feeling. Your behaviour not only creates an impression on other people, it also creates an impression on yourself. (This is an instance of the behaviour – attitude relationship described in Chapter 3.) Any good actor or actress knows this instinctively: if you start to behave as if you are angry by shouting, speaking quickly, glaring or gesticulating, it is quite easy to start to feel angry. If you start weeping, you soon feel quite sad. Similarly, if you start to speak authoritatively – slowly, in measured tones and slightly deeper voice than usual – generally, you soon stop feeling like a trapped rabbit and start to feel in control. Regulating your behaviour is, in many situations, easier than trying to regulate your thoughts and feelings directly.
3. Behaving assertively, covered in Chapter 6, may help boost your self-esteem.
4. If you receive negative feedback, focus on other favourable aspects of yourself, rate yourself highly on related or unrelated dimensions, behave in ways that contradict the feedback or behave in ways that highlight your other, positive, features. All these methods have been shown to work.
5. Make appropriate social comparisons. Comparing yourself with others who have performed better than or are better off than you (upward comparison) results in more negative feelings and lower self-esteem than comparing yourself with others who have performed worse than or are worse off than you (downward comparison). People with low self-esteem are most likely to make the mistake of comparing upwards after they fail. In contrast, people with high self-esteem are more likely to compare downwards after they fail (Wood *et al.*, 1999).
6. Try to emulate the other practices and attitudes of people with high self-esteem described in this section.

*Source*: Wood, J. V., M. Giordano-Beech and M. J. Ducharme (1999) 'Compensating for failure through social comparison', *Personality and Social Psychology Bulletin*, vol. 25, no. 11, pp. 1370–1386.

A factor closely linked to self-image and self-esteem that has been shown to influence interaction behaviour is 'perceived control'. This is the extent to which individuals perceive themselves as having control over what happens to them and hence of their environment, which, of course, includes the people at work. Perceived control includes self-control as well as control of external events. High perceived interpersonal control, over the processes and outcomes of interaction, influences individuals' sense of psychological well-being and creates expectations that lead to discovering how to act in different situations. Thus positive expectations can be 'an important component in the development and maintenance of competent communication patterns'.[21] Low perceived interpersonal control leads to avoidance and lack of relevant experience. These positive and negative effects of high and low perceived interpersonal control do not depend on the perceptions being accurate.

In contrast to the problem of low self-esteem, recent research has pointed to a different phenomenon connected to self-concepts, self-delusion. For instance, many people under-estimate their own and over-estimate others' task completion times.[22] This optimistic bias may occur because people focus on plans and intentions rather than on information such as past failures. Even in areas of chance, some people will readily exhibit an illusion of control. This self-deception increases when factors such as competition, choice, involvement and skill are present. For instance, the majority of drivers consider themselves more skilful than the average driver. The illusion of control affects our psychological functioning in some beneficial but some harmful ways. It can result in greater effort and persistence and so lead to greater success. On the other hand, people who are disinclined to believe that negative events can happen to themselves against their will are less likely to be self-protective and this can lead to rash experimentation with, for instance, trading securities.[23]

## SUMMARY – SELF-ESTEEM, PERCEIVED CONTROL AND SELF-DELUSION

Although in Western society most people have a positive self-concept, others suffer from low self-esteem. This undermines their social skills as well as making them miserable. Others, on the other hand, are self-deluded, especially about the level of control they have especially over the outcomes of their interactions with other people. These delusions can have both favourable and unfavourable results.

## COPING AND EFFICACY

It is unrealistic to pretend, as some do, that working life consists entirely of opportunities ('Every problem is an opportunity!') or that every situation can have a positive outcome. Some aspects of working life are inherently negative, give rise to negative responses in us and are problems with which, if we are realistic, we have to cope. Here, for illustrative purposes, I discuss two that are closely linked to our self: our own negative emotions and stress. The workplace is particularly stressful for members of minority groups and women, for whom coping presents the challenge of preserving their sense of 'selfhood'. Efficacy, or having confidence in one's ability to perform a task, is closely linked to effectiveness in the task and indirectly to coping and self-esteem.

## Coping with negative emotions

Effectiveness in interactions at work can require a high ability to keep negative emotions under control. Fear is one such negative emotion and there is more about it in the context of anxiety in Chapter 6 and communication apprehension in Chapter 7. Here, as an example of coping, ways of controlling the negative emotion of anger are considered.

Although the term 'control' is used, it is perhaps not the best word; most researchers and therapists now believe that the best way to deal with one's anger is to substitute adaptive responses for maladaptive responses. Maladaptive responses include direct aggression towards the target of the anger. Aggression may be physical (e.g. hitting, shoving, throwing things at the target), verbal (e.g. yelling, scolding, making a nasty remark) or symbolic (e.g. shaking a fist, slamming a door). Also maladaptive are indirect aggression such as malediction ('bad-mouthing' the target to a third party), indirect harm (harming something important to the target), displaced aggression (against an unconnected person or object), self-aggression (e.g. berating oneself for the situation) and anger held in (brooding, ruminating over the incident without expressing it).

Adaptive responses include rational, non-hostile discussions with the target of the anger and corrective action. There are two other kinds of response, which may be either adaptive or maladaptive, depending on the circumstances. One is escapist responses, such as attempts to defuse anger by distracting activities, minimising the importance of the incident, or leaving the situation. The other is reappraisals, such as reinterpreting the motives or actions of the target, e.g. 'He didn't mean it', 'She was just trying to help' or of one's own role, e.g. 'It was partly my fault; maybe I should have been more careful.'

## Coping with difficult situations and with stress

A supervisor in a shoe shop seized on every mistake made by a new recruit – criticising, blaming and ridiculing him to other staff. The recruit began to think seriously about leaving. However, the shop had staff shortages and, after a day or two, the shop manager, who had been noticing what was happening, said to the recruit 'She's moody', referring to the supervisor. I happened to interview the recruit at about this time, and he was understanding about the supervisor:

'She's got problems – basically, she's been working here for ten years, she's got a load too many things she has to do, she's hoping for promotion and it's not coming. All the same, it's not my fault, and I wish she wouldn't take it out on me. And, of course, she's probably dishing her chances of getting promotion because she keeps tearing into trainees.'

Here we have examples of both the problems posed in this section. One participant was stressed, while the other had a difficult situation to deal with, which might well have been an eventual stress inducer for him in turn. High stress levels have been found among managers. Work overload, time pressures and deadlines affect both male and female managers at all levels, while women at all levels additionally report being affected by Type A behaviour. Other pressures differ according to managerial level and gender. Senior women managers report a lack of consultation and communication, while senior men managers find under-promotion to be a major source of stress. Further down the seniority level, women's particular stress sources are mainly gender-related. They feel they have to perform better at the job than colleagues of the other sex, they face a career-related dilemma over whether to start a family, they find their sex a disadvantage in career prospects and they suffer from office politics. Men, by comparison, report fewer sources of stress, and those are more closely job-related. Sacking someone, disciplining subordinates and rate of pay get mentioned. Only at the supervisory level do men report more sources of major stress than women, citing long working hours, work overload, staff shortages, equipment failures, unclear career prospects, rate of pay and redundancy threat.[24] Some of the major effects of stress reported by managers and supervisors include sleep trouble, tiredness, being unable to cope well in conflict situations, wanting to be left alone, smoking, drinking and eating too much, being unable to influence or persuade people and finding it difficult to get up in the mornings.

## Gender issues in coping

Women's coping abilities are often seen as related to whether or not they have a strong sense of autonomy. There are two kinds of autonomy, emotional and instrumental. Emotional autonomy means being able to define oneself rather than be defined by others. Women have traditionally been raised to be more other-centred than autonomous, but without emotional autonomy, women inhibit the development of self-expression, self-knowledge and self-esteem and tend to see difficulties as their own fault or failure. Instrumental autonomy is the ability to act upon the world, carry on activities, cope with problems and take action to meet one's needs. For women to achieve this means combatting centuries of custom and stereotyping. Girls are often encouraged to nurture others and to be expressive of feelings rather than to be task-oriented, receiving little encouragement for achievement. However researchers have found that women who score

Box 4.3

### How to cope with difficult situations and stress

What can you do to help yourself cope, especially with stress? The following techniques are based on recognising that you are trying to modify internalised behaviour patterns which have been established for many years, so your expectations should not be too high, and you should be pleased with small increments of progress (Davidson and Cooper, 1983).

- Listen to other people. Stop trying to finish their sentences or hasten their speech rhythms.
- Try to reduce the pressure you feel to keep talking. Does it matter if you let this bit of the discussion go and do not contribute?
- Change obsessional and driven behaviour. Punish yourself, e.g. by making yourself turn right and go round the block if you jump the lights. Reward yourself, e.g. by going to see a good film when you resist working late.
- Assess the cause of your Type A behaviour from time to time. Is it a need to feel important? Is it designed to avoid some activity or person? Is it essential to achieving some personal or organisational goal? Will this matter be important five years from now? Must you do this right now, or do you have time to think about the best way to accomplish your goal?
- Undertake a slow-paced but absorbing activity – bowls, cricket, complex needlework, gardening, cooking. Some of these also provide exercise.
- Learn to say 'no'. Do not overload yourself.
- Be aware of activities that increase your own stress levels. These may be unexpected. For example, you may think that because writing reports, articles or long memos is a quiet activity, it is a low-stress one. However, counsellors have found that stress is particularly likely to arise during this activity, perhaps because of the pressure to perform well in a durable medium. You should interrupt your own stress activities frequently with bouts of other, relaxing, activities.
- Reduce your hostility to others. For example, give warm thanks to people who have done something for you. They are likely to reciprocate, leading to a more supportive climate in your relationships.
- A validated questionnaire used in much stress research suggests the following coping strategies are positive: informal relaxation techniques, exercise, talking to someone you know, leaving the work area and using humour. Negative stress-induced strategies include taking aspirin, using tranquillisers or other medication, drinking coffee, cola or eating frequently, smoking and drinking alcohol (Steinmetz, 1979).
- Coping is recognised to be intimately connected to our self-concepts and self-esteem. Study the section in this chapter on how to boost your self-esteem.

*Sources*: Davidson, M. and C. Cooper (1983) *Stress and the Woman Manager*. Oxford: Martin Robertson. Steinmetz, J. (1979) *Conflict/Stress Questionnaire*. San Diego: UC Medical Centre.

high on instrumental personality attributes such as 'active', 'independent' and 'competitive' improve their performance after success, do not deteriorate after failure and are better able to attribute success to ability and failure to external causes.[25] A successful top woman executive who was interviewed for research into coping suggested how she tries to do it. Her suggestions are listed in Box 4.4.

**Box 4.4**

### How to cope with stress – a woman executive's method

- Being in touch with my anxiety and searching for the cause.
- Deliberately thinking of people in the situation.
- Talking about my anxieties.
- Trying to take a long-term perspective of success and failure.
- Trying to ensure people get to know me as a person so they can't stereotype me.
- Making notes, learning from experience what I would do in the same situation again.
- Allowing 'gestation' time during problem-solving, i.e. trying to let my subconscious work things out.
- Feeling confident about my appearance when in risk-taking situations.
- Acknowledging my successes to myself.
- Reading something away from the immediate 'problem' but around work to lighten my mind and stimulate thinking.
- Doing one personal development or training activity a year – to take time to take stock, heighten awareness and get things into perspective.
- Keeping in touch with issues and problems outside work, e.g. family, politics, etc., to put my work problems into perspective.
- Looking for another door to push open when one has just closed.

*Source*: Davidson, M. and C. Cooper (1983) *Stress and the Woman Manager*. Oxford: Martin Robertson.

## Efficacy

People's confidence in their abilities to perform particular tasks, called 'efficacy', largely determines the extent to which they persevere with those tasks and how successful they are with them. Efficacy is the confidence that one can use one's capabilities to execute a course of action that will result in performance.[26] Efficacy theory states that people develop 'efficacy expectations', highly specific beliefs about their abilities to perform certain tasks in certain situations.[27] They do this by synthesising information from a variety of sources, including previous experience with the activity and setting, observations of other people's behaviour in similar situations, verbal information and interpretation of their own state of psychological arousal (for instance, interpreting increased heart beat as fear in the way described in Chapter 3). For their behaviour to be influenced, people must believe both that outcome 'Y' is desirable and that action 'X' will produce the outcome 'Y'. Efficacy beliefs have three important dimensions. These are magnitude (how taxing are the tasks people believe they can handle), generality (whether their sense of efficacy extends well beyond the particular task) and strength (a weak sense of efficacy is easily extinguished by disconfirming experiences, a strong one leads to continued striving in spite of disconfirming experiences).

Efficacy theory has been used to develop a series of 'treatments' for people with low efficacy expectations, by which their beliefs in their own ability to

**Table 4.1 Major sources of efficacy information and principal modes through which treatments operate**

| *Source* | *Mode of induction* |
|---|---|
| Performance accomplishments | Participant modelling<br>Performance desensitisation<br>Performance exposure<br>Self-instructed performance |
| Vicarious experience | Live modelling<br>Symbolic modelling |
| Verbal persuasion | Suggestion<br>Exhortation<br>Self-instruction<br>Interpretative treatments |
| Emotional arousal | Attribution<br>Relaxation, biofeedback<br>Symbolic desensitisation<br>Symbolic exposure |

Based on: Bandura, A. (1977) 'Self-efficacy theory: toward a unifying theory of behavioural change', *Psychological Review*, vol. 84, no. 2, pp. 191–215.

perform tasks can be enhanced. They are given in Table 4.1 in descending order of effectiveness. The most effective are those that give the most authentic information that mastery is achieved. Thus 'performance', actually carrying out a task successfully, is the most effective treatment. Emotional arousal, which gives little information, is least effective. Performance provides not just evidence of success, but ownership and internalisation. It also allows the person to adapt methods to suit themself. However, even carrying out the task successfully does not guarantee the sense of mastery for people with low self-esteem. Because of faulty appraisals of the circumstances under which they improve, they may credit their achievements to external factors rather than to their own capabilities. The more varied the circumstances in which they succeed in the task, though, the harder it is for them to doubt their ability to do it.

Gaining a sense of self-efficacy can be very beneficial for both individuals and their colleagues in group- or teamwork. A not uncommon response to such situations is 'Does my contribution really matter?' It has been shown that people over-generalise from experience with various sized groups and so generally presume that they are less efficacious in larger groups, even when they may not be. (They also over-generalise from past successes or failures of the group in solving problems without taking into account the relative difficulty of the task.) Thus, self-efficacy in groupwork is a judgement of the degree to which one's co-operative behaviour will increase the chances of the group achieving some valued collective outcome. It is therefore not surprising that it has been demonstrated that direct manipulation of perceived self-efficacy has a strong effect on willingness to co-operate.[28]

Box 4.5

**How to apply self-efficacy theory to gain self-confidence in your ability to carry out a task**

- Start by performing the task under close guidance, then do it without help, then do other related tasks using your own adaptation of the taught method. Once you have developed some sense of mastery you need plenty of practice, otherwise one or two disconfirming experiences will weaken your confidence.
- If you do not have the opportunity to actually perform the task, watching others perform is next best. Seeing others perform (without adverse consequences) activities that look too difficult is effective in making us expect that we too will improve if we intensify and persist in our efforts. The effect is greater the more effort is shown by models, the clearer their result, the more the persons modelling resemble us in ways relevant to the task, the more diversified the tasks using the same skill and the more varied the situations in which they are demonstrated.
- The effects of verbal persuasion are weak, because there is no authentic base of experience. Despite this, people who are targets of persuasion that they can master difficult situations and who are given aids for effective action try harder than those who receive only the performance aids. However, unless the conditions promote success, persuasion will only discredit the persuaders. Whether there is any real effect depends on the credibility of the persuaders, which is a function of their perceived prestige, trustworthiness, expertise and assuredness.
- It has sometimes been thought that if you get excited and keyed up you can do things you would normally find too threatening, but research findings do not support this. This is probably because high arousal usually undermines performance and therefore leads people to expect failure.

Individuals' need for self-efficacy, for feeling mastery over their environment, appears from research to be cross-cultural.[29] In both Chinese and US samples, people who attributed failures in relations with others to their own ability, strategy, personality, trait, effort or temporary mood state were more likely to suffer depression and loneliness than people who attributed such failures to external factors. Similarly, those who accepted credit for success were less depressed and lonely.

## SUMMARY – COPING AND EFFICACY

Our ability to cope with negative experiences at work, such as events or situations that cause us anger, or with stress, may be crucial to our effectiveness in interactions as well as to our own well-being and health. To cope with negative emotions such as anger, the best strategy is to substitute adaptive responses such as rational, non-hostile discussions with the target of anger for maladaptive strategies such as verbal or physical aggression. Strategies to cope with difficult situations and with stress, which is now widespread among people at work, include acting directly on Type A behaviour in a range of ways. Women's socialisation and the hostility of some work environments may present women with particular coping problems. Two sets of coping guidelines are given. Efficacy, or confidence in one's ability to perform a task, including an interpersonal task, strongly influences how effectively it is performed. Efficacy is best developed through practice under a range of conditions.

## PERSONAL DEVELOPMENT

Personal development is about fulfilling our potential, expanding our talents and progressing at work and through life with meaning and satisfaction. Ultimately we have to develop ourselves. Others can set the scene, supply role models, give encouragement, provide support, propose methods and means, set up mechanisms, give advice, impart knowledge and provide contacts but the learner is at the heart of the development process. Personal development includes developing appropriate qualities and skills, including independent learning skills, interpersonal skills and our own ethical systems.

### Qualities and skills

We need to develop qualities and skills that reflect the likely future world in which we will live out our lives or have our careers. In a fast-changing world, we need to develop ourselves for tomorrow's demands rather than just today's. American management writer Rosabeth Moss Kanter has argued that future work demands will require seven particular qualities:[30]

1. The ability to operate without relying on a hierarchy. Managers will have to rely on their personal capacities to achieve results rather than depending on the authority of their position.
2. The ability to compete in a way that enhances rather than undercuts co-operation.
3. A high standard of ethics: collaborations, joint ventures and so on depend on a high level of trust.
4. Humility – there will always be new things to learn.
5. Having a process focus – how things are done is just as important as what is done; making things happen is as important as deciding what should happen.
6. Multifaceted and ambidextrous abilities – to work across functions and business units to find synergies that multiply value, to form alliances when opportune but cut ties when necessary, to swim effectively in the mainstream and the 'newstreams'.

7. The ability to gain satisfaction from results, valuing the contribution rather than demanding status rewards.

**Box 4.6**

> 'Companies must have executives who are better informed of their own development needs, better apprised of the realism of their aspirations, and better equipped to feel in control of their destinies.'
>
> *Source*: Thorne, P. (1993) 'Lost leaders', *International Management*, Jan./Feb., p. 80. Paul Thorne was then head of Psycom, a UK-based corporate psychology partnership.

On a rather more down-to-earth level, in a book written with K. Tyler,[31] I suggested that the conditions of the late twentieth and early twenty-first centuries will require us to develop a set of enterprise skills. Enterprise skills are transferable from job to job. In addition to interpersonal skills, they consist of the following:

- Self management. Taking responsibility for our own lives, getting to know ourselves, becoming aware of our motives, feelings, values and abilities and our strong and weak points, setting personal goals and developing our ability to cope with difficult situations and stress.
- Learning. This is an active process driven forward by the learner, a continuous process, going on throughout life, a multifaceted process, drawing on cognitive, behaviourist and experiential learning theories.
- Obtaining and using good quality information. Working out what we need to know, accessing sources, analysing and interpreting information, presenting it in a user-friendly way, recording, storing and retrieving it.
- Decision-making and planning. Using a process that ensures we reflect our true values and preferences, consider all our alternatives, use information fully and systematically evaluate our options. Learning ways of planning to implement decisions effectively.
- Recognising, creating and evaluating opportunities. Making the most of opportunities is a key factor in succeeding in getting what we want from life and work. Environment scanning, networking and applying methods of boosting creativity all increase the number of opportunities open to us and the chances that we will recognise them; ways of assessing opportunities in terms of riskiness and value are then needed to ensure they are worthwhile.
- Performing. We can only make the most of our opportunities if we satisfy others by what we produce. Making our work user-friendly, maintaining high standards and working for continuous improvement are needed.
- Changing. Adapting to change introduced from outside, helping others to adapt, and ourselves spotting the need or the opportunity for change and knowing how to bring it about.

Some of these skills are too peripheral to the subject of this book to justify my covering them here; aspects of others appear in other places in the book – there is material on decision-making in groups in Chapter 11 and on networking and changing in Chapter 8. Here I concentrate on aspects of personal development that are necessary for working effectively with and through other people: learning, interpersonal skill development and developing an ethical framework.

## Learning

There are four models of learning that are particularly relevant to learning at work. These are the cognitive model, the behaviourist/associative model, the Kolb 'learning-from-experience' model and 'double-loop' learning. Although social scientists tend to adhere to one or other of these as 'the' learning model, for our purpose this is not necessary. It seems more likely that different individuals learn in different ways or that the same person may learn in different ways at different times or even simultaneously. At work it is wise to be prepared to apply all four models to improve our knowledge and skills.

### *Cognitive learning*

Cognitive learning includes the sort people are expected to achieve at school. It is sometimes also called information processing and involves interpreting present perceptions in the light of past information and storing the result in memory in such a way that it can easily be recalled or recollected. There are many different theories on memory structure and functioning and thus on cognitive learning. For the most part they can be regarded as variations on a theme. Figure 4.2 charts the main processes and influences that some researchers now believe to be involved in cognitive learning. According to the model shown in Figure 4.2, a piece of information, a stimulus, first enters sensory memory and is analysed there to establish its physical properties such as colour, loudness and shape. Entry into sensory memory is virtually instantaneous, but the information stored there is limited, in that no meaning is attached to the physical properties, and the 'memory' will normally be lost very quickly unless it is transferred to short-term memory.

Whether such transfer into short-term memory takes place depends on whether meaning can be assigned to the incoming information by combining it with the contents of long-term memory (cognitive schemas), categorising and interpreting it.[32] Information that is transferred to short-term memory is not, however, 'safe'. Short-term memory has limited storage and processing capacity, so the chunks of related information will rapidly be lost as they are displaced by new incoming information unless they are transferred to long-term memory. Long-term memory is generally viewed as an unlimited, permanent store of information.

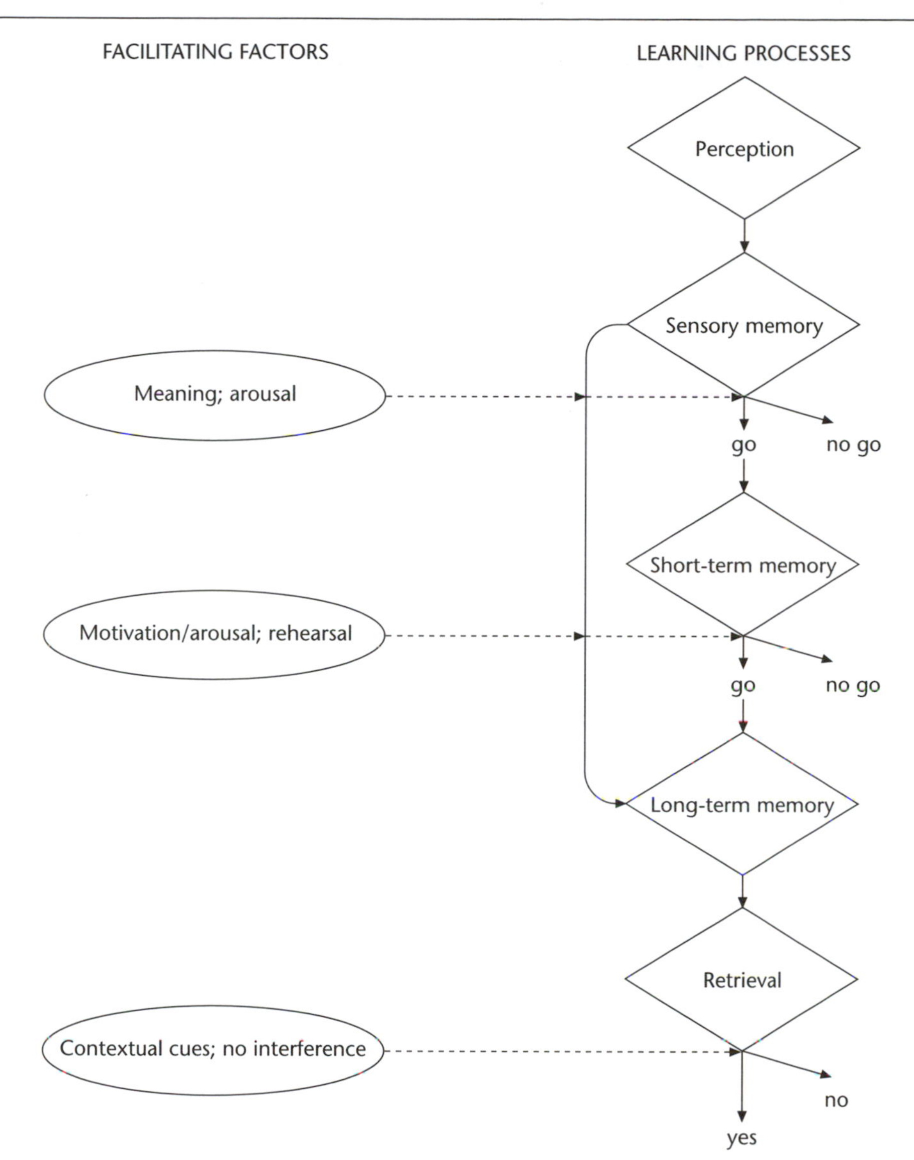


**Figure 4.2 A process model of cognitive learning and the factors that facilitate this type of learning.**

It consists of cognitive schemas, 'facts' about one's own personal history, semantic data, concepts that help interpret the world and procedures, which are the skills and knowledge needed to use stored facts, concepts and cognitive schemas.[33] Another version of the contents of long-term memory sees it as a network that relates concepts and facts in a structural way.[34] Information is constantly being organised and re-organised as new links are forged between chunks of information.

Studies of cognitive learning have explored why some information is easy to learn and some more difficult, why some is retained briefly but then forgotten (short-term memory) while some is retained and can be recalled for long periods of time or permanently (long-term memory). In Figure 4.2, the factors that are conducive to cognitive memorising are shown as 'facilitating factors'.

1. People actively select and process information, even though they are not always aware of doing so. They are more predisposed to learn some things than others, according to how well these things fit with their previous knowledge, i.e. according to the level of meaning they attach to the new information. Next, whether and how well people learn depends on their motivation. For example, it is widely recognised that interest in a subject or activity affects how quickly people learn. Interest is mainly affected by people's need for the knowledge on offer. Thus an ambitious junior executive will quickly absorb information needed for an imminent meeting with a top manager. Highly motivated people will pay more attention, i.e. select out fewer of the incoming stimuli and transfer more of what they attend to into memory. Inappropriate motivation may, however, lead them to distort information more.

Like other active human processes, learning requires energy, even if it is of a somewhat different kind from the energy used to run a race. Like muscular activity, though, learning activity is stimulated by arousal which can be triggered either by an appeal to a current motivation, as suggested above, or through more primitive reflexes, such as surprise, shock, fear or excitement. Finally, learners who can enjoy the immediate intellectual development of a topic, irrespective of any instrumental motive, learn faster. This capacity is known as cognitive playfulness and is abundant and pervasive in everyday life. Researchers have found that learning performance in microcomputer training is positively related to playfulness.

2. Rehearsing helps people learn. Normally, rehearsing refers to silent inner speech, as when someone mentally repeats a telephone number in order to learn it. Up to a point out-loud repetition such as chanting multiplication tables is also rehearsal and helps people learn, although when it is externally controlled, as by a teacher or advertiser, it is much less likely that the optimal level of any individual will be reached. Overdo it, boredom sets in and learning is reduced. Mere reiteration, however, usually produces transfer into short-term memory only, which is why the telephone number that was known perfectly last night is so often forgotten beyond recall this morning. For longer-term storage, associative rehearsal is more effective, because it locks the memory in with more connections and supplies more pathways to recalling it. This explains why it can be effective to use mnemonics and images, to link new data with previous experiences or knowledge, to identify similarities with or differences from other known cases,

to structure information input and to build logic paths from the known to the unknown.

3. Retrieval is the process by which we recover information from long-term storage. It is crucial to the usefulness of long-term memory. Current wisdom has it that the problem of forgetting is really one of being unable to retrieve information that is there: long-term memory is considered to have unlimited storage capacity. Two factors help retrieval efficiency: activation by an appropriate context, and lack of interference by other stored information.

### *Behaviourist learning*

Behaviourist learning is learning from experience in the same way that primitive animals such as amoebae do: i.e. learning that takes place as the result of observable responses to external stimuli. The theory, here, is that organisms of all kinds respond to stimuli from the environment and, in fact, that that is what we mean by stimuli and for that matter by organisms: they are stimulus–response mechanisms, variously elaborated. Humans, being organisms, respond to stimuli just as amoebae do, only being possessed of more sophisticated nervous systems their range of potential responses is wider. Once any particular response has been made to a given stimulus the two become, for that individual, associated, not mentally this time, but behaviourally, as a tendency to repeat the response whenever in future the same or a similar stimulus is experienced. Two stimulus–response theories of great relevance to interpersonal interaction at work are classical conditioning and instrumental conditioning.

In *classical conditioning*, so-called because it was the type of learning introduced by Ivan Pavlov, the creator of conditioned learning theory, an established relationship between a stimulus and a response is used to bring about the learning of the same response to a different stimulus. The 'natural', reflexive, or already-learned stimulus is called the unconditioned stimulus; the response to it is the unconditioned response. The stimulus that comes to be associated with the same response is the conditioned stimulus, and the response to it is the conditioned response. Factors that promote classical conditioning are repetition and stimulus generalisation.

Repeated exposure to the association between the unconditioned stimulus and the conditioned stimulus increases the chances that the association will be learned and the same response given when the conditioned stimulus is supplied on its own. For example, an international executive might enjoy her first transatlantic flight in Business Class but as the number of tiring flights she makes increases, might come to dislike the long-haul ones. There is plentiful evidence of the efficiency of sheer repetition to impart a message.

Stimulus generalisation refers to the ability of individuals to generalise. For instance, the salivating dogs, on whose behaviour Pavlov based his theory, could generalise from the sound of a bell to the sound of jangling keys. Learning is faster because of this ability, because it means that each association of a response with a stimulus does not have to be separately learned. This argues for grouping similar items to be learned together. In the adult human the capacity to generalise is large but not infinite. Using stimulus generalisation to promote learning depends on understanding which stimuli the individual learners do in fact generalise. There are also some sequencing effects that influence classical conditioning. For instance, if the learners are already familiar with either the conditioned or the unconditioned stimulus, they are less likely to form associations between them even when they are repeatedly presented together.

In *instrumental conditioning*, an individual attempts to gain rewards by responding to stimuli, initially on a trial-and-error basis. If the response produces a good result for the individual or, in behaviourist language, is rewarded, the tendency to repeat the response, already noted, will be greatly increased. If it produces a bad result, the tendency to repeat it will be reduced. This principle is called reinforcement.[35] Much interactive behaviour is learned by instrumental conditioning. People try out an interactive style, repeat it if it works and try something else if it does not work. Instrumental conditioning is promoted by offering reinforcements in appropriate form, amount and timing. One important way in which reinforcements can vary is between total reinforcement (always reinforcing the desired response) and partial reinforcement (reinforcing the desired response only some of the time, either systematically, or randomly). Studies have suggested that with animals, total reinforcement leads to faster learning, but partial reinforcement leads to more durable learning.[36]

There is much more to behaviourist learning theory than this; but from a self-developer's point of view the two main themes have emerged: the importance of repetition and the importance of reward and punishment. I do not know of any research that shows that self-granted rewards or self-imposed punishments work according to behaviourist theory, but the writers on self-development seem to assume they do.

### Kolb's model

According to Kolb's experiential learning model, we learn from experience through thinking and reflecting on what has happened.[37] After an experience we go through a cycle of processes, as illustrated in Figure 4.3. For example, a new consultant might be over-forceful in expressing negative views of a client company's advertising and find that his opinions caused dismay and disapproval. Then the following learning processes are likely to occur: first, he reflects on the experience, perhaps recalling additionally that he has been told that the company is proud of its advertising. From this reflection he concludes that the company's culture is one of uncritical loyalty, and that in future he will be more gradual. He has now completed the conceptualisation stage. On the next occasion he tests out this idea by expressing his views more cautiously.

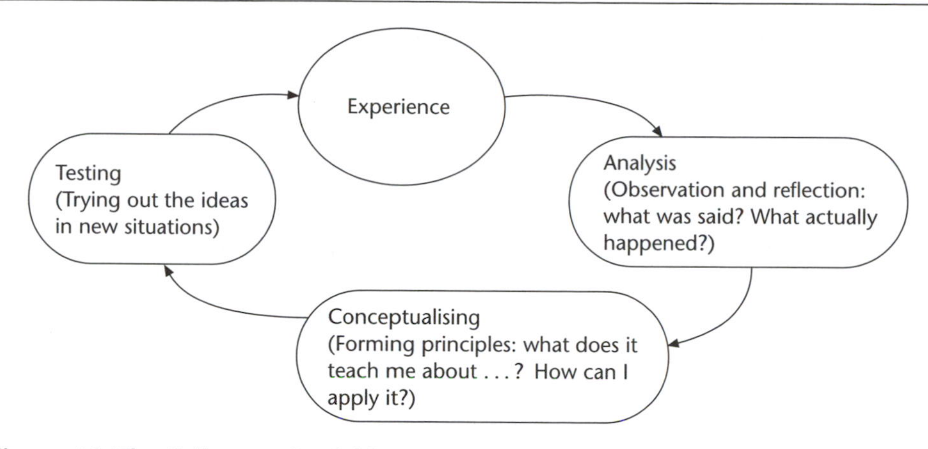

**Figure 4.3 The Kolb experiential learning model.**

### *Double-loop learning model*

The double-loop learning model is based on the idea that two kinds of learning are needed in all organisations. The first is single-loop learning, which is incremental and adaptive. It corrects errors by changing routine behaviour without, however, examining the appropriateness of current ways of learning. The second kind is double-loop learning, which corrects errors by examining underlying values and policies.[38] Thus a single-loop learning response to a drop in sales of a product would be to look at the data on all the variables that usually affect sales, from economic variables such as incomes and taxes to what the competition is up to and whether the company's own marketing efforts are as effective as they should be. Action would be taken to put right whatever this investigation found to be wrong, and some learning would happen which would lead to things being done differently in future. Such a process is often necessary and useful. Double-loop learning, though, would ask, 'Are these the right questions to be asking about this sales problem? Is it possible that something quite different is going on here, possibly a change in consumer preferences or a deep-seated loss of faith in our brand (such as UK retailer Marks & Spencer suffered around the year 2000)?'

According to Argyris, the originator of the double-loop learning concept, the capacity for double-loop learning is rare. Most people in organisations use 'master programmes' and 'defensive reasoning processes' that are counter-productive for learning and change and have to be unlearnt before double-loop learning is possible. He argues that it only becomes widespread in organisations if it is adopted by leaders who will both model and reward it. Learning should be in the service of action, rather than simply discovery or insight. The targets of double-loop learning are 'theories of action' – the sets of rules that individuals use to design and implement their behaviour. To change these theories of actions involves mapping defensive action rules applied to a live problem by dialoguing with a peer, creating productive action rules and applying them to the problem. The competencies required for double-loop learning are the same when dealing with individuals, groups, 'inter-groups' or organisations.

## Developing interpersonal skills

We know now that being 'good at dealing with people' is not just a capacity that someone either has or lacks, an unalterable facet of personality. Instead, learning is the key to how interpersonal skills develop. How to talk to different kinds of people, when to talk or be silent, what to say in different circumstances, with whom to associate for different purposes and where to hold certain kinds of conversations – all these skills and many more we acquire, without thinking about them, as we grow up. Learning how to interact is a key element in socialisation, so that the set of interpersonal skills we possess in adult life reflects the culture, social class, family, friends and institutions we have experienced while growing up. That means that our skills are appropriate for that set of social groups, and to some extent reflect their values, attitudes and tastes. It can also mean that a change of social setting requires a shift in ways of behaving that calls for new learning. For example, representatives of European companies trying to do business in Arab countries or in Japan have to learn new social conventions – how being kept waiting for half an hour or more after the time of an appointment is quite normal, and should not be resented, and how turning the discussion to 'business' before a prolonged period of social conversation is impossibly rude. For most people, starting college or work, even a change of job, requires new learning about how to behave – new socialisation. Figure 4.4 illustrates the

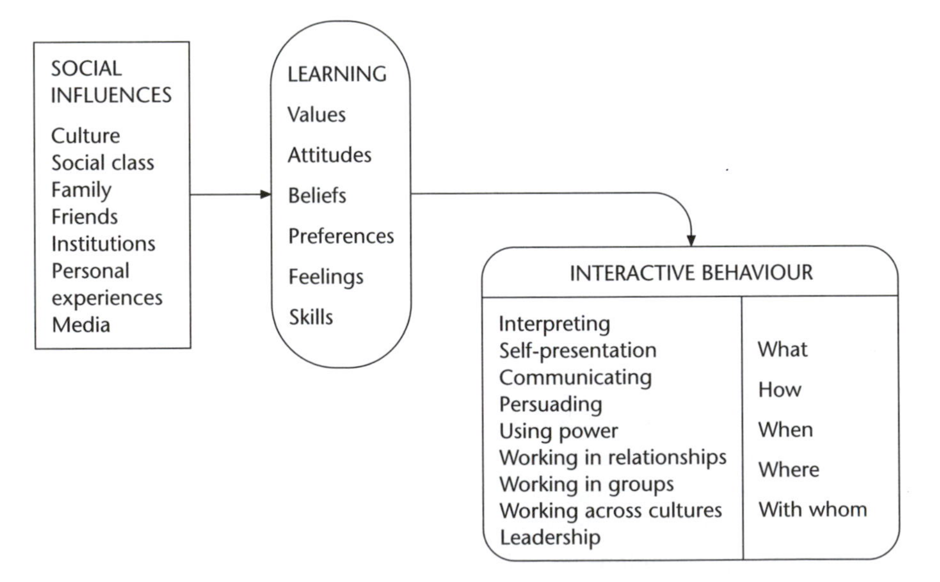


**Figure 4.4 Learning: how we acquire our interpersonal skills.**

relationships between skills and social influences that are developed through learning.

**Box 4.7**

### How to develop your interpersonal skills

If 'being good at dealing with people' is achieved by learning, what is it precisely that is learnt? The answer to this is a set of skills, approaches and attitudes that can be studied, understood and practised. In this way most people can improve considerably on their initial performance level.

- Aim to have a broad repertoire of ways of dealing with people, based on a good level of understanding and practice. Unfortunately, however, using a wide range of interactive behaviour does not come easily to most people, for the following reason. 'In an interaction, people will emit only certain selected behaviours, selected on the basis that they have been rewarded in the past' (Swenson, 1979). What this means is that we tend to keep on using the approaches and styles that worked well when we first tried them. This consistency has some value – it makes predicting one another's reactions and responses easier. However, there is a danger of becoming increasingly imprisoned in one or two ways of behaving and therefore of being unable to deal effectively with situations which really need a different approach. Using the appropriate skills well builds your credibility, maintains your influence and enables you to get effort and initiative from others without constant monitoring. It also builds your own self-confidence.
- Know about the factors that affect interpersonal behaviour and be aware of what goes on when people interact. (This is called 'mindfulness' and is described further in Chapter 12.)
- Know yourself better – be more aware of your own strengths, weaknesses, prejudices and the impressions you give.
- Be more aware of others – more sensitive to their emotions and attitudes and a better judge of their motives and abilities. Carefully observing others helps this learning once you know what to look out for.
- Practise your skills, ideally where there is little at risk and where feedback is available.

Your attitude to yourself needs to be confident. You need to feel, when you enter an interaction, that you are likely to handle it well. Following the guidance above will help increase your confidence.

*Source*: Swenson, C. H. (1979) *Introduction to Interpersonal Relations*. Glenview, Ill.: Scott, Foresman and Co.

## Developing an ethical framework

To interact confidently, people need to have a clear understanding of their own moral stance. Interacting as an employee may sometimes seem to require making moral compromises. Then the guidance of a clear moral framework can help us to decide our course of action. It can be argued that in principle moral compromise is morally acceptable. In the view of Goodstein,[39] moral compromise may affirm rather than undermine personal integrity, given a view of the self that is responsive to multiple commitments and grounded in an ethic of responsibility. This requires being responsive and reasonable in moral discourse and discerning in establishing moral limits on compromise. McElreath[40] pointed out that individual, interpersonal, small group and organisational factors influence an individual's perception of an ethical problem and the alternatives and consequences they consider. The same is equally true of cultural factors. A logical, interlocking procedure for moral decision-making has been proposed with four steps:

1. Define the situation, that is, evaluate the dilemma from perspectives other than one's own.
2. Identify the values that shape or affect the situation, that is, the standards by which individuals seek meanings and self-worth.
3. Identify relevant moral principles (or theory) that provide ethical contexts for the situation.
4. Identify publics, that is, publics to whom an institution or individual should be loyal.[41]

## SUMMARY – PERSONAL DEVELOPMENT

The topic of personal development has been divided into four: qualities and skills to develop, learning, interpersonal skill development and developing an ethical framework. The qualities and skills to develop should be those that will be required by the work environment of the twenty-first century; they should also be transferable. We learn by four methods – mental processes, associative learning, generalising from experience and double-loop learning. Understanding more about each of these methods produces ideas for learning more effectively. Skill development is a special case of learning where experiential learning predominates. Developing interpersonal skills depends also on having a suitable attitude and approach, an important part of which is having a clear ethical framework and process for moral decision-making.

## INTERACTION PLANNING

The idea of planning interactions in advance may be unfamiliar, although most people faced with what they fear will be a difficult meeting or interview think about what line they will take. A planned approach merely extends this type of thinking in three ways. It makes it more systematic, using a set of guidelines, applies it to a wider range of encounters, including those where no difficulty is anticipated, ultimately, in fact, making it routine, and analyses encounters more thoroughly after they happen. Interaction planning can be divided into two subtopics: interaction strategy and interaction tactics. Interaction strategy refers to deciding what interactions, with whom, in what order and when, are needed to achieve an objective. Planning the broad tenor of approaches to others in face-to-face meetings and deciding what type of behaviour is needed to deal with the current situation and what role to play is referred to as interaction tactics.

**Box 4.8**

A sales engineer described his strategy when negotiating a large order as follows:

> There were many stumbling blocks – over delivery, price, terms. Every time I came to a stumbling block I'd refer it back to the customer's purchasing rep. and push him to compromise. Usually he didn't want to compromise very much because he felt he'd got the whip hand – it is a competitive area of business. Then when he wouldn't budge any further, I could go back to my Head Office to give a bit more. On delivery, for instance. They wanted delivery in six weeks. I couldn't say to my Head Office 'It's got to be six weeks', because it's normally twelve. Then it's brinkmanship, and I had to take the customer to the point of saying 'It's got to be six weeks or no order'; then Head Office gave in.

An industrial buyer talking about negotiations with a sales representative, said:

> We got quite friendly by the end, although we had a confrontation or two along the way. At one time I staged a confrontation and I said, 'I can't accept what you are saying'; and I asked to take it over his head to his Section Leader. Then I could say to my boss that I'd seen the senior man. Otherwise if I went back to my boss to ask that we should budge, he'd just want me to go back to the senior man.

*Source*: Interviews, author's research.

## Interaction strategy

The quotes in Box 4.8 show that at least on some occasions the position taken was part of a strategy aimed at getting the speaker's own Head Office, or boss, to shift in the direction which would make the sale or purchase possible. The quote in Box 4.9 emphasises the timing aspect of interaction strategy, the application of a grasp of the other person's motivational state and the deployment of the norm of reciprocity.

The last paragraph of the quotation in Box 4.9 shows how not just a single meeting, but a whole series of meetings leading to an outcome, can be, and often at work need to be, treated strategically, as an episode in a relationship. Box 4.10 illustrates the importance of strategic persistence. In many situations it is repeated or regular contact which does more to help reach an objective even than the way the interactions themselves are handled.

Finally, Box 4.11 is an example of strategic planning which involves building on good relationships and deciding whom to approach and how to adjust the approach taken according to the individual.

### Box 4.9

An oil company Area Sales Manager spoke about gaining business from a Local Authority:

> I waited until there was a change of planning decision-maker: this is timing. Now a new man, they always say that he wants to evaluate, he wants to contribute, he wants to prove to somebody that he is doing a good job. So when I contacted him, I said that (a), I would like to supply (b), I was competent not to let him down and (c), I would like him to let me judge the moment. I said, 'I'll tell you exactly the moment when to trigger it, when we're looking'. For instance, if we lost the metropolitan authority's business, we'd be looking to replace a lot of business, so that my company would offer an unusually good price.
>
> And for the next parcel you remind him, you remind him that he owes you, that he benefited, that his business or Local Authority benefited, benefited from your judgement and your timing. Debts have to be paid. And you build; and while the customer will obey all the rules, what they will do is they'll make it easier for you; they'll concede things they won't concede to somebody else.

*Source*: Interview, author's research.

### Box 4.10

From a brand manager for a fast-moving consumer-goods company talking about his relationship with the advertising agency creative director who worked on the account for his brand:

> I've built up a good relation with him now. He comes to all the meetings, but I also ring him up a couple of times a week when he's working on some stuff for us. That way I make sure the guy who is actually creating the advertising really understands what we want, without someone else's interpretation in between. I can also check up that he keeps working on my stuff – they're under a lot of pressure in these agencies and if you don't watch out your stuff keeps getting put down the pile.

*Source*: Interview, author's research.

### Box 4.11

The media manager of an advertising agency, describing how they handled a crisis that arose when, owing to confusion within the agency, the wrong commercial was screened for a client, said:

> As an agency, this was our mistake, and we said to the client we would pay. But we, the media staff, were naturally asked how could the sum that would have to be paid be reduced. So we as a media department set to and we reduced that sum of money down to – it was less than 10 per cent of the original figure. Purely done on our good relations with the media, and the right tactics and strategy in approaching them in how to do it, and the person at the media one should approach.
>
> There were three of us involved – the head of TV buying, the media director and myself. We met, and I suggested we should find out how much money was involved, which particular spots. We discussed whom we should approach at each TV contractor and who would be best to approach them. We talked to them, explained that it was a lot of money for us, and would they do their best to try and retrieve the situation. And they did. We had to discuss with them the different ways of how they would do it. Each TV contractor we treated a bit differently, because we have different relationships with different people, in the TV companies, as to whom you went to and what you asked for.

*Source*: Interview, author's research.

The examples given in Boxes 4.8 to 4.11 show the following types of interaction strategy being activated:

- approaching the right people;
- building on good relations;
- persistence and regular contact;
- treating interactions as episodes in a relationship – being prepared to take several meetings to achieve an objective;
- timing;
- using the interaction with one person to structure the situation for a future interaction with another person.

Other possibilities include deploying third-party pressure and forming alliances and coalitions.

Developing interaction strategy, like developing any strategy, is a creative, unprogrammable process (though see the section on creative controversy in Chapter 11), but the above are some of the available options worth considering.

## Interaction tactics

This section describes the rigid approach to interactions that tends to develop 'naturally', sets out a model for more effective interactive behaviour and considers planning the detailed units of communication within interactions.

Borwick[42] suggests that most managers adopt one of five different orientations to interaction: acquiescence, defensiveness, compromise, conflict or problem-solving. Each of these orientations has an active and a passive mode. A conflict orientation, for instance, can be aggression (active) or resistance (passive). Each orientation is also associated with a need, a tone and a style. For example, an acquiescent orientation in interactions would be the behaviour of people who were primarily driven by the affiliation needs, to have good relationships with others, friendships and approval. Their tone in interactions would be good-natured and agreeable, and might be expressed by such phrases as 'To show our goodwill . . .', 'We want to co-operate' or 'Let's avoid haggling'. A defensive orientation would be driven by the needs for safety, security and survival. The tone would vacillate between anger 'Will this satisfy you?' and servility 'We'll do whatever you suggest'. The model is set out in Table 4.2, which is adapted from Borwick's article. Research has shown that most executives do indeed have a preferred approach to interactions.[43] This preferred approach is usually adopted because it is one that the individual is comfortable with and has found to 'work' rather than as the result of a thought-out analysis of alternatives and their likely outcomes. This finding implies that executives' approaches to interactions tend to be need-driven rather than adjusted to the situation and are probably therefore adhered to more consistently than is truly effective.

**Table 4.2 Management and interaction orientations at work**

| *Orientation* | *Need* | *Tone* | *Style – sample expressions* |
|---|---|---|---|
| Acquiescent | Good relations<br>Friendship<br>Approval | Good-natured<br>Agreeable | 'To show our goodwill'<br>'We want to co-operate'<br>'Let's avoid haggling' |
| Defensive | Security<br>Safety<br>Survival | Vacillation between anger and servility | 'Will *this* satisfy you?'<br>'We'll do whatever you suggest' |
| Compromise | Order, progress | Reason, logic | 'Let's split the difference'<br>'We'll trade this for . . .' |
| Conflict | Power<br>To win<br>To control | Hostility<br>Rigidity | 'I don't buy that'<br>'I insist'<br>'You are wrong' |
| Problem-solving | Achievement<br>Best solution | Balance of logic and concern | 'Will this help to accomplish our goal?'<br>'Is this the best way?' |

*Source*: Reprinted by permission of the publisher from Borwick, I. (1978) 'Management and interaction strategy', *Management Decision*, vol. 16, no. 6.

Leadership theorists have had much to say about the choice for managers among autocratic, democratic, participative, authoritarian, person-centred and task-centred approaches. At bottom, the distinctions among these styles are based on two dimensions: control and warmth.[44] Using these dimensions as a base, the styles approach can be adapted to help in planning approaches to a range of interactions, not just those with subordinates. The control dimension concerns the extent to which the direction taken by the interaction will be determined by one or the other party or shared. A high-control style is intended to ensure that the outcome of the interaction is according to the stylist's own prior plan. A low-control style anticipates that the outcome is to be largely determined by the intentions of the other party. A shared control style allows the outcome to emerge from the interaction, possibly as a compromise, or possibly as something entirely new and unthought of by either party beforehand. Clearly the choice of position on the control dimension is not unconstrained. As always with control, power may enter into it. In interactions with a superior or lateral superior, a high-control approach may not be feasible: the superiors may have determined on a high-control approach and their higher power position will ensure they get their way. For the subordinate to attempt it would simply make them look foolish. This situation points to a general rule for deciding control tactics: anticipate the approach that will be adopted by the other party and take it into account in deciding one's own.

On the other hand, power is not the only element in the case. Even for superiors, a low-control approach may be optimal on occasion, when subordinates

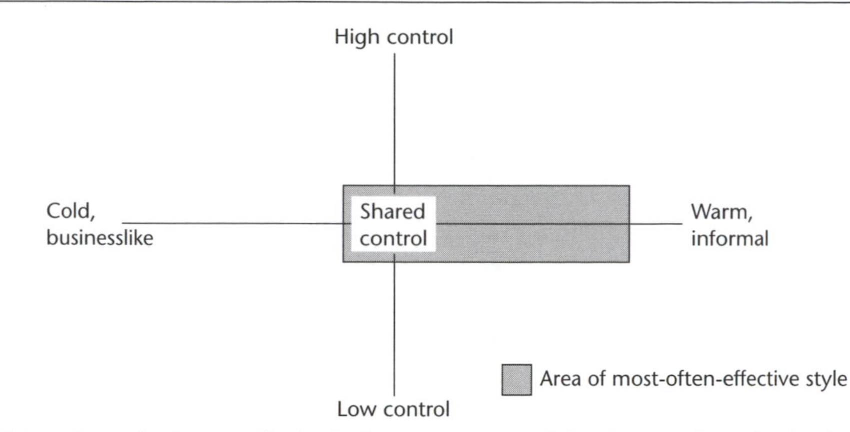


The interaction styles that are effective in the greatest range of situations are those that imply shared control, and are warm and informal or, at least, neutral.

**Figure 4.5 Control and warmth as dimensions of interaction styles.**

have more information or expertise on the issue to be discussed. Alternatively, if a manager wants to boost the subordinates' sense of responsibility and help them 'mature' in the task, a shared control approach may be best. Interaction can also be conducted in a warm, friendly manner or one that is cold and businesslike. Here more choice is available, since power cannot dictate the terms. For instance, it is not uncommon for managers to choose a cold style to emphasise their higher status, and their subordinates might be expected to exhibit greater warmth in order to collude in this game. However, a manager cannot force subordinates to be warm and friendly if they choose not to. Figure 4.5 shows how the control and warmth dimensions combine to yield different interaction styles. As the diagram indicates, a warm/shared-control style is probably the most effective in more interactions than any other. This does not mean, however, that the other styles should never be used. For example, a cold, high-control style may be required when the primary need is to appear strictly businesslike – for instance, when a customer is dismissing a supplier for flagrant and persistent breaches of contract. A warm, high-control style, which may for convenience be labelled as 'paternalistic', could be adopted, with success, towards a school-leaver recruit who is being socialised to work and coached in the tasks required for the job. A cold, low-control style may be needed by a subordinate with a grievance, to indicate that while they acknowledge that they must accept the position, they feel their rights have been infringed. Finally, a warm, low-control style may be the usual style adopted by subordinates of autocratic managers.

At the most detailed level, interaction planning involves deciding what to say and how to say it – in other words, how to communicate. Conversational plans (CPs) are units of thought with an actor–goal–action structure.[45] CPs vary in complexity (that is, in the number of planned actions, contingency statements and distinct arguments), specificity (how fully articulated they are) and sophistication – they may be rigid, capable of being adapted to different situations, or creative. The following are examples of CPs of different types:

- Simple: 'I was planning to explain how to improve the quality.'
- More complex: 'I was planning to say that quality should be more important than quantity and to stress the need for improved quality control systems.'
- Non-specific: 'As he was expressing his views, I was planning my response and forming my opinion on whether or not what he was saying was feasible or realistic.'
- More specific: 'I moderately disagree with what she is saying and I am planning a counter-point.'
- More specific again: 'I was hoping to change his mind by appealing to his sense of morality.'
- Rigid (knowledge-based): 'I told her we could increase sales if we improved the quality.'
- Accommodative: 'I wanted to get her to say more about that argument, so I asked a question. I was changing my views and wanted to show that I agreed with her.'
- Creative (proactive): 'I thought I would introduce the idea to show we agreed on that part, so she would listen to me when I talked about quality control.'

Plan-based models such as this have been put forward as explanations of human interaction behaviours. They imply active cognitive control processes, which are the 'mental processes by which individuals plan and direct, select and orchestrate the various cognitive structures and processes available to them for attaining some goal'.[46] Some research suggests that differences in interaction effectiveness can be traced to variations in interaction planning processes and/or variations in plan performance, and that it is the relative efficiency of a person's active cognitive control that can account for differences in planning and plan performance. However, some authorities consider that this analysis is too simplistic, because their findings suggest that plan-behaviour correspondence is a function of motivation as well as cognitive efficiency.[47]

## SUMMARY – INTERACTION PLANNING

Interaction planning means substituting a thought-out approach for habitual responses. It means developing work interaction strategies, that is deciding with whom, in what order and when to meet to achieve an objective. Interaction tactics means planning the broad tenor of approaches and detailed communication units in face-to-face meetings. This leads to choosing among acquiescence,

Box 4.12

### How to make your interaction tactics effective

- Decide what type of interaction is in train and what role to play.
- Work out who the other participants in the meeting are, in terms of the relationship structure. This is a major dimension of the organisational context of the interaction, which, as discussed in Chapters 2 and 3, strongly constrains and influences work behaviour.
- Decide whether what is primarily needed is to communicate information, persuade, mediate, negotiate, discuss, receive information, problem-solve, sell, present, interview, consult, advise, counsel, reprimand, direct or coach. Once that decision has been made, apply the appropriate interpersonal skills and knowledge to the interaction.
- Choose the most effective interaction mode. Often there is a choice of modes, of which one will be more successful than others. For instance, where a manager's first thought, or natural mode, might be to direct a subordinate to do something, their more considered approach might be to discuss with them what to do and how to do it, or vice versa. Again, whereas when entering a meeting without preplanning, people might launch straight into a negotiating mode, with preplanning they might decide to treat the matter as a joint problem to solve together – or vice versa. Ultimately, success in face-to-face dealings depends on correct judgement of the mode, because application of an inappropriate set of skills will have poor results, just as it would for any other kind of technique. Unfortunately, selecting the appropriate mode is not so obvious that people at work always get it right. For instance, it is a common failing of managers who are trying to introduce change, to develop their ideas in isolation and then launch them in 'selling' mode, whereas we know from research that change is more readily achieved through a combination of 'consultation' and 'communication'. To choose the best mode, judge carefully the requirements of the task and the behavioural context of the situation, especially the relationship structure and the likely behaviour of the other participants, 'forecast' from an analysis of their inner states and qualities as interpreted from their past behaviour.

defensiveness, compromise, conflict and problem-solving according to the perceived requirements of the situation and the likely behaviour of the other participants, rather than using the same approach each time because it comes most easily. Other tactics are to decide styles, on a warmth/control basis, and conversational plans, which vary in complexity, rigidity and sophistication.

## CHAPTER OVERVIEW

This chapter has been concerned with the self because in all our work interactions the self is central both to our experiences and to our performances. Self-related ways of improving interactive behaviour include understanding our self-concepts, including their cultural variations, gaining appropriate self-esteem while eschewing self-delusion, developing coping capabilities and confidence in our ability to perform tasks, learning how to learn and develop skills, especially interpersonal skills and interaction planning.

## EXERCISES

1. A self-image is a mental 'picture' of yourself, describing what sort of person you think you are. There are many components to this mental picture that you have of yourself. As an exercise you can make a list of words and phrases describing yourself. Most people find they can reach 20 descriptions without much hesitation.

2. (a) List words or phrases that describe how you see yourself at this time.
   (b) Starting with the list above, make changes so that it describes how you would like to be. You may add or remove items, or modify them, for instance by substituting 'fairly tall' for 'very tall'.
   (c) Compare the (a) and (b) lists. How far is your actual self-image from your ideal self-image?
   (d) List words or phrases that describe how you think other people see you at this time.
   (e) Compare the (a) and (d) lists. How differently do you see yourself from the way you think others see you? Why do you think these differences (if any) exist?
   (f) Change the (d) list (the social actual self-image) to describe how you would ideally like other people to see you. What differences are there?

3. Complete the questionnaire given in Table 4.3. *See the Appendix to find out how to analyse your responses to this questionnaire.*

4. Clarify your values, goals, feelings, beliefs, attitudes and traits. In seeking self-knowledge, you want to know about the relatively durable aspects of yourself, such as goals and the beliefs, motivational patterns and values to which they are related. When seeking self-knowledge, it is a good idea to use a range of techniques, which in combination reveal more than one alone. Some possibilities are as follows:

   (a) Event analysis. Take a number of major and minor events in your recent past, describe them in writing as precisely as possible, together with your responses, reactions and behaviour. Then re-examine them, looking for an understanding of what values were influencing you, what goals you were aiming at, what abilities you used, your feelings, thoughts and attitudes.
   (b) Repeat this exercise on a number of occasions, comparing your analyses for consistencies and contradictions until you build up a picture of yourself.
   (c) Getting feedback. Write out a list of adjectives and other ways of describing yourself, using a framework like that shown in Figure 4.1. Get an honest friend to complete the same description. Compare the two and discuss the differences with your friend. If your picture of yourself and your friend's are very different, consider whether it points to self-deception on your part.

**Table 4.3 Self-awareness questionnaire**

To indicate your level of agreement with the following statements, against each one place a tick on the appropriate section of the line.

| | *Strongly Agree* | *Agree* | *Neither Agree Nor Disagree* | *Disagree* | *Strongly Disagree* |
|---|---|---|---|---|---|
| 1. When I communicate with others, I am always aware of my relationship with them | X______X | ______X | ______X | ______X | ______X |
| 2. In communication with others, I am mainly concerned to have them understand where I am 'coming from' | X______X | ______X | ______X | ______X | ______X |
| 3. I like the people I meet to know my tastes and preferences at an early stage in our acquaintance | X______X | ______X | ______X | ______X | ______X |
| 4. When I communicate with others, I try to maintain an even balance between meeting my own needs and meeting theirs | X______X | ______X | ______X | ______X | ______X |
| 5. I place a high value on self-expression | X______X | ______X | ______X | ______X | ______X |
| 6. I like the people I meet to understand my important beliefs and values | X______X | ______X | ______X | ______X | ______X |
| 7. It is important to get across one's personality in social conversations | X______X | ______X | ______X | ______X | ______X |
| 8. I am generally concerned with how other people see me – what they think of me | X______X | ______X | ______X | ______X | ______X |
| 9. I am very concerned that my interactions with others should be at all times harmonious | X______X | ______X | ______X | ______X | ______X |
| 10. I use other people's attitudes and behaviours as ways of setting standards for my own | X______X | ______X | ______X | ______X | ______X |

(d) Interpersonal skills audit and difficult situations analysis. To develop your interpersonal skills, you need to know what your starting point is. One way is a listing of strengths and weaknesses which concentrates on social skills generally and work-relevant ones in particular; another is working out which kinds of encounters or social situations at work create most awkwardness, embarrassment or lack of self-confidence for you. If you failed to carry out the interpersonal skills audit or complete the Difficult Situations questionnaire in the Chapter 1 Exercises, now is the time to go back and do them.

(e) Biographical SWOT analysis. List your strengths, weaknesses, opportunities and threats, then look for ways to build on your strengths, correct your weaknesses, exploit your opportunities and counter your threats.

5. Consider, on your own or in a group, each of the suggestions for modifying internalised behaviour patterns listed in Box 4.3. Draw up a programme for implementing at least three of them that you feel will be most helpful to you.

6. Consider, on your own or in a group, each of the 13 coping strategies listed in Box 4.4. Draw up a programme for implementing at least five of them that you feel will be most helpful to you.

7. Goals Scale. Take a few moments to focus on yourself and what is going on in your life at this moment. Once you have this 'here and now' set, answer each item according to the following scale: 1 = Definitely False; 2 = Mostly False; 3 = Somewhat False; 4 = Slightly False; 5 = Slightly True; 6 = Somewhat True; 7 = Most True; and 8 = Definitely True.

   (a) If I should find myself in a jam, I could think of many ways to get out of it.
   (b) At the present time, I am energetically pursuing my goals.
   (c) There are lots of ways round any problem that I am facing now.
   (d) Right now I see myself as being pretty successful.
   (e) I can think of many ways to reach my current goals.
   (f) At this time, I am meeting the goals that I have set for myself.

   *To see how to score and analyse this scale, see the Appendix.*

8. Undertake a personal goal-setting exercise for yourself. This should end with you having established what you need and want out of life; recognising your important values; assessing the extent to which you live by those values; and outlining your main life and work goals.You can use one of the personal development books listed in Further Reading as a guide to this process.

9. Identify areas for self-development that will increase your ability to fulfil your goals; set up a personal development file based on a daily log of your interactions and other work experiences and use it as a tool for a self-development personal strengths exercise. Record whether you are 'satisfied' or 'dissatisfied' with each of your own core skills.

10. Give two examples of how you could use Kolb's learning model to acquire a skill, change a bad habit or work toward a goal. Do you foresee any problems? How could they be overcome?

11. Write a short self-history as if to support an application for a job. This, of course, will emphasise strengths and achievements. Then write a complementary statement, describing weaknesses and failures. Keep this self-history on file and update it from time to time. Use it as the foundation for a self-development exercise, with an action plan to address weaknesses and build on strengths.

12. Set personal targets for specific interpersonal skills development or improvement. These targets are to be achieved by the end of the course or by some other date. Then translate the targets into development strategies, which are

amplified into a series of activities to implement the strategies and achieve the targets. Self-monitoring and recording progress are intrinsic parts of the process.

13. List the key enterprise skills and describe them; show how these skills can 'empower' you; explain the concepts of empowerment and transferable skills.

14. In a group, think of some aspect of your course, its administration or the institution that you would like to have altered. (As examples, one group wanted to get a vegan menu made available in the college restaurant, while another wanted more flexibility about the deadline for assignments.) Undertake an interaction planning exercise to achieve this goal, covering allocating roles, approaching the right people, building good relations, persistence and regular contact, treating interactions as episodes in a relationship, timing, using the interaction with one person to structure the situation for a future interaction with another person and possibilities including deploying third-party pressure and forming alliances and coalitions.

15. A Board Director of an advertising agency intended to get a subordinate of his made an Assistant Director with a seat on the board, to reward her for an outstanding performance during the past year. He got the matter put on the agenda of the next Board meeting, which took place a week later. At the Board meeting, the issue was the subject of heated discussion, when the Director discovered to his surprise that there was a lot of opposition to putting his subordinate on the Board, that she was seen as his 'protégée' towards whom he was biased, and that there were others in the agency who had better or at least more long-standing claims to the seat. Eventually the Chairman of the Board halted the discussion and deferred the matter to the next meeting. The Director had to inform the woman, who was expecting that the matter would only require rubber-stamping, that her promotion was deferred and had met with a lot of opposition. In discussion afterwards the Chairman told him, 'You ignored the way we do these things around here, and as a result created a lot of ill-feeling. You should have spoken to each member of the Board individually, and got their agreement beforehand – really before you put it on the agenda.'

    What do you think of the Chairman's comment? What do you think of the way the Director went about his objective?

16. Following the appointment of two new Marketing lecturers at the University of Sundringford, the Head of the Marketing Teaching Unit wanted to ensure that the allocation of staff accommodation would facilitate rather than hinder the development of the unit's strength. She wanted to have all six full-time and part-time marketing lecturers accommodated together – owing to the

university's constrained accommodation position, there was a danger of them being scattered around different buildings – as she felt sure that would best promote both teaching and research in the subject. At the same time, she wanted to put each of the new members of staff in an office with an old hand, who could teach them the ropes.

Room allocations at Sundringford were the responsibility of the Dean of Faculty, rather than the Unit Head's immediate boss, the Head of Department, so she went to see the Dean, armed with a plan showing how her proposals could be made to work in practice. The Dean was very busy with the details of the Faculty Plan, but was able to spare ten minutes to look over the plans, and at the end agreed them. Staff were informed by letter of the new dispositions (a number of non-marketing staff as well as marketing staff had to move rooms under the plan), and the porters transferred their files, books and furniture in time for the start of the new academic year.

What do you think of the Marketing Head of Unit's interaction strategy for attaining his or her objective? What potential problems can you foresee? What alternative interaction strategy would you recommend? Why?

## FURTHER READING

Guirdham, M. and K. Tyler (1992) *Enterprise Skills for Students*. Oxford: Butterworth Heinemann.

Hogg, M. A. and D. Abrams (eds) (1999) *Social Identity and Social Cognition*. Oxford: Blackwell. Especially Chapters 1, 2, 9 and 10. Chapters 3 to 9 are relevant to Chapter 5 of this book and Chapters 12 to 14 to Chapter 8.

Hogg, M. A. and D. Abrams (1988) *Social Identifications*. London: Routledge.

## REFERENCES

1. Pyszczynski, T. A. and J. Greenberg (1987) 'Self regulatory perseveration and the depressive self-focusing style: a self-awareness theory of reactive depression', *Psychological Bulletin*, vol. 102, pp. 122–138.
2. Swann, W. B. Jr and S. J. Read (1981) 'Acquiring self-knowledge: the search for feedback that fits', *Journal of Personality and Social Psychology*, vol. 41, pp. 1119–1128.
3. Baumeister, R. F. (1996) 'Self' in A. S. R. Manstead and M. Hewstone (eds) *The Blackwell Encyclopaedia of Social Psychology*. Oxford: Blackwell.
4. Hogg, M. A. and D. Abrams (1988) *Social Identifications*. London: Routledge.
5. Ibid.
6. Simon, B. (1998) 'The self in minority–majority contexts', in W. Stroebe and M. Hewstone, *European Review of Social Psychology*, vol. 9. Chichester: John Wiley, pp. 1–30.
7. De Cremer, D. and M. van Vugt (1998) 'Collective identity and cooperation in a public goods dilemma: a matter of trust or self-efficacy?', *Current Research in Social Psychology*, vol. 3, no. 1, pp. 1–11.
8. Tajfel, H. (1974) 'Social identity and inter-group behavior', *Social Science Information*, vol. 13, pp. 65–93.

9. Tajfel, H. (1978) 'Social categorisation, social identity and social comparison' in H. Tajfel (ed.) *Differentiation Between Social Groups: Studies in the Social Psychology of Inter-group Relations*. London: Academic Press.
10. Martin, J. N., R. L. Krizek, T. K. Nakayama and L. Bradford (1996) 'Exploring whiteness: A study of self labels for white Americans', *Communication Quarterly*, vol. 44, no. 2, pp. 125–144.
11. Markus, H. R. and S. Kitayama (1998) 'The cultural psychology of personality', *Journal of Cross-Cultural Psychology*, vol. 29, no. 1, pp. 63–87.
12. Ibid.
13. Swann, W. B. Jr, B. W. Pelham and D. S. Krull (1989) 'Agreeable fancy or disagreeable truth? Reconciling self-enhancement and self-verification', *Journal of Personality and Social Psychology*, vol. 54, pp. 268–273.
14. Baumeister, R. F., D. M. Tice and D. G. Hutton (1989) 'Self-presentational motivation and personality differences in self-esteem', *Journal of Personality*, vol. 57, pp. 547–579.
15. Brewer, M. B. and W. Gardner (1996) 'Who is the "We"? Levels of collective identity and self representations', *Journal of Personality and Social Psychology*, vol. 71, no. 1, pp. 83–93.
16. Pelham, B. W. (1995) 'Self-investment and self-esteem: Evidence for a Jamesian model of self-worth', *Journal of Personality and Social Psychology*, vol. 69, pp. 1141–1150.
17. Markus, H. R. and S. Kitayama (1991) 'Culture and the self: implications for cognition, emotion and motivation', *Psychological Review*, vol. 98, pp. 224–253.
18. Turner, J. C., M. Hogg, P. Oakes, S. Reicher and M. Wetherell (1987) *Rediscovering the Social Group: A Self-categorisation Theory*. Oxford: Basil Blackwell.
19. Major, B., A.-M. Sciacchitano and J. Crocker (1993) 'In-group versus out-group comparisons and self-esteem', *Personality and Social Psychology Bulletin*, vol. 19, no. 6, pp. 711–721.
20. Mummendey, A., T. Kessler, A. Klink and R. Mielke (1999) 'Strategies to cope with negative social identity: predictions by social identity theory and relative deprivation theory', *Journal of Personality and Social Psychology*, vol. 76, no. 2, pp. 229–245.
21. Brenders, D. A. (1987) 'Perceived control: Foundations and directions for communication research', *Communication Yearbook*, vol. 10, pp. 86–116.
22. Buehler, R., D. Griffin and M. Ross (1995) 'It's about time: optimistic predictions in work and love' in W. Stroebe and M. Hewstone (eds) *European Review of Social Psychology*, vol. 6. Chichester: John Wiley.
23. Mckenna, F. P. (1993) 'It won't happen to me: unrealistic optimism or illusion of control?', *British Journal of Psychology*, vol. 84, pp. 39–50.
24. Lee, C. and F. Schmaman (1987) 'Self-efficacy as a predictor of clinical skills among speech pathology students', *Health Education*, vol. 16, pp. 407–416.
25. McBride, M. C. (1990) 'Autonomy and the struggle for female identity: implications for counseling women', *Journal of Counseling and Development*, vol. 69, pp. 22–26.
26. Alper, S., D. Tjosvold and K. S. Law (2000) 'Conflict management, efficacy and performance in organizational teams', *Personnel Psychology*, vol. 53, no. 3, pp. 625–642.
27. Bandura, A. (1977) 'Self efficacy theory: toward a unifying theory of behavioural change', *Psychological Review*, vol. 84, no. 2, pp. 191–215.
28. Kerr, N. L. (1996) '"Does my contribution really matter?" Efficacy in social dilemmas' in W. Stroebe and M. Hewstone (eds) *European Review of Social Psychology*, vol. 7, pp. 209–240.
29. Augsburger, D. (1986) *Pastoral Counseling Across Cultures*. Philadelphia: Westminster Press.
30. Kanter, R. M. (1989) *When Giants Learn to Dance*. London: Simon and Schuster.
31. Guirdham, M. and K. Tyler (1992) *Enterprise Skills for Students*. Oxford: Butterworth Heinemann.

32. Anderson, J. R. (1984) *The Architecture of Cognition*. Cambridge, Mass.: Harvard University Press.
33. Wickelgren, W. (1979) 'Human learning and memory', *Annual Review of Psychology*, vol. 32, pp. 21–52.
34. Anderson, op. cit.
35. Skinner, B. F. (1971) *Beyond Freedom and Dignity*. New York: Knopf.
36. Sawyer, A. G. (1974) 'The effects of repetition: conclusion and suggestions from experimental laboratory research' in G. D. Hughes and M. I. Ray (eds) *Buyer/Consumer Information Processing*. Chapel Hill, Carolina: University of North Carolina Press, pp. 190–219.
37. Kolb, D. A., I. M. Rubin and J. M. McIntyre (1973) *Organizational Psychology: An Experiential Approach*. Englewood Cliffs, New Jersey: Prentice Hall.
38. Argyris, C. (1993) 'Education for leading–learning', *Organizational Dynamics*, Winter, pp. 5–17.
39. Goodstein, J. D. (2000) 'Moral compromise and personal integrity: exploring the ethical issues of deciding together in organizations, *Business Ethics Quarterly*, vol. 10, no. 4, pp. 805–819.
40. McElreath, M. P. (1993) *Managing Systematic and Ethical Public Relations*, Dubuque, Iowa: Brown and Benchmark.
41. Christians, C. G., K. B. Rotzoll and M. Fackler (1991) *Media Ethics: Cases and Moral Reasoning*, 3rd edn. New York: Longman.
42. Borwick, I. (1978) 'Management and interaction strategies', *Management Decision*, vol. 16, no. 6, pp. 350–361.
43. Fleishman, E. A. and E. F. Harris (1962) 'Patterns of leadership behaviour related to employee grievances and turnover', *Personnel Psychology*, vol. 15, pp. 43–56.
44. Wright, P. L. and D. S. Taylor (1984) *Improving Leadership Performance*. Englewood Clifts, N.J.: Prentice-Hall.
45. Waldron, V. R. and J. L. Applegate (1994) 'Interpersonal construct differentiation and conversational planning: an examination of two cognitive accounts for the production of competent verbal disagreement tactics', *Human Communication Research*, vol. 21, pp. 3–35.
46. Schumacher, E. F. (1998) *Small is Beautiful: Economics as if People Mattered*. Vancouver, Canada: Hartley and Marks.
47. Jordan, J. M. (1998) 'Executive cognitive control in communication: extending plan-based theory', *Human Communication Research*, vol. 25, pp. 5–38.

# Part 2

# CORE PROCESSES

# 5 Understanding others

## CHAPTER INTRODUCTION

Interacting with other people is universally accompanied by the effort to understand their internal mental and emotional events.[1] The drive to explain and predict others' behaviour may be part of a general drive to reduce uncertainty. Social (or person) perception differs from perceiving objects or events, precisely because the emphasis is placed on the internal properties of the person or their traits.[2] It is true that there are occasions when we are mainly or equally concerned with people's appearance for its own sake, with what they say for its content and with what they do for its physical effect. But at work our interest in people's behaviour usually needs to, and does, go well beyond this. We try to give meaning to the other person.

The aim of this chapter is to help readers perceive how to understand others at work more effectively by explaining:

- why social perception is so important;
- the processes of perception in general, including attending, comprehending and applying cognitive schemas;
- the processes of perceiving people, including using cues and identification and association rules based on social comparison and categorisation, making attributions and judging, framing, stereotyping, expectations, forming impressions and detecting deceptions;
- causes of perceptual errors, such as over-reliance on stereotypes, applying our own frames of reference while ignoring other people's, attribution errors and the locked-in effect;
- how we interpret messages and non-verbal cues;
- how to learn more during interactions through active and empathic listening;
- how to allow for cultural, ethnic and gender influences on ways of communicating;
- cultural differences in perception;
- what happens when we are perceiving groups;
- work applications using skill in understanding others, which include interviewing and selection interviewing.

## THE SIGNIFICANCE OF SOCIAL PERCEPTION

Accurate and differentiated social perception is the basis of all skilled interpersonal interaction. For example, at work, selection interviewers need to understand the motives, work attitudes, abilities and personality traits of interviewees; international negotiators need to have a grasp of the values, motives, assumptions and attitudes of their opposite numbers. More generally, though, our own behaviour towards other people – what lines of conversation we open up, how we respond to what they say, whether we smile at them or frown, prolong a meeting with them or curtail it – are and inevitably must be governed by what we think we know about them. To the degree that we lack knowledge we are forced to make assumptions. For instance, if I cannot decide whether a person's attitude is friendly or hostile when they say to me 'Oh, there you are, Smithers', I will not know whether to explain where I have been or to simply smile and say, 'Yes'. If I explain where I've been and the person was, in fact, simply glad to see me, it might suggest to them that perhaps I had a guilty conscience. If I just say 'Yes', on the other hand, I might appear to be guileful or fatuous if the person's real attitude was to suspect that I had been wasting time. And yet I would be in a position where I had to do something.

All face-to-face skills, including self-presentation, communicating, using power, persuading, making presentations, working in groups, chairing discussions and so on are built up on a foundation of interpreting accurately what other people do and say. Understanding others is not, however, an elementary skill. People do not usually explain their deepest inner thoughts: conventions generally prevent them doing so. Even if asked, they may be unwilling or unable to do so. Unwillingness could stem from shame or feeling they will be put at a disadvantage, inability from low awareness. Thus other people's inner states and qualities generally have to be inferred from how they behave. This means that understanding others may be the most difficult to acquire of all the interpersonal skills.

There are two main criteria for successful people-perception: the accuracy of an interpretation, the need for which is obvious, and its complexity or differentiation. The more elements are taken into account in making an interpretation, the more useful it is likely to be. Cognitive complexity refers to how many constructs social perceivers use to interpret the behaviours of others and how those constructs are organised. From this viewpoint, people who have more complex systems of personal constructs should be more competent social perceivers.[3] This idea has been criticised for lacking a specific mechanism that links having complex personal construct systems to interaction behaviour. However, it is reasonable to expect individuals who are cognitively complex to be advantaged in situations that require a complex analysis of the partner as a precondition. For instance, when people are engaged in verbal disagreements at work, incompatible goals and the need to negotiate and co-ordinate one's own and the other person's actions mean that a conflict situation of great complexity is occurring. In such situations, disputants who are able to perceive the opponent's perspectives, goals, motives and interpretations and to anticipate their likely actions are more likely to attain their preferred solution.[4]

## SUMMARY – THE SIGNIFICANCE OF SOCIAL PERCEPTION

To interact effectively (present ourselves and communicate appropriately, influence others, work with them in relationships and groups or lead them) we must have a grasp of what others are thinking and feeling, including their motives, beliefs, attitudes and intentions. In social perception, accuracy and differentiation are essential but difficult. Achieving them may be linked to the complexity of a person's system of cognitive constructs.

## HOW WE PERCEIVE

One step forward in developing skilled person-perception is to know how it works – what the processes are – and to know how it is that those processes themselves can easily lead to errors in interpretation. Perceiving people differs from perceiving objects such as tables, or physical events such as stones rolling down a slope, because we interpret the cues we perceive about people – their appearance, what they say, how they say it, and so on – to infer meaning. Nevertheless, the process starts in the same way as simpler forms of perception and is subject to the same errors. General perception processes are shown in Figure 5.1.

### Attending and comprehending

At work, as elsewhere, our senses are exposed to a very large number of incoming stimuli – sounds, colours, shapes, smells and so on. It is not possible for us to process and use all these sensory impressions, so, largely unconsciously, we are selective about what we attend to and what we do not. The selection we make is not, however, random, but depends on a number of factors. These include the following:

- *Stimulus characteristics.* We are more likely to notice stimuli that stand out by contrast with their context, such as a woman in a room full of men, or that are unexpected, such as someone in a meeting suddenly shouting, or those that we have been primed beforehand to notice. Vivid stimuli are also noticed more easily, though not necessarily remembered.
- *Motivational state.* Someone who is very concerned about fire hazards is more likely to notice when a fire extinguisher needs servicing than someone who is less bothered about this matter. People with high relationship needs are more

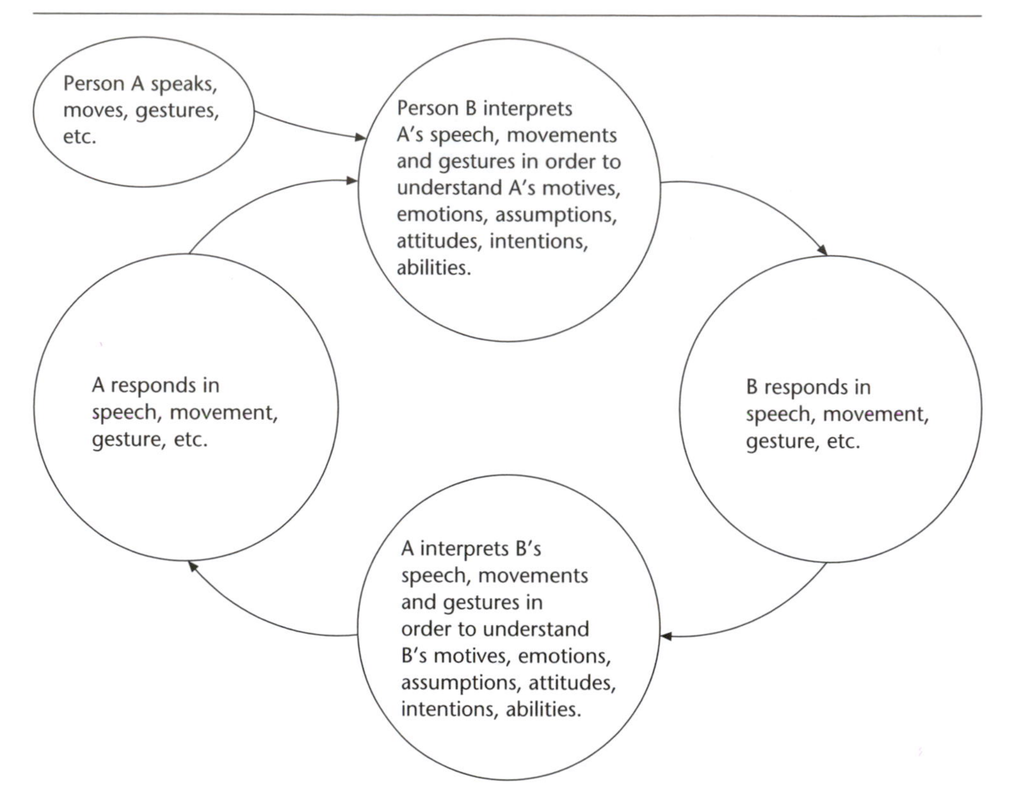


**Figure 5.1 The cycle of perception and behaviour.**

likely to notice a colleague's manner towards them than are people with low relationship needs. We are more receptive to stimuli that relate to our needs or goals and we tend to select out those that do not.

- *Maintaining cognitive consistency.* Human beings have a strong tendency to resist changes in strongly held attitudes and beliefs, especially when these are integrated with a whole network of other beliefs. (There is more about maintaining cognitive consistency in Chapter 8.) One way of resisting these changes is through selective attention. Therefore, we are more attentive to stimuli that are consistent with values that we already have and which are important to us and less to those which conflict with our values. For example, a strong Euro-sceptic would be less likely to notice newspaper stories or statistics reporting high growth rates for euro-currency countries than a strongly pro-Europe person would be.
- *Habituation.* Most people have been saddened by noticing how quickly the smell of a sweet perfume becomes undetectable or have been gladdened by noticing that even a loud steady humming noise eventually stops being annoying. These are both examples of habituation. The lower threshold above which a stimulus is sensed increases as a result of familiarity, probably because the

nerves become 'tired' of transmitting the same information. Habituation means we pay more attention to newer cues, although they may not necessarily be more important.

- *Ignoring details.* There is evidence that we perceive things holistically, rather than by a 'bottom-up' addition of perceptions of their parts. This may lead us to ignore details providing we can satisfactorily identify what the object is without them.

After attention the next process involved in both perception generally and perception of people is comprehension. The perceiver organises the observed stimuli in order to reach some conclusion about what they are. Is this complex of sounds the arrival of a dumper-truck or a fault in the grinding machinery? Is that pattern of light, shade, colour and line a design for this season's new products or just last season's from a different angle? Does that smell mean something is burning? Most of the time, of course, there is no mystery – the process occurs so quickly that we are not conscious of it, and we 'know' straight away what it is. Nevertheless, on each occasion we go through the process along the following lines: first, complexity is reduced as perceptions are formed into the simplest possible patterns. Then, we go beyond the evidence to produce a complete picture through a process known as closure.

## Applying cognitive schemas

Cognitive schemas, which were introduced in Chapter 3, affect perception in important ways. They exist before an instance of perception and affect both what stimuli we attend to and how we comprehend them. If they are strong and accessible, there is increased sensitivity to information that relates to them, it is processed efficiently, confidently and consistently and is remembered better. On the other hand, a strong cognitive schema may be used to over-interpret ambiguous information: a hesitation on the part of a candidate in an interview may be seen as a clear sign of an intention to deceive. When a particular cognitive schema is activated, related feelings may also become active.

**Box 5.1**

Some research has indicated that when individuals lack real-world experience, they may rely on media portrayals to create their cognitive schemas. Hall *et al.* (1999) found from interviews with Mexican, Turkish and American students in the United States that non-American viewers thought US television programming was more typical of Americans before, rather than after, they came to the United States. Once there, judgements by Mexicans and Turks of the typicality of media portrayals were not very different from those judgements by Americans.

*Source*: Hall, A., T. Anten and I. Cakim (1999) 'Perceived typicality: American television as seen by Mexicans, Turks, and Americans', *Critical Studies in Mass Communication*, vol. 16, no. 4, pp. 436–455.

## SUMMARY – HOW WE PERCEIVE

We perceive objects, events and people by noticing and interpreting stimuli, which are sensory impressions. What we notice is selective, but our selection is usually neither deliberate nor random. It is affected by our mood, current needs, existing beliefs and habituation as well as by characteristics of the stimulus. Comprehension is largely unconscious but, again, it is affected by our individual psychology, particularly by our cognitive schemas or mental representations of information on a subject.

## HOW WE PERCEIVE PEOPLE

In addition to those elements that are common to perceiving objects, events and people, there are special processes involved in perceiving other humans and what they do. First I will outline the general process and then describe some important particular aspects of it. We now know that perceiving even the simplest 'facts' about other people is a complex process. For example, to decide whether a face is male or female, we bring together at least three categories of information: the 3D shape of the face, superficial or local features (such as facial hair, skin texture and shape of eyebrows) and relationships among the features. All these types of information are vital. For instance, when laser scan technology is used on photographs to leave only the 2D layout of the features, identification of males and females is very poor, although when all three types of information are available it is almost 100 per cent.[5] Making more complex judgements than this simple categorisation of male/female is likely to be highly complex.[6] Thus the description of person-perception processes that follows is necessarily simplified.

### Perceiving people: general processes

The processes specific to perceiving people include using cues, applying identification and association rules based on social comparison and categorisation, making attributions and making trait judgements.

#### *Observing cues*

Cues are stimuli from which the receiver can infer meaning. Language reflects this idea: the phrase 'He smiled' has a sense reaching well beyond 'He moved his facial muscles in a particular way'. Cues may express meaning, as when the person intends to communicate, or reveal it without them intending to. In all cases, though, the receiver has to infer the meaning from the message given by the cue. In the case of verbal and pictorial messages, observing cues involves a prior stage, decoding, which means translating the symbols into the message.

In organisations, the language used can make this translation process quite difficult for outsiders or newcomers. For instance, a message such as 'Julia, the NEB meeting is at 3 p.m. Can you bring the RQU figures along?' could be difficult, not just because of the abbreviations, but also because the writer has omitted where the meeting will take place, wrongly assuming that 'everyone knows'.

### *Applying identification 'rules'*

To make inferences about others' moods, attitudes, intentions and so on, we apply our own personal identification rules. These are of the type, 'When people shout, frown and stamp their foot, they are angry', 'Domed foreheads show intelligence', 'Dressing like a punk indicates anti-Establishment values', 'Fat people are jolly' and 'People who talk a lot are nervous'. As these examples show, identification rules draw on the categories that we have in memory from earlier experiences. Some categories are more accessible than others – that is, they are more readily retrieved. This may be 'chronic' – some people may generally perceive others only in terms of how intelligent they are – or temporary, as the result of 'priming' (being alerted to the category before the stimulus is perceived). Few identification rules are based on the findings of scientific research. They come from making inductions from experiences, and from introspection, drawing analogies and believing things we have read or been told. Many identification rules organise the world into categories. We group people according to their gender, age, race, nationality, the language they speak, their accent, where they live, what they do for a living and so on. We often place people in these categories not on the basis of facts but by applying our identification rules to our superficial impressions of them.

### *Using association 'rules'*

Next, we link the inferred state or quality with others, using personal association rules. For instance, we may link nervousness with 'having something to hide' or intelligence with being well-educated. Quite different characteristics may be linked in this way – 'cunning' and 'cowardice', for example. Both identification and association rules may derive from cognitive schemas. When we perceive people, what we perceive is influenced at least by our schemas about ourselves, other people, events and situations, our relationships and interactions.

- About ourselves, our schemas include a representation of the self that is based on past experience of our own behaviour and our self-concept, which also covers goals, incentives, plans and 'scripts' for things to do and say.
- About other people, we usually have schemas consisting at least of our implicit personality theory, roles and stereotypes. 'Implicit personality theory'

refers to expectations about what traits typically occur together in the same person. When people are read lists of adjectives that describe certain types of people, such as extraverts, they later falsely recognise words that were not on the original list but are highly 'consistent' with the category of person described. Similarly, if someone is told a woman is a librarian, they will be better at recalling information conventionally consistent with that label, for example that she wears glasses, than at recalling other information, for instance that she usually wears trousers. This reflects their role schemas and stereotypes for librarians.

- We have schemas about events and situations. We tend to make these socially appropriate. For instance a 'networking' schema might include having a well-prepared excuse for making the contact when telephoning a new acquaintance. Such schemas are called scripts.
- Relational schemas are to do with our relationships with particular other people. A sense of how to respond to the other and expectations of satisfactions or frustrations in the relationship are some elements in our relational schemas.[7]
- Yet another type of schema is used to interpret what is going on in interactions that we observe or take part in. Individuals tend to focus on either dominance or affiliation in interpreting interactions.[8]

Figure 5.2 shows the range of cognitive schemas described above.

Identification and association rules are mainly based on social comparison and categorisation. People compare themselves with others to learn about themselves and to obtain confidence in their beliefs being true and useful. The need to compare oneself with others is very powerful; it is 'spontaneous, effortless and unintentional'.[9] However, circumstances and situations vary in the degree to which they call for social comparison, while individuals also have some choice of whom they will use to compare themselves with. Individuals vary in how much use they make of social comparisons.[10] They are made more often by people with low self-esteem or unstable self-concepts, or who are depressed, high in uncertainty about their own mood states or neurotic. These characteristics have a common component of high uncertainty. (In a comparison of large samples of North American and Dutch people, researchers found the US sample more comparison-oriented than the Dutch.)

Social comparisons underlie the determination of social categories. People fit other people and themselves into categories, corresponding to their own values and expectations. They also base their choice of categories and how to fit people into them on comparisons with other people they have known. They use comparisons, according to the theory, because no objective standards exist. For example, we have no objective standard for personal attractiveness, nor for friendliness. Social comparison and categorisation are self-protective and self-enhancing, and can therefore be applied to cope with damage to self-esteem.

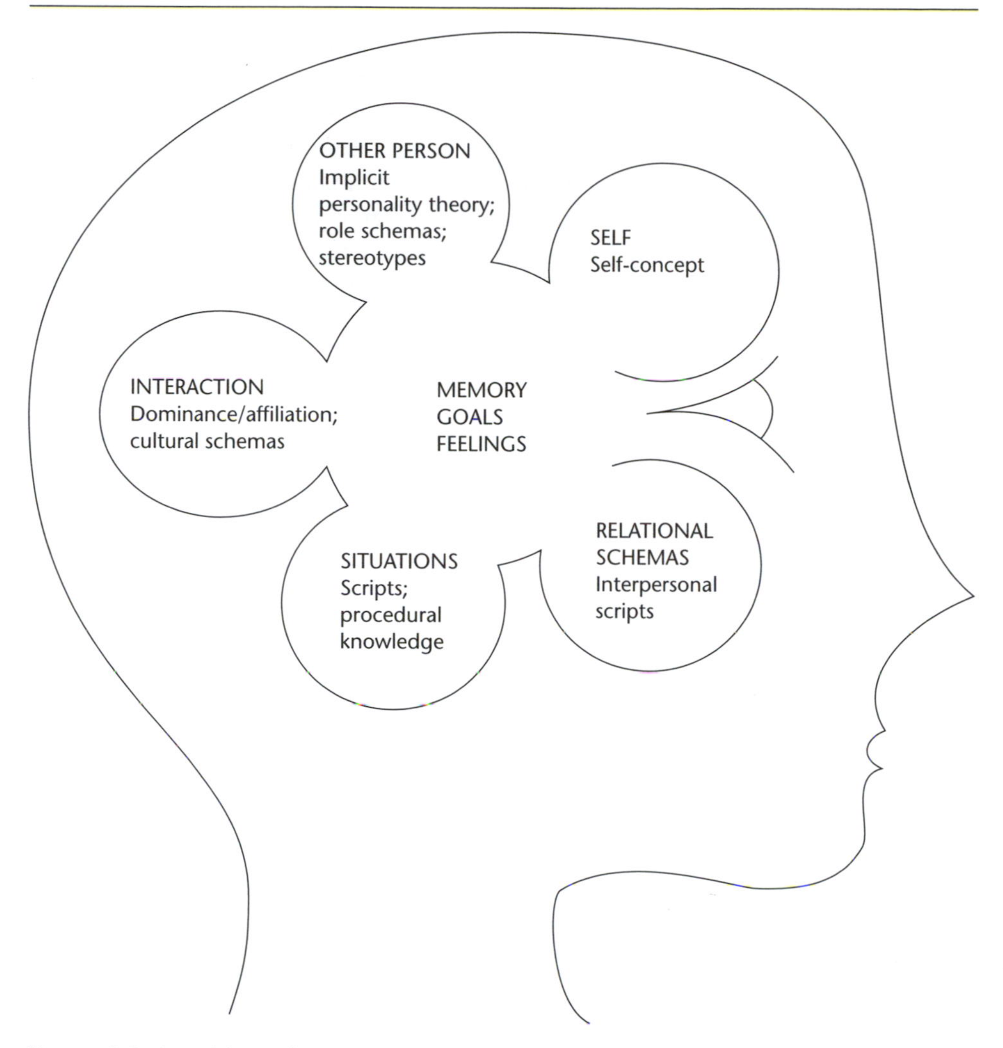


**Figure 5.2 Cognitive schemas in perceiving people.**

### *Making attributions*

Deciding the 'cause' of what someone is doing appears to be a near-universal process. (Attribution theory was introduced in Chapter 3.) In the West, attributions are often either to a person's own character or to their situation; in other cultures, attributions to the person's in-group have been found. Although sometimes we can be certain that someone's traits, skills or efforts are 'causing' their actions, at other times it can be difficult to distinguish whether it is these factors or features of the situation which are mainly responsible for how they are behaving. We often give little thought to these judgements but they are important because they affect our responses to people. So, to revert to our example of Chapter 3, if John knows that something Jane has just said to him is untrue, his future attitude to Jane is likely to be affected by whether he thinks Jane has been misinformed by her boss or is deliberately lying, assuming these are the only two options he considers. If he thinks Jane has been misinformed by her boss, he attributes her untruth to the situation, and would normally not blame her. If he thinks Jane is deliberately lying, he attributes her untruth to her as a person, and would normally regard it as evidence of a character defect or at least be sceptical of the truthfulness of things she says in future. Accuracy in making these judgements is important because misunderstandings lead to breakdowns in communication and are detrimental to work. Managers, who have to evaluate subordinates' performance as part of their job, need especially good judgement in deciding how responsible these subordinates are for what happens. Unfortunately, as we shall see, attribution errors are common.

### *Making trait judgements*

In the West, it is common to make trait judgements, which means 'deciding' that a person's behaviour reflects some aspect of their personality, such as honesty or kindness. Intelligence, warmth and conscientiousness are the most common trait judgements. However, in other cultures, such as India, Ethiopia and Japan, the most common judgements are of contextual characteristics, such as social roles and origins.[11]

Figure 5.3 shows a chart of these people-perception processes.

**Box 5.2**

**Perceiving how other people perceive us.**

What do others really think of us? How do we know? When we form a judgement of what others think of us, are we likely to be right? Research shows that when people interact with several other people and then say how they think each of those others viewed them, their perceptions are highly consistent. That is, people believe they convey similar impressions to the various people with whom they interact. In reality, however, other people's impressions of us, and particularly how much they like us, are variable. We are worse at judging how others in general perceive us than at judging their traits and still worse at judging how we are uniquely viewed by specific individuals.

*Source*: Kenny, D. A. and B. M. DePaulo (1993) 'Do people know how others view them? An empirical and theoretical account', *Psychological Bulletin*, vol. 114, no. 1, pp. 145–161.

## Perceiving people: ancillary processes

The section above has described the general processes by which we perceive other people. In many but not all cases, however, other ancillary processes also take place. The most important of these are framing, stereotyping, applying expectations, forming impressions and detecting deceptions.

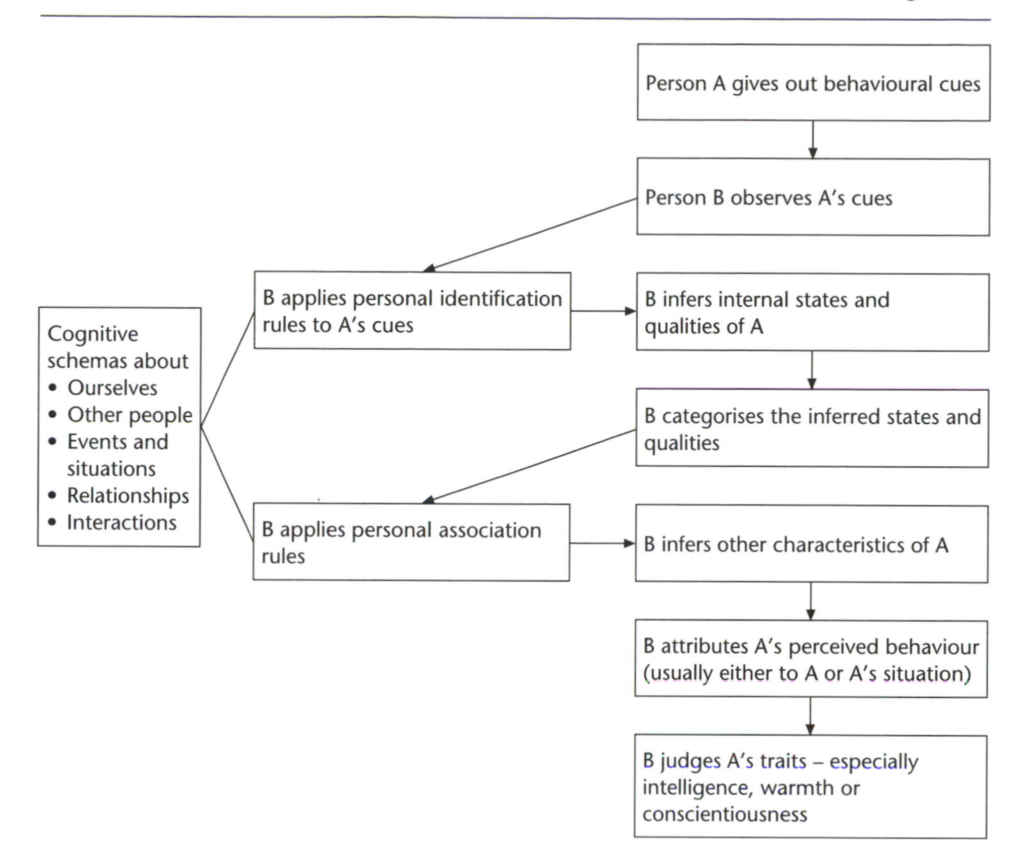


**Figure 5.3 Processes of perceiving people.**

### *Framing*

The universal need to make sense of our experiences has already been described in Chapter 3. It leads people to use 'frames' to interpret events. Frames are definitions of sequences of activities. Thus, someone might frame the activity of entering a colleague's office, talking with them for an hour and taking notes as 'working on the sales plan'; on the other hand, they might frame this same sequence as 'another hour of wasted time'. To understand the way individuals organise their experiences, therefore, 'frame analysis' is undertaken.[12] Communication activities, like all others, are viewed in the context of frame analysis. A sales encounter, for instance, is an interaction between two or more people who frame their meeting as buying and selling.

### *Stereotyping*

Use of association rules can lead to mentally creating or recalling a whole complex image, known as a stereotype. The concept of stereotype has gradually lost its earlier connotation of irrationality and prejudice. Instead, stereotyping is now considered an ordinary cognitive process in which people construct schemas to categorise people and entities in order to avoid 'information overload'. It is over-reliance on stereotypes which is now considered to prevent perceivers being accurate; I will discuss this issue later in this chapter.

#### *Expectations*

How we expect others to behave affects our ability to understand them accurately. Our expectations are influenced by what we think their role requires and how we think people should behave in general. We have expectations about both the verbal and the non-verbal behaviour of others. These expectations concern both how others do behave and how they should behave.[13]

#### *Forming impressions*

Perceivers organise even minimal displays of behaviour into unified personality impressions and sustain them by interpreting new data in the light of their initial impressions.[14] To demonstrate this, it has been shown that people recall more items describing another person when asked to form an impression than if they are asked simply to recall as many of the items as they can.[15] People forming an impression organise their perceptions into 'clusters' representing different categories of information (e.g. abilities and interests), whereas memory subjects do not do this to the same extent. Hamilton and Sherman[16] put forward four explanations of why we form impressions so readily and cling to them so firmly:

1. We expect people to have stable dispositions.
2. It is easier to remember organised information.
3. We try to avoid cognitive dissonance.
4. During interactions, we are able to retrieve the previously formed impression rather than details. This allows a quicker response.

There is, however, an ongoing debate about impression formation between structuralists and constructivists. Structuralists think impressions are 'data driven' – formed by combining observed elements. In support of their view there is evidence that non-verbal behaviour such as speed of speech and voice pitch do influence perceptions and that some impressions are accurate. Constructivists think the thoughts, goals and feelings of perceivers strongly influence their impressions of a target person. In support of their view, there is evidence that impressions are influenced by the perceiver's expectations and the accessibility of trait descriptions in their cognitive schemas.

Research shows that impressions once formed are resistant to change. For example, H. H. Kelley told half a class that a speaker would be 'warm' and told the other half that he would be 'cold'. The people who expected him to be cold saw him as cold, and participated less in the group discussion; those who expected him to be warm did the reverse.[17]

### *Detecting deceptions*

At work, knowing when someone is not telling the truth, or not the whole truth, is an important skill. Concealing information, exaggerating, covering up and plain lying do occur and it is important for lawyers, purchasers, interviewers, managers and negotiators to know how truthful clients, sales representatives, interviewees, subordinates and negotiators are being. To detect deceptions, most people use three criteria. These are how plausible is the message being communicated, how nervous is the communicator and whether the communicator's non-verbal behaviour breaches common expectations. Many people, though, use a fourth cue: is the source of the message socially attractive? Socially attractive message sources are perceived as less deceptive. In fact, discrepancies in deception attributions mainly vary between levels of attractiveness.[18] This may be part of the reason why, as research shows, lie detection rates barely exceed chance. One study found that subjects who were trying to detect deceptive communicators achieved only a 0.54 success rate. They did rather better in detecting truthful communicators, where accuracy was 0.70.[19] The researchers concluded that communicators attempting to deceive are difficult to detect and that a possible explanation is that receivers of messages have a bias towards believing that others are truthful, known as the 'veracity effect'.[20]

Figure 5.4 summarises these ancillary processes of person-perception.

**Box 5.3**

**How to improve your person-perception skills**

- Increase the number of cues you attend to, through active listening.
- Become more aware of your own identification and association rules.
- Become more aware of your implicit personality theory and the way it emerges in stereotyping.
- Practise postponing evaluative and trait inferences. Instead of thinking 'nice/nasty, cold/warm, likes me/dislikes me' try thinking 'lively expression', 'loud voice', 'fast speech', 'rapid gestures', 'sitting forward', etc. Concentrate on the cues to increase how observant you are, to make you more aware of which cues you over-use and which you neglect and to block out judgements. Then concentrate on a new range of cues from those you habitually use.
- Ask yourself if the person you need to understand is framing events and situations differently from you.
- Ask yourself if the person you need to understand is using inaccurate stereotypes. Are you?
- Are your expectations fair and realistic? Or are they culture-biased?
- Are you too keen to form an impression and so going too far beyond the evidence?
- In trying to detect deceptions, are you too influenced by how socially attractive the other person is? Are you biased in favour of believing people?
- Avoid the perceptual errors described in the next section.

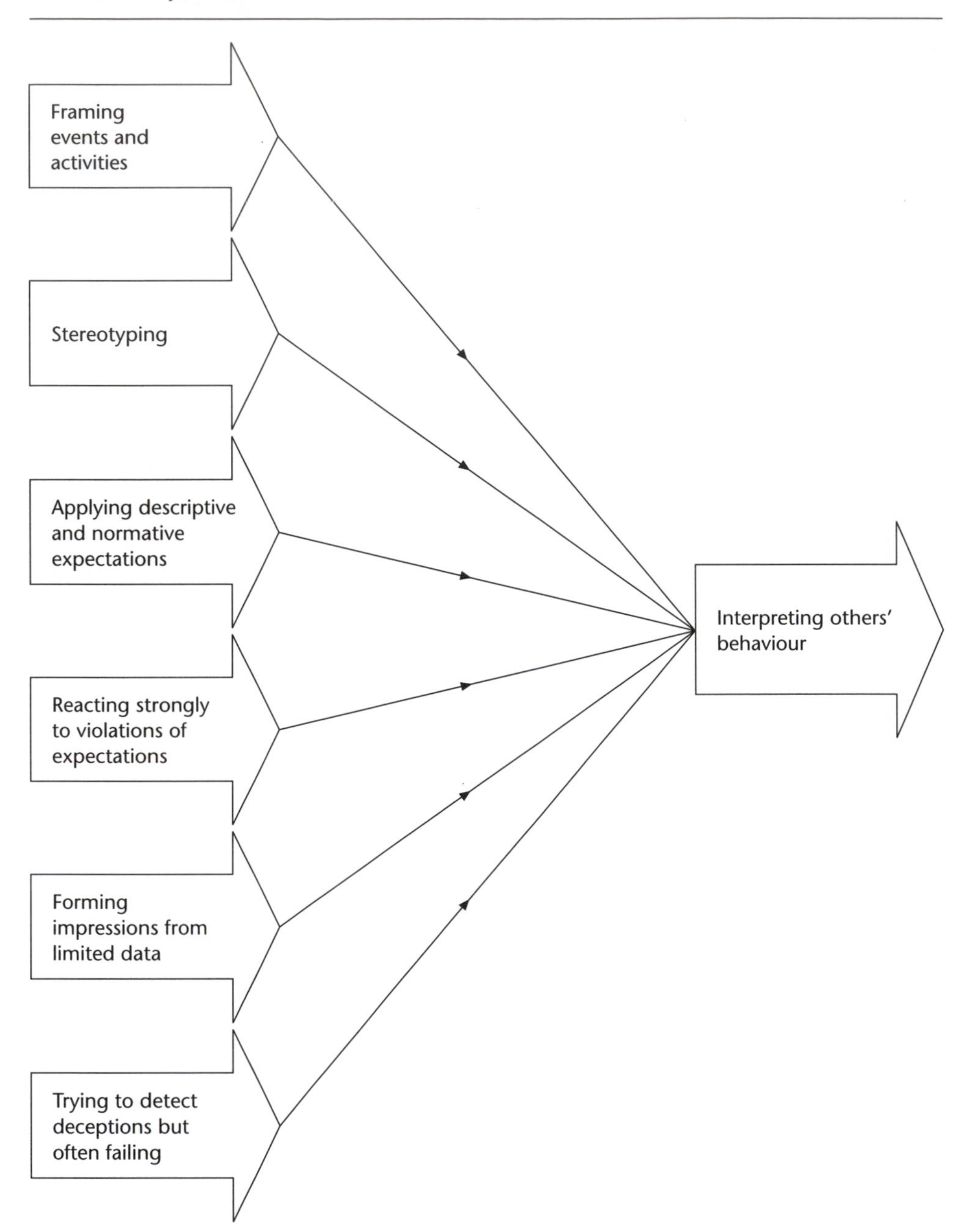


**Figure 5.4 Perceiving people: ancillary processes.**

## SUMMARY – HOW WE PERCEIVE PEOPLE

Understanding the 'inner meaning' of how other people behave is achieved through a set of highly skilled processes. These processes are learned, mainly from experience. They are carried out effectively when they produce accurate and sufficiently differentiated perceptions of others. The processes consist of observing a cue, identifying the cue with a value, motive, emotion, belief, attitude, intention, ability or trait, by using personal 'rules' and categories based on social comparison and categorisation, completing the picture by association, attributing a cause for the behaviour and making trait judgements. Ancillary processes in understanding others include framing, stereotyping, applying expectations, forming impressions and detecting deceptions.

## PERCEPTUAL ERRORS

Both general perception and social perception, including interpreting messages and non-verbal cues, are error-prone processes. General perception is affected by selective attention, perceptual distortion and cognitive errors. Social perceptions are further distorted by systematic biases, individual errors and the locked-in effect. Systematic biases are types of error that have been found to occur across a wide range of individuals. The commonest biases are over-reliance on stereotypes, assuming similarity, ignoring other people's different frames of reference, assuming intentionality and attribution, trait judgement, expectation and involvement errors.

What we attend to is affected by the characteristics of the stimulus, our motivational state, our need to maintain cognitive consistency and habituation. This is termed *selective attention.*

*Perceptual distortion* occurs during the process of comprehension. There are three main types:

1. Halo effects, which mean inferring the general qualities of an object from a specific characteristic. For example, a detergent that smells nice and lathers well will tend to be perceived as washing cleaner than one whose smell and lather level are less preferred.
2. We process information more efficiently but also distort it more if it is related to our strongest and most accessible cognitive schemas.[21]
3. To a large extent, we see what we expect to see, as in the case of illusions. For instance, people fill in information gaps about events with expected behaviours and thus mistakenly remember events that never took place.

*Cognitive errors* are widespread errors in the way we think. They include the following:

- Ignoring the prior probability of someone met with being a member of a particular category or group, such as lawyers or engineers, in favour of judging by how similar the target is to their stereotype.

- Treating the likelihood of a conjunction, for instance that someone is both a lawyer and an engineer, *P*(A & B), as more probable than its least typical constituent.
- Altering probability estimates when given information that is irrelevant to a judgement. For instance, our estimate of a colleague's chances of being promoted are likely to be reduced when 'has two brothers and once went on a blind date' is added to 'has been given added responsibilities and ran a successful marketing campaign'. This happens because we try to incorporate all given material as informative and relevant.
- Weighting information that comes first in a series more heavily than information that comes later.[22]
- When asked to test a rule, selecting rule-confirming opportunities over rule-falsifying opportunities.

However, recent research has strongly suggested that these may not all be 'errors'. In the words of Slugoski and Wilson[23]

> Much of what we once considered to reflect 'hardwired' information processing mechanisms in human judgement (cognitive biases, attitudinal shifts, causal attribution) actually reflects the operation of communicative goals and strategies people habitually rely on.

This point is explained further when the subject of conversation skills is discussed in Chapter 7.

Although stereotyping is unavoidable and generally functional, *over-reliance on stereotypes* distorts our understanding of others. For instance, people and groups are more likely to create stereotypes of people who are members of different groups from themselves. Stereotypes also tend to favour the in-group. Out-group members are believed to be less attractive, capable, trustworthy, honest, co-operative and deserving than members of the in-group.[24] Stereotypes influence the way information is processed. More favourable information is remembered about in-groups, less favourable about out-groups. Table 5.1 shows the effects of these factors on our use of stereotyping.

Our use of stereotypes is inconsistent. Evidence is emerging about conditions that lead to people making more or less use of stereotypes. Some people use stereotypes more than others do. The more control people think they have (over themselves and their environment, including other people) the more they tend to rely on stereotypes.[25] People who feel deprived of control usually seek diagnostic information about others. In contrast, people who feel they have social power, whether through their own position or that of their group, seek less diagnostic information. Possible reasons for this are that, for them, outcomes of interactions with others depend less on the others' attitudes and behaviour. In addition, they may suffer from information overload, because of the effects of a power hierarchy. The personality of people who gain power may also have an

**Table 5.1 Influences on the use of stereotyping**

| *Use of stereotyping* | *Influence* | *Research evidence* |
|---|---|---|
| Increased use | Positive mood | In a happy mood perceivers use more stereotypes than in a negative or neutral mood (Stroessner and Mackie, 1992). |
| Lowered use | Negative or neutral mood; Awareness of being influenced by stereotypes; Intention not to use stereotypes | Being in a sad mood increases perceivers' use of individuating information (Bless *et al.*, 1996). Perceivers use strategies to combat unwanted automatic influences on their responses, so long as they are not suffering from cognitive constraints such as overload or habit (Banaji and Greenwald, 1995; Blair and Banaji, 1996). |
| More positive stereotypes | Priming with positive exemplars | Priming with a well-liked African American led to more positive views of the entire social category (and stronger views that they were discriminated against) Bodenhausen *et al.* (1995). Similar views of politicians have also been found (Schwartz and Bless, 1992). |
| More negative stereotypes | Negative frame of reference; Negative social influence; Inter-group conflict | Australians' stereotype of Americans became more negative when the frame of reference was extended to Iraq (Haslam *et al.*, 1992). More negative stereotypes are reported when research subjects are told others have negative views. Inter-group conflict leads to more negative and extreme stereotypes of out-group members (Grant, 1991). |
| Less adjustment of stereotypes for new information | Cognitive overload | Garcia-Marques and Mackie (1999) found that when people had 'too much' to think about, either at the time when they were given information which was incongruent with their stereotype, or at the time when they were asked for their judgement, they adjusted their stereotype of a group much less than when they could concentrate. |

*Note: it may be that the inverse of these relationships holds (e.g. that positive social influence induces more positive stereotypes) but the table only shows those relationships found in research.*

*Sources*: Banaji, M. and A. Greenwald (1995). 'Implicit gender stereotyping in judgments of fame', *Journal of Personality and Social Psychology*, vol. 68, pp. 181–198.

Blair, I. V. and M. R. Banaji (1996) 'Automatic and controlled processes in stereotype priming', *Journal of Personality and Social Psychology*, vol. 70, no. 6, pp. 1142–1163.

Bless, H., N. Schwartz and M. Kemmelmeier (1996) 'Mood and stereotyping: affective states and the use of general knowledge structures' in W. Stroebe and M. Hewstone (eds) *European Review of Social Psychology*, vol. 7, pp. 63–94.

Bodenhausen, G. V., N. Schwartz, H. Bless, M. Wanke *et al.* (1995) 'Effects of atypical exemplars on racial beliefs: Enlightened racism or generalized appraisals?', *Journal of Experimental Psychology*, vol. 31, pp. 48–63.

Garcia-Marques, L. and D. Mackie (1999) 'The Impact of stereotype incongruent information on perceived group variability and stereotype change', *Journal of Personality and Social Psychology*, vol. 77, no. 5, pp. 979–990.

Grant, P. R. (1991) 'Ethnocentrism between groups of unequal power under threat in inter-group competition', *Journal of Social Psychology*, vol. 131, pp. 21–28.

Haslam, S. A., J. C. Turner, P. J. Oakes, C. McGarty and B. J. Hayes (1992) 'Context-dependent variation in social stereotyping: 1: the effects of inter-group relations as mediated by social change and frame of reference', *European Journal of Social Psychology*, vol. 22, pp. 3–20.

Schwartz, N. and H. Bless (1992) 'Scandals and the public's trust in politicians: Assimilation and contrast effects', *Personality and Social Psychology Bulletin*, vol. 18, pp. 574–579.

Stroessner, S. J. and D. M. Mackie (1992) 'The impact of induced affect on the perception of variability in social groups' *Personality and Social Psychology Bulletin*, vol. 18, pp. 546–554.

effect. Stereotypes reinforce the status quo and maintain social identities, including that of the power-holder. Changing stereotypic beliefs is 'costly'; power-holders may feel entitled to judge others based on their own expectations. Thus they are more prone to stereotyping.

People cling firmly to stereotypes in the face of disconfirming evidence. To do this they recast disconfirming evidence as an 'exception to the rule', form a separate representation of the deviant group member, or predict that people who act inconsistently with their stereotypes will in future act 'hyperconsistently' to compensate. When a person's behaviour is extremely inconsistent with the stereotype, observers adjust their expectations, but they still expect compensatory behaviour from another member of the person's social group.[26] The more cognitively accessible an idea is, the more it affects the inferences we make from what we observe. Thus the more readily a trait judgement such as 'stupid' comes to mind, the more likely we are to infer that a person we are observing is, indeed, stupid. Dijksterhuis and van Knippenberg,[27] basing their argument on associative learning theory, which was outlined in Chapter 4, hypothesised that the higher the frequency and the greater the consistency with which a social category and an attribute co-occur, the faster and further the association will develop and the more the effects of a stereotype on bias. Their research confirmed this. Inaccurate stereotypes continue to be used, they argued, because a person's learning history is generally quite predictive of his/her future encounters, partly from opportunity, partly from preference.

Misused stereotypes do damage. Stereotypes occupy a pivotal role in intergroup relations, bias individuals' information processing concerning in-group and out-group members, facilitate the creation of self-fulfilling prophecies, become incorporated in the ideology of in-groups and are used to justify and explain their behaviour towards out-groups.[28,29]

**Box 5.4**

Some scholars believe that computer-mediated communicators may be no more immune from stereotyping than face-to-face communicators are. A review of research found that even though computer-mediated communication allows social boundaries to be blurred, it may increase a communicator's susceptibility to the power of group influence, stereotyping and discrimination.

*Source*: Postmes, T., R. Spears and M. Lea (1998) 'Breaching or building social boundaries? Side-effects of computer-mediated communication', *Communication Research*, vol. 25, no. 6, pp. 689–715.

*Assuming similarity* means attributing to others characteristics we see ourselves as possessing. In extreme cases, people unconsciously assume that others have exactly the same values, motives and goals as they themselves have. At a lower extreme, many people assume that other people's reasons for what they do are similar to those they would have for doing the same thing. For instance, ambitious people will tend to think of everyone else as similarly ambitious and to feel competitive with them.

Another source of perceptual errors is ignoring other people's *different frames of reference*. When other people do things that surprise us, especially things that seem inappropriate or wrong, it may be because they perceive the situation differently from us. For instance, an accountant might think that ruthlessly pursuing every bad debt is safeguarding the financial health of the business, while a sales representative might think it is a good way to lose customers. We each perceive the world in different ways – from a different frame of reference. To understand what someone else does in a given situation we have to see it from their frame of reference, to perceive the situation as they do. If we are to understand each other's behaviour we have to understand each other's perceptions. Information about these influences is hard to come by and poses a barrier to our understanding of others, but similarities of basic needs and motives, sensory apparatus, some aspects of environment, and some experiences create at least the possibility of mutual understanding.

Most people tend to assume that other people have more *control of their situation* than they see themselves as having or than other people actually do have, and so think that everything others do is intentional. There is a temptation to think that other people do things such as giving the wrong change deliberately, and could have done differently, but to think that our own actions often result from accident, error or having no choice. More generally, researchers have found some widespread errors in the *attributions* people make. There is a strong tendency to attribute our own behaviour and other people's differently – our own more to the situation, others' more to their personality. This is probably because we know more about our own behaviour. We are more aware of the different ways we behave in different situations. Moreover, self-esteem leads us to see ourselves as complex and flexible, rather than locked into the kind of rigid responses that personality traits imply. Our need to reduce the quantity of incoming information, on the other hand, leads us to a simplifying 'personality' model of other people. The tendency to attribute other people's behaviour to their personality is greater still in certain circumstances:

- If the behaviour is 'inappropriate', such as wearing unsuitable clothes to work.
- When the perceiver is dependent on the other person, probably because they are motivated to know the other's 'character' in order to predict their future behaviour. Thus, interestingly, subordinates are more likely to attribute their boss's behaviour to the boss's personality than the boss is to do the same to the subordinate. However, when the attributions are highly relevant to predicting behaviour that could affect the perceiver's own outcomes and the potential costs of an inaccurate dispositional inference are high, this bias

decreases. This is probably because the situation motivates the perceiver to try to be accurate.[30]

- Generally, if the action is a success. On the whole, we credit others with their successes and blame the situation for their failures. This rather attractive quality is not, however, found among managers with regard to their subordinates. They tend to do the reverse, blaming the person for the failures and attributing the successes to the situation. Two reasons have been suggested for managers' biases in this direction. One is ease of response. It is easier to blame or in extreme cases dismiss an employee, than to investigate and correct external factors such as job design or organisational structure. The other is the managers' needs to maintain their own reputation and self-esteem. This might be achieved by attributing subordinates' successes to their own briefing, training or supervision and their failures to incorrigible personality defects. On the other hand, subordinates' 'positive' behaviours, those beneficial to the organisation, are regarded by managers as more stable than their 'negative' ones. This probably reflects reality. Selection of suitable individuals for jobs plus organisational pressures and norms make it likely.[31,32]
- If the person being perceived has high status. High-status people are assumed by others to be more responsible for their own actions.[33] If they conform to a group's norms or ideas, for instance, they will be seen as doing so for their own reasons, whereas low-status people will be seen as succumbing to pressure from others. High-status people are also more likely to be attributed favourably regarded motives for their actions.
- If the behaviour is enacted by an in-group member and is regarded as positive or by an out-group member and is regarded as negative. Positive in-group and negative out-group behaviour tend to be attributed to internal, stable or controllable causes. On the other hand, negative in-group and positive out-group behaviour tend to be attributed to external, unstable or uncontrollable causes. In this way, people are able to maintain a positive social identity.

*Trait judgements* often produce perceptual errors. First, in making inferences about people we tend to treat traits as if they were sharply distinct and dichotomous categories. We say that people are warm or cold, honest or dishonest, extravert or introvert. In reality, events and people usually fit along these dimensions at different points, some closer to one end, some to another. The Eysenck Personality Inventory lists 24 levels of extraversion. Most people use only three or four, such as extremely, very, somewhat and not at all. Second, we often emphasise the extremes of traits we value highly. For instance, someone who values intelligence very highly will tend to rate others as highly intelligent or stupid, rather than in the middle. Third, evidence is emerging that two key judgements we make about ourselves and others (and about our own in-group and out-groups) are concerned with 'competence' and 'moral desirability'. We use our perceptions of a person's intended goals – what they were trying to achieve – to judge the morality of their action and them as a person. We use the extent to which they attained the goals we believe them to have to decide their competence. It all starts to get us into making a lot of assumptions! We are also biased in our own favour. We prefer our own behaviour to be judged in terms of competence but tend to interpret the behaviour of others in moral rather than competence terms (because we are potential targets of what the others do).[34] When we judge other people as (in)sincere, (un)trustworthy, (un)conscientious, (un)reliable, modest or arrogant, we tend to make the mistake of forming positive and negative attitudes towards them from the scanty evidence of first impressions.

When someone's behaviour *violates our expectations* as perceivers beyond a certain point, we notice it, are aroused by it and may judge it and the other person in a more extreme way. This may be either more positively or more negatively. Our expectations are based on social (cultural) norms and, where applicable, previous experience of the situation and the other person. This means that, during first meetings with people from backgrounds different from our own, our expectations are particularly likely to be violated and we are particularly likely to make extreme judgements.[35]

According to Sherif's *involvement theory*, perceivers who are highly involved, either with the other person or with an issue that arises between them, interpret messages that they agree with as more positive than they really are.[36] For instance, sales representatives who are hoping to hear that their company has been awarded a major contract may interpret a casual smile from the buying organisation's Procurement Director as favourable news. This reaction is called an assimilation effect. On the other hand, messages that highly involved individuals disagree with are interpreted as more negative than they actually are. This reaction is called a contrast effect. Therefore, highly involved individuals are more likely to perceive messages in a distorted way, based on their preconceptions and biases. On the other hand, highly involved individuals will use more attributes in assessing another person or situation and will attend to more messages about them. The more involved someone is, the more they are likely to be trying to make a 'perfect' judgement or decision, so the more information they will want to have, and the more factors they will try to take into account. This may counter the distorting effects of polarisation. Putting together all these ideas about how someone's level of involvement affects their judgement produces the analysis shown in Table 5.2.

*Individual errors* result from the fact that individuals' perceptual worlds are influenced by their motives, goals, past experiences, social and cultural environment, physical environment, psychological characteristics and needs. If new information seems likely to make someone re-think their self-concept or their image of others who are important to them, they are likely to disregard or distort it.

**Table 5.2 Effects of different levels of involvement on social judgement**

| | *High involvement* | *Low involvement* |
|---|---|---|
| Number of attributes considered in judging the person or situation | Many | Few |
| Amount of information about the person or situation attended to | Much | Little |
| Interpretation of cues | Extreme (assimilation or contrast) | Not extreme |
| Perceptual selection errors | Low | High |
| Distortion of perception | High | Low |

> We do not take in, with our eyes or ears, exactly what is 'out there'. We constantly respond to cues that have meaning for us. We see what we want or need to see to defend ourselves or advance our aims. We select out cues below our perceptual threshold; we distort cues which are too threatening to our emotions. We do not see people for what they are or as they see themselves; we see them for what they signify to us.[37]

It is particularly hard to decipher people's values, motives and aspirations across the barriers of social class, occupation or culture. This means that:

> It is hard for the son of a successful middle class businessman to understand the values and career aspirations of the son of an immigrant or unskilled worker. It is hard for the general manager to understand the values and career aspirations of the technically-oriented person and vice-versa. It is hard for people in different functional areas of business to decipher each other's values and aspirations.[38]

Errors resulting from these individual variations have been shown to occur in, for example, the decoding of messages. Researchers Gallois and Callan concluded that the receiver's own goals and perceptions of the context as threatening may lead to an overall distortion of the sender's message.[39]

The *locked-in effect* refers to our tendency not to accept any information that does not fit with our existing ideas and beliefs.[40] We therefore select and distort our new observations, so that the initial impression can be preserved. Some practical consequences of the locked-in effect have been found: tape recordings of interviews showed that the interviewers had their ideas of what the interviewees meant to say and ignored or interrupted them if they tried to explain what they really meant.[41] The more rapidly we form our impressions of other people, the more subject they will be to the effects of biases. Then, the locked-in effect will operate to prevent us substituting more accurate impressions afterwards. The more time between a first meeting and forming a judgement, the more cues we will have at our disposal and the easier it will be to avoid forming prejudiced and inaccurate assessments. The result will probably be that we feel unsure of how to act. This state is one in which real learning can happen very quickly.

## SUMMARY – PERCEPTUAL ERRORS

General perception processes give rise to selective attention and distorted comprehension, while our ways of thinking produce a number of judgemental errors. The processes of perceiving people more specifically give rise to systematic biases, including over-reliance on stereotypes, assuming similarity, ignoring other people's different frames of reference, assuming intentionality and attribution, trait judgement, expectation and involvement errors. These are added to by individual errors caused by such factors as personal motives and experiences and by the locked-in effect.

## INTERPRETING MESSAGES AND NON-VERBAL CUES

Most of what we learn about others comes directly from what they say and how they say it or how they behave non-verbally in other ways. This section explains some of what we can learn from these sources, what errors they can give rise to and how to improve listening skills.

### Messages

Because meaning cannot be transmitted, it must be recreated by the receiver, using inference. It is easy to get it wrong. For instance, it might be easy for a market research interviewer to interpret the statement 'I prefer tabloid newspapers', as meaning that the interviewee prefers the popular press, when the person is expressing a preference for the convenient tabloid size but not their style or content. Messages are often complex and carry more than their surface meaning. For example, a selection interview question such as 'How ambitious are you?' could also mean 'Would you compete for my job?'; 'What do you do in your spare time?' often means 'Are you a team player or a loner?' and/or 'Do you have hobbies or family commitments which will consume more of your interest/time/energy than your work?' Being alert to multiple meanings is related to experience. Mixing with a wide range of people leads to receiving more diverse information, opinions and accounts that suggest that there can be more than one view of a situation. This in turn leads people to expect complexity in messages. Multiple meanings can, though, lead to ambiguity, either because the receiver is confused or uncertain about the meaning of a message, or because there are two or more possible meanings to a message but the receiver is unaware of this possibility. For example, if two executives, one from the United Kingdom and one from Germany were talking and both used the term 'business management', the UK executive would be referring to a shareholder-oriented management of assets, the German to management with an extensive worker input. However, in Europe, messages about task-related concerns are generally structured and explicit; background information is provided and what is being referred to is made clear. Because communication at work is mainly task-related, the barriers to understanding can be lower than they would otherwise be. In other cultures, on the other hand, this may not apply, as the section in this chapter on cultural differences in ways of communicating explains.

Work messages often include arguments in favour of or against an idea or proposal. How people judge an argument depends on whether they know enough about the subject of the message to allow them to think critically about it, their personal preference for critical thinking and their involvement with the issue. (It also depends on how many persuasive sources and different arguments are used.) On an issue on which they are involved and knowledgeable, critical thinkers will use elaborated and thoughtful processing. In other cases, arguments are evaluated casually, in which case factors such as liking for the person arguing have more influence than the strength of argument.[42] There is evidence that, to English-speaking senders and receivers, the rules for encoding and decoding negative messages are clearer and more accessible than rules for positive or neutral messages, which could significantly affect how, for instance, workforces respond to management announcements of their plans.[43] Edwards and Smith[44] found evidence for a disconfirmation bias in the evaluation of arguments. Arguments incompatible with prior beliefs are scrutinised longer, subject to more extensive refutational analyses and consequently are judged to be weaker than arguments compatible with prior beliefs. People are generally unable to evaluate evidence independently of their prior beliefs.

## Non-verbal cues

Knowing what can and what cannot be inferred validly from how other people speak and act physically – that is to say, from their non-verbal cues – improves understanding. There are wide individual variations, but some bodily and facial movements generally express the same thing whoever makes them, and research has contributed some useful pointers to these. Most of our knowledge of 'universal' expressions comes from laboratory studies which have used independent tests of internal states and properties, e.g. emotions and attitudes, and then measured how well these correlated with different verbal and non-verbal cues.[45] In other words, they measure to what extent the same cue expresses the same internal property or state in different people or in the same people at different times. Other studies have measured the interpretation process – the average extent to which different characteristics can be judged accurately by observers.

Each different type of non-verbal behaviour can indicate different inner states or qualities of an individual and many can be used for intentional communication as well as unintentional. The second column of Table 6.6 in Chapter 6 lists

**Table 5.3 Motivational patterns revealed by behavioural cues, based on Maslow's hierarchy**

| *Motive* | *Cue* | *Comment* |
|---|---|---|
| Biological | A range of physical cues, e.g. yawning, stomach rumbling, high concern with money or ambition | Concern with money and ambition can also be motivated by higher-order motives. |
| Security | How people respond to proposed change; repeatedly referring back to written rules and procedures; believing unquestioningly in 'experts'; working obsessionally hard | |
| Affiliation | Expressing sympathy, trying to help, giving support in arguments, bringing-in to conversations and discussions, advocating others' interests, smiling, eye contact, and choosing to sit or stand nearby | All these actions may be stimulated by an ulterior purpose, motivated by the power or security needs or by a sense of obligation. |
| Power | Being determined to win every point of an argument, or being set on convincing others, dominating, or being unusually affected by any appearance of weakness. Promising, threatening, citing authority or position, and demanding or confronting others; finger wagging, leaning forward to 'invade' another person's 'territory' and standing when others sit | |
| Esteem | As for power; behaviour designed to impress rather than win, e.g. referring to prestigious 'contacts' without any specific objective in view | |
| Achievement | Using absolute evaluative terms such as 'excellence', 'high attainment' or 'good quality'; opposing pragmatic solutions, lacking concern with consequences when judging performance, being unwilling to compromise | |

some meanings of non-verbal behaviour which have been tested in research. Table 5.3 shows some cues that may be linked to motivational patterns.

Burgoon and Le Poire[46] showed that non-verbal behaviour is ambiguous, so perceivers must rely on an array of imperfect indicators which in combination establish a probabilistic relationship with the characteristic in question. For example, eye contact accompanied by close proximity, direct body orientation, smiling, nodding and gentle touching is perceived as intimacy, whereas eye contact accompanied by close proximity, direct body orientation, facial grimacing and pointing at the other's chest is perceived as intimidation and danger. Thus the researchers conclude that non-verbal behaviours have multiple but discernible meanings, so amounting to a coding system not unlike that for verbal communication and that they have 'social meaning', which is relatively impervious to variability in the social context. This is in contrast to an earlier view that the meanings of non-verbal behaviours are deeply embedded in the particulars of a given social situation.[47]

Ekman and Friesen[48] watched people interacting, paying particular attention to their non-verbal behaviour. They concluded that non-verbal behaviour, while it does express meaning and reveal inner states and qualities as I have described, also fulfils different functions from verbal behaviour. They found the following:

- Non-verbal behaviour is basically a relationship language. It makes it possible to express things such as 'I trust you', 'I acknowledge that you are my superior' or 'You bore me', which would be too embarrassing or difficult to state directly.
- Many bodily movements perform other communication functions than expressive ones. Some are conscious signals. Others are used by speakers to amplify, clarify and punctuate their own speech. Some are used by listeners to 'regulate' another person's speaking by indicating interest or a desire for them to speed up or repeat something or change the subject. Still others are only habits.
- Certain non-verbal behaviours express a person's attitude to themself or their body image.
- Both emotions and attitudes, which may be concealed in the spoken words, tend to leak out in non-verbal behaviour.

## Active and empathetic listening

Several studies have shown that executives spend between 45 and 65 per cent of their time listening.[49] Changes in organisational forms and cultures, discussed in Chapter 2, are likely to increase this amount.

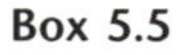

**Box 5.5**

In a television programme on Active Listening on 23 November 1993, the following people gave their comments on the importance of active listening.

Claire Rayner (agony aunt): You must listen to silences and what is not being said as well as what is said. Listening is complex.

Andrew Neil (newspaper editor): The worst interviewers in broadcasting have a list of questions and go through it regardless of what you say. For instance, if you were asked a question about how many unemployed you forecast for next year, and you answered 'about 50 million', with some interviewers the next question would be 'and what do you think about the money supply?'

Paul Booton (a doctor): I think the best doctors – especially GPs – are good at least in part because they are good listeners.

A Teacher: Teaching is a dialogue.

A Bishop: You've got to give people your undivided attention.

Good listening requires a series of skills. These include the ability to concentrate for a long time, an understanding for the other person's point of view, and an ability to read between the lines and grasp what is meant, which is often different from what is said. Box 5.6 is a guide to active listening.

**Box 5.6**

**How to listen actively**

- Your posture should be relaxed but alert. Sit back in your chair but upright, or stand comfortably but upright. Hold your head up and *look* alert.
- With a new acquaintance, break the ice with a smile or pleasant comment to put yourself as well as them at ease.
- Encourage the speaker to communicate more – say 'I'd like to hear more about that . . .' or 'That's interesting . . .', signal that you are paying attention with sounds like 'Mmmm', 'uh huh', 'Sure', and use non-verbals, especially eye contact and facial expressions.
- Concentrate:
  - Avoid thinking about yourself or the impression you are making;
  - Avoid day-dreaming: if someone else is talking at length, summarise or ask questions seeking clarification, even if you have to interrupt;
  - Avoid planning what you are going to say instead of listening to what is being said.
- Do not modify what is actually being said, because it is inconsistent, makes you angry or afraid or does not fit with your impression of the speaker. Be aware of these causes of reductive listening and overcome them.
- Do not evaluate the message or the speaker early in an interaction, as doing so will block your openness to new information.

Empathetic listening is very important for some work activities, such as mentoring and handling complaints; on occasion it is needed for a whole range of others. It means listening in order to understand the other person's point of view. To understand another person's behaviour, we must try to understand how they see the world around them – their frame of reference. The true meaning of what they do can only be understood in their own terms – not ours. Differences in past experience mean that another person's frame of reference is never the same as our own and rarely even similar. Seeing things from the other person's viewpoint – not necessarily with sympathy, just as objectively as possible, is difficult, but necessary.

There appear to be three key elements in listening empathetically: active emotional commitment to doing so, accepting the necessity of role-taking (as opposed to 'being yourself') and identification with the other person.[50] However, Hancock and Ickes[51] found that people are no more accurate in inferring the thoughts of a friend who is interacting with a stranger than they are at inferring the thoughts of the stranger. They concluded that the relationship between a perceiver and a 'target' does not affect empathetic accuracy. (They also found no reliable sex difference in receivers' empathy.)

Box 5.7

### How to interpret messages

- The content of what is said reveals a great deal but it is often misleading to draw inferences from a small sample. Early in a conversation, speakers' level of control can be so high that they distort and select at will to create a desired impression. Over a longer conversation or a three-way or more discussion, most people's control of what they say is lowered and the signs become easier to read.
- Messages, including questions, often have multiple meanings; you should be alert to these possibilities.
- If you are not highly involved with or informed on an issue, or you dislike critical thinking, your evaluation of arguments in favour or against ideas or proposals can be based on irrelevant factors rather than the strength of the argument. This is a weakness to guard against. On the other hand, if you are highly involved, you may perceive messages in a polarised way, based on your preconceptions and biases.
- Active listening will help you learn more from others' messages and get them to impart more. To listen actively, follow the prescriptions in Box 5.6.
- Empathetic listening will allow you to see things from the other person's point of view. To listen empathetically, practise examining other people's actions by trying to think about the thought processes which may have led to them. The more you find differences from what your own would have been, the more progress you are making. Even then, however, remember that it is improbable that you are fully understanding their perspective.

## SUMMARY – INTERPRETING MESSAGES AND NON-VERBAL CUES

Interpreting messages involves decoding symbols and inferring meaning, which are processes that can lead to errors of understanding. Messages often have multiple layers of meaning, which gives rise to ambiguity. Judging arguments gives rise to errors when the receiver processes them peripherally and so is influenced by factors other than the strength of the argument. Active and empathetic listening are techniques for improving understanding of messages.

Non-verbal behaviour gives a range of clues to people's inner states and qualities, though interpretation needs to be based on accurate understanding gained from research, as many common-sense interpretations are misleading. Although non-verbal behaviour can be deliberate, it is usually less subject to censorship than verbal behaviour. We use non-verbal behaviour to express things that would be difficult to say and to regulate the flow of talk.

## CULTURAL, ETHNIC AND GENDER INFLUENCES ON WAYS OF COMMUNICATING

Knowing how ways of communication vary according to social background helps us interpret the behaviour of people from other social categories than our own. A study of Chinese professionals working in corporate America found marked differences in these professionals' perceptions of interpersonal communication in Chinese organisations (blunt assertiveness, smooth amiability and surface humility) compared with American corporations (sophisticated kindness, manipulative 'stroking' and casual spontaneity).[52] This study shows not only that there are important cultural differences in work communication but that observers believe they can perceive them. However, to grasp the subtleties of ways of communicating in foreign languages and another culture is a major undertaking, even for good linguists. (It would be informative to know how closely the Chinese professionals' observations in American corporations corresponded to those of other groups.) When the time or opportunity to do this is lacking, an understanding of a core distinction in ways of communicating can be useful. This distinction, drawn by Edward T. Hall, is between low-context communication (LCC) and high-context communication (HCC) cultures. In LCC cultures, which predominate in Europe, people rely on the explicit verbal content of messages and 'the mass of the [communicated] information is vested in the explicit code.'[53] In contrast, in HCCs, which predominate in Asia, for instance, 'Most of the information [to be communicated] is either in the physical context or internalised in the person, while very little is in the coded, explicit, transmitted part of the message.' In comparison with members of LCCs, members of HCCs make more use of non-verbal cues, emphasise social roles and use different 'scripts' according to the role relationships and status of the participants.

There is evidence for significant cultural variation in non-verbal expression. Table 5.4 gives some examples of non-verbal expressions used in one country, Brazil. Ekman *et al.*[54] found that cultural display rules govern the show of emotion.

**Table 5.4 Brazilian body language**

| *Gesture* | *Meaning and function* |
|---|---|
| With the arm extended and the hand turned up or down, the fingers are flexed several times, accompanied by the words '*psiu, psiu*' | 'Come here' |
| Closed fist held to ear | To show that someone is speaking on the telephone |
| Finger and thumb of same hand rubbed together | Indicates that people referred to are intimate |
| Eyelid gently pulled downwards | Either: 'Watch out, be careful, keep your eyes open' or 'Do you think I'm stupid enough to believe that?' |
| Fingers tapped under chin | To show that a person doesn't know what he/she is talking about |

For instance, in some cultures men perform ceremonial weeping, intensifying the display of grief in a way that would be unseemly for a North American or Northern European. Culturally learned display rules over-ride natural expressions and therefore produce variations. What is more, this cultural effect applies to organisations, too: some require higher levels of suppression of feelings than others. (Table 5.5 gives some examples of culturally regulated display rules.) Culture may also determine how individuals use personal space. People from contact cultures choose closer distances, maintain more direct eye contact, touch each other more frequently and speak more loudly than those from non-contact cultures.[55] However, this analysis may ignore other variables – age, sex, relationship, environment and ethnic co-cultures. These variables may play equally important roles in determining use of personal space and, particularly in the cases of age and relationship, supercede any cultural aspects.[56]

**Table 5.5 Culturally regulated display rules**

| *Display rule* | *Example* |
|---|---|
| Intensification | Looking very happy on receiving a mildly pleasing gift |
| De-intensification | Looking mildly pleased when winning a very rewarding competition |
| Neutralisation | Maintaining a poker face or stiff upper lip |
| Masking | Showing anger in the presence of a bully when feeling fear |

Within cultures, there are gender differences in non-verbal behaviour. For instance, Mehrabian[57] found that when American men are intending to convey a positive attitude towards the person they are addressing, their most used signal is a high level of eye contact, followed by smaller distance and a relative absence of an arms-akimbo position. Women, however, signal positive attitudes most clearly by relative absence of the arms-akimbo position, then by smaller distance and then by eye contact. For signalling that they have lower status than the addressee, men make most use of tilting the head, followed by, in order of importance, not crossing their legs, more eye contact, a relative absence of the arms-akimbo position, less leg relaxation, less hand relaxation and more direct shoulder orientation. To signal the same subservience, women make most use of reduced hand relaxation, then absence of arms-akimbo, then less leg relaxation, head tilting and eye contact.

However valid in terms of their own culture, differences in how people communicate, such as dialect, frequency of interruption, story telling and conversational rules, can lead to them being perceived as disorganised and poor thinkers or as being insulting. Gender differences in style lead to women being wrongly perceived: soft-spoken women who use tags ('I think') or hesitations are usually perceived as non-assertive or relationship-oriented, whereas in fact some soft-spoken women are power-driven. Non-verbal behaviour is easily misinterpreted by members of different groups: how people move or hold themselves, how close they stand, how fast they speak, the amount of eye contact they seek, how much personal information they disclose and their use of verbal aggression differ by culture and are interpreted differently depending on culture, which leads to misunderstanding.[58]

## SUMMARY – CULTURAL, ETHNIC AND GENDER INFLUENCES ON WAYS OF COMMUNICATING

Although fully to take into account these influences requires an in-depth study of a particular language and culture, the distinction between high-context and low-context communication cultures usefully draws attention to the significance of the context in the one versus the explicit content in the other. Non-verbal behaviour is subject to culturally determined display rules, although some forms of expression do cross cultural boundaries. There are also gender differences in how people express themselves in speech and non-verbally. Unless the differences in how people from different backgrounds communicate, both verbally and non-verbally, are taken into account, misunderstanding is likely.

## CULTURAL AND GENDER DIFFERENCES IN HOW WE PERCEIVE

To avoid deluding ourselves that our own perceptions are always accurate, it helps to realise that people from different cultures, seeing the same piece of behaviour, may perceive, interpret and judge it differently. For example, East Asian cognition has been shown to be relatively holistic, that is, attention is paid to the field as a whole.[59] Western cognition, in contrast, has been shown to be object focused and control oriented. Furthermore, we have evidence that attributing observed actions to properties of the individual actor is less common in collectivist settings. For instance, when Hindu adults in India and adults from the United States described and then explained four behaviours from their recent, everyday experience, 40 per cent of Indian explanations were contextual in comparison with only 18 per cent of American.[60] In another study, American students explained an ambiguous outcome by emphasising properties of the individual, Chinese students by emphasising properties of the group. Collectivists make more use of contextual attributions (e.g. interpersonal relationships, situations, group associations and activities) and individualists use more context-free, dispositional, abstract information (e.g. abilities, traits, knowledge, cognitive-emotional style). There are various explanations for these differences. One is that North Americans have an inflated sense of individual control, whereas East Asians perceive that they cannot control their destinies independently of groups.[61] Another is that whereas perceivers from some cultures believe individuals have dispositions, perceivers from other cultures believe that groups have dispositions and individuals are controlled by situational forces including their group.[62] In contrast to these cultural differences in how we perceive, research subjects from ten different cultures agreed in their judgement of facial expression – particularly about which was the most and which the second most intense emotion signalled by an expression and about the relative intensity among expressions of the same emotion.[63]

On the interpretation of messages, women have been found to be slightly better decoders of feelings and attitudes (and considerably better encoders, especially with strangers). Overall, positive messages are decoded worst and negative messages best; but men are worse than women on both positive and negative messages. Similarly, a comparison of encoding and decoding of messages by people of Australian, British and Italian ethnicity found that positive messages by Australian and Italian men were decoded less accurately than positive messages by British men. On negative and neutral messages, Italian male speakers were decoded less accurately than Australian and British male speakers. There were fewer differences for female speakers.[64]

## SUMMARY – CULTURAL AND GENDER DIFFERENCES IN HOW WE PERCEIVE

Culture affects whether people perceive others holistically or by paying attention mainly to what is related to their goals or aspects they can control. It also affects whether attributions are made to individuals or to groups. On the other hand, emotion is interpreted similarly from facial expressions across a wide range of cultures. Gender affects accuracy of perception: women decode messages more accurately. Ethnicity also affects accuracy of perception but in this case the evidence points to some ethnic groups being decoded more accurately than others. An understanding of these cultural and gender differences in perception is useful in preventing us from treating our own perceptions as objective and those of others as erroneous. This understanding is also important for intercultural impression management and communication.

## PERCEIVING GROUPS AND MEMBERS OF SOCIAL CATEGORIES

In addition to trying to understand and predict the behaviour of individuals, people at work often need to comprehend and foretell how groups will act. This applies particularly to contact groups – the Board, the union, department, consultant firm X, customer organisation Y – but also to social categories, such as women or ethnic minorities. Social psychological research has shown that how we perceive and behave towards other people are influenced by what we believe about the groups of which they are members.[65] Table 5.6 summarises some of the biases that have been found in the way people perceive groups.

**Table 5.6 Forms of judgement bias**

| *Judgement bias* | *Description* |
|---|---|
| In-group favouritism/out-group derogation | Tendency to judge in-group more favourably than out-group |
| Out-group homogeneity effect | Perceived variability of out-groups low relative to in-group |
| In-group homogeneity effect | When the in-group is a minority and the attribute dimension is relevant to in-group identity, perceived variability of in-group low |
| Out-group polarisation | More extreme out-group than in-group ratings |
| Out-group co-variation effect | Tendency to more consistent ratings of attributes for out-groups as compared to in-groups |

- When the group to which a person belongs is seen as homogeneous, that is, all more or less similar, perceivers tend to ignore individual differences, no matter how obvious. Some groups are perceived as more homogeneous than others. Most people see out-groups as more homogeneous than their own in-group. However, members of minority groups, unlike majorities, perceive their in-group as more homogeneous than their out-groups.[66] Equally, low-status groups are seen as more homogeneous than high-status groups, both by members and non-members. In fact, whereas members of high-status groups are especially likely to see low-status groups as homogeneous, members of low-status groups are aware of the individual differences among high-status group members to the point of eliminating the out-group homogeneity effect.[67] Thus, whereas top managers of a business may see the workers on the factory floor as all alike, the factory-floor workers will probably distinguish individual members of the top management team from one another. People who identify strongly with their in-group, especially if it is a low-status one, will tend to see both their in-group and any out-group as not homogeneous.[68]
- Stereotypes are central to perception of groups. Contradicting earlier ideas that stereotypes are based on abstract representations, Smith and Zarate[69] showed in 1990 that judgements tend to be based on the target's similarity to specific exemplars rather than to average group-typical information. Thus, a person's stereotype of 'accountants' would be based on accountants they had met or seen represented in books or films, rather than on an abstract idea of accountants. More recently, mixed models have gained acceptance: a person's 'knowledge' of social groups is based on both abstract and exemplar-based information and different conditions may lead one type of information to be relied on more heavily than the other.[70–72] Exemplars have more influence on judgements of in-groups than out-groups, for instance.[73] People's stereotypes of their in-group contain a large number of weakly associated characteristics whereas out-group stereotypes contain a small number of strongly associated characteristics.

**Box 5.8**

There may be an in-group bias in the interpretation of media events. Priming perceivers with counter-stereotypic representations of women and African Americans increased the likelihood that they would make internal attributions of responsibility. Priming counter-stereotypic representations tended to elicit external attributions, portraying African-Americans and women more credibly.

*Source*: Power, J. G., S. T. Murphy and G. Coover (1996) 'How stereotypes and counter-stereotypes influence attribution of responsibility and credibility among in-groups and out-groups', *Human Communication Research*, vol. 23, no. 1, pp. 36–58.

- Relative group size affects how group members are perceived. Members of minority groups are both categorised to a larger extent and better individually recalled than members of majority groups.[74] The likely explanation is that perceivers' attention is drawn towards relatively infrequent, novel or distinctive phenomena of any kind. When reliable data are lacking, group members tend to overestimate both the relative size and the status of their in-group.[75]
- Perceivers do not expect the same degree of coherence in the actions of a group as in those of an individual person and, accordingly, are less likely to draw inferences about group dispositions.[76] (However, as we have seen, this finding may not apply outside Western cultures.)
- When forming an impression of a group, perceivers make less extreme trait judgements, make those judgements less quickly and with less confidence, and recall less information than when the subject is an individual.[77]
- The level of people's own self-esteem affects their judgement. People with high collective self-esteem may be mainly concerned with enhancing the self, leading to positive in-group evaluation rather than derogation of out-groups.[78] In contrast, because low self-esteem makes self-enhancement implausible to them, people with low collective self-esteem may be primarily concerned with protecting the self, making out-group derogation more likely than positive in-group evaluation. Verkuyten[79] found these predictions confirmed among Dutch youth members of ethnic minorities.

Inter-group biases such as these are usually explained in terms of biased processes, different representations or motivational assumptions. However, Fiedler *et al.*[80] dispute the need for such explanations. Instead, they argue that they are the result of the fact that people typically have large samples of individuals from which to judge members of their in-group but smaller samples to assess their out-groups.

Biases in perceiving groups are important because people respond differently to the same action according to whether they perceive it to be carried out by an individual, a non-cohesive group or a cohesive group. In the last case, the cohesive group, they are more likely to express negative judgements and also to prefer collective forms of redress to acting alone if, for instance, they are insulted.[81] However, being accountable (see Chapter 3) can reduce judgemental biases by motivating people to think in more nuanced, self-critical and differentiated ways about the stimulus evidence.[82]

## SUMMARY – PERCEIVING GROUPS AND MEMBERS OF SOCIAL CATEGORIES

There is clear evidence that a focus on a person's group or social category membership alters the way they are seen. Out-groups are seen as more homogeneous, and regarded less favourably and in more extreme terms than in-groups, except that members of minority and low-status groups tend to see their in-groups as homogeneous. Identification with the in-group increases the chances that it will be seen as heterogeneous. Minority out-groups are less often perceived as homogeneous. Both stereotypes of, and behavioural responses to, an out-group are affected by how cohesive it seems, but the response varies. If the perceiver's collective self-esteem is high, the response is to elevate the in-group. If it is low, the response is to derogate the out-group. There are various explanations for these inter-group perceptual biases. Recently it has been argued that they and their resulting cognitive and behavioural effects arise simply from people having larger samples from which to judge their in-group.

## WORK APPLICATIONS FOR UNDERSTANDING OTHERS

All interactive work activities call for using people-perception skills. Interviewing and selection interviewing are just two in which those skills are particularly focal.

### Interviewing

Interviews serve many different work-related purposes, including research, consultancy, fact-finding generally, diagnosis, selection, giving performance feedback, reprimanding and firing a subordinate. Some of these types of interview are treated in this book as applications of other core skills. Giving performance feedback, for example, is closely linked with communicating effectively. However, as they are all interviews, they share certain characteristics and skill requirements. The following remarks apply to all types of flexible interview, in which the interviewers adjust their questions and give explanations according to the responses of the interviewee; they apply less in standardised interviewing.[83]

In an interview, two people meet, face to face, to accomplish a known purpose by talking together. An interview is different from many work interactions because it is explicitly one-sided, as the words 'interviewer' and 'interviewee' suggest. Whether the 'known purpose' is personnel selection or market research, it is the interviewer's purpose that is explicitly acknowledged and the success or failure of the interview is judged by whether or not that purpose is achieved. Interviewees may have a purpose in interviews – in job selection interviews they certainly do – but that is not the acknowledged purpose of the interview. This one-sidedness means that interviewers should try to maximise the benefit and minimise the disbenefit to the interviewee arising during or from the fact of the interview. Normal human interaction is an exchange into which both parties enter to get satisfaction.[84] If artificial interactions such as interviews shift too far from this natural balance, open communication is prevented. Interviewers also take responsibility for conducting the interview. There are many lists of rules of thumb for conducting interviews. One is given later in this chapter. However, such rules can be applied and adapted better if interviewers have thought about their task and the relationship they are trying to establish. One way of regarding the interviewer's task is that it is to keep the interviewee both willing and able to disclose the required information. An unwilling interviewee will distort and disguise; an 'unable' one will omit and confuse.

**Box 5.9**

**How to keep interviewees willing and able to give you the information you need**

- Are they unsure of the facts? Provide reassurance, but also check what they say.
- Do they feel that you do not have the right to be given the information? Establish your legitimacy.
- Are they covering for someone, or sensing danger to themselves? Establish trust (refer to Box 9.9).
- Do they know just what information it is that you need, or realise what information they have that could be useful to you? Since you may not know what information they do in fact have, this situation is quite problematic. Use an open style of questioning, be alert to any hints or suggestions of useful information and follow them up.

The relationship between an interviewer and interviewee can be thought of in terms of a contract, a climate and content. The contract means the understood, though often unstated, 'terms and conditions' governing the parties in and after an interview. It determines what counts as breaches of good manners, unfair questioning, unfair use of the information and unfair treatment, such as making the interviewees feel that they are being interrogated, exploited or poured scorn on. The climate can be supportive or threatening. A threatening climate will reduce a speaker's willingness to disclose. The content refers to the nature and style of the questions. Table 5.7 shows how task and relationship factors should be combined to guide the interviewer's conduct in an interview and emphasises

**Table 5.7 Combining task and relationship factors in an interview**

| *Task* | *Relationship* | | |
|---|---|---|---|
| | *Contract* | *Content* | *Climate* |
| To keep the interviewee willing to disclose the required information | Total confidentiality (never disclose things learnt elsewhere)<br>An exchange | No threatening or blaming<br>No leading or trick questions<br>No questions revealing bias<br>The best guide to the next question is the answer to the one before | The interviewer brings the gift of attentiveness, so active listening<br>Egalitarian; not a one-sided extortion; not stronger to weaker, or superior to inferior |
| To help the interviewee to be able to disclose the required information | Interviewer takes responsibility for guiding the process | Questions should be short, single, not too demanding of memory<br>Questions should be open ended – inviting discursive answers not monosyllabic ones | Active listening |

the use of active listening skills to establish the right climate for an interview. Research supports this idea. A study compared how three interviewing techniques affected the amount of information obtained. (The interviews dealt with recall of incidents of family illness, but the lessons from the research apply to all interviews.) The three techniques were active listening, sensitising the interviewee in the form of reading out a list of symptoms at the beginning of the interview and, as a control, administering the questionnaire without using any extra words or non-verbal cues, and without the prior 'sensitising' process. More symptoms, conditions and illnesses were recorded when the active listening technique was used. 'In this study the reinforcement technique elicited about 29 per cent more reports of symptoms than did the sensitisation techniques.' Sensitising had little greater effect than just administering the questionnaire.[85]

Box 5.10 is a checklist of more specific points on interviewing.

## Selection interviewing

Interviewing job applicants and choosing the 'right' candidate for the job is probably the work activity that depends most directly on understanding people. The purpose of selection interviewing is to assess abilities, motives, attitudes and traits. As this chapter has already discussed, this is also the main purpose in interpreting other people's behaviour generally. Furthermore, the main interpersonal skills required for selection interviewing, as for all fact-finding interviewing, are

Box 5.10

## Interviewing checklist

### Before the interview

1. Prepare yourself mentally for the meeting.
2. Know the interviewee's language.
3. Think about the situation and the environment in which the interview will take place.
4. Consider the interests and values of the interviewee.
5. How will you be seen, what will you represent to the interviewee?
6. Think through your interview objective and write it down. It should state what information you intend to discover, bearing in mind the constraints that may be present. These include limited time, the complexity of the subject, the interviewee's likely frame of mind and powers of expression and the difficulty of establishing a relationship with the interviewee.

### On entering the interview

1. Make the contract clear with the interviewee: who you are, why you are there and what you are going to do with the information.
2. Your role as interviewer is essentially that of a listener, and you must therefore do all in your power to encourage the interviewee to talk to you. This will almost certainly mean devoting some time at the beginning to an introduction, when your aim will be to establish a relationship that encourages communication. You may decide to achieve this by talking about something quite unconnected with the subject of the interview. After this you should aim for a listening/talking ratio of about 80 : 20. Roles in an interview are interdependent: an interviewer encourages the interviewee to talk freely by listening actively.

### Get the process going

1. Ask these kinds of questions:
   - (a) Short, open questions, starting with how, why, what and when.
   - (b) Probes to get extra information or evidence after open questions. This combination of short initial questions followed by probes is called a pyramid technique.
   - (c) Closed questions to establish simple points of fact – such as dates or quantities. Closed questions can be misused, however, as in the following example: 'Do you like your work?' If a sensitive point like this is the one you want to establish, open questions and probes are the best approach.
   - (d) Comparisons: 'Which would be better, to raise the price or reduce the quantity?'
   - (e) Hypotheticals: 'If we raised the price by 5 per cent, how would that affect our sales?'
2. If you need precise facts and figures it is better not to rely on the interviewee's memory. Get them to look them up and ask for a copy, or copy them out for yourself.
3. Avoid, as far as possible, the following types of question:
   - (a) Leading questions – those in which the answer is implicit in the question, e.g. 'You find stock-taking difficult, don't you?'
   - (b) Questions the interviewee is not qualified to answer or cannot understand.
   - (c) Multiple questions, e.g. 'Can you use word-processing packages or are you familiar with spreadsheets and databases?'
   - (d) Prejudiced or discriminatory questions.

**Box 5.10** *continued*

(e) Non-questions disguised as questions, e.g. 'Are you really telling me that your prices are fixed six months in advance?' (This is really an expression of disbelief, not a question.)

4. Avoid asking questions too fast so that it seems like an interrogation.

**Keep the process going**

1. Do not attempt to work through an exhaustive list of prepared questions – interviewees dislike 'shopping lists'. Your main guide to what to ask next is always the answer to the last question, though it may be useful to have planned some key questions that will steer the interview into important areas.
2. Show that you are interested in what is being said and are absorbing the answers. Repeat part of the answer in an animated way; or link the next question verbally with the last: 'So do you think that . . .' or 'Does that mean . . . ?'
3. Show that you are involved in what is going on.
4. Signal active listening by eye contact, slight nodding, occasional smiling, 'mmm', 'Yes, I see. . . .', alert posture, attentive expression, being comfortable with silence.
5. Do not rebuke. For instance, do not say, 'You should know the answer to that question!'
6. Do not overlook unclear, inadequate answers. Ask the question again in a different way.
7. Accept responsibility for misunderstood questions. Do not blame the respondent.
8. When interviewees cannot answer a question, do not imply that it was not important anyway.

**Possible problems in the interview and how to deal with them**

The interviewee is untruthful, withholds information, attempts to control the situation through over-talking, an appeal to technical expertise or concealed information, questions the legitimacy of the interviewer, intellectualises everything or emits empty noise, tries to shock the interviewer, is aggressive or cuts off the interview by physical movement or asking 'Have I told you what you want to know?'

1. Both deliberate lying and evasion occur less often in extended free-answer interviews, providing the right climate is established. All the same, be alert for them, and when they happen make a mental note to return to the subject, if it is important, later in the interview from a different tack.
2. Provide reassurance by your manner (or explicitly) that you are not going to extract information by tricks.
3. Reassure about confidentiality. Never refer to what you have learnt elsewhere – if you disclose what others told you, how can this interviewee trust you?
4. Minimise your 'threat'. Think about which questions will seem threatening, and if you must ask them, keep them for late in the interview. Do not be defensive.
5. Be patient. When you tell your interviewee in advance how long you expect to take, allow for digressions, so that they will not make you anxious when they occur.

**Concluding**

Give the interviewee a chance to add anything they wish or to ask any questions they wish. Thank the interviewee. Explain what will happen after the interview and how the material will be used. Try to arrange another meeting, by telephone or in person, if needed to fill any gaps.

person-perception, active listening, interpreting messages and keeping the interviewee willing and able to disclose the information you seek. (Boxes 5.3, 5.6, 5.7 and 5.9 summarise guidance on these skills.) Naturally, impression management, communicating, even using power and persuading, are also important in selection interviewing but the core skill in this activity is coming to understand others' qualities and traits.

**Box 5.11**

### Selection practices

1. Recruiters tend to use knowledge, skills and abilities to assess person–job fit and values and personality traits to assess person–organisation fit (Kristof-Brown, 2000).
2. A survey of 959 organisations in 20 countries found that cultural differences in uncertainty avoidance and, to a lesser extent, power distance, explained some of the national differences observed in the extensiveness of the method used for recruitment (Ryan *et al.*, 1999).
3. Research on 60 specialist recruiters found that they work with sets of social rules to judge applicants' behaviour in terms of hireability and communication competence. The rules divide into two categories. One is general interpersonal competence, including interpersonal skills, self-confidence and taking an active role. The other is interview presentation skills, covering positive language, future career goals, verbal fluency, self-awareness, preparation and giving focused answers. Interviewers attributed breaches of the general interpersonal competence 'rules' by candidates mainly to the interview situation, but breaches of specific interview 'rules' mainly internally, to lack of ability or effort of the candidate (Ramsay *et al.*, 1997).

*Sources*: Kristof-Brown, A. L. (2000) 'Perceived applicant fit: distinguishing between recruiters' perceptions of person–job and person–organization fit', *Personnel Psychology*, vol. 53, pp. 643–672.
Ramsay, S., C. Gallois and V. J. Callan (1997) 'Social rules and attributions in the personnel selection interview', *Journal of Occupational and Organizational Psychology*, vol. 70, pp. 189–203.
Ryan, A. M., L. McFarland and R. Page (1999) 'An international look at selection practices: Nation and culture as explanations for variability in practice', *Personnel Psychology*, vol. 52, pp. 359–392.

Interviewing is only one part of the selection process, which also includes drawing up the job description and the person specification, designing the application form, taking up references, and deciding on, conducting and assessing the results of standardised tests or assessment centre findings. (Some approaches even treat the interview as a negotiation over any divergent expectations, resulting in a plan for the candidate's training and career.)[86] However, because it can be crucial to the appointment decision, and is expensive, time consuming and often atrociously executed, selection interviewing merits special attention in this book. As Figure 5.5 shows, the role of assessing others and interpreting their behaviour is even greater in selection interviews than in diagnostic or fact-finding interviews. Only certain points can be covered in the space available; a selection of other sources is given in the Further Reading section.

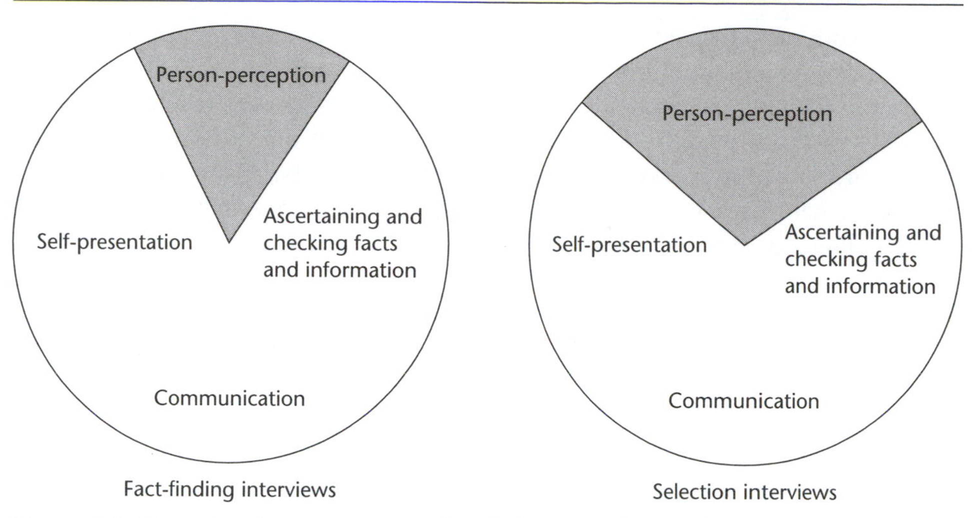


**Figure 5.5 The role of person-perception in interviewing and selection interviewing.**

***Objectives***

What is it that is valuable to the organisation and the candidate that can come out of an interview, but not out of the curriculum vitae or application form?

- Usually, some information is missing from the application documents.
- Certain items in the application documents may need to be explained. For instance, it is quite common for candidates to submit applications with periods of months or even years not accounted for. What were they doing? Again, there may be obvious weaknesses in the CV, such as exam failure or long periods without promotion in one job.
- After the interview, selectors assess the candidates against a person specification that describes the characteristics of the 'ideal' appointee under a number of headings. These headings will be specific to the job. Those for a sales representative will be different from those for a market researcher. The following, however, usually appear: impact on others, abilities, motivation and adjustment. These points are judged from the information obtained at the interview by open-ended questioning about the candidates' past experiences and actions.

***Preparation***

A systematic process is less vulnerable to bias and in particular is more likely to lead to selection which is consistent with equal-opportunities legislation and policies. When managers use subjective criteria to evaluate job candidates, they often favour candidates who appear to be like themselves. It makes them feel that they understand the person and can trust him or her. They often use words such as 'comfort', 'fit' and 'team' to express that desire; those are codewords for the 'in' group or the 'old boy network'. Concern about teamwork is, of course, legitimate, but personal prejudice can often cause managers to underestimate the skills of those who are 'different'. In fact, people from minority groups are often more skilled in working with others; they have to be, to survive in a world of work where they continuously face prejudice. African-American managers say they have to use collaboration to exert influence in order to avoid having the majority group label them as 'pushy', 'too aggressive' or 'difficult to work with'. However, as Box 5.12 shows, over-concern with legal topics can reduce selection interviewers' effectiveness.

**Box 5.12**

A study found that training of recruiters reduced applicants' perceptions of the recruiters' interpersonal skills. The researcher commented:

> Given the legal climate that exists today, training on equal employment opportunity concerns and other legal topics is necessary. However, given the negative impact that focusing on legal issues had on applicants' perceptions of recruiters' interpersonal skills, organisations may want to re-examine how they are training recruiters on legal issues. Recruiters may become so preoccupied with worrying about saying the wrong thing, or giving an applicant the wrong impression, that the interpersonal skills which are so important in applicant attraction are negatively affected.

*Source*: Connerley, M. L. (1997) 'The influence of training on perceptions of recruiters' interpersonal skills and effectiveness', *Journal of Occupational and Organizational Psychology*, vol. 70, pp. 259–272.

**Box 5.13**

### How to prepare for conducting a selection interview

1. Using the person specification derived from the job description, draw up a selection interviewing checklist of points to cover. Do not make it too long for the time you will have in the interview. Space the checklist out so that you can write on it.
2. Plan how to divide the time across the interview topics.
3. Read and make notes on the candidates' application forms, CVs and references.
4. Arrange the room furniture so as to put the candidates at ease and to give a sense of exchange rather than interrogation. Try to make sure that the candidate will not feel that they are intruding on 'your' territory. Some people prefer to use the 'neutral' territory of interviewing rooms for this reason.
5. Think about your greeting (non-verbal as well as verbal content), your introduction and how to make the changeover to 'business'.

#### *Conduct*

The answers to the following questions are a guide to conducting the selection interview.

1. *What questions should be asked?* The starting point should be the selection criteria listed on the person specification. These should cover the knowledge, skills and abilities of candidates that are needed for the vacancy. A skill is the ability to do something; skills should be defined carefully and phrased concisely but so as to avoid ambiguity. Describing skills in one word, such as numeracy or literacy, is ambiguous. It is better to use a phrase such as 'ability to calculate wages from standard input data'. Attributes, which are the ability to be something, such as pleasant, cheerful or acceptable to clients, are poor criteria as they lead to over-subjective assessments.

2. *What types of questions should be asked?* The points made about questioning techniques in interviewing generally apply in selection interviews but there are additional considerations. First, there is the danger that discriminatory questions may be asked. Questions such as 'How would you respond to instructions from a white supervisor?', asked of a black person, or 'Do you intend to have a family?', asked of a young married woman, or 'Are you likely to have to take a lot of sick leave?', asked of a disabled person, may be illegal and are certainly unfair. Second, a selection interview is generally a more nerve-racking occasion for the candidates than most interviews, and it is easy to ask questions that make them feel ill at ease and so not do themselves justice. For this reason it is especially important not to use the kinds of questions listed as to be avoided in Box 5.10.

3. *Should there be any attempt in a selection interview to imitate the job conditions?* For example, when interviewing for a supervisory job in which being able to tolerate stress is important, should an interviewer try to evaluate how well the candidate withstands pressure by aggressive questioning, interrupting, appearing annoyed or restless, or other similar methods? How a candidate acts during the interview itself is of use in assessing their impact on others, appearance and ability to express themselves, but it is poor evidence for the crucial factors of motivation, energy and adjustment, because people rarely act 'normally' in interviews. An applicant who is nervous when 'selling' himself may be perfectly confident when selling the company's product; an individual who is generally lethargic may be stimulated by the challenge of the interview into seeming energetic and enthusiastic; a trained or experienced interviewee may appear relaxed under a hail of questions but crack under the pressure of work overload or role conflict. Thus it is now generally accepted that the best evidence for what candidates can and will do is what they have done previously and how earlier employers regarded them. A steady promotion record is a good sign but so is having been given increased responsibility or discretion, even when no promotion was involved. Here the interview data add to or sometimes contradict what the references show. The candidates' own choices and the reasons for them can show a great deal about their motivation and judgement.

4. *Should the interviewer cover all aspects of an applicant's history equally?* More recent events tend to be given more importance, because applicants would often

**Box 5.14**

Selection interviewers need to allow for cultural influences on interviewees' behaviour. For instance, Chinese applicants in Singapore tend to defer to the interviewer, whom they treat as 'superior', and to focus on the group or family, besides avoiding self-assertion. All these behaviours are consistent with national Chinese culture, which is rated high in power distance and low in individualism (using Hofstede's dimensions of national cultures). Hence, applicants from a Chinese background may be disadvantaged when being interviewed for jobs with multinational companies that are heavily influenced by Anglo-American culture.

*Source*: Ryan, A. M., L. McFarland and R. Page (1999) 'An international look at selection practices: nation and culture as explanations for variability in practice', *Personnel Psychology*, vol. 52, pp. 359–392.

act differently in the future from how they did in the distant past. There is another issue, however: whether to aim for comprehensive coverage or to concentrate on the obvious weak spots, such as an employment gap, a sideways move or a series of short stays with a number of employers. Ideally both would receive full coverage, but interviewers are often short of time. In these cases, weak points should not be over-emphasised, partly because it is demoralising for the candidate, and partly because weak points, like strong points or indifferent points, are part of a pattern and not especially indicative. They should be treated as events in the candidate's history, and when the interviewer is satisfied that what happened is understood as well as the other events, the subject should be left. There may be exceptions where a weak point alone suggests a problem that would be fatal to a candidate's performance but these will be rare.

5. *What significance can be attached to a candidate's own questions and knowledge of the organisation?* This depends on the job and the age of the applicants. When 17-year-old applicants for a naval officers' training course were asked about such matters as the worldwide distribution of year-round naval ports and the meaning of different flags, some were rejected with the comment that it was an insult to apply with so little knowledge of the service. The problem here is that to discriminate among such young candidates on these grounds is simply to bias selection in favour of people with a family connection or a childhood interest in the organisation, although neither of these categories necessarily provides the best material. With older candidates, however, especially for executive posts, evidence that they have not 'done their homework' by researching the organisation's history and thinking up sensible questions to ask at the interview may predict how they will perform in certain jobs.

6. *What information should applicants be given about the job and the company?* Candidates need enough relevant information to make a decision about whether to take a job if offered. Selection is a two-way process (though as Ralston and Kirkwood[87] have shown, most employment interviewers do not treat it as such. They consider primarily the interests of management, not of both parties. By

doing so, they neglect the point that it is not in the best interest of the organisation to recruit people who will be discontented in the job.) But what is 'enough relevant information'? Obviously it varies among candidates and it is up to the applicant to ask about any unusual concerns. They should not, however, be left to ask about all their legitimate interests – for instance, many candidates do not like to ask about salary. Interviewers should think about what candidates need to know about this particular job and organisation.

7. *How can selection interviewing skills be improved 'on the job'?* Studies have shown that experience does not improve the way managers interview, unless they get training or instruction. Therefore, to improve performance, active steps are needed. The suggestions in Box 5.15 are all based on selection interviewing research.

**Box 5.15**

**How to improve your selection interviewing performance 'on the job'**

1. Use a structured interview guide and take notes. Managers who do this are better at recognising data that distinguish applicants who can do the job from those who cannot. They are also better at recalling information afterwards.
2. Record candidates' answers, not your interpretation or assessment of them. There is a halo effect – a favourable bias towards candidates – unless notes are taken in this form. Recording the answers to open-ended questions is difficult, but jotting key phrases, preferably in the interviewee's own words, is enough to help you recall after the interview most of what was said.
3. Wait until after the interview to make your decision. Untrained interviewers tend to reach a decision to accept or reject a candidate after four or five minutes. This means that they are really judging from the application form data and the candidate's appearance and initial impact. It is a particular instance of the tendency to form first impressions too quickly for accuracy. It means that most of the remaining time of the interview is wasted.
4. Be aware of the pressures on you that will tend to bias your judgement, and try to allow for them. Needing to fill a vacancy urgently and being short of time for interviewing both tend to bias managers in candidates' favour. Internal candidates can have an advantage because they know the organisation, know what jargon to use, and may know the 'preferences and prejudices' of the selector. This needs to be guarded against when there are both internal and external applicants for a job.
5. Use a systematic process. Check the information you have received against the person specification drawn up before the interview. This process is called 'validating'. Missing information can lead to wrong choices. Ideally candidates should be re-interviewed where there is information missing but if that is impractical, only information that is available for all candidates should be taken into account.
6. Whenever possible, analyse your own selection interviewing performance soon after completing the interview. Other pressures will probably prevent you doing this for more than a small percentage of interviews, but you must make time to do it regularly if you are to improve or to maintain a high standard. A guide to help you analyse how well you selection interview is given in the Exercises.

## SUMMARY – WORK APPLICATIONS FOR UNDERSTANDING OTHERS

Interviewing generally refers to a face-to-face situation in which the interviewee supplies the interviewer with information so that the interviewer may accomplish a known purpose. The one-sidedness of interviews places responsibility on interviewers to be ethical and to control the interview process. Interviewing skill can be thought of in terms of a task and a relationship. Task skills keep interviewees willing and able to disclose the required information. Relationship skills involve ensuring that the psychological contract between interviewer and interviewee is adhered to, that the content (the questions) are appropriate and that the climate is not threatening. Successful interviewing of all types depends on applying active listening skills.

Selection interviewing is part of a broader selection process, which leads to having clear aims for the interview itself and using a systematic approach involving a 'person specification' such that different interviewees are treated consistently. Methods of improving selection interviewing skills include taking care over the types of questions used, especially to avoid discrimination, using the interview to obtain information and evidence, not placing too much reliance on how the interviewee behaves during the interview itself, recording answers and waiting until after the interview to make decisions.

## CHAPTER OVERVIEW

To work well with other people, we need to learn how to understand what motivates them, how they see the world and how they feel about things. Understanding other people involves both general and social perception processes. These include attending, comprehending and applying cognitive schemas, on the one hand and observing cues, both verbal and non-verbal, applying identification and association rules, making attributions, judging, framing, stereotyping, applying expectations, forming impressions, interpreting messages and detecting deceptions on the other.

Perception processes are error-prone. Errors include expectation effects, distortions to meet emotional needs, over-use of stereotypes, a range of attribution biases and getting locked into first impressions. Recognising and trying to eliminate these biases, active listening, practising empathy and trying to postpone judgements are techniques for increasing interpretation skills. We also need to be aware of the distortions that can occur in perceiving groups generally and members of different cultural, ethnic and gender groups particularly.

These techniques and knowledge sets underlie successful interviewing and selection interviewing.

## EXERCISES

1. 'Tell me . . .' Work in pairs. One speaks on any subject of his/her choice for ten minutes. The other is not allowed to interrupt or contribute more than prompts such as, 'Tell me more about . . .', 'How do you feel about . . . ?'
2. Working individually, write down your interpretations of the non-verbal behaviours described in (a) to (c). Then compare your interpretations with those of others in your group and discuss the reasons for any differences.
   (a) Peter nodded at Mark, smiled at him, leaned towards him, moved a little closer and increased the amount of eye contact with him. Mark stepped back, shifted his gaze away, and raised his hand to his mouth.
   (b) During a ten-minute conversation between Mary and Sara, Sara looked at Mary most of the time, but Mary frequently looked around, particularly when Sara was speaking. When Mary replied to Sara, there was often a pause before she began speaking, but then she spoke fairly continuously; Sara, however, began her replies to Mary immediately Mary finished speaking, but then often paused or hesitated during her reply.
   (c) In a group of three men Simon was speaking. He had been doing so for about three minutes. Philip started to lift his arm in a sharp gesture, inhaled audibly, and tried to catch William's eye; William, however, was looking towards Simon, nodding and occasionally saying 'mm-hmmm'. How would you interpret these different non-verbal behaviours of Philip and William?
3. Harry failed to arrive for the meeting this morning, or to send an apology. Afterwards his boss asked him what happened. 'I thought it was tomorrow', said Harry, 'I'm sorry'. Afterwards, he wondered how it could have happened. The meeting was entered in his diary, and he always looked through his engagements for the day when he first came in to the office. He thought he could remember doing so this morning as usual, although he had had his thoughts elsewhere, on the problems of absenteeism on the 'C' shift. Deep down Harry was not sorry to have missed the meeting, however; although he disliked getting into his boss's bad books by this kind of thing, it gave him another week to prepare the report on safety regulations he'd been asked to prepare, and which he really did not have fully ready.

   What concepts of perception theory might help explain Harry's non-attendance at the meeting?
4. What types of perceptual errors might be involved in the following common judgements?
   (a) A talkative person is judged less responsible than a quieter individual.
   (b) Attractiveness increased the performance evaluations, pay rises and promotions of women in non-managerial positions, but decreased the same

outcomes for women in managerial positions. No differences occurred in the evaluation or compensation of men.

(c) An older worker who fears that his skills may be becoming obsolete states that the new recruits have no respect for experience.

(d) A manager ignores the signs of stubbornness and rejection coming from Joe, who is normally compliant, but immediately registers any indications of lack of acceptance from Sue, who is normally difficult.

5. How might making the kinds of perceptual error described in exercise 4 above lead managers to mishandle their subordinates?

6. Complete the questionnaire given in Table 5.8. *See the Appendix to find out how to analyse your responses to this questionnaire.*

7. How would you interpret the facial expressions shown in Figure 5.6? What moods or attitudes do you initially attribute to a person who exhibits these facial expressions? What other moods or attitudes may they convey?

**Table 5.8 Attribution errors questionnaire**

| | *Strongly Agree* | *Agree* | *Neither Agree Nor Disagree* | *Disagree* | *Strongly Disagree* |
|---|---|---|---|---|---|
| 1. When things go wrong with tasks I am trying to accomplish, I am more likely to blame myself than the situation | X______X | X______X | X______X | X______X | X______X |
| 2. I feel personally responsible for whether work activities result in success or failure | X______X | X______X | X______X | X______X | X______X |
| 3. If something people are working on turns out well, I believe that to be a personal success for them | X______X | X______X | X______X | X______X | X______X |
| 4. I usually think that my colleagues' successes are due to their abilities and their failures to their weaknesses | X______X | X______X | X______X | X______X | X______X |
| 5. I believe that most people's attitudes are similar to my own | X______X | X______X | X______X | X______X | X______X |
| 6. In general, I consider that my colleagues feel about things at work much as I do | X______X | X______X | X______X | X______X | X______X |
| 7. Usually, I can persuade others at work to see my point of view | X______X | X______X | X______X | X______X | X______X |
| 8. I find that few people at work have the same attributes as myself | X______X | X______X | X______X | X______X | X______X |
| 9. In general, my good qualities are unusual | X______X | X______X | X______X | X______X | X______X |
| 10. Usually when things go wrong with my work, it is because of factors outside my control | X______X | X______X | X______X | X______X | X______X |
| 11. Lack of resources, information, too little time or lack of co-operation from others are usually the causes of things going wrong in my work | X______X | X______X | X______X | X______X | X______X |

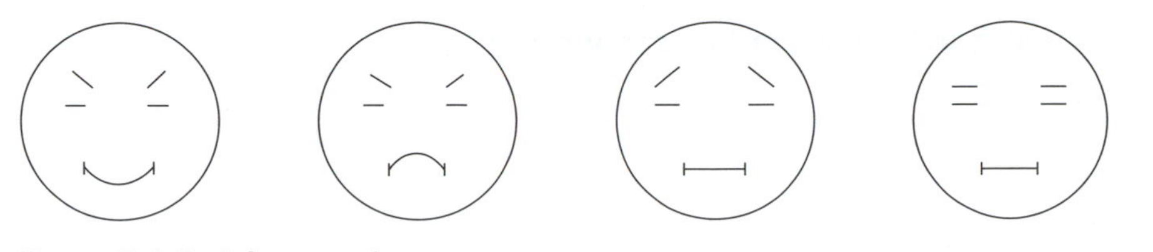

**Figure 5.6 Facial expressions.**

Compare your interpretations with those of others, preferably in a mixed-culture group.

8. To which groups, if any, are the following descriptions commonly applied? To which groups are they very rarely applied? Working individually, write down your ideas. Then compare your ideas with those of others in your group and discuss the reasons for any differences: aggressive; conceited; extraverted; ambitious; independent; emotional; active; illogical; competitive; easily hurt; unemotional; insecure; neurotic; easily influenced; objective; self-confident; easy going; indecisive; dependent; scientific bent; always interested in sex; passive; direct; knows the ways of the world; excitable; exploit the system; adventurous; submissive; hard-working; introverted.

   Groups may be the whole of one of the following categories or a subordinate-category such as American men or French managers.

   Ethnic: Americans, Irish, Italians, Jews, Germans, French, English, Swedes, Danes, Indians, Pakistanis, Chinese, Japanese.
   Gender: men, women.
   Sexual orientation: male homosexuals, lesbians, heterosexuals.
   Socio-economic: the homeless, single-parent families, the poor, the unemployed, manual workers, white-collar workers, professionals, managers.
   Job-related: accountants, computer specialists, business school lecturers, marketing managers, investment bankers, journalists.

9. Role plays of fact-finding or diagnostic interviews can be conducted between the following:

   (a) lawyer and client (e.g. divorce, contract, crime);
   (b) market research interviewer and interviewee (e.g. concerning the interviewee's travel habits and preferences or brand purchases, using a specific brand);
   (c) doctor and patient (e.g. a general practitioner and patient reporting a set of symptoms);
   (d) auditor and auditee, management consultant and manager, systems analyst and colleague involved in the information system being reviewed (e.g. using the following case material:

**Table 5.9 Rating scale on interaction performance**

| In the interview/meeting/negotiation just completed, I feel I | *Strongly Agree* | *Agree* | *Neither Agree Nor Disagree* | *Disagree* | *Strongly Disagree* |
|---|---|---|---|---|---|
| 1. Asked questions and listened until I had a good understanding of the other participants' viewpoint | X______X______X______X______X______X | | | | |
| 2. Asked open questions instead of closed questions | X______X______X______X______X______X | | | | |
| 3. Sought explanations of others' behaviours that might be rooted in their culture | X______X______X______X______X______X | | | | |
| 4. Made it clear that any views I express are only opinions that may be disagreed with | X______X______X______X______X______X | | | | |
| 5. Acknowledged that values, beliefs and opinions that are different from my own may be equally valid | X______X______X______X______X______X | | | | |
| 6. Avoided over-generalising | X______X______X______X______X______X | | | | |
| 7. Distinguished my own subjective feelings from objective facts | X______X______X______X______X______X | | | | |
| 8. Withheld judgement until I had a good understanding of the other participants' viewpoint | X______X______X______X______X______X | | | | |

*Since this scale is transparent, no scoring guide is needed.*

The subject of the audit / management consultancy / systems analysis is the two-person travel department of an export business. The department has responsibility for organising all the travel and accommodation arrangements as well as visas for a staff of 35 international executives and sales representatives.)

10. Complete the rating scales in Table 5.9 for any work interaction you have just completed.

11. Interviewing task. Persuade an acquaintance whose job is not known to you in any detail to allow you to interview them. Interview them for half an hour to determine:

- the duties and nature of the job in question;
- the kinds of abilities, skills and characteristics required to perform the job;
- what kinds of information and resources are needed to perform the job;
- what range of reporting relationships and supervisory responsibilities the job involves;
- the position of the job in an organisation chart of the organisation.

As soon as possible after the interview, write up your findings in the form of a job description and person specification. Then consider the following questions:

(a) What information that would have been useful did you miss?
(b) What kind of questioning was most productive? What was less successful?
(c) What worked best and worst for you in terms of interviewing techniques such as note-taking, the 'warm-up', concluding, keeping the process going and so on?

Report back to your class on the experience and compare with the parallel experiences of other members of the class.

12. Work through this exercise individually and then discuss each item in your group.

(a) Could any of the following questions be considered discriminatory in a selection interview?
(b) Do you consider the following questions to be good and effective questions, or not?

- Why do you want this job?
- What qualities do you think will be required for this job?
- Tell me about yourself.
- Why do you want to work for this company?
- What do you know about this company?
- What interests you about our product (or service)?
- What can our company offer you that your present company cannot offer?
- You have not done this sort of job before. How will you cope/succeed?
- Why should we employ you?
- How long do you think it would be before you were making a significant contribution to the team/company?
- What do you like and dislike about your present job?
- Why did you choose a career in . . . ?
- Why are you changing careers?
- How much does your last job resemble the one you are applying for? What are the differences?
- What do you think of the last company you worked for?
- Why did you join your previous company? Did it live up to your expectations? Why are you leaving now?
- What was the organisational structure in your last company and how did you fit into it?
- How long have you been looking for a new job?

- Do you prefer to work in a small, medium or large company?
- How often are you off sick?
- Are you considering any other positions at the moment?
- Aren't you too young for this job?
- Did you increase sales or profits in your last job?
- How would you describe yourself? How would others describe you?
- Do you consider yourself successful?
- What has been your biggest failure?
- How could you improve yourself?
- Are you a leader?
- How do you handle criticism?
- What sort of manager are you?
- What makes a good manager?
- Do you work well with others? Or are you a loner?
- Do you need other people around to stimulate you or are you self-motivated?
- Are you accepted into a team quickly?
- Can you act on your own initiative?
- How do you run a meeting?
- What motivates you?
- What management style gets the best results out of you?
- Do you know how to motivate other people?
- Are you competitive?
- Are you aggressive?
- Will you need any special holidays for religious observance?
- What do you dislike doing?
- What problems did you encounter in your last job?
- What would you like to avoid in your next job?
- How do you think you will get on with the white members of the department?
- Do you feel you are ready to take on greater responsibilities?
- Can you work under pressure?
- How many hours are you prepared to work?
- Do you mind working for someone older than yourself? Younger than you? Of the opposite sex?
- What are your career goals?
- How did you get on with your previous manager/supervisor, co-workers and subordinates?
- Have you been responsible for implementing ISO9000/BS5750?
- What interests do you have outside work?
- You have changed jobs a lot. How long would you stay in the new job?

- Have you ever been fired?
- Aren't you too old for this job?
- Aren't you over-qualified for this position?
- Are you prepared to relocate?
- Are you willing to travel?
- What did you earn in your last job?
- What level of salary are you looking for now?
- How does your husband feel about your applying for this job?
- What will your referees say about you?
- What do you do in your present job?
- Would your personal commitments allow you to work these hours?
- There is a lot of routine work in this job; how do you feel about that?
- How did you set about that task?
- You said you set up a liaison committee. Why did you do that?
- If we were to offer you this job, what is the first thing you would do?
- What is your experience of figure work in finance?
- Will you be able to fit in with the rest of the staff?
- Do you find that men respond as well to a female professional?
- What do you do in your spare time?

*Note: this questionnaire was originally devised by Elizabeth Kennedy of the University of Westminster (though the specific questions have been altered). It is used with her permission.*

13. Using a job description and person specification (for instance those devised for exercise 5 on p. 500, corrected and supplemented by the trainer), conduct a selection interview. This can be a panel or a person-to-person interview.

    Applicants will need to prepare and submit their CV.

    All participants should be supplied with the three documents – job description, person specification and applicant's CV.

14. An EU-funded course in business planning is being offered to enterprises in a city in one of the transition economies. It is substantially oversubscribed. Those who apply are interviewed and screened for the following:

    - having a thought-through project which requires commercial (bank) funding of $600,000 to $5,000,000;
    - having the support of the top management of the enterprise (there is a tendency for junior managers to apply without the backing of their chiefs).

    The role play is the interview to select the applicants. The interviewer is from an EU country, the interviewee is from a transition economy.

15. Complete the selection interviewing self-rating scale (Table 5.10).

**Table 5.10 Selection interviewing self-analysis questionnaire**

| | Yes | | | | | No |
|---|---|---|---|---|---|---|
| Did my introductory remarks create an open, relaxed but businesslike climate? | × | × | × | × | × | × |
| Did I give the candidate the chance to do some talking before the transition to the selection process? | × | × | × | × | × | × |
| Did I describe the environment, the organisation and the job thoroughly? | × | × | × | × | × | × |
| During the interview, was I patient and unhurried? | × | × | × | × | × | × |
| During the interview, was I sincere and friendly? | × | × | × | × | × | × |
| Did the candidate behave as if at ease? | × | × | × | × | × | × |
| Did I use my interview structure fully? | × | × | × | × | × | × |
| Did I cover all the areas in enough detail? | × | × | × | × | × | × |
| Did I ask open questions? | × | × | × | × | × | × |
| Did I avoid leading questions? | × | × | × | × | × | × |
| Did I avoid discriminatory questions? | × | × | × | × | × | × |
| Did I get the listening/talking ratio right? | × | × | × | × | × | × |
| Did I record the candidate's answers? | × | × | × | × | × | × |
| Did I avoid recording my interpretations and judgements? | × | × | × | × | × | × |
| Towards the end of the interview, did I encourage the candidate to ask questions about the organisation, the job, the rewards and the prospects? | × | × | × | × | × | × |
| Did I ensure the candidate had the information needed to decide whether to take the job if offered? | × | × | × | × | × | × |
| Did I make it clear what was to happen next? | × | × | × | × | × | × |
| Did I bring the interview to an end on the right note? | × | × | × | × | × | × |
| After the interview, could I recall from notes and memory the information needed to make the right decision? | × | × | × | × | × | × |

For every question answered in the right-hand two sections (the 'no' sections), analyse 'why not?' and develop a strategy to overcome this problem in future.

## FURTHER READING

Fiske, S. T. and S. E. Taylor (1991) *Social Cognition.* New York: McGraw Hill.

Gudykunst, W. B. (ed.) (1986) *Intergroup Communication.* London: Edward Arnold.

Jones, E. E. (1990) *Interpersonal Perception.* New York: W. H. Freeman.

Kahn, R. L. and C. F. Cannell (1983) *The Dynamics of Interviewing.* Melbourne, FLA: Krieger.

## REFERENCES

1. Rosenberg, M. (1990) 'Reflexivity and emotions', *Social Psychology Quarterly,* vol. 53, no. 1, pp. 3–12.
2. Heider, F. (1958) *The Psychology of Interpersonal Relations.* New York: Wiley.
3. Delia, J. G., B. J. O'Keefe and D. J. O'Keefe (1982) 'The constructivist approach to communication' in F. E. X. Dance (ed.) *Human Communication Theory, Comparative Essays.* New York: Harper and Row, pp. 147–191.

4. Waldron, V. R. and J. L. Applegate (1994) 'Interpersonal construct differentiation and conversational planning: an examination of two cognitive accounts for the production of competent verbal disagreement tactics', *Human Communication Research*, vol. 21, pp. 3–35.
5. Bruce, V., A. M. Burton, E. Hanna, P. Healey, A. Mason, R. Coombes, R. Fright and A. Linney (1994) 'Sex discrimination: how do we tell the difference between male and female faces?', *Perception*, vol. 22, pp. 131–152.
6. Martin, C. L. (1996) 'Gender' in A. S. R. Manstead and M. Hewstone (eds) *Blackwell Encyclopaedia of Social Psychology*. Oxford: Blackwell.
7. Baldwin, M. W. (1992) 'Relational schemas and the processing of social information', *Psychological Bulletin*, vol. 112, no. 3, pp. 461–484.
8. Dillard, J. P., D. H. Solomon and J. A. Samp (1996) 'Framing social reality: The relevance of relational judgments', *Communication Research*, vol. 23, no. 6, pp. 703–723.
9. Gilbert, P., J. Price and S. Allan (1995) 'Social comparison, social attractiveness and evolution: How might they be related?', *New Ideas in Psychology*, vol. 13, pp. 149–165.
10. Gibbons, F. X. and B. P. Buunk (1999) 'Individual differences in social comparison: Development of a scale of social comparison orientation', *Journal of Personality and Social Psychology*, vol. 76, no. 1, pp. 129–142.
11. Markus, R. H. and Kitayama S. (1991) 'Culture and the self: implications for cognition, emotion and motivation', *Psychological Review*, vol. 98, pp. 224–253.
12. Goffman, E. (1972) *Interaction Ritual: Essays on Face-to-Face Behaviour*. Harmondsworth, Middlesex: Penguin Books.
13. Asch, S. E. (1965) 'Effects of group pressure upon the modification and distortion of judgments' in H. Proshansky and B. Seidenberg (eds) *Basic Studies in Social Psychology*. New York: Rinehart and Winston, pp. 393–401.
14. Berger, C. R. and M. Zelditch (1985) *Status, Rewards and Influence*. San Francisco: Jossey-Bass.
15. Hamilton, D. L., L. B. Katz and V. O. Leirer (1980) 'Cognitive representation of personality impressions: Organisational processes in first impression formation', *Journal of Personality and Social Psychology*, vol. 39, pp. 1050–1063.
16. Hamilton, D. L. and S. J. Sherman (1996) 'Perceiving persons and groups', *Psychological Review*, vol. 103, pp. 336–355.
17. Kelley, H. H. (1951) 'Communication in experimentally-created hierarchies', *Human Relations*, vol. 4, pp. 39–56.
18. Aune, R. K., P. U. Ching and T. R. Levine (1996) 'Attributions of deception as a function of reward value: A test of two explanations', *Communication Quarterly*, vol. 44, no. 4, pp. 478–486.
19. Feeley, T. H. and M. A. deTurck (1995) 'Global cue usage in behavioral lie detection', *Communication Quarterly*, vol. 43, pp. 420–430.
20. Levine, T. R., S. P. Hee and S. A. McCormack (1999) 'Accuracy in detecting truths and lies; documenting the "veracity effect"', *Communication Monographs*, vol. 66, no. 2, pp. 125–144.
21. Baldwin, op. cit.
22. Asch, op. cit.
23. Slugoski, B. R. and A. E. Wilson (1998) 'Contribution of conversation skills to the production of judgmental errors', *European Journal of Social Psychology*, vol. 28, pp. 575–601.
24. Hewstone, M. and H. Giles (1986) 'Social groups and social stereotypes in intergroup communication: Review and model of intergroup communication breakdown' in W. B. Gudykunst (ed.) *Intergroup Communication*. London: Edward Arnold.

25. Fiske, S. and E. Depret (1996) 'Control, interdependence and power: Understanding social cognition in its social context' in W. Stroebe and M. Hewstone (eds) *European Review of Social Psychology*, vol. 7. Chichester: John Wiley, pp. 31–62.
26. Seta, J. J. and C. E. Seta (1993) 'Stereotypes and the generation of compensatory and non-compensatory expectancies of group members', *Personality and Social Psychology Bulletin*, vol. 19, no. 6, pp. 722–731.
27. Dijksterhuis, A. and A. van Knippenberg (1999) 'On the parameters of associative strength: central tendency and variability as determinants of stereotype accessibility', *Personality and Social Psychology Bulletin*, vol. 25, no. 4, pp. 527–536.
28. Stephan, W. G., C. W. Stephan, T. Stefanenko, V. Ageyev, M. Abalakina and L. Coates-Shrider (1993) 'Measuring stereotypes: a comparison of methods using Russian and American samples', *Social Psychology Quarterly*, vol. 56, no. 1, pp. 54–64.
29. Warr, P. B. and C. K. Knapper (1968) *The Perception of People and Events*. London: Wiley.
30. Vonk, R. (1999) 'Effects of outcome dependency on correspondence bias', *Personality and Social Psychology Bulletin*, vol. 25, pp. 382–389.
31. Green, S. G. and T. R. Mitchell (1979) 'Attributional processes of leaders in leader–member relations', *Organizational Behavior and Human Performance*, vol. 13, pp. 429–458.
32. Bizman, A. and S. Fox (1984) 'Managers' perceptions of workers' behaviour', *Journal of Applied Psychology*, vol. 69, no. 1, pp. 40–43.
33. Pepitone, A. (1958) 'Attributions of causality, social attitudes and cognitive matching processes' in R. Tagiuri and L. Petrullo (eds) *Person Perception and Interpersonal Behaviour*. Stanford, Calif.: Stanford University Press.
34. Phalet, K. and E. Poppe (1997) 'Competence and morality dimensions of national and ethnic stereotypes', *European Journal of Social Psychology*, vol. 27, pp. 703–723.
35. Burgoon, J. K. and B. A. Le Poire (1993) 'Effects of communication expectancies, actual communication and expectancy disconfirmation evaluations of communicators and their communication behaviour', *Human Communication Research*, vol. 20, no. 1, pp. 67–96.
36. Sherif, M. and C. E. Hovland (1964) *Social Judgment*. New Haven: Yale University Press.
37. Kolb, D. A., I. M. Rubin and J. M. McIntyre (1971) *Organizational Psychology – An Experiential Approach*. Englewood Cliffs, New Jersey: Prentice-Hall.
38. Schein, E. H. (1981) 'SMR Forum: Improving face-to-face relationships', *Sloan Management Review*, Winter, pp. 43–52.
39. Gallois, C. and V. J. Callan (1986) 'Decoding emotional messages: Influence of ethnicity, sex, message type and channel', *Journal of Personality and Social Psychology*, vol. 51, no. 4, pp. 755–762.
40. Warr and Knapper, op. cit.
41. Kahn, R. L. and C. F. Cannell (1957) *The Dynamics of Interviewing*. New York: Wiley.
42. Petty, R. E. and J. T. Cacioppo (1986) *Communication and Persuasion: Central and Peripheral Routes to Attitude Change*. New York: Springer-Verlag.
43. Gallois and Callan, op. cit.
44. Edwards, K. and E. E. Smith (1999) 'A disconfirmation bias in the evaluation of arguments', *Journal of Personality and Social Psychology*, vol. 71, no. 1, pp. 5–24.
45. Argyle, M. (1973) *The Psychology of Interpersonal Behaviour*. Harmondsworth, Middlesex: Penguin.
46. Burgoon and Le Poire, op. cit.
47. Heider, op. cit.

48. Ekman, P. and W. V. Friesen (1968) 'Non-verbal behaviour in psychotherapy research' in J. M. Schlien (ed.) *Research in Psychotherapy*, vol. 3. Washington DC: American Psychological Association.
49. Keefe, W. F. (1971) *Listen, Management*. New York: McGraw-Hill, p. 10.
50. Walker, K. L. (1997) 'Do you ever listen? Discovering the theoretical underpinnings of empathic listening', *International Journal of Listening*, vol. 11, pp. 127–137.
51. Hancock, M. and W. Ickes (1996) 'Empathic accuracy: When does the perceiver–target relationship make a difference?', *Journal of Social and Personal Relationships*, vol. 13, no. 2, pp. 179–199.
52. Wang, S. H.-Y. and H.-C. Chang (1999) 'Chinese professionals' perceptions of interpersonal communication in corporate America: A multidimensional scaling analysis', *The Howard Journal of Communications*, vol. 10, no. 4, pp. 297–315.
53. Hall, E. T. (1976) *Beyond Culture*. New York: Doubleday.
54. Ekman, P., W. V. Friesen, M. O'Sullivan, I. Diacoyanni-Tarlatzis, R. Krause, T. Pitcairn, K. Scherer, A. Chan, K. Heider, W. Ayhan Le Compte, P. E. Ricci-Bitti and M. Tomita (1987) 'Universals and cultural differences in the judgments of facial expressions of emotion', *Journal of Personality and Social Psychology*, vol. 53, no. 4, pp. 712–717.
55. Hall, op. cit.
56. Dolphin, C. Z. (1988) 'Beyond Hall: Variables in the use of personal space in intercultural transactions', *Howard Journal of Communications*, vol. 1, no. 1, pp. 23–38.
57. Mehrabian, A. (1968) 'Inferences of attitudes from the posture, orientation and distance of a communicator', *Journal of Consulting and Clinical Psychology*, vol. 32, pp. 296–308.
58. Olaniran, B. A. and D. E. Williams (1995) 'Communication distortion: An intercultural lesson from the Visa application process', *Communication Quarterly*, vol. 43, no. 2, pp. 225–240.
59. Li-Jun, J., P. Kaiping and R. E. Nisbett (2000) 'Culture, control and perception of relationships in the environment', *Journal of Personality and Social Psychology*, vol. 78, no. 5, pp. 943–955.
60. Miller, J. G. (1984) 'Culture and the development of everyday social explanation', *Journal of Personality and Social Psychology*, vol. 46, pp. 961–978.
61. Fiske, A. P., S. Kitayama, H. R. Markus and R. E. Nisbett (1998) 'The cultural matrix of social psychology', in D. Gilbert, S. T. Fiske and G. Lindzey (eds) *Handbook of Social Psychology*, 4th edn. Boston, Mass.: McGraw Hill, pp. 189–211.
62. Menon, T., M. W. Morris, C.-Y. Chiu and H. Ying-yi (1999) 'Culture and the construal of agency: attribution to individual versus group dispositions', *Journal of Personality and Social Psychology*, vol. 76, no. 5, pp. 701–717.
63. Ekman *et al.*, op. cit.
64. Gallois and Callan, op. cit.
65. Simon, B. (1992) 'Intragroup differentiation in terms of ingroup and outgroup attributes', *European Journal of Social Psychology*, vol. 22, pp. 407–413.
66. Simon, B. and R. Brown (1987) 'Perceived intragroup homogeneity in minority–majority contexts', *Journal of Personality and Social Psychology*, vol. 53, no. 4, pp. 703–711.
67. Lorenzi-Cioldi, F. (1998) 'Group status and perceptions of homogeneity', in W. Stroebe and M. Hewstone (eds) *European Review of Social Psychology*, vol. 9. Chichester: John, Wiley, pp. 1–30.
68. Doosje, B., R. Spears, N. Ellemers and W. Koomen (1999) 'Perceived group variability in inter-group relations: the distinctive role of social identity' in W. Stroebe and M. Hewstone (eds) *European Review of Social Psychology*, vol. 10. Chichester: John Wiley, pp. 41–74.

69. Smith, E. R. and M. A. Zarate (1990) 'Exemplar-based models of social judgement', *Psychological Review*, vol. 99, pp. 3–21.
70. Sherman, J. W. (1996) 'Development of mental representations of stereotypes', *Journal of Personality and Social Psychology*, vol. 70, pp. 1126–1141.
71. Klein, S. B., J. Loftus, J. G. Trafton and R. W. Fuhrman (1992) 'Use of exemplars and abstractions in trait judgements: A model of trait knowledge about the self and others', *Journal of Personality and Social Psychology*, vol. 63, pp. 739–753.
72. Park, B., C. M. Judd and C. S. Ryan (1991) 'Social categorisation and the representation of variability information', in W. Stroebe and M. Hewstone (eds) *European Review of Social Psychology*, vol. 6. Chichester: John Wiley, pp. 553–667.
73. Coats, S. and E. R. Smith (1999) 'Perceptions of gender subtypes: sensitivity to recent exemplar activation and in-group/out-group differences', *Personality and Social Psychology Bulletin*, vol. 25, pp. 515–526.
74. van Twuyer, M. and A. van Knippenberg (1999) 'Social categorisation as a function of relative group size', *British Journal of Social Psychology*, vol. 38, pp. 135–156.
75. Simon, B. and A. Mummendey (1990) 'Perceptions of relative group size and group homogeneity: We are the majority and they are all the same', *European Journal of Social Psychology*, vol. 20, pp. 269–286.
76. Hamilton and Sherman, op. cit.
77. Susskind, J., K. Maurer, V. Thakkar, D. L. Hamilton and J. W. Sherman (1999) 'Perceiving individuals and groups: expectancies, dispositional inferences and causal attributions', *Journal of Personality and Social Psychology*, vol. 76, no. 2, pp. 181–191.
78. Crocker, J. R., B. Luhtanen and Z. Broadnax (1994) 'Collective self-esteem and psychological well-being among White, Black and Asian college students', *Personality and Social Psychology Bulletin*, vol. 20, pp. 503–513.
79. Verkuyten, M. (1997) 'Intergroup evaluation and self-esteem motivations: self-enhancement and self-protection', *European Journal of Social Psychology*, vol. 27, pp. 115–119.
80. Fiedler, K., M. Kemmelmeier and P. Freytag (1999) 'Explaining asymmetric group judgements through differential aggregation: Computer simulations and some new evidence' in W. Stroebe and M. Hewstone (eds) *European Review of Social Psychology*, vol. 10. Chichester: John Wiley, pp. 1–40.
81. Abelson, R. P., N. Dasgupta, J. Park and M. R. Banaji (1998) 'Perceptions of the collective other', *Personality and Social Psychology Review*, vol. 2, pp. 243–250.
82. Tetlock, P. E. and R. Boettger (1989) 'Accountability: A social magnifier of the dilution effect', *Journal of Personality and Social Psychology: Attitudes and Cognition*, vol. 57, pp. 388–398.
83. Schober, M. F. and F. G. Conrad (1997) 'Does conversational interviewing reduce survey measurement error?', *Public Opinion Quarterly*, vol. 61, no. 4, pp. 576–602.
84. Keefe, op. cit.
85. Marquis, K. H. and C. F. Cannell (1971) *Effects of Some Experimental Interviewing Techniques of Reporting in the Health Interview Survey*, Washington, DC: US Department of Health, Education and Welfare.
86. Herriot, P. (1989) 'Recruitment in the 90s', Institute of Personnel Management, London.
87. Ralston, S. M. and W. G. Kirkwood (1995) 'Overcoming managerial bias in employment interviewing', *Journal of Applied Communication*, vol. 23, no. 1, pp. 75–92.

# 6 Self-presentation at work

## CHAPTER INTRODUCTION

To interact effectively at work, we need to be known as well as know, be understood as well as understand. In this chapter, self-presentation and impression management (which are used here synonymously) are mainly meant in this sense of being known and understood. They are also used in the sense of creating a desired impression but not at all in the sense of manipulating others by creating false impressions. Impression management is either inborn or learned early in life:

> One of our chief life activities, I believe, is the constant effort to insert, implant, displace or otherwise alter the contents of others' minds. The types of effects we wish to produce are extremely varied: we may wish to console, inform, excite, impress, persuade, or produce other effects on the person to whom we are speaking.[1]

Motives for self-presentation include the following: to gain approval or respect, optimise self-esteem, socially validate idealised self-images, verify existing self-beliefs, gain material advantages and meet needs for power and control over (social) environments. Both inner-oriented and outer-oriented people self-present. However, whereas inner-oriented people aim to create their preferred impression, outer-oriented people aim to create the impression they think their audience will prefer. It should be clear from a reading of Chapter 5 that we have no choice other than to give an impression, but also that it takes just as much interpersonal skill to create a desired, sincere impression as a desired, false one.[2] It is very easy for us to give a wrong impression of our thoughts, feelings and intentions, because the same cues are interpreted differently by different people and by the same people in different circumstances. This chapter is concerned with how we produce intended and unintended effects on the minds of those with whom we interact at work. It aims to help readers achieve effective self-presentation at work by describing:

- ethical issues, which are a concern to many;
- models of how impressions are created, including facework and politeness theories, the self-presentation model of the American sociologist Erving Goffman, general impression management models and a model more specifically tailored to work;

- different goals and strategies for managing impressions at work and the techniques by which they can be achieved;
- cultural and sub-cultural differences in self-presentation, which are important for working in diverse organisations and internationally;
- work applications of impression management, including self-introductions, team presentations, expressing opinions assertively and making and handling complaints.

## ETHICAL ISSUES

Some people are very concerned about the morality of impression management. They feel that there is an element of deceit in trying to manage the impression we make on others. For example, they might feel that newly appointed managers, when introducing themselves to their staff, should aim to be themselves, rather than try to create an impression that corresponds to the way they intend to manage. The position taken in this chapter is that impression management is in itself morally neutral. The choice of whether to portray ourselves as different from what we really feel we are is ours, providing we have the skill. Without skill, we may be unable to avoid giving an impression which we do not want or intend to.

Despite the above, important moral issues concerning impression management undoubtedly remain. A variety of codes have been suggested. These include:

- avoiding conflicts of interest which may tempt us to give a false impression of our attitude;
- not claiming objectivity on matters in which we are emotionally engaged;
- respecting (even protecting) the personal identity of the target of our impression management;
- acting in accordance with the precept that mutual understanding and trust are the basis for interpersonal ethics.[3]

In public relations, which can be regarded as impression management writ large, the ethics of impression management are more often discussed than in most other fields. There are many ethical codes operating in the public relations field, a situation that has led to complaints that they have confused the market. One response has come from the International Association of Business Communicators; some readers might welcome the guidance provided by this code, which is given in Box 6.1.

## SUMMARY – ETHICAL ISSUES

Although in itself inevitable and morally neutral, impression management can be misused and should be governed by an ethical code.

**Box 6.1**

Because hundreds of thousands of business communicators worldwide engage in activities that affect the lives of millions of people, and because this power carries with it significant social responsibilities, the International Association of Business Communicators developed the Code of Ethics for Professional Communicators. The Code is based on three different yet interrelated principles of professional communication that apply throughout the world. These principles assume that just societies are governed by a profound respect for human rights and the rule of law; that ethics, the criteria for determining what is right and wrong, can be agreed upon by members of an organisation; and that understanding matters of taste requires sensitivity to cultural norms.

Recognizing these principles, members of IABC will:

1. uphold the credibility and dignity of their profession by practicing honest, candid and timely communication and by fostering the free flow of essential information in accord with the public interest.
2. disseminate accurate information and promptly correct any erroneous communication for which they may be responsible.
3. understand and support the principles of free speech, freedom of assembly, and access to an open marketplace of ideas and act accordingly.
4. be sensitive to cultural values and beliefs and engage in fair and balanced communication activities that foster and encourage mutual understanding.
5. refrain from taking part in any undertaking which the communicator considers to be unethical.
6. obey laws and public policies governing their professional activities and be sensitive to the spirit of all laws and regulations and, should any law or public policy be violated, for whatever reason, act promptly to correct the situation.
7. give credit for unique expressions borrowed from others and identify the sources and purposes of all information disseminated to the public.
8. protect confidential information and, at the same time, comply with all legal requirements for the disclosure of information affecting the welfare of others.
9. not use confidential information gained as a result of professional activities for personal benefit and not represent conflicting or competing interests without written consent of those involved.
10. not accept undisclosed gifts or payments for professional services from anyone other than a client or employer.
11. not guarantee results that are beyond the power of the practitioner to deliver.
12. be honest not only with others but also, and most importantly, with themselves as individuals; for a professional communicator seeks the truth and speaks that truth first to the self.

*Source*: The International Association of Business Communicators.

## IMPRESSION MANAGEMENT MODELS

There are three strands of theory and research that dominate the self-presentation literature. The first, facework, originates in cross-cultural research, the second in the theorising of Erving Goffman and the third in impression management models. All have been fruitful in producing practical guidance on how to manage the impressions made on others.

## Facework and politeness

We all, when interacting with others, engage in facework. 'Face' is 'a claimed sense of identity in an interactive situation' – that is, it describes the person someone projects themself as being when dealing with others.[4] Face claims are of two kinds: a claim to personal space, privacy and the right not to be distracted, which is called a negative face claim; and a claim to be associated with and approved of by others, which is a positive face claim. People may be concerned with supporting the negative or positive face of the person(s) with whom they are interacting as well as their own. Table 6.1 shows the face concerns that are present in interactions. For most people, whether their self-esteem is enhanced or diminished during an interaction depends on whether or not their face and face claims are honoured and maintained: if not, they may feel they have lost face. Therefore, during the course of interactions, they may feel exposed to face threats. For example, a fashion department buyer in a planning meeting with other store buyers might feel threatened with face loss if he or she had not been at the latest designer shows and feared that this might be exposed during the discussion.

**Table 6.1 Face concerns in an interaction**

| | *Own face* | *Other's face* |
|---|---|---|
| Negative face concerns | Protecting own space, privacy and right not to be imposed on | Respecting other's space, privacy and right not to be imposed on |
| Positive face concerns | Seeking to be accepted and approved of by others | Understanding other's desire to be accepted and approved of |

Facework is the process of using communication devices to support face claims – in other words to maintain or save face, recover from face loss or support another person's face. Apologising, building up to making requests and refusing requests with a recognised formula, such as 'Sorry, I'll be away on business on that date', are negative facework, supporting negative face claims. To support positive face claims, people use positive facework, such as self-disclosure, paying compliments and making promises. Supporting another person's face is done, for example, by being tactful, showing solidarity with the other person or showing approbation of them.

According to the emerging theory of 'politeness', virtually all communication involves a face threat. To ask for something, explain or excuse something, disagree with somebody, or tell someone something about ourselves involves a threat to either the receiver or the sender of the message. The threats arise because of

**Table 6.2 Threats to receiver's and speaker's desires for autonomy and approval created by different types of communication**

| | *Desire for autonomy* | *Desire for approval* |
|---|---|---|
| Threaten receiver | Requests<br>Self-disclosures | Disagreements |
| Threaten speaker | Promises<br>Explanations | Apologies<br>Explanations |

**Table 6.3 Varying degrees of threat to hearer's face, and hence of politeness, of different request-making strategies**

| | *Strategy* | *Defining feature* | *Example of request to close the door* |
|---|---|---|---|
| Least threatening (most polite) | Not doing anything | | |
| | Off-record act | Intent is deniable | 'It seems cold in here' |
| | Negative politeness | Indicates respect for hearer's autonomy | 'Could you shut the door?' |
| | Positive politeness | Indicates solidarity with the hearer | 'How about shutting the door for us?' |
| Most threatening (least polite) | Bald on-record act | No attention is given to hearer's face | 'Shut the door' |

our face needs and claims as just described. For example, addressing a remark to someone imposes on them by requiring a response; hence there is potentially a threat to their desire not to be impinged on (i.e. their negative face claim). Table 6.2 shows the types of threats created by different types of communication: requests, disagreements and self-disclosures all threaten the receiver's face. However, they can all be expressed in ways that communicate different degrees of threat. For example, a request to close the door can be made using any one of five different strategies. These strategies vary in the degree of threat they offer to the receiver's face, as shown in Table 6.3. The lower the degree of threat to the receiver's face, the greater the level of politeness of the communication. In addition, the level of threat to the receiver depends on three further factors. These are the degree of imposition (asking for the time is less imposing than asking for a loan), the receiver's power in relation to the sender (it is more threatening for a Private to disagree with a General than vice versa) and how well the receiver and the sender know one another. Between strangers, the potential for aggression is unknown and so the potential for threat is greater. Such a concern is assumed to be less important among people who know one another well.

Politeness theory asserts that people will use more politeness the higher the intrinsic level of threat in the communication.[5] Thus the theory predicts that in making a comment involving a high degree of imposition, from a relatively low-power position to an unknown work acquaintance, most people would use a low threat form. For example, they would use an off-the-record act such as 'There seems to be a problem with the accounts'. On the other hand, in making a comment when they are the more powerful party and they have worked in the same office as the person they are addressing for many years, a bald on-the-record act such as 'You've made some errors with the accounts' would be predicted. The evidence to date provides support for all aspects of politeness theory except for inconsistent findings for the effects of how well the sender and receiver know one another. Most research has been done on requests, which are the most threatening acts – worse than disagreements, for instance. There is some evidence that politeness theory applies cross-culturally. For instance, there is a finding that, among both American and Korean subjects, the perceived politeness of a strategy was, with one exception, as predicted by the theory.

## Erving Goffman's model of self-presentation

Erving Goffman originated much of the study of self-presentation.[6] Goffman argued that in order to interact, people must define the situation and the roles each will play. Thus, the opening impression we give is not just an impression of what kind of person we are, it also conveys our definition of the situation. As Goffman put it: 'Each individual entering a conversation projects by dress, manner and opening remarks a proposal for what the basis of the interaction shall be.' This might be equal-to-equal, superior-to-inferior, follower-to-leader, teacher-to-learner, or any other of a great many bases. Clearly, if this projected definition is quite unacceptable to the other person, the interaction may break down. For instance, graduate trainees who project to a senior manager a definition of equal-to-equal may get categorised as cheeky young devils and quickly be put in their place.

The interactors must then keep behaving in a way that sustains these definitions. For example, one new member of a committee might well perform in such a way as to define the situation and their role as 'I am new and inexperienced and my contributions, if any, are of lower value than those of other committee members.' Someone else, though, in the same situation, might act in such a way as to imply, 'Although I am new to this committee, I am an expert in its subject matter and very experienced in other committees so that my contributions are at least equal in value to those of other members.' As this example shows, maintaining our definition of the situation involves face. For Goffman, face is the positive social value we assume for ourselves. Face has a promissory quality, and involves us in the risk of losing face by saying the wrong thing, or not having the information we might be expected to have, or otherwise behaving inappropriately. For example, a civil servant engaged in a work-related discussion with a colleague might say 'The Minister's mind is completely made up on this issue.' If the colleague responds 'Oh, have you been discussing it with her then?' and the first speaker has to answer 'No', he or she loses face, no matter how the 'No' is qualified in terms of 'Johnny told me' or 'But it's obvious from the minutes' or in other ways. The opening statement about the state of the Minister's mind carried the implication that the speaker had had direct discussions with the Minister. That 'promise' was not fulfilled, and so face was lost, even though no actual falsehood occurred.

To sustain an impression we have to regulate how much information we give out and control the level and type of contact we have with the other party. For example, to appear trusting we must be willing to tell others something about ourselves, even if we would rather not, perhaps because of a feeling that we are boring. On the other hand, if we are over-intimate, talk too much of the time and too privately to one person in a meeting, we will have trouble conveying authority to them or observers. Goffman notes that one implication of his work is that managers need to maintain some dignity – not to behave like 'one of the boys'. 'Whatever lowers the dignity of a superior position makes it more difficult for the subordinates to accept the difference of position. Also, where a single organisation is involved in which the superior position is symbolic of the whole organisation, the prestige of the latter is thought to be injured.' In Goffman's model, tact, or protecting other people's faces, is very important. He wrote: 'Few impressions could survive if those who received the impression did not exert tact in their reception of it.'[7] This mutual dependence also, naturally, brings power into play.

Four kinds of influences, which Goffman calls forms of alienation,[8] can easily undermine self-presentation, and prevent us making the impression we intend:

1. External preoccupation. Our attention slips, we are thinking of something other than the conversation in hand and we give the game away, either by committing a solecism, or because the mere fact of being preoccupied is itself incompatible with giving an impression of interest and concern.
2. Self-consciousness. This makes us awkward and nervous. It too is incompatible with the impression we are trying to give.
3. Over-consciousness of the other person. This form of alienation most often happens on the job if we are sexually attracted to someone with whom we are working, or over-aware of them as high-status individuals. Again it makes it difficult to keep the mask of concentration in place.
4. Both 2 and 3 above are likely to lead to over-consciousness of the interaction processes themselves. 'If I say that, how will it make me appear?' 'How will she respond?'

Under the influence of any of these distracting concerns we are likely to show too much or too little attention, involvement, concern or emotion, lose muscular control, for instance by yawning when our face requires us to be interested, or

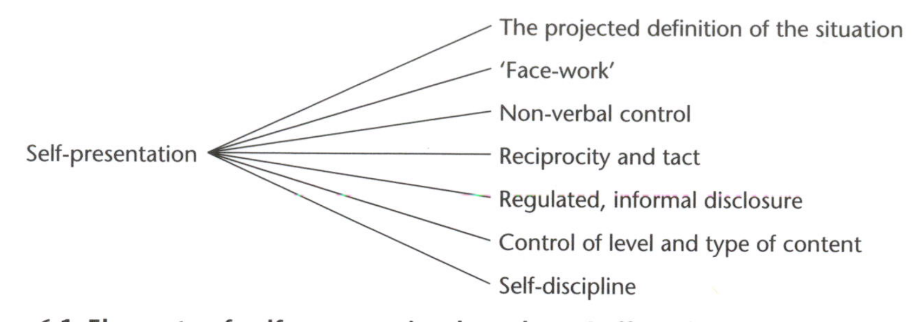


**Figure 6.1 Elements of self-presentation based on Goffman's performance approach.**

make timing and other errors such as embarrassing silences or over-talking. Note that often our anxiety over the last two of these, losing muscular control or timing errors, itself leads us to create the wrong impression of how involved or emotional we are. This, however, can be most important. For instance, if a person is embarrassed by any silence on a first meeting, they may talk too much and so appear over-eager. All this means that performing well requires not only skill, but also self-discipline. It is necessary to suppress inappropriate responses, such as desires to laugh about matters that are defined as serious or to take seriously matters that are defined as funny. Figure 6.1 shows the elements in self-presentation based on Goffman's model.

There are three situations that seem to give rise to special problems in self-presentation. One is making the transfer from the social chit-chat at the start of a meeting to its business and vice versa, another is where two parties have discrepant roles and a third is in dealing with third parties.

1. Many people feel awkward at having to make the transition from, for instance, the social warm-up at the start of an interview to the real business, or from the formality of a meeting to the informal chat as people leave their chairs. Goffman accounts for the difficulty by explaining that what is involved is to negotiate a shift to a different 'social distance', set of roles or definition of the situation. This negotiation inevitably jeopardises the existing agreement which sustains present performances. To negotiate this shift, overtures must be made, involving the risk that they will be rejected: if they are, the person making the overture may feel worse off in face terms than if they had not been made.
2. There is a particular difficulty for both parties in handling discrepant roles. Where one party is high in status but low in power, and the other is the reverse, both parties find the situation difficult. For example, internal auditors often have low status but substantial power – their reports can lead to far-reaching changes being introduced in the departments that they audit. Auditees, on the other hand, have little power over auditors, since otherwise the auditors' independence could not be guaranteed, but may be high in

**Box 6.2**

### How to negotiate social transitions, such as from business to socialising

- Make only small overtures at a time.
- Use incrementalism. For instance, instead of inviting the chairperson of a just-finished meeting to the bar immediately, you start by some comment on the date of the next meeting – 'Just as well to get another one in before the Christmas period.' Then, when contact is established, it is easier to introduce the invitation.
- Use ambiguity so that face can be saved by your demand or invitation being taken in its innocuous sense. For example, 'Some people are suggesting an adjournment to the bar, Chair, but'; Chairperson: 'Not for me, thank you: I've got work to do'; 'Oh, good, that lets me off the hook, too, I'm tied up myself.' Here it is the distancing of yourself from the situation by 'Some people' and the introduction of ambiguity with the word 'but' that can save your face. If the chairperson adopts the suggestion, your 'but' can conveniently be ignored by both parties. There are innumerable variations on the ambiguity theme, many of them enhanced by euphemisms.
- Use guarded disclosure. When negotiating a social transition, you can sometimes use an indirect reference instead of a direct invitation or request with less risk to face. Instead of 'Can I do X?' use 'I was wondering how it would be if I did X'.
- Use hints. Requests and suggestions should sometimes be hinted at, not made openly.
- Use non-verbal signals. A 1987 study by Glenn and Knapp examined how adults signal 'Let's play' during face-to-face interactions. It found that 'Let's play' was signalled non-verbally, as well as with topic shifts and humour.

*Source*: Glenn, P. J. and L. Knapp (1987) 'The interactive framing of play in adult conversations', *Communication Quarterly*, vol. 35, no. 1, pp. 48–66.

status and position within the organisation. Some auditors and auditees find this discrepancy the most difficult social aspect of their job. The relative positions of auditor and auditee are shown diagrammatically in Figure 6.2.

3. When a third person is present whom either or both parties want to impress, they can be tempted to try to put themselves in a good light and the other party in a poor one. Goffman comments: 'It is these covert forces of self-elevation and other-derogation that often introduce a dreary compulsive rigidity to sociable encounters.' It applies to work encounters, too.

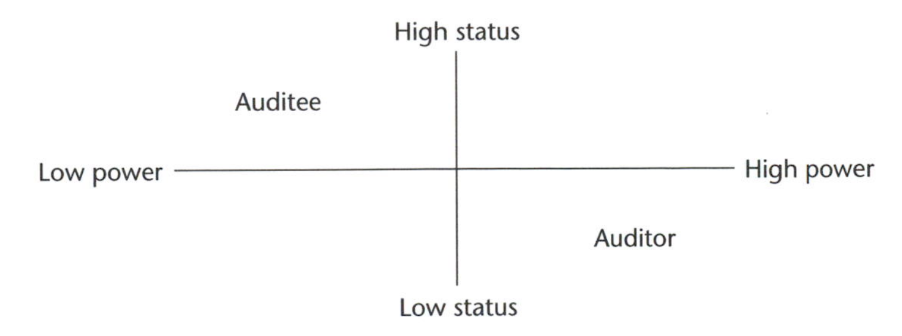


**Figure 6.2 Discrepant roles: auditor and auditee.**

Box 6.3

**How to handle discrepant roles**

- Acknowledge the other person's claims throughout your discussions without waiting to be asked.
- At the same time, your own claims or power bases will often have more effect if you leave them unstated.
- If the attitudes of the other party seem appropriate, bring the problem out into the open: 'We are both likely to feel a certain awkwardness about this, because you are so much higher in the organisation, but in this matter I have a lot of influence. I'm sure we can get round this difficulty, though, aren't you?' or 'Can we start by talking about any worries we may have as a result of the fact that I have a lot of influence in this matter although you are so much higher in the organisation?'

Freedom to choose a self-presentation style is constrained by our role.[9] If, for instance, someone wished to ingratiate themself with another person, he or she might use one of several tactics. These include flattery, agreeing with the other, getting the other to talk about themself, doing them a favour or showing off their own best qualities. However, if the other person is a boss or subordinate then some of these tactics may be ineffective or may even backfire. The more subordinates agree with their boss, the more they seem to the boss to be agreeing simply because of their dependence. The more bosses agree with subordinates, the more they appear to be weak characters. Often the most important constraint is fulfilling other people's expectations. Doctors who dispense with physical examination are perceived as negligent. Lawyers often argue long and hard over hopeless cases. They know it is a waste of time and so does the judge – they do it to make the client feel s/he has been well served. An important part of impression management is conveying the accepted attitude.[10] In self-presentation at work, it is better not to deviate more than a certain amount from the behaviour generally considered appropriate for the role.

## Impression management approaches

Several theories share the central idea that people communicate strategically to facilitate goal achievement and must take into account the varying perspectives and agendas of the audience. This applies not only in initial or early encounters but over the duration of life-long relationships. Chambliss,[11] in his social exchange-based theory of impression management, assumed that, in any interaction and whatever its goals, people seek information about one another and attempt to convey personal images to one another of the kind of person they want the other to think they are. This impression need not correspond to how people see themselves, nor with how they want most others to judge them. Chambliss added three concepts to our understanding of impression management:

1. It is effective or ineffective according to whether the other person's impression is what the actor intended.
2. It is successful or unsuccessful according to whether the other person's reaction to the self that is being presented is positive or negative. The other person is assumed to be evaluating the impression giver.
3. If the other sees the person as they see themself, the encounter is validating. Validation necessarily involves self-disclosure.

Interaction goals of success and validation can conflict. For example, a sales representative's success goal might be to present themself as uncritically enthusiastic about their product at a time when their validation goal would have them show a more balanced view. Any interaction represents some combination of these variables. Chambliss's theory is that people seek out social relationships that they perceive as effective, successful and validating and avoid those that produce an unacceptable combination of those variables.

## The Gardner and Matinko model of work-based impression management

How a work environment affects impression management is taken into account in a model in which individuals define the situation and their role, just as Goffman described, but their definitions are shaped by three sets of factors:

1. Demographic attributes of the other party, such as sex, nationality, ethnicity and class.
2. Personal attributes of the other party, such as status, power, abilities and attractiveness, plus those attributes which come from the other party's group membership.
3. Organisation structure and work-based social systems.

How people interpret such cues, however, depends on several factors internal to the individual. These include their self-system (social identity, gender identity, self-esteem, self-efficacy and self-monitoring), social perceptions, beliefs, feelings and motives for interacting. Thus, whether the audience's definition of the situation corresponds to the actor's definition is highly variable, but strongly affected by two core aspects, called situational dimensions. These are relational similarity and situational ambiguity.[12] Relational similarity has been found to influence strongly how positively (or negatively) individuals feel towards one another.[13] Thus, targets of impression managerment are predisposed to like and hence form favourable impressions of people whom they see as similar to themselves. The more ambiguous the situation is, the less information the target has for forming an impression, so the greater the chance that stereotypes will be used. Figure 6.3 shows the core processes of the Gardner and Matinko model.

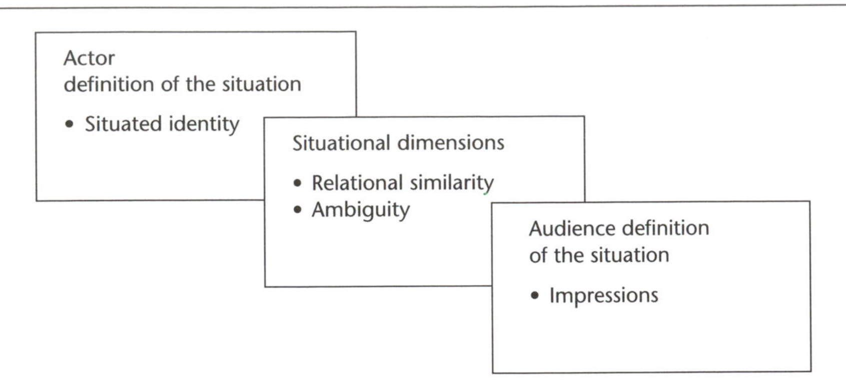


**Figure 6.3 Core processes of the Gardner and Matinko work-based impression management model.**

**Box 6.4**

## Critique of self-presentation theories

The concept of positive face has been criticised for conflating two kinds of wants, the desires to be included and to have one's abilities respected. Instead, it is suggested, three types of politeness are used, corresponding to threats to three kinds of want and face: inclusion, competence (both corresponding to aspects of positive face) and autonomy (corresponding to negative face). Thus, for threats to another person's competence face, expressed by, for instance, negative comments on their work or requests for them to do it again, approbation is the mode of politeness used. Table 6.4 gives examples of threats and their related polite, less polite and impolite expressions. Research shows that high power difference reduces and low perceived legitimacy of the request increases solidarity and tact politeness in socially distant relationships such as those at work (Lim and Bowers, 1991).

Goffman's theory has been criticised on the following grounds:

- While people do indulge in more or less deliberate playacting at times, they more often act spontaneously and unreflectingly, showing different degrees of intimacy or laying claim to expertise by means of a stream of verbal and non-verbal signs.
- Not all presentations aim at being creditable. People might want to present a negative image and would still use skill to do it (Danziger, 1976).
- The approach de-emphasises the psychology of the individual.
- It focuses on what often seemed to be illicit behaviours designed to manipulate others.

Despite these criticisms, Goffman's insights are generally credited with providing a springboard for the entire study of impression management and some have lasting value.

The shared assumptions of the impression management models are criticised because not all self-presentation is goal-directed and strategic or consciously considers the attitudes of the audience. Other factors than those given in the Chambliss model affect which interactions people seek out and avoid – instrumental purposes, for instance.

*Sources*: Danziger, K. (1976) *Interpersonal Communication*. Oxford: Pergamon.
Lim, T.-S. and J. W. Bowers (1991) 'Facework: Solidarity, approbation, and tact', *Human Communication Research*, vol. 17, no. 3, pp. 415–450.

**Box 6.4** *continued*

**Table 6.4 Politeness of different expressions in relation to different types of threat to the receiver's face**

| *Politeness dimension* | *For threats to others* | *Least polite expression* | *Medium polite expression* | *Most polite expression* |
|---|---|---|---|---|
| Approbation | Inclusion face | It's none of your business | I had a similar thought | I know I can trust you |
| Solidarity | Competence face | Please do this again | It's not the best work you can do | It's an excellent piece of work |
| Tact | Autonomy face | You'd better let me do it | Do you think you could do it? | Could we work together on . . . |

**Box 6.5**

### How to apply the four impression management models to self-present at work

- Be sensitive to the negative and positive face claims of others in an interaction and, where possible, honour those claims to support their face and ingratiate yourself with them.
- Apply an understanding of politeness theory to avoid communicating unintended threats.
- Remember that all social interactions are essentially performances in which it is legitimate and reasonable to expect the co-operation of the other parties. They are more likely than not to help you enact your role, i.e. to be tactful.
- Do not project by your opening remarks or manner an image that you cannot maintain.
- Do not allow preoccupations or fatigue to lead to losses of attention and be aware of the importance of and stay in control of your non-verbal behaviour.
- At work, remember the constraints on self-presentation imposed by your role and others' expectations and by the need to convey the accepted attitude.
- Follow the suggestions on how to handle transitions and discrepant roles.
- Avoid self-elevation and other-derogation in the presence of a third party.
- Take into account the criteria for making self-presentations effective, successful and validating.
- Bear in mind the likelihood that your audience's definition of the situation will differ from yours.
- To increase the chances of your definition of the situation and that of your audience being similar, emphasise similarity with them and try to reduce situational ambiguity, by, for instance, giving your business card on first introduction.

## SUMMARY – IMPRESSION MANAGEMENT MODELS

This section has introduced four models of impression management. Face concerns are universal and relate on the one hand to needs for autonomy and privacy and on the other to needs for acceptance and relationships.

Facework is the process of using communication devices to support our own and others' face claims. We also use politeness to manage the threat to our own and others' face of such communications as requests, orders and self-disclosures.

According to self-presentation models, originating with Goffman, in interactions we aim to sustain a particular definition of ourselves and the situation. Our ability to do this is constrained by the context and by errors that undermine performances.

Impression management approaches share the idea that people have communication goals and strategies and must take their audience into consideration. One such model accounts for how people select those relationships they seek out and those they avoid according to how effective, successful and validating they think they will be. Another emphasises how the context including, at work, organisation structure and work-based social systems, influence both how people self-present and how likely it is that the impression that they try to give is the one that will be received.

## IMPRESSION MANAGEMENT GOALS AND STRATEGIES

Goffman's approach played down the idea that people might have differing goals in impression management. However, later research has shown that people do have varying goals. They do not always try to present themselves positively. Impression management strategies can be separated into 'assertive behaviours, used proactively to achieve particular goals' and 'defensive behaviours, intended to protect and maintain a desired identity, especially in cases of event failures'.[14] An example of an event failure would be a missed meeting or a failure to produce a report on time.

Five basic classes of impression management goals and strategies have been identified in the literature.[15] They are ingratiation (aimed at being likeable), intimidation (to appear dangerous, ruthless or powerful), self-promotion (to seem competent), exemplification or justification (to show integrity and moral worthiness) and supplication (to exploit one's own weakness or dependence on others). As this list suggests, if our goal requires it, we may choose to try to create a modest or even unflattering impression. Our choice will probably be influenced by what attributes we think our audience values and what impression we think we can make credible to them.[16] Most people's self-presentations are held in check by reality and are consistent with publicly known information about them. However, like other behaviours, self-presentations come to influence beliefs and attitudes. Research has shown that people will change their self-beliefs and self-evaluations to bring them in line with their prior strategic self-presentations.

Gordon[17] found that ingratiation led to perceivers judging the ingratiator as likeable. However, exactly how likeable depended on the specific ingratiation tactic used, how transparent it seemed, the direction of the influence attempt (upward, downward or lateral), whether perceivers were targets of the influence attempt or simply observed it, the gender of the perceiver and the setting. For instance, in the case of the flattery used by a customer to a service adviser (see Box 6.6), the ingratiation was not perceived as transparent or motivated, the perceiver was the target, both target and perceiver were female and the impersonal setting of a telephone call avoided embarrassment. It is not surprising that the ingratiation attempt had clearly led to liking and a willingness to be helpful.

**Box 6.6**

The bank customer service adviser had received a call from a customer who had found, from the automated service, that an expected credit had not, apparently, been received. When told the due date and the amount, the adviser confirmed that no such credit had been received. Then she noticed and told the customer that two credits, each for half the amount, had been received on the right date. 'Ah', said the customer, 'We still need you. You can still do things computers can't.'

*Source*: Given as an example of a satisfying interaction in an interview with a bank's customer service adviser, author's research.

Organisations use different impression management strategies in different forums to legitimise their actions. Ingratiation strategies are often used in public statements while justification strategies are used in interviews.[18] Ingratiation appears to be the most effective strategy.[19]

## SUMMARY – IMPRESSION MANAGEMENT GOALS AND STRATEGIES

Impression management goals and strategies include giving negative impressions, such as being intimidating, as well as positive ones, such as being likeable. The choice usually depends on the individual's wider objective, their assessment of the target's attitudes and their beliefs about what impression they can make credible. The success of one common impression management strategy, ingratiation, has been shown to depend on a number of factors, some within, some outside the ingratiator's control. It seems likely that the same applies to other strategies.

## IMPRESSION MANAGEMENT TECHNIQUES

To achieve their impression management goals and strategies, people use both verbal and non-verbal self-presentation. Using them well is related to self-monitoring, assertiveness, conquering nervousness and being able to handle others' aggression.

## Verbal self-presentation: messages, communicator styles and framing

*Messages* may be speaker-oriented, non-responsive or receiver-oriented.[20] Not surprisingly, receiver-oriented messages convey a more positive impression of the speaker, especially in terms of empathy, than the other kinds. Asking questions and seeking information has been shown in some situations to create a more empathetic impression.

Successful *communicator styles* include dominant, relaxed and open styles. Dominant communicators take charge; they are perceived as assertive. Relaxed communicators exude confidence. Open communicators disclose personal information to others. The underlying variable in these successful styles appears to be having self-confidence. Communicator styles are partly controllable, but individuals tend to use one style or set of styles more than others. This tendency is partly influenced by social background.[21] Two major social dimensions underlying impressions of communicators are status (or social position) and solidarity (or approachability). Both these are affected by stylistic features – for instance, non-standard dialects lead to people being assessed as lower in status and competence, but higher in solidarity and warmth.

*Framing* was introduced in Chapter 5, where it was pointed out that interpreting events and relationships involves imposing a schema or frame on them. However, framing also refers to an impression management activity, used especially of politicians and media. In this context, framing is 'a quality of communication that causes others to accept one meaning over another'.[22] In some contexts the uses made of framing are highly dubious, but framing itself is inevitable. (In children, the framing of talk activities has been shown to change with age, which suggests an underlying developmental process.)[23] Within organisations, framing can be used to set agendas, generate consensus, give prominence to issues, and focus staff on particular issues. Framing techniques include:

- choice of angle, for instance, health and safety at work issues can be framed as welfare concerns, legal concerns, macro-economic concerns (impact on the enterprise) or insurance concerns;
- choice of topic;
- the devices listed in Table 6.5, which were found by Gail Fairhurst,[24] who showed how framing was used in work conversations between leaders and staff in five manufacturing plants during implementation of a Total Quality programme.

## Non-verbal self-presentation

As we saw in Chapter 5, only a few valid interpretations can be made from someone's appearance, voice or movements. However, the fact is that non-verbal

**Table 6.5 Framing devices in vision implementation**

| *Framing device* | *Definition* | *Linguistic features* | *Examples* |
|---|---|---|---|
| Communicated predicaments | Articulated confusion about the vision | Expression of doubt, confusion or misunderstanding about the vision | 'I'm just trying to understand. If I looked at a Pareto chart, what would I want to be seeing with that chart?' |
| Possible futures | Sense-making that makes the vision actionable | | |
| P–f1 Specification | Making the assumptions of the vision or its tools explicit | Distinctions drawn between tools or concepts of the vision | A Pareto or pie chart or one of those are not time dependent. |
| P–f2 Personalisation | Tying the vision to the recurring activities of the role incumbent | Labelling role behaviour as consistent with the vision | 'Now in your job . . . ultimately you're trying to focus on customers.' |
| P–f3 Reconciliation | Confronting the real or perceived differences between the vision and culture | Linking the vision to old or existing visions' values, norms or other political realities; clarifiying seeming contradictions; dismissing/rejecting the old for new | 'What's going on here is against TQA, OK? He's trying to instil fear in folk to force them to do something that's just not right.' |
| Jargon and themes of the vision | Using the vision as a lens; seeing the work context in terms of the vision | Use of jargon and themes of the vision | 'The work teams . . . were filled with people doing their best you know, willing workers.' |
| Positive spin | Partisan critique and selling of the vision | Articulating advantages associated with the vision and its solutions to problems | 'What does it cost us? If it hadn't been for this incident we would have upset customers who might not buy the product.' |
| (Local) Agenda setting | Identification of unaddressed vision activities | Identifying needs, next steps, issues, challenges | 'They don't have anyone in the leadership role so to me that is a challenge.' |
| Motivational agenda | Identification of unaddressed vision activities with strong encouragement to address them | 'Coaching' and use of motivational language | 'We gotta do a lot of managing around it. I mean just manage the hell out of it.' |

*Source*: Fairhurst, G. T. (1993) 'Echoes of the vision: when the rest of the organization talks total quality', *Management Communication Quarterly*, vol. 6, no. 4, pp. 331–371.

behaviours strongly affect impressions. Observers and participants both perceive the same messages from non-verbal behaviours, although participants tend to see them more intensely.[25] Clearly, then, the non-verbal cues we give out are important. However, we cannot assume that producing the non-verbal expression we intend to, will be non-problematic. Non-verbal behaviour can be divided into three categories: communicative acts, used deliberately to convey meaning, interactive acts intended to influence the behaviour of others, and informative acts, which are not intended to communicate, but actually do provide others with information – like yawning during a lecture.[26] We have little control over informative acts. For example, suppose someone wants to appear competent, they may care so deeply about it that they become, and appear, nervous. Motivation and confidence are just two of a wide array of factors that affect how successfully we self-present non-verbally.[27] Table 6.6 shows what non-verbal behaviour generally expresses and how it is usually interpreted.

The following aspects of non-verbal behaviour have special significance for impression management:

- Non-verbal behaviour is involuntary. When people suddenly become fearful, for example, non-verbal signs of fear begin to appear on their faces involuntarily. There is no comparable process whereby a particular, predictable set of words begins to be formed at the same time. Trying to suppress non-verbal behaviour makes people seem passive, inhibited, rigid, unexpressive or withdrawn.[28]
- The kind of information that non-verbal behaviour conveys is more intense and personal than that conveyed by what we say. There may be certain automatic links between experiencing and expressing emotion that are present for non-verbal, but not for verbal, behaviour. It may also be that facial expressions of emotion are directly perceived; that is, that our perceptual apparatus is hard-wired to pick up emotional information without needing any additional contribution of higher-order cognitive processes.
- Non-verbal behaviour is less accessible to participants in interactions than to observers.[29] In most ways people know more about themselves and know it more directly than others could ever know. Awareness of non-verbal behaviour is an important exception to this rule. Facial expressions are not normally even visible to those who make them, and they are not very conscious of other aspects such as gestures.
- There are cross-cultural consistencies in how facial expressions of emotions are perceived.
- Most people's judgements about the significance of non-verbal behaviour fall along three dimensions: evaluation, status and interest.[30] Research suggests that people observe others' facial expressions, body movements, voice tone and so on, in order to answer three questions: 'Is he or she pleasant or unpleasant?',

**Table 6.6 Non-verbal cues – a comparison of interpretations and expressions**

| | *What the cues really express* | *How the cues are usually interpreted* |
|---|---|---|
| The face at rest | Age and ethnicity ranges, gender | Often thought to reveal personality and intelligence but does not |
| Clothes, accessories, hairstyle and make-up | Some attitudes and aspirations<br>The image the person wants to project | Used as major clues<br>Conventions are important |
| Facial expression | Emotions, especially fear, joy, anger, shock; but there are display rules controlling this | As conveying mood or emotion<br>Many expressions are seen as showing apprehensiveness; no expressions seen as showing neutrality; also seen as showing attitudes: e.g. liking, superiority |
| Gaze | Interest and attention; looking up indicates end of speaking | Conveys interest and attention, or the lack of them |
| Eye contact | Shows interest. Low amount indicates dislike or awkwardness; used to express a range of feelings and attitudes | As showing a desire to advance the relationship; sincerity; short bursts are distrusted; people are generally good at interpreting eye contact messages |
| Gestures | Degree of involvement. Learnt and controllable – can be deceptive | Convey arousal, animation; head nodding reinforces speakers; uncontrolled gestures are seen as betraying emotion – e.g. foot-tapping as impatience, hand over mouth or folded arms as defensiveness |
| Handshake | Most people are aware that handshakes are 'read' so gives few real cues | Often assumed to reveal personality but this is unproven in research |
| Changes in body language – faster breathing, more gestures | Heightened emotion, more involvement<br>Changes are often more revealing than content | Heightened emotion, more involvement |
| Postures and orientation | Affected by behavioural contagion; not easily controlled; show emotions, attitudes to interlocutor and the encounter<br>Affected by culture | As showing personality and attitudes |
| Voice and accent | National or regional origins, class, age, gender and physique | National or regional origins, class, age, gender and physique |
| Voice timbre and average pitch | Lasting features give little away | As showing personality and leadership qualities |
| Voice tone, speed and variability | Degree of certainty about what is being said<br>Slowness shows thinking<br>Speech disturbance shows emotion or fatigue | As showing friendliness/hostility, confidence, aggressiveness |

'Where does he or she rank on a status hierarchy?' and 'Is he or she interesting to me?' The particular content of the dimensions varies. For instance, for status judgements, some people will be more concerned with education, others, especially at work, with organisational position or job prospects. Sometimes 'interesting' means sexually attractive, sometimes potentially useful, sometimes, even, just having interesting things to say. These perceived attributes are combined to derive overall favourable or unfavourable impressions.

**Box 6.7**

### How to manage the impression given by your non-verbal behaviour

- Work at ensuring consistency between different non-verbal signals. For instance, it is not effective to smile with your mouth but not your eyes.
- Work at ensuring consistency between non-verbal signals and speech content. Inconsistency leads to the person who receives the conflicting messages feeling confused. He or she will dislike being in this confused state and may transfer the dislike to you. Your body language will over-ride what you say. Your inner states and qualities will be interpreted more from what your voice and body movements seem to indicate than from what you say (Williams and Sundene, 1965; Mehrabian, 1969).
- Relax. You can only do so much. First, much non-verbal behaviour is uncontrollable. Second, how people perceive one another is strongly influenced by their own character and situation. Third, many people are using stereotypes relating appearance to personality. Stereotypes can be based on facial type or physique. High brows 'mean' intellect, lines mean a worrier, fat people are jolly, thin people nervous. Voice timbre is often taken to reveal leadership potential (Mehrabian, 1968).

*Sources*: Mehrabian, A. (1968) 'Inference of attitudes from the posture, orientation and distance of a communicator', *Journal of Consulting and Clinical Psychology*, vol. 32, pp. 296–308.
Mehrabian, A. (1969) 'A semantic space for non-verbal behaviour', *Journal of Consulting and Clinical Psychology*, vol. 35, pp. 248–257.
Williams, F. and B. Sundene (1965) 'Dimensions of recognition: visual versus vocal expression of emotion', *Audiovisual Communication Review*, vol. 13, pp. 44–52.

## Self-monitoring

People differ in how sensitive they are to cues about how appropriate their own social behaviour is and in how willing and able they are to use these cues to regulate their self-presentations.[31] High self-monitors are concerned with how others respond to them and so adjust their self-presentations in response to social and interpersonal cues. In contrast, the expressive behaviours of low self-monitors reflect their own inner states and dispositions, including their attitudes, emotions and self-concepts. Research suggests that self-monitoring is more a matter of attitude than ability.[32] However, self-monitoring is a state as well as a trait – we all do more and less self-monitoring at different times. High self-monitors are effective social participants who adapt their behaviour to others' expectations, but tend to be inconsistent across different situations.

## Assertiveness

To give the impression we want, we often need to act assertively. One definition of assertiveness is 'the behaviours that enable an individual to act in his or her best interest, or to stand up for him- or herself without undue anxiety; or to express his or her rights without denying the rights of others.'[33] Basic rights that individuals might want to assert at work include the following: the right to make mistakes, to set their own priorities, to have their own needs considered as important as those of other people, to refuse requests without feeling guilty, to express themselves as long as they do not violate the rights of others and to judge their own behaviour, thoughts and emotions and take responsibility for the consequences.[34]

Assertiveness can be contrasted with two other ways of behaving. Over-submissive behaviour means failing to stand up for our own rights, or doing so in such a way that other people can easily disregard them. Aggressive behaviour means violating other people's rights in pursuit of our own rights or interests. Acting assertively means holding a steady middle course between the two extremes of over-submission and aggression. It is because the alternatives are so undesirable that assertiveness is worth working for. People who are usually over-submissive get trampled on and can lose their self-respect. Consistent aggression gets people into all sorts of trouble and leads to other people avoiding them. Few people are consistently aggressive or over-submissive, though, and a common pattern is to veer between the two extreme behaviours without entering the middle state at all. This can happen when someone allows themself to be trampled on for a time, bottling up their anger at the treatment, until it finally explodes in a burst of temper and rage. In reverse, it occurs when someone is attacking or bullying another, and eventually starts to notice their own behaviour and, in a fit of contrition or distaste for their own conduct, abases themself or concedes more than is reasonable.

**Box 6.8**

### How to behave assertively

- Assertive behaviour is natural behaviour – what we all do in situations that do not seem difficult or threatening. The trick is to extend that behaviour to situations that do worry us.
- Basic assertion is a simple expression of standing up for your rights. It can be explicit: 'Excuse me, I'd like to finish what I'm saying' or, less directly, a firm statement of information: 'The presentation starts at nine o'clock.' If the other person ignores or over-talks you, repeat your main point in the same tone as before but a little louder. Do not get angry or shout. Refuse to allow yourself to be distracted or angered by side issues.

**Box 6.8** *continued*

Eventually they will attend to your concern. However, guard against the other person feeling that you are being aggressive by showing empathy for them at the same time: 'I appreciate that you feel you have something important to say at this point, and I will listen to you, but first I'd like to finish what I'm saying', or 'I know you have strong views on presentation start times and I would like to discuss them with you, but this presentation starts at nine o'clock.' This technique can be especially effective when you are asking for something. Requests are often turned down the first time but later conceded.

- Fogging is used when the response to your assertion is personal criticism. Fogging means not challenging the criticism, which is a common side-trap, just saying 'You could be right, but . . .' and repeating your assertion. Criticism does not deprive you of your rights. If you are confident of your skill at fogging, you can invite the other person's criticism, which may help disarm them, and may help bring their hidden agenda into the open.
- If you are not sure about why another person is behaving in a way that seems unfair or unreasonable, the assertive behaviour is to ask questions to find out. Non-assertive behaviour is to be afraid of being intrusive or in breach of some convention and therefore to shy away from getting the information on which to base your response. Aggressive behaviour is simply to assume the worst about the other person's reasons and counter-attack. Assertive questions are aimed at finding out the other person's thoughts and feelings, any information they may have and their reactions to your ideas: 'Why did that happen?', 'Are you saying . . . ?', 'How do you feel about that?', 'What do you want to do?' You want the other person to see your questions as assertive, and not aggressive, and respond assertively to them; therefore, so your tone and expression must be clearly assertive, not aggressive. 'Why did that error in the sales figures happen?', for instance, though clearly less aggressive than 'Why did you make that mistake in the sales figures?', can easily be perceived as blaming if spoken in the wrong tone.
- If you find that an earlier agreement is being ignored, act assertively to draw attention, without rudeness, to the discrepancy between words and actions. For instance: 'I understood from our last appraisal that you were going to delegate more of the correspondence work to me. I'm still very keen to do that.'
- If you have failed to get any change in another person's behaviour using other types of assertion, you may decide to remind them of the consequences for them of continuing to act as they are: 'If you continue to withhold the information, I'm left with no alternative but to bring in the Production Director. I'd prefer not to do it.' Only use this type of assertion when you do have sanctions to use and as a last resort because it is so difficult to distinguish from threatening. The trick is to wait until the psychological moment when they, too, must realise that your patience has been tried too far. Then you need to impress on them that you mean business and referring to sanctions is the best way to do it. It should, however, be accompanied by a genuine offer of a chance to change or it is bound to seem aggressive.
- Make your non-verbal behaviour assertive by using a firm, steady voice and matter-of-fact tone and by steadying your voice when you start, with a slow weighing of words, like 'W-e-ll'. Practise saying phrases that are easy to say followed by ones that are difficult to say, both in the same tone, e.g. 'Peter, what is the mileage to Warrington?', 'Peter, what did you do on your visit last week?'
- Use a rating scale, like the one in Exercise 5, to assess whether you behaved assertively in a situation which you afterwards feel, or beforehand felt, called for it. Complete it as soon as possible after the interaction is over.

Assertion in private life is often a matter of ourselves recognising, and asking other people to recognise, that our feelings and the way we react to how we are treated are legitimately part of the equation. At work the emphasis is different. However desirable it might be that personal needs and feelings should be recognised, the fact is that in most organisations they have little legitimacy. On the job, assertiveness needs to be recast in terms of facts, action and achievement rather than feelings.[35] Sadly, women and members of ethnic minorities may find that behaving assertively can provoke negative reactions. Their assertive responses are seen as less sympathetic, friendly and kind than those of white males (especially by traditional men), but more competent and appropriate. Many minority members find, however, that the gain in self-esteem that comes from acting assertively more than compensates for the sacrifice of some liking from people who are applying outdated and oppressive stereotypes.

Argumentativeness, which is a subset of assertiveness, is defined as willingness to engage in constructive, persuasive debate.[36] It is distinguished from verbal aggression by the object of attack. Argumentativeness attacks position, aggression attacks the self-concept of others. Argumentativeness is an individual trait connected to a person's attitudes about arguing and their beliefs concerning how important others feel about arguing.[37] Managers have been shown to be more satisfied with subordinates who are argumentative, providing they can put their point of view tactfully, have a constructive disagreement style, which is one that is sensitive to rules and what is sanctioned, and know what will and what will not offend others.[38] Complainers, who are disliked by their managers, are seen as low in argumentativeness.[39] This research on the constructive effects of argumentativeness in work communication is consistent with argumentativeness research in other contexts, where it has been associated with more learning, less egocentric thinking, more accurate social perspective-taking, more creativity and better problem-solving and decision-making.[40]

## Conquering nervousness

Nervousness in interaction often stems from the fear of being unable to control the impression we make, but itself can mar self-presentations. Another, more deep-seated, source, is anxiety. One analysis of the effects of anxiety on interactions treats encounters between people as taking place when they have complementary needs to satisfy.[41] For instance, what leads us to interact might be my need to make a sale and your need to make a purchase, or, on another level, my need for security (money) and your biological need for food. In a successful interaction, these complementary needs are resolved. I sell, you buy; I gain money, you gain food. Other things are achieved as well. First, we set up 'reciprocal patterns of activity'. For instance, if I praise, you show pleasure; if I ask questions, you give constructive answers. What is more, our success in this interaction leads us to believe that future meetings will also work out well and enable us to satisfy future complementary needs. If, however, either or both persons are feeling anxious, the outcome may be quite different. The anxiety inhibits effective interpersonal behaviour, leading to inappropriate statements and responses. The person is driven by anxiety to assuage that, rather than to satisfy the needs that the interaction is supposed to be about. And, while needs can often be complementary, and so reciprocally met, there is rarely a complement to anxiety, so frustration results. Not only do the two parties fail to reach their goals but the chances are that the interaction itself breaks down, creating further embarrassment and anxiety.

Anxiety can produce a range of ways of behaving, from obvious nervousness to obstinate defensiveness or outright aggression. Some anxiety phenomena are overt, others the anxious person conceals. To sustain interactions with anxious people we must provide reassurance and stroking. We cannot, and should not, attempt to psychoanalyse or treat them – the source of the anxiety may be quite deep-seated – but irritation, nervousness or aggression on our own part are likely to compound their problem. Unfortunately, anxiety is catching. If one person is feeling anxious the other is quite likely to end up feeling that way through behavioural contagion.

Important though it is to be able to handle other people's anxiety in interactions, we will often be more urgently concerned with dealing with our own. The general rule applies here as elsewhere – break into the cycle by acting on the behaviour. By concentrating on behaving in a relaxed and confident way, usually the feeling of anxiety will diminish. For some people, however, anxiety takes the form of a self-destructive inner conversation. When this is the case, a more cognitive approach may work, or at least complement the behaviour-control approach.[42] According to this cognitive approach, there are three kinds of anxiety-driven inner talk:

1. 'I'm not old enough/experienced enough/clever enough to ask for that/claim that/express my opinion.' In other words, I am deficient relative to other people I deal with, and therefore do not have any rights to assert myself.
2. 'If I am wrong, my colleagues will think I'm a fool.' This anxiety is linked to a neurotic over-concern with self-presentation.
3. 'We'll just get into an argument.' These worries are a fear about essentially unpredictable consequences.

There are occasions when an objective assessment would lead to the same conclusions as self-destructive talk. It sometimes is inappropriate for the youngest or least-experienced person present to hold the floor, at least for long. More often, however, it is an expression of a lack of self-confidence. The cognitive analysis suggests ways of overcoming interaction anxiety, shown in Box 6.9.

**Box 6.9**

### How to overcome interaction anxiety

- Recognise if your anxiety is an expression of a lack of self-confidence.
- Analyse which of the three kinds of anxiety it is: self-deprecating, over-concern with impressions or the fear of consequences.
- Practise empathy on your own behalf. To do this, you ask yourself: 'If I were the other person, e.g. the boss, would I feel that the person who is myself has no right/is a fool for making a mistake? Would I argue over it?'
- Concentrate full-time on what you are saying and doing, not on your feelings. Act 'OK' and you will start to feel more 'OK'.

## Aggression

The manager of a branch of an estate agent returned from escorting prospective purchasers one Sunday, just before the agency's Sunday closing time of 2 p.m. He found the branch's receptionist/administrator quite upset. While he was out, a client who was buying three properties to let, with a total value of £1 million, had rung to demand a final viewing of all three that afternoon. The receptionist/administrator said that when she pointed out the fact that the branch was about to close and the difficulties of arranging viewings at such short notice, he grew abusive and threatened to cancel all the deals, on which he was due to exchange legally binding contracts on the following Tuesday.

Few people have any difficulty in recognising the signs of aggression, which include threats, raised voice or an audibly controlled and steely one, frowning or stony countenance, jabbing or prodding gestures, unflinching eye contact and invading someone else's personal space. What is much less clear to most people, however, is what such behaviour means and what lies behind it. Research has thrown up quite a long list of what those third factors might be, as Table 6.7 shows.

## SUMMARY – IMPRESSION MANAGEMENT TECHNIQUES

Verbal impression management includes the use of messages, communicator styles and framing. Receiver-oriented messages can give an impression of empathy. By controlling their style, communicators can give a range of impressions, including openness, dominance and being relaxed. Style also affects impressions of status and warmth. Framing is 'a quality of communication that causes others to accept one meaning over another.' Framing techniques include choice of angle, choice of topic, and a range of framing devices such as positive spin and agenda setting. Non-verbal impression management depends most of all on consistency between the different cues.

Box 6.10

## How to deal with another person's aggression

- Make sure that you have correctly identified the other person's behaviour in calling it aggressive. Duncan (1976, 1979) found that both white and black American subjects were far more likely to label the same video-recorded act as 'violent behaviour' if they believed it was performed by a black person than if performed by a white person. This shows, apart from further depressing evidence of prejudice, that our perceptions of aggression levels in others are not objective.
- Ask yourself whether you are really the target or just happen to be there.
- Use silence. Do not add fuel to the flames by trying to interrupt or shout the aggressor down. Let any emotion that may be causing the aggression or caused by it die down naturally, as emotion tends to. Listen, and look as if you are listening, but keep tight control of your non-verbal behaviour to avoid appearing to concede anything. Use the time while you are not speaking to work out what is causing this attack. Are they counter-attacking because they feel you have attacked them? Is it instrumental aggression? Is it driven by some need of theirs? Is it caused by frustration? Or imitation? Or simply, and commonly, fatigue? When you have worked this out, you will know whether you need to deal with the underlying causes or only with the symptoms – or if all you need do is administer a stroke or two.
- Do not let your silence be so noticeable that it is simply provocative. If, nevertheless, they throw an angry question at you, 'Well, haven't you got anything to say for yourself then?', explain that you are listening carefully to make sure you understand what the matter is. Follow that up with a question or suggestion. 'I'm afraid I missed the bit when you were explaining about such and such. Could you go over it again?'
- Anger from another person can easily hook us into what is essentially someone else's problem. If their anger provokes you into anger, you will have a problem you need not have had. This can happen through contagion – their mood affecting you – as much as your reacting to what they say.
- It can help to acknowledge their anger and express willingness to listen; it can sometimes help to acknowledge the effect of their emotion on you and that your own tenseness may lead to misunderstanding. It can help to clarify and diagnose wants and needs, expectations and 'who owns what' in the situation.
- Ultimately, success in dealing with others' verbal aggression is only possible if your own attitude is a genuine wish to resolve the conflict; otherwise there will probably be an edge to your voice, or an expression, however fleeting, on your face, which will inflame it.
- If the antagonism is directed against you because you are a member of an out-group against whom the aggressor is prejudiced, remember the finding given in the last chapter (Abelson, *et al.*, 1998), that the more cohesive, similar and closely linked the members of an out-group are perceived to be, the more they may, unfairly, provoke negative reactions. Therefore, the researchers suggest: 'Emphasis on the out-group's variability of attitudes, or perhaps their internal disagreements, should discourage perceptions of entitivity (cohesiveness).'

*Source*: Abelson, R. P., N. Dasgupta, J. Park and M. R. Banaji (1998) 'Perceptions of the collective other', *Personality and Social Psychology Review*, vol. 2, pp. 243–250.
Duncan, B. L. (1976) 'Differential social perceptions and attributes of intergroup violence: Testing the lower limits of stereotyping of blacks', *Journal of Personality and Social Psychology*, vol. 34, pp. 590–598.
Duncan, B. L. (1979) 'The effects of race of harm-doer and victim on social perception and attributional behavior', *Journal of Psychology*, vol. 101, pp. 103–105.

**Table 6.7 Likely sources of aggressive behaviour**

| *Source* | *Comment* |
|---|---|
| Experiencing aggression | Feeling they have been attacked or unfairly treated is probably the most common cause (Infante *et al.*, 1992), may be inborn and can only be controlled, not unlearnt.[43] |
| Instrumental aggression | This is intimidation. It is most frequent in contractual relationships, when the intimidator can inflict real harm and does not mind the target's dislike and the target cannot easily retaliate (Gardner, 1992).[44] |
| Instinct | Whether aggression is instinctive is debated, but the drive to meet needs can certainly lead to aggression among both animals and people (Tedeschi *et al.*, 1974).[45] |
| Frustration | Freudian theory treats aggression as displacement of energy when goal-directed behaviour is frustrated. The target may be randomly selected. This source is controversial (De Charms and Wilkim, 1963).[46] |
| Imitation | Research has shown that imitation is powerful in leading to aggression (Bandura *et al.*, 1965).[47] |
| Justification | Verbal aggressiveness is related to believing verbal aggression is justified (Martin *et al.*, 1996).[48] |
| Anger | Though often correlated with aggression, anger is not proven to cause it – instead, the aggression may 'cause' the anger. Research shows that hostility and hatred are not linked to aggression (Manning and Taylor, 1975).[49] |

Assertiveness recognises other people's rights, but also requires them to respect our own. Assertion techniques include basic statements of position, assertive questioning, pointing out discrepancies between others' statements and actions and warning of the consequences of continuing to over-ride our rights. Argumentativeness, or willingness to engage in constructive persuasive debate, is valued, for instance by superiors in their subordinates, so long as it is accompanied by an affirming communication style.

Anxiety, which may be caused by past experience of hurtful interactions, is often expressed in self-defeating inner talk. Reassurance and stroking can help other people control their anxiety-ridden behaviour. If we ourselves suffer from anxiety in social or business interactions, our performance at self-presentation is likely to suffer, but there are step we can take to help overcome it.

Aggressive behaviour has many causes, including reacting to perceived attack, attempts to intimidate to gain objectives, ungratified needs, frustration and imitation. Most people who act aggressively believe that aggression is justified. Using silence, waiting, acknowledging the other's anger without showing

**Box 6.11**

### How to create a generally favourable impression

- Use a degree of openness. Make a disclosure, but avoid intimate revelations too soon in a relationship.
- Show liking for the other person. This is undoubtedly the most powerful way of being liked in return. It works with everybody, but especially with people who are insecure (Byrne, 1969).
- Show similarity with the other person. Agreement works, but expressing similar attitudes as if spontaneously, is even more effective.
- Try stroking. This can be done through body language – visibly listening, nodding, not interrupting and keeping your gaze under control.
- Adopt some aspects of the communication style of other person.
- Assess and confirm the other person's expectations about yourself, or at least do not prove them wrong.
- Resist the temptation to put the other person right on small, irrelevant facts.
- Allow for cultural differences.
- You can make an inventory of your strengths and weaknesses in managing the impression you make on others. It is best to use it repeatedly about different interactions soon after they are completed, rather than to complete it on the basis of your current self-image. When you have a sample of ten or more inventories, you can compile a fairly realistic analysis of your own performances.

*Source*: Byrne, D. (1969) 'Attitudes and attraction' in L. Berkowitz (ed.) *Advances in Experimental Social Psychology*, vol. 4. New York: Academic Press.

fear, and appropriate stroking can help others retreat from their aggression. It is important, though sometimes difficult, to avoid letting their aggression provoke us into retaliating.

## CULTURAL AND GENDER DIFFERENCES IN IMPRESSION MANAGEMENT

Self-presentation is a concern that exists in all cultures, but its goal varies.[50] In individualist cultures, such as those of north European countries, maintaining consistency between the private and public self-images, and maintaining one's own face, is paramount. Things are different, however, in more collectivist cultures, such as those of Greece and central Europe. In a collectivist culture, the goal is to present the self as an appropriate member of the social network and to help others maintain a similarly appropriate face. At a more detailed level, the precise behaviours implied by the appropriate self-presentation vary from culture to culture. For instance, Collier[51] found that politeness is a rule of appropriate

**Box 6.12**

## European variations in expectations of self-presentation

Germans expect formal work attire, and terms of address (except among computer specialists) and seriousness. They also expect others to conform, and to avoid stepping out of their prescribed role or behaving at all eccentrically. They may take this to the extent of commenting on deviations. To watch over each other's behaviour is seen as a social duty. In Italy, a good dress sense, dignified style and being cultured are important in giving a good impression. For Spaniards, breeding and manners are important; others' personal qualities (rather than competence) must be honoured; modesty is expected rather than assertiveness. Among younger people in the United Kingdom, traditional British deference is giving way to assertive individualism but understatement still predominates and self-aggrandisement is frowned on. The use of humour is common, sometimes as a cover for embarrassment. However, this should not be mistaken for a lack of seriousness about the task. Dutch people accommodate highly to people from other cultures, but look for directness and straightforwardness, while disliking pretentiousness or self-aggrandisement. In Sweden, egalitarian values mean that status markers are little used: first names are used early and universally. Conversational style is direct and can seem abrupt. Interrupting a speaker is not done but the non-speaker may give no signs of listening.

behaviour in different ethnic groups across the United States but the particular behaviours which are defined as polite vary.

The work context can over-ride cultural variations in self-presentations. Cai and Donohue[52] found that during intercultural negotiations between Taiwanese and US Americans, the effects of culture on facework were limited. In fact, they concluded, contextual factors of the interaction have a stronger influence than shared cultural values on the overall use of facework. Similarly, Dinges and Lieberman[53] showed that the differences between work situations such as firing, selection and promotion interviews had more influence on what was judged to be communication competence than the culture or gender of the participants.

Being noticeable and different makes impression management particularly important for women and other minorities at work. Women managers are more inclined than men to try to act as good examples, which places them under extra pressure to perform, ingratiate and possibly to supplicate. These self-presentations in turn reinforce gender stereotypes of women as weak and dependent, leading to the impression that they lack some of the abilities required for higher-level positions. Women are less likely than men to intimidate or to self-promote. They tend not to claim credit for success but report low performance expectations and attribute failure to lack of ability, which can result in them being taken at their own valuation.[54] The most effective members of both sexes adopt aspects of the styles of the other sex, according to a study of mixed sex groups discussing business problems over 15 weeks. In the study, the most effective men softened their speech with tag questions and qualifications, changed topics less abruptly and were more self-disclosing than the other men. The most effective women used more slang, more third-person pronouns and longer, more complex sentences, refused to be interrupted and addressed the whole group rather than the person who asked the last question or made the last comment.[55]

## SUMMARY – CULTURAL AND GENDER DIFFERENCES IN IMPRESSION MANAGEMENT

Impression management is a concern in all cultures but has different goals and is enacted differently in different cultures. Adopting elements of the style of the opposite sex is the most effective work self-presentation; this may also apply to intercultural impression management at work.

## WORK APPLICATIONS FOR SELF-PRESENTATION

Giving an impression is unavoidable in all interactions at work but skilled self-presentation is particularly important for self-introduction, team presentations, expressing opinions and making and handling complaints. Boxes 6.2, 6.3, 6.5, 6.7, 6.8, 6.9, 6.10 and 6.11 give summary guidance on different aspects of skilled self-presentation.

### Self-introduction

Because first impressions are important, the first few minutes of the first meeting are vital for job-interviewees, executives first meeting colleagues in a new department, managers introducing themselves to subordinates or organisational representatives greeting customers or clients for the first time. When two people first approach one another or are introduced, both try to gather information as a means of categorising one another. Both then infer traits from what they observe, gauge the attractiveness and similarity of the new acquaintance and decide whether to progress the relationship. Basically, both are deciding what level and degree of reinforcement they can expect from knowing each other better.[56] At work, though, new acquaintances are equally or more concerned with how to work together; personal preferences may have to be set aside. Even so, providing people newly met at work with the information that shows social compatibility lubricates the early stages of a work relationship.

**Box 6.13**

### How to apply a knowledge of self-presentation to introduce yourself

- Your manner in the meeting will be taken, however unreasonably, as typical of how you generally behave, though some allowance may be made for your situation. What is more, your manner and style will outweigh anything you can say. So if, for instance, you intend as a manager to operate democratically and to invite a great deal of participation from your subordinates, you must not dominate the discussion when you first meet them.
- Do not express opinions too forcefully on first meeting. Playing it low-key reduces the risk of solecisms and errors based on lack of knowledge. It allows time for you to obtain the information on which to base your approach.
- An appearance of energy, enthusiasm and enterprise (the three Es) always seems to be the most effective. This is particularly important if you are being interviewed for a job or promotion.
- With people who are of lower status than yourself, emphasise the things you have in common, rather than your differences. A more neutral position is better when meeting bosses or other higher-status people. In either case, keep careful control of any non-verbal mannerisms that may convey that you think you are superior, or that you are less than friendly.
- If your role requires that you exercise authority, you have to establish that authority right at the start. Expertise and experience are generally the most acceptable bases of authority at this stage. It always pays to talk briefly and modestly, but tellingly, of what you have done before. To achieve this, keep your recital as factual as possible.
- On the whole, it is easier to soften later the edges of an over-firm first impression than to harden up an over-soft one.
- Ask questions and listen to the answers. Show interest, but do not get embroiled in any debates or fights that people try to involve you with. Just say it is too soon for you to discuss this and you will be looking into every aspect of the job or relationship as soon as possible.
- Think through your first few sentences in advance. Think even harder about your initial non-verbal behaviour.
- When introducing yourself to someone from another culture, you will need to adjust your behaviour for their different expectations. For instance, if you are from Sweden (a low power distance culture) and are meeting your French manager (who is from a higher power distance culture), you should expect to show more deference than usual. Similarly, the French manager should expect to show less social distance towards a Swedish subordinate than usual. To get this right, you need to study cultural differences (Chapter 2 and boxes throughout this book), ways of communicating interculturally (Chapter 7) and ways of working interculturally (Chapter 12).

## Team presentations

When a group of people is acting as a team with an audience, for instance as a negotiating or presentation team, it has two sets of images to project. There is the particular image required by the occasion, which may be one of professionalism, disdain for the offer on the table or business-like understanding of the client's needs. But there is also, and especially, a need to project a set of images about the team itself: that it is united (not to be split up by opposite-party manoeuvres), unanimous in its opinions and that there is no skeleton in its shared cupboard. To achieve this impression requires teamwork, which here means a high level of co-operation and co-ordination up front brought about by behind-the-scenes communication and consultation. Goffman's suggestion that 'an impression does not have to be sincere but it helps'[57] applies particularly to team impressions. For this reason among others it is advisable to build teams before public occasions arise. It takes time to develop smooth interaction patterns.[58]

Choice of team members is crucial. For impression management they must all be loyal, disciplined and circumspect. In addition, the team must be composed of members undertaking different roles. At least one member should be socially skilled and self-disciplined, prepared to offer a plausible reason for any disruptive event or to take blame in order to protect another team member. Another useful team member is someone who can be presented as an independent expert, one whose specialist knowledge has led her or him to a position supporting the team's case, and whose integrity makes it impossible that s/he should have any other reason for endorsing it. A certain distance must be kept between the other team members and this specialist, who should not participate fully in the discussion. S/he comes in only or mainly when asked for his or her expert opinion. There should be one team member who can plausibly be built up as authoritative, whose pronouncements are treated by all present as having additional weight. This person's authority has to be built up not only by their personal skill but also by the way the rest of the team treat them – with an obvious respect, even deference, with attentive listening whenever they speak, and some visible signs of agreement such as slight nodding. It should be taken for granted in anything said by other team members that the authority figure's judgement is right. Team performance depends on setting aside individual differences. For instance, normal status or positional differences may have to be sacrificed, though it is often easier, because more natural, to sustain the performance if these differences are taken into account in constructing the team.

Team members must be able to communicate with one another without endangering the impression that their unity is spontaneous, their public line independently reached. Whispering does not work well for this purpose. Word codes or non-verbal signals can be effective, if carefully designed, thoroughly learnt and subtly applied. The best communication systems within teams, though, really derive from the team members knowing one another's minds so well that they develop a sixth sense for what other team members are thinking. Though this may sound unrealistically mystical, it is not. It is what usually happens when the team that is presenting a proposal is also the team that has worked together on developing it over a period of time.

Team performances necessitate back-stage consultations about the position that will be taken publicly. Each team member must clearly understand his or her role, the team objectives, strategies and positions, and the signalling system. They must all agree to put aside disputes and conflict all the time the team is presenting. Thorough discussion and planning of roles and tactics are required but as the team approaches the time to meet the audience it must adopt the roles that will be enacted up front. Last-minute disagreements, for instance, must be avoided or suppressed, or the illusion of solidarity will not be created in the team members' own minds and the performance may seem insincere.

The members of the team who are speaking, or the team chairperson, should bring in the contributions of other team members. This is both to draw on the full range of member abilities, knowledge and experience and to reinforce the team impression. Having one spokesperson, or even two, will not help create an impression of team cohesion. Every team member should be allocated an aspect of the proposal on which they are prepared to speak and every attempt within reason should be made to ensure that that happens. The non-verbal behaviour of members of the team who are not, for the time being, speaking, is crucial in sustaining the face of the spokesperson. They should help focus attention on the speaker, by looking towards him or her with an attentive expression, showing agreement and enhancing his or her authority, for example by occasional nods. They should never show disagreement or derogate from the speaker's authority, as by frowning or head shaking. The team's spokesperson should not have to fear being interrupted by fellow members.

There are two recurring problems in team presentations and negotiations. One is how to pass information (ammunition) to the team members who are currently speaking. The difficulties here are that the impression that the speaker is master of their subject may be dented and that they may be distracted from their train of thought. If the information is really vital, the usual written note is the least clumsy way, assuming the voice-in-the-ear technique used in broadcasting to be impractical. If it is possible for the team's chairs to be placed in a shallow crescent shape rather than a straight line, it may be possible to communicate non-verbally, but along the side of a straight-edged table this looks artificial. The most important point, however, is to keep such occasions to the very minimum. Non-speaking team members should take a very conservative view of the value of their stray thoughts and remembered data and exercise self-discipline in the matter. The other common problem occurs when the speaking member makes a significant error. Once again, it is better that minor mistakes go uncorrected and ignored in front of an audience. If amendment is unavoidable, a modification is better than a flat contradiction, and, above all, the speaker's face must be preserved.

To determine the strengths and weaknesses of your team presentation, use the guide given in Exercise 12.

## Expressing opinions

It is quite common at work to have to carry out courses of action which do not seem likely to be effective, nor, perhaps, ethical. Clearly most of us have a bottom line, a sticking-point beyond which we would have to say 'No', but short of that point many compromises are necessary and should be seen as part of the give and take of any organisational life. Some people find working life very difficult, and their colleagues find them very difficult, because they simply lack this reasonableness of attitude, this willingness to compromise. Others, however, have an appropriate attitude, but lack the interpersonal skill to enact it, and therefore find themselves either playing the 'Yes' man or woman or isolated because they seem unable to meet others half way.

Expressing opinions assertively helps to avoid these kinds of difficulties. This means stating views at the right pitch, neither too forcefully nor apologetically. People who can only express opinions in a dogmatic manner create the impression that they are so committed to their viewpoint that they can only change under duress. It is true that at work some points do need to made forcefully. For instance, a management team that has to present a plan to staff must maintain a united front if the staff are to be convinced and motivated to carry out the plan, whatever individuals' private doubts. In other circumstances a forceful presentation can be a source of strength because it mobilises the 'power of commitment'.[59] Usually, however, over-forceful expressions of opinions are harmful. Often, indeed, the very fact of having expressed an opinion very forcefully, and the reactions of others to that forceful expression can lead to losing an argument. At the other extreme from being over-dogmatic and over-forceful is non-assertiveness – expressing views so feebly that in effect the person says, 'Although I think this, I fully expect and accept that my view will be disregarded.' This is not the same as having no opinion on the matter, and stating that fact assertively. It is having an opinion, but attaching little or no importance to it and so to oneself.

**Box 6.14**

### How to express an opinion assertively

- Make clear what your opinion is and how strongly you are committed to it.
- Recognise that other people have other views that are equally worth being heard and considered as your own, but not more so.
- Communicate a willingness to change your opinion if you hear a better argument, or to set your opinion aside in the interest of, for instance, keeping the team united.

## Making and handling complaints

The key skill to use for making complaints is assertiveness. The objective is above all to have rights accepted and to achieve this without behaving aggressively.

Opening statements of complaints should therefore be in basic assertion mode. This means a clear statement of the problem and its consequences. The tone should be factual and unemotional. What is said should be concrete and precise, not vague. It is better to come directly to the point rather than beat about the bush, but to show some empathy with the position of the person receiving the complaint. For instance, the opening words might be, 'I'm sorry to tell you that I have a complaint to make about . . .'. It can be useful to plan the opening statement beforehand; this may mean writing it down and rehearsing it.

Expressing complaints in blaming mode should be avoided, as it is likely to provoke resistance and counter-attack. For this reason, it may be better to avoid any account of how the problem arose in the opening statement. Subsequently, the history should be discussed only if it is likely to contribute to working out a solution. The objective is to get the situation put right, not to express anger. It may be appropriate to describe anger as one of the consequences of the problem but it will not be appropriate to get angry during the complaint discussion. It is important to make clear right from the start that the person being addressed is being asked to deal with the problem. However, it is better to leave open the question of what they should do. This is partly because the discussion may generate more favourable solutions but also because an approach which seems to dictate to the other person, leaving them no room for contribution or discussion, is likely to generate a defensive climate in which antagonism can quickly surface. Defensive climates are considered more fully in Box 7.10.

Complaining assertively means giving the other person a fair chance to speak, listening to what they have to say, and showing that they have been heard. It does not mean accepting their argument, or being 'fobbed off' or bullied out of rights. If new information is revealed which seems to undermine a complaint, it is better to call an adjournment ('I'll need to think this over') than to concede, as concessions make it hard to re-open the issue. Assertive questioning should be used to fill any information gaps. A questionnaire for analysing and improving complaint-making behaviour is given in Table 6.10.

**Box 6.15**

1990 data from the UK Office of Fair Trading show that 51 per cent of a sample who had complained about a service and 23 per cent who had complained about goods they had bought were less than completely satisfied with the response they received. Other data suggest that dissatisfied customers tell twice as many people of their experience as satisfied customers and European motor industry data show that satisfied complainants talk to 5 others, the mollified to 10 and the dissatisfied to 14 (Mitchell, 1995). Clearly there is some way to go before complaint-handling skills are uniformly high and equally clearly there is a good deal at stake.

*Source*: Mitchell, V.-W. (1995) 'Handling consumer complaint information: why and how?', *Management Decision*, vol. 31, no. 3, pp. 21–28.

Handling complaints is a skill often needed at work. The complaint may be from a customer about delivery or product quality, from a client about service, from the manager of another department about lack of co-operation or inefficiency from staff, or any other of a long list. Many executives find these unexpected attacks, which is how they often appear to their target, among the most difficult interactions they have to deal with.

The objective when handling complaints, especially those that arise unexpectedly, is containment. Occasionally the matter can be resolved then and there, but often this can only be achieved by giving away something that should not be conceded. On the other hand, simply refusing to acknowledge the complaint or trying to pass the buck is only likely to lead to the complainer escalating the matter.[60] There are two kinds of escalation. The first is in the form of the complaint. For instance, what started out as an oral complaint may, if mishandled, subsequently be put in writing or raised with a higher authority. Preventing escalation of the form of the complaint calls for providing plenty of incremental steps. The complaint should be broken down into smaller parts in such a way that there is at least one that can be presented as the larger part and satisfied. It is better to suggest what the complainer should do next than to leave them to decide to escalate the matter in a major way. Particularly if they seem dissatisfied at the time when they are about to ring off, or walk away, options should be suggested for the next stage. Containment also calls for discretion. The case in Box 6.16 illustrates why. The second kind of escalation is in the level of aggression shown by the complainer. People who are dissatisfied with the response to a complaint usually feel frustrated, which may make them aggressive. Ways of dealing with aggression were discussed earlier in this chapter.

**Box 6.16**

**Mishandling a complaint – an example**

The case concerned problems that had arisen with controls installed by an interviewee's firm.

> We had a typical example of that last year where a control failed and the service engineer went in and said, 'There's a lot of inclusions [rough protrusions] in the chamber. It's a very rough surface, and maybe the float has jammed on a bit of metal sticking out.' Well, there was no way that could have happened, all the chambers have a rough finish anyway [*therefore floats are designed to cope*], he was just speaking in ignorance. It worked out that we had to machine all these chambers for this certain Hospital Board; there was nothing wrong in fact with our control and it turned out that someone had oiled the electrical switch, thinking it would work better with a bit of grease over it. But that one remark cost us a lot of money and time and written work, and could have got quite nasty.

*Source*: Interview with a sales manager for a boiler control manufacturer, author's research.

Research has shown that institutions and their representatives tend to handle complaints by first attempting the response which is least costly to the institution

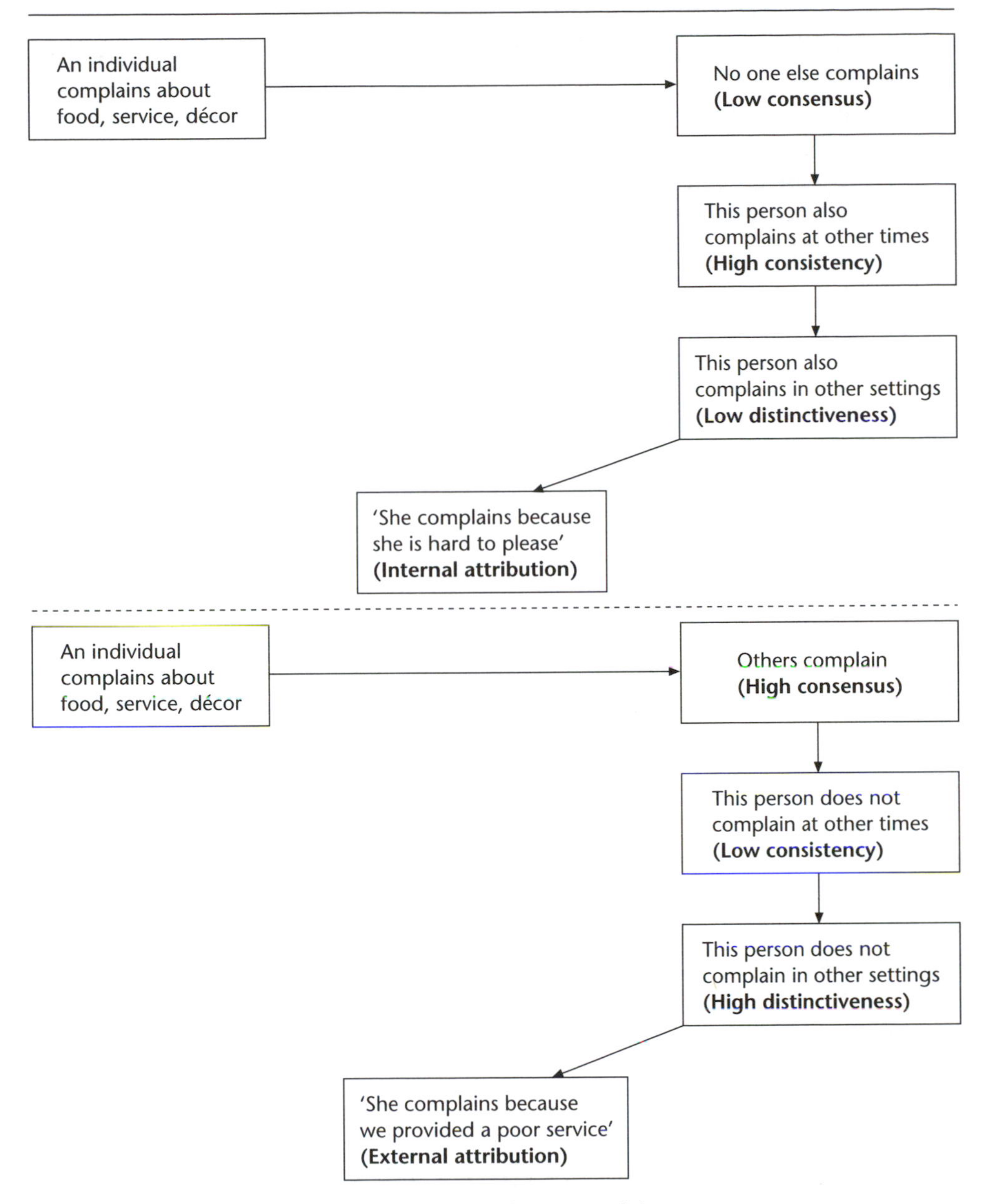


**Figure 6.4 Using attribution theory to analyse complaints.**

*Source*: Based on Greenberg, J. and R. A. Baron (1993) *Behaviour in Organizations*, 4th edn. Boston, Mass.: Allyn and Bacon.

– avoidance.[61] For example, a call centre assistant, confronted with an accusation of poor service by a caller, might say 'That is not my responsibility.' Only when avoidance fails and the complainer escalates the complaint does the institution respond more actively, following up by counter-persuasion, adjustment and finally suppression. The order is determined by the relative cost to the complaint receiver of each course of action. The weakness in this approach is that both avoidance and counter-persuasion increase the likelihood that the complainer will be driven to escalate the matter. By the time the institution is prepared to adjust, the complainer's demands may have increased.

**Box 6.17**

The woman was irate as she spoke to the national representative of the window-replacement service supplied by an insurance company. She had waited in the previous day for a fitter who never arrived; now, she had been kept waiting over an hour to learn when he was coming. The local service centre had promised over an hour before to try to rearrange his appointments to accommodate her and to ring her back. Now she was waiting in once more, afraid to use the telephone in case they called and not knowing what was happening. She began to threaten to complain to the insurance company.

Immediately she ended the call, the door bell rang. It was the fitter. The local service centre had rearranged his appointments as promised, but they had failed to communicate with the customer and so had lost the goodwill that their efforts could have created.

*Source*: Interview, author's research.

Containing the complainer's anger in fact implies going straight away to a degree of adjustment. The adjustment required, however, is not, initially at least, on the substantive issue – not money refunds, compensation or extra service. After all, many complaints are unjustified or unreasonable. Holiday tour operators, for instance, are plagued by people who routinely complain about their room or the hotel food in the hope of refunds. Figure 6.4 shows how attribution theory can be applied to decide when a complaint is reasonable. The adjustment needed for containment is in how the complaint receiver responds. Box 6.18 gives some suggestions.

## SUMMARY – WORK APPLICATIONS FOR SELF-PRESENTATION

Self-introductions to colleagues or others at work calls for constructing a sustainable face that will serve in future performances. Non-verbal behaviour is especially important in creating this first impression. Showing expertise and referring to experience help create an impression of authority, shared interests or experiences give an impression of friendliness, modest disclosures one of openness, questions and listening one of being a participative leader. The differing expectations of the new colleagues, based on cultural differences, should be taken into account.

Box 6.18

### How to contain complaints

- Do not try to avoid or counter-persuade.
- Show careful listening to the complainer's account.
- If possible, show understanding of the basis of the complaint.
- Show that the main points are being recorded and check back that the complainer accepts the version in the record.
- Show concern about the issue. Never belittle it.
- Take responsibility for action. That means consideration or investigation. Do not take responsibility for the problem. Do not take responsibility for putting the matter right. Never mention possible solutions, even without any hint of promise attached, until the next contact, after the investigation.
- Remember that handling complaints is an exercise in impression management: it is as important to make the complainer aware that you are doing these things as it is to do them.
- If the complainer is angry or aggressive, encourage them to talk, to allow emotional release. Do not interrupt but use probing questions, if necessary, to keep the flow of talk going. After a while most angry people, if not interrupted, start to repeat themselves and to exaggerate. They also gradually come to listen to themselves and to dislike what they hear. They then swing rapidly into a reasonable, often very reasonable, frame of mind.

A questionnaire to help you analyse your complaint-handling performances is given in Exercise 22.

To present well, a team must appear united because its individual members are each independently in agreement with the team position on an issue. This requires careful behind-the-scenes preparation. Thought must be given to the choice of team members, the allocation of roles such as chairperson and authority figure, the set of signals to be used, and what the team position is.

Expressing opinions in a way that asserts one's own rights while respecting those of others creates a good basis for work discussion and relationships.

Making and handling complaints are direct applications of assertion skills. In the case of making complaints the approach is aimed towards getting what is wrong put right, or obtaining redress, not expressing anger or blame. In the case of handling complaints the objective is containment and preventing escalation while avoiding getting hooked in by the complainer's anger or aggression.

## CHAPTER OVERVIEW

The purpose of studying self-presentation is to increase control over the impression given to others, rather than to project any particular image. We do not have a choice about whether to give impressions or not. Other people are bound to form impressions of us.

One useful way of conceptualising impression management is as performances, in which we act to sustain our own definition of the situation and of our role in it. We attempt to preserve our face against marring influences, such as losing concentration; fortunately others usually exercise tact towards us, as we do towards them. This chapter suggested ways of dealing with three special performance problems: negotiating social transitions, handling discrepant roles and being tempted to show off. Many people can improve their self-presentation by learning to act assertively. Assertiveness is a middle way between over-submissiveness and aggression. There are specific techniques for behaving assertively, both in the spoken words and in body language, and these can be developed through practice. Anxiety and aggressiveness, either other people's or one's own, undermine assertiveness; their sources and ways of controlling them are discussed.

Self-introduction, presenting and negotiating as a team, expressing opinions and making and handling complaints all call for special skill in self-presentation.

## EXERCISES

1. You are a public relations assistant account executive for a small but highly regarded agency with about 40 employees. During your two years with the agency, you have worked successfully on three different accounts. Last year you spent eight months working for one of the agency's oldest clients, the Chamber of Commerce. Now the Chamber has specially requested you to work on a new account for them – opposing extending paternity leave. You have ethical objections to working on such an account. Meet your boss and extricate yourself from the situation.

2. Describe the appearance, verbal and non-verbal behaviour of the sales representative/counter clerk/receptionist that would make you feel confident when:

   (a) buying a second-hand car;
   (b) making a first-time appointment with a hairdresser;
   (c) booking a hotel room over the telephone in an overseas country you have not visited before;
   (d) buying potted flowers from a garden centre;
   (e) opening a savings account in a bank you have not used before.

3. What would you say in order to bring about the following:

   (a) borrow something from a bad-tempered colleague.
   (b) ask the same bad-tempered colleague to return something you lent that should have been returned days ago.
   (c) refuse to donate to a leaving present.

4. Make a list of everyday situations in which you normally find it easy to act assertively. Next list everyday situations in which you have difficulty in acting assertively. Try to distinguish those in which you are liable to act aggressively and those in which you are liable to act non-assertively.

   *As a private-study exercise,* identify the emotional and interpersonal differences in the three types of situation and work on ways of handling more situations assertively.

   *As a group exercise,* bring this list to class and discuss it in your group. The object of the discussion is to identify the emotional and interpersonal differences between the three types of situation and to work on ways of handling more situations assertively.

5. The scale in Table 6.8 can be used to self-assess whether you communicate assertiveness, submissiveness or aggressiveness and whether you adjust for the cultural expectations of the person with whom you are interacting. It can be used for assessing performance in a wide range of work activities, including making and handling complaints, apologising and all kinds of meetings. *See the Appendix to find out how to analyse your responses to this questionnaire.*

6. Think of four positive work-related qualities you have.

**Table 6.8 How assertive was your behaviour?**

| In the interaction (meeting/interview/negotiation) just completed, I feel I: | *Strongly Agree* | *Agree* | *Neither Agree Nor Disagree* | *Disagree* | *Strongly Disagree* |
|---|---|---|---|---|---|
| 1. Gave a clear, unemotional description of the facts as I saw them | X______ | X______ | X______ | X______ | X______X |
| 2. Showed that I understood the other person's position | X______ | X______ | X______ | X______ | X______X |
| 3. Stated my feelings about the situation* | X______ | X______ | X______ | X______ | X______X |
| 4. Asked questions about the other person's thoughts (and feelings*) | X______ | X______ | X______ | X______ | X______X |
| 5. Was sensitive to the other person's cultural attitude to assertiveness | X______ | X______ | X______ | X______ | X______X |
| 6. Mentioned sanctions or threatened the other person | X______ | X______ | X______ | X______ | X______X |
| 7. Gave long explanations justifying my conduct | X______ | X______ | X______ | X______ | X______X |
| 8. Put the other person down | X______ | X______ | X______ | X______ | X______X |
| 9. Allowed the other person to put me down | X______ | X______ | X______ | X______ | X______X |
| 10. Adjusted my level of assertiveness to allow for the cultural attitudes of the other person | X______ | X______ | X______ | X______ | X______X |

* optional for work interactions

*As a private study exercise*, write down how you would describe those qualities in yourself:

(a) to a new social acquaintance;
(b) in a selection interview;
(c) as a newly appointed manager introducing yourself to a meeting of your subordinates.

*As a role play*, enact (b) and/or (c).

7. Nowadays it is common for people at work meetings to be asked to say a few words of self-description at the start, whenever there are 'new' members present.

   *As a private study or group discussion exercise*: What would you say about yourself? What impression would you try to convey? What verbal and non-verbal behaviour would help you to create that impression?

   *As a role play* enact the scene, with each person speaking in turn, either from a seated position or by standing and coming to the front of the room before speaking.

8. You are at a work gathering of colleagues where you have not previously met most of the people present. You notice one person you recognise as a manager in another department, and would like to meet, as there are problems regarding some overlapping aspects to your work (you are both on the same small e-mail circulation list). The person is standing and talking with a small group of people. You walk over to this group and become a part of the conversation so that you can get to know the person better.

   *As a private study or group discussion exercise*: What would you say to introduce yourself? Would you excuse yourself for breaking into their conversation? How would you create an opening for talking about your concerns to the person you want to meet?

   *As a role play* enact the scene. The roles are the self-introducer, the 'target' manager and two or more others in the group with whom s/he is speaking. The members of the group can help or hinder the self-introducer according to the needs of the course.

9. You are talking with your boss at the gathering described in Exercise 8 when you notice a person come in to whom you need to speak. You want to terminate your present conversation and go over to see them.

   Use this scenario for a private study, group discussion or role play exercise.

10. Introductory visit role play.

    *Role A*: You represent PQR, one of a number of companies that supply computer equipment to schools and manage their information technology needs. Your company has a strong position (about a 20 per cent market share) because it redesigns existing software into simple packages that can be used as teaching aids for reading and arithmetic. Its main rival, STU, with an about 33 per cent market share, does the same, but also supplies follow-up services direct, which your company does not do. The rest of the market is fragmented among a large number of smaller companies. PQR Co. is negotiating with Jurg Krahn Publishing, Germany's largest educational publisher, over a deal that will give the publisher the right to adapt your company's mathematics package to the German mathematics curriculum and distribute it to German-speaking schools and Germany's large after-school market. This could be the route for the company to establish a base on the Continent.

You have made an appointment to introduce yourself to the executive from the publishing company official who will decide whether or not the deal will go ahead. You are new to the company but experienced in the field.

*Role B:* You represent Jurg Krahn Publishing, Germany's largest educational publisher. You are about to receive an introductory visit from the new representative of PQR, a company that supplies computer equipment to schools. This company has a strong position (about a 20 per cent market share) because it redesigns existing software into simple packages that can be used as teaching aids for reading and arithmetic. Its main rival, STU, with an about 33 per cent market share, does the same, but also supplies follow-up services direct, which this company does not do. Another problem with this company is that it tries to sell overpowered and sophisticated equipment. However, their products are good and, most importantly in this market, reliable. The rest of the market is fragmented among a large number of smaller companies.

PQR and Jurg Krahn are negotiating over a deal that will give the publisher the right to adapt your company's mathematics package to the German mathematics curriculum and distribute it to German-speaking schools and Germany's large after-school market. You believe PQR's mathematics package to be the best in the field, but there have been difficulties in the negotiations over the royalty to be paid.

11. Team presentation role play.

The setting is a local authority. A team of three internal auditors enters a room in which two chairs are placed on each side of a square table; at the far side from the door two members of the Travel Department are seated. They get up, and hand-shakes and introductions are exchanged over the table. They all sit down, with the two auditors facing the two auditees. The auditors introduce themselves, explain the purpose of their audit, their roles and the process. They are faced with immediate aggression from one of the auditees, who is upset by the outcomes of past audits and the interference with the work of the department.

Role play the meeting. Use the team presentation questionnaire given at Table 6.9 to guide, analyse and get feedback on the performances.

**Table 6.9 How effectively does your team present itself?**

Each member of a team needs a well-defined job such as main spokesperson, chairperson, recorder and analyser, independent expert or authority figure.

1. Were the jobs of your team members suitable for the task in this meeting?
   Very suitable ——×——×——×——×—— Not at all suitable
2. Were the jobs appropriately allocated to individuals?
   Very appropriately ——×——×——×——×—— Not at all appropriately
3. Were their jobs clearly understood by the individual team members?
   Clearly understood ——×——×——×——×—— Not understood
4. Were the team objectives fully understood by each team member?
   Fully understood ——×——×——×——×—— Not understood
5. Did each team member accept and feel committed to the team objectives?
   Full commitment ——×——×——×——×—— No commitment
6. Were the strategies fully understood by each team member?
   Fully understood ——×——×——×——×—— Not understood
7. During the meeting, how effectively were member resources (abilities, knowledge and experience) deployed?
   With full effect ——×——×——×——×—— Poorly
8. Was signalling within the team effective?
   Yes ——×——×——×——×—— No
9. Was your signalling visible to the other parties?
   Not visible ——×——×——×——×—— Conspicuous
10. How much open conflict between team members surfaced during the meeting?
    Hardly any ——×——×——×——×—— A great deal
11. How much conflict was there within the team, that was suppressed but affected team performance?
    Hardly any ——×——×——×——×—— A great deal

Rate the behaviour of non-speaking members of the team on the following scales:

12. Non-verbal behaviour helping to focus attention on the speaker.
    High ——×——×——×——×—— Low
13. Non-verbal behaviour distracting attention from the team's speaker.
    Low ——×——×——×——×—— High
14. Non-verbal behaviour showing agreement with the team's speaker.
    High ——×——×——×——×—— Low
15. Non-verbal behaviour suggesting disagreement with the team's speaker.
    Low ——×——×——×——×—— High
16. Non-verbal behaviour enhancing the authority of the team's speaker.
    High ——×——×——×——×—— Low
17. Non-verbal behaviour derogating from the authority of the team's speaker.
    Low ——×——×——×——×—— High
18. Were there any interruptions by team members when other team members were speaking?
    None ——×——×——×——×—— Ten or more

Rate the contributions of speaking team members:

19. Bringing in contributions from other team members.
    Good ——×——×——×——×—— Poor
20. Boosting the authority of expert or spokesperson members.
    Good ——×——×——×——×—— Poor

*Note*: The more your team's 'profile' in this analysis tends towards the right of the scales, the worse, overall, you have diagnosed its performance to have been.

12. Complete the rating scale in Table 6.9 for a recently-completed team presentation.

13. You work for a small venue hire business. Your boss, who is passionate about theatre, wants to hire your largest space to a children's theatre group for a peppercorn rent for the three weeks starting on 26 December. This is your peak season for corporate entertaining. Role play telling your boss that you disagree with him/her and why.

14. Yesterday evening you saw your colleague drinking heavily at a party and then driving off in his company car. His/her conduct was not only illegal but contrary to company policy, which does not allow private use of company cars. Role play telling him/her that you saw the incident and that you disapprove.

15. It has long been the custom at your new workplace for staff to take a three hour lunch break on Fridays; in effect, it means that staff are working only a four and a half day week. You have been invited to join them, but you do not drink and do not approve. Role play refusing the invitation.

16. Your co-worker, off sick for two weeks, has agreed to your opening his/her e-mail at work. You find that a number of them contain racist jokes and it is clear that your colleague belongs to an e-mail group that circulates these. Role play telling your colleague that his/her behaviour is offensive and unacceptable.

17. You are busy at work when a manager from another department comes in to your office and accuses you of making an error in a cost calculation for a contract which the firm won on price. You realise that such an error would be very costly for the firm and embarrassing to him/her. At this point you are not sure whether you did in fact make this error.

    *As a private study or group discussion exercise*: What would you say? What impression would you aim to convey by your verbal and non-verbal behaviour? How?

18. A junior colleague has made an error in a cost calculation for a contract that the firm won on price. Such an error will be very costly for the firm and embarrassing to you. You have long suspected that this person is slapdash in their work. You go to their office to find out more.

    *As a private study exercise*: What would you say? What impression would you aim to convey by your verbal and non-verbal behaviour? How?

19. The cases at Exercises 17 and 18 can be used as the briefings for the two roles in a role play.

20. Handling complaints role play.

### Table 6.10 How well did you make your complaint?

This questionnaire is to help you analyse how well you make complaints. It should be completed shortly after you have in fact made or practised making a complaint. Circle the numbers that most closely match your feeling about the conversation. Think carefully before doing so, and give an example of the behaviour on which your judgement is based.

I feel that in making this complaint I:

1. Was sufficiently specific about the problem:

   True 1 2 3 4 5 False

   For example:

2. Gave the other person a fair chance to speak:

   True 1 2 3 4 5 False

   For example:

3. Was blaming the other person:

   True 1 2 3 4 5 False

   For example:

4. Was most interested in expressing angry feeling — 1 2 3 4 5 — Was most interested in solving the problem

   For example:

5. Was most interested in solving the problem — 1 2 3 4 5 — Was most interested in getting the other person to admit responsibility

   For example:

6. Used (tick one):
   Assertiveness (asserting my rights and position but acknowledging theirs).
   Non-assertiveness (failure to assert my rights adequately).
   Aggressiveness (refusing to acknowledge their rights and position).

*Role A* is a customer services agent at an airport, working for a ground services handling company. Late arrival of three planes has led to delays in unloading baggage; now the luggage of about 50 passengers from a ten-hour flight is missing an hour after their plane landed. The rest of the luggage from that plane arrived in the baggage hall late, but over 20 minutes ago. The passengers are tired and angry and feel obscurely unfairly treated. They take their complaint to the customer services agent, eventually reaching the front of a long queue.

*Roles B, C, D* (as required) are the angry passengers.

21. The scales in Table 6.10 can be used to assess how well you made a complaint.
22. The scales in Table 6.11 can be used to assess how well you dealt with a complaint.

**Table 6.11 How well did you deal with a complaint?**

This is a questionnaire to help you analyse how skilfully you deal with people who are making a complaint. It is best to use it with regard to a particular complaint, preferably just after the event.

Circle the numbers which most closely represent your feeling about the interaction. Think carefully before doing so and give an example of the behaviour on which your judgement is based:

I feel that in handling this complaint I:

1. Listened carefully to the complainer's account:

   True 1 2 3 4 5 False

   For example:

2. Probed for further details:

   True 1 2 3 4 5 False

   For example:

3. Fed back summaries of what the complainer said:

   True 1 2 3 4 5 False

   For example:

4. Listened actively:

   True 1 2 3 4 5 False

   For example:

5. Used (tick one):
   Assertiveness (asserting my rights and position but acknowledging theirs).
   Non-assertiveness (failure to assert my rights and position adequately).
   Aggressiveness (refusing to acknowledge their rights and position).

6. Took responsibility for (tick any that apply):
   The problem.
   Action – consideration or investigation.
   Action – putting the matter right.

## FURTHER READING


Back, K. and K. Back (1996) *Assertiveness at Work*, 3rd edn. Maidenhead: McGraw-Hill.

Fairhurst, G. T. and R. A. Sarr (1996) *The Art of Framing: Managing the Language of Leadership*. San Francisco: Jossey-Bass. Also relevant to Chapter 13 of this book.

Giaccalone, R. A. and P. Rosenfeld (1989) *Impression Management in Organizations*. Newbury Park, Calif.: Sage.

Giaccalone, R. A. and P. Rosenfeld (1991) *Applied Impression Management*. Newbury Park, Calif.: Sage.

Goffman, E. (1972) *Interaction Ritual: Essays on face-to-face behaviour*. Harmondsworth, Middlesex: Penguin Books.

Jones, E. E. (1964) *Ingratiation*. New York: Appleton-Century Crofts.

Leary, M. R. (1995) *Self-presentation: Impression Management and Interpersonal Behaviour*. Wisconsin: Brown and Benchmark.

## REFERENCES

1. Schlenker, B. R. (1996) 'Impression management' in A. S. R. Manstead and M. Hewstone (eds) *Blackwell Encyclopaedia of Social Psychology*. Oxford: Blackwell.
2. Rosenberg, M. (1990) 'Reflexivity and emotions', *Social Psychology Quarterly*, vol. 53, no. 1, pp. 3–12.
3. Deetz, S. (1990) 'Reclaiming the subject matter as a guide to mutual understanding: Effectiveness and ethics in interpersonal interaction', *Communication Quarterly*, vol. 38, no. 3, pp. 226–243.
4. Ting-Toomey, S. (1988) 'A face negotiation theory' in Y. Y. Kim and W. Gudykunst (eds) *Theories in Intercultural Communication*. Newbury Park, Calif.: Sage.
5. Levinson, S. C. (1983) *Pragmatics*. Cambridge: Cambridge University Press.
6. Goffman, E. (1959) *The Presentation of Self in Everyday Life*. New York: Doubleday.
7. Ibid.
8. Goffman, E. (1972) *Interaction Ritual: Essays on face-to-face behaviour*. Harmondsworth, Middlesex: Penguin Books.
9. Jones, E. E. (1964) *Ingratiation*. New York: Appleton-Century Crofts.
10. Drummond, H. (1993) 'The power of impression management', *Management Decision*, vol. 31, no. 3, pp. 16–20.
11. Chambliss, W. J. (1965) 'The selection of friends', *Social Forces*, vol. 43, pp. 370–380.
12. Gardner, W. L. and M. J. Matinko (1988) 'Impression management in organizations', *Journal of Management*, vol. 14, pp. 321–338.
13. Byrne, D. (1969) 'Attitudes and attraction' in L. Berkowitz (ed.) *Advances in Experimental Social Psychology*, vol. 4. New York: Academic Press.
14. Tedeschi, J. (1990) 'Self-presentation and social influence: an interactionist perspective' in M. J. Cody and M. L. McLaughlin (eds) *The Psychology of Tactical Communication*. Clevedon: Multilingual Matters, pp. 299–323.
15. Jones, E. E. and T. S. Pittman (1982) 'Toward a general theory of strategic self-presentation' in J. Suls (ed.) *Psychological Perspectives on the Self*. Glenview, Ill.: Scott, Foresman, pp. 231–296.
16. Schlenker, B. R. and M. F. Weigold (1992) 'Interpersonal processes involving impression regulation and management', *Annual Review of Psychology*, vol. 43, pp. 133–168.
17. Gordon, R. A. (1996) 'Impact of ingratiation on judgment and evaluations: A meta-analytic investigation', *Journal of Personality and Social Psychology*, vol. 71, pp. 54–70.
18. Allen, M.W. and R.H. Caillouet (1994) 'Legitimation endeavors: Impression management strategies used by an organization in crisis', *Communication Monographs*, vol. 61, no. 1, pp. 44–62.
19. Caillouet, R. H. and M. W. Allen (1996) 'Impression management strategies employees use when discussing their organization's public image', *Journal of Public Relations Research*, vol. 8, no. 4, pp. 211–227.
20. Arnold, W. E. and J. Johnson (1992) 'Perceptions of empathic messages and message sources', *International Journal of Listening*, vol. 6, pp. 83–88.
21. Norton, R. (1983) *Communicator Style: Theory, Applications and Measures*. Beverley Hills, Calif.: Sage.
22. Fairhurst, G. T. and R. A. Sarr (1996) *The Art of Framing: Managing the Language of Leadership*. San Francisco: Jossey-Bass.
23. Dumesnil, J. and B. Dorval (1989) 'The development of talk-activity frames that foster perspective-focused talk among peers', *Discourse Processes*, vol. 12, no. 2, pp. 193–225.

24. Fairhurst, G. T. (1993) 'Echoes of the vision: When the rest of the organization talks total quality', *Management Communication Quarterly*, vol. 6, no. 4, pp. 331–371.
25. Burgoon, J. K. and B. A. Le Poire (1999) 'Nonverbal cues and interpersonal judgments: Participants and observer perceptions of intimacy, dominance, composure and formality', *Communication Monographs*, vol. 66, no. 2, pp. 105–124.
26. Ekman, P. and W. V. Friesen (1968) 'Non-verbal behaviour in psychotherapy research' in J. M. Schlien (ed.) *Research in Psychotherapy*, vol. 3. Washington DC: American Psychological Association.
27. De Paulo, B. M. (1992) 'Nonverbal behavior and self-presentation', *Psychological Bulletin*, vol. 111, no. 2, pp. 203–243.
28. Ibid.
29. Jones, E. E. and R. E. Nisbett (1972) 'The actor and the observer: Divergent perceptions of the causes of behaviour' in E. E. Jones, D. E. Kanouse, H. H. Kelley, R. E. Nisbett, S. Valins and B. Weiner (eds) *Attribution: Perceiving the Causes of Behaviour*. Morristown, New Jersey: General Learning Press.
30. Osgood, C. E. (1966) 'Dimensionality of semantic space for communication via facial expressions', *Scandinavian Journal of Psychology*, vol. 7, pp. 1–30.
31. Snyder, M. (1974) 'Self-monitoring of expressive behavior', *Journal of Personality and Social Psychology*, vol. 30, pp. 526–537.
32. Snyder, M. (1987) *Public Appearances, Private Realities: The Psychology of Self-Monitoring*. New York: W. H. Freeman.
33. Kelley, C. (1979) *Assertion Training: A Facilitator's Guide*. San Diego, Calif.: University Associates, p. 14.
34. Langrish, S. (1981) 'Assertive training' in C. L. Cooper (ed.) *Improving Interpersonal Relations: Some Approaches to Social Skill Training*. London: Gower.
35. Stubbs, D. (1985) *How to Assert Yourself At Work*. London: Gower.
36. Waldron, V. R. (1999) 'Communication practices of followers, members, and protégés: The case of upward influence tactics', *Communication Yearbook*, vol. 22, pp. 251–299.
37. Stewart, R. A. and K. D. Roach (1998) 'Argumentativeness and the theory of reasoned action', *Communication Quarterly*, vol. 46, no. 2, pp. 177–193.
38. Gorden, W. I., D. A. Infante and J. Izzo (1988) 'Variations in voice pertaining to dissatisfaction/satisfaction with subordinate', *Management Communication Quarterly*, vol. 2, pp. 6–22.
39. Infante, D. A. and W. I. Gorden (1989) 'Argumentativeness and affirming communicator style as predictors of satisfaction/dissatisfaction with subordinates', *Communication Quarterly*, vol. 37, pp. 81–90.
40. Johnson, D. W. and R. T. Johnson (1979) 'Conflict in the classroom: controversy and learning', *Review of Educational Research*, vol. 49, pp. 51–70.
41. Sullivan, H. S. (1953) *The Interpersonal Theory of Psychiatry*. New York: Norton.
42. Bullmer, K. (1975) *The Art of Empathy*. New York: Human Sciences Press.
43. Bandura, A., D. Ross and S. Ross (1961) 'Transmission of aggression through imitation of aggressive models', *Journal of Abnormal and Social Psychology*, vol. 63, pp. 575–582.
44. De Charms, R. and E. S. Wilkins (1963) 'Some effects of verbal expressions of hostility', *Journal of Abnormal and Social Psychology*, vol. 66, pp. 462–470.
45. Gardner, W. L. III (1992) 'Lessons in organizational dramaturgy: The art of impression management', *Organizational Dynamics*, Summer, pp. 33–46.

46. Infante, D. A., K. C. Hartley, M. M. Martin, M. A. Higgins, S. D. Bruning and G. Hur (1992) 'Initiating and reciprocating verbal aggression: Effects on credibility and credited valid arguments', *Communication Studies*, vol. 43, no. 3, pp. 182–190.
47. Manning, S. A. and D. A. Taylor (1975) 'Effects of viewed violence and aggression: stimulation and catharsis', *Journal of Personality and Social Psychology*, vol. 31, 180–188.
48. Martin, M. M., C. M. Anderson and C. L. Horvath (1996) 'Feelings about verbal aggression: Justifications for sending and hurt from receiving verbally aggressive messages', *Communication Research Reports*, vol. 13, pp. 19–26.
49. Tedeschi, J. T., R. B. Smith and R. C. Brown Jr (1974) 'A reinterpretation of research on aggression', *Psychological Bulletin*, vol. 81, pp. 540–562.
50. Ting-Toomey, S. (1988) 'Intercultural conflict styles: A face-negotiation theory' in Y. K. Young and W. B. Gudykunst (eds) *Theories in Intercultural Communication*. Thousand Oaks Calif.: Sage.
51. Collier, M. J. (1989) 'Cultural and intercultural communication competence: current approaches and directions', *International Journal of Intercultural Relations*, vol. 13, pp. 287–302.
52. Cai, D. and W. A. Donohue (1997) 'Determinants of facework in intercultural negotiation', *Asian Journal of Communication*, vol. 7, no. 1, pp. 85–110.
53. Dinges, N. G. and D. A. Lieberman (1989) 'Intercultural communication competence: coping with stressful work situations', *International Journal of Intercultural Relations*, vol. 13, pp. 371–385.
54. Gardner, W. L. III, J. V.-E. Peluchette and S. K. Clinebell (1994) 'Valuing women in management: An impression management perspective of gender diversity', *Management Communication Quarterly*, vol. 8, no. 2, pp. 115–164.
55. Case, S. S. (1993) 'The collaborative advantage: The usefulness of women's language to contemporary business problems', *Business and the Contemporary World*, vol. 5, no. 3, pp. 81–105.
56. Mehrabian, A. (1969) 'A semantic space for non-verbal behavior', *Journal of Consulting and Clinical Psychology*, vol. 32, pp. 296–308.
57. Goffman (1972), op. cit.
58. Lau, J. B. and A. B. Shani (1988) *Behaviour in Organizations: An Experiential Approach*, 4th edn. Homewood, Ill.: Richard D. Irwin.
59. Schelling, T. C. (1960) *The Strategy of Conflict*. Cambridge, Mass.: Harvard University Press.
60. Mitchell, V.-W. (1993) 'Handling consumer complaint information: why and how?' *Management Decision*, vol. 31, no. 3, pp. 21–28.
61. Bowers, J. W. (1974) 'Communication strategies in conflicts between institutions and their clients' in G. R. Miller and H. W. Simons (eds) *Perspectives on Communications in Social Conflict*. Englewood Cliffs, New Jersey: Prentice Hall.

# 7 Communicating at work

## CHAPTER INTRODUCTION

Whether measured by job level, upward mobility, performance appraisal ratings or current salary divided by age, communication abilities help people to progress in organisations.[1] In small businesses, the owners' communication abilities affect how well they are regarded by their employees. To communicate is to send and receive messages using a mutually intelligible symbol system. Communication may be one- or two-way, face-to-face or indirect, formal or informal, and messages can be transmitted verbally or non-verbally. One-way communication, as when the Chief Executive Officer (CEO) sends a 'round-robin' e-mail to all staff, has taken place if the message is received and comprehended by those to whom it is addressed. If a staff member replies, and is read and comprehended by the CEO, two-way communication has taken place. In this book we are mainly concerned with face-to-face communication, which, unlike mass-media communication, allows instant feedback. It allows the sender to detect almost at once how the receiver is reacting to his or her message. In formal communication, the sender speaks in a professional or commercial capacity – for instance, as a salesperson to a prospect. Informal communication at work can also be directly job-related. For example, two colleagues may happen to meet in the corridor and stop to discuss next week's production schedule or next year's staff budget. Informal communication that is not job-related, such as an over-lunch discussion about summer holiday resorts, can also be valuable because it allows colleagues and, on occasion, representatives of different organisations, to get to know one another better and build better work relationships. Communicating involves both verbal and non-verbal behaviour. Disagreement may be expressed by saying, 'I don't agree with you there' or by a frown. A customer may express indifference to a sales pitch by saying, 'That's all very well, but it's not much use to me' or by a yawn. The emphasis, though, switches to the intentional transmission of messages by a sender, in contrast to self-presentation, which covers conveying information both intentionally and unintentionally.

High-quality communication is effective and appropriate. This means it is able to produce the effects intended by the communicator and makes sense to the receiver in terms of wording, statements and logic. The aim of this chapter is to help readers to understand how to communicate effectively and appropriately at work by describing:

**Box 7.1**

> A Business Development Manager for a firm of solicitors said, 'I used to sit in my office, working away, and feel that no one ever let me know what was going on. Then I realised that everyone was too busy to make sure I was kept in the picture, and I was too busy to read all the paperwork that might have told me. So I started making it my business to find out, mainly by talking to people informally, being willing to ask naive questions and so on. It was hard at first, because I felt I was showing ignorance about things people would expect me to be aware of. But once I got past that, I found I not only got to hear about opportunities I would have missed, but my work became much more enjoyable.'
>
> *Source*: Interview, author's research.

- the functions of communication;
- the effects on communication of language, speech acts and one- or two-way communication;
- differences in how people from different social categories and groups communicate;
- how to overcome the barriers to good communication (some are intrinsic, some are set up by individual-level influences or group differences in communication, others arise from inter-group communication);
- the importance of following an accepted ethical code;
- the meaning of communication competence and how to achieve it both intra- and interculturally by applying facework and politeness to communication elements, accommodating, grounding and managing anxiety and uncertainty;
- how to apply communication skills to work activities including coaching, mentoring, consultancy, employee communications and service encounters.

## FUNCTIONS OF COMMUNICATION

When people communicate, certain consequences follow almost inevitably. These consequences include the following:

- Content data are communicated. Though perhaps uppermost in most Europeans' minds, this function is not universal. In non-Western cultures, the emphasis on content is less. Even in Western cultures, greetings, for instance, contain virtually no content data. Their purpose is to acknowledge that another person is recognised and affirm that the relationship with that person remains in being.
- Signals show how literal meaning should be taken, interpreted, filtered or understood. Signalling is achieved both verbally and para-verbally (by voice tone or facial expression linked to content).[2] For example, an industrial sales representative might quote a price, then laugh to signal the possibility of discounts and rebates.

- Relationship data are communicated. Senders inescapably transmit messages about their view of their relationship with the receiver.[3] Two key dimensions here are the sender's perceived levels of superiority/equality/inferiority and of intimacy/friendliness/neutrality/hostility towards the receiver.

  In the West, self-disclosure has been shown to be the most powerful strategy available to promote both egalitarianism and affiliation. Disclosure means voluntarily making available information about the self that would not normally be accessible to the other at that moment. It serves to escalate a relationship towards positive affiliation because of the norm of reciprocity – the social pressure on people to produce equivalent responses.[4] Reciprocating self-disclosures at a similar level is the norm in most situations, but in the work context, subordinates, clients and patients do most of the disclosing. Even though in some cultures, such as the Japanese, people generally favour a low level of self-disclosure,[5] it is still one of the main components in effective communication with people from different cultures.[6]
- Communicative control is distributed. Usually, in Western cultures, how 'air time' is allocated is determined in one of two ways. One is a competitive process in which each participant transmits messages implicitly designed to obtain control. In the other, one participant claims control and the other or others implicitly concede. Messages designed to obtain control include using formal terms of address and pronouns (*vous* rather than *tu* in French), doing most of the talking, initiating 90 per cent of the topics, posing 90 per cent of the questions raised, asking further questions before the last one has been answered, interrupting more, determining the 'agenda' and when to end the encounter and exhibiting a relaxed posture (arms-akimbo, reclining or leaning backwards, open legs).[7,8] These control messages limit the options available to other participants. It is likely that communicators usually seek optimal control distribution rather than dominance but there are exceptions, which may occur more frequently at work.
- Participants experience a subjective sense of social identity and community membership. For example, by using 'organisation-speak', people may reinforce their sense of membership in their company.

Figure 7.1 shows these functions of communication in diagrammatic form.

## SUMMARY – FUNCTIONS OF COMMUNICATION

When people communicate, content and relationship data are transmitted, plus signals to show how the literal meaning should be interpreted. Communicative control is distributed. Participants experience a subjective sense of social identity. These consequences have received the label of communication functions.

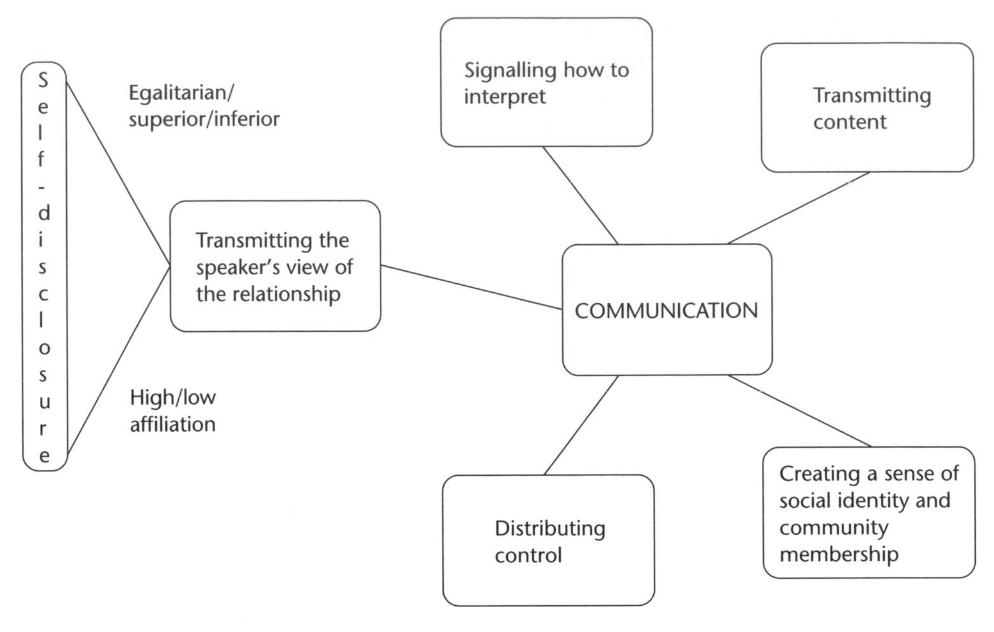


**Figure 7.1 Functions of communication.**

## COMMUNICATION PROCESSES

Interacting effectively depends on understanding the impact of language, communication rules, speech acts, communicator style and the differences between one- and two-way communication.

### The impact of language

Only messages can be transmitted and received. Meanings cannot be transmitted but must be inferred by the receiver. Senders must encode their meanings into symbols, choosing those that are likely to be familiar to their audience both in themselves and in what they stand for. Thus communicating entails the use of language, though the language may be verbal or non-verbal. The language used affects people's responses to situations. For instance, receivers may see the same situation as a strength or a weakness, a problem or an opportunity, depending on how the sender expresses it.[9]

### Communication rules

Language, whether verbal or non-verbal, follows rules of coherence and efficiency. Communication occurs only if the rules are followed by both sender and understood by the receiver. To be coherent, a message must be framed in a way that will make sense within the perspective of the receiver and be seen by them as a sincere move in a plan to achieve a goal.[10] For example, if someone says in the presence of the person with whom they share an office, 'Now, where did I put that blue folder?' the spoken words will make sense to the receiver only if they know which blue folder is referred to. Furthermore, it will work as a question (and not a rhetorical question) only if the receiver believes that the sender wants an answer. For efficiency, communicators must follow the rules of relevance, quality (being truthful), quantity (providing enough but not too much information) and manner (not being obscure, disorganised or ambiguous). Applying these rules is required in order to follow a 'co-operative principle'. This principle allows listeners to assume that speakers are being co-operative and so make a wide range of inferences which would otherwise not be possible.[11] This, in turn, allows speakers to imply a wide range of meanings without explicitly stating them. For example, if a speaker says, 'The XYZ Company has 35 per cent of the market', while it would be logically impossible for the statement to be true if the XYZ Company has less than 35 per cent of the market, it could be true if it has more than 35 per cent. Therefore, to tell a listener explicitly what XYZ Company's market share is, the speaker would have to say, 'The XYZ Company has exactly 35 per cent of the market.' The principle of co-operativeness, however, allows the receiver to assume that if the speaker means that the XYZ Company has more than 35 per cent, s/he would say so (e.g. by saying 'The XYZ Company has at least 35 per cent of the market') and so to understand that s/he means that the company has just exactly 35 per cent. These efficiency rules, it is claimed, are never violated without disrupting the flow of conversation or affecting the perceptions of others in the conversation. However, the violations may be seen as intentional and receivers may read inferences into that interpretation, such as an intention to deceive.

## Speech acts

To speak is not only to state or describe something, it is actually to *do* something. Speakers do not speak only to give information. They may have one or more of a range of intentions, including requesting, disagreeing, qualifying, ordering, promising or a number of other possibilities.[12] If the receiver does not understand what action the speaker is performing, what their intention is, the communication will fail. For instance, if when Person A asks a question, the receiver, Person B, understands the words, but not that A intends to ask a question, B is unlikely to give an answer, and the communication will fail. Speech act theory identifies what it takes to have an intention understood. There are guidelines for how to use speech to accomplish a particular intention. For instance, if A wants something, s/he makes a request, and does it in a form that B will understand to obligate him or her either to grant it or to turn it down.

## Communicator style

People transmit messages on two levels: an informative level and one that transmits how the speaker expects the message to be responded to (the style message). Receivers have such a strong tendency to expect others to send a style message that they will infer one even if none is transmitted (an abnormal situation) and will try to identify one using their previous perceptions of the speaker's usual style. Inability to detect or infer a style message will make a listener uneasy and disrupt communication, it has been argued.[13]

Figure 7.2 shows these basic process rules for making communication work.

## One- and two-way communication

One-way communication has different characteristics from two-way, as shown in Table 7.1. Each type of communication has its uses, depending on the requirements of the situation, but here we shall be concerned mainly with two-way communication. Some comments on one-way communication are given in the section on making presentations in Chapter 8.

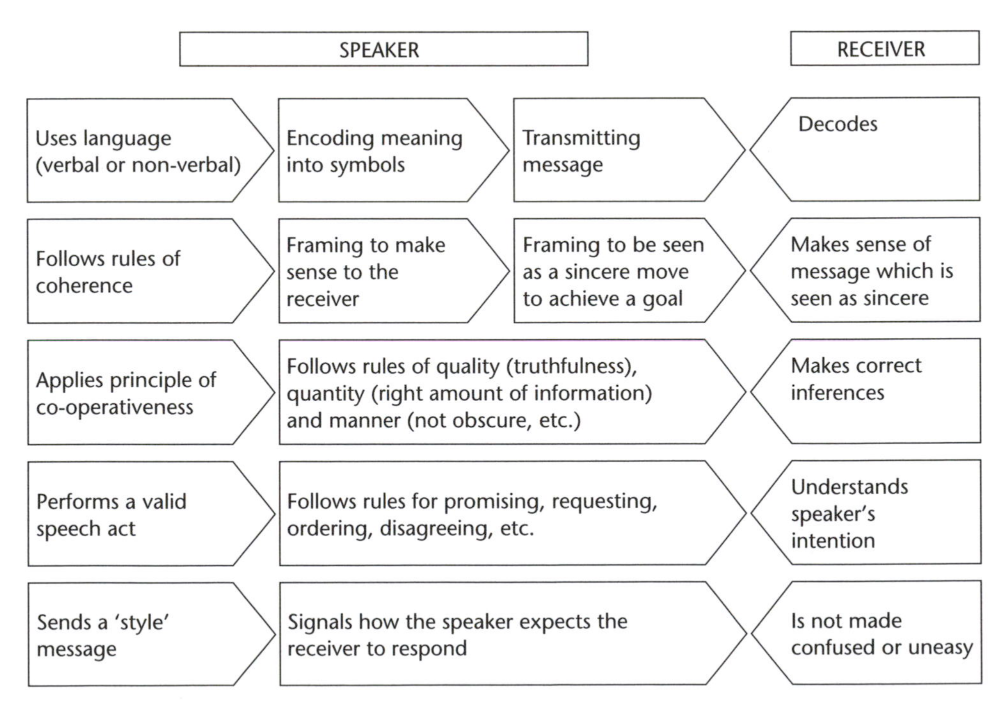


**Figure 7.2 Basic process rules for communicating.**

**Table 7.1 Characteristics of one- and two-way communication**

| *One-way communication* | *Two-way communication* |
|---|---|
| Is fast | Is slow |
| Looks efficient but is often inaccurate because of lack of feedback about how the receiver perceives the message | Looks noisy and disorderly but is often more accurate – possible misunderstandings can be checked out and corrected |
| Needs planning | Planning is less essential |
| Is less threatening to the sender | The sender is vulnerable |
| The receiver can feel frustrated | The receiver often feels more confident |

## SUMMARY – COMMUNICATION PROCESSES

Very different messages can be transmitted about the same situation according to the language used by the sender. Spoken messages must follow rules for coherence and efficiency, including the principle of co-operativeness. Speech acts must allow receivers to infer the type of communicative act intended by the speaker. Communicators' style messages must let receivers know what type of response the speaker expects. Two-way communication has different characteristics and uses from one-way communication.

## COMMUNICATION PRACTICES OF DIFFERENT SOCIAL CATEGORIES AND GROUPS

There are differences in the communication practices of members of different social categories and groups. These differences are relatively minor. Nevertheless, they affect how the members of some groups are responded to and how they are treated more generally. Status, culture, gender and disability are the variables whose effects on communication have received most attention to date.

### Status and communication

Members of lower-status groups often acknowledge in-group inferiority in public situations, while privately believing that their group is just as good as or better than others. This is a strategic response to avoid conflict.[14] These findings show that the apparent attitudes of members of low-status groups cannot be taken at face value.

### Culture and communication

Culture conditions attitudes towards communication, communication processes and information systems,[15] communication functions, uses and styles.

The communication functions described in an earlier section of this chapter are believed to apply universally. However, the emphasis varies from culture to culture. There are differences in the relative value placed by different cultures on control, affiliation, content and relationship in communication. Japanese culture, for instance, places a very high value on communicating subtle aspects of feeling and relationship and a much lower value on communicating information. Most Japanese people also believe that the most important things cannot be communicated in language. Most Western cultures, despite some recent shifts, are the opposite. Not only do they emphasise communicating content at the expense of relationship but they tend to treat what cannot be expressed in language as not worth attending to. (Women from Western cultures, though, are closer to the Japanese in this respect.) How speech functions to affirm social identities also varies across speech communities (which can include work organisations). A study of four communities found four different ways: to reveal and reinforce the sender's place in a hierarchical social structure, to reaffirm membership of a culture that values the unique self, to affirm equality of persons and to bond.[16]

In different cultures there are differences in whether language is normally used for negotiation or ratification. In some societies relationships are thought of as spontaneously created by individuals and language is used to negotiate those relationships. In other societies, however, relationships are thought of as predetermined and set. In these cultures, language performs the function of ratifying pre-existing relationships. In business negotiations, Asians, who follow the ratification model, may state their positions less extremely if they feel that not to do so would disrupt the harmony of the relationship. In contrast, Westerners may assume that each party has only in mind achieving their own best advantage and may state their positions strongly even if it should cause a feeling of disharmony. These differences can lead to misunderstandings and conflict.

Low-context cultures (LCCs) and high-context cultures (HCCs) are ways of differentiating cultures on the basis of their preferred communication styles.[17] LCCs, such as those of most European countries, value linear logic, direct verbal interaction and verbal and non-verbal styles that express the individual and his or her own values. HCCs, like that of Japan, value spiral logic, indirect verbal interaction and verbal and non-verbal styles that express group and cultural values. In HCCs, understanding one another depends much more on the shared knowledge of the cultural context. This means that to communicate effectively with people from high context cultures, greater awareness of their culture is required. HCC is 'the process of drawing meaning from the social context'. Meaning may be found purely in the context – in Japan, silence can be interpreted as disagreement – or the context may modify the spoken message, as when saying, 'That may be difficult' but meaning 'That's impossible'.

Tables 7.2 and 7.3 analyse cultural differences in ways of communicating.

**Box 7.2**

## Cultural variations in communication practices

- Perceptions differ on what is going on in the course of a conversation or discussion. For example, Chinese immigrants' and North Americans' perceptions of interactions were shown to differ on six dimensions to do with paying compliments, including how many compliments were paid and which adjectives were complimentary (Fong, 1998).
- Western (individualist) cultures emphasise speaking skills and sender strategies, whereas Eastern (collectivist) cultures emphasise listening and interpretation (Okabe, 1983). In collectivist cultures, both sender and receiver focus on, and are sensitive to, each other. Receiver orientation allows the sender to formulate indirect messages to avoid disturbing smooth relations, knowing that the receiver will determine the underlying meaning by weighing the message and the context appropriately. Markus and Kitayama (1994) called this phenomenon mind reading.
- In international organisations, the overall patterns of communication with in- and out-group members differ for workers from different countries. For instance, Japanese workers, who identify strongly with other in-group members, communicate more social distance from out-group members than US workers do (Suzuki, 1998).
- When making requests, individuals high in interdependence are more likely to use hint strategies on the first and second occasions, when individuals high in independence are more likely to use direct strategies. However, when non-compliance is high, both inter-dependent and independent individuals resort to using direct strategies (Kim *et al.*, 1998).
- In potentially offending situations, Japanese respondents are more likely than their US counterparts to use statements of remorse, reparation, compensation and requests for forgiveness. However, both cultures share the basic norm of offenders feeling compelled to respond to potentially offending situations (Sugimoto, 1997).
- Compared with Americans, Japanese communicators differentiate criticism more finely as a function of how close their relation is to the target person. Japanese (but not Americans) associate critical accounts or treating a decision affecting the target person as impersonal with a lower value of maintaining the relationship (Saeki and O'Keefe, 1994).
- Min-Sun Kim (1994) found that the perceived importance of clarity is higher in individualist cultures, whereas the perceived importance of not hurting the receiver's feelings and minimising imposition is higher in more collectivist cultures. All three (Korean, Hawaiian, US students) rated equally the importance of effectiveness and avoiding negative evaluation by the receiver.

*Sources*: Fong, M. (1998) 'Chinese immigrants' perceptions of semantic dimensions of direct/indirect communication in intercultural compliment interactions with North Americans', *The Howard Journal of Communications*, vol. 9, no. 3, pp. 245–262.

Kim, M.-S. (1994) 'Cross-cultural comparisons of the perceived importance of conversational constraints', *Human Communication Research*, vol. 21, pp. 128–151.

Kim, M.-S., H.-C. Shin and D. Cai (1998) 'Cultural influences on the preferred forms of requesting and re-requesting', *Communication Monographs*, vol. 65, no. 1, pp. 47–66.

Markus, H. R. and S. Kitayama (1994) 'The cultural construction of self and emotion: Implications for social behaviour' in S. Kitayama and H. R. Markus (eds) *Culture, Self and Emotion*. Washington, DC: American Psychological Association, pp. 1–19.

Okabe, R. (1983) 'Cultural assumptions of East and West: Japan and the United States' in W. Gudykunst (ed.) *Intercultural Communication Theory: Current Perspectives*. Beverly Hills: Sage, pp. 21–44.

Saeki, M. and B. J. O'Keefe (1994) 'Refusals and rejections; designing messages to serve multiple goals', *Human Communication Research*, vol. 21, pp. 67–102.

Sugimoto, N. (1997) 'A Japan–U.S. comparison of apology styles', *Communication Research*, vol. 24, no. 4, pp. 349–369.

Suzuki, S. (1998) 'In-group and out-group communication patterns in international organisations: Implications for social identity theory', *Communication Research*, vol. 25, no. 2, pp. 154–182.

**Table 7.2 Relations among different cultural values and communication styles**

| *Cultural values* | *Communication styles* | *Comment* |
|---|---|---|
| High uncertainty reduction | Expressive | |
| Low uncertainty reduction | Phlegmatic | |
| High masculinity | Assertive, competitive | Except among Japanese |
| High femininity | Supportive, co-operative | |
| High power distance | High formality, low disclosure and openness | This applies to manager–subordinate interactions; depends on power balance |
| Low power distance | Low formality, high disclosure and openness | |
| High individualism | Competitive | Mediated by self-concepts |
| High collectivism | Co-operative with in-group | Mediated by self-concepts |

**Table 7.3 Differences in communication practices of people from collectivist and individualist cultures**

| *Collectivism* | *Individualism* |
|---|---|
| High context | Low context |
| Ratification | Negotiation |
| Emphasis on relationship data | Emphasis on content data |
| Emphasis on listening and interpretation | Emphasis on speaking skills and strategies |
| More social distance communicated with out-group members | Less difference in speaking to in-group versus out-group members |
| Hinting preferred in seeking compliance | Directness preferred in seeking compliance |
| Remorse readily expressed | Remorse not readily expressed |
| Criticism adjusted for relationships | Criticism not adjusted for relationships |
| Emphasis on minimising imposition | Emphasis on clarity |
| Emphasis on showing respect | Domination and subordination often feature |

**Box 7.3**

When Americans write letters, they go from major to minor, from generalities to specifics. They immediately state what they're planning to speak about and then proceed to fill in the details. Azerbaijanis approach from the opposite direction – developing ideas from minor to major. The point we want to emphasize always comes at the end – like an accumulative whole. American letters puzzle Azerbaijanis. We wonder why anyone would want to write two or three pages if they've already said everything in the first sentence?

*Source*: Mammadov, G. (1994) 'Traditions in transition across cultures: Western logic, Eastern passions', *Azerbaijan International*, vol. 2, no. 2, pp. 46–48.

Servaes[18] argues that because each culture operates out of its own logic, each culture has to be analysed on the basis of its own logical structure. Cross-cultural and intercultural communications are only successful when these logical foundations are understood and accepted as equal by the people concerned.

Box 7.4

**European variations in work communication practices**

In France there is an emphasis on written reports rather than oral presentations and on formality in work communication. However, informal networking and 'politicking' are important in actually making things happen. The Dutch, on the other hand, practise widespread dissemination of information and 'behind the scenes' influence is discouraged. In Germany, there is a tendency for everything to be put in writing (e-mail flourishes), while use of the telephone is inhibited. In contrast, in Italy there is extensive use of all personal channels of communication, including telephone and e-mail, that can be used to bypass the formal structure. In Spain, communication is mainly oral, face-to-face and one-to-one, especially with the boss.

## Gender and communication

Work-based communication presents women with particular problems, such as the fact that they inevitably communicate difference, risk, marginality and potential disruption. Forms of address are used to level (lower) the status of senior women. The dominant language forms are man-made and stereotype women: 'Interpreting speaking longest and with more dominant features as powerful speech is so firmly established as an assumption, that women's strategies for maintaining affiliation and encouraging others to contribute are often devalued.'[19] Women are often excluded from informal networks, especially of those in more senior positions.[20] Partly as a result of these difficulties, women are more likely than men to use a form of communication that minimises threat to the receiver's face. They may give their orders as requests, such as 'Please would you mind finishing this letter first?', make their statements sound provisional by using qualifiers, such as 'Perhaps we should cut our prices', use tag questions, as in 'We need to call a meeting, don't we?', use disclaimers, 'I may be wrong, but . . .' and use supportive rather than powerful vocabulary.[21]

## Disability and communication

People with disabilities suffer communication problems, often because of the prejudiced attitudes of those with whom they are interacting. 'Conversations with visibly disabled strangers entail unequivocally higher uncertainty and relatively more negative predicted outcome values compared to conversations with able-bodied strangers.'[22] When people without disabilities interact for five minutes with strangers with visible disabilities, they become significantly less aware of the stranger's vocal, verbal and overall non-verbal activity than usual. They also ask significantly fewer questions. Such reduced levels of awareness could explain continued and increasing uncertainty and discomfort, early termination and many of the other dysfunctional effects reported in past research into communication with visibly disabled individuals. Coleman and De Paulo[23] showed that anxiety, as well as negative stereotypes and expectations, affect both parties in such encounters and lead to miscommunication.

## SUMMARY – COMMUNICATION PRACTICES OF DIFFERENT SOCIAL CATEGORIES AND GROUPS

There are cultural differences in communication at both the general level of the importance of the context in collectivist and individualist cultures and the detailed level of such matters as the perceived importance of clarity or the use of hinting. At work, within Europe, there are national differences in communication practices. Women and people with disabilities experience communication problems because of the attitudes of others, problems that can lead to communication styles that reinforce others' prejudices.

## BARRIERS TO COMMUNICATION

> Human communication is intrinsically fallible, whether we are aware of it or not. Miscommunication occurs between conversationalists who share the same language and cultural backgrounds, and particularly in intercultural interactions in which one participant speaks a second language and functions in a foreign culture.[24]

As Figure 7.3 shows, some barriers to communication are intrinsic to the process. Some, though, are caused by individual differences, some by differences in the communication practices of different social categories and groups and some by the emotional and cognitive challenges of inter-group encounters themselves.

### Intrinsic barriers

Few people now think of communication as being a straightforward process where A says or writes something to B and B hears or reads precisely what A said or wrote and vice versa. Most people agree that this is over-simplified. Some of the complications are as follows:

- The messages may be obscure, ambiguous or in other ways badly encoded.
- Environmental 'noise', such as a mobile phone user entering a tunnel, may prevent A's message reaching B or B's message reaching A.
- The medium used to send the message can change it.[25] For instance, the same words can mean different things when they are heard in the sender's presence, over the telephone, or read.
- Both A and B will sometimes select, distort, decode inaccurately, categorise indiscriminately or wrongly interpret the messages reaching them. This will happen even more if they are suffering from information overload.

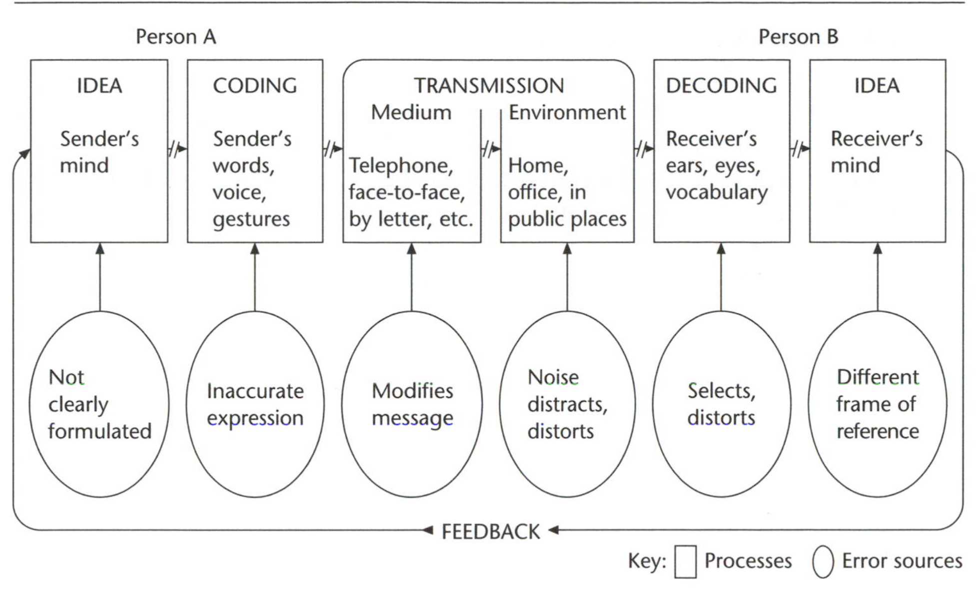


The many sources of error in communication make feedback a vital part of the process. Feedback enables Person A to check that the intended message has been received and understood by Person B.

**Figure 7.3 Communication processes and error sources.**

- Communications are much more than just the words that flow between people. All behaviour conveys some message.
- Communication is highly interactive on all levels: messages, language and non-verbals are all adapted, to varying degrees, as encounters proceed. For instance, LePoire and Yoshimura[26] found that pleasant communication behaviour was reciprocated. (However, rather to their surprise, they found that unpleasant communication behaviour was not reciprocated but instead elicited involvement, expressiveness and pleasantness. It seems that people try to maintain a viable communication environment despite the difficulties sometimes presented by others.)

## Barriers set up by individual-level influences

Individuals may create or be affected by personal barriers to communicating, including apprehension, uncertainty and negative expectations, or by their reactions to having their (positive or neutral) expectations violated.

### *Communication motives*

Whether people seek out or avoid communicating and how they act communicatively are affected by their motivations and needs. Communication apprehension (CA) and global uncertainty are two that create barriers. CA, which is based on the fear that encounters will turn awkward or even hostile, is increased by situations containing new, atypical and/or conspicuously different stimuli. It may be limited to interactions with particular people, for example, members of the opposite sex or it may be 'global'. William Douglas[27] found that individuals who experience high CA ask few questions during the first minute of an interaction, engage in high levels of self-disclosure, lack expertise when playing out acquaintance scenarios and are considered less competent by their communication partners. Self-reports suggest that individuals who experience high CA are also high in global uncertainty. The people most satisfied with their jobs may be low in CA and work in jobs with high communication requirements.[28] Global uncertainty (GU) refers to being uncertain about acquaintanceship in general. People high in GU define initial meetings with others in negative ways, attempt to avoid conversations with unfamiliar others, perform less effectively when meeting others for the first time and develop less satisfactory long-term relationships than people low in GU.[29]

**Box 7.5**

**Critique of communication motivation theorising and research**

Kim (1999) criticised this work for being biased by the assumption that communication approach is more desirable than communication avoidance. The author agrees that extreme forms of communication avoidance and lack of verbal assertiveness can be a handicap in any culture. However she is critical of the ethnocentric preoccupation with the Western view which sees communication avoidance solely as a deficit. For instance, assertiveness, which was described in Chapter 6, is sometimes defined as communication approach. Within the US context, people perceived as low in assertiveness are characterised as uncompetitive, risk avoiders, slow to take action, 'go-along' persons, non-directive and incompetent communicators. Kim points out that this is probably not true for people from different cultures. A large amount of research shows that Asians, such as Koreans, are lower on assertiveness than Americans, yet other research demonstrates that they include at least the usual proportion of entrepreneurs. The collectivist view is that communication 'avoidance' stems from being sensitive to social context.

*Source*: Kim, M.-S. (1999) 'Cross-cultural perspectives on motivations of verbal communication: Review, critique, and a theoretical framework', *Communication Yearbook*, vol. 22, pp. 51–89.

### *Expectations*

As Chapter 5 discussed, expectations about how other people will behave influence our perceptions about them, especially if what they do violates the expectations. Not surprisingly, therefore, expectations and their violations affect people's responses and ongoing communication. For instance, videotaped conversations between 46 American students and research confederates from India showed significant differences in the communication behaviours of the Americans according to what they previously believed about India.[30] Similarly, Honeycutt[31] found that when an interlocutor displayed friendly non-verbal behaviour, subjects who were previously given to believe that their interlocutor was friendly, reciprocated and accommodated their own behaviour accordingly. The reverse was also found. However, when the subjects were given no previous expectations about the interlocutor, the impact of his/her non-verbal behaviour during the interaction was much less.

## Barriers set up by group differences

Differences in the ways different groups communicate mean that, to understand a message fully, we must know a great deal about the relevant social conventions. It is not enough just to understand the words. There is a large body of social and cultural knowledge that users of a language need to have. This includes what to say to whom and how to say it appropriately in any situation.

- In HCC cultures, communicators have to know what is going on in order to function: 'HCC transactions feature preprogrammed information that is in the receiver and in the setting, with only minimal information in the transmitted message. In general, they are more predictable, if, and only if, one is familiar with the system.'[32] When a speaker uses HCC, the problem for an LCC receiver is literally to grasp their meaning. The receiver is neither attuned to the large amount that is left unsaid nor to the extensive use of non-verbal communication, nor to the emphasis on relationship data. When the speaker uses LCC, the problem for an HCC receiver is to avoid seeing inferences which may not be present, being affronted by directness and the concentration on hard content or suffering from information overload.
- Barriers are created by cultural differences in the order in which people express their points. For instance, speakers may first give the context of what they want to say and then their main point or vice versa. In some cultures it would be more 'natural' to say, 'Protecting our market share requires us to make a price cut' than 'We should cut our prices to protect our market share', while in others the reverse is the case. This difference can cause confusion, especially in languages such as English that (unlike Japanese) have no semantic way of marking the main subject.
- Further barriers are created by group differences in the functions to which communication is put, such as distributing control and communicating relationship data. For instance, women tend to see talk as the essence of a relationship, men to see it as a way to exert control, preserve independence and enhance status. The amount of content data versus relationship data varies

cross-culturally, so that Greeks are liable to find Northern Europeans abrupt and Swedes are likely to find Southern Italians slow to get to the point.

- Other difficulties are caused by group differences in directness and indirectness, especially in paying compliments or making negative observations. For instance, Germans, while generally more formal than the British, regard it as a kindness to tell an acquaintance that their tie is askew. The British tend to pretend it isn't so. Directness viewed positively is honesty, negatively rudeness. Indirectness viewed positively is politeness, negatively is insincerity.
- Differences in culturally inculcated rules for emotional display can cause problems. English men, famous for their 'stiff upper lip', fear the emotionalism of Italian men. However, it may be that there are no great differences in the amount of emotion felt, only differences in display rules.
- Body language not only varies cross-culturally, it may also give rise to more misunderstanding than spoken or written messages. Lack of a common verbal language just means there is no verbal communication. In body language, on the other hand, Arabs and Americans, for instance, have different expectations about distance, facing, touching, loudness and eye contact.

Barriers set up by social category or group differences in communication can lead to discrimination at work. In 1997 Clark[33] found that members of some cultures working in Australia use what in terms of the local culture is 'inappropriate' deference behaviour and that doing so may lead to disadvantage, for example in the loss of promotion opportunities.

## Barriers arising from inter-group interaction

Evidence for difficulties in intercultural communication comes from a study that found lower levels of involvement and lower use of alignment talk in initial interactions between Americans talking with East-Asian non-native speakers of English compared with when they were talking with other Americans.[34] Full communication across groups, especially cultures, is made more difficult by the following factors:

- With people familiar to them, people use a restricted code to communicate, leaving out explanations and background facts, using abbreviations, and so on.[35] In contrast, for people from different backgrounds to understand one another, they must use an 'elaborated' code, spelling things out and explaining rather than assuming that they will be understood. This necessary elaboration slows the pace of communication, can seem awkward and, for people from some cultures, such as the American, appears unfriendly and unaccommodating.

- Disobeying the social rules of another culture, for instance by speaking loudly and forcefully in Japan, alienates people from the 'offended' culture. On the other hand, trying to adjust, for instance by using simplified 'foreigner talk', can be equally or more offensive.
- Cultural meanings of behaviour are invisible to outsiders. Therefore, before intercultural communication can even begin, there needs to be a recognition that we each carry a particular mental software because of the way we were brought up, and that others carry a different mental software for equally good reasons. Many, perhaps most, people still lack that awareness.
- Chapter 3 has shown how at times, particularly in dealing with strangers, we tend to deal with others not as individuals but as representatives of their group, so creating the following barriers:

  - Group membership is often not obvious but must be inferred, creating scope for errors.
  - Inter-group encounters are complex: interpersonal factors cannot be ignored and therefore two dimensions need to be juggled. It can be difficult to get the right balance.
  - Interactions between strangers can create anxiety and often are experienced by both parties as a series of crises.[36]
  - When people treat an encounter as inter-group they commonly use their knowledge of the group to make their attributions of the causes of the other person's behaviour. They may know little about the culture of the other's group, leading them to make false attributions or, if they are aware of the problem, limited and provisional attributions that inhibit openness.
  - Using stereotypes constrains others' patterns of communication. Politeness may prevent people who realise they are being treated in accordance with a stereotype from refuting it. Even if they do react, this is likely to distract them from the discussion. Moreover, members of groups often feel a pressure to confirm the expectations created by others' stereotypes, as when women use disempowered ways of speaking. This leads to them being rated as less intelligent and less well informed than other people who do not use them (and also than men who do use them).[37] In other cases, the individual violates the expectations about their group, provoking an extreme response. In either case communication is impaired.
  - 'Subtle and systematic linguistic biases' transmit and help maintain stereotypes.[38] For instance, when they are describing an in-group member doing something desirable or an out-group member doing something undesirable, people generally speak in a relatively abstract way. The in-group member is 'helpful', the out-group member is 'aggressive'. In contrast, when describing undesirable in-group member behaviour or desirable out-group

member behaviour, people are specific: the in-group member 'pushes someone', the out-group member 'opens the door for someone'.[39] Speaking like this implies that desirable behaviour is typical for an in-group member, atypical for an out-group member and vice versa for undesirable behaviour.

- In uncertain situations, such as meeting people from another culture for the first time, especially in important work meetings, negotiations or interviews, aligning facework strategies is problematic. The classic case of the Western businessman who offends his Arab counterpart by being in too much of a hurry to 'get down to business' is an example. The Arab's positive face needs for a relationship to exist as the context for negotiation are ignored. Non-alignment of facework strategies leads to mis-communication – the people misread each others' signals and so respond inappropriately. This can lead to spiralling conflict.
- Negative emotions during the intercultural encounter itself can give rise to problems. These include:

  - disconfirmed expectations – a person may be upset not because a situation is bad but because it is not what was expected;
  - a feeling of alienation, being an outsider;
  - ambiguity – not knowing how to interpret events;
  - being confronted with one's own prejudices;
  - anxiety over whether a given behaviour is appropriate, what is safe, how to negotiate a situation and so on.[40]

  These negative feelings experienced during intercultural encounters may feed into intercultural communication apprehension (ICA) about future encounters.

## SUMMARY – BARRIERS TO COMMUNICATION

Barriers arising from four different sources need to be overcome for people to communicate fully, especially if they are members of different social categories or groups (including cultures). These are, first, poor encoding, noise, channel distortion and perceptual blocking or distortion; second, communication apprehension, global uncertainty and expectations and their violations; third, in intergroup encounters, group differences in the importance of context, the accepted sequence of types of content, directness, relative emphasis on content or relationship, emotional display rules and body language; and fourth, the necessity of using an elaborated code, the cognitive difficulties of following the communication rules of other cultures and understanding other groups' values, the tendency to treat members of other groups as representative of their groups, linguistic bias and the negative emotions of intercultural encounters.

## MAKING COMMUNICATION WORK

Despite the difficulties described above, we do in fact communicate with some success in work contexts, including intercultural ones. This may be because we do in fact get more practice than is at first apparent:

> All communication is fundamentally intercultural, in the sense that each participant in an act of communication brings to it a specific repertoire of identities, positions and expectations formed through complex relationships with their own and other cultures. . . . Effective communication is closely related to the participants' understanding and management of these different cultural identities and positions.[41]

In line with this perspective, the intercultural and other contents of this section will be integrated. It begins with ethical issues, then discusses what we mean by (intercultural) communication competence, and how we achieve it through using facework and politeness, communication accommodation, grounding and anxiety/uncertainty reduction.

### Communication ethics

An important factor in making communication work is to operate according to a mutually agreed set of ethics. Communicating entails making choices, for instance of what to omit, and choices imply the possibility of ethics.[42] Ethics may be particularly important in face-to-face interaction, because we are so vulnerable there. Ethical concerns set limits to message invention. Unethical messages limit the ability to engage in genuine conversation. Examples include the following:

- Calling the other person a racist, sexist or Marxist or by other terms that stop further expression by the other.
- Disqualifying the other, as by saying. 'You're just saying that because you are a woman' or calling someone 'naive'.
- Basing a claim beyond evaluation, for example by suggesting that differences between male and female emotional reactions are inborn.
- Treating value-laden processes as if they were value-free, as by just giving the facts or data, which hides both the criteria used to choose these rather than other observations and the conceptual frame that produced the data in the first place.
- Ruling out some topics, as in the way that some big business organisations make it 'illegitimate' for employees to talk about problems at home and so essentially hide the home.
- Proclaiming that an issue is 'a matter of opinion' to terminate the discussion.
- Denying intent, as by making an inappropriate sexual innuendo then denying it meant anything in order to disempower the receiver.[43]

For Habermas, ethical communication is the attempt to reach mutual understanding, not to transmit already formed thoughts. That is, he proposed a productive rather than reproductive approach to communication. In line with this conception, Habermas[44] lists four conditions necessary for ethical communication:

1. Speakers choose the appropriate verbalisation of their ideas to reflect a mutually recognised background of values.
2. Parties intend to be truthful.
3. They believe the information that they reveal to each other is true.
4. They comprehend what each other is really saying. This condition is the most basic of all.

## Communication competence

Competent communication is effective and appropriate. Effectiveness depends on a set of abilities to formulate and achieve interaction objectives, collaborate with others and adapt to different situations. Effectiveness increases as people become more aware of relevant factors.[45,46] To be appropriate, message type and style must be structured to match the particular relationship at hand and environmental constraints must be taken into account.[47]

**Box 7.6**

### How to communicate clearly

Communicating clearly is often (though not universally) important, especially where the work requires it, as when coaching others in how to perform a task. In order to be clear, you should:

- state your points clearly and precisely;
- adjust to the other person's level of understanding without being demeaning;
- use simple language;
- explain jargon;
- where possible and acceptable use the idiom of the other (sub)culture;
- avoid slang;
- slow down (but not speak more loudly);
- start from where the other person is 'at';
- use progressive approximations to impart difficult ideas;
- divide projects and explanations into smaller, more specific pieces;
- repeat in alternative ways;
- get the other person to ask questions;
- give short answers (stopping after a partial reply and waiting for their response);
- check understanding, for example by asking 'Am I being clear?', 'Will you say it back to me in your own words?', 'Let me show you what I mean', 'Why don't you give it a try now?'

At work, competent communication is adapted at least in part to the organisation's preferred style. To adapt successfully, a person must understand the accepted guidelines. When Wellmon[48] got 20 employees to talk about 'critical incidents' as a way of accessing what they saw as important behaviours, 13 categories of guidelines for organisational communication emerged. These are shown in Box 7.7. Wellmon concluded that the employees clearly recognised the rules for competent communication in their organisation.

**Box 7.7**

**Categories of perceived competent behaviours that relate directly to communication, from interviews with employees of an organisation (1st number = number of interviews, 2nd number = number of incidents)**

1. Listening (15/37) – strong listening skills, ability to paraphrase while listening versus not listening to the other's point of view, formulates responses while you are talking, no empathic communication.
2. Friendly, personable behaviour (13/30) – sense of humour, sensitive, reasonable, warm.
3. Successful behaviour (13/26) – dedicated, enthusiastic, persistent.
4. Good leadership skills (11/15) – works by example, uses innovation, successful delegator, maintains authority without distance, effective goal-setting abilities, knows how to hire competent people versus 'can't implement the concept', makes promises he can't keep, 'doesn't hire super employees because they're afraid for their own job'.
5. Understanding human nature (10/21) – consistency, dealing with people versus 'can't work with women, is racist and is sexist'.
6. Motivation (8/18) – ability to motivate self and others – can energise people, creates positive environment, is a team player/builds team spirit.
7. Professionalism (8/15) – maintains a professional demeanour, has a professional air versus brash, rude, intimidating, manipulative, jokes are offensive.
8. Organisational involvement (7/18) – willingness to learn, knowledgeable about the job, values training for self and employees versus doesn't go beyond the job, doesn't take chances, doesn't seize the opportunity to grow professionally.
9. Organised (6/17) – pays attention to details, complete preparation.
10. Feedback (6/12) – responds with positive before negative statement, uses compliments and constructive criticism well, keeps others informed of the progress of the project, gives information without getting into minutiae and telling more than they need to know versus can't see the value of telling others what you see and hear, no positive feedback, telling others what they want to hear, not aware of others' feedback.
11. Interaction skills (6/12) – ability to negotiate and co-ordinate; also to socialise; ease at communication, communication focuses on the situation, no games playing; versus little or no interpersonal skills, socially inept, doesn't know how to talk to people, doesn't convey changes in the contract to those who would carry them out.
12. Effective verbal style (8/18) – comes to the point, articulate, clear and concise, doesn't raise voice, doesn't lose emotions, succinct in verbal style.
13. Ability to demonstrate knowledge of the business to superiors.

*Source*: Based on Wellmon, T. A. (1988) 'Conceptualizing organisational communication competence: A rules-based perspective', *Management Communication Quarterly*, vol. 1, no. 4, pp. 515–534.

Appropriateness and effectiveness are also the two indispensable elements for conceptualising intercultural communication competence, according to Chen and Starosta.[49] Chen's research found significant and positive relations among a large number of dimensions of intercultural communication competence and their components, including personal attributes, communication skills, psychological adaptation, cultural awareness, self-disclosure, flexibility, stress and social values.[50] Figure 7.4 shows the findings.

People from different cultures have different views on what constitutes (intercultural) communication competence. For instance, verbal behaviours are more

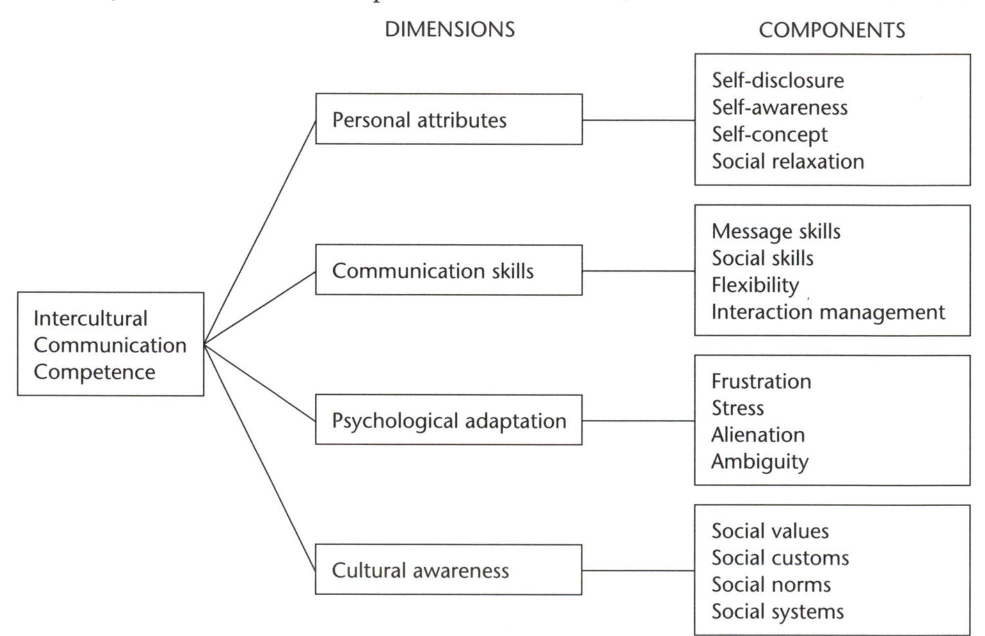


Personal attributes – competent communicators must know themselves well and, through their self-awareness abilities, initiate positive attitudes.
Self-awareness is linked to self-monitoring, which is linked to adaptability.
Social relaxation – showing low levels of anxiety, in postural cues, speech and object manipulation as well as experiencing low levels.
Communication skills – competence in verbal and non-verbal behaviours.
Message skills – linguistic, descriptive, supportiveness, oral message evaluation, basic speech skills; ability to execute the language appropriately.
Interaction management – turn taking, knowing how to initiate and terminate a conversation, interaction involvement.
Social skills – empathy or taking the role of the other in interaction, identity maintenance, human relations skills (describing and expressing different viewpoints).
Psychological adaptation – ability to acclimatise to a new environment.
Cultural awareness – understanding.

**Figure 7.4 Findings on relations among intercultural communication competence dimensions and components.**

*Source*: Based on Chen, G.-M. (1989) 'Relationships of the dimensions of intercultural communication competence', *Communication Quarterly*, vol. 37, no. 2, pp. 118–133.

highly valued by Americans than their Chinese counterparts.[51] Mexican, black and white Americans have similar expectations of politeness and role fulfilment norms in intercultural communication competence, but white Americans emphasise verbal content, black Americans individuality and Mexican Americans relational climate. Of these three groups, only Mexican Americans think rules for inter- and intra-cultural conversations are similar.[52]

## Applying communication theories

To achieve competent communication, it helps to understand and apply the theories of facework and politeness, communication accommodation, grounding and anxiety/uncertainty management.

Facework and politeness, introduced in Chapter 6, are major contributions to our understanding of how we communicate successfully, including across cultures. For example, politeness theory helps explain how people who feel called on to give explanations (or accounts) because an act of theirs has or might have given offence, choose among the four possible types of explanation: apologies, excuses, justifications and denials. These vary in the degree to which they support the receiver's or the sender's face, and hence in politeness, as Table 7.4 shows. Having to explain threatens the sender's face and so politeness theory predicts that the more severe the offence, the more elaborated the explanation.[53] This idea is confirmed by a study that found that when people pile on reproaches they tend to follow up with explanations that provide little or no face support for the receiver, suggesting that in these circumstances senders have an over-riding need to support their own face. There are gender differences in explanations giving. Women give politer explanations than men; this may be a function of status differences.

Like criticisms or complaints, disagreements and self-disclosures threaten the receiver's face. Clearly, people know this. When discussing subjects on which they disagree, they generally use positive politeness strategies. So, for instance,

**Table 7.4 Types of explanation, with their defining features and levels of politeness**

| *Explanation type* | *Defining feature* | *Politeness (face support)* |
|---|---|---|
| Concession | Admits offensiveness and responsibility | Most receiver support/least sender support |
| Excuse | Admits offensiveness but minimises responsibility | |
| Justification | Admits responsibility but minimises offensiveness | |
| Refusal | Admits nothing | Least receiver support/most sender support |

if people are talking about insider trading, they might focus on the current law, which, being neutral and objective, avoids overt disagreements. They also hedge their opinions ('Yes, but', 'I tend to think', 'It might be') or ask for the previous speaker to say more. The receiver of a self-disclosure is placed in the role of helping to manage the sender's identity, which is an imposition. Politeness is exercised by the discloser introducing the topic gradually, in a series of moves that allow the receiver to signal resistance. Self-disclosures are also usually disclosed indirectly, made in a cheerful manner, or balanced – positive disclosures are made, as well as negative. The receiver often exercises tact by reciprocity, expressions of concern, being attentive or not joining in the discloser's own self-mocking laughter.

### *Communication accommodation*

When two people are absorbed in a conversation or discussion, over time they often adjust aspects of their speech or non-verbal behaviour. Sometimes they adjust to be more like the other person, at others to be more unlike them. Accent, speed, loudness, vocabulary, grammar, voice tone and gestures are all among the aspects they may adjust. These adjustments are labelled accommodation and those to be more like the other person are 'converging' while those to be more unlike them are 'diverging'. Explanations of why people converge or diverge are that these are ways for senders to signal their attitudes towards each other,[54] or to achieve smoother or clearer communication. Alternatively, people may converge to gain approval or identify and diverge to distinguish themselves or to accentuate their own group membership. Converging can create a favourable impression through the attempt to highlight similarities.

Convergence and divergence may or may not be mutual. Sometimes Person A will be converging while Person B is diverging, which creates certain difficulties for both parties. It is thought that people are largely unaware of these processes. When people converge accurately on another person's speech qualities, it may make them more attractive to the other by increasing their predictability and intelligibility; this leads to higher mutual involvement. When they get it wrong, so that their accommodation is perceived as inappropriate, it can be evaluated as patronising, ingratiating or humiliating. When convergence is seen as violating norms, it is evaluated as negatively as divergence.[55] Figure 7.5 illustrates communication accommodation.

### *Grounding*

Communicators continuously update their shared understanding of an ongoing conversation in a process called conversational grounding. To communicate, people must have a common understanding of content (e.g. that a reference to 'the cap' is actually to 'the CAP', that is to the EU's Common Agricultural

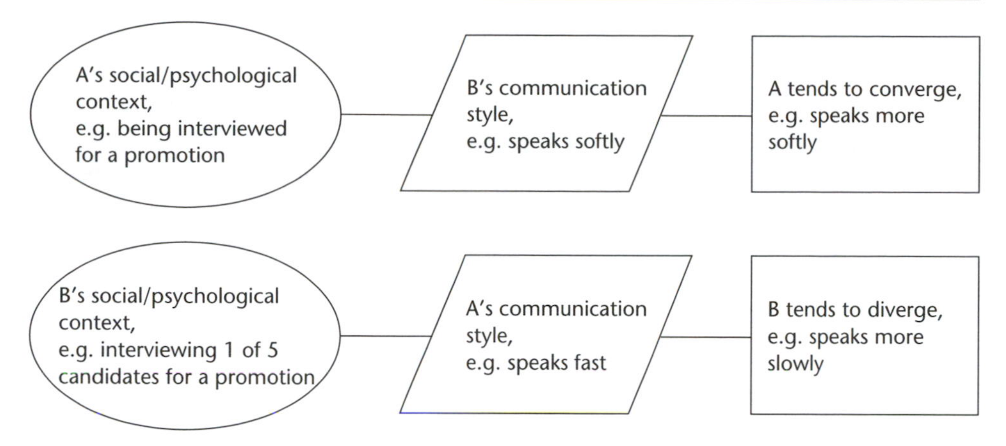


**Figure 7.5 Communication accommodation theory.**

Policy). They must also co-ordinate on process, so that each person only speaks when the receiver is attending to, hearing and trying to understand what is said. The receiver must guide by giving evidence of this.[56] In the example of successful grounding given in Table 7.5, B obtains an accurate account of what happened because s/he asks questions to test his or her understanding and A gives informative responses. In the example of unsuccessful grounding, although A presents successfully to begin with, B's questions only invite A to confirm or deny and A fails to give enough extra information for B to understand.

**Table 7.5 Examples of unsuccessful and successful grounding**

**Unsuccessful grounding (but with successful presentation)**
A: When we were taken over, a lot of good people left.
B: Okay.
A: It was a year ago we were taken over.
B: So that was when the good people left?
A: Some left then.

*Several turns later*
B: Um, you say the good people left a year ago?
A: Not all of them.

**Successful grounding**
A: When we were taken over, a lot of good people left.
B: Uh.
A: A year ago, we were taken over.
B: A year ago?
A: Yes, a year ago.
B: Didn't you say your top technician left last month?
A: Yes, but some other good people left earlier . . .
B: . . . oh, some people took longer to make the decision?
A: Yes.

Grounding has been shown to be a central process in exchanges between a caller and a telephone operator, between two persons who have a shared task and in everyday conversations. Grounding helps receivers to understand better than people who simply overhear. By asking questions, the receiver gets the speaker to concentrate, dialogue and accommodate, rather than just present information. One advantage of grounding, especially in intercultural settings, is that it overcomes the problem that two people in a discussion 'may not have a vast amount of shared information or common ground'.[57] Research shows that the more intercultural pairs engage in grounding, the better they communicate. It has been argued that although intercultural communicators need to do more grounding, to overcome lack of shared knowledge, they nevertheless do less, because questioning or admitting non-understanding or misunderstanding raises anxiety and threatens face. However, studies found more grounding taking place in conversations between Canadians and Chinese than in monocultural conversations. It was, though, found that more grounding occurred when the language used was the receiver's native language rather than vice versa, probably because most grounding is receiver-initiated. Receivers using a non-native language may not realise the problem or may have more anxiety.

### *Anxiety/uncertainty management*

Managing the emotions and cognitions of encounters is the concern of anxiety/uncertainty management (AUM) theory. Its origins lie in the hypotheses of Berger[58] that individuals attempt to reduce uncertainty in initial interactions with strangers, especially when the strangers will be encountered in future, can provide rewards and act in a deviant fashion in the terms of the individual's own culture or sub-culture. Berger put forward 7 axioms and 21 theorems about the relations among uncertainty and the amount of communication, the degree to which people show warmth to one another by body language, information seeking, intimacy level of communication, reciprocity, similarity and liking. In general each of these relations is inverse – thus, the greater the amount of communication and the higher the similarity, the lower the uncertainty – but information seeking is higher in the presence of high uncertainty. Berger also suggested that people adopt one of three general strategies for reducing uncertainty. A passive strategy means doing nothing in the hope that as time passes things will become clearer, an active strategy means finding out as much as possible from outside sources and an interactive strategy means seeking out opportunities to interact with people about whom uncertainty exists and using those occasions to obtain as much information as possible. An interactive strategy is generally most effective.

Core elements of AUM theory include the concepts of the stranger, uncertainty, anxiety and initial encounters.

- Strangers are people who are different because they are members of other groups. When strangers act in a way that is deviant in terms of an individual's own culture, the individual experiences uncertainty and, especially when those strangers will be encountered in future or can provide rewards, anxiety.
- Uncertainty is of two distinct types: not being able to predict what strangers' attitudes, feelings, beliefs, values and behaviour will be and not being able to explain why they behave in the way they do. When uncertainty is too high for comfort, people will either try to reduce it by gaining information or end the interaction. When uncertainty is too low, people may be too bored to interact effectively.
- Anxiety refers to the feeling of being apprehensive about what might happen. This is an emotional response, whereas uncertainty is a cognitive one. Anxiety is usually based on people's negative expectations, such as that their self-concepts will be damaged or that they will be negatively evaluated. When anxiety is too high for comfort, people either avoid encounters or their attention is distracted from the communication. Then they rely on information such as stereotypes to predict other people's behaviour and may misinterpret it. When anxiety is too low, people may not care what happens in the interaction, not pay attention and miss important cues.

  Thus optimal levels of uncertainty and anxiety are intermediate between too high and too low. However, in interactions with strangers, both are normally too high. In these cases, communicating effectively is a matter of reducing uncertainty by information seeking and controlling anxiety through tension-reducing behaviour. In other words, attempts to adapt to the ambiguity of new situations involve a cyclical pattern of tension-reducing and information-seeking behaviours.
- Initial encounters. Culture forms an implicit theory (about the rules being followed and the game being played) that individuals use to guide their behaviour and interpret others' behaviour. Much within cultural behaviour is habitual and therefore not conscious.[59] The matter is different, though, in the initial stages of intercultural communication. When interacting with a stranger, individuals become aware that the stranger does not share their own implicit theory about the rules or the game. Therefore they become more conscious of that implicit theory. The result is that interactions between strangers take place at high levels of behavioural awareness, known as mindfulness.

Figure 7.6 shows the elements of AUM theory.

AUM theory has attracted a considerable effort of research and testing, although it is so complex that most areas remain untested. Research has shown that uncertainty reduction applies to both low-context and high-context communication cultures,[60] friendship relations across cultures,[61] ethnic differences in interactions between blacks and whites in the United States[62] and inter-ethnic communication generally in the United States.[63]

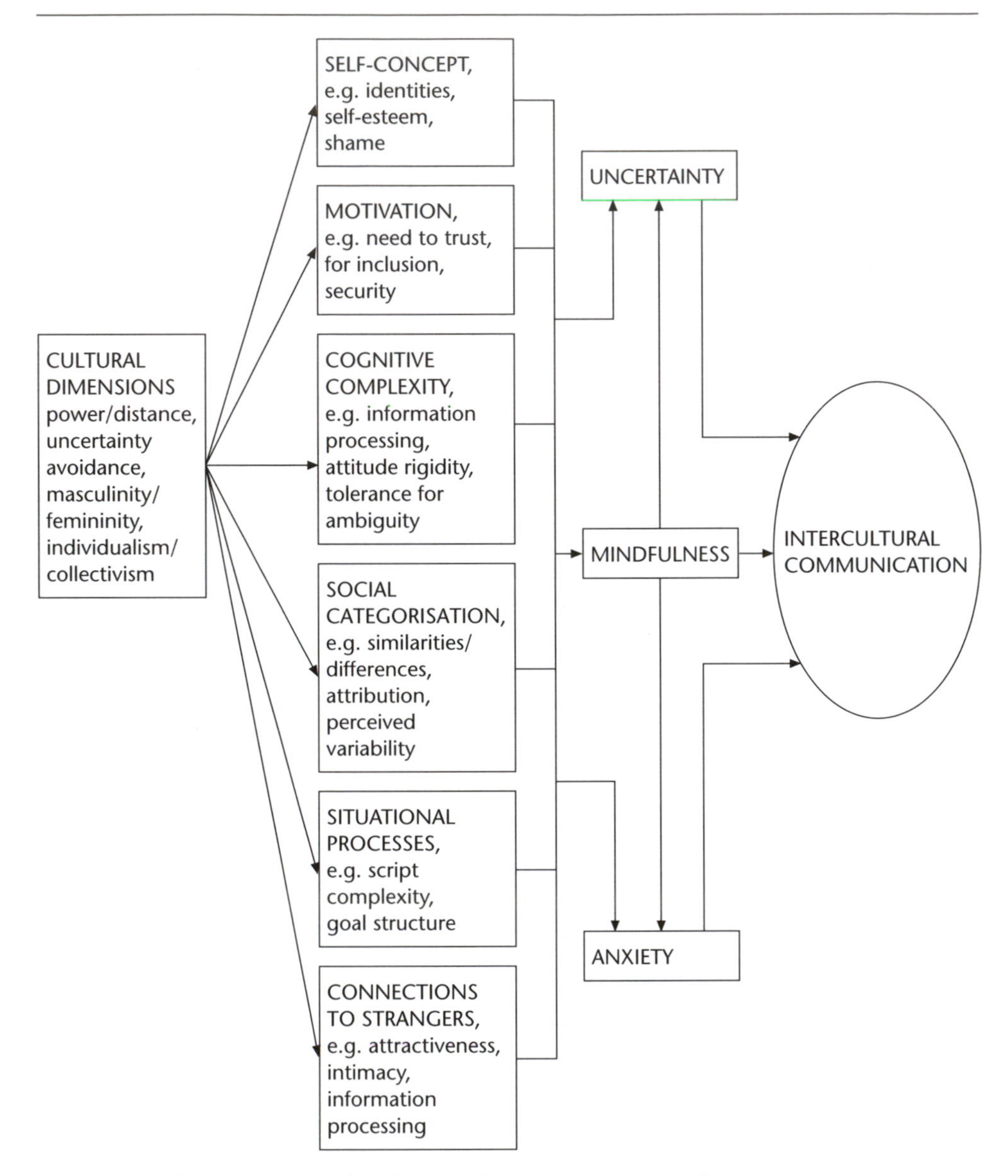


**Figure 7.6 Elements of anxiety/uncertainty management theory.**

## SUMMARY – MAKING COMMUNICATION WORK

An agreed set of ethics governing communication enhances mutual understanding. Competence in communication can be defined in terms of effectiveness (achieving goals) and appropriateness (matching others' expectations and behaviours). These may apply to communication both within and between cultures. However, competence embraces a wide range of dimensions and

**Box 7.8**

### How to reduce your uncertainty and anxiety in intercultural encounters

- Cultivate positive expectations about people from other cultures.
- Network with members of other cultures.
- Make friends with members of other groups.
- Learn to speak a second language.
- Gain confidence in the attributions you make for others' behaviour.
- Work on decreasing communication apprehension generally.
- If you are high in individualism, an increase in collectivism will produce a decrease in uncertainty in out-group communication relative to in-group communication.

*Source*: Gudykunst, W. B. (1988) 'Uncertainty and anxiety' in Y. Y. Kim and W. B. Gudykunst (eds) *Theories in Intercultural Communication*. Newbury Park, Calif.: Sage, pp. 123–156.

**Box 7.9**

### Critique of (intercultural) communication theories

- Intercultural communication theorising and research have been criticised for looseness in the theorised links between culture and individual interactive behaviour as well as for the concept of culture as values (Bond *et al.*, 2000).
- AUM theory's focus on initial interactions and the early stages of acquaintanceship makes it valuable for understanding those aspects of communicating across barriers at work which involve meeting strangers, such as introductory interviews between professionals and clients or international negotiations. However, this theory can be criticised for being static and taking the individual interactor as the only unit of analysis, when what is needed are theories that are processual, include dynamic elements and take both the individual interactor and the interaction itself as the units of analysis.
- Casmir and Ascuncion-Lande (1989) commented that we should seek to build a 'third culture' in our interactions with people from other cultures, aiming to create opportunities for mutual development and synthesis, where cultural domination and subjugation are rejected.

*Sources*:

Bond, M. H., V. Zegerac and H. Spencer-Oatey (2000) 'Culture as an explanatory variable: problems and possibilities' in H. Spencer-Oatey (ed.) *Culturally Speaking: Managing Rapport Through Talk Across Cultures*. New York: Continuum, pp. 47–71.

Casmir, F. L. and N. C. Ascuncion-Lande (1989) 'Intercultural communication revisited: Conceptualization, paradigm building and methodological approaches', *Communication Yearbook*, vol. 12, pp. 278–309.

components. What is regarded as competent communication may differ from organisation to organisation and from culture to culture.

There are many communication theories that can be applied to improve both intracultural and intercultural communication. Facework and politeness theory can be applied to communication elements such as explanations, disagreements and self-disclosures. Accommodating to the other party's way of communicating can increase attractiveness and mutual involvement. Grounding can support mutual understanding even in the absence of a shared pool of (social) knowledge. Anxiety and uncertainty can be reduced in initial encounters with strangers and so allow people to adapt better.

Exercise 23 gives a questionnaire that can be used to help assess communication performances.

## WORK APPLICATIONS FOR COMMUNICATION

Coaching, mentoring, consultancy, employee communications and service encounters are the work activities treated in this book as primarily applications of communication. The guidance given in Boxes 7.6, 7.8 and 7.10 will be especially helpful for communicating competently in these work activities.

### Coaching

In Anglo-American cultures, coaching is now seen as a managerial role and a crucial aspect of leadership. Advice such as the following has become commonplace: 'Include coaching in your checklists of core competencies and behaviors' and 'Coaching and leadership go hand in hand. From creating trust through discipline, reward and mentorship, coaching behaviors exemplify leadership behaviors; in fact, they are leadership behaviors.'[64] Coaching is about helping others learn. Ideally, learning is an active process. The coach's role is to guide, support and provide information inputs into a process that is driven forward by the learner. The first stage, then, in improving coaching skills is to understand how learning works. Coaches should aim to develop their coaching skills by basing them on the four approaches to learning theory given in Chapter 4. A coach also needs to have a supportive attitude towards learners. The coach must see them as a 'human resource who brings assets to the work situation that need to be nurtured if the employee is to grow and be productive.'[65] It helps if the coach prefers to think of managers as nurturing their subordinates rather than controlling them. Coaches need also to have a feeling of equality with the learners, whatever the differences in education or organisational position. They need to be sensitive to how people see themselves in terms of their strengths, what goals they are aiming for and what they can be induced to aim for.

Coaches should combine warmth and firmness. Trainees instructed in a warm, directive way have been shown to be most productive, motivated to the task, willing to work again and satisfied with the relationship with their leader. Warmth without direction leads to low productivity, coldness to low satisfaction with the relationship and unwillingness to work again.[66] On top of all these attitudinal

Box 7.10

## How to be a successful communicator

- Allow for receivers being distracted by a less than 100 per cent level of concentration or a possibly emotional state of mind as well as for distracting 'noise' from the environment. These factors can lead to messages not being received, not being attended to or being distorted by the receivers. This applies to your attention to what others say as much as to how well they receive your messages.
- Get the 'basics' right: knowing what to say; using language that will be understood, avoiding both jargon and long, rambling sentences; adjusting the pace to the state of the receiver and introducing new ideas or a change of subject by signalling intentions, e.g. 'Let me make a suggestion' or 'May I ask you a question?'
- Realise that not all worthwhile communication at work is rational, 'up-front' and directed towards organisational goals.
- Convey a 'you' attitude, which wherever possible uses 'We' instead of 'I', is positive about the other's role and contribution and avoids blaming.
- Avoid creating defensive climates by transmitting attitudes such as 'I'm judging you', 'I'm in charge', 'I can manipulate you', 'I don't give a damn about you', 'I'm superior to you' or 'My mind is made up. Nothing you can say will alter it.' These attitudes inhibit and frustrate open or genuine communication. Reduce others' defensiveness by substituting understanding for evaluating, co-operating for controlling, explaining for manipulating, commitment and enthusiasm for neutrality, showing respect for a sense of superiority and open-mindedness for rigidity.
- Increase your range of responses to the statements and questions of others. Avoid over-use of evaluative responses (which express judgements) or interpretive responses (which 'read between the lines'). Instead increase the proportion of responses you use which simply indicate 'This is what I think you are saying' without adding or interpreting anything, probing responses, which ask for more information, and supportive responses, which agree, back up or offer psychological or material support.
- Allow for cultural variations in both verbal and non-verbal expression.
- Give careful thought to the concepts of effectiveness and appropriateness and how to apply them in your own interactions.
- Use facework and politeness to support the other person's positive and negative face as well as your own.
- Use convergence to the other person's communication style to increase mutuality but make sure your understanding of their style is accurate.
- Ground your conversations to ensure mutual understanding. Especially as the receiver of information initiated by others and if you come from an individualist background, increase the amount of probing you normally undertake.
- Recognise the negative effects of anxiety and uncertainty on initial encounters (especially intercultural ones) and follow the guidance in Box 7.8 to reduce them.
- Use inclusive language, such as sales representative instead of salesman, Chairperson instead of Chairman, people instead of men, the plural instead of he or him.
- Follow an ethical framework for your communications.
- Remember that though communication can usefully be analysed, people experience it as an undifferentiated whole.

requirements, coaches need a well-developed set of listening skills on the lines of those outlined previously.

Many management training courses include an exercise in which participants practise directing by giving instructions to a team of 'subordinates' on how to carry out a task – assemble a paper boat, organise cards in a complicated sequence, or work out a puzzle. In these exercises some of the main differences between the successful and unsuccessful instructors are these:

- Successful instructors give out very full instructions, first in outline and then in detail, for each stage of the task. They break down the task into units of a suitable size for the learners to absorb. They also reinterpret the instructions given to them in a way that makes them easily grasped by the learners. Less successful instructors prepare less carefully and interfere more readily when the task is in progress.
- Successful instructors get the delegating/doing balance right, neither taking over from the learners nor distancing themselves too far from the problems of execution.
- Successful instructors interpret any constraints built into the exercise, such as time limits, as significant pressure. Less successful instructors are often very relaxed about these constraints. On the other hand, successful instructors do not introduce constraints that do not exist in the rubric of the exercise.
- Successful instructors exercise self-control. Less successful instructors often increase the already heightened anxiety of those they are instructing by showing their own worry. The author of this book once heard an instructor say 'I'm completely confused.' It is not difficult to imagine how the learners who were depending on him felt!

The new emphasis on coaching as a leadership skill has refocused it on problem areas in subordinates' performance. The purpose is to help those being coached to identify their weaknesses and patterns of thinking and behaviour they are not aware of that will lead to repeated mistakes. Precisely because of low awareness and possible blocking, this process is often difficult. The following is some guidance on how to coach people through this process:

- The subordinates are asked to talk about a recent time when they were stuck or ineffective. These instances should be as specific and concrete as possible. These incidents can reveal gaps or inconsistencies in people's thinking or where their action did not work.
- Prompts are used to get them to recap on details such as their intentions, who did what, how they felt as a result and their consequent actions.
- Often these accounts reveal that the subordinates are deluded about their performance. For example, 'We made a great presentation but didn't get the boss to sign off. He says he cares about quality but he is a liar and a phoney.

On the other hand, I feel like a failure.' To penetrate these illusions, they are asked to give examples of the assessments they have made. This process helps people to see where they have jumped to conclusions, been inconsistent in their thinking or camouflaged error with defensive reasoning. It is important to listen not only to what happened but also to the assessments people made about it. In this example, a coach might ask, 'What led you to conclude you made a good presentation?' 'What evidence or examples do you have to support your contention that the boss is a liar and a phoney?' 'Does this really mean you are a failure?'

To improve at coaching, feedback must be obtained from those who have been on the receiving end. Many teachers and coaches are afraid that asking for feedback in this way will undermine their authority. It need not. If that authority is genuinely based on expertise, showing willingness to learn about how to communicate it better and how to meet the learners' needs usually increases their respect for their coach. For those who are willing to try, a specimen feedback questionnaire is given in Exercise 17. Guidance on 'How to coach' is given in Box 7.11.

## Mentoring

As Box 7.12 shows, mentoring can be valuable across a wide range of work situations. Generally, a mentor is someone senior and experienced in an organisation who undertakes to provide information, advice and support for a junior person in a relationship lasting over an extended period of time. The mentor need not be the junior person's line manager. An American study found that individuals who were mentored reported having more advantageous career and job outcomes than individuals who were not mentored, regardless of sex or level. Mentors' contributions to staff development and to helping junior staff become effective more quickly are very valuable to their organisations, as well as to the mentored individuals. Mentors themselves often gain great satisfaction from passing on the fruits of their experience, and can find the 'coaching' aspect helps their own development.

Research in several private firms and public service agencies revealed seven types of mentor assistance that are particularly helpful:

1. Helping a person to shift her or his mental context.
2. Listening when the mentoree has a problem.
3. Identifying mentoree feelings and verifying them.
4. Effectively confronting negative intentions or behaviour.
5. Providing appropriate information when needed.
6. Delegating authority or giving permission.
7. Encouraging exploration of options.[67]

**Box 7.11**

## How to coach

- Help subordinates recognise patterns of thinking and behaviour that produce performance weaknesses. Get them to focus on specific incidents, probe them in depth and assess them.
- Direct, by setting objectives, breaking down the task into units, but ensuring that the whole is understood. Agree individuals' targets and standards of performance.
- Motivate, by referring to the rewards and benefits to the individual or organisation from learning the skill or carrying out the task.
- Apply the techniques derived from the four models of learning described in Chapter 4:

  (i) cognitive: facilitate arousal, rehearsal, coding, transfer to memory and appropriate placement in memory;
  (ii) behaviourist: use repetition and reward;
  (iii) involvement: guide learners through the processes of experience, analysis, conceptualisation and testing;
  (iv) double-loop: map defensive action rules applied to a live problem by dialoguing with a peer, creating productive action rules and applying them to the problem.

- See the task as the learner will see it.
- Aim to help learners progress from dependence to being able to perform their task independently.
- Build a trusting relationship based on learners' belief in the coach's expertise and good intentions towards themselves.
- Show confidence in the learner's ability to learn and to succeed in the task. Most learners are anxious about what happens if they fail to learn or perform to the required standard. This anxiety interferes with learning. The coach should try to reduce anxiety about personal consequences, and to make learning as risk-free as possible. A very few learners, however, benefit from having their anxiety increased to an appropriate level, because they are lazy or over-confident.
- Give timely and constructive feedback in a skilled way.
- Handle the contextual issues, e.g. make sure the physical environment is as suitable as possible.
- Increase your own speed of learning by actively seeking feedback.

Mentoring is a process whereby mentor and mentoree work together to discover and develop the mentoree's latent abilities, provide the mentoree with knowledge and skills as opportunities and needs arise and enable the mentoree to sharpen skills and hone her or his thinking.

Mentors should:

- communicate explicitly what works for them and why;
- encourage mentorees to develop a repertoire of role models, judging these by effectiveness (Is the role model successful?), feasibility (Would her behaviour work for me?) and attractiveness (Do I want to be like her?);

**Box 7.12**

- Ibarra (2000) argued that professional organisations, such as investment banks and law firms, are buyers in a seller's market for talent, competing with Internet companies especially. Instead of letting 'natural selection' determine who makes it to partner or lowering standards, seniors should mentor juniors, understanding that the transition is a difficult one.
- A young subordinate was giving his new manager a lot of trouble. Although enthusiastic and very good at the part of his job that involved external relations, within the organisation he was resentful of authority, poor at co-operating with colleagues and passively resistant to carrying out those aspects of his job description that did not appeal to him. Eventually, after a series of unsuccessful attempts to get him to improve, his manager spoke to the person who had mentored him in his previous organisation. The mentor agreed to see the young subordinate, a session took place and the young man returned contrite, with raised awareness of his weaknesses and expressing the intention of acting differently.

*Sources*: Ibarra, H. (2000) 'Making partner: a mentor's guide to the psychological journey', *Harvard Business Review*, March–April, pp. 147–155.
Interview with a manager, author's research.

- provide emotional and practical support at the most difficult moments.

People who make good mentors:

- are confident of their own position in the organisation and do not feel threatened by or resentful of the mentoree's opportunities;
- are perceptive and sufficiently senior to be well-informed about the organisation and able to facilitate the mentoree's opportunities;
- are knowledgeable about the mentoree's area of work;
- are committed to fulfilling their own particular responsibilities to the mentoree;
- are easily accessible to the mentoree and willing to negotiate a planned timetable;
- treat their mentoring role as an integral part of their own job responsibilities, not an add-on.

How far-reaching the relationship between mentor and junior is can vary. Some writers distinguish mentors from sponsors (for a protégé), who provide career support such as advocacy for promotions, feedback and coaching, on the grounds that a mentor offers psychosocial support and friendship as well as instrumental career support. Mentoring may be marked by substantial emotional commitment from both partners, and this can be enriching, but there are dangers. The mentoree may become dependent and suffer from fear of not meeting the mentor's expectations, of the relationship being ended and of gossip.

Mentoring can be particularly valuable to people from minority groups. It can go some way to helping them overcome the obstacles caused by prejudice. One woman described what her mentor did for her as assigning her work so she could get experience in that particular area in order to get on, refusing job transfers for her that were not to her advantage, introducing her to the network of power relations in the organisation, encouraging her, boosting her confidence and providing a role model, helping to overcome the shortage of women role models.

## Consultancy

The function of a consultant is to provide advice on work-related problems. The advice should be based on a wider experience than may be available to the people facing the problem and should have the benefit of an outsider's perspective. Since consultants are often involved in introducing change, the section on that in Chapter 8 is relevant. There are now many different models of consultancy, both internal and external, including process consultancy, and they cannot all be covered; this section will be confined to some basic points about how to behave in the face-to-face relations implied by consultancy. The process is divided into ten stages, following Bellman.[68]

### *1. Entry*

The fact that consultants have been called in suggests that the client has defined the problem, and probably the solution, in his or her own mind but his or her definition may be wrong and the consultants are not bound by it. They should, however:

- respect the client's willingness to act on the problem, not ignore it;
- start where the client wants to begin, not where they want to begin, with the parts of the problem that seem particularly important to the client;
- demonstrate their understanding by, for instance, body language;
- check that they have understood the problem by repeating their understanding in their own words;
- show their commitment to helping solve the problem, but not take it over – it remains the client's problem;
- explain what resources they have to draw on, including expertise, time, equipment, money and so on;
- describe real experiences they have had, to provide reassurance about their ability to handle this problem;
- negotiate a way of working which suits both – Will everything be discussed? How much will be put in writing?;
- ask for copies of readily available materials;
- arrange for meetings with two or three others who could give them perspective on the problem;
- schedule their next meeting with the client before they leave this one, telling him or her that next time they get together they will propose a way of attacking

the problem. The client may want earlier action, but consultants cannot suggest solutions until they have more information;

- as they close the meeting ask the client if s/he is getting what s/he expected, in order to legitimate discussing the consulting process.

### *2. Contract*

After entry, a meeting takes place to agree what the problem is, the consultants' approach, how they will collect information, who from, how much time it will take, when each step will happen and the estimated cost. At this meeting, the consultants should:

- make the meeting business-like, emphasising clarity, structure and understanding and getting the customer's support for all the main points. The contract meeting is difficult to handle well as it should not be over-formal, because that will reduce the ease of the future working relationship but without formality it is hard to get all these points clear and firmly agreed;
- follow up the meeting with a memo setting out the agreement, check that this is agreed and create opportunities for changing the contract as they progress and new information points to a need for change.

### *3. Data collection and 4. Analysis*

Except for the section on 'interviewing' in Chapter 5 the skills required for Stages 3 and 4 are beyond the scope of this book as they are not primarily interpersonal.

### *5. Reporting back*

Data must be presented in a way that the client can understand and accept. Bellman suggests data first and analysis second, only after the data are accepted. This is in order to build towards acceptance of the consultants' analysis. The consultants report back to a meeting of people who are crucial to initiating action, so that they will be involved; the consultants run the meeting. They should anticipate defensive behaviours from those present, as consultants' data can often seem critical of their past performance. However, the data come from their organisation, and the implications are their concern. When people challenge the data as false or distorted, the consultants should ask them for the real data and add them to what they have already collected.

### *6. Recommendations*

Consultants can either develop alternatives of their own, help clients develop alternatives, which is better, or recommend their preferred alternative. Decisions that are chosen from alternatives give the decision-makers increased confidence – they feel they are in control.

**Box 7.13**

> 'When you are working as an adviser', said the small business consultant, 'In principle you should get all the information out and then start to think about solutions. In practice, it often doesn't work like that because the person with the information cannot or will not readily articulate all he or she knows. For instance, recently I was advising a manager in a small business with a personnel problem. A key member of staff had a long record of short-term work absences for sickness. We had all the relevant documentation (over 100 pages) in front of us to guide our attempts to find a solution. However, the manager was very unforthcoming with details. So I began making suggestions, based on what I knew and the guidelines. Time after time, the manager, without rejecting my ideas, showed by her silence and expression that, in some respect or other, my suggestion did not fit the bill. Then my task was to probe until I found what information it was that she had, but had not disclosed, that made my suggestion unworkable. Finally, after about three hours, I had enough knowledge to put forward a proposal that she thought would work. It was slow and unorthodox, but I do not think in that case any other method would have worked.'
>
> *Source*: Interview, author's research.

When preparing their presentation, the consultants should find out how this is done in the organisation and what the client is likely to expect based on past experience, and then do it better. Above all, they should keep in mind the client's focus on action and results and avoid getting involved with the data or the analysis. The section on Making presentations in Chapter 8 gives more guidance for this stage.

### *7. Decision*

This meeting should involve people with relevant expertise, people with the necessary authority, those who are affected by the decision, those who need to be committed to the decision and those who need to support the decision. The meeting can be advisory only, if the organisational culture requires a one-person decision. The consultants make sure the people know what is being decided and its potential impact on them and the organisation – costs, benefits, consequences and potential problems. They allow for full discussion but are firm in getting a decision before the meeting ends.

### *8. Action*

Momentum is built by urging immediate action. The consultants carry out their part of the action promptly as an example. In the early stages they monitor action closely to make sure that management is committed to the project. They also support and reinforce people who are trying new behaviours as a result of the changes being instituted. Review meetings are held. Consultants anticipate problems and develop contingency approaches.

### *9. Evaluation*

Evaluation must be embedded in the overall plan. People should be told that their project will be evaluated, as this delivers better results. Checkpoints and a progress review are built in along the way. Source credibility is important in evaluators.

### *10. Exit*

Consultants should ensure that the client is satisfied before ending the consultancy arrangement and that the way is left open for future consultation.

## Employee communications

The two studies in Box 7.14 indicate the wide range of situations in which employee communications are important. Many organisations now stress the centrality of face-to-face communication with employees: 'An effective ongoing practice, the face-to-face meeting plays a crucial role during times of uncertainty and change.'[69] Based on feedback from employees, one business learned that face-to-face encounters had made a critical difference in how it managed a major acquisition. The business had sent senior managers to every major installation of the organisation it had acquired, so that 75 per cent of employees had an opportunity to meet the Chief Executive Officer and other top officials. 'We stood there for hours, until every question was answered', one commented. This gave employees the chance to 'take a measure of you, look you in the eye, ask some questions and see how you responded.' However, as Box 7.15 indicates, cultural differences within Europe affect the prevailing approach to employee communications in different countries.

**Box 7.14**

- A longitudinal study of 91 transferred employees showed that how well they adjusted was related to how much sense they made of the ways in which tasks were communicated in their new environment. Once employees moved to a new site, those whose expectations for organisational support and communication were unmet experienced negative adjustment beyond that explained by their initial expectations and background traits (Jablin and Kramer, 1998).
- Another study found that using appropriate impression management messages can increase how fair employees consider reward allocations and how responsibly they react to those rewards (Tata and Rhodes, 1996).

*Sources*: Jablin, F. M. and M. W. Kramer (1998) 'Communication-related sense-making and adjustment during job transfers', *Management Communication Quarterly*, vol. 12, no. 2, pp. 155–182.
Tata, J. and S. R. Rhodes (1996) 'Impression management messages and reactions to organizational reward allocations: The mediating influence of fairness and responsibility', *Communication Quarterly*, vol. 44, no. 3, pp. 379–393.

Box 7.15

### European variations in employee communication practices

A study of six leading companies highlighted the role played by national culture in European employee communication policy and practices. Comments included the following:

- Unilever: 'Northern Europe management is much more open. Southern European management is a lot more paternalistic in its approach to employees.'
- British Airways: 'Meetings are more prevalent in some areas, and both content and degree of formality vary. In general, German employee communications are most formal, in contrast to the Mediterranean preference for informal face to face communication.'
- Henkel: 'In Southern Europe, the social distance between managers and staff is greater.'

*Source*: Fourboul, C. V. and F. Bournois (1999) 'Strategic communication with employees in large European companies: a typology', *European Management Journal*, vol. 17, no. 2, pp. 204–217.

Employee communications should:

- communicate not only what is happening, but why and how it is happening;
- be timely – telling people what is known as soon as it is known, rather than waiting until every detail is resolved;
- be continuous, especially during periods of change or crisis;
- link the 'big picture' with the 'little picture';
- avoid trying to dictate the way people should feel about the news.

## Service encounters

'Already there are more people working in ethnic restaurants than in the coal, steel, automobile and ship-building industries put together.' This quote from Charles Handy[70] suggests the importance of service encounters in the UK economy. Service encounters are also fertile ground for overt and suppressed conflict, especially when there are cultural and linguistic differences between the provider and the customer.[71] For service providers, who include cashiers, food servers, bank tellers, receptionists, physicians, lawyers, counsellors, hairdressers, flight attendants, teachers, consultants, investment brokers, insurance brokers and more, interacting with the public either face-to-face or by telephone is a central part of their role. While in some cases their functions may include personal selling, which is described in Chapter 8, the service provision encounter itself is distinct. Research has shown that service providers typically engage in one or more of three types of communication behaviour: courteous, personalised or manipulative.

- Courteous communication includes greetings, smiles, eye contact, small talk, humour and use of names.
- Personalised communication attempts to address the particular needs of individual customers. It involves asking questions to identify customer concerns, offering options and advice, listening attentively, responding sensitively, explaining complex issues in simple language and providing informal support.

**Box 7.16**

- Sir Brian Pitman, Chairman of Lloyds TSB Bank, talking about a new call centre in Sunderland, said that some people have 'smiling' voices and others have sour voices: 'We need people with smiling voices,' he said.
- A negotiator for a lettings agency sent out the agency agreement, with its terms, to only the male co-owner of a flat owned by a couple. He did this despite having been told clearly by the male co-owner to send it to both parties, and despite his computer records from previous business showing the female as the main owner. When the female co-owner telephoned to object, the negotiator told her she was 'over-reacting' – a classic male chauvinist expression, used only for women, meaning being over-emotional. He lost the business.

*Sources*: Interview, BBC1 TV News, 14 March 2001; experience of the author.

- Manipulative communication attempts to control customers. It includes fake smiles, sales pitches, threats and rewards, bureaucratic routines, emotional detachment, reliance on standardised 'scripts' and attempts to dominate.

These three can be combined. For example, a postal service counter clerk might smile at a new customer, give a greeting and listen attentively but use standard scripts and procedures to process customers quickly and accurately.[72] However, most service providers tend to rely more heavily on one than the others in different interactions, depending on the following:

- The service provider's training and experience.
- The service provider's role. Fast food servers, for instance, are not expected to act as individuals but to be 'functionally equivalent'.[73]
- The perceived social status of the customer. Rafaeli[74] found that supermarket check-out operators show more courtesy to men and that men get served before women in department stores, regardless of the gender of the assistant or the type of store or department. This applied especially to men in suits, not casual clothes. How well female customers dressed affected how quickly and courteously they were served.
- Time pressure. The longer the time allowed to the service provider for interactions, the more courtesy they showed; the shorter the time, the more they used manipulative behaviours.
- The effects of technology. Fast-growing telephone service operations have led to an increase in routine (i.e. manipulative) interactions, but on the other hand the use of sophisticated technology backing the human being enables them to identify and address customers' unique situations, so increasing personal service.

Customers' long-term satisfaction is strongly affected when expectations for courtesy, efficiency and caring are not satisfied. To gain customers' compliance, service providers (such as doctors) need to give enough information. Prompting and showing a customer orientation can be effective in cross-selling other products but sales pitches give mixed results.[75] When service employees exhibit emotional intelligence, consumer attitudes, intentions, and behaviours in service encounters are positively affected.[76] In general, accountability (which was introduced in Chapter 3) increases employees' performance, leading them to work harder and attend to clients' needs more carefully. However, in service encounters it has been shown that accountability can create apprehension about being able to justify their actions, and so reduce efficiency and effectiveness.[77]

## SUMMARY – WORK APPLICATIONS FOR COMMUNICATION

Coaching can be seen as a training activity or as helping subordinates to deal with performance weaknesses. In either case, it depends on applying learning theory appropriately, providing support and listening with empathy. To improve their own performances, coaches need feedback from those they coach.

Mentors need to combine expertise in the mentoree's task area with social perceptiveness and the communication skills that will enable them to coach, facilitate and support.

A basic consultancy process has ten separate stages: entry, contract, data collection, analysis, reporting back, recommendations decision, action, evaluation and exit. Most of these stages involve face-to-face interaction with the client. There is a checklist of points to remember at each stage.

The new emphasis in employee communications on face-to-face meetings places demands on managers' skills in responding to employees' questions and assertions.

Service encounters, which are of increasing importance in European economies, depend on a combination of courteous, personalised and manipulative communication skills.

## CHAPTER OVERVIEW

Interpersonal communication at work may be face-to-face or indirect, formal or informal, and transmitted verbally or non-verbally. Communication is affected by language, communicator style, the differences between one- and two-way communication, power and status, culture, gender and disability. These effects on communication give rise to barriers, which can be analysed as intrinsic, individual-level and inter-group. To be high in quality, communication must overcome these barriers. Competence in communication can be defined in terms of effectiveness (achieving goals) and appropriateness (matching others' expectations and behaviours) but there are cultural differences in what counts as competent. Making communication work results from having an agreed ethical framework and applying facework and politeness, communication accommodation, grounding and overcoming anxiety and uncertainty. Coaching, mentoring, consultancy, employee communications and service encounters are work activities that rely particularly on applying communication skills.

## EXERCISES

1. Think of two recent intercultural encounters at work. If possible, one should be an instance when communication did not go well and the other when it did go well. Compare the two encounters.
2. Watch a video of a business interaction, such as a sales encounter or an interview. Identify examples of communicating content, signalling, communicating relationship data and distributing communicative control.
3. Give examples of how a major downsizing could be expressed as either a problem or an opportunity.
4. Watch a video to identify instances of:
   (a) appropriate/inappropriate assertiveness;
   (b) aggression and submission.
5. Construct three examples that break the rules of coherence for messages.
6. Construct five examples that break the rules of efficiency for messages, state which rule each breaks and explain your reasoning.
7. In a mixed-culture group, discuss whether the following five basic rules for making a promise apply in and constitute a complete set of the rules required for each culture represented.
   (a) A promise must include a sentence indicating that the speaker will do some act in the future.
   (b) The receiver would rather that the speaker do the act than not do it.
   (c) It should not be obvious that the act would be done in the normal course of events.
   (d) The speaker must intend to do the act.
   (e) It establishes an obligation for the speaker to do the act.
8. Work alone to identify some basic rules for requesting or ordering. Then, in a mixed-culture group, compare your rules, to see if they are the same in different cultures.
9. In some cultures, to admire an object in someone's home obligates them to give it. Working in a mixed-culture group, identify more rules like this.
10. Analyse a video-recorded intercultural work interaction for examples of low-context and high-context communication, and record who used them.
11. Analyse a video-recorded mixed gender work interaction for examples of 'feminine' and 'masculine' ways of speaking, and record who used them.
12. In each of the following statements, identify one or more hidden messages that may produce a defensive climate:

(a) 'I can't understand the high level of vehicle breakdown we're getting. Are you sure you're keeping to the proper maintenance schedule?'
(b) 'Just make sure you don't let this stock level drop so low again next month.'
(c) 'Whether you like it or not, this is the way the Managing Director likes it done.'
(d) In response to an expressed grievance: 'I'm sorry you feel that way, but now could we get on with the job?'

13. A supermarket has three checkouts. During one busy Saturday morning half-hour, three announcements were made over the tannoy system, dealing with a reduced price offer, a sales promotion and a late-night opening. At the end of the half-hour, recall of the announcements by the checkout operators was 33 per cent – two remembered the late-night opening and one of these two remembered the reduced-price offer. The third checkout operator thought they recalled an announcement of a new product line, although in fact no such announcement was made. What factors might have influenced these recall rates?

14. Complete the rating scale given in Table 7.6. *See the Appendix to find out how to analyse your responses to this questionnaire.*

15. The text gives examples of how differences in communication practices can lead to misunderstanding and even conflict. Collect a list of other examples. Produce examples of differences in:

(a) directness/indirectness;
(b) non-verbal behaviour;

**Table 7.6 Communicating scale**

| In the interaction (meeting/interview/negotiation) just completed, I feel I: | *Strongly Agree* | | | | *Strongly Disagree* |
|---|---|---|---|---|---|
| 1. Stated my points clearly and precisely | X | X | X | X | X |
| 2. Adjusted to the other person's level of understanding without being demeaning | X | X | X | X | X |
| 3. Explained any jargon that might be unfamiliar to the other person | X | X | X | X | X |
| 4. Started from the other person's position rather than my own | X | X | X | X | X |
| 5. Used progressive approximations to explain points causing difficulty | X | X | X | X | X |
| 6. Divided difficult points into smaller pieces | X | X | X | X | X |
| 7. Used concrete terms, not abstract ones | X | X | X | X | X |
| 8. Gave examples | X | X | X | X | X |
| 9. Repeated difficult points in different ways | X | X | X | X | X |
| 10. Encouraged the other person to ask questions | X | X | X | X | X |
| 11. Gave short answers | X | X | X | X | X |
| 12. Waited for responses to short answers before enlarging | X | X | X | X | X |
| 13. Asked questions to check for understanding | X | X | X | X | X |

(c) style;
(d) encoding and decoding;
(e) face.

16. Work in threes (two participants and an observer). In turn, each participant chooses a topic on which they are knowledgeable and on which the other participant knows much less. They have five minutes for the speaker to impart as much information as possible to the other person. The objective is to practise grounding. Use the examples of successful and unsuccessful grounding given in Table 7.5, together with the comments on it in the text, to guide the activity and the observer's feedback.

17. Instruct a learner in how to perform a simple task such as knitting or changing a fuse. It should be a task that the instructor has, and the learner has not, done before. The instructor gives all instructions verbally in advance; s/he may not demonstrate how to perform the task. Then the learner attempts to perform the task. The instructor may not intervene while the learner tries. At the end of the exercise, the learner uses the 'Coaching feedback rating scale' given in Table 7.7 to report back on how the learning experience felt. If possible, the exercise should be video-recorded and watched as part of the debrief.

18. Counselling is an important face-to-face aspect of mentoring. It is closely related to coaching, but with a greater emphasis on getting the person concerned to confront their own problem. Active listening skills are vital. The aim of the exercise is to let participants experience how it feels to be helped to confront a problem, to examine a range of counselling styles and to develop flexibility and sensitivity in helping another person confront a problem. Procedure:

    (a) Participants are divided into pairs and named as A and B; each notes down a problem or failing they have noticed in someone else (who should be unknown to the rest of the class).
    (b) A describes his or her 'case' to B, then for five minutes B role plays counselling A as if it were A's problem or failing. A gives B feedback on how B's counselling 'felt'.
    (c) Each pair in turn repeats the exercise – A describing the case and B counselling A on the problem – for three minutes in front of the class. After each role play, the class notes down what counselling style they thought B was using, how they think that style might affect the outcome and different approaches that might have been used.
    (d) There is a class discussion of the counselling incidents presented, drawing on the notes made after each role play.
    (e) B describes his or her case to A, then A role plays counselling B on the problem for five minutes. If preferred, at this stage some pairs can be reallocated as observers to other pairs, to ensure that they receive feedback.

**Table 7.7 Coaching feedback rating scale**

Rate your instructor on the following scale:

| | | |
|---|---|---|
| S/he knew exactly how to perform the task | ×—×—×—×—×—× | S/he had no idea how to perform the task |
| S/he told us our purpose and our objective | ×—×—×—×—×—× | S/he failed to tell us what we were trying to do and why |
| S/he explained clearly how to perform the task | ×—×—×—×—×—× | S/he was confusing about how to perform the task |
| S/he told us the standards of performance | ×—×—×—×—×—× | S/he did not tell us the performance standards |
| S/he was understanding about our difficulties in learning or executing the task and helped us overcome them | ×—×—×—×—×—× | S/he was not helpful in overcoming difficulties and seemed not to understand |
| S/he rewarded and encouraged our efforts | ×—×—×—×—×—× | S/he blamed us for our errors |
| While I was learning I had confidence in the instructor's ability to bring about a successful outcome | ×—×—×—×—×—× | While I was learning, I was mistrustful of the instructor's ability to bring about a successful outcome |
| I finished the session with a sense of achievement and well-being | ×—×—×—×—×—× | I finished the session with a sense of failure and lack of self-confidence |

19. This exercise concerns the meeting between managers and a group of staff of Mattey Tractors, a European farm equipment manufacturer and distributor, about an agreed takeover by an American corporation. Mattey Tractors is one of the most famous names in the world tractor industry and employs 3500 people in factories in its domestic and neighbouring countries. The agreed bid has thwarted a rival offer from a domestic consortium; there are rumours that the American bid has been accepted because of close links between the two companies in North American distribution and agricultural credit markets. The buyer has been expanding fast in the domestic farm equipment market, but has publicly announced that it is looking for opportunities for rationalisation and cost savings.

    *As a private study or group discussion exercise,* draft the statement that the managers will make at the start of the meeting with the employees of Mattey Tractors. What questions should they anticipate? How should these questions be answered?

    *As a role play,* enact the meeting. Ideally, the managers should be represented by a three-person team and the employees by as many people as possible (e.g. the rest of the class), allowing for at least two observers.

20. A motor insurance customer telephones his broker, which is a large national agency. He wants to extend his car insurance to cover a van which he is borrowing for a few days; in the course of looking for his policy number, he finds that he has no policy document and only a temporary cover note, even though he paid for the insurance three months before. He telephones to sort out both matters.

    *As a private study or group discussion exercise*:

    (a) Imagine that you are a customer service representative for the broker. What would you say to the customer following his initial explanation?
    (b) The customer says that he is convinced that the broker failed to issue the necessary documents, although there are, in fact, other possibilities – they have been lost in the post or he received them and mislaid them. What would you say in answer to this accusation?
    (c) There is no doubt that the cover is in place – the computer record shows it. However, the policy cannot be extended to cover a van – the underwriters have excluded it. What would you say about these points?
    (d) What kind of telephone manner would help you in this service encounter?

    *As a role play*, conduct the telephone call.

21. In this exercise, a bank customer service representative writes to or telephones a customer who has had a postdated cheque debited from her account a week before it was dated, resulting in an apparent substantial overdraft. The problem is explained in the following letter from the customer:

21, Crichton Road,<br>London SW10 1NQ<br>4.1.2002

Northern Wool Bank,
Smithfield
re: a/c 55554444

I am writing because I note with concern that my bank statement shows that the cheque for £52,618.19 to Porter Dodge, which my records show was dated 16.12.2001, was paid out on 11.12.2001, resulting in a negative balance from 11.12.2001 to 14.12.2001 of £13,127. Although, because I was going abroad on 9th December, I had to send the cheque to Porter Dodge in advance of the required date, my own records show that I had postdated it, to allow time for the funds being credited from various sources to be received into my account. I am therefore unwilling either to pay any charges on the overdraft or to have my record stand as having incurred one, when the cause is an error on the part of the bank. I look forward to hearing from you.

Yours faithfully,

Investigation has shown that there undoubtedly was an error on the part of the bank. Role A will write to or telephone Role B to apologise and explain what the bank will do to correct matters. It is not possible to alter the record that shows an overdraft.

*As a private study or group discussion exercise,* draft the letter that Role A will send to Role B.

*As a role play*: Role A telephones Role B.

22. A is a negotiator for a lettings agency. In regard to one property, s/he has followed the agency's practice of taking a 'holding' deposit from the potential tenant without prior consultation with the landlord, even though s/he knew that the landlord had placed the business with two other agents. S/he has begun the process of taking up references. Now the landlord has telephoned to say that she has a suitable tenant through another agency.

    A has to explain the situation to the tenant.

23. The scale in Table 7.8 can be used to assess performance in a range of work activities, including making complaints, making presentations, delegating,

**Table 7.8 Inter-group interaction scale**

| In the interaction (meeting/interview/negotiation) just completed, I feel I: | *Strongly Agree* | *Agree* | *Neither Agree Nor Disagree* | *Disagree* | *Strongly Disagree* |
|---|---|---|---|---|---|
| 1. was aware that the other party might be treating the encounter as an inter-group one | X______X______X______X______X______X | | | | |
| 2. was aware that the other party might be affected by ethnocentrism | X______X______X______X______X______X | | | | |
| 3. was conscious of my own stereotypes of the others in the encounter and the barriers they can create | X______X______X______X______X______X | | | | |
| 4. was aware that the other party might be seeing me in stereotypical terms | X______X______X______X______X______X | | | | |
| 5. was conscious of the possible presence of sexism, racism and other forms of group prejudice among the participants | X______X______X______X______X______X | | | | |
| 6. was conscious of the barriers to communication that might be created by sexism, racism and other forms of group prejudice among the participants | X______X______X______X______X______X | | | | |
| 7. was alert to barriers arising from differences in surface culture | X______X______X______X______X______X | | | | |
| 8. was alert to barriers arising from differences in values | X______X______X______X______X______X | | | | |
| 9. was alert to barriers arising from differences in beliefs or assumptions | X______X______X______X______X______X | | | | |

giving feedback and reprimanding. *See the Appendix to find out how to analyse your responses to this questionnaire.*

## FURTHER READING

Bellman, G. M. (1992) *Getting Things Done When You Are Not In Charge*. San Francisco, Calif.: Barrett-Koehler.

Evans, D. W. (1990) *People, Communication and Organisations*, 2nd edn. London: Pitman.

Gudykunst, W. B. and Y. Y. Kim (1997) *Communicating with Strangers: An Approach to Intercultural Communication*. 3rd edn. Boston, Mass.: McGraw-Hill.

Gutek, B. A. (1995) *The Dynamics of Service: Reflections on the Changing Nature of Customer / Provider Interactions*. San Francisco: Jossey-Bass.

Hall, E. T. (1976) *Beyond Culture*. Garden City, New York: Anchor.

Reid, M. and R. Hammersley (2000) *Communicating Successfully in Groups*. London: Routledge. Chapters 7–12 are relevant to Chapter 11 of this book.

Shea, G. F. (1992) *Mentoring: A Guide to the Basics*. London: Kogan Page.

Thorne, K. (2001) *Personal Coaching: Releasing Potential at Work*. London: Kogan Page.

Ting-Toomey, S. and F. Korzenny (eds) (1989) *Language, Communication and Culture: Current Directions*. Newbury Park, Calif.: Sage.

## REFERENCES

1. Zorn, M. T. and M. T. Violanti (1996) 'Communication abilities and individual achievement in organizations', *Management Communication Quarterly*, vol. 10, no. 2, pp. 139–167.
2. Norton, R. W. (1983) *Communicator Style: Theory, Applications and Measures*. Beverley Hills, Calif.: Sage.
3. Bateson, G. (1958) *Naven*. Stanford, Calif.: Stanford University Press. *For a fuller exploration see* Watzlawick, P., J. Beavin and D. Jackson (1967) *Pragmatics of Human Communication: A Study of Interactional Patterns, Pathologies and Paradoxes*. New York: Norton.
4. Gouldner, A. M. (1960) 'The norm of reciprocity', *American Sociological Review*, vol. 25, no. 2, pp. 161–178.
5. Nakanishi, M. (1986) 'Perceptions of self-disclosure in initial interaction: A Japanese sample', *Human Communication Research*, vol. 13, no. 2, pp. 167–190.
6. Chen, G.-M. (1989) 'Relationships of the dimensions of intercultural communication competence', *Communication Quarterly*, vol. 37, no. 2, pp. 118–133.
7. Argyle, M. (1973) *The Psychology of Interpersonal Behavior*. Harmondsworth: Penguin.
8. Argyle, M., V. Salter, N. C. Nicholson, M. Williams and P. Burgess (1970) 'The communication of inferior and superior attitudes by verbal and non-verbal signals', *British Journal of the Society of Clinical Psychology*, vol. 9, pp. 222–31.
9. Marshak, R. J. (1993) 'Managing the metaphors of change', *Organizational Dynamics*, Summer, pp. 44–56.
10. Jacobs, S. and S. Jackson (1983) 'Strategy and structure in conversational influence attempts', *Communication Monographs*, vol. 50, pp. 285–304.
11. Grice, H. P. (1975) 'Logic and conversation' in P. Cole and J. Morgan (eds) *Syntax and Semantics*, vol. 3. NewYork: Academic Press.
12. Searle, J. (1969) *Speech Acts: An Essay in the Philosophy of Language*. Cambridge: Cambridge University Press

13. Norton, op. cit.
14. Ellemers, N., C. van Dyck, S. Hinkle and A. Jacobs (2000) 'Inter-group differentiation in social context: identity needs versus audience constraints', *Social Psychology Quarterly*, vol. 63, no. 1, pp. 60–74.
15. Brown, A. D. and K. Starkey (1994) 'The effect of organisational culture on communication and information', *Journal of Management Studies*, vol. 31, no. 6, pp. 807–828.
16. Philipsen, G. (1989) 'Speech and the communal function' in S. Ting-Toomey and F. Korzenny (eds) *Language, Communication and Culture: Current Directions*. Newbury Park, Calif.: Sage.
17. Hall, E. T. (1976) *Beyond Culture*. New York: Doubleday.
18. Servaes, J. (1988) 'Cultural identity in East and West', *Howard Journal of Communications*, vol. 1, no. 2, pp. 58–71.
19. Alban-Metcalfe, B. and M. A. West (1991) 'Women managers' in J. Firth-Cozens and M. A. West (eds) *Women at Work*. Milton Keynes: Open University Press.
20. Marshall, J. (1993) 'Viewing organizational communication from a feminist perspective: A critique and some offerings', *Communication Yearbook*, vol. 16, pp. 122–143.
21. Colwill, N. and T. I. Sztaba (1986) 'Organizational genderlect: the problem of two different languages', *Business Quarterly*, vol. 3, pp. 64–66.
22. Grove, T. G. and D. L. Werkman (1991) 'Conversations with able-bodied and visibly disabled strangers: An adversarial test of predicted outcome value and uncertainty reduction theories', *Human Communication Research*, vol. 17, pp. 507–534.
23. Coleman, L. and B. De Paulo (1991) 'Uncovering the human spirit: moving beyond disability and "missed" communication' in N. Coupland, H. Giles and J. Wiemann (eds) *'Miscommunication' and Problematic Talk*. Newbury Park, Calif.: Sage.
24. Han, Z. L. (1999) 'Grounding and information communication in intercultural and intracultural dyadic discourse', *Discourse Processes*, vol. 28, no. 3, pp. 195–221.
25. McLuhan, M. (1964) *Understanding Media: The Extensions of Man*. London: Routledge and Kegan Paul.
26. LePoire, B. A. and S. M. Yoshimura (1999) 'The effects of expectancies and actual communication on nonverbal adaptation and communication outcomes: A test of interaction adaptation theory', *Communication Monographs*, vol. 66, no. 1, pp. 1–30.
27. Douglas, W. (1991) 'Expectations about initial interaction: an examination of the effects of global uncertainty', *Human Communication Research*, vol. 17, pp. 355–384.
28. Harville, D. L. (1993) 'Person/job fit model of communication apprehension in organisations', *Management Communication Quarterly*, vol. 6, pp. 150–165.
29. Douglas, op. cit.
30. Manusov, V. and R. Hegde (1993) 'Communicative outcomes of stereotype-based expectancies: An observational study of cross-cultural dyads', *Communication Quarterly*, vol. 41, no. 3, pp. 338–354.
31. Honeycutt, J. M. (1991) 'The role of nonverbal behaviors in modifying expectancies during initial encounters', *Southern Communication Journal*, vol. 56, no. 3, pp. 161–177.
32. Hall, op. cit.
33. Clark, J. (1997) 'Some discriminatory consequences of cultural difference in communication behaviour in the Australian workplace', *Australian Journal of Communication*, vol. 24, no. 1, pp. 70–81.
34. Chen, L. (1997) 'Verbal adaptive strategies in U.S. American dyadic interactions with U.S. American or East-Asian partners', *Communication Monographs*, vol. 64, no. 4, pp. 302–323.

35. Bernstein, B. (1971) *Class, Codes and Control: Theoretical Studies Toward a Sociology of Language*. London: Routledge and Kegan Paul.
36. Gudykunst, W. B. (1988) 'Uncertainty and anxiety' in Y. Y. Kim and W. B. Gudykunst (eds) *Theories in Intercultural Communication*. Newbury Park, Calif.: Sage, pp. 123–156.
37. Kim, M.-S. and M. Bresnahan (1996) 'Cognitive basis of gender communication: a cross-cultural investigation of perceived constraints in requesting', *Communication Quarterly*, vol. 44, pp. 53–69.
38. Wigboldus, D. H. J., G. R. Semin and R. Spears (2000) 'How do we communicate stereotypes? Linguistic bases and inferential consequences', *Journal of Personality and Social Psychology*, vol. 78, no. 1, pp. 5–18.
39. Maass, A. D., D. Salvi, L. Arcuri and G. R. Semin (1989) 'Language use in inter-group contexts: The linguistic inter-group bias', *Journal of Personality and Social Psychology*, vol. 57, pp. 981–993.
40. Brislin, R., K. Cushner, C. Cherrie and M. Yong (1986) *Intercultural Interactions*. Beverly Hills, Calif.: Sage.
41. *Berlin Declaration: Language Studies in Higher Education: A Key Contribution to European Education*. Berlin: European Language Council.
42. Reinsch, N. L. Jr (1996) 'Management communication ethics research: Finding the bull's-eye', *Management Communication Quarterly*, vol. 9, no. 3, pp. 349–358.
43. Deetz, S. (1990) 'Reclaiming the subject matter as a guide to mutual understanding: Effectiveness and ethics in interpersonal interaction', *Communication Quarterly*, vol. 38, no. 3, pp. 226–243.
44. Habermas, J. (1998) *On the Pragmatics of Communication*. Cambridge, Mass.: MIT Press.
45. Argyris, C. (1965) 'Explorations in intercultural competence I', *Journal of Applied Behavioural Science*, vol. 1, pp. 58–83.
46. Argyris, C. (1965) 'Explorations in intercultural competence II', *Journal of Applied Behavioural Science*, vol. 1, pp. 255–269.
47. Bochner, A. P. and C. W. Kelly (1974) 'Interpersonal competence: rationale, philosophy and implementation of a conceptual framework', *Speech Teacher*, vol. 23, pp. 279–301.
48. Wellmon, T. A. (1988) 'Conceptualizing organizational communication competence: A rules-based perspective', *Management Communication Quarterly*, vol. 1, no. 4, pp. 515–534.
49. Chen, G.-M. and W. J. Starosta (2000) 'The development and validation of the intercultural sensitivity scale', *Human Communication*, vol. 3, no. 1, pp. 1–14.
50. Chen, op. cit.
51. Zhong, M. (1997) 'Report on Perceived Intercultural Communication Competence of Chinese and Americans', Unpublished MA Dissertation, Kent State University.
52. Collier, M. J. (1988) 'A comparison of conversations among and between domestic culture groups: How intra- and intercultural competencies vary', *Communication Quarterly*, vol. 36, no. 2, pp. 122–144.
53. Holtgraves, T. (1992) 'Linguistic realisation of face management: implications for language production and comprehension, person perception and cross-cultural communication', *Social Psychological Quarterly*, vol. 55, no. 2, pp. 141–159.
54. Giles, H. (1977) *Language, Ethnicity and Intergroup Relations*. London: Academic Press.
55. Giles, H., A. Mulac, J. L. Bradac and P. Johnson (1987) 'Speech accommodation theory: The first decade and beyond', *Communication Yearbook*, vol. 10, pp. 13–48.
56. Clark, H. H. and E. F. Schaefer (1989) 'Collaborating on contributions to conversations' in R. Dietrich and C. F. Graumann (eds) *Language Processing in Social Context*. Amsterdam: Elsevier, pp. 123–149.

57. Li, H. Z. (1999) 'Grounding and information communication in intercultural and intracultural dyadic discourse', *Discourse Processes*, vol. 28, no. 3, pp. 195–215.
58. Berger, C. R. and R. J. Calabrese (1975) 'Some explorations in initial interactions and beyond', *Human Communication Research*, vol. 1, pp. 99–112. *See also*: Berger, C. R. (1987) 'Communicating under uncertainty' in M. E. Roloff and G. R. Miller (eds) *Interpersonal Processes*. Newbury Park, Calif.: Sage.
59. Triandis, H. C. (1980) 'Values, attitudes and interpersonal behavior' in M. Page (ed.) *Nebraska Symposium on Motivation 1979*, vol. 27. Lincoln: University of Nebraska Press.
60. Gudykunst, W. B., T. Nishida, H. Koike and N. Shiino (1986) 'The influence of language on uncertainty reduction: An exploratory study of Japanese–Japanese and Japanese–North American interactions', in M. McLaughlin (ed.) *Communication Yearbook*, vol. 9. Beverly Hills, Calif.: Sage.
61. Gudykunst, W. B., S. M. Yang and T. Nishida (1985) 'A cross-cultural test of uncertainty reduction theory: Comparisons of acquaintance, friend and dating relationships in Japan, Korea and the US', *Human Communication Research*, vol. 11, pp. 407–455.
62. Gudykunst, W. B. and M. R. Hammer (1988) 'Strangers and hosts: An uncertainty reduction based theory of intercultural adaptation' in Y. Y. Kim and W. B. Gudykunst (eds) *Intercultural Adaptation*. Newbury Park, Calif.: Sage.
63. Gudykunst, W. B., T. Nishida and E. Chua (1986) 'Uncertainty reduction in Japanese–North American dyads', *Communication Research Reports*, vol. 3, pp. 39–46.
64. Baldoni, J. (1999) *Leader as Coach*, lc21.com/directions/practice2.html.
65. Argyris, C. (1990) *Overcoming Organizational Defences*. New York: Prentice Hall.
66. Lau, J. B. and A. B. Shani (1988) *Behaviour in Organizations: An Experiential Approach*, 4th edn. Homewood, Ill.: Richard D. Irwin.
67. Shea, G. F. (1992) *Mentoring: A Guide to the Basics*. London: Kogan Page.
68. Bellman, G. M. (1992) *Getting Things Done When You Are Not In Charge*. San Francisco, Calif.: Barrett-Koehler.
69. Young, M. J. E. P. (1993) 'How leading companies communicate with employees', *Organizational Dynamics*, Summer, pp. 31–43.
70. Handy, C. (2001) 'The workers' revolution', *The Times* magazine, 28 April, p. 15.
71. Bailey, B. (2000) 'Communicative behavior and conflict between African-American customers and Korean immigrant retailers in Los Angeles', *Discourse & Society*, vol. 11, no. 1, pp. 86–108.
72. Goodsell, C. T. (1976) 'Cross-cultural comparisons of behaviours of postal clerks towards clients', *Administrative Science Quarterly*, vol. 21, pp. 140–150.
73. Gutek, B. A. (1995) *The Dynamics of Service: Reflections on the Changing Nature of Customer/Provider Interactions*. San Francisco: Jossey-Bass.
74. Rafaeli, A. (1989) 'When clerks meet customers: A test of variables related to emotional expressions on the job', *Journal of Applied Psychology*, vol. 74, pp. 385–393.
75. Ford, W. S. Z. (1999) 'Communication and customer service', *Communication Yearbook*, vol. 22, pp. 341–375.
76. Hartel, C.-E. J., S. Barker and N. J. Baker (1999) 'The role of emotional intelligence in service encounters: A model for predicting the effects of employee-customer interactions on consumer attitudes, intentions, and behaviors', *Australian Journal of Communication*, vol. 26, no. 2, pp. 77–87.
77. Adelberg, S. and C. D. Batson (1978) 'Accountability and helping: When needs exceed resources', *Journal of Personality and Social Psychology*, vol. 36, pp. 342–350.

# 8 Persuading

## CHAPTER INTRODUCTION

The next two chapters are both about influencing. Success in business and many other kinds of work depends on exerting influence. In the words of Turner and Henzl[1] 'Actually, everyone in organisations is influencing everyone else.' Perhaps it would be more accurate to say that everyone in organisations is trying to influence everyone else. As Chapter 2 showed, new forms of organisation have led to influencing being substituted for 'directing' and opened up influence possibilities to a wide range of the organisation's personnel. Influence means changes in people's behaviour or attitudes that result from yielding to interpersonal or social pressure. This chapter covers influencing by persuasion, while Chapter 9 focuses on influencing by exercising power.

The aim of this chapter is to help readers understand how to persuade others by explaining:

- influence;
- ethical issues in influencing;
- compliance gaining, which means influencing behaviour but not necessarily attitudes;
- attitude change, including the theories of self-perception, dissonance and involvement (social judgement) and how uncertainty, intelligence, the basis of an attitude and source credibility affect ease of attitude change;
- persuasion theories and techniques, covering general reward theory, balance theory, reinforcement, satisfying needs and adoption models;
- persuasive messages, including persuasive language, elaboration likelihood, heuristic-systematic processing, repetition, fear appeals, guilt-arousing appeals, two-sided appeals, using exemplars and framing techniques;
- different personal influencing styles;
- commitment gaining;
- work applications of persuasion, which include personal selling, networking, making presentations, introducing change and subordinate–manager influence.

Persuading builds on skill in understanding others, impression management and communicating.

## GENERAL POINTS ABOUT INFLUENCING

Influence may be direct or indirect, brought about by persuading or using power, and ethical or unethical.

*Direct influence* means convincing others to accept advice or ideas and to change their beliefs or behaviour accordingly.[2] The likelihood of direct influence generally corresponds to the status and expertise of the source and the value of the knowledge imparted, which can be a function of its rarity. If knowledge is widely available, it is less usable as a source of influence than if it is hard to obtain.[3] Indirect influence refers to changes in how rather than what the influence target thinks. When a person's beliefs change in ways that are only secondary to the content of the message they receive, that is a case of indirect influence.[4,5] For instance, someone from Germany might argue that an organisation should have written-down rules governing every possible sickness absence contingency. A British person might not accept the possibility or the necessity of so elaborate a set of rules. However, if the British person were induced in future to think more about guarding against contingencies (i.e. of reducing uncertainty) they would have been indirectly influenced.

Most accounts of influencing do not distinguish *persuading* and *power*. For example, a classic typology lists reward, punishment, legitimacy, expertise and charisma as the bases of social power.[6] Another, which is focused on influence within organisations, has the following breakdown in which persuasion and power overlap:

- Assertiveness – demanding, ordering and setting deadlines: 'This work must be done this week and there's an end to it'.
- Ingratiation – unobtrusive flattery: 'Only you have the brains . . .'.
- Rationality – logic or offering a compromise.
- Sanctions – use of administrative sanctions: 'This will reflect negatively on your next performance evaluation'.
- Exchange – 'If you let me go to the conference, I'll work overtime before and after'.
- Upward appeal – 'You'll have to see my boss about that'.
- Blocking – threatening.
- Coalition – support of others: 'I know the other workers will put in some time for me . . .'.[7]

Although no hard and fast line can be drawn between persuading and exerting power, for clarity it helps to distinguish the two. Persuading then becomes exerting influence over others by means other than using power, including discussion, argument, conveying liking and other communication actions covered in this chapter. Power means influencing others through using the ability to 'control their outcomes',[8] in other words, to affect what happens to them, for example through rewards or punishments. Power can be used to influence others, but persuasion can work just as well, and may have fewer undesirable consequences. Also, anyone can try to persuade others, and if s/he is skilled, can often succeed. Persuading does not depend on having authority or the power to reward or punish.

Influencing raises *ethical issues*, on which we have more opinions than evidence. The use of power is potentially more problematic ethically than persuading, for which the guidelines given in Chapters 6 and 7 may suffice. However, some persuasive techniques may be thought questionable. For example, some people would have moral scruples about using fear appeals and guilt-arousing appeals although they can be very effective. Box 8.1 gives some suggestions for ethical frameworks for influencing.

**Box 8.1**

**Ethical frameworks for influencing**

- The concept that sharing influence is more ethical than exercising it unilaterally.
- The argument that the ethics of advocacy differ from those of reporting – i.e. that objectivity is not required so long as the target clearly understands (and the advocate takes steps to ensure they understand) that what is in train is persuasion. This argument derives from the model of press news coverage, where a common principle is that comment should be distinguished from reporting (McBride, 1989). Barney and Black (1994) go further, arguing, in the context of public relations, that the persuasion ethic can be defensible and even laudable in a participatory democracy where, similar to the social role of the lawyer, the public relations practitioner can be expected to be an advocate and distribute 'selective truth'.
- Baker (1999) presents a framework consisting of five baselines of ethical justification for professional persuasive communications. The models are self-interest, entitlement, enlightened self-interest, social responsibility and kingdom of ends (justified purposes).

*Sources*: Baker, S. (1999) 'Five baselines for justification in persuasion', *Journal of Mass Media Ethics*, vol. 14, no. 2, pp. 69–81.
Barney, R. D. and J. Black (1994) 'Ethics and professional persuasive communications', *Public Relations Review*, vol. 20, no. 3, pp. 233–248.
McBride, G. (1989) 'Ethical thought in public relations history: Seeking a relevant perspective', *Journal of Mass Media Ethics*, vol. 4, no. 1, pp. 5–20.

## SUMMARY – GENERAL POINTS ABOUT INFLUENCING

It is useful to distinguish direct influence from indirect and persuasion from power. Direct influence refers to changes in what targets do or believe, indirect means changes in how they approach issues. Persuading relies on communicative acts, power on the ability to control others' outcomes. Influencing raises ethical issues about others' rights to autonomy. Most issues are covered in the chapters on impression management, communication and power but some persuasive techniques can be questioned.

## COMPLIANCE GAINING

In some work contexts, compliance – performing what is asked – is all that is required. For example, in market research, interviewers who intercept passers-by only need to influence the people they approach to take part in a survey. Within organisations, power is often available for obtaining compliance but in other work situations, such as getting passers-by to be interviewed, power is not available. Hornik and Ellis[9] investigated strategies to secure compliance in such cases. Among their findings was that when potential respondents were touched and gazed at by interviewers, they were both more likely to participate and said that they found the process less burdensome. Their replies were no more likely to be biased than those of other respondents, so using non-verbal techniques to obtain compliance produced a net gain for the interviewers. Touching and gazing were more effective for women interviewers than for men but both men and women interviewees were equally influenced.

Compliance-gaining strategies are affected by the influencer's goals, power, culture and ethical beliefs.

*Particular compliance goals*, such as giving advice, asking favours and enforcing obligations, differ in several ways. These differences include whether or not there is an obligation on the influence target to comply before the influence attempt is made, whether or not there are benefits to both parties if compliance occurs and what level of resistance is likely. Wilson *et al.*[10] used a politeness framework (see Chapter 6) to research people's compliance-gaining efforts and found the following:

- When giving advice, influencers were more likely to provide reasons to justify their attempts than when pursuing other influence goals. This was because they anticipated threats to both their own positive and the target's negative face (because they might appear to be butting into the target's affairs).
- When asking favours, influencers anticipated threats to both parties' negative face and to their own positive face (because they might appear too lazy to handle their own problems) and rated themselves less likely to persist if the other party resisted than for other influence goals.
- When enforcing unfulfilled obligations, influencers anticipated threats to the other party's negative and positive face, but were more concerned about the primary goal of compliance. Thus they expressed less approval and exerted stronger pressure, provided fewer reasons and said they would persist despite resistance.

Although this research studied compliance gaining between friends, and so the findings themselves may not apply in quite the same way to work situations, they do give indications of the way particular compliance goals can influence how people go about getting others to comply.

**Table 8.1 Factors affecting compliance-gaining strategies**

| *Factors* | *Strategies* |
|---|---|
| Influencer's goals | |
| *e.g. to give advice* → | Explaining reasons |
| *to ask a favour* → | Persisting despite resistance |
| *to enforce an obligation* → | Exerting strong pressure and persisting despite resistance |
| Influencer's power → | (Managers') use of punishment versus 'altruism' or reasoning |
| Influencer's culture → | e.g. use of punishment, authority, moral pressure and modelling |
| Influencer's ethics → | Can promote use of prosocial strategies |
| Influencer's perception of target's ethics → | Can promote use of altruistic arguments |

It is almost certainly the case that other factors affect the choice – for instance the influencer's beliefs about the target's attitudes.

*Power* affects compliance-gaining strategies but gender may not. Hirokawa *et al.*[11] found that both male and female managers with high power resorted to punishment strategies to secure their subordinates' compliance, while low-power managers of both genders used altruism or rationale-based strategies.

Compliance-gaining strategies are also affected by *culture*. For instance, Lu[12] found that Chinese teachers' compliance-gaining techniques emphasise punishment, authority, morality and modelling. He argues that these teacher techniques are similar to other values in Chinese culture.

The *ethical beliefs* of the influencer can affect their choice of compliance-gaining strategy. Baglan *et al.*[13] showed that environmental activists were more likely to say they would use prosocial strategies (such as arguing their case) than anti-social strategies (for example destructive acts) across a range of 12 different situations. The strategy most often used was expertise. The research also showed that choice of strategy was influenced by the perceived level of moral development of the influence target. Where this was high, the influencers would be more likely to use altruism as a compliance-gaining argument than where it was low.

Table 8.1 summarises the factors that affect choice of compliance-gaining strategies.

## Effects of compliance-gaining attempts

In general, the stronger the pressure on people, the more they will comply outwardly. This pressure need not be direct or explicit. For example, when people are members of a group, team or department, they are more likely to comply when the unit is facing external threats or competition than at other times. People reach agreement more easily, compromise more readily and back one another more consistently when their unit confronts external difficulties. Another way of saying this is that under these circumstances the group is more cohesive. However, compliance in behaviour alone may not last long, often only while the person is being watched. Long-lasting influence is likely only when people's attitudes also change. Strong pressure, far from increasing the chances that others will change their private attitudes, can have the opposite effect. It may only produce 'reactance'. Reactance means that someone will oppose what is asked of him or her and even do the opposite just because they feel that whoever asked exceeded the limits of formal or legitimate rights.[14] For instance, a secretary with more than one boss may put urgent work for one to the bottom of the pile, because that boss repeatedly leaves dealing with matters to the last minute and then insists that they are done instantly. Thus a lower degree of pressure may be more effective. It may work better to ask the secretary apologetically for the work to be done as soon as possible. Some recent research findings support this theory that strong pressure can be counter-productive. More forceful language actually increased the resistance of parents to messages about family sun safety.[15] In a work context, when supervisors used warm, supportive methods for getting their subordinates to comply with directions, they were rated by those subordinates as more competent than they were if they used forceful or 'antisocial' methods.[16]

## SUMMARY – COMPLIANCE GAINING

If the goal of an influence attempt is limited to getting the other person to act in a certain way, without necessarily changing any attitudes, then a range of strategies, listed in the right hand column of Table 8.1, is available. Research has shown how factors such as the influencer's power, culture, ethics and so on, listed in the left hand column of Table 8.1, affect choice of compliance-gaining strategy. Evidence on the effects of compliance-gaining attempts seems clear: strong pressure generally produces changes of behaviour, but the influence may not last long and reactance may occur.

## ATTITUDE CHANGE AND INFLUENCE THEORIES

Attitude change refers to a change in the psychological tendency to evaluate a particular entity favourably or unfavourably.[17] Four theories of attitude change – self-perception theory, dissonance theory, balance theory and involvement (or social judgment) theory – are first discussed; then theories of the relationship between liking and influence and the adoption of innovations are looked at.

## Theories of attitude change

### *Self-perception theory*

> To produce change, it is useful to employ just enough pressure to induce people to take action or make an explicit decision, but not enough to provide them with a justification for taking that decision. With insufficient justification from outside, private attitudes change in order to psychologically justify what has been done.[18]

This quotation is based on self-perception theory, which argues that people know they have an attitude partly because they see themselves acting in a way consistent with having that attitude. According to this theory, in the example given above concerning the secretary, an apologetic request would be more effective in the long run than an insistent demand, because if the secretary acceded to it, she would perceive the reason as being a forgiving and sympathetic response to her boss's dilemma, an attitude that is likely to persist. If she acceded to imperious demands, however, she can think she was forced to act as she did, and feel no pressure to bring her attitudes to the boss into line with her behaviour. Self-perception theory is part of attribution theory, which was discussed in Chapters 3 and 5.

### *Dissonance theory*

High dissonance in the receiver of a persuasive message increases the chance of attitude change. We experience dissonance when two or more beliefs we have are in conflict.[19] This could happen because we have an existing attitude yet act in a way that seems to ourselves inconsistent with that attitude. This inconsistent act might result from a deliberate decision, submitting to outside pressure or a loss of self-control. For instance, if a person held strongly the attitude that 'honesty is the best policy' and then a severe personal financial crisis led him to start fiddling his expenses, he would experience dissonance. Figure 8.1 illustrates another example of how dissonance can arise.

Dissonance is psychologically uncomfortable and so people try to reduce it. The stronger the dissonance, the harder they try to lower it. Equally important, the way in which people reduce dissonance is to change the element least resistant to change. In the example given above, the person might simply stop fiddling his expenses and find some other way out of his financial crisis, so as to preserve his previous attitudes both towards honesty and towards himself. However, if someone is 'locked in' to a position, it will probably be the attitude that changes. An example of this would be a company director who strongly believed that a proposed profit-sharing scheme was a good and fair one, but who voted against it at a Board meeting in order not to rock the boat, because her fellow directors were against it. After the vote, if it was too late to revise the Board's decision, the chances are that she would begin to revise her attitude to the scheme, seeing difficulties where she saw none before, or reassessing the potential benefits.

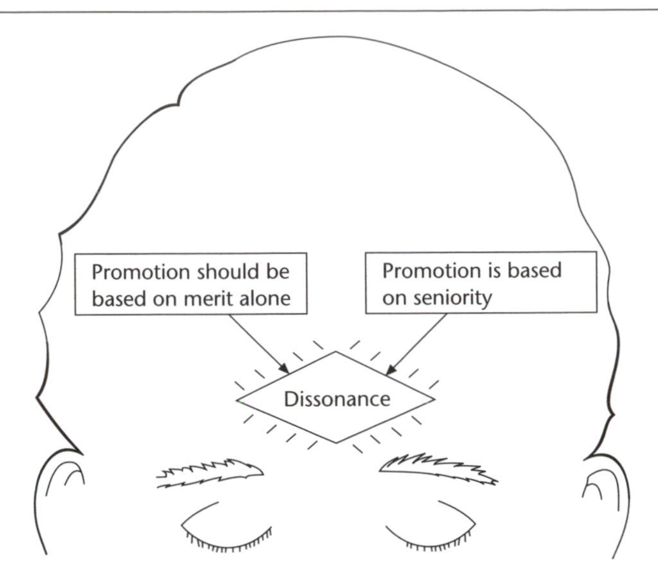


Mr Smith, a middle manager, believes that promotion should be based on merit alone. He joins Company X, where seniority is the main determinant of promotion. He experiences dissonance between his initial attitude, and his need to conform in order to gain acceptance in his new organisation.

**Figure 8.1 Example of dissonance arousal.**

Dissonance is raised and attitude change becomes more likely when incentives are lower, when personal responsibility is higher and when an action turns out badly. These findings, which are by no means self-evident, can be explained in the following ways:

- High incentives, whether threats or rewards, make the case abnormal, so the person feels that the usual 'rules' implied by their pre-existing attitudes do not apply. When the incentive is low, however, and the person still goes ahead with the behaviour or decision, there is less excuse for the deviation, so dissonance is higher.
- If people have no choice, they cannot blame themselves. This means that the more freely someone chooses an action (the higher their sense of personal responsibility), the more dissonance they experience. In fact, Joule and Beauvois[20] argued that dissonance is unlikely to be aroused at all unless the person feels free to refuse or comply with a request.
- If the action turns out badly, even though the person did not and could not have anticipated that it would, dissonance is higher. Presumably, if it did not turn out badly, even though it was inconsistent with previous attitudes, then the person feels that the end justifies the means.

In principle, dissonance theory provides a clear guide to anyone trying to change other people's attitudes. By getting them to change their behaviour in a way that is inconsistent with those attitudes, powerful pressure builds up to get them to change the attitudes. For example, if someone who is becoming discontented with their job because they feel their workload is excessive can be persuaded to volunteer to take on an extra task, perhaps because it particularly interests them, they may become less discontented, not more so. There is evidence that attitude change is more likely to be brought about by personal interaction and word of mouth than by formal presentations or advertising. Part of the reason for this may be because talking gives the influencer information. It tells them whether a given behaviour would arouse dissonance in a particular individual and if so how the person is likely to handle it.[21] Even face to face, though, getting people to change their attitudes takes skill. A person who anticipates that doing X will cause them to feel high dissonance will probably avoid that action.

### *Balance theory*

Balance theory is similar in some ways to cognitive dissonance theory in that a state of imbalance is regarded as psychologically uncomfortable and likely to lead a person to seek to restore balance. However, balance theory relates particularly to attitudes to other people. Attitudes towards a person and towards an act by that person are seen as inter-related.[22] For example, if a manager thinks highly of one new subordinate's technical competence, then she may take a tolerant, even amused, view of his lack of punctuality, whereas if another subordinate, whom she thinks less of, has this same habit of unpunctuality, she will disapprove. On the other hand, if she feels a strong concern about office tidiness, and the first subordinate's desk is always squalid, her initial liking for him may diminish, while her attitude to the second subordinate may soften if he turns out to be neat and tidy about the office. In other words, an attitude towards a person can alter the attitude towards his or her actions, while an attitude towards an event or situation can alter the attitude towards the person who is seen as having caused it.

These changes, according to balance theory, come about because the attitudes towards the person and the event form a mental cluster. So long as the attitude towards the person and the attitude towards the related event are similar, the position is balanced and the holder of the attitudes feels no pressure to change either. If, however, the attitude towards the person and that towards the linked event are dissimilar, there is a state of imbalance that produces tensions. The person then tries to reduce these tensions by changing his or her attitude towards the event (or the person) to re-establish balance. A third possibility is to divorce the two attitudes. For instance, the manager could reason that the state of the first subordinate's desk is not really his fault because he is working so hard. The second subordinate may receive the same treatment. It is easy for him to be tidy as he works on a computer rather than with paper. In this way the manager's attitudinal balance can be restored without any attitude change. One

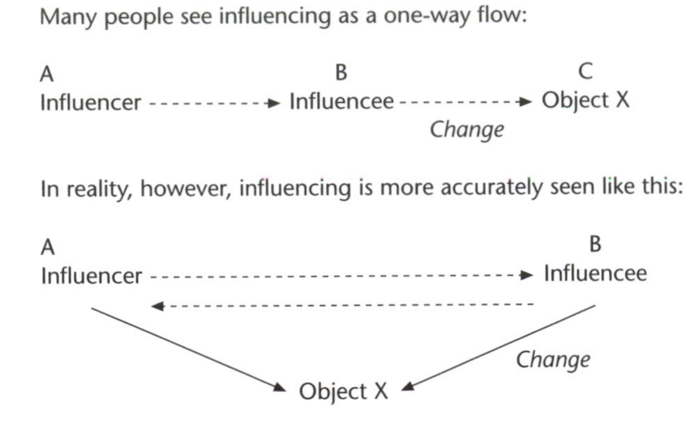


For A to persuade B to change his/her attitude or behaviour towards X, B's attitude towards A is most important: the more strongly positive it is, the more the influence attempt by A is likely to succeed. A needs to pay as much attention to B's attitude to A as to B's attitude to the object; and B's attitude to A will usually be strongly affected by what B thinks of A's attitude to him or her: that is, if A can convey to B that s/he likes him/her, A's chances of influencing B are much greater.

**Figure 8.2 Balance model of influencing.**

of the practical implications of balance theory is to change the common-sense model of influencing, as shown in Figure 8.2.

### *Involvement theory*

Sherif's involvement (social judgement) theory,[23] introduced in Chapter 5, states that a person who is highly involved in a situation or issue will tend to reject most of the possible positions on the issue and accept very few positions. This means, in the language of the theory, that that person has a narrow latitude of acceptance and a wide latitude of rejections. An extreme case of involvement would mean that the person said, in effect, 'Nothing you can say or do can change me.' Their latitude of acceptance includes only the present attitude and all other possibilities fall into the latitude of rejection. Conversely, a person who is not much involved with an issue would find a number of positions acceptable and be against few positions.

A central assumption of social judgement theory is that when people are highly involved with an issue, they distort messages about that issue which are outside their latitude of acceptance. The distortion may be one of assimilation – judging it as closer to their own position than it actually is. This enhances its impact. Alternatively there may be a contrast distortion, exaggerating how different it is from their position. This reduces its impact. Some recent research has shown that whether a message is assimilated or distorted depends on how far from the individual's latitude of acceptance the position of the message is. Not far, and assimilation follows, far and it will be contrasted. The persuasive impact of a discrepant communication is greater the lower the contrast effect. Therefore, for messages that advocate positions outside the latitude of acceptance, the greater the difference between the target's own position and the judged position of the message, the smaller the attitude change, eventually resulting in changes away from the position.[24] When someone is highly involved with an attitude, the most persuasive strategy is to design a series of messages in such a way that each falls towards the outer edge of the target's latitude of acceptance. This has the effect of shifting that edge progressively in the desired direction.[25] Once the first message, which has been positioned to just avoid rejection, is accepted, the person's attitude position shifts, accompanied by a new set of latitudes. Then a new message may well be accepted, which would previously have been within the rejection latitude, and so on. Figure 8.3 gives an example of how this process could produce

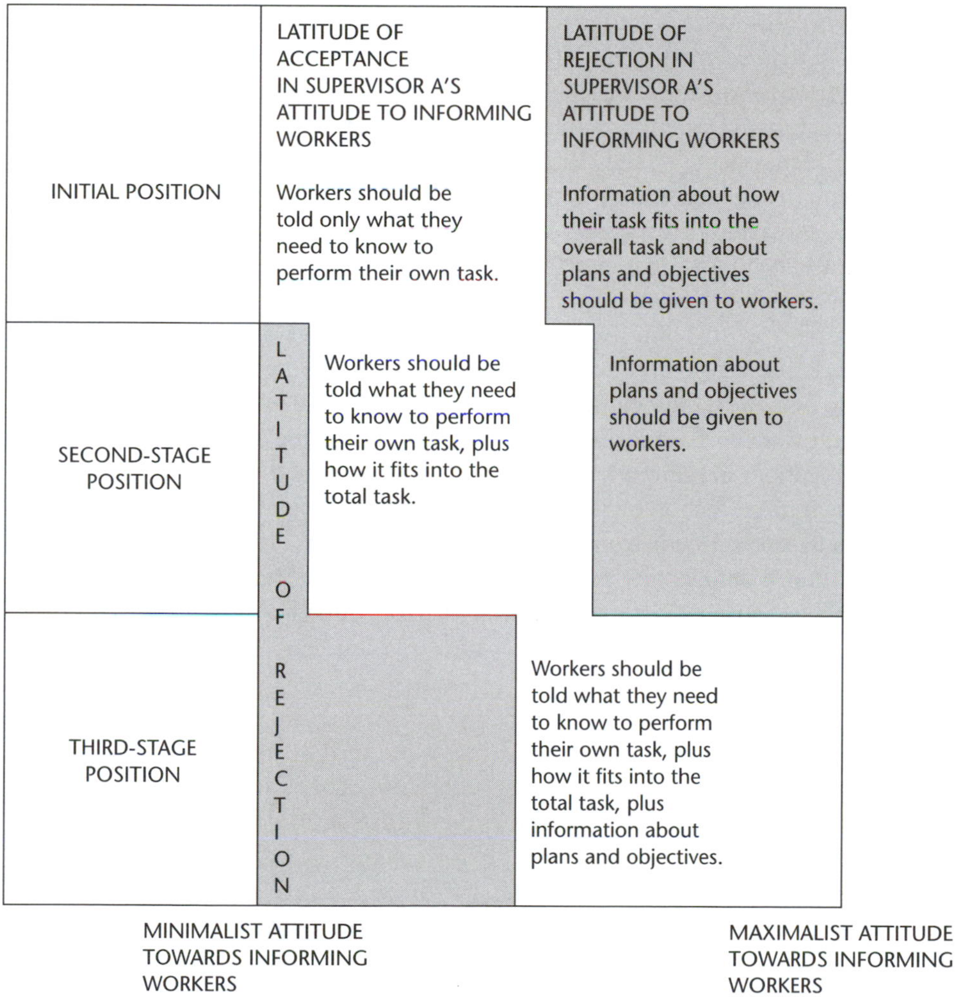

| | | |
|---|---|---|
| INITIAL POSITION | LATITUDE OF ACCEPTANCE IN SUPERVISOR A'S ATTITUDE TO INFORMING WORKERS<br><br>Workers should be told only what they need to know to perform their own task. | LATITUDE OF REJECTION IN SUPERVISOR A'S ATTITUDE TO INFORMING WORKERS<br><br>Information about how their task fits into the overall task and about plans and objectives should be given to workers. |
| SECOND-STAGE POSITION | LATITUDE OF REJECTION<br><br>Workers should be told what they need to know to perform their own task, plus how it fits into the total task. | Information about plans and objectives should be given to workers. |
| THIRD-STAGE POSITION | LATITUDE OF REJECTION | Workers should be told what they need to know to perform their own task, plus how it fits into the total task, plus information about plans and objectives. |

MINIMALIST ATTITUDE TOWARDS INFORMING WORKERS — MAXIMALIST ATTITUDE TOWARDS INFORMING WORKERS

**Figure 8.3 Attitude shifts within latitudes of acceptance.**

a change in attitude – in this case of a supervisor towards informing workers about their role and the organisation.

## General reward theory

Several research studies have shown that liking and influence are linked. In fact one study showed that the influence of someone who was liked was greater than that of somebody who had the power to reward and punish.[26] Another study showed that as pairs of people became better acquainted, those who came to like one another more came to have strikingly more similar attitudes and shared values than they had initially. Those who had come to dislike one another had also diverged further in their attitudes and values.[27] Research into opinion leaders, who influence a number of other people, has shown that they are often people who seem approachable – who will not make others feel uncomfortable or inferior for asking.[28] People say that they like others with rewarding personal characteristics such as sincerity, competence, intelligence, energy and physical attractiveness.[29,30] They also feel more attracted towards those who seem to like them,[31] or to those they see as being similar to themselves.[32] These findings are all consistent with general reward theory, which states that people like and are influenced by people who provide them with social rewards at low cost to themselves. Recent research suggests that giving out cues of liking another person is to some extent controllable. Palmer and Simmons[33] found that research subjects who were instructed to vary their non-verbal displays to increase or decrease another person's liking for them were successful at doing so, although they could not describe what they had done.

A modification of general reward theory proposes that a gain or loss of reward has more effect on attraction than a constant level, however high or low. Thus a small compliment from a stranger may have more effect on our liking for them than a lavish one from someone who has already said nice things about us several times before. Research has produced some support for this idea.[34]

## 'Adopting innovations' theory

Some valuable insights into influencing people to accept ideas or ways of behaving that may be new to them come from studies that show that in adopting innovations people usually go through four stages – knowledge, persuasion, decision and adoption.[35] Later, they may go through a confirmation stage. Knowledge means being aware of and having some understanding of the innovation. Persuasion refers to forming favourable or unfavourable attitudes towards it. The decision stage involves activities that lead to choosing between trying or not trying the innovation. Adoption means going beyond trial to regular use –

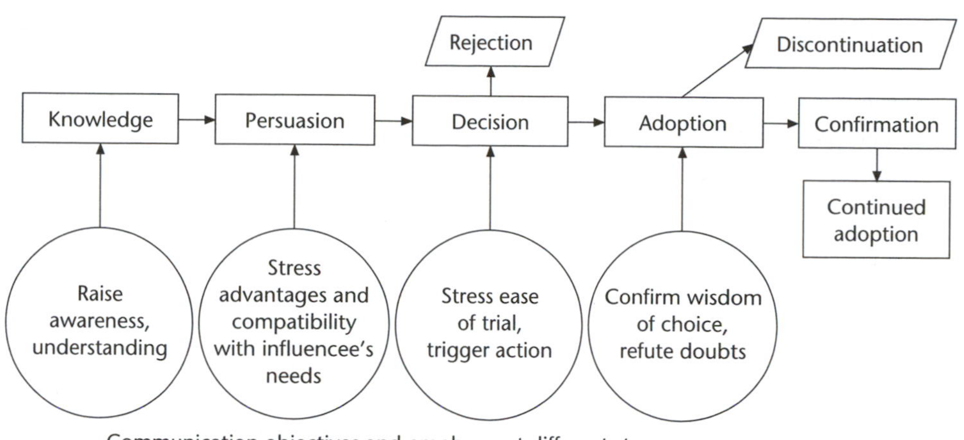


**Figure 8.4 Stages of the innovation–adoption process.**

absorbing the innovation into normal behaviour. In the confirmation stage, if it occurs, the adopter seeks reinforcement for the adoption decision. It may be reversed at this time. At each stage of this process the content and style of communication received have to be appropriate. What is suited to creating awareness and understanding is not suited to encouraging someone to form favourable attitudes. Introducing persuasive messages too early in the process, therefore, can be counter-productive. It is especially ineffective to try to trigger a decision before the idea is fully understood. 'Don't rush me' is how the person receiving such messages is likely to feel, and the sense of being hustled may lead them to reject ideas that they might otherwise welcome. Figure 8.4 shows the adoption process and appropriate communication objectives for each stage.

The adoption model identifies five characteristics of new ideas that make them more likely to lead someone to adopt them.[36] These five are relative advantage, compatibility, complexity, trialability and observability.

1. The more benefits someone can see in a new idea, especially for themselves, but also more broadly, the more easily they will be persuaded.
2. The less adopting a new idea means disrupting existing ideas or ways of behaving, the more easily a favourable attitude to it will be formed.
3. Simple ideas are more favourably received.
4. When people are faced with doing, using or buying something new, they see potential risks in the situation. For example, if a manager is considering setting up a B2B (business to business) subsidiary, they may be worried about costs escalating beyond control, low revenues in the early years and the effect on their personal reputation if it all goes wrong. These kinds of 'perceived risk' inhibit people from adopting innovations. The more a new idea can be

tried in small stages, with a low commitment, or in a way that seems reversible, the more likely it is to be tried at all.
5. If the use of a new idea, process or product is highly visible to others, potential adopters may think they will gain prestige from being seen as innovative. This can encourage them to make a trial, although visibility also increases perceived risk.

These five characteristics of easily adopted ideas mean that persuasive communications should stress the benefits as much as the contents of the ideas themselves, be introduced by small stages, each preferably with few ramifications for other aspects of behaviour and with possibilities for reversing, and use social pressure and word-of-mouth. The rate at which people adopt new ideas varies according to such things as their age and their general attitudes towards change and also according to the values of the social system, such as the culture of the organisation.[37] People are likely to be more easily persuaded to try new ideas in companies in which there is more reward for being creative and active than for being always right.

**Box 8.2**

### Critique of influencing research and theory

- Reinforcement theorists criticise balance theory for over-emphasising the relations between attitudes and liking. They consider that any behaviour from one person which another finds rewarding will tend to make them like them, for example 'stroking', humour, listening, courtesy or deference. Equally, other forms of negative reinforcement apart from disagreement over attitudes can promote dislike. These would include criticising, interrupting, ignoring or rudeness.
- General reward theory is too simple to predict all the cases of liking (Aronson, 1980). For instance, though competence leads to liking, evidence of some fallibility on the part of the competent leads to even more. Though flattery is appreciated, it is not if an ulterior motive or manipulative intent is suspected (Jones, 1964). Though physical beauty is attractive, it is less so if the persons concerned seem to misuse their beauty (Sigall and Ostrove, 1969). Getting someone else to do a favour may be more effective in gaining their liking than doing one for them (Benjamin Franklin, quoted in Aronson, 1980).
- Influencing models are generally located in a Western cultural frame of reference that ignores cultural differences in harmony, loyalty, social obligations and the role of the individual.
- There is a lack of theorising and research on outcomes for the collectivity, such as the organisation, as opposed to the individual.
- There is a lack of research on resistance and particularly how targets' efforts to protect their self-concept lead them to resist.

*Sources*: Aronson, E. (1980) *The Social Animal*, 3rd edn. San Francisco: W. H. Freeman and Co.
Jones, E. E. (1964) *Ingratiation*. New York: Appleton-Century-Crofts.
Sigall, H. and N. Ostrove (1969) 'Beautiful but dangerous: Effects of offender attractiveness and nature of the crime on juridic judgment', *Journal of Personality and Social Psychology*, vol. 5, pp. 93–100.

## SUMMARY – ATTITUDE CHANGE AND INFLUENCE THEORIES

Persuading can get people to change their attitudes. Self-perception theory suggests that moderate pressure is more effective than extreme. Dissonance theory argues that, given a high level of dissonance between an influence target's attitude and their other beliefs or behaviour, they will change the attitude if doing so is easier than changing the other beliefs or behaviour. There are certain non-obvious ways in which dissonance can be raised. Balance theory argues that people strive for consistency between their attitudes to a person and an associated attitude object. Therefore, influencers should pay as much attention to the target's attitude to themselves as to the target's attitudes to changes they are advocating. Involvement theory puts forward the ideas that people have 'latitudes of acceptance' around their attitudes and that advocacy messages are more persuasive the closer they are to those latitudes. Positioning a series of messages just inside the target's latitude of acceptance can cause those latitudes to shift progressively in the desired direction. Reward theory supports the idea that a target's liking for an influencer makes it easier for the latter to persuade them. Adoption of innovations theory identifies characteristics of new ideas which give them persuasive appeal.

## FACTORS AFFECTING ATTITUDE CHANGE

Certain factors make some attitudes easier to change than others or affect how change is brought about. These factors include the attitude's components and dimensions, the attitude holder's level of certainty about the attitude, intelligence and needs and the credibility of the source of the persuasive message.

Chapter 3 introduced the idea that most attitudes have three *components*, beliefs, affects and action tendencies. This analysis is helpful when considering how hard or easy an attitude will be to change. An attitude may well alter if new information causes a rethink of its belief component, but when the attitude is part of a larger, consistent, complex it is more likely that new information will be ignored or disbelieved.[38] In some cases, moreover, attitude change will come about only through a change in the affect component. For instance, if someone feels that advertising copywriting is a trivial activity unworthy of professional status, i.e. if they have a strongly negative affect towards it, no amount of information on the contribution of advertising to the success of the firm or on salaries and career prospects in the industry is likely to change their attitude. Attitudes that are mainly based on affect are more likely to be changed by emotional appeals, whereas those more strongly based on beliefs are more susceptible to information or argument-based persuasion.[39] Chapter 3 also introduced the idea that attitudes can be seen as having three *dimensions* – centrality, consistency and intensity. These three dimensions can also be used to identify how difficult attitude change will be in different cases. Attitudes that are high in centrality, consistency and intensity are hardest to change; those that are low on all three dimensions are easier. For instance, it will be harder to change the attitudes of secretaries who feel that the secretarial provision in the department in which they work is inappropriate than the attitudes of outsiders, because of the greater centrality and intensity of the formers' attitudes. The values on these dimensions will not always be consistent however, not all high or all low.

When the *influence targets* feel unsure about the subject of the influence attempt, their attitudes may be changed by supplying information. For example, many people who were antagonistic at first to the idea of using computers, nevertheless felt uneasy about being left behind by the technological revolution. When they realised that they could use software packages, instead of having to learn to program, their attitudes changed. Some kinds of people are easier to influence than others. People who are low in self-esteem are easier to influence than those who value themselves more. People higher in the middle and upper ranges of the IQ scale are harder to persuade than those below them, while people higher in the lower portion of the scale are easier to persuade, as Figure 8.5 shows.

Being attractive to another person, and so having a basis for influencing them, may be a function of complementary needs.[40] According to this view, people who have, for example, a strong need to dominate are attracted to people who behave submissively; generally, this means people who have the need to be dominated. Equally, people who want to 'teach', 'mother' or otherwise nurture other people are attracted to those who are receptive to such treatment and vice versa. Although much of the research into this theory has concerned people's private lives, especially choice of marriage partner, some has confirmed that the theory can operate in work relationships. One interesting point about these

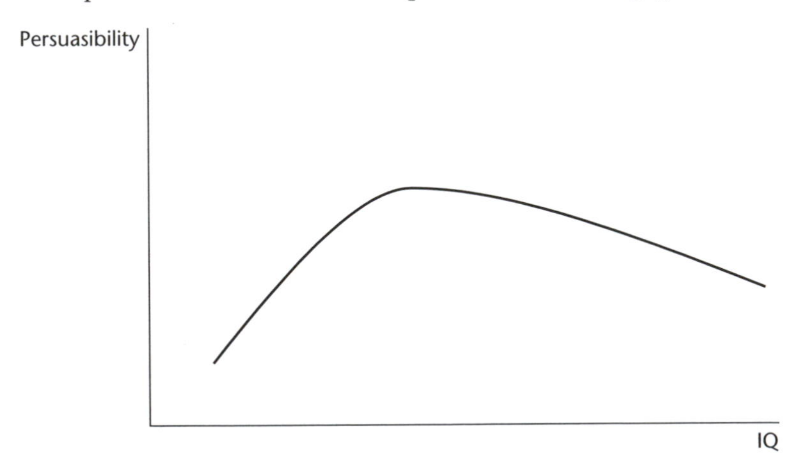


People with medium IQ levels are easier to persuade than people of lower IQ levels, but beyond a certain IQ level, people's persuasibility decreases.

**Figure 8.5 The relation between intelligence and persuasibility.**

concepts is that they suggest ways to 'dominate' the dominant or 'teach' the didactic. Because their dominating or nurturing behaviour is based on their own needs, not on a thought-out strategy for getting their way, they can, paradoxically, be influenced by people whose submissiveness or receptivity gratifies their need.

Attitude change is more likely when the *persuader* is highly *credible* to the target person. Credibility is related to recognised expertise, being a reliable information source, the perceived motives and intentions of the influencers, how friendly they seem to the target, their attractiveness and social status. There is some evidence that these source credibility variables apply cross-culturally. Yoon *et al.*[41] found little difference between Americans and Koreans when they measured which of perceived source expertise, trustworthiness and attractiveness had more influence on response to advertising. On the other hand, people with interdependent self-concepts change their attitudes more in response to a high-status source than individuals with independent self-concepts.[42] Other factors include the point that it is easier to exert influence if the persuader is not seen as trying to influence. However, energy, confidence and forcefulness increase credibility, whereas low-energy communication styles reduce it.

## SUMMARY – FACTORS AFFECTING ATTITUDE CHANGE

The belief component of attitudes can be changed by new information. The affect component responds more to emotional appeals. High centrality, consistency and intensity make an attitude harder to change. The level of certainty the influence target feels about an existing attitude, their intelligence and in some cases their motivational pattern affect how easily they can be influenced. The credibility of the source of the persuasive attempt is another important factor.

## PERSUASIVE MESSAGES AND STYLES

Naive persuaders sometimes think that the right message can persuade anyone to do anything. Although, as this chapter shows, they are wrong, the characteristics of persuasive messages undoubtedly affect the outcome. Findings from research on persuasive messages include the following:

1. Comprehensibility is vital. (Thus the effectiveness of subliminal advocacy and advertising has probably been over-rated.)
2. There is no clear link from the number of arguments to the message's effectiveness.
3. Repetition has mixed effects. Hearing or seeing a message over and over often does lead people to have a more positive attitude towards it.[43] On the other hand, there may be no effect at all. Over-repetition is counter-productive, leading to loss of attention, boredom and disregard of the communication. Repetition is most effective for non-central attitudes. An example might be a

**Box 8.3**

### How to increase your effectiveness at changing others' attitudes

- Apply moderate rather than extreme pressure.
- Raise dissonance by keeping incentives low and the target's sense of personal responsibility high.
- Pay attention to the target person's attitude to yourself, not just the attitude change object; emphasise similarity.
- Provide rewards and increases in reward.
- Position messages just inside the target's latitude of acceptance.
- Stress the benefits of new ideas and introduce them incrementally.
- Supply new information to change the belief component of an attitude and emotional appeals to change the affective component.
- Avoid trying to change attitudes that are central, consistent and intense.
- Adjust your persuasive appeals to allow for the intelligence and self-esteem of the target.
- Identify the target's needs that could be met by an attitude change.
- Work to increase your credibility as a persuasive source.
- Use social pressure and word-of-mouth.
- Use common sense. Make it easy for people to do what you want. Explain why the person should do as you ask, don't make them hunt for reasons. Avoid running up against impossible obstacles, for instance, asking for treatment that contradicts company policies or will create a precedent that will bring the shop floor out on strike. On the other hand do not take excuses at face value, either when given by others or to stop you asking in the first place.
- Rehearse. If possible try role-playing with a friend.
- Be persistent. People are often refused what they ask for the first time but get it in the end because they keep trying. Some recruitment officers even use it as a sort of test. When they are in doubt about whether a candidate is suitable, they wait to see if they will keep trying despite refusals or lack of reply. Those who do keep trying get accepted.

telephone receptionist's attitude to dealing with callers. Few, probably, are actively antagonistic to callers, so that leaving them for long periods in silence not knowing whether their call has been cut off is merely the result of an attitude of indifference that is habitual rather than central. In such cases it can work well to simply repeat the persuasive message, saying, 'Please make sure that when you are waiting to put a call through to an extension you keep talking to the caller every 30 seconds.' For more central attitudes it is more effective to repeat the basic theme with variations. With this approach, it seems, the listener gets reward from receiving the message itself, which increases the appeal. Many communicators are afraid of repetition. They feel uncomfortable saying the same thing twice, even in different ways. However, research has shown that in general it is not until the fourth repetition of a message that it starts to become less effective.

4. Receivers respond cognitively in different ways to different messages. They may engage in thinking carefully about the message and attempt to evaluate

the arguments it raises. This is known as systematic or central processing. It is used when receivers want to have confidence in their judgement, are not too concerned about the effort required to process systematically, know enough about the subject matter to allow critical thinking about it, and the topic is important to them. On the other hand, they may rely on peripheral/heuristic assessment, using rules of thumb, schemas and other implicit theories about the world,[44] or being influenced by extraneous factors, such as source credibility, liking for the source, fear or guilt.[45] Which the receivers use depends in part on the message arguments. Systematic processing is more likely when the message arguments are many, strong and unambiguous. Figure 8.6 shows this logic in a diagram. For instance, 'I'm going to show you how a £1,000

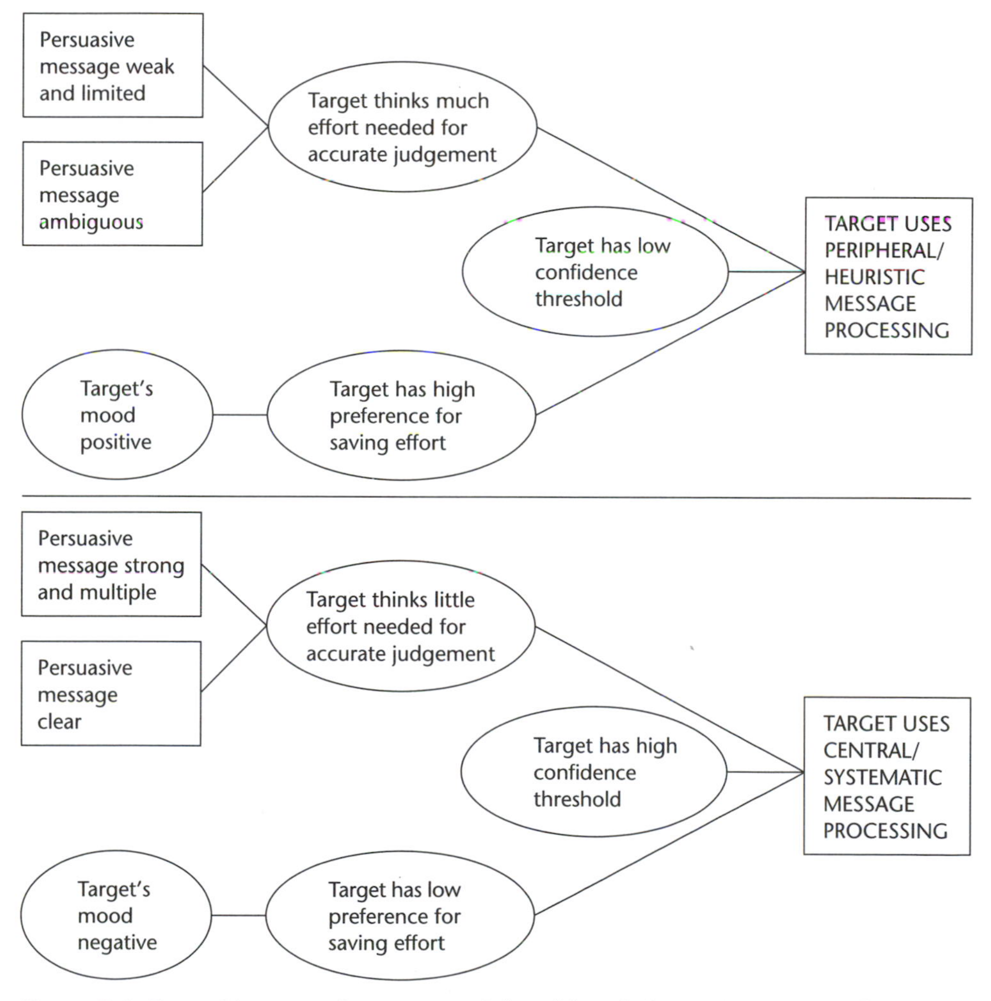


**Figure 8.6 Central/systematic versus peripheral/heuristic message processing.**

investment could turn into £1 million, how one single share purchase could make you hundreds of thousands, how you can enjoy the thrill of receiving "live" share tips from those at the Centre of the Stock Market and the excitement of receiving your first £10,000 cheque from your stockbroker' is, other things being equal, more likely to be processed systematically than 'A small investment may grow up to 1,000 fold.' There is no clear evidence on whether central/systematic or peripheral/heuristic processing is more likely to produce influence. What is clear, though, is that attempts to persuade that are aimed at central/systematic processing are only likely to be effective if the arguments in favour of a position are genuinely strong.

5. Fear of consequences can be persuasive. An example might be a colleague's warning to a poor time-keeper, 'You're risking the sack if you go on getting in so late.' Of a total of more than 100 studies, the great majority show that fear arousal and persuasion are linked.[46] While a fear appeal may be a threat based on power, 'If you go on getting in so late I'm going to give you the sack', it can be just a friendly warning. In either case, how much effect it has depends on how credible it is.[47] In the case of a threat it will only work if the person issuing it has the power and the intention to use it and in the case of a friendly warning only if the warner is seen as well intentioned and well informed.
6. Guilt makes people comply more readily with a request for help. When people break rules or behave 'badly' they are often much more compliant afterwards. Anticipating feeling guilty can also make people compliant. However, although more explicit guilt appeals successfully arouse greater guilt than less explicit appeals, they are significantly less persuasive.[48] On the other hand, messages that convey the opportunity to stop feeling guilty are more effective than straightforward requests, if (and only if), the target is feeling guilty ('It's something that you could feel really good about if you help us out this time'). Shaming and inducing guilt have been shown to work better than threats of sanctions, which can provoke reactance. Messages that focus on the problem, rather than blaming the wrongdoer, are more persuasive. However, guilt can lead to cover-ups and so can the fear of being shamed.[49]
7. The more aware the influence targets are of the other side of the story, the more important it is for persuaders to show that they have taken both sides into account by using two-sided appeals. For example, experienced sales representatives who know that their company's products are more expensive than those of the competition will not wait for the customer to point this out. They will refer to it early on, before mentioning that their company has a more durable and reliable product, better delivery, more extensive spare parts and so on. Two-sided persuasive messages increase the target's resistance to future attempts to undermine their impact. Two-sided appeals may either present the other point of view and then answer it (refutational messages), or

simply state both, leaving the greater strength of the favoured message to win over the recipients' minds unaided (non-refutational messages). Refutational two-sided messages are generally more persuasive than one-sided messages but non-refutational two-sided messages are less persuasive than one-sided messages.[50] It is not the case that one-sided messages work better with uneducated targets or those initially favourable to the idea but two-sided messages work better with educated targets or those initially opposed. Nor does sequencing – using favourable or opposing messages first – have any effect. However, the background expectations of targets do need to be taken into account. For example, where a communicator might be expected to discuss only risks or benefits (e.g. of a given technology), their credibility might be enhanced by a non-refutational discussion of both sides.

8. Exemplars are short quotations (verbal or visual) from concerned or interested people that illustrate a particular problem or view on a problem. (They are frequently used by journalists because of their apparent authenticity and their vividness.) Research shows that exemplars influence opinions and attitudes more strongly than statistics, comprehensive overviews or official information, although they may often be less valid. To date, we have no real knowledge of why exemplars are so persuasive, though one study has shown that the strategy appears to work on a range of targets, regardless of any similarity between them and the exemplar.[51]
9. It is clear that framing techniques, described in Chapter 6, hold considerable potential for persuading.

## Persuasive language and styles

Language styles have been characterised as powerful or powerless. Hesitations and tag questions characterise the powerless style. Research suggests that the power of the language style used by a speaker influences both the target's evaluation of the speaker and their attitudes towards his or her recommendations. However, this applies only when the message is spoken and the audience can either hear or both hear and see the speaker. For written persuasion, the power of the language style does not appear to have any effect on how persuasive it is.[52] Subtlety is an alternative to powerful language to achieve influence goals at work. For example, suppose a supervisor says to a subordinate, 'Working on anything interesting these days?' If the answer is, as the supervisor plans it to be, 'It's mainly routine', then the supervisor's request to take on additional work appears as a solution to a problem of the subordinate rather than a demand for compliance.[53]

There are two main dimensions of persuasive styles – a dominative–dependent dimension and a high–low affiliative dimension. These two combine to give four types of influencing style,[54] shown in Figure 8.7. For instance, some people offer

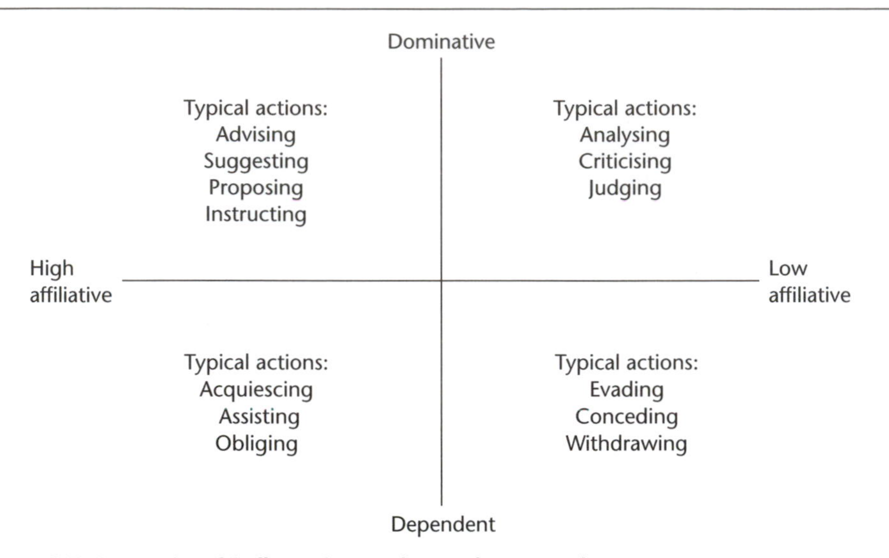


**Figure 8.7 A matrix of influencing styles and approaches.**

advice, give directions and initiate ideas. This style, which combines a degree of dominating with being warm and supportive, and is therefore labelled dominative–high affiliative, is most generally effective. Less effective is a dominative–low affiliative style, which is based on analysing, criticising and judging, or one marked by acquiescing, assisting and obliging, called a dependent–high affiliative style. Least likely of all to bring success in influencing others is a dependent–low affiliative style, marked by evasion, concession and withdrawal. Although it is probable that influencing styles are effective in this order, the best influencing style, like the best leadership style, depends on the situation. Especially important will be the character and attitudes of the influence target. If they have high needs for autonomy a less dominative style will be appropriate. The best approach is to judge the requirements of the situation and adopt a suitable style.

## SUMMARY – PERSUASIVE MESSAGES AND STYLES

Persuasive messages only persuade if they are understood. The effects of number of arguments and repetition are not clear cut. How the receiver is likely to process the message – centrally, systematically or heuristically, peripherally – should be taken into account. Messages can convey a range of different types of persuasive appeal, all with different effects. Powerful language can be persuasive face-to-face but so can more subtle language use. Persuasive styles have been analysed in terms of a 'dominative–dependent' and 'high- and low-affiliative' typology. Switching style according to the situation works better than having a consistent style.

Box 8.4

### How to make your persuasive messages and styles effective

- Make sure your target understands your message.
- Use repetition of favourable messages when the target's existing attitude is not strongly held but not when it is central. Avoid over-repetition.
- Do not rely too much on having several arguments. More arguments will be better if the target is more likely to process the message centrally, but not if s/he is using rules of thumb or peripheral factors such as liking the message source.
- Use fear appeals with care to avoid reactance; friendly warnings may be more effective than threats.
- Use guilt and shame appeals but focus on the problem rather than blaming and show the target how the advocated behaviour can overcome the guilt or shame.
- Use refutational two-sided appeals.
- Place more reliance on exemplars than statistics.
- Use powerful language when persuading face to face. Alternatively, aim for subtlety in persuasive language.
- Adjust your persuasive style to the influence target but if in doubt aim for a dominative–high affiliative style.

Exercise 6 gives a rating scale designed to help you analyse your persuasive performances.

## GAINING COMMITMENT

Often the level of influence sought at work amounts to commitment – a psychological state in which a person feels tied or connected to someone or something.[55] For instance, consumer brand loyalty is sought by marketers, 'goodwill' is considered an intangible but significant business asset and commitment of staff to the organisation has long been valued and is coming back into fashion as the costs to loyalty of downsizing and re-engineering come to be felt. Fey and Beamish[56] quoted the general manager of an advertising agency joint venture in Moscow as saying that commitment to the joint venture makes all the difference to resolving conflicts. Degree of commitment has been linked to how publicly the person has adopted an attitude,[57] the amount of an individual's 'investment' or 'sunken costs' in a situation or relationship,[58] to what extent an individual feels personal responsibility for costs that have been incurred[59] and meaning and values. People feel especially committed to relationships and other life goals that express their own beliefs,[60] values[61,62] and identities.[63] Box 8.5 lists the factors shown by research to influence commitment. The factors influencing commitment suggest that the effects of influencing techniques are likely to be limited unless there is a match between the target's beliefs, values and identity and the influence object. Because commitment most often occurs in a time-extended relationship, interdependence theory, described in Chapter 10, may provide a better account than either persuading or using power.

Box 8.5

**Factors influencing degree of commitment of an individual to a project/relationship/attitude**

- Extent of public support they have given.
- Amount of influencee's 'investment'.
- How personally responsible the influencee feels for the situation.
- Degree of match to the influencee's beliefs and goals.
- The amount of adversity involved for the influencee in maintaining the commitment.

There are cultural variations in how commitment is conceptualised. Guzley *et al.*[64] found that commitment is conceptualised differently in the United States and Japan. To the US sample of respondents, commitment implied themes of dedication, obligation, integrity and determination. In contrast, for the Japanese respondents, it implied connection, membership, responsibility and co-operation. The researchers concluded that the cultural values of individualism and collectivism accounted for these differences.

## SUMMARY – GAINING COMMITMENT

Gaining commitment – getting others to feel ties of loyalty – goes beyond the normal range of influence. The factors influencing commitment include the targets' beliefs, values and identities. To gain real commitment, these must be matched by the influence object. What commitment means may vary cross-culturally.

## WORK APPLICATIONS FOR PERSUADING

Success in personal selling, networking, making presentations, introducing changes and subordinates' attempts to influence their managers depends on exercising effective persuasive skills. In most cases of these work activities, the person trying to influence another has little or no power over the influence target. Thus to perform these work activities well, the understanding learnt from this chapter needs to be applied, and the guidance given in Boxes 8.3 and 8.4 followed, in addition to the points made in this section.

### Personal selling

Sales representatives are prime examples of people who use persuasive skills at work. How they work is still somewhat mysterious. In a survey of over one hundred studies which analysed the behavioural and organisational factors associated with salespersons' effectiveness, it was found that no single factor was able to explain as much as 10 per cent of the variation in performance.[65] However, a new perspective on sales talk has started to emerge, which suggests that the kinds of selling techniques taught on sales courses are little used or substantially modified by many experienced and successful sales personnel. Instead, the salesperson is a dynamic processor of information, able to respond to client cues by selecting the most appropriate learned script.[66] The sales dialogue is more like an ordinary conversation, though one with a purpose. From research in which more than 40 live industrial sales calls were unobtrusively tape-recorded, Peter Gorley concluded:

> Each interaction has a balance, a consistency, a unique equilibrium, and within each interaction we can detect similar mechanisms, similar negotiations of a definition of the situation . . . by the end of a call, the verbal behaviour of one actor . . . will approximate to the verbal behaviour of the other actor. Thus it is likely that, if at some point the salesman [sic] tells a story, the buyer will at some time later tell one too. If a buyer obstinately refuses to buy a product, the salesman will attempt at a later stage to dominate the interaction. What is commonly called the 'give and take' of a personal relationship is very much a feature of the talk in a sales call, an interaction involving two people who are usually strangers to one another. . . . The relationship between the salesman and the buyer is collusive, not conflictive. By this I mean that they play into one another's hands, as opposed to a relationship in which each tries to maximise his own gains at the expense of the other, which I would describe as 'conflictive'. This finding is at odds with the stereotype of the salesman as 'high-pressure', 'fast-talker' which I found by informal research with a group of civil servants to be still current. This finding is the more surprising if it is remembered that the salesmen in my study are working on a commission-only basis: if they do not sell, they make no money, so one would have thought the compulsion to sell would be acute.

Gorley finally interpreted the findings of his study as follows:

> The sales call remains a social interaction based on human communication behaviour, with all the mutual adjustments that this entails; and . . . it is not, nor can it be, a form of instrumental action based on technical rules for achieving success.[67]

Other research confirms that the ways of behaving which work well in other types of interaction help determine success or failure in selling. Riordan *et al.*[68] showed that the number of co-operative responses in a sales dialogue was related to the probability of a sale resulting. They found that people who eventually bought were more likely than those who did not buy to have attitudes similar to the sales representatives.

Perceived similarity of sales representatives to buyers emerges again and again as a positive influence in selling. Insurance agents who achieved high levels of sales were seen by prospects as similar in outlook and personal situation,[69] paint salespersons were more likely to influence purchasers when buyers saw them as liking and buying similar things[70] and sales of a tape cleaner increased significantly

Box 8.6

An understanding of and sensitivity to the motivational pattern of sales prospects is crucial to personal selling. One motive of particular interest for negotiators or sales personnel is the need for closure. This involves a desire for knowledge on some issues as opposed to confusion or uncertainty. It derives from situational or personality factors that influence how people weigh the subjective costs or benefits of certainty. It operates through two general tendencies, one to attain closure quickly and seize on early information potentially leading to closure, the other to maintain closure once achieved by, for instance, locking out new information. The need for closure leads to less extensive information processing and hypothesis generation, raised judgemental confidence and preference for prototypical over diagnostic evidence. All these effects mean that triggering the customer's need for closure at the right point can be a powerful tool in personal selling.

*Source*: Webster, D. M. and A. W. Kruglanski (1997) 'Cognitive and social consequences of the need for cognitive closure' in W. Stroebe and M. Hewstone (eds) *European Review of Social Psychology*, vol. 8. Chichester: John Wiley, pp. 133–174.

when the salesperson was perceived as having similar musical taste to the buyer.[71] Other studies show that the more similar the buyer and seller in their clothing, language and other symbols of social background, the more likely it is that a sale will occur. It also helps if a seller has similar occupational status to the person representing the buyer. It is for this reason that it works better when sales directors interact with procurement directors and ordinary sales representatives with ordinary buyers. Equally, a sales engineer is more effective at selling to a works or production engineer, not only because of having the necessary technical expertise but also because their common educational background gives them an affinity.

Being friendly, showing personal interest in the buyer and being seen as different from the typical negative stereotype all help in selling.[72] So does fulfilling prospects' role expectations. For instance, when wholesale drug salespeople's actual behaviour differs from the expectations of retail pharmacists' buyers, loyalty to the supplier is lower.[73] Being perceived as expert increases the trust customers have in salespeople. Using reward power and the norm of reciprocity also appear to help sell. All these findings support Pruden and Reese's conclusion that 'Salesmen [sic] set up a patterned interaction with members of customer organisations, such patterns of interaction being an extension of the human relations that take place within an organisation.'[74]

## Networking

Another example of influencing skills in organisational and inter-organisational life is networking. This means getting things achieved politically, through networks of contacts. While 'office politics' in the sense of self-seeking intrigue has rightly acquired a bad name, political activity directed towards organisational goals is an essential part of the role of most executives. Politics has been defined as the activity 'by which government is made possible when differing interests in an area to be governed grow powerful enough to need to be conciliated.'[75] The ability to conciliate powerful interests can be vital to getting things done within and between organisations, just as it is in wider society. In the new types of organisation described in Chapter 2, networking is built into the system. An intensive study of the hidden economy has shown how the system functions almost entirely through the activities of fixers and networkers.[76]

Political skills enable managers to deviate from accepted practices and to introduce new ideas with less protest or resistance than managers who lack them. They therefore contribute to helping organisations adapt and change. In the words of one writer, 'Effective participation in the political process can lead to a better definition of organisational problems and the generation and implementation of more successful solutions.'[77] For individuals, political skills enable them to get round the rigidities and obstacles of the 'system', especially in large hierarchies, and to operate more effectively. Executives can feel frustrated and powerless to influence events. By acquiring or improving their political skills they increase their sense of their own control and are encouraged to become more pro-active.

**Box 8.7**

In some organisations, the requirement for representativeness creates opportunities for women and members of ethnic minorities to network. A woman middle manager in a public service organisation, where appointments and promotions are decided by a panel of at least four staff, one of whom has to be a woman and another from an ethnic minority (or the two roles can be combined) said the following: 'I'm often asked and I usually accept', she said, 'although it takes a lot of time. It gives me an inside view of other departments and makes friends. You get to be friends with your fellow-panel members after two days together round a table interviewing, and anyone you appoint or promote always remembers.'

*Source*: Interview, author's research.

Networkers cultivate the people they want to influence all the time. They cannot succeed by turning charm, interest and consideration on and off like a tap. Networkers are sensitive to other people's motivations, attitudes and so on. They know who has influence and how to build contacts with them. Skilled politicians place themselves in positions to mobilise the support of other influential people or to neutralise their influence if it is likely to run counter to their own objectives. Networkers believe in themselves and in their ability to change things. Some people have a determinist view of the social world; they think of it as governed by impersonal forces too powerful and too indifferent for individuals to make changes happen. Others lack faith in their own influence because, they feel, they lack status or authority. These beliefs can lead to a fatalistic resignation, an expectation that if an influence attempt is made, it will fail. They are examples of self-fulfilling prophecies. Networkers are free of them.

**Box 8.8**

Medlab, a medium-sized Dutch subsidiary of a large American industrial firm, uses inter-organisational networking as a strategy. The business distinguishes three types of co-operation that differ in their degree of intensity. These are half yearly contacts with universities and hospitals to stay in touch with important developments; sponsoring research projects through the provision of services and/or the payment of salaries; and intensive collaboration by means of joint research projects. For inter-organisational networking such as this to work well, 'Both parties need to establish and maintain properly functioning personal relationships. Despite all formal agreements, the ultimate success of the co-operation project largely depends on the people involved.'

*Source*: Biemans, J. (1990) 'The managerial implications of networking', *European Management Journal*, vol. 8, no. 4, pp. 529–540.

## Making presentations

Many people with successful careers owe a great deal to their ability to make good presentations. More than most other activities it gives a chance for relatively junior staff to stand out from their peers and bring themselves to the attention of those who can influence their progress. For senior managers it has a central role in employee communications (see Chapter 7) as well as in influencing policy decisions through informal presentations to superiors and colleagues. Formal presentation to the sales force, for instance, has for a long time been accepted as one way to get commitment behind a new sales drive. Managers who lack confidence in their presentation skills tend to fall back on e-mails or memoranda. The result is that work relationships become more formal and rigid and they lose control of an important channel of communication within the organisation. In external relations, the need to make presentations often arises. Throughout the growing professional, investment banking and consultancy sectors, presentations of varying degrees of formality are an integral part of new business approaches. In marketing research and advertising, presentations, backed up by a written report, are the main way of communicating plans, campaigns, research programmes and findings to clients.

There is plenty of reading available on the mechanics of presentation, such as structuring the material, the form of diagrams, the use of visual aids and how to set up the physical environment. These are important matters and an excellent book on them is listed in Further Reading. The main objective in the mechanics of presentation is how to communicate clearly, but more emphasis will be placed here on how to influence an audience. How can presenters get their audience to believe their findings, understand their proposals, react favourably to their ideas and plans, feel motivated and committed towards their objective or buy their service? By understanding these, the presenter's skills can be increased and their approach can be linked to their objective.

### *Preparing to present*

There are three key preparation areas, deciding the purpose, researching the subject and rehearsal.

1. Presentation purposes are concerned with audience response. They range from getting the audience to listen and learn to getting them to modify their attitudes or to 'buy' something they otherwise might not. Audience learning is most important when reporting data or identifying problems and opportunities and trying to stimulate creative thinking. Most presenters, however, need their audience to go through the processes of being influenced or persuaded.
2. Researching the subject is essential to convince the audience but also allows the presenter to feel secure enough about the material to make a confident presentation. Digesting the material, that is thinking about it, is as important as assembling it. Presenters of ill-digested material often confuse their audience by attempting to tell them everything they know. Being selective matters.
3. Rehearsal is vital for getting content order right (it often turns out that the 'logical' order is not the best), adjusting timing, memorising, deciding what to emphasise, practising variations in voice tone and body language, and making sure the visual aids are visible. The best sort of rehearsal is in front of a supportive audience. To be most helpful, such a rehearsal audience should offer a very limited number of constructive criticisms but should also provide reinforcement by praising the good points. Presenters who lack a rehearsal audience should practise live in front of a mirror and with some form of recorder – ideally video, but otherwise audio. Figure 8.8 shows the relationships between preparation, practice and rehearsal and presenters' control in front of the audience.

### *Interacting with an audience*

There are five key factors in audience interaction, and good presenters pay attention to all of them. They are shown in Figure 8.9. Box 8.9 gives some detailed guidance.

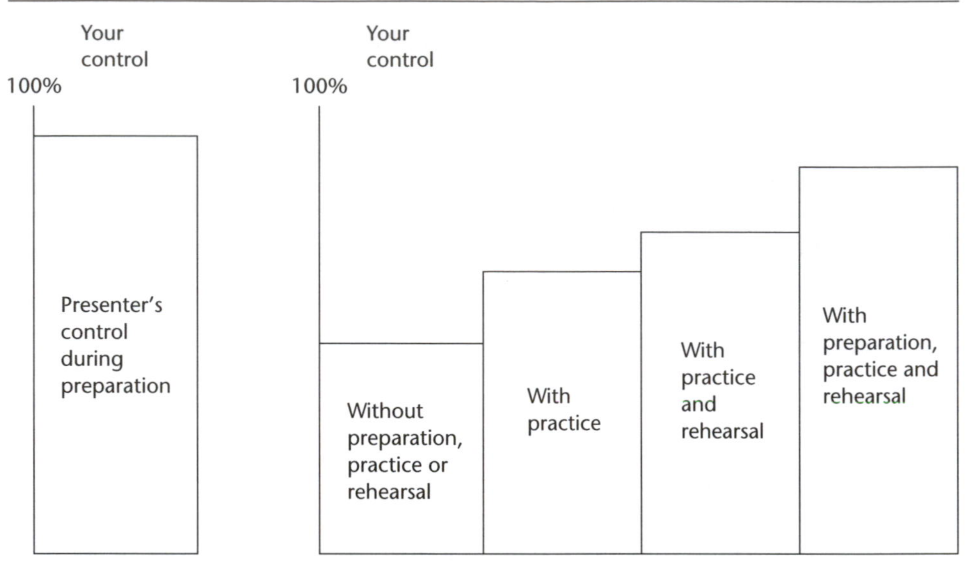


**Figure 8.8 Controlling a presentation.**

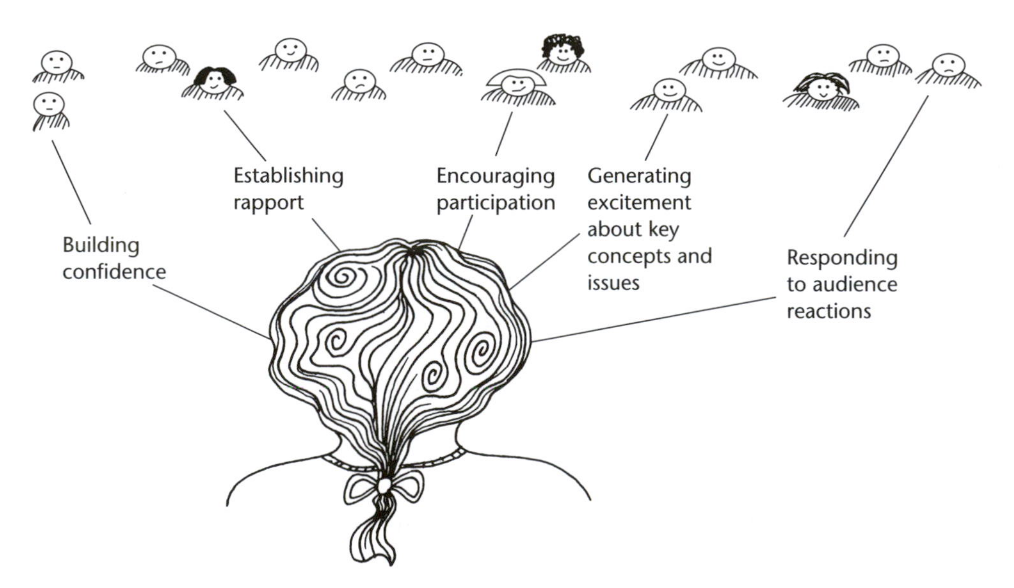


**Figure 8.9 Five keys to successful interaction with an audience.**

### *Presentation stages*

There are five rather well-defined stages: the opening, the positive arguments, dealing with objections, drawing conclusions and the question and answer session.

**Box 8.9**

## How to make effective presentations

**Stimulate active listening**

- Pay attention to the non-verbal signals you give out.
- Avoid arousing ego-defences by appearing superior, manipulative, over-certain or over-judgemental.

**Stimulate learning**

- Provoke 'unlearning' by raising your audience's uncertainty level. Instead of entitling your talk 'How advertising works', call it 'So you think you know how advertising works'; instead of 'How to get rich', 'Do you sincerely want to be rich?'
- Relate your subject to your audience's needs, motivations and background. Grab them – 'THIS is why you MUST listen'.
- If you have a list of points or figures, perhaps on a slide or flipchart, sort out which are the important ones and tell your audience that they are important – do not leave them to guess. Figure 8.10 gives an example of how to do this. Explain the implications of any statistical data or research findings you use or any illustrations or examples you quote. Most of your audience will be too busy following what is being presented to work out its implications, so if you do not tell them they will be confused about its meaning and dissatisfied with your argument. Some of your audience, on the other hand, may be distracted into trying to think through the implications of what you have said and you will have lost their attention for what you are saying now.
- Help people to remember important points by arousal and repetition. Remind them at each stage about the structure of your talk, where you are now, where you are going and any major points. Use the three S's – structure, signposts and summaries.

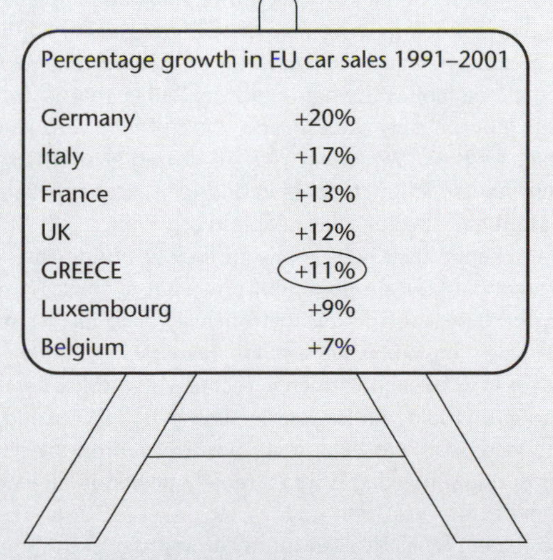


Visual aids should highlight, and presenters should emphasise, the facts which are important to the argument – in this case the growth of the Greek car market. Without such highlighting it is a struggle for the audience to find the important statistic – not many will bother.

**Figure 8.10 Helping an audience to follow a presentation.**

- Ask questions, if possible, to get your audience to participate. Reward those who reply with 'Good point', 'Yes' (even if you mean 'No'). Wrong answers should be accepted and only then gently put right; otherwise you stop anyone answering your questions.
- Give a positive welcome to audience questions that show that learning has happened: 'That's a good question' (especially if it isn't); 'Ah, I'm pleased you picked up that point' (especially if you were dreading that they would).
- Stroke your audience with occasional smiles, a voice tone which conveys interest, and little verbal pats on the back such as: 'Of course, you'll have realised by now', 'Now I know you're ahead of me here', 'I don't have to tell this audience'. Do not, however, overdo it.

**Stimulate change**

- Present yourself as likeable, through humour or non-verbals, but not, generally, through jokes.
- Present yourself as similar to your audience. Clothes and grooming should be like theirs. Presenters are more effective if they are seen not only as expert, but also as members of the group on equal terms with the audience (Argyle, 1967) and as having the same broad attitudes as themselves.
- Messages that audiences perceive as sincere and meant to benefit them are more likely to be believed. Show the audience that you have thought about the issue from their point of view, and are concerned with their interests. If possible take some prior soundings to make sure you get it right. Even unpalatable messages can be made acceptable if presented from this perspective. You can help your audience 'separate the people from the problem'.
- Audience participation increases the probability of change. If the audience is not too large, if the conventions do not forbid, if you have enough confidence, encourage contributions from the floor. Otherwise, keep the formal presentation to a minimum, leaving plenty of time for floor discussion. Get the audience participating in their thoughts, even if not aloud, by saying, for instance, 'At this point, I'd like you to think about a question – and that is how you could use this technology in your own business', *pause*, 'One way might be . . .'.
- Keep the audience mentally saying 'Yes'. Leave disputable points until you have built an image of a shared basic outlook with your audience. Rather than trying to impress or challenge the audience in the early stages, carry the audience with you and give them the pleasure of seeing for themselves what you are driving at shortly before you state it. Satisfaction from this mental act of completion and identification will spill over onto your proposal and increase the chance of a favourable reception.
- Get your audience to change their behaviour and they will bring their attitudes into line. Tell them what to do about your proposal, not just what to think. What you recommend them to do should not appear to commit them heavily or to involve much risk, but should be typical of an action expressing a mildly favourable attitude, such as interest. You can get your audience to make appointments, record your address and telephone number or agree to the question 'Would you like me to send you . . .?' Making an affirmative act of this kind tends to lead people to think more positively about the next step.
- Public commitment during a meeting is an extremely powerful influence on subsequent behaviour. Get people to say 'Yes', and nod.
- Avoid spoken disagreement which is even more committing to the speaker and can influence others in the audience. Do not invite it and if you get it anyway, temporise: 'That's an interesting point, but perhaps of rather specialised interest / but we'd need to go into it at some length. I'd like to talk to you about it afterwards.' Alternatively, unless it's an important client or the boss, politely, but firmly, put them down.

**Box 8.9 *continued***

- Do not over-estimate the power of rational argument, or facts and figures, to persuade others. Powerful arguments can provoke mental counter-argument. Facts and figures can be disbelieved – 'You can make statistics tell any story.'
- Put group pressure for conformity to work (Asch, 1956). A small audience, up to about 20 people, can work as a group, especially if seating arrangements are appropriate, as with a circle round a table rather than rows of chairs.
- Do not over-address yourself to members of the audience who show by their facial expression or by nodding that they are following and supporting you. If you do you will probably lose their backing through embarrassment or a sense of undue pressure, while the rest of the audience may take offence at their comparative neglect. Instead, mobilise the support of those nodding, if possible: 'What do you think about such-and-such, so-and-so?' or 'Does this fit in with your experience, so-and-so?' With luck, their positive comments in answer to such a question will have a considerable impact on the rest of your audience.

**Create interest and excitement about your message**

Learning, influence and taking affirmative action all happen more readily when an audience is mentally aroused.

- Be more animated when you are making interesting points. Use livelier gestures, faster and higher-pitched speech and physical movement.
- Selectively tell your audience that you are excited by this research, study or concept, 'I think this is incredibly interesting because . . .', 'When I learned about this, it seemed to me a most important development'.
- Use visual aids that emphasise, through colour, underlining or diagrams, the points you want special attention paid to.

**Respond to the audience's reactions**

Reactions can include not understanding, boredom and over-excitement.

- If you are not being understood, repeat the point with the visual aids. Introduce your repetition by, 'This is a difficult point, so I'll run over it again . . .', in order not to insult or confuse your audience. Speak more slowly and louder. Maybe they didn't hear you the first time. About 15 per cent of most audiences are partially deaf. You may have unintentionally speeded up or dropped your voice.
- If the audience is bored, do not be tempted by the desire to escape into speeding up. The need is variety – of voice tone, gesture and your position; this is usually more practical than a panicky attempt to vary the content. Have a suitable 'arouser' up your sleeve when you start, such as an anecdote or a dramatic statistic, a challenging question or 'I would like you to imagine . . .'.
- Audience over-excitement is a problem if you have limited time and are in a competitive situation. For instance, if you are making a presentation for new business, someone from the client may interrupt your speech with an aside, or you may make a Freudian slip, which can produce gales of time-consuming laughter. In that state, you will not be heard, so you need to quieten them down both literally and metaphorically. Don't try to talk above a hubbub. Wait patiently and with a smile for quiet. As soon as the noise dies down resume firmly and slowly, repeating the bit just before you left off.

*Sources*: Argyle, M. (1967) *The Psychology of Interpersonal Behaviour*. Harmondsworth, Middlesex: Penguin Books.

Asch, S. E. (1956) 'Studies of independence and conformity', *Psychological Monographs*, vol. 70, no. 9.

*The opening*: four things need to be done at the start:

1. Make contact with the audience and secure their attention. Unless introduced by somebody else, it is important for speakers to give their names. It is very difficult for an audience to relate to an anonymous speaker. Even if they have been given the name in writing, the act of speaking it is a small 'gift' which starts to create trust.
2. Establish the mood of the presentation – serious? intellectual? polemical? matter-of-fact? light-hearted?
3. Establish links with the audience.
4. Outline the talk, why, in what order and hint at pleasant, interesting or important items to come.

*The positive arguments*: the first statement of a line of reasoning, case or finding should be uncluttered, unqualified and affirmative. It should be carefully structured. Sometimes the best structure will be logical, a version of $2 + 2 = 4$; at other times chronological. We all like to listen to a good story. Often, though, something less obvious is effective. For instance, when presenting research results, give the results summary immediately after setting the scene, then mention methodology and finish by restating recommendations and conclusions. This can work better than the 'logical' order, methodology first, because by knowing the broad results the audience has been given a reason for taking interest in the methodology description.

Later elaborations of positive arguments should use plenty of examples and carefully designed visual aids. These should be simple and varied. The argument should be geared to the needs, interests and attitudes of the audience, especially its influential members. Only a case that is oriented towards them is likely to convince them. Ideas that are likely to be unfamiliar to the audience need careful handling. They must be led up to, not thrown like a stone into a pond. If the argument is in any way complex, if, as a rough guide, it will take more than ten minutes to present, the audience will need reminding at suitable junctures of its structure, with signposts showing the point reached. Re-using the original 'structure' overhead for this purpose gives the audience a comforting sense of familiarity and confidence.

The third stage of presenting *deals with objections* that prior thinking and discussions have brought to light. This stage should be kept short. Some people think it should be left out altogether as it is difficult to make it sound positive.

The fourth stage of the formal presentation is to summarise, *draw conclusions* and make recommendations, thank the audience and invite questions.

Finally, in the *question-and-answer session*, questions come in three categories – supportive, neutral and hostile. From observation, most speakers get roughly 25 per cent supportive questions, 50 per cent neutral and 25 per cent hostile. Many, however, treat a much higher proportion of them as hostile – responding as if the distribution were 25 : 25 : 50 or even 0 : 0 : 100. Treating a question that is actually supportive or neutral as hostile, i.e. responding defensively to it, is a bad mistake. Other members of the audience are generally quite sensitive to the intent or attitude behind a question, and a put-down, counter-attack or even unresponsive answer to what was in fact a supportive or information-seeking question loses the presenter sympathy. It is therefore much better to assume that no questioners are hostile until they are conclusively proved to be. The same applies to questioners who raise red herrings, ramble on inconclusively, or are clearly interested, not in asking questions about the talk, but in making a speech of their own. All audience contributions should be treated seriously and sympathetically up to the point where the audience is becoming impatient with the questioners or upset by them. Then it is essential to take firm control and stop them, or the rest of the audience will blame the presenter for their embarrassment and see them as weak and ineffectual.

Making a presentation can be quite exhilarating and usually creates tension. When they conclude some speakers are 'hyped up'. They often fail to listen carefully to questions, and sometimes they even interrupt. This should never be done except to extreme ramblers or hostiles. Interrupting can lead to misunderstanding the question and having to be corrected. It also insults the questioner by implying that their train of thought was obvious. Listening attentively and visibly is essential and it may pay to repeat the question in summary form to show understanding. Doing this can be presented as for the benefit of the rest of the audience, 'I'll just repeat that in case anyone could not hear', and, indeed it does help them. Questioners should be rewarded for speaking up, 'Thank you', 'That's an interesting question' and so on.

To ensure getting questions, the best technique is to implant ideas for them in the course of the formal presentation: 'You may want to ask me some more about this at the end.' Some public-spirited person is bound to raise this point if no other questions are quickly forthcoming. After all, a prolonged silence is uncomfortable for most of the audience as well as for the presenter.

Consider the way the following two questions were handled. They came after a presentation proposing a new type of international mailing service, which concluded with the possibility of a remail service whereby bulk postings from overseas would be split up and remailed to continental Europe from the United Kingdom.

Questioner: Do you have that capability right now – of going remail into Europe?

Presenter (laughing): No, no, what we want to do is, no, that would be giving the business to the UK Mail. No, what I meant by remail is. . . .

Questioner: What basis for pricing will you use?

Presenter: Now, there is a pricing complication in all this because of something called imbalance charges which means that the country which is delivering – in a relationship between two countries both with postal services – the company which is receiving is paid an imbalance charge and that relationship between UK and Europe means that we are not very interested.

In both of these examples, the presenter committed a cardinal error. In the first, he somewhat ridiculed the questioner for not understanding the position, and used the word 'No' four times, thus giving the questioner four negative 'strokes'. In the second, instead of answering the simple question that was put, he introduced what may well be a preoccupation of his own, but one that was unknown to his audience and was not the focus of the question; in this way, rather than clarifying an issue, he created further confusion. Here, however, is an example of a question that is handled well:

Presenter (answering the previous question): It's a very versatile technology. . . .

Questioner (interrupts): You could go for the institutional market as well.

Presenter: Yes, I should think we might be able to, in a limited way. I would like to begin by going for the affluent consumer market, both in the US and the UK, and then later we could perhaps look at the institutional, corporate market.

Here the presenter has not allowed the fact that he has been interrupted to 'rattle' him, and has tactfully avoided rejecting a suggestion which is in fact inappropriate, without, on the other hand, falling into the trap of accepting it.

## Introducing changes

In business, and work generally, a wide range of problem situations, concerning individual behaviour, business, marketing, or performance, call for people to change. That is, there is a need to unfreeze the current or problem situation, intervene, and then refreeze the resultant future state (which, it is hoped, is the one defined as the solved state). As Box 8.10 implies, subordinate members of organisations may have considerable power to subvert planned change if they disagree with it. The following are some of the sources of resistance to change:[78]

- Parochial self-interest – people make an understandable attempt to protect a status quo with which they are content and which they see as advantageous to themselves.
- Vested interests – most change threatens someone with a real loss of power, prestige or security.
- The disturbance of established relationships, which give people social support at work.
- Dislike of disruption, as when change will impose a geographical move.
- Loyalty to a subunit, which perhaps will be disbanded during change implementation; misunderstanding and lack of trust, possibly caused by lack of consultation.

- Poor information leading to people not seeing the reasons for the change.
- Contradictory analyses of change leading to different views on its potential consequences.
- Low tolerance of uncertainty or anxiety.

Change agents need to take into account the variety of individuals' responses to news of planned changes. These can be analysed along three dimensions: positive versus negative, decided versus undecided and self-focused versus other-focused.[79]

**Box 8.10**

An average German worker costs over than 50 per cent more than a North American to employ and is often less productive. There are likely to be huge barriers to change. These barriers include trade unionism, residual nationalism and the corporate culture, which could be major impediments in both Germany and France. In Germany, bosses tend to regard themselves as corporate father-figures, while French bosses have not caught up with the idea that the customer is king.

*Source*: Hammer, M. and J. Champy (1994) *Re-engineering the Corporation*, New York: Harper Business.

Presenting changes to staff should be preceded by analysing the forces for and against the change. Force field analysis (see Further Reading) is a useful tool. However, the analytic stage is beyond the scope of this book, which is concerned with interactive behaviour.

**Box 8.11**

- A study found that knowing what to do and making a public commitment to change predicted actual behavioural adaptation and that these in turn were affected by the social resources and interpersonal expectations of the change targets (Parrott *et al.* 1998).
- A worldwide survey by consultants 'Atticus' found, on the basis of 400 replies, that for companies in the top 5 per cent, top management are more than twice as likely to be involved in change projects as they are in the bottom 10 per cent. Also the top 5 per cent of companies are three times as likely as the bottom 10 per cent to have pro-active policies on communicating change (*The Economist*, 2000).

*Sources*: Parrott, R., J. Monahan, S. Ainsworth and C. Steiner (1998) 'Communicating to farmers about skin cancer: The behavior adaptation model', *Human Communication Research*, vol. 24, no. 3, pp. 386–409.
*The Economist*, 15 July 2000, p. 87.

Here are two examples of situations where change had to be presented to people who would be affected by it and where resistance might be expected.

1. Promo Public Relations decided to change its pricing system to come into line with the rest of the industry. Up to then Promo clients were charged a flat fee,

out of which all normal expenditure on printing, telephones, travel, etc. was met by the agency. The rest of the industry billed the client for these 'rechargeables', and thus Promo often lost business to competitors on price, because the agency's fees looked more than the competition. The change, however, was resisted by the agency's account executives. They disliked having to explain the change to clients and to do additional billing work. They also feared that the unpleasant task of chasing up clients who were slow to pay would be greatly increased when large numbers of bills for rechargeables were added to the invoices for fees.

2. An oil company had a large number of small commercial customers such as builders' merchants, builders, small-scale furniture or garment manufacturers and so on, to which it made 'small-drop' deliveries into their own tanks. Analysis had shown that overall these deliveries were unprofitable, and also that in many cases the contractual conditions were not being adhered to. For example, deliveries were being made in quantities of half the minimum contractual volume. An exercise was launched to improve the profitability of this business by enforcing the contractual conditions and by persuading as many customers as possible to accept changes such as taking deliveries at night, widening gates for the entry of larger vehicles, and giving longer notice of their orders. The managerial problem here was to motivate the sales force to persuade their customers to make these changes. The sales representatives feared that their customers would resist making costly changes from which they could expect no direct benefit.

People who are trying to get others to accept change often launch into advocating the change too soon. Instead they should listen and ask questions to determine the needs, understanding and concerns of the person to be changed, then use this information to guide their approach. The questions should be open ones plus probes, not closed ones that limit the possible answers. Part of the benefit of introducing change by questioning and listening is establishing a relationship leading to more friendliness and trust. The persons being asked to change will probably have to trust the change agent. The effect of the change will be felt in the future, so they cannot fully weigh it up. In accepting the arguments for change they have to trust the change agent's judgement about future effects, or their information about how it has worked out in other cases. Thus it is important that a trust-based relationship is built between the change agent and the change target.

Change agents often meet with resistance. Pushing harder, using more facts and figures, appeals to fair play, loyalty, references to power and status, guilt, self-interest and benefits for the person resisting can all just increase resistance and reduce trust. It often works better to get the opponents to express all their reservations, eliciting the frankest possible statements, and only argue in favour

**Box 8.12**

### How to present changes to the people affected

You may need to do a lot of changing yourself:

- Do you need to change your assumptions: to find out the reality of the prospect's beliefs, not just assume them?
- Do you need to change your perspective: to see the advantages and disadvantages from the prospect's point of view, not just your own?
- Do you need to change your style: use more listening, less advocacy?
- Do you need to change your attitude to the person you are trying to get to change? Do not criticise them for being not open to change; you probably are not yourself in many areas.
- Do you need to change your approach to a holistic one? There is a temptation to concentrate just on the one issue or aspect that you are concerned to change, but the situation as it impinges on the person you are trying to change is a whole. It may be that aspects of the environment of the issue, or of the circumstances of your interaction, are impeding the change. For instance, you can spend lots and time persuading someone of the benefits of a new idea, only to find out afterwards that it is their boss, not they, who is resistant to the idea.
- Remember also, that the physical set-up in the place where you are introducing the change is important. If it is wrong for the occasion, rearrange it.
- Do not assume that if you can provide the resister with appropriate data or information, he or she will change – information may not be enough. Be sensitive to the moment of psychological unfreezing. The 'sale' must be made when the 'prospect' is ready, not when the salesperson is ready.
- Do not treat what can and cannot be discussed as fixed. Consider the following extract from an interview with the commercial distillates marketing manager of an oil company, who was discussing relations with authorised distributors of oil products:

> Some of the discussions on the allowances we give them to operate and make a profit are quite tough nowadays. If we think the person has got too many resources, and isn't cutting them down, and he's running two Rolls-Royces where he should be running one, this is all talked about; whereas before it was never talked about, now it is, and some of the discussions can be quite uncomfortable. But so long as it was 'not done' to discuss their personal spending, the dice were loaded against getting them to cut their costs. And we are all learning from it.

*Source*: Interview with an oil company manager, author's research.

of the proposed change when asked to do so. Talking about any aspects of implementing the change should be postponed until all the opponents have expressed all their objections and negative feelings. If the resistance is too strong, it is better to leave things as they are for now – the opponents may be right. Even if they are wrong, it is important to avoid getting unwilling consent which turns to lack of support after the change agent is committed to the change. There may, however, be cases where it will work better to enforce the change despite resistance, trusting to the normal human capacity to adapt to what cannot be prevented or altered by adjusting attitudes. This is a high-risk approach and requires a good knowledge of the people involved. It is also more likely to be the best alternative where the situation does not leave time for consultative processes, and where the change does not require a high level of commitment from those affected in the early stages of its implementation.

**Box 8.13**

**European variations in how to present change**

In France, the emphasis should be on logic. The French prefer radical restructuring to gradual reform. They like technological novelty.

In Italy, new ideas, if poorly presented, will often be opposed automatically but if the change target can be given a sense of contributing or ownership, will usually be embraced just because they are novel.

In the Netherlands, change proposals should be well thought out, clearly presented and based on facts.

## Subordinate–manager influence

Individuals can exert upward influence, to promote their own interest or to get agreement to do things they want to do, or in the way they want them done. In many European countries, changes are increasing opportunities for subordinates to influence their managers. Decentralisation, team-based organising and downsizing increase the influencing opportunities for subordinates.

**Box 8.14**

**European variations in subordinate–manager relations**

In Sweden, since a main function of leaders is to listen and unanimity is sought, subordinate–manager influence is very high. Similarly, in the Netherlands, there is an expectation that upward communication will be treated with respect. In Germany and the United Kingdom, however, relations are too distant, even awkward, for feedback from subordinates to managers to be given or received comfortably. In Spain, subordinates expect their managers to solve their problems and answer their questions.

'Followers and members increasingly practice influence as part of team work, coaching relationships, mentor–protégé interactions and other less-hierarchical relationships.'[80] Despite the increased opportunities, however, 'Upward influence is inherently risky for low-power followers. Procedural structure, work roles, job stress etc. can limit scope for upward influence. So do organization culture, economic situation (ease of getting another job).' Thus, to exercise upward influence, subordinates use tactics, including:

- rationality/reasoning, such as providing job-related information and explanations – these create impressions of reasonableness;
- ingratiation, such as praise, flattery, approbation, opinion conformity – these enhance the subordinate's perceived qualities or motives;
- exchange/bargaining – reminding of past favours, offering rewards or sacrifices;
- assertiveness, based on technical expertise, information or social capital;
- coalitions;
- upward appeals over the head of the immediate supervisor or manager;
- inspirational appeals to arouse enthusiasm or increase the manager's confidence;
- consultation tactics.[81]

To gain influence in the longer run, subordinates have been found to volunteer first, undertake trouble shooting, adhere more closely than normal to organisational rules and procedures, accentuate similarities with their boss, give good explanations for any failures, seek feedback and give feedback. Which tactics subordinates use does not appear to be influenced by the gender of the subordinate.

Most of these tactics are aimed at positive impression management, to establish perceptions of competence early in the leader–member relationship. In time these may lead to patterns of reciprocal influence. High-quality leader–subordinate exchanges show language patterns indicating mutual rather than one-way influence. In such exchanges, followers question and challenge rather than listening passively.[82] Less work has been done on the outcomes of different influencing tactics used by subordinates. However, it does seem clear that subordinates' 'soft' tactics increase managers' evaluations, while assertiveness and repetition rebound negatively. In addition, supervisors have been shown to change their behaviour in response to negative feedback from subordinates.

## SUMMARY – WORK APPLICATIONS FOR PERSUADING

Personal selling is closer to normal social interaction than to the use of traditional sales techniques.

Networking means operating with political skill, that is, creating and maintaining contacts, gathering information through the grapevine, operating through reciprocity and mobilising support. It depends on having a view of the world as capable of being moulded without relying on authority.

Good presentations involve preparation by deciding the purpose, researching the subject and rehearsing. Successful interaction with an audience is achieved by building confidence, establishing rapport, encouraging participation, generating excitement and responding to audience reactions. There are different tasks to carry out and skills to apply at each of the five stages of a presentation – the opening, stating the positive arguments, dealing with objections, concluding and answering questions.

Successfully introducing change proposals involves beginning by asking questions and listening, instead of advocacy. It also depends on building a trust-based relationship, thinking about what aspects of the situation are open to discussion and handling resistance not by simply pushing harder for the change but by first eliciting all the objections and reservations of those resisting.

A wide range of tactics is available for subordinates to use to influence managers. However, the subordinate's position, which may be low in power, and the resulting risks favour soft tactics. Over time these may produce reciprocal influence.

## CHAPTER OVERVIEW

Persuading means influencing people by getting them to change their attitudes and beliefs. It relies on communicating reasons for these changes, as distinct from using power, which relies on the ability to control others' outcomes. Compliance can be brought about by strong pressure but long-term attitude change requires more subtle methods. These include using moderate pressure, raising dissonance, advocacy within the target's latitudes of acceptance and applying lessons from the adoption of innovations.

Adjusting for the characteristics of the target's existing attitudes, certainty about the influence object, intelligence and motivations underlie persuasive techniques. Being a credible source is important. Persuasive messages can convey a wide range of appeals but they need to be understood by the target and adjusted for the likelihood of heuristic or peripheral versus systematic information processing. Varying affiliation and domination levels according to the influence target, the influence object and the situation provide the most effective persuasive style. Gaining commitment requires high levels of adjustment to the influence target. The underlying factors affecting persuasion are probably universal, but techniques, messages and style need to be adjusted for cultural differences.

Applications of persuasive methods can be seen in personal selling, where research is pointing to the prevalence and effectiveness of normal social interaction, as opposed to sales techniques, and in networking, as well as in making presentations, introducing change and subordinate–manager influence.

## EXERCISES

1. Persuade a person you know only slightly to lend you £10 for a week.
2. Convince a friend or relative to go to see a film you know they do not want to see.

3. Persuade a small shopkeeper to drop his or her price.

4. Work in pairs. The influence target selects a topic from a given list and states his or her position in not more than 30 words. The persuader then attempts to change the target's mind.

5. This exercise concerns the encounter between a Web editor with a team of four journalists, over whom s/he has editorial, but not line management, responsibility and one of the journalists. This person works faster than the other three, completes five or six reports a day (the same number as they do) and then spends his/her time in Internet chat rooms. The team as a whole is under-performing and management is complaining. All four are paid the same. The Web editor must persuade the journalist to do more.

   *As a private study or group discussion exercise,* plan how the Web editor should approach the journalist. What should s/he say? How should s/he apply the persuasive strategies and tactics described in this chapter? How should s/he deal with the likely objections from the journalist?

   *As a role play,* enact the meeting between the Web editor and the journalist.

6. Complete the persuading performance self-rating scale given in Table 8.2.

7. Make a conscious effort to observe the interactions in a sales transaction. Look for all the nuances of interactive behaviour such as gestures, posturing, speech variations, noises such as 'hum' or 'tut', pauses, stares and signs indicating a change in mood or feeling.

   After you have made your observations write down how you believe the salesperson impressed the target. Use your knowledge of persuasive theories and techniques to analyse the salesperson's performance. (Did s/he create liking for him/herself? Offer rewards? What persuasive messages did s/he use? etc.) Why did the salesperson succeed (or fail)?

8. Imagine you are a salesperson in a shoe shop. You show the customer a pair of shoes and he or she responds by saying emphatically that they do not need the product. How would you respond? You are aware that the customer is hiding the true nature of their objection from you and is resisting purchase. How would you deal with this?

9. This exercise is a role play that gives practice in a combined selling/coaching situation.

   *Role A* is a lettings negotiator for a firm of estate agents in a high-prestige sector of the market. S/he covers a metropolitan area that attracts a large number of foreign clients seeking to rent a house or flat for a few months.

   *Role B* is one such potential client.

   The role play consists of their initial meeting to identify properties for B to view; A also needs to ensure that (i) B fully understands the contract s/he

**Table 8.2 Persuading performance self-rating scates**

To complete this questionnaire, place a tick on the section of the line following each question that most clearly represents the strength of your agreement or disagreement with the statement implied in each question.

| | *Yes* | | | | | *No* |
|---|---|---|---|---|---|---|
| Did my introductory remarks create an open and relaxed climate? | × | × | × | × | × | × |
| Did I use a questioning, participatory introductory approach? | × | × | × | × | × | × |
| Did I try to stimulate 'unlearning' – to create some uncertainty in the influencee's mind? | × | × | × | × | × | × |
| Did I apply cognitive dissonance theory? | × | × | × | × | × | × |
| Did I apply social judgement theory? | × | × | × | × | × | × |
| Did I pay as much attention to the influencee's attitude to myself as to their attitude to the matter I was trying to influence them about? | × | × | × | × | × | × |
| Was I sincere and friendly? | × | × | × | × | × | × |
| Did I reward any shifts of attitude in the direction I was seeking? | × | × | × | × | × | × |
| Did I use repetition appropriately? | × | × | × | × | × | × |
| Did I use fear appeals? | × | × | × | × | × | × |
| Did I use two-sided messages? | × | × | × | × | × | × |
| Did I stress the benefits to the influencee? | × | × | × | × | × | × |
| Did I introduce my ideas incrementally? | × | × | × | × | × | × |
| Did I attempt to mobilise social pressure? | × | × | × | × | × | × |
| Did I get the balance between friendliness, toughness and logic about right? | × | × | × | × | × | × |
| Did I get the balance between warmth and coldness, dominance and submission right? | × | × | × | × | × | × |

will be bound to if s/he takes on the flat and (ii) that B is able to supply references that can be checked in this country.

10. This exercise concerns the meeting between the Board of Smythe's, a books and stationery high street retail chain operator, and a group of staff of Quotient, a video publisher, about an agreed takeover of Quotient by Smythe's. Quotient is an established player in its sector, which is at the quality end of the market. It employs 350 largely specialised staff – editors, film makers and technicians. There is a rumour that the new owner will be quitting the quality product range that has been carefully built up and will be buying in product rather than making it, leading to possible redundancies. The agreed bid has thwarted a rival offer from a broadcaster and publisher, Crew Media

Group, which had announced plans to develop the existing profile of Quotient's business if its acquisition went ahead. The staff of Quotient are suspicious about the motives of the Quotient Board in accepting Smythe's offer.

*As a private study or group discussion exercise,* plan the presentation that the Smythe's Board will make at the start of the meeting with the employees of Quotient. What questions should they anticipate? How should these questions be answered?

*As a role play,* enact the meeting. Ideally, the Smythe's Board should be represented by a three-person team and the employees by as many people as possible (e.g. the rest of the class), allowing for at least two observers.

11. 'Managing change' said Sir John Harvey-Jones, 'is the most desirable management skill for the 1990s' (quoted in *The Observer*, 20 February 1994). Is it still true for the 2000s? Why?

12. This exercise concerns the meeting between the Communications Director for Multiplex Developments and a large group of the public. Multiplex has obtained planning consent from the local council to develop the site of a former historic building, which is an area of some four acres in a public park, by building an 11-screen cinema and leisure complex with eight restaurants and car parking on the roof. A campaign of opposition from local people has gradually built up over traffic congestion, the despoliation, as they see it, of the park, the ugliness of the design, anticipated litter, vandalism and late-night noise in a residential area, competition for the flourishing restaurants in the nearby High Street and so on. The level of support has driven Multiplex to hold a public meeting to hear the objections and try to reach some agreement. Arguments for the development include the extra jobs it will bring to the area, the lack of entertainment facilities in the area and the expected associated 'urban renewal' of the locality. It is the job of the Communications Director for Multiplex to present this case and respond to the audience's questions and objections.

    *As a private study or group discussion exercise,* plan how the Communications Director for Multiplex should make his/her initial presentation to the public meeting. What should s/he say? How should s/he apply the persuasive strategies and tactics described in this chapter, and the particular guidance given on making presentations? How should s/he deal with the likely objections from the public?

    *As a role play,* enact the presentation by the Communications Director for Multiplex to the public meeting.

13. This exercise concerns the meeting between the Chief Executive for a small charity engaged in vocational education for teenagers at risk and a manager for a major accounting firm. The charity needs to appoint a firm of auditors. Its previous auditors, who worked on a 'pro bono' basis (unpaid, in order to

perform charitable services), have resigned because the workload became excessive. The reason for this was that the charity's accounts became extremely confused owing to the incompetence of the in-house accountant who dealt with them previously. This person has now been replaced with agency staff. Charities need accounts not only for statutory reasons but because grant awarders and major donors increasingly demand satisfactory accounts for the previous two years before they will make or continue awards and donations. The payment of two large grants, which are vital for the continuation of the charity's work, is now suspended until satisfactory accounts are produced. The charity needs the auditing firm concerned to be a well-known one, as its prestige will assist with the donors. In addition, it is vital that they do their work pro bono – the charity cannot afford auditing fees.

One firm of accountants is well known for its charitable attitude and its interest in the kind of field in which the charity operates. However, it is widely known that the firm already has close to its full complement of pro bono auditing work and there are, of course, many charities that seek this type of support. The charity's Chief Executive has an appointment with the manager responsible for the accounting firm's decision.

*As a private study or group discussion exercise,* plan how the charity's Chief Executive should put his/her request to the accounting firm manager. What should s/he say? How should s/he apply the persuasive strategies and tactics described in this chapter, and the particular guidance given on networking? How should s/he deal with the likely objections from the accounting firm's manager?

*As a role play,* enact the meeting between the Chief Executive and the accounting firm's manager.

14. This exercise concerns a discussion between the Chief Executive and the Web Managing Editor of Airshop.com. The Web Managing Editor is in charge of the four-person Web Design and Journalism section. The company's results and trading forecast show that the company is in difficulties. There is a recession looming, hundreds of dot.com companies have gone out of business and the company's revenues are scarcely growing. However, the Web Managing Editor believes that long-term survival depends on the site being more attractive than its competitors. Currently, the site has a static front page, which does not change and provides only one link to the rest of the site. The Web Managing Editor wants to substitute an active front page, with multiple links and hourly changes of news stories. S/he believes that this change would give the firm a number of benefits. In the short term it would mean that the firm would have to invest in development but would also mean that the company would retain its two valuable technical staff. In the medium to longer term, s/he believes, the changes will improve the attractiveness and competitiveness of the site. On the other hand it is well known

in the company that the Chief Executive, though not unsympathetic to new ideas, considers there will be no scope for additional expenditure in the near future. S/he does not claim to be well up on technical matters. However, s/he does not think it is time for expensive changes but for planning for a bad recession that can be expected to last for some time. That could mean putting all plans and growth proposals on the back burner – maybe long term.

The Web Managing Editor has arranged an appointment with the Chief Executive at which s/he will try to persuade her or him to consider the redesign proposal for inclusion in the forthcoming quarter's plans and budgets.

*As a private study or group discussion exercise,* plan how the Web Managing Editor should put his/her suggestion to the Chief Executive. What should s/he say? How should s/he apply the persuasive strategies and tactics described in this chapter, and the particular guidance given on introducing change and subordinate/manager influence? How should s/he deal with the likely objections from the Chief Executive?

*As a role play,* enact the meeting between the Web Managing Editor and the Chief Executive.

15. In order to remain competitive, Postworthy Mail Order has decided to introduce an Internet ordering system. This means that the company's millions of catalogue order customers will be able to order on the Net, pay by credit card, and have their orders dispatched the same day. In effect, the company is introducing a real-time response system. The implications for the packing and dispatch staff are quite major: instead of working at a steady rate, subject to daily targets, they will have to adapt the dispatch rate to meet the demand so that the company's promise of same-day dispatch can be met. In addition they will have to use new technology to check stock availability positions and process orders. If you had the job of presenting this change to the 200-strong workforce (a) how would you organise the presentation meetings and (b) how would you approach the meetings and what points would you make?

16. What do you think of the following openings for presentations to gain new business?

    (a) 'Good morning, Ladies and Gentlemen. I stand before you this morning to talk about one project, but in actual fact I've been chasing three this past few weeks, so it's all been rather hectic. My first remit was from. . . .'
    (b) 'Well, as usual it falls to me to take the difficult part, but the subject I shall be talking about today is. . . .'
    (c) 'Well, I'm very glad we've had the break before I do my presentation, because I must say that was a hard act to follow. . . .'

17. Analyse the good and bad points about each of the following extracts from a presentation of a business plan for a new company to market specialist DVD recordings, e.g. wine guides, antique guides, operas.
    (a) 'Good morning, Ladies and Gentlemen, I will briefly tell you what I'm going to talk about this morning by giving you an outline of my speech. First of all. . . .'
    (b) 'What kind of person is buying or renting DVD recordings? (Puts up overhead.) In Europe, it's a fairly affluent market; 70 per cent own their own house, are young, married, primarily they're using it for time shift of broadcast programmes and pre-recorded usage equally. DVD rentals – right now they're occurring in the music/feature film area, but this is the area that I'm interested in (points to overhead) the 2 per cent educational/informational market. Now, the rental market is 1.2 billion euros at retail, so 2 per cent is a large amount of money.'
    (c) 'What sort of things do I mean by informational-educational? This is not the best example, but it will help to illustrate the idea: Sotheby's has produced a video guide to eighteenth-century French furniture.'
    (d) 'Now I'd like to talk about where I see the opportunities in this market. I see them at the high end – the affluent – I think it's a defined target, it has a lot of discretionary income, and its interests lie in the areas I want to market into.'
    (e) 'The project would investigate the viability of starting a production and distribution outfit in Europe; it would investigate the potential product portfolio in the market, and would essentially turn an idea into a business proposition that can be put to a bank to raise capital.'
    (f) 'The types of questions I want answers for are these (puts up overhead and reads from it):

        - How is the market structured?
        - What alternative distribution systems are there in the market?
        - How are products presently distributed?
        - And, most important, what makes for a successful product? Is it the pricing? Is it the quality of production? Is it the content? Or is it re-usability? For example, an exercise tape that you can go on using and amortising your costs on.

        These questions are listed in the file I gave you to take away and study.'
    (g) 'I'm running over a bit in time but (*smiles at audience*) I hope you'll allow me that. . . .'
    (h) 'So, in conclusion, I would say that this is a very fast-growing market, with a very interesting market opportunity; there is ample room for good new ideas on distribution and that's where the key problem lies in the market right now. There is, with this, a need for some real solid

information on how large this market is, how it is structured, where it is going, what shape it is assuming.'

(i) 'At this point I'd like to hand over to you for some questioning.'

Questioner: What I would like to know is how you are going to go about meeting all the information requirements that you've identified as needed for your plan.

Presenter: Right. Er, there is tons of desk research because there's lots of material written on this market. Some of it is in Germany, so I'm probably going to go there for some of it; um, I think at some point I'm going to have to do some primary research on what are the motivations behind buying patterns, what price are people prepared to pay, those sort of questions. . . .

Questioner: Do you see it as an international market?

Presenter: Very much so – it is already an international market, but what I see as happening is that there are some very good products out there that have a lot of investment put into the production but with little into the marketing. And I think that's what's killing the market right now. . . .

Questioner: The main question I have is to do with competition. Do you expect some of the other companies like TVmatic or. . . .

Presenter: (interrupts): They already are – they're already in it. . . .

## FURTHER READING


Eales-White, R. (1992) *The Power of Persuasion*. London: Kogan Page.

Petty, R. E. and J. T. Cacioppo (1986) *Communication and Persuasion: Central and Peripheral Routes to Attitude Change*. New York: Springer-Verlag.

Whetten, D. and P. C. Godfrey (1998) *Identity in Organizations: Building Theory Through Conversations*. Thousand Oaks, Calif.: Sage. Especially Chapter 7, 'How do people identify with organizations?'

Williams, J. S. (1996) *Presentations*. London: Elliott Right Way Books.


## REFERENCES


1. Turner, L. H. and S. A. Henzl (1987) 'Influence attempts in organizational conflict: The effects of biological sex, psychological gender and power position', *Management Communication Quarterly*, vol. 1, no. 1, pp. 32–57.
2. Ancona, D. G. and D. F. Caldwell (1998) 'Rethinking team composition from the outside in' in M. A. Neale, E. A. Mannix and D. H. Gruendfeld (eds) *Research on Managing Groups and Teams*, vol. 1. Greenwich, Conn.: JAI Press, pp. 21–38.
3. Levine, J. M. (1989) 'Reactions to opinion deviance in small groups' in P. B. Paulus (ed.) *Psychology of Group Influence*, 2nd edn. Hillsdale, New Jersey: Erlbaum, pp. 187–231.
4. Moscovici, S. (1985) 'Social influence and conformity' in G. Lindzey and E. Aronson (eds) *The Handbook of Social Psychology*, 3rd edn, Vol. 2. New York: Random House, pp. 347–412.
5. Nemeth, C. J. (1986) 'Differential contributions of majority and minority influence', *Psychological Review*, vol. 93, pp. 23–32.
6. French, J. R. P. Jr and B. Raven (1959) 'The bases of social power' in D. Cartwright (ed.) *Studies in Social Power*. Ann Arbor: University of Michigan Press.

7. Kipnis, D., S. M. Schmidt and I. Wilkinson (1980) 'Intraorganisational influence tactics: Explorations in getting one's way', *Journal of Applied Psychology*, vol. 65, pp. 440–457.
8. Depret, E. F. and S. T. Fiske (1993) 'Social cognition and power: some cognitive consequences of social structure as a source of control deprivation' in G. Weary, F. Gleicher and K. Marsh (eds) *Control Motivation and Social Cognition*. New York: Springer-Verlag, pp. 176–202.
9. Hornik, J. and S. Ellis (1988) 'Strategies to secure compliance for a mall intercept interview', *Public Opinion Quarterly*, vol. 52, no. 4, pp. 539–551.
10. Wilson, S. R., C. G. Aleman and G. B. Leatham (1998) 'Identity implications of influence goals: A revised analysis of face-threatening acts and application to seeking compliance with same-sex friends', *Human Communication Research*, vol. 25, no. 1, pp. 64–96.
11. Hirokawa, R. Y., R. A. Kodama and N. L. Harper (1990) 'Impact of managerial power on persuasive strategy selection by female and male managers', *Management Communication Quarterly*, vol. 4, no. 1, pp. 30–50.
12. Lu, S. (1997) 'Culture and compliance gaining in the classroom: A preliminary investigation of Chinese college teachers' use of behavior alteration techniques', *Communication Education*, vol. 46, no. 1, pp. 10–28.
13. Baglan, T., J. Lalumia and O. L. Bayless (1986) 'Utilization of compliance-gaining strategies: A research note', *Communication Monographs*, vol. 53, no. 3, pp. 289–293.
14. Brehm, J. (1966) *A Theory of Psychological Reactance*. New York: Academic Press.
15. Buller, D. B., R. Borland and M. Burgoon (1998) 'Impact of behavioral intention on effectiveness of message features: Evidence from the family sun safety project', *Human Communication Research*, vol. 24, no. 3, pp. 433–453.
16. Johnson, G. M. (1992) 'Subordinate perceptions of superior's communication competence and task attraction related to superior's use of compliance-gaining tactics', *Western Journal of Communication*, vol. 56, no. 1, pp. 54–67.
17. Manstead, A. S. R. (1996) 'Attitude change' in A. S. R. Manstead and M. Hewstone (1996) *The Blackwell Encyclopaedia of Social Psychology*. Oxford: Blackwell.
18. Kiesler, S. (1978) *Interpersonal Processes in Groups and Organizations*. Arlington Heights, Ill.: AHM Publishing Corporation.
19. Festinger, L. (1957) *A Theory of Cognitive Dissonance*. Evanston, Ill.: Rob Peterson.
20. Joule, R.-V. and J.-L. Beauvois (1997) 'Cognitive-dissonance theory: A radical view' in W. Stroebe and M. Hewstone (eds) *European Review of Social Psychology*, vol. 8. Chichester: John Wiley, pp. 1–32.
21. Brehm, J. and S. Cohen (1962) *Explorations in Cognitive Dissonance*. New York: Wiley.
22. Heider, F. (1958) *The Psychology of Interpersonal Relations*. New York: Wiley.
23. Sherif, M. and C. E. Hovland (1964) *Social Judgment*. New Haven: Yale University Press.
24. Sarup, G., R. W. Suchner and G. Gaylord (1991) 'Contrast effects and attitude change: A test of the two-stage hypothesis of Social Judgment Theory', *Social Psychology Quarterly*, vol. 54, no. 4, pp. 364–372.
25. Sherif, C. W., K. Kelley, H. L. Rodgers Jr, G. Sarup and B. T. Tittler (1973) 'Personal involvement, social judgment and action', *Journal of Personality and Social Psychology*, vol. 27, pp. 311–327.
26. Lewin, K. (1943) 'Forces behind food habits and methods of change', *Bulletin of the National Research Council*, vol. 108, pp. 35–65.
27. Newcombe, T. M. (1961) *The Acquaintance Process*. New York: Holt, Rinehart, Winston.
28. Summers, J. O. (1970) 'The identity of women's clothing fashion opinion leaders', *Journal of Marketing Research*, May, pp. 178–185.

29. Lott, A. J., M. A. Bright, P. Weinstein and B. E. Lott (1970) 'Liking for persons as a function of incentive and drive during acquisition', *Journal of Personality and Social Psychology*, vol. 14, no. 1, pp. 66–76.
30. Berscheid, E. and E. H. Walster (1978) *Interpersonal Attraction*. Reading, Mass.: Addison-Wesley.
31. Byrne, D. (1969) 'Attitudes and attraction' in L. Berkowitz (ed.) *Advances in Experimental Social Psychology*. New York: Academic Press.
32. Sekord, P. and C. Backman (1964) 'Interpersonal congruency, perceived similarity and friendship', *Sociometry*, vol. 27, pp. 115–127.
33. Palmer, M. T. and K. B. Simmons (1995) 'Communicating intentions through nonverbal behaviors: Conscious and nonconscious encoding of liking', *Human Communication Research*, vol. 22, no. 1, pp. 128–160.
34. Aronson, E. (1980) *The Social Animal*, 3rd edn. San Francisco: W. H. Freeman and Co.
35. Rogers, E. and F. Shoemaker (1971) *Communications Innovations*. New York: The Free Press.
36. Rogers, E. (1965) *The Diffusion of Innovations*. Glencoe, Ill.: The Free Press.
37. Ibid.
38. Festinger, op. cit.
39. Fabriger, L. R. and R. E. Petty (1999) 'The role of the affective and cognitive bases of attitudes in susceptibility to affectively and cognitively based persuasion', *Personality and Social Psychology Bulletin*, vol. 25, p. 363–381.
40. Rychlak, J. F. (1965) 'The similarity, compatibility or incompatibility of needs in interpersonal selection', *Journal of Personality and Social Psychology*, vol. 12, pp. 334–340.
41. Yoon, K., C. K. Kim and M.-S. Kim (1998) 'A cross-cultural comparison of the effects of source credibility on attitudes and behavioral intentions', *Mass Communication and Society*, vol. 1, no. 3/4, pp. 153–173.
42. Tasaki, K., M.-S. Kim and M. D. Miller (1999) 'The effects of social status on cognitive elaboration and post-message attitude: Focusing on self-construals', *Communication Quarterly*, vol. 47, no. 2, pp. 196–214.
43. Sawyer, A. (1972) 'The effects of repetition: Conclusions and suggestions about experimental laboratory research', Paper presented at the workshop on consumer information processing, University of Chicago, November.
44. Bohner, G., G. B. Moskowitz and S. Chaiken (1995) 'The Interplay of heuristic and systematic processing of social information' in W. Stroebe and M. Hewstone (eds) *European Review of Social Psychology*, vol. 6. Chichester: John Wiley, pp. 33–68.
45. Petty, R. E. and J. T. Cacioppo (1986) *Communication and Persuasion: Central and Peripheral Routes to Attitude Change*. New York: Springer-Verlag.
46. Janis, I. L. and S. Feshbach (1953) 'Effects of fear-arousing communication', *Journal of Abnormal and Social Psychology*, vol. 48, pp. 78–92.
47. Burnett, J. J. and R. L. Oliver (1979) 'Fear appeal effects in the field: Segmentation approach', *Journal of Marketing Research*, vol. 16, pp. 181–190.
48. O'Keefe, D. J. (2000) 'Guilt and social influence', *Communication Yearbook*, vol. 23, pp. 67–101.
49. Planalp, S., S. Hafen and A. D. Adkins (2000) 'Messages of shame and guilt', *Communication Yearbook*, vol. 23, pp. 1–65.
50. O'Keefe, D. J. (1999) 'How to handle opposing arguments in persuasive messages: a meta-analytic review of the effects of one-sided and two-sided messages', *Communication Yearbook*, vol. 22, pp. 209–249.
51. Brosius, H.-B. (1999) 'Research note: The influence of exemplars on recipients' judgments', *European Journal of Communication*, vol. 14, no. 2, pp. 213–224.

52. Sparks, J. R., C. S. Areni and K. C. Cox (1998) 'An investigation of the effects of language style and communication modality on persuasion', *Communication Monographs*, vol. 65, no. 2, pp. 108–125.
53. Waldron, V. R. (1999) 'Communication practices of followers, members, and protégés: The case of upward influence tactics', *Communication Yearbook*, vol. 22, pp. 251–259.
54. Argyle, M. (1967) *The Psychology of Interpersonal Behaviour*. Harmondsworth, Middlesex: Penguin Books.
55. Lydon, J. (1996) 'Toward a theory of commitment' in C. Seligman, J. Olson and M. Zanna (eds) *Values: the 8th Ontario Symposium*. Hillsdale, New Jersey: Lawrence Erlbaum, pp. 191–213.
56. Fey, C. J. and P. W. Beamish (1999) 'Strategies for managing Russian international joint venture conflict', *European Management Journal*, vol. 17, no. 1, pp. 99–106.
57. Kiesler, C. (1971) *The Psychology of Commitment*. New York: Academic Press.
58. Rusbult, C. E. (1983) 'A longitudinal test of the investment model: the development and deterioration of satisfaction and commitment in heterosexual involvement', *Journal of Personality and Social Psychology*, vol. 45, pp. 101–117.
59. Staw, B. (1976) 'Knee-deep in the big muddy: A study of escalating commitment to a chosen course of action', *Organisational Behaviour and Human Performance*, vol. 16, pp. 27–44.
60. Janoff-Bulman, R. (1989) 'Assumptive worlds and the stress of traumatic events: Applications of the schema construct', *Social Cognition*, vol. 7, pp. 113–136.
61. Rokeach, M. (1980) 'Some unresolved issues in theories of beliefs, attitudes and values' in H. Howe Jr and M. M. Page (eds) *1979 Nebraska Symposium of Motivation*. Lincoln: University of Nebraska.
62. Schwartz, S. (1992) 'Universals in the content and structure of values: Theoretical advances and empirical tests in 20 countries' in M. Zanna (ed.) *Advances in Experimental Social Psychology*, vol. 25. San Diego, Calif.: Academic Press, pp. 1–65.
63. Thoits, P. A. (1982) 'Conceptual, methodological and theoretical problems in studying social support as a buffer against life stress', *Journal of Health and Social Behaviour*, vol. 23, pp. 145–159.
64. Guzley, R. M., F. Araki and L. E. Chalmers (1998) 'Cross-cultural perspectives of commitment: Individualism and collectivism as a framework for conceptualization', *Southern Communication Journal*, vol. 64, no. 1, pp. 1–19.
65. Churchill, G. A. Jr (1985) 'The determinants of salesperson performance: A meta-analysis', *Journal of Marketing Research*, vol. 122, pp. 103–118.
66. Szymanski, D. M. and G. A. Churchill Jr (1990) 'Client evaluation cues: A comparison of successful and unsuccessful salespeople', *Journal of Marketing Research*, vol. 27, pp. 163–174.
67. Gorley, P. J. (1975) 'In the sales call. A study of the industrial sales interview'. London: London Business School, unpublished PhD dissertation.
68. Riordan, E. A., R. L. Oliver and J. H. Donnelly Jr (1977) 'The unsold prospect: Dyadic and attitudinal determinants', *Journal of Market Research*, vol. 14, pp. 530–537.
69. Evans, F. B. (1963) 'Dyadic interactions in selling – a new approach', *The American Behavioural Scientist*, vol. 6, pp. 76–79.
70. Brock, T. (1965) 'Communicator–recipient similarity and decision change', *Journal of Personality and Social Psychology*, vol. 1, pp. 650–654.
71. Woodside, A. G. and J. W. Davenport Jr (1974) 'The effect of salesman similarity and expertise on consumer purchasing', *Journal of Market Research*, vol. 11, pp. 198–202.

72. Busch, P. and D. T. Wilson (1976) 'An experimental analysis of a salesman's expert and referent bases of social power in the buyer–seller dyad', *Journal of Marketing Research*, vol. 13, pp. 3–11.
73. Tosi, H. L. (1966) 'The effects of expectation levels and role consensus on the buyer–seller dyad', *Journal of Business*, vol. 39, pp. 516–529.
74. Pruden, H. O. and R. M. Reese (1972) 'Inter-organizational role-set relations and the performance and satisfaction of industrial salesmen', *Administrative Science Quarterly*, vol. 17, pp. 601–609.
75. Crick, B. (1962) *In Defence of Politics*. Harmondsworth, Middlesex: Penguin.
76. Pym, D. (1980) 'Individual development: problems and possibilities', *Proceedings of the International Training and Development Conference, Dublin, Eire*.
77. Hayes, J. (1984) 'The politically competent manager', *Journal of General Management Studies*, vol. 10, no. 1, pp. 24–33.
78. Bedeian, A. G. (1980) *Organization Theory and Analysis*. Fort Worth, Tex.: The Dryden Press.
79. Lewis, L. K. (1996) 'Users' individual communicative responses to intra-organisationally implemented innovations and other planned changes', *Management Communication Quarterly*, vol. 10, pp. 455–490.
80. Waldron, op. cit.
81. Ibid.
82. Fairhurst, G. T. (1993) 'Echoes of the vision: When the rest of the organization talks total quality', *Management Communication Quarterly*, vol. 6, no. 4, pp. 331–371.

# 9 Using power

## CHAPTER INTRODUCTION

As Box 9.1 shows, opinions vary on what power is but there is general agreement that it allows people to influence others.[1] In support of this, we have evidence that in small groups, low-power individuals behave in a more deferential and approval-seeking manner than high-power individuals. In the workplace, people perceive themselves to be more submissive and less dominant when interacting with a supervisor as opposed to a subordinate. Sequential analyses have shown that one person's behaviour is often submissive following another's dominant behaviour. Lower-power individuals may be particularly attentive to high-power individuals' behaviours.

Power is usually associated with greater status, where status refers to 'the differentiation of prestige and deference among individuals'.[2] Status differences may not only influence low- and high-status individuals' behaviour, but also the attributions made by observers. Low-status individuals may be perceived as deferential and interpersonally sensitive, while high-status individuals may be perceived as assertive and dominant. Conway *et al.*[3] found that others' expectations of people in high-status occupations were that they would be less communally-minded but more effective in action. Thus status and power can have effects well beyond influencing others in regard to a particular purpose or action.

The aim of this chapter is to help readers understand how to handle power successfully by explaining:

- the nature of power – interpersonal approaches, structural power theories and cognitive/structural power theories;
- certain techniques and methods of power exercise, including knowing what power base to use, factors affecting success in influencing attempts and how to choose among various ways of mobilising power;
- what is involved in handling other people's power assertions;
- how to gain and retain power;
- how to exercise power in work activities, including business meetings and negotiations.

## UNDERSTANDING THE NATURE OF POWER

One review of the literature on power concluded that it was 'scattered, heterogeneous and chaotic',[4] while another pointed out numerous contradictions and ambiguities in five formal definitions of power, each of which has been widely used.[5] Van Dijk[6] commented, 'The complex notion of power cannot simply be accounted for in a single definition' and contended that writers and researchers

**Box 9.1**

### Views from the literature on power

- Dahrendorf (1990): The existence of a power structure is intrinsic to society, because any community needs to regulate the conduct of its members; so a power structure is necessary for the application of sanctions.
- Russell (1938): Power is the production of intended effects.
- Weber (1947): Power is the ability to obtain one's will despite resistance.
- Moscovici (1976): Power is domination and coercion leading to compliance (and hence is a less-preferred alternative to persuasion).
- Lukes (1990): Power operates to shape desires and beliefs in a manner that can be directly contrary to people's interests.
- Huston (1983): Power is a theoretical construct that accounts for the portion of social influence that is under the actor's control, 'the ability to achieve ends through influence'.
- Raven (1992): Social power is the different bases of interpersonal influence.
- In social exchange theory (Thibaut and Kelley, 1959) A has power over B when A controls B's outcomes, regardless of influence processes. Power relations are asymmetrical outcome-dependency situations. Defining social power as control over others' outcomes suggests some necessary cross-fertilisation between issues of power relations and research on psychological control.
- Fiske and Depret: Feelings of power not only reflect individual but also group power positions. Experiments by Depret support the idea that, when people perceive themselves as group members, their personal feelings of control are derived from their social locus of control as in-group or out-group. People report feeling unhappy with increases in (perceived) out-group power, especially if the group categorisation is salient and they have no personal control over their outcomes (Fiske and Depret, 1996).

*Sources*: Dahrendorf, R. (1990) *Class and Conflict in Industrial Society*. Stanford, Calif.: Stanford University Press.
Fiske, S. and E. Depret (1996) 'Control, interdependence and power: Understanding social cognition in its social context' in W. Stroebe and M. Hewstone (eds) *European Review of Social Psychology*, vol. 7. Chichester: John Wiley, pp. 31–62.
Huston, T. L. (1983) 'Power' in H. H. Kelley *et al.* (eds) *Close Relationships*. New York: Freeman, pp. 169–219.
Lukes, S. (1990) *Power*. New York: New York University Press.
Moscovici, S. (1976) *Social Influence and Social Change*. London: Academic Press.
Raven, B. H. (1992) 'A power/interaction model of interpersonal influence: French and Raven thirty years later', *Journal of Social Behavior and Personality*, vol. 7, pp. 217–244.
Russell, B. (1938) *Power: A New Social Analysis*. London: George Allen & Unwin.
Thibaut, J. W. and H. H. Kelley (1959) *The Social Psychology of Groups*. New York: Wiley.
Weber, M. (1947) *The Theory of Social and Economic Organisation*, translated by T. Parsons and A. M. Henderson. Chicago: Free Press.

should choose the most relevant for their purpose from among the 'major properties' of power. Here I set out the approach taken to power in this book. This approach is in conflict with some current views of power but consistent with others.

According to one approach, trait-factor theory,[7] certain individuals, such as the rich or heads of governments and businesses, can exert power in any of their relationships, while other, powerless individuals, can exert none. A different approach, dynamic-interdependence theory,[8] considers, on the contrary, that most people are able to exert power over some other people under some circumstances, but not over others or under different circumstances. While some people do have more sources of power than others, there are always circumstances and behaviours, either their own or other people's, that can act to constrain the exercise of power and to allow more autonomy and influence to those with fewer sources of power. A second question concerns how wide the scope of the concept of power should be taken to be. This is partly a question of semantics, especially of differentiating between 'power', 'influence' and 'control'. Some writers draw no distinctions between these terms; others treat power and influence as the same but differentiate them from control. As Chapter 8 has already suggested, here influence and control are treated as outcomes, i.e. as changes in other people's behaviour, which differ from each other in degree. Control implies a greater effect than influence. Power, or rather exercising power, is then one way of bringing about influence or control, while persuading is another way. Getting people to comply by physical coercion, promising them rewards or threatening punishment, are exercises of power; they are treated as analytically different from persuading them. A third issue is whether power has some kind of objective existence or exists only in people's minds, subjectively. For example, if someone controls information which others need or is in a position to raise another person's salary, do they automatically possess power over the people who need the information or the salary rise? Or does their power depend on those others believing that those factors mean that they must modify their behaviour in the way required? Again, if persons who are offered a reward to get them to change their behaviour do not see the reward as desirable, does the promiser still have power over them? In this book, power is treated as 'in the mind', existing only when it is recognised as relevant to their behaviour by those over whom it may be wielded. Objective factors, such as the ability to raise salaries, are treated as potential sources of power, which may or may not lead to the successful exercise of power.

Conversely, there is evidence that, in spite of all the pitfalls in the way of our perceiving others accurately, we do in fact seem to take notice of the objective circumstances of our interactions and particularly to our relative standing. We do often perceive the structure of power in an interaction accurately, as well as the levels of inputs and outcomes of the participants. This does not change the

**Box 9.2**

> Baroness Park, a former spy for MI6, the UK government intelligence body, showed a very good practical understanding that power is in the mind of the perceiver when, during an interview, she was asked 'How good is MI6 at disruptive intelligence?' She replied, 'Very good, if only because, once you get inside intelligence, you get a hold over the levers of power, *on what each . . . fears of the others and what each will credit that the others will do*' (author's italics).

point that power exists only as it is perceived but means that we can more often assume potential power and perceived power to be co-extensive.

## Structural power theories

There is a considerable literature, based on social exchange theory, which adopts a structural approach to power. In the words of Edward Lawler:

> Power capabilities are based on the social structure in which the relationship of parties is embedded, a variety of specific tactical actions can use power, and successful use produces actual or realised power at a given point in time. For example, unions negotiating with management have some structurally-based capability to apply leverage (e.g. workers difficult to replace, a sizeable strike fund), make tactical decisions about whether and how to use such capability, and achieve variable degrees of influence through such tactics.[9]

For structuralists, the primary units of social structure are 'positions'. Positions entail interests that occupants represent in interaction with others. Interests have more effect than the behaviour of the people. There is, of course, substantial evidence for the impact of organisational positions on influence and control. For instance, Schlueter *et al.*[10] found that how managers tried to exert influence (e.g. by persuasion or exerting power) was consistently connected to hierarchical level (whereas gender seemed to make only a marginal overall difference).

Lawler points out some key differences that arise from interpersonal and structural premises. Within the interpersonal paradigm, negotiation is a form of co-operative decision-making in a mixed-motive setting. Conflict resolution reconciles individual needs or opinions, with an emphasis on the co-operative over the competitive tendencies present. Structuralists see negotiating as inherently conflictual, owing to the different interests of the bargainers being irreconcilable. Conflict resolution needs a structural change. For structuralists, bargaining is an integral component of important social processes. Most bargaining, therefore, is tacit, not explicit. Explicit bargaining entails a prior decision by parties to consider, if not actively seek, a compromise solution to the conflict. Tacit bargaining refers primarily to parties' efforts to outmanoeuvre each other and reach an unstated, implicit bargain favouring their own interests. Parties do not consent

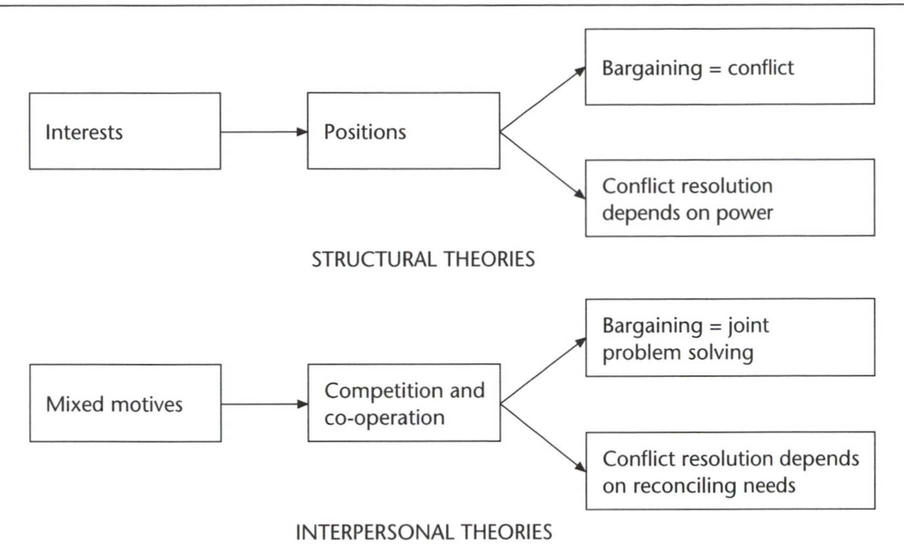


**Figure 9.1 A comparison of structural and interpersonal theories of bargaining.**

(or are unable) to sit at a bargaining table, do not see clearly a range of possible solutions and resolve or manage the conflict through some form of tacit co-ordination. Figure 9.1 illustrates the differences.

Within this framework, there are two theories of power with some useful implications for behaviour, even to holders of an interpersonal perspective. These are deterrence theory and network exchange theory.

**Box 9.3**

> A manager in a public service agency was in a permanent post but with a three-year fixed-term appointment giving higher status, responsibilities and salary. At the end of this term, his senior managers were dissatisfied with his performance. Therefore, instead of reappointing him, they insisted on the post being readvertised internally. He was forced to reapply. He made it known to anyone who would listen that if he was not reappointed, he would perform the duties of his permanent post at a minimum level. It was, in the words of one of his colleagues, 'blackmail'. The organisation had recently lost a case of unfair dismissal and been heavily criticised by the court. Although there was no comparison, the senior management would be reluctant to risk another such case. The manager was reappointed.

Deterrence theory is concerned with the effects of the power balance on the behaviour of people who interact. The majority of the work in this area has been done in the context of explicit bargaining. Deterrence theory states that the use of conciliatory versus hostile tactics is a function of the total amount of power in a relationship and how equal or unequal the power balance is. More particularly, it states that:

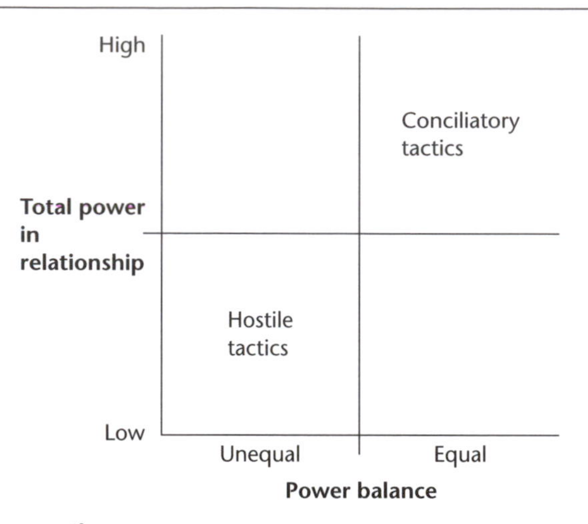


**Figure 9.2 Deterrence theory.**

- Given equal power between two parties, higher levels of total power in the relationship decrease hostility and increase conciliation. This is because each has an equal and high capacity for harming the other, or for retaliation, and therefore both sides abstain.
- When there is a power difference, lower-power parties resist efforts to coerce them into an agreement if they have some capability of punitive action that will be significant to the higher-power party.

So the theory suggests that unequal power relationships are less stable and escalate conflict. Figure 9.2 shows the relationships between power and tactics in deterrence theory.

Network exchange theory is a recent effort to go beyond looking at A/B dyads, and to look instead at the structure of relationships among numbers of people, in other words in networks. The theory explains the observation that within formally constituted structures, such as monopolistic markets and hierarchies, power differentials tend to be greater than in informal structures such as friendship groups. Markets and hierarchies are sparsely connected. Their linkages have many fewer strands compared with the more densely connected networks of friendship groups. For instance, in a market, connections may be limited to those required to buy and sell a single category of products, whereas most friendship groups will have links ranging from sharing pastimes and spending time together to providing emotional support or material help. The correlation of these two variables, density of connectedness and size of power difference, has led network exchange theorists to suggest that the heart of 'strong' power lies in the absence of exchange opportunities for the weak. All else being equal, higher connectivity provides more opportunities for people in weak positions to 'short-circuit' the structural advantages of the strong and thus create a greater

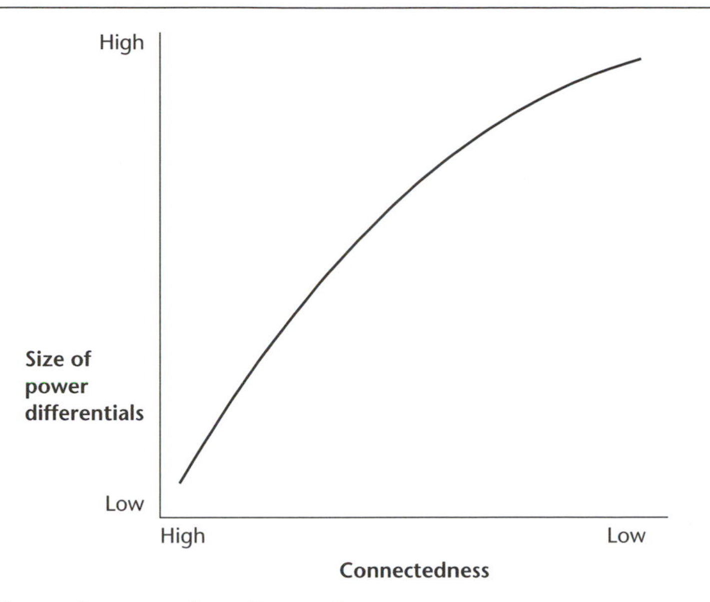


**Figure 9.3 Power in network exchange theory.**

likelihood of small resource differentials, i.e. weak power.[11,12] Figure 9.3 shows the relationship between power and connectedness in network exchange theory.

These two theories, deterrence and network exchange theory, have obtained a good measure of support from the considerable research efforts devoted to them.

## Cognitive adaptations of structural theories

Some researchers have been attracted by the conclusions of the structural theories but wished to give them a more cognitive emphasis. For instance, Ford and Blegen[13] developed and tested a modified version of deterrence theory, based on Schelling's argument[14] that if deterrence is to succeed in a dyad, two conditions must be met: (1) both parties fear retaliation and (2) each believes the other is unlikely to initiate an unprovoked attack. Deterrence also implies that conflicting parties can use punitive tactics (i.e. action damaging to the other party) either offensively (to gain advantage or to intimidate) or defensively (in response to, or anticipation of, the other's use of punitive tactics). Ford and Blegen argue that the use of punitive tactics is decreased by higher fear of retaliation but increased by higher expectation of attack. Moreover, if one party perceives the other's use of punitive tactics as defensive, they are less likely to respond in kind than if they perceive the other's use of them as offensive. The way in which a punitive tactic is used communicates the priority given by bargainers to different goals. In explicit bargaining, each party sees the ideal agreement as one that favours their party but satisfies the other. Thus parties typically direct their action towards two potentially inconsistent goals. Each sees the need to concede in order to reach some sort of agreement (co-operative orientation) but each desires a favourable agreement (competitive orientation). Offensive use of punitive tactics communicates a tilt towards competition, defensive tactics a tilt towards co-operation.

These researchers also examined the differences between low- and high-power positions. They found that those in high-power positions used damage tactics more than those in low-power positions, they were more likely to carry out their threats and they were less likely to reciprocate non-aggression. However, low-power parties were equally as likely as high-power ones to use punitive tactics both offensively and defensively. That is, the low-power parties showed relatively high levels of resistance, with a high rate of punitive tactic use, a low rate of concession making and an unwillingness to accept unfavourable agreements that still were more beneficial than non-agreements. They also did not decrease their use of punitive tactics over time.

Ford and Blegen's study provides support for the claim that actors interpret and respond to opponents' offensive use of punitive tactics differently from their defensive use. Thus, in bargaining, strategies high on the defensive dimension and low on the offensive dimension are most effective at deterring hostile action. Also, although high-power parties' may use more punitive tactics than low-power parties, the latter still offer substantial and persistent resistance to high-power parties' efforts to coerce them into unfavourable agreements.

Figure 9.4 illustrates a cognitive approach to structural power.

According to a theory proposed by Emerson,[15] power is closely related to dependence. If Person A has power over Person B, that situation is the result of the 'netting out' of two factors, B's dependence on A and A's dependence on B. Dependence, in turn, is a function both of the subjective value that the dependent person places on goals mediated by the other person (their 'motivational investment' in the goal) and of the ease or difficulty they would have in attaining

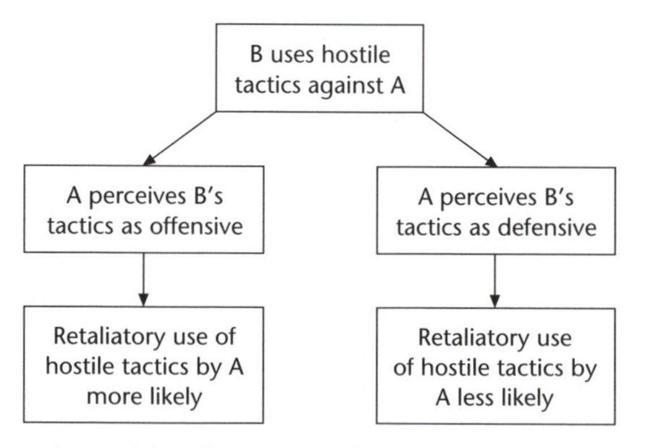


**Figure 9.4 Aspects of cognitive deterrence theory.**

the goal without the other person. For example, suppose Coral is Etienne's manager and can determine whether or not Etienne gets promoted to a particular post. If Etienne places a high value on gaining promotion, and really wants this particular one, power/dependence theory would assert that Coral will have substantial power over Etienne. On the other hand, Coral may have some source of dependence on Etienne which gives him some countervailing power. This would be the case if, for instance, she needs to appoint someone to the post, places a high value on it being one of her own staff rather than an outside appointment and Etienne is the best-qualified applicant. Thus power/dependence theory introduces the cognitive concept of 'subjective value' into an otherwise structural analysis.

Power/dependence theory suggests that unequal power relationships tend towards equality through one or both of the following processes. First the higher-power (less dependent) party will use power, thereby inflicting costs (loss of value) on the weaker (more dependent) party. Over time this will reduce the lower-power party's dependence. Second, the lower-power party will adopt tactics that either increase the higher-power party's dependence (e.g. by forming coalitions) or decrease their own dependence.[16]

Power/dependence theory has implications for gaining power, which are set out in a later section of this chapter. Figure 9.5 shows how a combination of dependence, deterrence and network exchange could product hostile or conciliatory tactics.

## SUMMARY – UNDERSTANDING THE NATURE OF POWER

Different people have power in different relationships. Influencing by persuasion is not an example of power exercise and requires a different behavioural analysis. Power can lead to influence only when it is perceived by the target but, if it exists structurally, there is a real possibility that it will be so perceived. Structuralist theories are based on the view that power inheres in social positions. One, deterrence theory, puts forward propositions about how the total amount of power and the power balance in a relationship affect the use of conciliatory or hostile bargaining tactics. A second, network exchange theory, considers power in networks rather than dyads and proposes that weaker parties are less weak in circumstances where they have multiple links to their environment. These theories have implications for face-to-face handling of power, subject to the proviso that allowance is made for perceptual effects. Some adaptations to structuralist theories specifically allow for cognitive intervening variables. One, cognitive deterrence theory, shows that people respond differently to the offensive and defensive use of punitive tactics, not just to the structural power position. Another, power/dependence theory, argues that one person's power is another person's dependence, which is in part a function of the subjective value they place on goals mediated by the other.

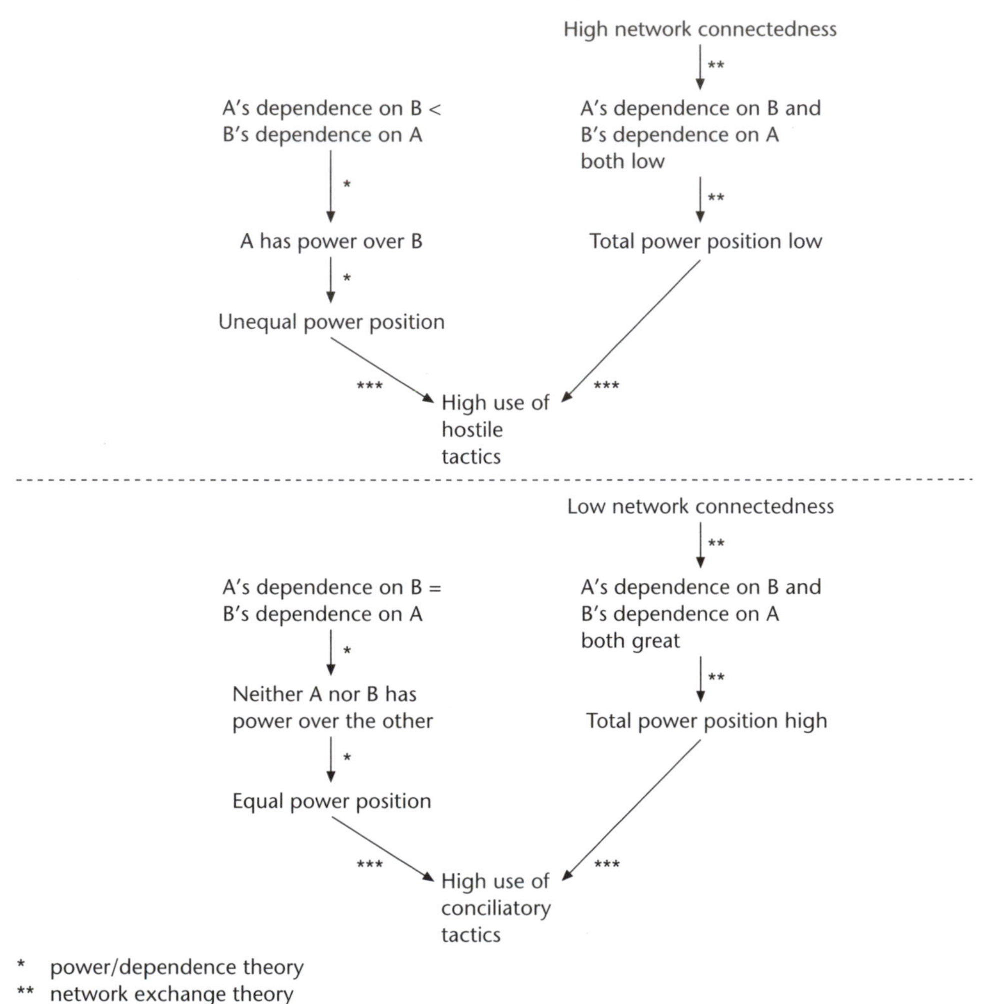


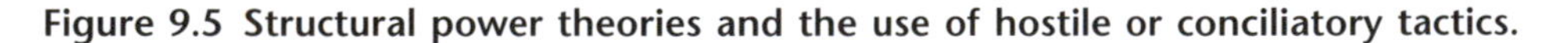

**Figure 9.5 Structural power theories and the use of hostile or conciliatory tactics.**

## EXERCISING POWER

What do the points made so far mean for using power in face-to-face interactions? They mean that the structural power position will affect the outcomes of attempts to exercise or restrain power, and therefore needs to be realistically assessed, but will be mediated through the beliefs, attitudes and motivations of the parties. Using power successfully depends, therefore, as shown in Figure 9.6, first of all on the user's credibility, secondly on the influence target's beliefs, attitudes and motives and thirdly on the skill with which the user exerts power. These, as well as the structural power position, affect the perceived power position, which in turn affects behaviour.

Box 9.4

## Critique of power theory and research

- Different disciplines have concentrated on some aspects of power and ignored others. For instance, organisational behaviour studies have emphasised hierarchical and structural aspects of power, but ignored social interaction and perceptual effects. Social psychologists have done the reverse, ignoring the structural links that bind people together.
- Structuralists have given a great deal of attention to analysing 'sources of power' but have ignored the target's beliefs. It may be that the target (B's) belief that s/he 'must' obey the influencer A is ill-founded; perhaps another person would see the position quite differently. However, that does not alter the fact that B is in A's power. Equally, B may be in real danger from A, but if B does not think s/he is, A will have no power to affect B's behaviour. A will only be able to punish B or to withdraw a reward, neither of which may be what A wants to do at all.
- Power/dependence theory ignores perceptual effects but has merit in identifying variables in the power dynamic, thus in pointing to ways in which power relationships are likely to develop.
- Some social psychologists define power as social influence. This definition can be criticised for making one of the two concepts redundant: power would only exist if it produced influence.
- There has been too little attention to how communication practices reflect, reproduce, constitute or lead to change in power relationships.
- Most analyses (but not power/dependence theory) have treated power relations as static, whereas they change and should be seen as able to be changed.

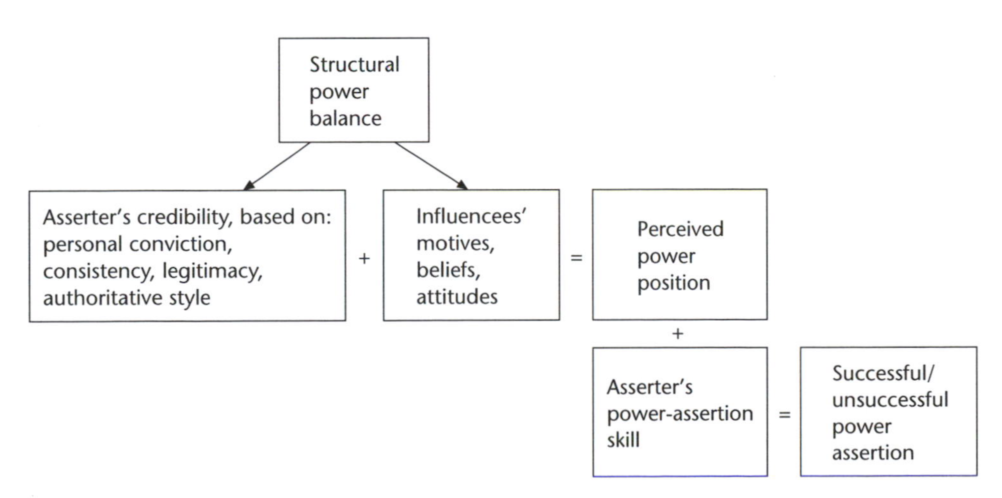


**Figure 9.6 Factors in successful power assertion.**

## Asserter's credibility

Credibility depends first and foremost on the power user's own personal conviction of the strength of their case, that what they are asking is legitimate, and that they actually do have power over the other party. The power user must believe that the target would hate to lose the reward on offer, such as the contract being negotiated, in spite of their professed indifference, that the 'competitor's offer' the target keeps talking about is a myth, that the target does need the information the power user can give them.

Some people are inhibited from using power when they could do so successfully because they are over-conscious of the risks. There are risks and costs attached to using power, especially in the form of threats. An unsuccessful attempt will expose weakness as well as damage the relationship with the person who has been threatened. However, if the risks always prevent us from using our power, then we have not got any power. If it is never used, it will wither away. Instead, the risks should be assessed and minimised, for instance by checking that the law is favourable. Then it is sometimes necessary to act in spite of the risks, accepting that occasionally the outcome will be unfavourable.

Second, credibility is affected by consistency. This means having a clear-cut policy and sticking to it. From the point of view of using power, it is better if that policy is a tough one. A marketing manager for a brand of consumer goods that had only a low market share, so that his company had little 'franchise' (i.e. power) with retail distributors, said this about how he dealt with chains of outlets which paid late:

> On credit we have a tough policy, and it's worked and it's worked and it's worked. People pay us first, because they know that if they don't we'll be on the phone badgering them day and night.

Being consistent does not mean refusing to negotiate: people fight shy of those who do not give and take. It does mean having a bottom line that is clearly visible.

Having a consistent policy is one way of creating legitimacy, of establishing a sense of 'rightness' or 'fittingness' about orders or demands. Other ways are by personal style. Books on management usually distinguish between an authoritarian style ('I'm boss around here') and democratic style ('Let's all get together and work this thing out'). Each has its merits and demerits, and is appropriate or otherwise according to the situation. Neither, however, is entirely suitable when dealing with people from outside organisations – customers or distributors, for instance. That is because these dealings take place in an unstructured context where there are no hierarchies, no career progressions and few procedures or regulations binding on both parties. However, in dealing with outside organisations, as well as in one's own, an authoritative (not authoritarian) style usually pays dividends in creating legitimacy. This is a style that 'speaks' of expertise, experience and influence.

**Box 9.5**

### How to appear authoritative

- Have available relevant information, problem analyses or, at worst, ideas, to bring forward at the judicious moment.
- Be relaxed, but alert. Sit upright but back in your chair, with both feet on the ground and one arm on the table to claim 'territory'.
- Speak slowly and deliberately.
- Do not take detailed notes, but have a pad in front of you. Jot down only the really important points.
- Authoritative and powerful people receive more communication than they initiate. Their opinions are sought, they are asked for guidance and instructions, no agreement is ratified until they have accepted it. They themselves direct very few of these types of communication at other people. They do ask for information, but only to a limited extent (Hurwitz *et al.*, 1968). Of course, the problem here is that any individual who tries to establish his or her own authority by this means risks merely being isolated – left out of the discussion. The best solution to this is to have a team of, say, three people, two of whom will so direct their communication as to build up the authority of the third. (See the discussion of team impression management in Chapter 6.)
- To gain authority in an unstructured situation you must be ready to take the initiative. You must arrive prepared to propose the agenda, the order of priorities, decision criteria, etc. If there is a previously arranged agenda, even if you prepared it, you might arrive with constructive suggestions for amending it.
- Thibaut and Kelley (1959) suggest that a person may increase the impression of power by 'seeming to undergo little variation in outcomes as a result of the actions of others and that his [sic] behaviours are largely internally rather than externally caused.' In other words, you can appear powerful by acting independently, because people confuse the two.
- A successful exercise of power, especially if it is conspicuous, builds your credibility for future occasions. This is often taken to mean imposing a punishment '*pour encourager les autres*', but actually punishing is a confession of weakness. It amounts to admitting that someone has not acted in the way you asked, and that your power is not equal to the occasion nor as great as your behaviour implied. On the other hand, rewarding demonstrates the opposite. Others have done what you wanted and have earned a reward. You demonstrate that you have the power to make that reward. Unfortunately, just as exercising power successfully builds future power, so a visible and unsuccessful attempt to exert power reduces your credibility for next time. This is one of many reasons why good judgement is needed in using power.

*Sources*: Hurwitz, J. I., A. F. Zander and B. Hymovitch (1968) 'Some effects of power on the relations among group members' in D. Cartwright and A. Zander (eds) *Group Dynamics: Research and Theory*. New York: Harper and Row, pp. 291–300.
Thibaut, J. W. and H. H. Kelley (1959) *The Social Psychology of Groups*. New York: Wiley.

## Motives, beliefs and attitudes of the influence targets

Just as much as persuading, exercising power depends on correctly interpreting and understanding what underlies other people's behaviour. Reward and punishment power only exist insofar as the person at whom they are directed has needs that can be satisfied through the reward or left unsatisfied through the punishment. (For example, during the period when an employee who has obtained another post elsewhere is serving out their notice, the current employer's reward and punishment power are virtually non-existent.) The target's power needs are particularly important. Individuals vary in their level of need for power. Some authorities believe that people with high needs for power are more ready than others to accept power assertion from others.[17] Thus those who are very ambitious may take orders willingly because they accept the hierarchical principle by which they hope to gain power themselves. On the other hand, the people who resent orders may be those who are low in needs for power themselves. They are motivated to seek autonomy. Paradoxically, therefore, it may prove easier to assert power over someone with a high power need. People with high needs for power will make concessions more readily to others who have a position of authority that they regard as conferring legitimacy on their demands.

One 'goal' of the power motive is to feel powerful,[18] so it may be possible to exert influence without giving much away, by flattering some people's sense of their own power. That is what status symbols, titles and honours are largely about. Finally, people with high power needs usually believe that 'might is right'. They are likely to be more susceptible to the strength of the power user's power base than to the justice of their case. With people who are low in needs for power but high in needs for autonomy, however, a different strategy may be more effective. They are more likely to respond to arguments or appeals based on the justice of the case (i.e. to persuasion). Trying to get them to comply by any explicit pressure based on power may lead them to try to frustrate the power user's wishes.

With either type of individual it is important when exerting power to minimise the damage to their self-esteem. Most people will feel a strong urge to repair such damage, which could lead them to disruptive actions or to taking effective counteraction. It is far better, therefore, to gratify their need for esteem, for instance by acknowledging their expertise, competence or moral superiority. Exercising power over somebody inevitably risks doing some damage to their self-esteem, but many people inflict unnecessary damage at the same time, contrary to their own best interest. For instance, in dismissing someone for poor performance due to unsuitability, managers sometimes feel driven to justify what they are doing. This can lead them to produce a long catalogue of the inadequacies of the subordinate who is being dismissed. If, instead, the manager presents the problem as one of a round peg in a square hole, praises roundness and suggests careers in which roundness is a valuable attribute, the damage to the individual's self-esteem is minimised and the potential damage to both the individual and the organisation is limited.

## Asserter's skill

Asserting power skilfully face-to-face calls for preplanning. It is difficult to think through all the implications of a threat or promise while at the same time assessing the influence target, speaking and following the argument. There are situations when power assertion should be avoided. These include its use by a weaker party who obviously lacks all significant power resources. Using intimacy or the norm of fairness or reciprocity may well be more effective. As power can be diminished by use (though can also be increased by it), over-use should be avoided. A third case is when using power would be a zero-sum game, such that what one side gains, the other loses. In this case a better approach would be one from which both may gain. Thinking about winning and losing stops people thinking creatively about win–win solutions.

A condition for power exercise is suggested by Van Dijk[19] who asserts that, except in cases of bodily force, B must know about A's wishes, wants, preferences or intentions. Apart from direct communication, for instance in the form of commands, requests or threats, this knowledge may be inferred from cultural beliefs, norms or values or from interpreting A's social actions. A further condition is that B believes that s/he has to or had better comply with A's directives, meet A's demands, or anticipate and satisfy A's wishes. (This condition is based on Weber's point that power is the ability to obtain one's will *despite resistance*.) B's sense of 'having to comply' can have many sources. It may be moral, as a devout Catholic would feel about a Papal edict. It may be social-utilitarian, as in the feeling that the law, even 'bad' law, must be obeyed. It may be authoritarian, as when B feels that A 'knows better' than he does. Often it is due to B's feeling that the consequences of not complying, whether punishment or loss of reward, are not acceptable. Unacceptable consequences might, for instance, be either that an existing contract will be lost (punishment) or a hoped-for new contract will not be gained (loss of reward).

Since, as Table 9.1 shows, there are several different power bases that may be present, and since ordinarily several of them could apply in any one situation, a person who wishes to use power has to decide which to use. Of the various sources of power that have been identified, the most useful in meetings at work

**Table 9.1 Power sources**

| *Source of power* | *Referred to as* |
|---|---|
| Ability to apply sanctions | Coercive power |
| Status and formal position | Legitimate power |
| Ability to give valued resources – pay, contracts, etc. | Reward power |
| Superior knowledge and experience | Expert power |
| Personal relationships; charisma | Relationship power |
| Access to inside information | Information power |
| 'Who you know' | Connection power |

are legitimate, reward and punishment power, information and connection power.[20] (Two other sources, expert and relationship power, are treated in this book as bases for persuading rather than exerting power.) There are differences in ways of mobilising these power sources and in their consequences. For instance, using connection power may involve asking contacts for their support and may create obligations to them, while using information power can require careful decision-making about what to impart and what to conceal, as this power is often lost when the information is shared.

Managers who give orders to subordinates, establish guidelines for their decision-making, approve or reject subordinates' decisions or allocate resources to them are mainly using their legitimate power. This is the power that they have by reason of the authority with which the organisation has endowed them along with the responsibility to get things done, and which is acknowledged by their subordinates. Other forms of power, those to reward and punish, usually underpin this legitimate power. Sometimes the power to reward or punish is applied directly. Many managers are also able to benefit from having access to information that their subordinates do not have, and connection power – better contacts. All in all, most managers are able to rely on a complex of power sources in order to obtain compliance from subordinates in their requests and demands.

Mere compliance, however, may not be enough. Managers often need their subordinates to be motivated to perform well, to try hard, to throw their mental and physical energies behind the task. (Imagine if a sales manager could only obtain compliance from the sales force in their job. They would make the calls on customers required by the manager, go through the routine of showing the products and advocating them, ask for orders, but make no real effort to persuade, and if no order was forthcoming, walk out and shrug their shoulders with indifference.) That is why, in spite of their many seeming power bases, managers sometimes feel powerless and also why it may be better for management to offer some direct reward, rather than rely on authority, in order to increase the subordinates' motivation.

Managers exerting power over subordinates are not the only example of power assertions in organisations. Lateral influence can occur as well. Peers can give or withhold needed co-operation, thus using reward or punishment power. They may also have needed information or connections in the form of better access to a shared boss. A person who is newly appointed to a post may often find that lateral colleagues are attempting to influence how s/he does the job, based on their better knowledge of how the system works or the preferences of the boss. Such attempts are often benevolent, and it may well be in the interests of the new appointee to listen carefully to them, while recognising them for power assertions. Power can also be exerted in an upward direction (though, as the section on Subordinate–manager influence in Chapter 8 noted, upward influence attempts carry risks). People low down in hierarchies often have information needed by those higher up and can exercise control through deciding whether and when to release it. Lower participants in organisations may also have 'legitimate' power.[21] For instance, in some companies the porter can refuse to move electrical equipment for the Chief Executive, because the regulations say it is not his job.

Many factors influence what power base people try to use. Unfortunately, while there are usually good reasons for choosing one rather than another, people are often driven by emotions to choose power sources that will be detrimental to their influence attempt. Box 9.6 shows the factors that should and should not determine this choice.

**Box 9.6**

### How to choose the best power bases

Take the following into account:

- The costs of the power attempt. For example, if you promise someone a promotion in return for co-operation, will you be able to and will you want to promote them when the time comes?
- The likely reaction of the other person. For instance, if you threaten, will they comply or walk out?
- The legitimacy of the power attempt. How will important third parties view it? Will it be seen as fair or unfair?
- How long lasting a change is needed and how likely it is that long-lasting change will be brought about by the chosen method. For instance, while threats can often be effective in the short run, their effect tends to wear off and may not last unless the person is closely monitored to make sure they keep complying. Threatening to dismiss someone who persistently arrives late for work may produce results in the first week or two but there will be a danger of backsliding. They will have to be watched. If they do start to slip, but dismissing them would be undesirable, it would have been better not to threaten the punishment in the first place.
- Whether as influencer you can afford to use up power in the influence attempt (Harsanyi, 1962) or need to keep the target person in a state of continuing dependence. Information, as noted above, is only a power source until the influence target has the information too.
- Avoid being influenced by factors that sometimes have more effect than they should, such as the following:
  - Attitudes to the target person. Distrust or dislike may lead to an attempt to coerce them, when promising a reward or convincing them through expertise would work better.
  - Similarly frustration, anger or stress can lead people to threaten when other ways would work better or when the threat cannot be carried out.
  - The need to boost their own self-esteem or to gratify their own power need. Both of these tend to lead people to use those power sources that are conspicuous when a more subtle choice would be more effective. Exercising power can of itself become so reinforcing that powerful people become increasingly insensitive to the needs of others, sometimes to the point where they find themselves faced with a rebellion, a strike or a 'night of the long knives'.

*Source*: Harsanyi, J. C. (1962) 'Measurement of social power, opportunity costs and the theory of two-person bargaining games', *Behavioural Science*, vol. 7, pp. 67–80.

**Table 9.2 A planning tool for using power in meetings and negotiations**

| *Ways of using power in order of increasing riskiness* | *Their probable response/ reaction* | *Benefits and costs to us* | *Circumstances in which we would probably take this action* | *Circumstances in which we would not take this action* |
|---|---|---|---|---|
| Drawing their attention to our power resources (specify) | | | | |
| Making promises (specify) | | | | |
| Making threats (specify) | | | | |

Once influencers have made sure they have power available, want to use it and have chosen which source to use, they still have to communicate to others that they possess it and intend to use it.[22] (Carrying out the analysis shown in Table 9.2 is one way to help decide this.) Face-to-face, power is asserted through talk. However, except in military or penal situations, power is rarely asserted by naked commands. In form, power is mostly asserted persuasively (thus power holders need the understanding and skills described in Chapter 8): 'Powerful individuals, groups or institutions only rarely have to prescribe (command) what the less powerful should do. Rather, they argue by providing economic, political, social or moral reasons and by managing the control of relevant information.'[23]

The more powerful speaker may control turn-taking, choice of topic, when the topic is changed and style of dialogue. As Chapter 8 showed, language itself can be characterised as powerful or powerless. Low-power individuals and groups are subordinated in talk. For example, women generally do more 'work' than men do in conversation, by giving more support, showing more interest or withdrawing in situations of conflict; men tend to interrupt women more often.[24] A sense of superiority towards members of ethnic minorities may be shown by use of simplified 'foreigner talk'. Dittmar and von Stutterheim[25] showed that the German language used with '*Gastarbeiter*' was often of this kind. In job interviews, power differences show up in interviewers controlling the pace and progress. For example, interviewers use more side sequences and digressions, while interviewees use more explanations, qualifiers and 'You know's'. In conversations with subordinates, managers dominate the content, use verbal symbols (e.g. military metaphors), myths, jokes, legends and game metaphors which express possible sanctions, receive more deference and use first names non-reciprocally. Often, in organisations, stories are focused on the boss, legitimating hierarchy.

Box 9.7

**How to exert power successfully at work**

- Analyse your own and others' power bases and how people's beliefs affect the power balance.
- Apply the lessons of deterrence and network exchange theory in a cognitive and power/dependence framework.
- Be sensitive to other people's needs and motives (especially about power and self-esteem).
- Think through the consequences of different means of power assertions before making them.
- Understand the uses and effects of social distance, formality, the appearance of authority and their reverse.
- Use power to influence rather than to coerce and to serve your interests rather than to gain your point or beat your opponent.
- Build towards agreements. Be prepared to make concessions, reward other people's concessions and stroke the influence target.
- Operate a consistent, tough, policy.
- Act assertively when you want to resist other people's power assertions.
- Co-opt other powerful people or groups or form coalitions.
- Handle your own 'psychology of power' – for instance, be prepared to lock yourself in, suppress closure anxiety, tolerate uncertainty and ambiguity and use silence. Resist the impulse to dominate for its own sake rather than to achieve important objectives.

## SUMMARY – EXERCISING POWER

The availability of power bases underlies power assertions but other factors also decide how successful they will be. These factors include the power user's beliefs, such as that the power exercise is legitimate and their power bases adequate for the purpose and their credibility, which is built by making their demands consistently and appearing powerful (authoritative). Success also depends on the motives of the influence target, especially their power needs, and on their beliefs in the legitimacy and strength of the power user's power. Therefore, successful power assertion depends on skill in all the following: assessing the target and the costs and benefits of the exercise, protecting the target's self-esteem, choosing the appropriate power bases and communicating the demands.

## RESISTING OTHER PEOPLE'S POWER

At work it can happen that a person is asked to do something they do not want to do, or do not think it best for the organisation to do, by someone who appears to have the power to make them do it. For instance, an Area Sales Manager might be required by his or her Regional Manager to get the sales representatives to fill in a new form for each sales call, giving a long list of details about the call. The Area Sales Manager might be strongly opposed to this idea on the grounds that the sales force already feel they have so much paperwork to do that it is impeding their effectiveness and reducing their ability to earn a good level of commission. This extra burden will be very bad for morale. Despite being in a low power position, there are things the Area Sales Manager can do to resist:

1. First, the low-power member should remember that the amount of power needed to prevent something happening and preserve the status quo may be very much less than that required to introduce change. The low-power member is not entirely powerless, and may have enough for the former, if not for the latter. One way is to increase the costs to the powerful of using their power. One researcher has shown that the powerless increase their power by making malevolent actions by the powerful too costly, so reducing the alternatives available to them.[26] The threat of exposure is the great threat here: an example is the way that the power of consumers who have complaints against builders or tour operators has been increased by the possibility of exposure on television or in the press.

2. In other cases, however, low-power members may do better to use those influencing techniques that do not depend on power and that were described in Chapter 8.[27] These include avoiding excessive pressure, which can produce reactance, increasing the target's uncertainty, promoting dissonance, emphasising similarity with the target, promoting liking, rewarding incremental change and using fear appeals, guilt appeals or two-sided appeals where appropriate.

3. Power-holders' own behaviour norms may inhibit them. According to London,[28] many power-holders have an aversion to the use of coercion, based on three 'rules'. These are that people should not be forced to do what others want, but should be free to refuse them; they should not be seduced into compliance but should be told what is wanted of them; and they should be free to decide for themselves how they want to guide their lives. The values on which these rules are based are increasingly accepted in the new types of organisation described in Chapter 2. They can inhibit people from using the power they theoretically possess and can be brought into play by low-power colleagues to thwart power-holders' intentions.

4. In cases where being inhibited about using power does not apply to the high-power member, and s/he is not susceptible to positive feelings nor easy to persuade, then as a low-power member there may be no short-term remedy but to accede to her or his demands. In that case, two rules apply: first, to do it as gracefully as possible, avoiding creating an enemy, and second, to try to avoid the very fact of compliance increasing future dependence. It can happen that if, as the Area Manager feared, the sales force do go up in arms at the extra paperwork, it is the Area Manager who will get the blame and his or her own future

position will be weakened. One way to avoid this is to 'put in writing' who is in fact responsible for the decision. This should not be done crudely, in the form of a position statement, but in the form of an e-mail or memo naturally generated in the course of the work. Ideally the e-mail or memo should be copied to other relevant people in the organisation. Another point similar to one that has been made in other contexts arises here. The action of putting it in writing will seem less significant, less of a power play, if it is done by someone who regularly sends e-mails or memos to colleagues, to confirm verbal agreements or communicate when they can't be reached. This does not mean that everything should be put in writing. Some people hide behind written communications because they are reluctant to face people in person, which reduces their effectiveness at work.

5. Power play has been shown to be less where connectedness is greater, that is where there is more frequent and richer contact, possibly because it produces more positive feelings.[29] These in turn produce more 'stay-behaviour', which means the tendency to stick with relationships, and more 'gift-giving'. Both these modify the naked power play.[30] In this way, low-power members can make the effect of any action on themselves a more important factor in the situation from the high-power member's perspective.

6. In the longer run, low-power members have a range of strategies available. These include alliances, becoming protégés of other high-power people and changing the attitudes of the high-power member through 'education'.[31] To appreciate how effective these can be, consider the following 'admission' from the Retail Planning Operation Manager of a large and powerful oil company:

> There is no doubt that from our initial stance of wanting to eliminate the small-volume rural retail petrol stations from our dealer network, we've had to amend our policy very significantly as time went by, due to mounting pressure from the site owners themselves, from their Members of Parliament, from the Department of Energy, from the Office of Fair Trading.

It is difficult not to suppose that the parliamentary representatives and civil servants were mobilised, not by any preference of their own for tangling with a large oil supplier, but by the pressure of the dealers who saw their livelihood threatened.

Many of the other long-run strategies for resisting other people's power amount to ways of gaining power, which is the next topic in this chapter.

## SUMMARY – RESISTING OTHER PEOPLE'S POWER

Even weak parties have powers of resistance, partly because it takes less power to resist than to assert. Short-run resistance measures include using persuasive skills and mobilising the power-asserter's own behaviour norms against using power. In the longer run, alliances, attachments and building richer connectedness help low-power members to resist.

## GAINING AND RETAINING POWER

The main ways of gaining power are to get hold of more of its sources, for instance an increased ability to reward others or apply sanctions. Improved status or position, becoming an expert in some important area or getting control of needed information bring increases in power. Charisma can be developed and networks of contacts cultivated. Power can be gained by undertaking roles that yield power. For example, if someone takes on the task of Secretary of a committee, they gain access to information and the chance to write the minutes and correspondence and thus to influence them. People who act as liaison officers between two departments or organisations control the information flow between the two. This 'gate-keeping' role can give them power over any activities involving the boundary between the two.

Some of these methods have the objective of increasing other people's dependence, others to increase their incentive for staying in the relationship and hence their willingness to comply or co-operate. People can also increase their own relative power by reducing their own dependence. If someone has another job lined up, it may work wonders when they ask for a rise. If Department X is reluctant to release data someone needs but it could be obtained from a survey and moves are made towards setting up such a survey, the chances are Department X staff will change their minds.

According to Emerson's power/dependence theory, a person B has four ways of gaining power relative to another person A:

1. Decreasing the subjective value s/he places on the goals that A mediates. For example, if B is an industrial sales representative trying to win an order because s/he is in the running for an incentive prize s/he might, if the negotiations with the customer turn sour, decide that the incentive is not very attractive after all.
2. Cultivating alternative sources for the goals that A mediates. Thus another possibility for the industrial sales representative would be to put more effort into sales opportunities with customers other than A.
3. Increasing the subjective value that A places on the goals B mediates. For instance, the sales representative might have customer incentives at his/her disposal and might indicate this to the customer's Buyer.
4. Denying A alternative sources to attain his/her goals. This is the method of the cartel and is so effective a way of gaining power that in some countries legislation against restraint of competition would deny it to the sales representative in this example.[32]

A different possibility for power gain is to make less of the opponent's power usable.[33] Another has been suggested by UK politician Ken Livingstone, who said in one of his speeches, 'Political power is not so much about mobilizing your own support as tactical moves to exploit the mistakes of the other side.' This tactic is similar to that of the tennis player who has good ground strokes, and who makes no attempt actively to win the point, but concentrates on returning the ball in court, confident that sooner or later the opponent will make a mistake that can be exploited.

Power gain also comes from appearing powerful. This chapter began with the point that social power is perceived power – it exists only insofar as it is believed to exist. Successful strategies for maintaining or increasing power over another person can be founded on this knowledge: 'These strategies depend upon an understanding of the cues which people employ in making judgements of power.'[34] Two such strategies are showing no emotion at events, thus suggesting that others have no power to affect one's outcomes, and appearing as if all actions are under one's control, not externally caused. Charisma or personal power, at least in men, is often associated with highly dominant assertive behaviour, as well as with humour, energy, warmth and being articulate.[35] Charismatic leaders may have charisma because they arouse the power motive and feelings of powerfulness in their followers.[36] Finally, what someone does has an influence on how they appear. Being good at solving problems or presenting a good idea at the right time may help a person appear powerful.

How do the powerful retain power, that is how do they consolidate their position so that the power balance is a stable one rather than one that can be easily upset by unexpected contingencies?

- One way is to use their power successfully, i.e. to use it to bring about outcomes that are favourable for the organisation so that their reputation is enhanced.
- Powerful positions usually carry with them the opportunity for information control. The person in power has access to information that his or her subordinates and other colleagues can only obtain if he or she releases it. By choosing what to reveal and what to conceal with the goal of consolidating their own power, such a person can keep others in a weak position. This way of retaining power is often dysfunctional for the organisation, which might be served better if more or different information were more widely dispersed.
- Another way is to set up regulations and norms that make any change in the existing power relationships seem illegitimate to followers and colleagues. For example, someone who has an elected or ex-officio position on a powerful committee might take the opportunity to get the committee to lay down an approach to an activity, such as the vetting of Research and Development proposals, which enhances their own role in the process. Once laid down by

the committee, the approach gets embodied in regulations and procedures. This helps secure the individual's power base.

- Yet another way is to make any attempt to change the status quo by low-power members so risky as to deter them, or alternatively to reward them for support. Of the two, the second has usually been found to be most effective.

## SUMMARY – GAINING AND RETAINING POWER

Power can be increased by getting hold of more of its sources and/or by decreasing one's own dependence or increasing that of other parties, provided the changes can be successfully communicated to the influence targets. Appearing powerful may be as effective as actually having power sources. Strategies for retaining power include using it successfully, using it for information control, setting up regulations that preserve the individual's power base, fostering norms that make changes seem illegitimate and rewarding supporters.

## WORK APPLICATIONS FOR USING POWER

In business meetings, representatives of two or more parties meet together to exchange information, solve shared problems or discuss issues. Negotiation is the process by which two or more parties attempt to resolve a perceived divergence of interest.[37] Many business meetings, by which is meant mainly those between potential or actual suppliers and customers or advisers and clients, contain elements of negotiation or bargaining. Similarly, all pure or formal negotiations are meetings and resemble business meetings in the following ways:

- Distinct parties with divergent interests are present or represented.
- There are differences in power between the parties: in the amount each has relative to that of the others, their sources of power, their attitudes towards using it and their skill in applying it to achieve their objectives.
- There are personal interests, motives, beliefs, values and emotions attached to the matters under discussion. These have to be reconciled, satisfied or otherwise dealt with if successful outcomes are to be achieved.
- There may be no Chairperson and therefore no one to impose procedures.
- There is usually no one to adjudicate. Issues can only be resolved by agreement of both or all parties, not by taking a vote.

Nevertheless, many business meetings mainly involve joint problem-solving, discussing ideas or exchanging information. They are not all about bargaining or negotiating. Treating them as if they are always adversarial means losing chances for co-operation and increases the amount of confrontation and competitiveness, because other people will react adversely to this approach. Therefore, in this section business meetings and negotiations are discussed separately.

## Business meetings

Preparing for meetings by planning beforehand is time well spent. This means thinking, preferably with others who will be present at the meeting, about likely contingencies and how to handle them. Pre-planning should not, however, prevent people from being flexible or lock them into positions that stop them thinking about alternative solutions. What planning should do, in fact, is free people to interact creatively in the meeting itself by reducing their fears of making mistakes. The following points should be covered in pre-planning:

- Choice of approach. If the issues are capable of win–win solutions, problem-solving is the best approach, aimed at expanding the 'pie', exchanging concessions on different issues and/or finding new solutions that satisfy the underlying interests of both parties.[38] In other cases, a conflict of interest is present and 'distributive bargaining', usually using adversarial tactics, is unavoidable.
- The other party's objectives, interests (what would benefit them), the strengths and weaknesses of their case, their likely strategy and tactics and the likely character profiles, assumptions, beliefs, attitudes and authority of their representatives and, in multi-party meetings, relations with other parties. The other party's interests may be different from either their objectives or their position. It may be possible to help them realise this, and so perhaps change the entire direction of the meeting. It is also important to recognise different levels of authority that other parties can have within their own organisations. Some will have the power to make decisions that commit their organisations irrevocably, others will be influential members of an organisation's decision team or management group, still others will be representatives authorised to make commitments up to a certain level, and some may be delegates without discretion or authority.
- The party's own objectives, interests, case (preparations should include collecting and analysing supporting data), strategy, tactics and team. There are at least three roles to be covered by the team during a meeting. One is a spokesperson, who presents ideas and arguments, responds to the other side's statements, initiates tactics and judges how immediate progress is to be made. A second is an observer/analyst/recorder, who keeps a step-by-step account of the development of events and tries to avoid bias. The third is a chairperson, who manages the team, structures the proceedings, signals changes of plan and approach, evaluates progress, selects trade-offs, requests adjournments and acts as 'referee' for the spokesperson. It is difficult for these roles to be combined, which suggests a team of at least three persons.

The beginning, middle and end phases of a business meeting show clear differences in spoken communication, non-verbal behaviour, climate and tasks.

Box 9.8

### Tactics of information exchange

1. Decide in advance the following
   - what information you will give in order to 'stroke' other parties;
   - what to use as a quid pro quo for information received;
   - what you might give to surprise or upset the other parties, and whether such a use of information is compatible with your overall approach;
   - what must not be disclosed;
   - what information is essential to gain from the other parties;
   - what information you will seek as a quid pro quo for information given;
   - what information would lead you to ask for an adjournment because it would surprise you or upset your strategy.
2. Remember that the most important information can be about people, concerning their motives, beliefs and relationships.
3. Signal clearly when you want to give out information, make sure your targets are noticing and listen carefully to the points they make. At the same time analyse what is going on.
4. Listen and watch for behavioural cues. Be sensitive to the group forces at work.
5. Look for inconsistencies between different speakers, but be cautious. Do you want to push them apart or push them together?
6. Keep asking yourself, 'What is their hidden message?', 'What may they be trying to tell me apart from just the meaning of the words they use?' and 'What may they inadvertently be telling me by non-verbal behaviour?'

In the *first phase*, there are two tasks: to establish a procedure and to establish a relationship and an atmosphere. Setting up a procedure involves getting agreement on an agenda, procedures, timing and location. These discussions can serve as a warm-up for the real thing. They should be used to trade information and to build relationships. When there are many complex issues, agendas that prioritise the discussion should be formed and it is often useful to agree on broad preliminary formulas before filling in the details. The style of communication to be used in the meeting is usually set by the end of the first phase. The more formal the communication method, the more likely it is that the outcome will reflect the relative power of the parties.

In the *second phase*, there are three further tasks: to exchange information, to make progress towards decisions and to reach and record decisions. In a meeting with a multi-item agenda, this phase, with its tasks, may be repeated several times. Each party wants information from the others. To get it they must offer information. Undisclosed information can be a source of power but it is risky. If it has to be revealed at a later stage, it may be an excuse for the other parties to revoke agreements or open up new issues. In addition, concealing information undermines trust.

**Box 9.9**

### How to establish trust in business meetings

- Start by running through the areas of agreement. These are always considerable or you would not be meeting but are often ignored in favour of launching straight into a discussion of points of disagreement or dispute. Time spent on shared interests or views is not wasted as it builds towards agreement on other matters.
- Use information disclosure as a gift.
- Stroke. Listen and show you understand. Remember this does not have to mean you accept. Praise if you can with sincerity. Smile sometimes and make eye contact. Use humour but not, necessarily, jokes.
- Avoid anything that might be interpreted, as threatening or over-assertive. For instance, sit well back from the table to ensure your gestures do not invade other people's 'territory' or seem to seek to dominate.

Making progress involves exploring issues, thinking up possible solutions, evaluating them and moving towards a decision. If in the first stage an atmosphere of joint problem-solving has been created, then this stage can be quick, productive and positive. The factors that influence how effective groups are at problem-solving, described in Chapter 11, then become the main behavioural aspects to pay attention to. If the atmosphere is one of bargaining verging on confrontation, however, the parties may engage in adversarial tactics. These might include applying time pressure (either delaying or rushing to create a sense of urgency and inevitability behind their demands), attempts to get concessions or disclosures of information by tricks, surprise revelations to throw the other party off balance, personal attacks, power mobilisation (threats or promises), attempts to 'buy off' representatives from their organisations or clients, process tactics such as adjournments, distracting rituals, lies and coalitions.

**Box 9.10**

### How to handle adversarial tactics in business meetings

- Do not be stung into retaliating.
- Stay calm and slow the pace of your speech.
- Show that you are fully aware of the tactic.
- Do not ignore any hostile emotions, interpersonal conflict or aggression that arise at this stage. They must be dealt with. In team or multi-party meetings, try to identify the person with the social skills and orientation to handle interpersonal conflict, and trigger their efforts.
- Keep concentrating on interests rather than positions and on problems rather than disputes.

The commitment of all necessary parties is needed to whatever decision is made. Even if no solution can be found on which all parties will agree, sometimes people will accept a compromise on particular agenda items for the sake of overarching goals, such as keeping the other parties' goodwill.

The *third phase* of a meeting is the concluding one. At this meeting preparations are made for the next meeting if one is to take place. The meeting itself should end as a social event, in which any breaches in good relations can be repaired. The main events of the meeting should be minuted. Notes should be made on how the other parties acted. A report on the meeting should go to staff who may have to deal with customers or clients who will expect them to know what went on.

## Negotiating

### *Negotiating strategies and tactics*

Negotiating strategies and tactics are usually analysed as problem-solving or adversarial. Both types of behaviour have been described in the section on business meetings. In negotiations, the two tend to be alternatives. It is hard to commit to a particular demand while also sustaining an image of flexibility, although different sets of tactics can be pursued at different times or, in team negotiating, by different people. Research has identified the following factors as influences on individual negotiators who pursue adversarial tactics: having ambitious goals, seeing attractive alternatives to agreement, expecting low costs if no agreement is reached, framing issues negatively, having strong principles (e.g. of religion) underlying their demands, being an accountable representative and being high in self-concern as opposed to concern for the other. The following paragraph expands on three of these factors.

Issues are framed negatively when the available options are seen as involving various degrees of loss, positively when they are seen as involving various degrees of gain. Negotiators with a loss frame will demand more, concede less, settle less easily and the language they use will communicate more about costs and losses than profits and gains.[39] The opposing negotiators tend to adopt their opponent's communicated gain or loss frame. However, when negotiators know in advance that the opponent has a loss frame, they show an increase in altruistic motives and see the opponent's concession-making as more co-operative.[40] When negotiators' constituents are in a position to reward and punish them, the negotiators are motivated to behave so as to gain the approval of their constituents, rather than serving their constituents' best interests.[41] Benton and Druckman[42] found that negotiations between accountable representatives took longer to finish, involved more rejections of offers and fewer concessions and resulted in more unequal outcomes than negotiations between representatives who were not accountable. The most effective problem-solving negotiators are usually high in both self-concern and other-concern.[43]

Other influences on tactical choice include time pressure (which encourages both concession making and adversarial behaviour), the inferences the negotiators draw about their opponent's attitudes, judgements and preferences, trust (which fosters a problem-solving approach by increasing the perceived likelihood of the opponent joining in) and relative power. (High threat capacity encourages adversarial bargaining.)

**Box 9.11**

**European variations in negotiating styles**

The Dutch, perhaps unexpectedly, are assertive, stubborn and tough negotiators, whereas among the Swedes, negotiating skills are based on a combination of personal conviction and self-restraint.

### *Negotiation outcomes*

Negotiation outcomes are affected by the readiness of the parties to reach agreement, their relative power, the formality with which the negotiation is conducted, whether the negotiation takes place in the context of a continuing relationship, whether the parties are represented by single individuals or teams, whether interests, beliefs or values are mainly at issue, whether an orderly progression of stages is gone through and the skills of the negotiators.

- Readiness theory holds that all kinds of progress towards conflict resolution result from the existence, on both sides, of motivational ripeness (motivation to achieve de-escalation) and optimism about finding a mutually acceptable agreement. Optimism mainly develops during the talks themselves, by a circular process that involves a steady growth in working trust, a perception that the other side is represented by a valid spokesman, perceived common ground, assurances of absolute secrecy, provision of facilities that encourage intimacy between the delegates and arranging for meetings over a long enough period of time for the components of optimism to emerge.
- In formal bargaining, power impacts strongly on the messages conveyed, communicative persistence, the diversity of strategic compliance gaining employed and bargaining outcomes,[44] although persuasive messages moderate power effects and tenacious behaviour is a substitute to some extent for power.
- Strictly formal approaches – putting all offers in writing, minuting everything – prevent informal understandings being reached, lead to the parties not revealing information because it can only be done 'on the record'. This, in turn, leads to contracts being interpreted according to their letter rather than the spirit of

the agreement. Formality in bargaining also increases the degree to which power determines the outcome.

- In contract negotiations, both parties want an agreement that will be implemented by the other party with a degree of willingness. Neither wants to have to take or threaten legal action in order to enforce the contract. Macaulay[45] has shown how rarely legal moves are made to resolve disputes arising under the terms of an agreement, mainly because the costs are too high. Negotiators are not, therefore, usually aiming to beat an opponent or to extract an exploitative deal: they want one that satisfies their requirements and serves their interests.[46]
- Team negotiators increase the productivity of negotiation. Teams, more than solos, develop mutually beneficial trade-offs among issues, discover compatible interests, exchange information and judge the opponent's interests more accurately. The benefits do not flow only to the party that is composed of a team, nor does being a team give negotiators a relative advantage over solo opponents; instead, the benefit of both parties increases.[47]
- When interests, as opposed to beliefs or values, are the negotiation issues, negotiators tend to develop fixed-pie perceptions – the belief that their own preferences in a negotiation are diametrically opposed to those of the other party. This belief has been shown to reduce negotiators' tendency to search for win–win solutions.[48] However, Harinck *et al.*[49] found that parties in interest-based negotiations show greater willingness to engage in trade-offs of less important items for more. (Trade-offs are seen as inappropriate for belief- or value-based issues.) Trade-offs allow negotiators to attain significantly higher joint outcomes in interest-based negotiations than in the other two types of bargaining.
- In negotiations leading to settlements, the first phase consists of 'a thorough and exhaustive determination of the outer limits of the range in which they (the parties) will have to do business with each other'. The second phase contains 'official' statements of positions and unofficial interpersonal exchanges which do not commit the parties but reconnoitre the most promising areas of the bargaining range in which agreement might be reached. In the third phase, the negotiators try to force the opponent to make a decision, by precipitating a decision-making crisis. Timing is all-important: 'So far as the actions of the parties are concerned, the main imperative is that the movements of the two sides be synchronised to take on the phases of the bargaining sequence concurrently.'[50]

### *Multilateral negotiations*

In multilateral negotiations, there is an advantage in drawing on a metaphor of coalition building,[51] which highlights the commonality of interests among parties who have differing values, priorities or goals but have general or limited common objectives. Multicultural and international negotiations are treated more fully in Chapter 12.

**Box 9.12**

### How to be a skilled negotiator

- Practise self-monitoring. Self-monitoring is the habit of self-observation and analysis before, during and after interactions (Snyder, 1974). It is linked to goal commitment prior to negotiation, impression management strategies, choice of integrative tactics and plan complexity. High self-monitors are particularly well suited to negotiation, probably because they plan ahead (Jordan and Roloff, 1997).
- If you have a stronger power base than your opponents, increase the formality of the negotiations, perhaps by the presence of a senior member of staff. If yours is the weaker power base, and so reliant on the strength of your case, try to ensure that bargaining takes place in a friendly atmosphere between people who know and like one another.
- Take into account the impact on both parties of 'strategic misrepresentation'. To decide their tactics, the other party will make inferences about your attitudes, judgements and preferences (Pruitt, 1972). While in general individuals become more accurate about each other's preferences over time, in face-to-face negotiations accuracy seems to decrease, probably because of strategic misrepresentation (Harinck *et al.*, 2000).
- Set your objectives in terms of a range of targets and a resistance point, which is the worst position you would accept. The resistance point should be based on your best alternative to a negotiated agreement (BATNA). If that cannot be obtained it would be better to break off the negotiations.
- Successful negotiating is only possible if the resistance points of the parties overlap. Try to discover whether this settlement range exists by probing to find out more about the targets and the resistance point of your opponent, while trying to keep your own objectives concealed.
- The opening position of each side has more effect on the final outcome than any of the later moves. Pitch yours at least high enough to allow you to make concessions during the bargaining and still reach your target. Always demand more than you expect to get and offer less than you expect to give. If you pitch your opening offer low, your opponent will still treat it as the starting point for extracting concessions from you.
- Since it is a convention to ask for more than you want, assume that the other party has done so and reject the opening offer, no matter how excellent a deal it seems.
- A concession is a revision of a position you have held previously and justified publicly. Concessions are always expected in negotiations. Not to offer them is to signal that you are not really interested in reaching a settlement or that you are unskilled. On the other hand, do not make concessions except under specific pressure from the other party, decide the timing with care and keep them small to avoid undermining your credibility.
- Do not be affected by 'closure anxiety'. An extended process of bargaining allows both parties to test the other's limits and to be satisfied that no better bargain could have been made. This increases commitment to the outcome.
- Push for concessions from the other side. For instance, you may emphasise similarity: 'I think you approach this in the same way that I do', suggest adjournments: 'Now that you've heard what we've got to say, you will probably want to go away and decide', use an ally: 'Let's look again at the point raised some time ago by John Brown', appeal to good nature: 'Come on, help me out on this one' or put on pressure: 'Come on. Come on. I've made all the running. When are you going to start negotiating?'
- Receive concessions after a pause, with a low-response style, to restrict the information to the other side on your targets and resistance points. Part of a low-response style is

**Box 9.12 *continued***

responding slowly. This also reduces the risk that you will make a mistake in your response.

- Stimulate the other party's closure needs to get an agreement. For instance, you may mention an inducement: 'I know I can get my company to put more business your way if only we can agree on this one', assume agreement: 'Good, so we've agreed', or provoke a decision-making crisis, which places everything agreed so far in the balance: 'If we can't settle this last remaining issue, then I'm afraid the whole deal is off'. If, however, your closure tactics do not succeed, you must continue with determination to negotiate to a finish.
- Signal your final offer by making it with the minimum of argument, as simply as possible, in a tone of finality and with an impassive demeanour. Alternatively, put your final offer in writing, if previous ones have been made orally. Have it issued by the most senior negotiator. Answers to questions about the offer should be brief and no shifting of position should be made. All this is to demonstrate that this offer is different from your earlier concessions – it is final.
- Avoid these mistakes, recently identified by research: irrationally escalating commitment to a position out of self-justification, irrational competitiveness, assuming the negotiation is a win–lose affair (that there is a fixed pie) when there are win–win possibilities, errors in assessing risks, costs or outcome values when considering a concession or offer, over-using readily available information just because it is readily available and over-confidence.

*Sources*: Harinck, F., C. K. W. De Dreu and A. E. M. van Vianen (2000) 'The impact of conflict issues on fixed-pie perceptions, problem-solving and integrative outcomes in negotiation', *Organizational Behaviour and Human Decision Processes*, vol. 81, no. 2, pp. 329–358.
Jordan, J. M. and M. E. Roloff (1997) 'Planning skills and negotiator goal accomplishment: The relationship between self-monitoring and plan generation, plan enactment, and plan consequences', *Communication Research*, vol. 24, no. 1, pp. 31–63.
Pruitt, D. G. (1972) 'Methods for resolving differences of interest: A theoretical analysis', *Journal of Social Problems*, vol. 28, pp. 133–154.
Snyder, M. (1974) 'Self-monitoring of expressive behavior', *Journal of Personality and Social Psychology*, vol. 30, pp. 526–537.

**Box 9.13**

## Critique of negotiating research

Further study is needed on the following:

- the impact of pre-existing relationships;
- organisational (constituency) pressures;
- multilateral negotiating;
- the impact of social norms (especially fairness);
- cultural differences;
- individual differences.

## SUMMARY – WORK APPLICATIONS FOR USING POWER

Business meetings and negotiations have many similarities of tasks, phases and behaviours, but there is a greater element of distributive bargaining in formal negotiations and negotiating conventions apply.

Preparations for business meetings include in-depth research into and thinking about the attitudes, bargaining positions and inter-relations of the other parties; planning positions, cases and tactics, and allocating team members to the roles of spokesperson, observer, recorder and 'chair'. There are distinct phases, with different tasks, in a business meeting.

In negotiations, adversarial tactics are often used and are appropriate in negotiations over win–lose issues. For win–win issues and negotiations that are part of, or intended as the start of, a long-term business relationship, problem-solving tactics are better as they are more likely to produce a workable agreement. The parties' compositions, motives, relative power and skills, the negotiation issues and the formality and orderliness of the process all affect the negotiation outcomes.

Negotiating skills should be applied to setting targets and resistance points, opening offers, making concessions, encouraging movement, getting closure and making final offers. Opening offers should be pitched well above targets to allow room for making concessions, which should be small in scale and well timed. There are various ways of encouraging concessions from the other party and for getting closure on a position. A key skill is to use a low-response style. The way in which the final offer is made must convince the other party that no further concessions are possible.

## CHAPTER OVERVIEW

Social power (the probability of influencing others despite their resistance) depends on the influence targets believing, for whatever reason, that they have to or need to comply. Thus power exercise depends on the target's motives, attitudes and beliefs as well as the influencer's credibility and skill. Structuralist theories of power, including deterrence theory and network exchange theory, do not accept that power is mediated through perceptions. However, there are versions of structuralist theories that allow for the effect of cognitions and subjective values. In this book the view is taken that the so-called bases of power, the ability to reward or punish, information control, access to important people and so on have their effect by influencing the influencer's and target's beliefs about the latter having to comply with the former's demands. Stylistic factors, such as a convincing appearance of being authoritative, can also be effective.

Asserting power can be both costly and risky. A failed power attempt can endanger important goals and relationships as well as damage the influencer's credibility. Therefore power exercise needs to be planned ahead, thinking in a systematic way about the various ways of mobilising power, about the other party's probable responses and about benefits, costs and the circumstances in which to use each method.

Applications of power handling skills arise particularly during business meetings and negotiations, though all the skills covered so far are important. Pre-planning and skilled handling of timing, concession-making and closing are particularly needed.

## EXERCISES

1. Read the newspapers, especially the business press, to find examples of 'politicking'.
2. Interview a manager and describe the role s/he perceives that politics plays in managers' work.
3. Draw up an action plan to improve your career progression.
4. The weekly management meeting of the Marketing Department of the South-West Electrical Company has just been completed. The Marketing Director (MD) asks one of the four product managers in his department to stay behind. 'Lesley, we really cannot delay introducing car phones for the sales force any longer. All our main competitors have them, and the greater efficiency they allow them is beginning to show up in our sales figures. I want you to undertake a study of our needs, find out what systems there are on the market, get some costings done, and come up with your recommendation as soon as possible.'

   Lesley's immediate reaction is 'Why me?' She knows for a fact that she is more overloaded than her colleagues, it is always she who is still in the office hours after the others have gone home. Before this new MD took over, being in charge of the White Goods Marketing Section, as she was, had been recognised as the most demanding of the four product managers' jobs, but the new man just disregarded this and seemed to load every special project on to her. Plus, car phones are nothing to do with her area. Peter actually sells the things in his role as Product Manager for Office Communications products (mainly telephone systems and electronic mail).

   Lesley is determined to refuse this assignment, as she is entitled to. The culture of the company is explicitly consensual and democratic; in imposing his wishes on his staff, instead of settling such matters through general discussion and agreement, the MD is in breach of corporate management guidelines. However, Lesley knows that the MD requires careful handling; his personality means that he uses his power to great effect:

   (a) He is an older man, whose long years of experience make him a credible authority on a variety of matters. He understands the working of the firm inside out. Usually he is calm and soft-spoken, but occasional outbursts of anger mean that people fear to provoke him.

(b) He is very forceful in argument, loud and domineering. He does not hesitate to shout down any opposition, though does not often appear to be made actually angry by the exchange – he just acts as if shouting and being rude would bully people into compliance, which it often does. He is quick to attack any emotional arguments or hint of personal considerations.

(c) He rarely listens to other people's points of view once he has committed himself to a position. He lets them speak but then just goes on and on repeating his statement of position, looking his opponents straight in the eye. Most people find this so unnerving that they give in.

*As a private study or group discussion exercise,* plan Lesley's arguments and approach. How should she deal with the Marketing Director if he behaves in the way suggested in (a), (b) and (c) above?

*As a role play,* enact the discussion between Lesley and the Marketing Director which follows his instruction to her to investigate the supply of car phones for the sales force.

5. Complete the business meeting self-analysis rating scale in Table 9.3.

6. This exercise concerns the contract for baggage handling at an airport in a former communist country. The airport has a new international terminal with modern baggage handling facilities but retains its old terminal for domestic flights, with only the most primitive of facilities. Both international and domestic business were growing fast until recently, but there has been a downturn due to the Asian recession.

The contract is for one year. This negotiation is between the Airport Authority and XYZ Airport Services which has held the contract for the past year. There is a presumption in favour of renewal, but certain issues must be sorted out first; in particular, there have been complaints about long delays in the delivery of luggage in both the domestic and the international terminal. On one occasion a government minister was delayed for over an hour and on another a visiting UN dignitary had to wait an hour and a quarter: this led to an article in a Western news magazine describing the country as still disorganised. XYZ has blamed the poor facilities in the domestic terminal and a high rate of belt breakdown in the international terminal, owing to poor equipment having been purchased. The Airport Authority believes, however, that the problem lies in poor management of the local workforce by XYZ.

*As a private study or group discussion exercise,* plan the case, negotiating strategy and approach that each side will use in this negotiation.

*As a role play,* enact the negotiation. *Role A,* which can be a team, represents XYZ. *Role B,* which can also be a team, represents the Airport Authority.

**Table 9.3 A questionnaire to help analyse behavioural performance in the last business meeting attended**

In the course of the meeting just completed:

1. How concerned did you feel about the impression you were creating?

   Extremely concerned ×——×——×——×——×——× Not at all concerned

2. How often did this affect your concentration?

   Very often ×——×——×——×——×——× Very little

3. How often did your attention wander from what was being said?

   Four times or more ×——×——×——×——×——× Not once

4. How often were you planning your reply while another party was speaking?

   Four times ×——×——×——×——×——× Not once

5. Did the atmosphere (joint problem solving/negotiating/confrontation) you preplanned for the meeting prevail? If not, why not? Was there any way you could have altered that? In what way?
6. What attempts did you make to build trust?
   List here:

   How successful were they? Why?
7. Did you attempt to steer the meeting through its phases to a successful conclusion? If so, how successful were your attempts? Why?
8. Did you attempt to assert power at any points? How? (referring to your power bases/making promises/threatening). Did your power assertions follow your plan before the meeting? What effects did they have? Why?
9. Were you aware of any attempts by other parties to assert power over you? How did you deal with them? Were these ways of handling them successful? Why?
10. List here any statements, questions, comments or criticisms made by other people in the meeting which aroused anxiety or anger in you.

    How did you handle these emotions on each occasion?
11. Did you get involved in any interpersonal conflict yourself? Why? How can you avoid it next time?
12. Did you help resolve any interpersonal conflicts between others? How?

*Note*: If the meeting was, in effect, a negotiation, the rating scales in Table 9.4 will help you analyse your performance.

7. In this exercise, the representatives of the Chambers of Commerce of the four districts of a metropolis are meeting to plan their contribution to the forthcoming celebration of the two hundredth anniversary of the country's independence. This will take place in two years' time. The recent fiasco of the country's celebrations of the 'millennium' – a huge dome with a range of 'future-oriented' exhibitions inside, which 80 per cent of people thought was a waste of money – has made the issue sensitive. There are four parties:

**Table 9.4 How well did you negotiate?**

| | *Very Weak* | | | | *Very Strong* |
|---|---|---|---|---|---|
| I rate my performance in the last negotiation I conducted as: | | | | | |
| 1. Giving out the information I planned to | 1 | 2 | 3 | 4 | 5 |
| 2. Retaining the information I planned to | 1 | 2 | 3 | 4 | 5 |
| 3. Obtaining the information I sought | 1 | 2 | 3 | 4 | 5 |
| 4. Setting an appropriate initial offer | 1 | 2 | 3 | 4 | 5 |
| 5. Making the subsequent concessions at the right rate and amount | 1 | 2 | 3 | 4 | 5 |
| 6. 'Rewarding' the opponent's concessions | 1 | 2 | 3 | 4 | 5 |
| 7. Encouraging movement | 1 | 2 | 3 | 4 | 5 |
| 8. Pushing for closure | 1 | 2 | 3 | 4 | 5 |
| 9. Controlling my own need for closure | 1 | 2 | 3 | 4 | 5 |
| 10. Making my final offer convincing | 1 | 2 | 3 | 4 | 5 |

(a) The representatives of the businesses of the financial district, which is the country's major foreign exchange earner.

(b) The representatives of the businesses of the shopping and entertainments district, which attracts large numbers of tourists and is both a major foreign exchange earner and has high visibility in the eyes of the rest of the country and the world generally.

(c) The representatives of the declining manufacturing district, where unemployment is high and bankruptcies are many.

(d) The representatives of the businesses of a mixed district of small businesses and poorer residential areas with a large ethnic minority community.

Naturally, each Chamber would like the independence celebrations, and the resources and publicity they will attract, to be centred in their district. However, only by presenting a united front are they likely to win the backing of the government, the media and the public for any proposal they put forward.

*As a private study or group discussion exercise,* plan the case, negotiating strategy and approach that each party will use in this negotiation.

*As a role play,* enact this multi-party negotiation.

8. Complete the negotiating self-rating scale in Table 9.4. *See the Appendix to find out how to analyse your responses to this questionnaire.*

## FURTHER READING

Fowler, A. (1996) *Negotiation Skills and Strategies,* 2nd edn. London: Institute of Personnel and Development.

Kramer, R. M. and M. A. Neale (eds) (1998) *Power and Influence in Organizations.* Thousand Oaks, Calif.: Sage. Especially Chapters 4, 5 and 9. Chapters 1–4 for Chapter 7 of this book, Chapter 13 (Impression Management) for Chapter 6, Chapter 12 (Teams) for Chapter 11.

Lax, D. A. and J. K. Sebenius (1986) *The Manager As Negotiator: Bargaining for Cooperation and Competitive Gain*. New York: The Free Press.

Susskind, L., P. C. Foster and R. H. Mnookin (1999) *Negotiating on Behalf of Others; Advice to Lawyers, Business Executives, Sports Agents, Diplomats, Politicians and Everybody Else*. Thousand Oaks, Calif.: Sage. Especially the Introduction and Chapters 1 and 4.

Neale, M. and M. H. Bazerman (1993) *Cognition and Rationality in Negotiation*. New York: Free Press.

Pruitt, D. G. and P. J. Carnevale (1993) *Negotiation in Social Conflict*. Buckingham: Open University Press.

## REFERENCES


1. White, R. and R. Lippitt (1960) *Autocracy and Democracy*. New York: Harper and Row.
2. Buckley, W. (1970) 'Society as a complex adptive system' in W. Buckley (ed.) *Modern Systems Research for the Behavioural Scientist*. Chicago, Ill.: Aldine Publishing Company.
3. Conway, M., M. T. Pizzamiglio and L. Mount (1996) 'Status, communality, and agency: Implications for stereotypes of gender and other groups', *Journal of Personality and Social Psychology*, vol. 71, pp. 25–38.
4. Cartwright, D. P. (1965) 'Influence, leadership and control' in J. G. March (ed.) *Handbook of Organisations*, Chicago: Rand McNally.
5. Riker, W. H. (1964) 'Some ambiguities in the notion of power', *American Political Science Review*, vol. 58, pp. 341–349.
6. Van Dijk, T. A. (1989) 'Structures of discourse and structures of power', *Communication Yearbook*, vol. 12, pp. 18–59.
7. Hovland, C. I., A. A. Lumsdaine and F. D. Sheffield (1949) *Experiments in Mass Communication*. Princeton, New Jersey: Princeton University Press.
8. Cartwright, D. (1959) 'A field theoretical conception of power' in D. Cartwright (ed.) *Studies in Social Power*. Ann Arbor, Mich.: University of Michigan Press.
9. Lawler, E. J. (1992) 'Power processes in bargaining', *Sociological Quarterly*, vol. 33, no. 1, pp. 17–34.
10. Schlueter, D. W., J. K. Barge and D. Blankenship (1990) 'A comparative analysis of influence strategies used by upper and lower-level male and female managers', *Western Journal of Speech Communication*, vol. 54, no. 1, pp. 42–65.
11. Markovsky, B., D. Willer and T. Patton (1988) 'Power relations in exchange networks', *American Sociological Review*, vol. 53, pp. 220–236.
12. Markovsky, B., D. Willer and T. Patton (1993) 'The seeds of weak power: An extension of network exchange theory', *American Sociological Review*, vol. 58, pp. 197–209.
13. Ford, R. and M. A. Blegen (1992) 'Offensive and defensive use of punitive tactics in explicit bargaining', *Social Psychology Quarterly*, vol. 55, no. 4, pp. 351–362.
14. Schelling, T. C. (1960) *The Strategy of Conflict*. Cambridge Mass: Harvard University Press.
15. Emerson, R. E. (1962) 'Power-dependence relations', *American Sociological Review*, vol. 27, pp. 31–41.
16. Blalock, H. M. Jr (1989) *Conflict and Power*. Beverley Hills, Calif.: Sage.
17. McClelland, D. C. (1975) *Power: The Inner Experience*. New York: Wiley.
18. McClelland, D. C. and D. H. Burnham (1976) 'Power is the great motivator', *Harvard Business Review*, March–April, pp. 100–115.
19. Van Dijk, op. cit.

20. Ibarra, H. and S. B. Andrews (1993) 'Power, social influence and sense making: Effects of network centrality and proximity on employee perceptions', *Administrative Science Quarterly*, vol. 38, pp. 277–303.
21. Mechanic, D. (1962) 'Sources of power of lower participants in organizations', *Administrative Science Quarterly*, vol. 7, pp. 349–364.
22. Mulder, M. (1960) 'The power variable in communication experiments', *Human Relations*, vol. 13, pp. 241–257.
23. Boster, F. J., D. Kazoleas, T. Levine, R. G. Rogan and K. H. Kang (1995) 'The impact of power on communicative persistence, strategic diversity and bargaining outcomes', *Communication Reports*, vol. 8, no. 2, pp. 136–144.
24. Eakins, B. W. and R. G. Eakins (1978) *Sex Differences in Human Conversation*. Boston, Mass.: Houghton Mifflin.
25. Dittmar, N. and C. von Stutterheim (1985) 'On the discourse of immigrant workers' in T. A. van Dijk (ed.) *Handbook of Discourse Analysis*, vol. 4: *Discourse Analysis in Society*. London: Academic Press, pp. 125–152.
26. Van Dijk, op. cit.
27. Ibid.
28. London, P. (1969) *Behaviour Control*. New York: Harper and Row.
29. Neale, M. and M. H. Bazerman (1993) *Cognition and Rationality in Negotiation*. New York: Free Press.
30. Raven, B. H. and A. W. Kruglanski (1970) 'Conflict and power' in P. Swingle (ed.) *The Structure of Conflict*. New York: Academic Press.
31. Deutsch, M. (1969) 'Conflicts: productive and destructive', *Journal of Social Issues*, vol. 25, pp. 7–41.
32. Emerson, op. cit.
33. Bowers, J. W. (1974) 'Communication strategies in conflicts between institutions and their clients' in G. R. Miller and H. W. Simons (eds) *Perspectives on Communication in Social Conflict*. Englewood Cliffs, New Jersey: Prentice Hall.
34. Thibaut, J. W. and H. H. Kelley (1959) *The Social Psychology of Groups*. New York: Wiley.
35. Lieberman, M., I. Yalom and M. B. Miller (1973) *Encounter Groups: First Facts*. New York: Basic Books.
36. McClelland, op. cit.
37. Pruitt, D. G. (1996) 'Bargaining' in A. S. R. Manstead, M. Hewstone, S. T. Fiske, M. A. Hogg and G. R. Semin (eds) *The Blackwell Encyclopaedia of Social Psychology*. Oxford: Blackwell, pp. 81–85.
38. Pruitt, op. cit.
39. Neale and Bazerman, op. cit.
40. De Dreu, C. K. W., P. J. D. Carnevale, B. J. M. Emans and E. van de Vliert (1994) 'Effects of gain-loss frames in negotiation: Loss aversion, mismatching, and frame adoption', *Organizational Behavior and Human Decision Processes*, vol. 60, pp. 90–107.
41. Adelberg, S. and C. D. Batson (1978) 'Accountability and helping: When needs exceed resources', *Journal of Personality and Social Psychology*, vol. 36, pp. 342–350.
42. Benton, A. A. and D. Druckman (1974) 'Constituents bargaining orientation and intergroup negotiations', *Journal of Applied Psychology*, vol. 4, pp. 141–150.
43. Pruitt, D. G. and P. J. Carnevale (1993) *Negotiation in Social Conflict*. Buckingham: Open University Press.
44. Boster *et al.*, op. cit.

45. Macaulay, S. (1963) 'Non-contractual relations in business', *American Sociological Review*, vol. 28, pp. 55–67.
46. Pruitt and Carnevale, op. cit.
47. Thompson, L., E. Peterson and S. E. Brodt (1996) 'Team negotiation: An examination of integrative and distributive bargaining', *Journal of Personality and Social Psychology*, vol. 70, no. 1, pp. 66–78.
48. Pinkley, R. L., T. L. Griffith and G. B. Northcraft (1995)' "Fixed-pie" a la mode: Information availability, information processing and the negotiation of suboptimal agreements', *Organizational Behavior and Human Decision Processes*, vol. 62, pp. 101–112.
49. Harinck, F., C. K. W. De Dreu and A. E. M. van Vianen (2000) 'The impact of conflict issues on fixed-pie perceptions, problem-solving and integrative outcomes in negotiation', *Organizational Behavior and Human Decision Processes*, vol. 81, no. 2, pp. 329–358.
50. Douglas, A. (1957) 'The peaceful settlement of industrial and inter-group disputes', *Journal of Conflict Resolution*, vol. 1, pp. 69–81.
51. Dupont, C. (1996) 'Negotiation as coalition building', *International Negotiation Journal*, vol. 1, no. 1, pp. 37–44.

# Part 3

# PROCESS EXTENSIONS

# 10 Work relationships

## CHAPTER INTRODUCTION

So far this book has concentrated on 'one-off' person-to-person interactions and the skills needed for them, though with exceptions such as mediating, making presentations and team impression management, which relate particularly closely to core skills covered earlier. The next three chapters extend this analysis in three directions, to cover work relationships, which are time-extended, sometimes over many years, working in groups and working across cultures. The same core skills of understanding others, impression management, communicating, persuading and using power are required and applied in these three new areas, but with significant differences. In the case of work relationships, the difference is made by the history of the relationship, the familiarity of the participants, the expectation of continuity and the stronger influence of the organisational context. In the case of groups, the difference is due to the effects of multiple simultaneous and sequential interactions that produce group dynamics. In the case of working across cultures, the variations in participants' worldviews, values and ways of communicating are among the significant differences. However, there are overlaps among all these areas, so that material in one chapter is often relevant to the others.

To support readers' effectiveness in work relationships, this chapter describes:

- the nature of work relationships;
- how patterns of organisational communication, roles and norms affect work relationships;
- co-operation, competition, conflict and conflict resolution at work;
- trust and its effects on co-operation;
- the impact of cultural diversity at work;
- dealing with prejudice, discrimination and harassment at work;
- work activities including giving performance feedback and reprimand interviewing, customer relations and mediating.

## THE NATURE OF WORK RELATIONSHIPS

In this section, I discuss relationship theories in general, including interdependence and social orientations theory, and the special nature of work relationships, communication, role behaviour and norms.

## Relationship theories

Work relationships are, of course, relationships, which are the subject of a large body of theory and research. The term relationship here refers to an enduring association between two persons. Interaction between persons who are related even in this limited sense differs from interaction between unrelated persons. It typically involves mutual influence. Reciprocity may only occur across multiple events, spaced out in time. Within relationships, there exists a set of understandings about the nature of the relationship and what each side can expect from the other.[1]

Arguably the most comprehensive account of interaction patterns in relationships is given by interdependence and social orientations theory.[2] These theories relate interactive behaviour to the outcomes that people achieve through interaction and to those they attempt to achieve.

- The outcomes of each of two or more persons depend both on their own and the other participants' actions. Outcomes affect the level of satisfaction a person experiences with an interaction and so their motivation to continue the relationship. Expectations about the relationship, based on the early stages of the interaction or on experiences with previous relationships, also affect how satisfied people are with their outcomes. These expectations provide a comparison level or standard. A person's satisfaction equates to their outcome minus their comparison level. An individual will (or, in some versions, should) remain in a relationship only if their satisfaction level exceeds the satisfaction they would get from an alternative. People are dependent on any relationship to the extent that their outcomes from it exceed the satisfaction they would get from their best alternative.

  Rusbult[3] added the concept of 'investments', which represent resources put into a relationship that would be lost if the relationship ended. These consist of time, effort, money or other inputs. A person's dependence on (commitment to) a relationship is seen as equal to their outcome satisfaction plus investments minus their best alternative. So, for instance, if an employee in a small firm finds the work interesting and well paid, if they have moved their family in order to do the job and if there is not much alternative employment available for them, they are likely to be more willing to compromise in disagreements with the owner than if the opposite conditions, or some of them, apply.
- Interactive behaviour is linked to outcome goals. Co-operative behaviour stems from the attempt to maximise joint outcomes, competitive behaviour from the attempt to maximise one's own outcomes relative to the other. There are other possibilities, such as 'minimise the difference between participants' outcomes'.
- A later version of the theory considers how people reconcile their self-interested priorities and interests with the need to co-ordinate action and take into account the responses they receive from other participants. The theory asserts that they do it by transforming their personal desires and goals into behavioural tendencies through characteristic patterns of responding to the other participants'

interests. The later theory drops the assumption that outcome allocation criteria, such as 'maximise joint outcomes' or 'minimise the difference' are the only ones used by an interacting individual. Instead, s/he adopts a whole set of decision rules, known as social orientations, to decide whether and how to proceed. These rules may cover orientations as varied as trust, control, courage, dependence and power sharing. Social orientations are habits, formed as solutions to each individual's repeatedly encountered patterns of interdependence – solutions that on average yield desirable outcomes. For example, a person who has been made redundant several times may develop a social orientation of distrust or devaluation of loyalty and so avoid future feelings of being 'let down' if it happens again. This low-trust orientation will affect the person's behaviour in interactions with his or her employer. Whether that low-trust orientation will focus only on relationships with employers or be generalised more widely depends on whether they have also been let down in other relationships of their lives.[4]

- Satisfaction from outcomes and achieving interaction goals depend in part on how the interactor interprets their partner's behaviour and on their emotional response to the partner's behaviour. Thus interdependence theory incorporates attribution theory and various hypotheses on how emotions influence interactive behaviour. Self-presentation plays the part of communicating goals, values and motivations to interaction partners – either accurately or deceptively.

**Box 10.1**

### Critique of the interdependence model of work relationships

- It attends to precise, clearly articulated patterns of outcome interdependence.
- It is content free. It can apply to all shared activities.
- It captures the dynamic and interactive nature of relationship behaviour better than traditional reward/cost notions (e.g. social exchange). Nevertheless, it is at base an exchange model of interaction and some of the criticisms made in relation to interaction theory in Chapter 3 still apply.
- It allows for a sophisticated calculation of outcomes by interactors and hence for their having complex motives. For instance, they may aim for maximising the joint outcomes of both parties. It also recasts power in a dependence framework.
- Grzelak (1997) comments that the theory broadens our view of interactions and draws attention to their complexity and dynamics. For example, it reflects the fact that choices made early in an encounter may constrain choices later in it. On the other hand, it treats people as processing information in a systematic way, perceiving long-term outcomes and controlling the interaction to achieve desirable outcomes. Grzelak argues that many choices made in interaction with others are spontaneous and emotion-driven rather than a result of careful information-processing. However, task-based interaction choices may be more instrumental.

*Source*: Grzelak, J. L. (1997) 'Walking through interaction: comments on H.H. Kelley's "Expanding the analysis of social interaction by reference to the sequential-temporal structures of situations"', *European Journal of Social Psychology*, vol. 27, pp. 405–413.

## Work relationships

Relationships between people at work have a special quality. They differ from relationships between friends and relations, because they arise out of the work setting, which means the difference made by being alongside the same people day by day, working on the same or related tasks and having specified positions and roles. Although people who work together often share some purely social activities, they interact mainly in dealing with the task. In addition, people at work value each other partly for their competence, which is less of a concern between friends and relations. In particular, colleagues value others who are helpful to their own work goals, such as promotion prospects, or who support them in some project.[5] Although work relationships are first brought about by the formal system of work, they are elaborated in several ways by informal contacts of different kinds. (Social relationships support co-operation at work.) The informal system then affects the work itself. Norms are formed, for example about how much work to do, people split up into informal subgroups and there emerges a status hierarchy not recognised by management.[6] Argyle and Henderson[7] distinguished among four kinds of relationships at work, at different levels of closeness: friends outside work, friends at work, friendly working relationship and work relationship only. They researched the extent to which people who placed their relationships in each of these categories engaged together in a range of activities at work, subdivided into more work-related and more personal activities. Typical work-related activities would be showing the other person something, or asking or giving advice about a task. Personal activities would include chatting casually, joking with the other person or asking or giving personal advice. Argyle and Henderson found that the closer the perceived relationship with another person, the more likely people were to engage in all types of activity with them, work-related as well as personal.

**Box 10.2**

During the late 1990s US economic boom, it was reported that 25 per cent of the American labour force worked in businesses with annual staff turnover rates of 100 per cent or over. One of the main reasons employees gave for leaving was the poor quality of their co-workers.

*Source*: *The Economist*, 15 July 2000, p. 91.

At work, individuals must relate to one another simultaneously as sources of power and influence, of resources that need to be shared and of personal satisfaction. How we 'measure' the quality of our work relationships may be based on these three aspects. Table 10.1 sets out the correspondences. During interactions, people express these fundamental aspects of their relationship to one another in

**Table 10.1 Measures of work relationships and corresponding bases of interactions**

| *Measure* | *Base* |
|---|---|
| Relative social status and differences in the degree of prominence, control, influence and activity that go with it | Power and influence |
| Solidarity, pulling together to achieve a common goal or maintain a common commitment in the face of competition | Limited, shared resources |
| Person-to-person socio-emotional satisfaction, which involves relative closeness or intimacy rather than distance and impersonality | Personal satisfaction |

non-verbal behaviour, in how actively they participate in group discussions and in the way they address one another. For example, there is a great difference between the three greetings, 'Hi, Bill', 'Good morning, Bill' and 'Good morning, Mr Smith'. The first is familiar and egalitarian, the second conveys distance and superiority, the third distance and deference.

**Box 10.3**

**European variations in work relations**

Work relations in France have been described as primarily competitive. The French, it is said, do not seek to solve problems co-operatively or wait for a group consensus before taking action. At social events with colleagues, status remains important. In the Netherlands, in contrast, work relations are generally open and tolerant between all levels, effective co-operation is more valued than individual performance and concern for 'other face' is high. However, covert rivalry exists there as elsewhere. In Spain, work relationships are highly valued and often marked by trust and friendship. Similarly, in some Italian organisations, especially the large number of family businesses, work relationships go beyond the contractual to engage the emotions and a high sense of commitment. In others, colleagues can be mainly rivals, but on individual projects will co-operate well if given a chance to demonstrate their own skills.

## Work communication

Patterns of communication have a strong influence on all work relationships. There are significant differences between vertical and horizontal communication and the relative importance of these in turn depends, as Chapter 2 showed, on organisational structures and cultures. Downward communication in traditional organisations consists largely of job directives, feedback on performances, statements of organisational policies and practices and such information about the broader corporate picture as those higher up feel it appropriate for their subordinates to know. Much of this is transmitted impersonally, in newsletters or round-robin memoranda, and it is difficult for its originators to know how it is interpreted or received. Information or instructions that are passed person-to-person down the chain of command are also subject to distortion. There is thus a considerable gap in knowledge and understanding between superiors and subordinates, though it is often underestimated by both parties. Upward communications, too, are often inaccurate, especially when senders are keen to be promoted, do not trust their supervisor or feel insecure. Bad news is often likely to be ill received and may reflect on the competence of the person who brings it. For this reason, it is often delayed and distorted. Supervisors and managers are told what they want to hear, when they are thought to be in a good mood to hear it.

It might be expected that workers would often seek help from the most knowledgeable and experienced person available, their immediate supervisor. It has been found, however, that it is more common for help to be sought from equals, apparently because this avoids loss of reputation.[8] People at lower levels do, however, like to be consulted, to air their grievances and have their ideas heard at higher levels.[9] It is found in US firms that 41 per cent of messages sent or received by line production managers are with other managers at the same level. These contacts with other departments are needed to get the work done and may be quicker than using official channels, but they involve conflicts of interest, so people try to protect themselves. The protective devices they use include appealing to rules or a common authority, evading the rules (e.g. by ignoring requests), relying on friendships or past or future favours, using political allies, persuading, showing the other person the nature of the problem and trying to change the work-flow or other aspects of the organisational arrangements in an advantageous way.[10]

Matrixes, federations, networks and adhocracies require high levels of communication so that information and expertise can be pooled. High levels of communication are also needed for issues or ideas to be discussed by the members of the teams that mainly compose these organisations. On the other hand more of the communication required is 'natural' in the sense of arising out of the joint task. This contrasts with traditional organisations where more of it consists of reporting back, supplying information to managers or passing policy statements down the line, the usefulness of which is often unclear to those who have to do it.

There are cultural differences in work communication expectations. When Sheryl Lindsley[11] studied Mexican communication in US-owned assembly plants in Mexico (*maquiladoras*), she found that while Mexicans perceive 'stability' and 'trust' as organising constructs contributing to satisfying work relationships, they evaluate US communicative behaviours as eroding these core ideals.

## Work role behaviour

In work relationships, such as those between sales staff and customers, or between managers and subordinates, those concerned interact partly as individual personalities but also as occupants of positions and performers of roles. The term 'position holders' describes members of an organisation in terms of their responsibilities and rights. Examples are secretary, production manager and wages clerk. For every position there is a role, that is a pattern of behaviour that is both typical of the people in that position and expected of them. Work roles primarily include the requirements of the job – the task to be performed, the way it should be done and the speed and quality required. (In many organisations, a large part of people's work roles are formalised in job descriptions.) Work roles may also, however, include broader aspects of behaviour, such as verbal and non-verbal ways of behaving towards people in other positions, clothes or uniforms worn and style of life outside work, such as the kind of car to drive and where to have lunch. To make clear what their particular role is, people adopt role signs, which include what colour and style of clothes they wear. Office size, decor and furniture are role signs that will probably be determined for them by the organisation. These fine distinctions can be irritating, but without them there can be confused or differing expectations of roles, known as role ambiguity. This leads to uncertainty about the scope of responsibility and others' expectations, and can lead in turn to insecurity and lack of confidence. However, increasing informality in the workplace, such as wearing 'smart casual', is eroding some former distinctions.

The pressure to conform to a role can be very strong but higher-status roles are less programmed. Sometimes individuals are exposed to role pressures from others that differ from their own beliefs about their role. This can lead to role conflict, which can also result from being required to carry out more than one role at the same time, where the requirements of one role are incompatible with those of the other. Role conflict or role overload, which results from having too much work, can lead to role stress. Role stress most affects people who carry responsibility for the work of others, or who work in innovative functions that produce conflicting priorities or in roles that span boundaries between departments and organisations. Low sociability, emotional sensitivity and perceived flexibility (which leads to more people applying pressure) are personality factors linked to role stress. Role stress causes tension, low morale and communication difficulties. It significantly diminishes interactive work performances. On the other hand, some individuals get satisfaction from multiple roles that allow them to exert influence and display status.[12]

## Work norms

To maintain good relations with colleagues, people at work need to know and in general obey the 'rules' or norms governing interactions as well as those governing other aspects of the work. Among other matters, interaction norms are likely to cover how the right to speak should be allocated, how long speakers can legitimately hold the floor, when they can fairly be interrupted, what subjects can and cannot be raised, what counts as an offence for which apology is due, how disagreements will be settled, how decisions will be taken and so on. Work discussions and meetings proceed more smoothly when they are governed by such a set of norms. In work relationships, norms help resolve interpersonal problems and avoid conflicts over such matters as helping, how rewards should be divided and how work should be allocated. There are norms about such matters as clothes and language, such as the use of swearing, private slang and jargon.

Norms are not usually set up by open discussion. In new organisations they are usually those accepted by the founders, or they may be worked out in a series of disputes about concrete issues. When these are settled, either by agreement between the contestants or by other members intervening, they become precedents that eventually become norms. Afterwards, the norms become standards to which members of the organisation, including new members joining it, are expected to conform. Conforming to norms is rewarded, for example by being accepted, but breaching them is punished. Most people initially comply externally with the norms of the organisations they join in order to be accepted, but later 'internalise' them so that breaches make them feel ill at ease with themselves. Learning, expectations, sanctions and internalisation are key features of the ways in which norms are generated and operated. The more agreed-upon the norms, and the more they are adhered to, the lower the costs and the higher the rewards of organisational membership for individuals who find these norms acceptable and, generally, the more productive the organisation. Not surprisingly, organisations for which members feel little loyalty, or to which they have little motivation to belong, tend to have more difficulty in getting their norms adhered to.

Apart from those governing the details of face-to-face behaviour, there are some common norms governing interactions in many work or business settings. Some of the more important of these are fairness, reciprocity, reasonableness and role expectations.

### *Fairness*

'That's always the problem – to devise an incentive scheme that is fair and is seen to be fair, so that you don't get a salesman who gets thoroughly demotivated because he comes off badly out of it.' This remark, made by a sales manager, illustrates how important fairness can be in organisations. There is some evidence that behaving fairly is applied to the self and also expected of others. Not behaving equitably causes distress to the perpetrator and is punished in others.[13] Recognising that there is a general fairness norm does not have to mean believing that people are generally unselfish. The norm could be sustained by people's belief that they will be punished for acting unfairly and rewarded in the long run for equitable behaviour. Equity theory, explained in Chapter 3, entails certain predictions about fairness expectations. For instance, if the potential outcomes for all members of a work group are equal, the group will expect less effort from an experienced member who is able to contribute, and in fact does so contribute, by virtue of their experience than from one who is inexperienced in the task confronting the group. The operation of the equity norm all depends, though, on what are regarded as inputs and outputs by the people involved.

Breaches of the equity norm may be redressed either by compensation or, when no exact compensation is possible, when no future meeting with the 'victim' is expected and the 'victim' cannot retaliate, by self-justification. So, for instance, if Daphne's bonus is low although she worked extremely hard, because the rest of her work group was slow and idle, they are likely to try to compensate her. They might work harder in the next period, or make some gesture of friendship. If, however, Daphne leaves and moves away as soon as the bonus is declared, the other work group members when they discuss the matter will probably make excuses such as, 'We couldn't help it. After all, that was when the machines kept breaking down/the accounts department kept making errors/the 'flu epidemic struck.' It is likely, however, that work groups more frequently enforce compensation for breaches of the fairness norm by one member against another, than is the case in social life generally.[14]

### *Reciprocity*

Reciprocity means that the right of person A against person B implies a duty of person A towards person B. (The commonplace notion that if you take you should give is close enough.) However, the concrete demands made by the reciprocity norm vary from one situation to another. In particular, how it operates depends on what the recipient of a favour considers to be the donor's motives.[15] For example, the author's research among business executives showed that most of them treated the norm as not applying in most business relations because they thought that there were usually ulterior motives for apparently generous actions by trading partners. In one instance a consignment sent by post had gone missing. The customer had not notified the supplier within the time stipulated but the supplier replaced it without a quibble. The customer's reaction was that the supplier had done this 'to keep our goodwill' and implied that this meant that they (the customer) were under no obligation to reciprocate in any way. Even where it was recognised as applying, the norm seemed to dictate that some reciprocal act was required, but not necessarily an equivalent one. Finally, most respondents seemed much more inclined to apply the norm in evaluating other people's behaviour than in regulating their own.

Gouldner,[16] who made a close study of reciprocity, saw its flexibility as an advantage. He thought it meant that it could provide a moral sanction for transactions that would otherwise not be covered by any guiding principle. Gouldner also considered that reciprocity is a virtually universal and very strong norm, and that many social relationships would be unstable without it. His reason was that without it the more powerful parties in relationships would behave exploitatively more often than they in fact do and so increase the probability that the weaker parties would break off the relationship. Applying the reciprocity norm to restrict power exercises by others was mentioned in Chapter 9.

Reciprocity norms encourage people to initiate contacts. Opening up an exchange is likely to be seen as risky, as the other person may be rude or frosty, but if the norm of reciprocity is well established there is a better chance that people who are approached in a friendly way will be friendly too. Buunk and Schaufeli[17] reviewed research showing the importance of reciprocity for mental health and well-being in a wide range of relationships from marital to organisational employees. Lack of reciprocity was shown to be associated with burnout, loneliness, marital dissatisfaction and depression. Because it appears so important, these authors suggest that a basic psychological mechanism is involved, perhaps rooted in evolution. Despite these large claims it would be unwise to place too much reliance on the reciprocity norm. It undoubtedly takes experience to know what to do or what to expect in different cultures or sub-cultures, and certainly in Western urban societies its effects can be quite limited.

#### *Reasonableness*

The author's own research found that business executives show some belief in a norm of reasonableness. For instance, they might believe that if customers, no matter how powerful, are behaving 'unreasonably' they may be shamed into changing their ways. Unreasonableness means inflicting significant undeserved damage on another party or over-exploiting a power position. An example of the latter would be taking excessive credit, through late payment, from a supplier who really needs the business. In the case referred to, this behaviour was regarded as even more unreasonable because the customer knew that the supplier had previously had to pay the duty on the goods (spirits) for which extended credit was being taken. This norm may act as a brake on the exercise of power in circumstances where reciprocity would not apply.

#### *Role expectations*

Finally, role expectations have most of the characteristics of norms. In fact some authors consider that roles are 'a special case of norms'.[18] Like norms, role expectations tend to be enforced by the behaviour of others, who give rewards for conformity and punishments for flagrant breach. However, where most norms are rules that apply to all members of a group, particular role expectations apply only to a subset. Role expectations are more likely to be rigid in traditional, hierarchical organisations and between managers and subordinates rather than lateral colleagues. Equipped with formal authority, higher status and higher

**Table 10.2 Cultural values and work norms**

| *Cultural values* | *Work norms* |
|---|---|
| High power distance | Penalties for breaches apply more to lower members; higher ones are 'above the law'; norms are imposed by leaders rather than emerge by consensus |
| High masculinity | Norm adherence is more enforced and methods of norm enforcement are more punitive |
| High uncertainty avoidance | Norms are more rigid with less scope for different interpretations |
| High collectivism | There is special emphasis on norms concerned with loyalty to the group; treatment of in-group and out-group members differs |

power, managers can often impose their role expectations on their subordinates, even when this produces the seeming illogicality of imposing participation. Where role expectations are generally firm, but unclear in particular instances, as between non-line seniors and juniors in some bureaucracies, there is more scope for role ambiguity and role stress. In more fluid organisations of the newer type, while the lack of clear role expectations does not suit all types of personality, some enjoy the scope and the opportunity to negotiate and change their role.

Work roles and norms are extensively affected by cultural values. High power distance leads to steep hierarchies and narrow spans of control (and vice versa for low power distance). High uncertainty avoidance leads to strict adherence to job descriptions and formality (and vice versa for low uncertainty avoidance), individualism to an emphasis on personal responsibility, collectivism to an emphasis on group responsibility, high achievement orientation to prioritising task completion, high relationship orientation to concern with maintaining relationships. Table 10.2 shows the effects of different cultural values on work norms.

## SUMMARY – THE NATURE OF WORK RELATIONSHIPS

Interdependence theory helps explain important aspects of relationships, such as people's level of commitment, which is seen as a function of their satisfaction with their outcomes and equal to their outcomes plus inputs (or 'investments') minus their best alternative. To deal with the complexity of relationships, people develop social orientations or habitual solutions to interactive problems or situations.

Although work relationships develop out of the need to co-operate and co-ordinate over tasks, they come to acquire social and psychological meanings for work colleagues. How friendly two colleagues are has been shown to be reflected in the extent of their work-related as well as their personal interaction, while the perceived quality of work relationships is linked to how far they meet affiliation and power needs as well as those for resources.

Good communication both vertically and horizontally is vital to effective work in organisations but in hierarchies and bureaucracies is often undermined by self-protective behaviours. New forms of organisation make more demands on the communication skills of members but may benefit from making fewer attempts to impose artificial communication patterns.

Work interactions are constrained by work roles and norms. For any organisational position there is a work role, which is an accepted set of expectations about how the work will be done and about related aspects of behaviour. Pressure to conform to roles is considerable, though less for people of higher status. Role ambiguity, role conflict and role overload can make working life stressful and impair the interactive behaviour of those affected. Norms are implicit rules governing how to behave.[19] In most work organisations there are norms about fairness, reciprocity and reasonableness among others. Role expectations also function like norms. Paths at work are eased for those who are aware of the organisation's norms, as they are able to avoid the sanctions for unintended breaches and to bring normative pressure to bear to influence the behaviour of their colleagues.

## CO-OPERATION, COMPETITION, CONFLICT AND CONFLICT RESOLUTION

Co-operation is working together to maximise joint outcomes, competition is the attempt to maximise own outcomes relative to the other. Some influential writers have argued that co-operation is as natural a human and animal activity as competition is, and perhaps more essential to survival and growth for both the individual and his or her larger grouping. On the other hand, if people are aiming at maximising their personal outcomes (as some people at work undoubtedly do and as some theories of rationality say they should), they will frequently be motivated to compete, as there are situations where they can gain more from taking a larger share of the 'cake' than from helping to enlarge it. The structuralist writer Edward Lawler has pointed out that in some long-term relationships there is a continuous struggle for power, which leads to constant competition or conflict. Moreover, the motivation to compete is often amplified in organisations where, for instance, the hierarchy leads to competition for promotion.[20]

### Co-operative behaviour

Behaving co-operatively implies acting with openness, interacting flexibly but without springing surprises, not defending weak positions, considering new ideas on their merits, not on the basis of who originated them, and trying to improve work relationships. Many of the norms adopted by co-workers are designed to support co-operative behaviour, as the list given in Table 10.3 clearly

**Table 10.3 Rules for co-workers**

1. Accept one's fair share of the workload.
2. Respect others' privacy.
3. Be co-operative with regard to the shared physical working conditions (e.g. temperature, light, noise).
4. Be willing to help when requested.
5. Keep confidence.
6. Work co-operatively despite feelings of dislike.
7. Do not denigrate co-workers to superiors.
8. Address the co-worker by first name.
9. Ask for advice and help when necessary.
10. Look the co-worker in the eye during conversations.
11. Do not be overinquisitive about each other's private lives.
12. Repay debts, favours and compliments, no matter how small.
13. Do not engage in sexual activity with the co-worker.
14. Stand up for the co-worker in his or her absence.
15. Do not criticise the co-worker publicly.

*Source*: Argyle, M. and N. Henderson (1985) *The Anatomy of Relationships*. London: Heinemann and Penguin.

shows. Naturally these 'rules' were not pinned up on the notice-board, but that did not prevent them being powerful.[21] However, it could be that the need for powerful norms to support co-operative behaviour at work itself indicates that strong forces often pull in the direction of competition or conflict. Like most types of social interaction, work can give rise to situations where either co-operative or competitive behaviour may be appropriate.

Co-operative behaviour is not most appropriate when there is only a limited amount of reward available, such that if one person wins another must lose. It is most appropriate when it is possible for all participants to achieve their goals, and especially when if one person achieves his or her goal, the others may also gain. This suggests that co-operation is more often needed within organisations than competitiveness.

Trust can be considered as an essential underpinning for co-operative behaviour. Trust is the expectation by one person, group or firm that the other person, group or firm in a joint endeavour or economic exchange will not act in a way that will cause them painful consequences.[22] Trust is a component of organisational social capital, which was explained in Chapter 2. Trust is both an antecedent to and a result of successful collective action. It is needed if people are to work on common projects but also likely to be increased if they work together successfully.[23] Fragile or instrumental trust, based on the likelihood of rewards, can be distinguished from resilient trust, based on stronger and more numerous links, which can survive some transactions in which benefits and costs are not balanced. Fragile trust is concerned with developing a workable strategy of reciprocity, but resilient trust rests upon ongoing reciprocity norms. Equally, dyadic trust, between two parties who have direct knowledge of one another, is different from generalised trust that rests on affiliation or reputation.

Is it wise to trust others? Trustfulness may be a sign of discernment or 'social intelligence', not gullibility. For people who are good judges of character, sensitive to reliable signals of trustworthiness and wise to fraudulent imitations, it pays to trust. Indiscriminate distrustfulness is prudent only for the undiscerning. Some theorists, generalising from the example of reputation, claim that trust will flourish wherever people have good information and effective incentives to be trustworthy. Others argue that trust is deeply ingrained within a culture and is inherited, not calculated, by members of that culture. The corollary is that there are cultures where trust is widely lacking.[24] Dirks[25] found that in high-trust relationships motivation is transformed into joint efforts, in low-trust relationships into individual efforts. For example, distrust might cause individuals to be distrustful towards co-workers because of the perceived risks of co-operating. This anxiety, in turn, would be likely to cause individuals to lose focus on achieving the group outcome as they attempted to protect themselves by monitoring their co-workers' actions, focusing on personal success and so on. They might re-orient towards personal goals away from group goals that could be impeded by fellow workers. Parks and Hulbert[26] found that high trusters co-operate even when they risk receiving no pay-off from doing so but low trusters are less likely to co-operate in these circumstances.

There are instrumental arguments in favour of fostering trust. A moral commitment to trustworthiness is a less costly way to control opportunism (self-interest-seeking with guile) than by monitoring or performance incentives. However, to Wicks *et al.*[27] trust is a conditional good. They argue that it is possible to trust too much or invest in trusting relationships that have little value for the firm with the result that resources are misallocated. Optimal trust, they say, exists within prudent economic relationships biased by a willingness to trust. Optimal trust is shaped by a variety of factors, such as trustworthiness of the agent and local or broader social norms concerning trust, etc. 'The willingness of managers to create mutually trusting relationships is a matter of strategic choice. That is, managers can, through their behavior, help determine levels of trust in relationships between the firm and its various stakeholders.' Charles Handy,[28] despite considering the 'problem of trust' as impeding full acceptance of new technology, also regards trust as conditional. He argues that there are rules for trust. It is not blind, needs boundaries, demands learning (change), is tough (gets rid of those who do not match expectations), needs bonding, requires leaders and also requires small organisational units – a person can know a maximum of only 50 people well enough to trust them.

## Competitive behaviour

Many work situations are mixed and the people involved have mixed motives. They want the organisation to succeed but they also want to get their own way. 'Selfish' motives can lead people to compete against their colleagues, especially if for them personally competitive behaviour will reap greater advantages, even though for the organisation as a whole the outcome is worse. Second, difficulty in anticipating the behaviour of others leads to competitiveness. If others are about to behave in a competitive way, this may make the situation one where co-operative behaviour will lead to losses for the individual. Co-operating requires people to trust one another, and trust takes time to build up. Competition can be beneficial, leading people to try harder and be more creative. Misplaced competitiveness, however, leads to behaving secretively, springing surprises, using threats and bluffs, defending all positions, if necessary by non-rational arguments, and derogating rivals.[29] When people do engage in misplaced competitive behaviour, both the organisation and individuals suffer. The opposing members are seen as inferior, judgement is distorted, so that 'own' contributions are seen as better than others, and there is a tendency to think that others' points of view are understood, when in fact they are not. They are distorted in a polarised way and areas of common ground often go unrecognised.

**Box 10.4**

In non-intimate (e.g. work) relationships, women rated their male opponent in a conflict as less co-operative and more competitive, whereas men rated their female opponent as more co-operative and less competitive. However, as the authors pointed out, these ratings may be strongly influenced by men's and women's different stereotypes.

*Source*: Kluwer, E. S., C. K. W. de Dreu and B. P. Buunk (1998) 'Conflict in intimate vs non-intimate relationships: When gender role stereotyping overrides biased self-other judgment', *Journal of Social and Personal Relationships*, vol. 15, no. 5, pp. 637–650.

## Conflict and conflict resolution

When work relationships break down, it can be hard to restore peace. Neither party may wish to make overtures of peace, because doing so can seem like a concession involving a loss of face. The result, on the job as in private life, can be that for long periods people fail to work together or communicate. Sometimes other people get dragged into the dispute as supporters of those in contention. Then rivalry and conflict between groups is set up. For instance, a consultant who analysed the Research and Development Department of a well-known electronics manufacturer found that an entire group of six research scientists for several years regularly walked round three sides of a hollow square building. Their reason was that they did not want to walk through the open-plan offices on the fourth side of the square. It turned out that this was where their 'enemy' group worked. It is not difficult to imagine how this disrupted the work of the organisation. Thus, as well as co-operation and competition, there can be a lot of conflict in organisations. The difference between competition and conflict can be kept clear by thinking of competition as a race and conflict as a war. In both the parties are trying to win, but whereas in competition they will not actively hurt the other, in conflict they will. Conflict can be defined as 'the tension between two or more social entities – individuals, groups or larger organisations – which arises from the incompatibility of actual or desired responses'.[30] This definition is useful because it emphasises the communication aspect of conflict, which is important. Also it does not limit the subject to open conflict. The tensions between two people may be significantly affecting their behaviour without emerging in the form of a stand-up or verbal fight. Hunt's[31] description of conflict is also helpful because it draws attention to the role of perception in conflict: 'Interpersonal conflict occurs between two or more persons when attitudes, motives, values, expectations or activities are incompatible and if those people perceive themselves to be in disagreement.' Adjusting communication and changing perceptions are key elements in resolving conflict face-to-face. Both the definitions of conflict given above are broad enough to include conflicts of interest, which occur when one person or group cannot gain an objective in its entirety except at the expense of other persons or groups. The term 'interest' covers a broad range of objectives: profit, advantage, concern, right or claim. Conflicts of interest can inhibit creative, high-quality decision-making.

**Box 10.5**

In a committee meeting, tempers exploded under a surface of control. The first agenda item, to do with arrangements for a foreign visitor, passed peacefully. The next agenda item, to all appearances equally innocuous, concerned an application for funding for a training project in the former USSR. The Head of the Department (HoD) that had made the application reported as follows: 'We put in an application at very short notice, not really expecting to succeed in this case, but wanting to put down a marker that we are active in this area.'

Then someone from another department commented, 'I am afraid that we did ourselves no good at all by this application, which was a weak one. Really we showed how weak a basis we have for doing work in this area, and that is why I wrote a memorandum criticising it.'

Most committee members had not seen this memorandum, which apparently was circulated only to the chairperson of the committee and the aforesaid HoD, who quickly replied, 'I would like to say that I thought that memo was extremely unhelpful. A great deal of work had gone into that application, under acute time pressure, and to receive negative comments when it is too late to do anything is demotivating for staff, to say the least.'

'I did offer at our last meeting to help with the application.'

'And I accepted your offer; however, as I wrote in my memo replying to yours, the member of staff who drafted the application told me that you made no attempt to contact her, although you must have known that the deadline had been reached, and you never responded to the messages she left on your answerphone.'

Here the chairperson intervened, saying that in future memos should not be used to conduct slanging matches but only to record agreements reached face-to-face. The meeting moved on. All knew, however, that this was merely an episode in a long history of antagonism between these two combatants.

*Source*: Interview, author's research.

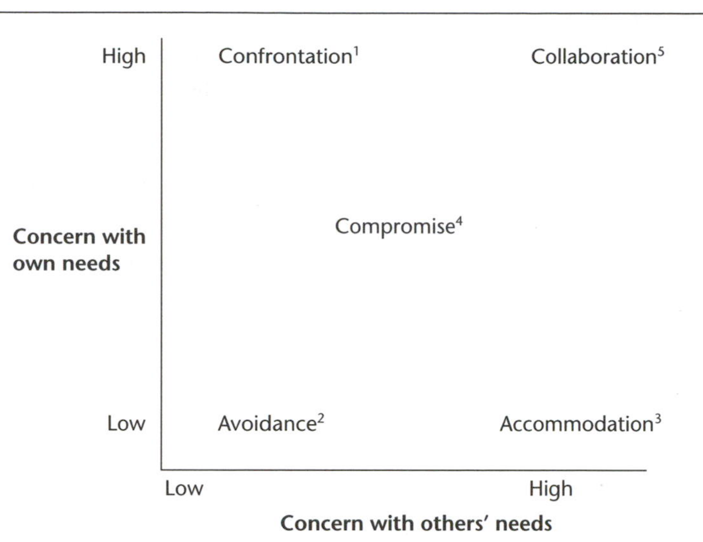


1. Confrontation involves, for example, demanding apologies from others and redress of perceived wrongs.
2. Avoidance means refusing to acknowledge that a problem exists, while reducing interaction with the other persons as far as possible.
3. Accommodation means apologising and conceding the issue to the other person regardless of the 'rights and wrongs' of the matter.
4. Compromise means bargaining, explicitly or implicitly, with the other person until a compromise is reached.
5. Collaboration involves an approach that treats the conflict as a problem that the parties need to solve together.

**Figure 10.1 Five conflict-handling styles.**

*Source*: Adapted from Thomas, K. W. (1976) 'Conflict and conflict management' in M. D. Dunette (ed.) *Handbook of Industrial and Organization Psychology*. Chicago, Ill.: Rand McNally. With permission from Houghton Mifflin Co.

Whatever its source, how those involved in conflict handle it affects its outcome. Blake and Mouton[32] set out a two-dimensional model of conflict handling based on concern for self and concern for others. The two dimensions frame five styles of conflict management – forcing, confrontation, compromise, withdrawal and smoothing – each differing in its location along one or both dimensions. K. W. Thomas[33] identified different conflict-handling styles used by different individuals and showed that people's tendency to adopt one style rather than another is a function of how concerned they are with meeting their own and other people's needs. Figure 10.1 illustrates the five styles and their relationship to concern with needs. Confrontation, avoidance and accommodation are all, in their different ways, undesirable, tending to reinforce the conflict and create more ill-feeling, to prolong it below the surface or to encourage further aggression in others. Both compromising and collaborative styles are more effective than these, though in compromises there is the well-known danger that the actual compromise agreed on will be the worst of all worlds.

Nicotera[34] labelled three different dimensions of the ways in which individuals approach conflict as 'attention to one's own view', 'attention to the views of others' and 'relational disruptiveness'. These dimensions are independent. It is possible to have an approach that is high in attention both to one's own view and to the views of others. Her research showed that in terms of these dimensions many individuals seem to follow particular sequences of conflict-handling behaviours as interaction over a conflict proceeds, regardless of the responses of the other party. Typical individual sequences are:

- starting and remaining high on attention to own-view, while switching on attention to other-view and relational disruptiveness;
- beginning low and switching to high on attention to own-view;
- starting and remaining low on attention to other-view, while switching on attention to own view and relational disruptiveness;
- starting high and switching to low on attention to other-view;
- changing from disruptive to non-disruptive or starting and remaining non-disruptive as the other dimensions change.

However, King and Miles[35] found evidence that contradicts the idea of personal conflict styles that remain stable across situations. Instead they found that people's conflict management choices depend on the interplay of the individual and, especially, the context. Their research was only exploratory but their findings seem to correspond to the idea of Knapp *et al.*[36] that conflict-handling research should consider all the following factors: the interdependence of the parties, 'subtle and rigid patterns of interlocking behaviour', the dynamic, fluid, non-rational nature of conflict and how it is influenced by both individual differences and context, larger frameworks than 'concern for self and others' and the organisation as the centre stage of conflict activity. Other research has shown that in conflict situations full-time and long-term employees are much more likely to use verbalisation responses than part-time or short-term employees are. The response to superior–subordinate conflict is more likely than others to be helplessness or verbalisation; when both parties are male, the response is more likely to be competitive. Findings such as these support the idea that the context influences conflict behaviour.[37]

People involved in workplace conflicts often talk to co-workers and outsiders as a means of making sense of the situation. How often and when people discuss workplace conflicts with third parties is affected by the relative power of the participants and how intense the conflict is. Low-power workers are more likely to consult both inside and outside and to do it earlier, especially internally. This is probably because they stand to gain support by pre-empting moves by their opponents, whereas managers would lose face as their position is supposed to allow them to resolve conflicts. Higher conflict intensity is associated with consulting outsiders, probably because such outsiders are free of the hierarchy and politics of the organisation and can be counted on to give emotional support. Consulting outsiders is associated with higher assertiveness and lower co-operativeness on the part of the disputant.[38] Emotion plays a major part in fuelling and sustaining conflict, including those in organisational settings. Gayle and Preiss[39] analysed reported memories of work-related conflicts discussed by 174 employees and supervisors from 11 different companies. Participants recalled more emotional interactions when they judged conflicts as unresolved, remembered conflicts as related events, or noted discussing conflicts with other employees who were also involved. Participants also typically recalled conflict interactions as emotionally intense when participants were supervisors or if others involved were administrators. As Gayle and Preiss pointed out, recalled emotions associated with past conflicts can influence future conflict interactions and organisational relations generally. Cloven and Roloff[40] found that in major conflicts 'mulling' over disputes and arguing over them increased the perceived severity of conflicts and the likelihood of blaming, whereas talking to one another often and doing things together reduced these negative effects.

Writers on conflict often argue that conflict is both inevitable and constructive. Franz and Jin,[41] for example, showed by research the importance of conflict in facilitating learning and building consensus during the stages of group development of an information system. It can lead to more creative solutions to problems and can force people to tackle socio-emotional issues, so clearing the air for more concentrated attention on tasks. Managers, we are told, should not automatically attempt to eliminate conflict. There are, however, two difficulties: a good deal of conflict is destructive, and even constructive conflict often feels acutely uncomfortable both to the participants and to the onlookers. Drawing a line between destructive and constructive conflict is not always easy, because it depends on the situation and who is involved. It is often a matter of 'feel' or instinctive recognition. Here, though, is a guide to when conflict may be, or may be becoming, destructive:

- When there is a threat of a whole organisation or group disintegrating or splitting into camps.
- When the goals of the organisation or group are being subverted by the conflict.
- When one member is being attacked persistently, either by a coalition of several other members or by one who is exploiting a power or position advantage. The person under attack may be prevented by differences in power and status from defending themself. He or she may be provoked into lying – deliberate distortion to preserve position or save face – or may withdraw by sulking or pretending to lose interest. Such conflict is always destructive, but especially so if the person being attacked could otherwise contribute skill or information needed for a task.

- When the conflict, no matter how constructive initially, goes on too long without progress towards being settled. Participants in conflict typically dispute many facets of the conflict process, not just the substantive issue – for instance, values, goals, facts and processes. Conflict can be very disturbing to some people's self-esteem and sense of identity.
- When one or both of the parties are culturally disposed to see conflict as destructive. Many people from collectivist cultures seek harmony in relationships as a fundamental value and for them the concept of constructive conflict is entirely alien.

How can conflicts be resolved? There is a theory, the contact hypothesis, that states that increased contact between actually or potentially disputing parties may lead to better understanding and hence to reduced conflict. Even as originally proposed by Allport,[42] this was not a simplistic hypothesis. The quality as well as the quantity of contact was understood to be important. Quality referred to status and role aspects and to the social atmosphere surrounding the contact, whether equal or unequal, forced or voluntary, superficial or intimate, competitive or co-operative. Moreover, where prejudice was involved in conflict, it was recognised that the contact situation needed to have four main characteristics before it would lead to positive change. These were that the parties had equal status, shared goals, co-operative interdependence (i.e. neither party being able to achieve their goals independently of the other) and socially authorised interaction. However, later work qualified the contact hypothesis. Contact enhances existing processes. Hostile attitudes may become more extreme through contact.[43] The outcome depends on the prior situation – some lead to trust, others to distrust.[44]

Many conflicts respond well to attempts to find integrative solutions, which means the following. The disputants try to create solutions jointly rather than to force a predetermined position or simply accept the partner's position in order to avoid confrontation. They also link their objectives with those of their opponent, eschew destructive personal attacks and offer persuasive arguments.[45] For conflict participants to pursue integrative solutions in these tactics, they must also meet the cognitive requirements, which include:

- seeing conflict situations as having many perspectives, motives and interpretations;
- thinking about the opponent's perspectives and goals;
- anticipating likely opponent actions;
- retrieving from memory multiple specific and effective arguments;
- constructing new arguments 'on-line' to accommodate to opponents and integrate their concerns;
- developing contingency plans.

Such requirements point to the likelihood that cognitively complex participants in conflict are more likely to pursue integrative tactics. However, Waldron and

Applegate[46] found that the use of integrative tactics was not closely linked to cognitive complexity but to how complex, specific and sophisticated the participants' conflict planning was.

Edgar Schein[47] is an authority on organisational behaviour who has looked at the question of how to repair our work relationships after breakdown. The main requirement is to come to terms with our own psychological blockages. Being afraid that unpleasant events will be repeated may often prevent us from starting to build bridges. For instance, we may be afraid that when we make an overture, such as a friendly or helpful remark, to someone else, we will be snubbed. Alternatively, it may seem easier to blame others than to work out how to renegotiate relationships with them.

There are cultural variations in conflict and conflict resolution. Studies have shown considerable variation in how people from different backgrounds behave when they are at loggerheads. German adolescents prefer confrontational styles of conflict resolution whereas Indonesian adolescents prefer submissive styles. Culture over-rides gender. The normative expectations – accepting responsibility for others in Indonesia, growing independence in Germans – are similar for both genders.[48] Black North Americans tend to use more controlling styles and strategies than do American whites,[49] Chinese use more passive strategies than North Americans, Japanese people prefer collaborative, face-saving styles, Yugoslavians value the equality norm and prefer a compromise style, while North Americans prefer a competitive style, consistently with their competitive values. People from collectivist countries show more conflict avoidance than those from individualist countries.[50] Confrontation is used more frequently in Western societies, whereas more subtle negotiation strategies are preferred, in, for example, Japan. More 'feminine' societies, such as the Swedish, prefer harmony-enhancing procedures, such as mediation and negotiation, over confrontational procedures, such as threats and accusations.

A study that compared Latino(a) and European Americans showed that:

- whether people have independent or interdependent self-concepts is a better predictor of their conflict styles than ethnic/cultural background itself;
- dominating conflict styles are associated with independent self-concepts while avoiding, obliging and compromising conflict styles are associated with interdependent self-concepts;
- integrating conflict styles are associated strongly and positively with interdependent self-concepts and weakly but still positively with independent self-concepts.[51]

Conflict is a communication process, and therefore requires active face-work. In individualist, low-context cultures, such as the United States and Western Europe, people often fight one another in a comparatively direct way. In conflict, as in other interactions, they will be mainly concerned with their own face. They

Box 10.6

## How to build bridges in conflict situations

### Overcome your own psychological barriers

- Look for new elements in the situation that you may not have noticed before: for one thing, the other people in the situation may have changed in significant ways. Other people tend to be more flexible and adaptive than our assumptions about them allow; our impressions become straitjackets or self-fulfilling prophecies. The confrontation itself is likely to have affected them in some way: often, it is true, people become more rigid after such an experience, but some may wish to change even if they lack the skill to do so.
- Look to superordinate goals around which a new set of relationships can be built. If you needed to keep in touch with this person before, you still need to even though you have quarrelled.
- Force yourself to see what happened from the other person's point of view. A friend or sympathetic colleague can often help to make this process less painful than it would otherwise be.
- A colleague who is a good listener can also be very helpful if your blockage is emotional – hurt or anger. Talking it through, if necessary over and over, blunts the edges of emotions which otherwise may prevent you being skilled in handling the repair interaction. Allowing some time to pass also helps in this, because, as Chapter 2 demonstrated, emotions tend to recede over time.
- More generally, aim to improve your own skills in conflict resolution before conflict arises, and learn how to listen, communicate, analyse issues, evaluate alternatives and make decisions more effectively than you could before. This is known as skills-based empowerment.

### Handle the situation, using an integrative approach

- Set up a meeting that is explicitly for the purpose of making the repair. This approach, which can be thought of as confronting the problem, is more likely to succeed than either evading it or attempting to build bridges in the course of other business. The best way to set up the meeting is to telephone the person with whom your relationship has broken down or intercept them in the corridor. Then say something on the lines of 'Look, Andrew, do you think we should get together to sort out why we are at loggerheads like this? I do, because it's affecting my work, and making me miserable – I very much dislike being on bad terms with colleagues.' You may need to persist to get agreement to the meeting, but usually you can get it in the end, because the other party is aware that it is unreasonable to refuse. It is important not to be dragged into discussing the cause of the dispute itself at this stage, because your objective is to get agreement to the meeting, this agreement itself being the first stage in the bridge-building process. An intermediary may be used to set up the meeting if someone really suitable is available, but this is less satisfactory because it reduces the amount of repair achieved by this first overture.
- In the meeting, allow the other person to express their negative emotions about what has happened, while keeping close control on your own. If you detect that they are in the grip of emotion which is not being expressed at the start, encourage them to bring it into the open. This may be painful for you, but is an essential first step in the bridge-building process. Make it clear that you are listening to and understanding what they say, though you do not necessarily accept that they are right.

**Box 10.6** ***continued***

- Make it clear that you do not intend the repair process to lead to further loss of face for either party.
- Treat the repair as a problem to solve jointly rather than a self-abasement: your objective is to reach agreement on a new basis for the relationship, but your offer is not unconditional. You are trying to explore differences creatively and locate some common ground but you do need to protect yourself from any attempt by the other person to exploit your overture, perhaps to gain, unfairly, the point on which you differed before. If their position was unjustified before, it remains so now, even if you do want to apologise for having lost your temper. You will need to be articulate and assertive to clarify what you are and are not conceding.

**Table 10.4 Cultural conflict-handling styles**

| | *Within same culture* | *With different culture* |
|---|---|---|
| European Americans | Dominating | Integrating/Obliging |
| Chinese Americans | Avoiding | Avoiding |
| Hong Kong Chinese | Avoiding/Obliging | Compromising/Integrating |

Based on: Khoo, G. P. S. (1994) 'The role of assumptions in intercultural research and consulting: examining the interplay of culture and conflict at work', Paper given at the David See Chai Lam Centre for International Communication Pacific Region Forum on Business and Management Communication.

will also feel a need to disassociate themselves from the other party. In collectivist, high-context cultures, people are more likely to be indirect in their struggle, concerned to preserve the other party's face and to maintain the relationship.[52] Khoo[53] found that there were marked differences in the conflict-handling styles of people from three different cultures according to whether they were in conflict with others from their own culture or from a different culture (see Table 10.4). She concluded that the ways in which culturally similar individuals behave in conflict situations cannot be simply generalised to how they will behave in conflict situations with culturally different individuals.

Third party involvement in conflict resolution is more typical for collectivist cultures. For instance, in Indian organisations, superior–subordinate conflict is typically handled by third party involvement.[54] Chinese respondents favoured mediation in response to conflict situations and considered it to be more successful in reducing hostility between the conflict partners. Turkish subjects were found to prefer to use an intermediary for negotiation, even where the conflict situation favoured co-operation, whereas US subjects chose direct communication in all cases.[55] In collectivist cultures, third party roles are significant because disputes are seen as a problem of the collectivity rather than as a problem concerning the two parties alone. This view is shared by third parties and disputants alike. Intermediaries also help save face for both parties. Concessions made in response to mediator suggestions are not seen as weak. In addition, privacy concerns are lower in collectivist cultures. On the other hand, Japanese managers have been found to perceive the level of trust to be higher when a North American partner requested a mutual conferral to resolve disputes rather than binding arbitration.[57]

To be successful in individualistic societies, intervening third parties must be expert in social processes, have little power over the personal futures of the contending individuals, have a high level of control over confrontation-settling procedures and moderate knowledge about the principles, issues and background factors. They must be neutral with respect to substantive outcomes, personal relationships and conflict-resolution procedures. Equally important, intervening third parties must be seen by the contending parties as disinterested, wise and knowledgeable. Depending on their standing and the needs of the contenders, third parties can act as arbitrators, mediators or fact-finders/reporters. As arbitrators, they choose among the contenders. This may settle the conflict, providing they are recognised as impartial and wise, but the arbitration route does little to help the self-development of the contenders. Mediation helps the parties to negotiate their own resolution, and is a clear advance, in terms of their future effectiveness, over arbitration, but still demonstrates the contenders' immaturity and inability to negotiate a resolution without mediation. Fact-finding and reporting back is the lowest level of external intervention of the three, and hence implies least about any lack of capability or trust between the contenders.

In intercultural or international disputes, conflict resolution must either overcome cultural differences or take them into account. Unilateral initiatives (UIs), such as offering concessions, may be a universally effective way to produce concessions by another party. They were used during the Cold War and found to diminish the tensions of the arms race. However, the effectiveness of such tactics depends on the impressions given, which are shaped in part by the relative power of the parties. Under equal power, UIs increase concession-making, the degree to which the other party regards the UI maker as trustworthy and the concern of the receiving party about appearing fair and trustworthy. They decrease punitive behaviour by the receiving party but also the degree to which they regard the UI maker as strong. Smaller UIs produce more concessions by the receiving party and create a higher probability of agreement than larger ones do. When used by a lower-power party, UIs are more effective than reciprocity, because the other party infers that the UI indicates that the lower-power party has begun to accept its inferior position. However, UIs are less effective than reciprocity when used by a higher-power party because, especially when following a period in which the higher-power party exploited their strength, UIs from the stronger party are distrusted.[56,57]

A conflict resolution model that aims to take cultural differences into account in international joint ventures includes the following elements:

- Align the parties' objectives.
- Ensure adequate communication between involved parties.

- Develop standard procedures for resolving conflict.
- Consider the gain of all involved parties not just own-gain maximisation.
- Express understanding of the other party's view.
- Develop high tolerance and understanding for different national cultures.
- Discuss ways to avoid future conflict.[58]

## SUMMARY – CO-OPERATION, COMPETITION, CONFLICT AND CONFLICT RESOLUTION

Much work behaviour is co-operative and many of the norms applied by co-workers are directed towards sustaining co-operation. Trust, especially generalised rather than fragile trust, underpins co-operative behaviour. Neither generalised distrust nor unconditional trust is optimal.

Both competitive behaviour and conflict are common. These can lead people to try harder and stimulate creativity, but misplaced competitiveness is harmful and conflict can easily be destructive. Some indicators were given for which types are damaging. Conflict-handling styles include confrontation, avoidance, accommodation, compromise and collaboration. Compromise and, especially, collaboration are more effective than the first three. Preferences for different conflict-handling styles seem to be culturally influenced and the same applies to conflict resolution, with people from collectivist cultures preferring third party interventions, while people from individualist cultures opt for direct methods such as confrontation. Intercultural conflict resolution may use 'universal' methods, such as offering unilateral initiatives or may attempt to take cultural difference into account, as in a model used in international joint ventures.

## DEALING WITH PREJUDICE, DISCRIMINATION AND HARASSMENT

The incidence of prejudice, discrimination and harassment at work has been described in Chapter 2. Dealing with these negative behaviours must not be seen exclusively, nor even primarily, as a problem for the victims. They are first and foremost a problem for the perpetrators and secondly for the organisation. Laws in most European countries recognise the responsibility of organisations to protect their employees against discrimination. However, in many organisations, in practice, individuals are left to cope with prejudice and harassment more or less alone.

There are no easy answers to the problems of coping with other people's discriminatory, harassing or prejudiced behaviour. Someone could follow all the advice given in Box 10.9, which is culled from a variety of sources, and still be a persistent victim and trapped by needing the job in which they are being victimised. All the same, this advice, from people who have been there, will help some people to cope.

**Box 10.7**

Karen is faced by a major problem at work. She is a woman in her mid-thirties, buying a house with a mortgage. She has to commute for an hour and a half to her job at an accommodation agency. Her problem is with her boss, who owns the agency. He has no management training. He has a very off-hand manner with everybody – in fact, in the last week one flat-owner has told Karen that if she had to deal with him she would take her business elsewhere. However, he appears to pick particularly on Karen. He is highly critical of every little thing, and especially of the fact that she has to travel so far to the job, even though to date she has always arrived on time. Today he has told her that a 'Britney Spears look-alike' wants her job. This has really frightened her. With her mortgage to pay, she needs to earn well and is afraid that 'at my age' she would be unable to get another equally well-paid job.

*Source*: Interview, author's research.

**Box 10.8**

### How to help people with disabilities (and avoid hindering them)

- Avoid using disabling language, e.g. the expression 'the disabled' which confirms stereotypes. 'People with disabilities' places the emphasis more appropriately. There is even a case for the clumsy but accurate 'differentially abled'.
- Always consider the effects of environments and individual perceptions when planning interventions.
- Emphasise abilities rather than limitations.
- Recognise the complexity of disability and consider referring to or consulting with a specialist (e.g. rehabilitation counsellor) when necessary.
- Accept that people with disabilities have the same rights to community participation as their peers without obvious disabilities.

*Source*: Humes, C. W., E. M. Szymanski and T. H. Hohenshil (1989) 'Roles of counseling in enabling persons with disabilities', *Journal of Counseling and Development*, Nov./Dec., vol. 68, pp. 145–150.

**Box 10.9**

### How to cope with prejudice, discrimination and harassment

- Establish clear parameters. Show clear and consistent commitment to your career. Take it for granted that you are entitled to equal treatment.
- You have to be better qualified, where qualifications matter, more technically competent, where that is valued, as in the computer industry, and more experienced, where experience is what counts. Getting more experience if you are in a prejudice-victim category is often difficult. (For instance, when the author joined the oil industry, sales experience was needed for career progress, and no woman was ever allowed into sales, so she left.) Many women gain experience by taking assignments others spurn, or by adopting the next recommendation (Davidson and Cooper, 1992).
- Be prepared to move on. Many people's careers get stuck, regardless of gender or ethnicity, but it happens less easily to people who expect to change jobs every three or four years, and who, if they cannot do it within their own organisation, will go outside.

**Box 10.9** ***continued***

Nine of the eleven successful women featured in Jane White's book *A Few Good Women: Breaking the Barriers to Top Management* (1992) had to change bosses within the company, leave the company or threaten to leave it in order to improve their job situations.

- Be discerning about when to get tough about prejudice and when to let the issue slide. An ambitious salesperson cannot reprimand a major client for calling her Lass or Love, however offensive she finds it.

> It's a horrible way to have to face the issues, but if a problematic person doesn't work for your company, it's not within your control to change a person who is not ready for equality. If women are going to succeed in the corporate world they have to be bright enough to recognize that there are things over which they have no power, that you can't remake the world in a moment. So the best approach is to play their game – but by your rules (Karen Reimer, Director of Corporate Transactions, Honeywell).

- Reduce your sensitivity to hostility or displays of prejudice that are not damaging. Women who act authoritatively will be seen by some as unfeminine, even butch, and treated accordingly. Members of ethnic minorities who act authoritatively will be seen by some as 'uppity'. However, both groups have to act authoritatively to get anywhere. Successful women such as Reimer often take the view that prejudice is '*their* problem, ignore it; realise that men are victims of their conditioning – it takes time and effort by men to accept women.'
- Be prepared to prove yourself over and over. You cannot rely on your job title, no matter how elevated, to establish your authority. When prejudiced men hear elevated job titles for women or members of other minorities, they downgrade the title to fit their notion of the kind of work these groups usually do, rather than upgrading their view of women or minorities (Harlan and Weiss, 1980).
- Get a mentor, a man or woman who will give you good advice, to help you think things through, and who might bring your name to the fore when opportunities arise. How? Lorraine Binion of Levi-Strauss, who is an African-American woman, suggests

> You'll run into someone at a meeting and you'll call them up and say 'I heard you say this at the meeting, it sounds interesting. Can you tell me more about it, would you mind giving me some help?' . . . You show an interest in the person's responsibilities and you ask for advice. Older men have an ego and they like acting as big brothers and giving advice. You talk to two or three people – you don't put all your eggs in one basket. Some people will be receptive, others will put you off. If they do, you just try to find someone else.

- Do not assume that all men, members of dominant ethnic groups or people without disabilities are your enemy. Frequently a woman's male colleagues will be the ones who 'blow the whistle', especially in cases of harassment, because they are affronted by the behaviour. And white men have often been the most supportive mentors for both women and members of ethnic minorities.
- Take comfort in knowing that, if you get there, seniority helps. Liz Neville, Assistant Chief Constable of Sussex in the UK at the age of 40, said in an interview in *The Times*, 'At this level, what sex you are really does not matter so much because from the point of view of other officers you are so senior, and to them removed and remote that rank gets in the way of sex.' Getting older helps women, too.
- On dealing with harassment, most women recommend starting by ignoring it, providing it is verbal and at a low level, then firmly saying, 'No' and changing the subject back to business. However, if it persists or is at a dangerous level, be prepared to confront it with

**Box 10.9** ***continued***

anger, screams, threats or whistle-blowing. Nancy Faunce, Head of Kodak Legal Systems, is quoted in Jane White's book as saying,

> If it [harassment] comes from a customer, you are forced to at least try to reason with the individual before resorting to confrontation, because your primary responsibility is to make the sale. In the beginning you try to find ways to avoid the conflict. You try to put down the behaviour without 'slamming it'. I'd head it off and then I'd talk business and I'd think 'Okay, I put it down'. And an hour later he'd bring the subject up again. It's when you reach the point two hours later when you realise diplomacy is not going to work, then you say, 'Screw you. Get out of my face.'

Figure 10.2 shows these suggestions.

*Sources*: Davidson M. and C. Cooper (1992) *Shattering the Glass Ceiling: The Woman Manager*. London: Paul Chapman.
Harlan, A. and C. Weiss (1980) *Moving Up: Women in Managerial Careers – 3rd Progress Report*. Wellesley, Mass.: Wellesley Centre for Research on Women.
White, J. (1992) *A Few Good Women: Breaking the Barriers to Top Management*. Englewood Cliffs, New Jersey: Prentice-Hall.

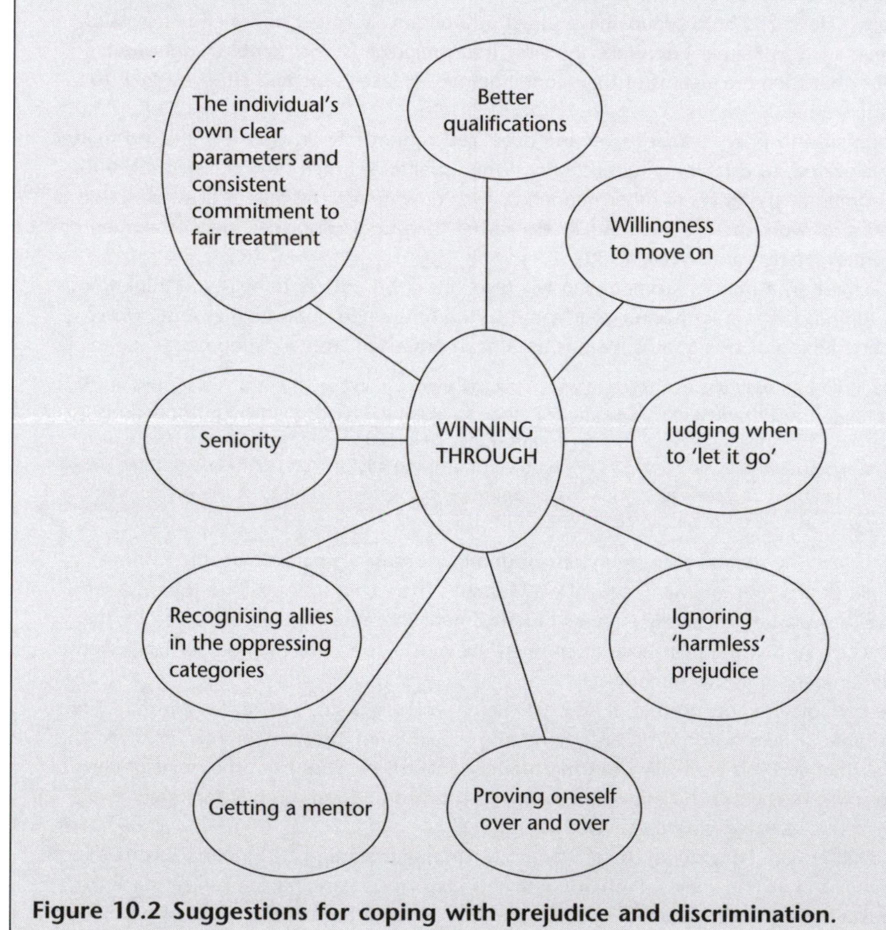


**Figure 10.2 Suggestions for coping with prejudice and discrimination.**

## SUMMARY – DEALING WITH PREJUDICE, DISCRIMINATION AND HARASSMENT

There are, unfortunately, no easy solutions to the problem of dealing with prejudice, discrimination or harassment, but we can learn from others' experience and take comfort from the fact that they've 'been there'.

## WORK APPLICATIONS FOR RELATIONSHIP SKILLS

The understanding and skills covered in this and earlier chapters are essential in all interactions which are part of a time-extended work relationship. This section provides additional guidance on giving performance feedback and reprimand interviewing, customer relations and mediating.

### Giving performance feedback

In some European countries it is part of all managers' responsibilities to help their staff improve their individual performance by recognition and guidance. They also have to ensure that staff know what the organisation expects them to achieve. Managers carry out these responsibilities by giving feedback, which can be done formally in a 'progress interview' or informally by well-timed conversations on the job. (The situation in some other European countries is shown in Box 10.10.)

**Box 10.10**

**European variations in attitudes to feedback**

In France, performance is seen as closely linked to the individual's personal qualities, so it is difficult to separate feedback from criticism. In Germany, feedback must be precise and demonstrably objective. Criticism is neither given nor received easily. In Italy, feedback is rarely given openly, as criticism is difficult for either side to manage, except in a kind of mentoring relationship. In Spain, criticism from a manager to a subordinate is seen as an exercise of power rather than useful information. Positive feedback and the reason for giving it are not understood.

Some managers find giving feedback so difficult that they shirk it altogether or do it only when forced to by the company appraisal scheme. The result can be that for long periods their subordinates have no clear idea of how they are regarded or how they could improve. Learning and job satisfaction are both endangered. In addition, when feedback is given only at the time of an annual appraisal, it is likely to be mishandled by the manager and misunderstood by the subordinate. This is because the annual appraisal is associated in both the subordinate's and the manager's minds with career prospects, so that it can be a time of anxiety. Feedback should be given fairly frequently and in a way that separates it from too close a link with career prospects. The most valuable feedback is positive feedback – praise and thanks. Recognition of the contribution they are making by their efforts motivates most people to try even harder. Reinforcing a behaviour tends to lead to it being repeated. Rewards of this kind earn the manager the 'right' to point out failures and omissions when necessary.

**Box 10.11**

Studies show that women's self-evaluations are more responsive to the evaluative feedback they receive than are men's. Men are less likely to think that others' evaluations of them are right. Women's responses may be affected by their lower status or they may be more likely to approach each situation as an opportunity to gain information about their abilities. Men may be more likely to be competitive about being evaluated and so adopt a self-confident approach that leads them to deny the evaluator's criticism.

*Source*: Roberts, T. A. (1991) 'Gender and the influence of evaluations on self-assessments in achievement settings', *Psychological Bulletin*, vol. 109, no. 2, pp. 297–308.

Feedback will only be understood and accepted if the receiver trusts the giver. One way of gaining trust is to show 'unconditional positive regard' for the other person – that is, to convey liking for them even when pointing out faults.[59] Giving feedback or progress interviewing cannot be a one-way flow. Encouraging the person receiving feedback to self-evaluate helps remove causes of conflict in these meetings. Higher commitment comes from encouraging staff to develop ways to improve their performance, because the solutions are largely their own solutions. Managers can also coach staff in analysing and solving their own performance problems. This may well be the aspect of feedback that has most impact on performance in the long run. Two-way feedback, however, means more than this. In truly open relationships between managers and their staff, informal feedback sessions can be an exchange. Subordinates report on their satisfaction with their job and the company, responses to recent changes, how well informed they feel about what is happening in the organisation and how easy they find it to get the information they need to do their job properly. Truthful answers to some of these questions will only be given when relationships between managers and their staff are based on trust; they should be sought by gentle probing based on a free flow of talk, never by insistent questioning. Some of the answers may be distasteful to the manager, perhaps reflecting badly on his or her own performance. Receiving and responding to these negative comments demand a mature approach, which is usually only available to managers who recognise and acknowledge areas of weakness in their own performance.

Formal performance reviews should be systematic. Only facts that can be substantiated should be used. For this reason, quite a bit of preparation is necessary,

**Box 10.12**

## How to give good and helpful feedback

- Base feedback on publicly observed behaviour: do not reveal secrets.
- Describe before judging. People become defensive and wary when they feel they are being judged. When giving judgements, first say something like 'It seems to me . . .' or 'Do you think it would be better if . . . ?' It is better to appear open-minded than dogmatic, although it is essential to make certain of any facts.
- Avoid blaming people for their errors or weaknesses. Instead, use 'causal analysis', which asks a series of questions to lead subordinates to see their errors or weaknesses for themselves. For instance: 'When you did X, what effect did it have?', 'Was that the effect you wanted to have?', 'What could you have done that would have produced the effect you wanted?' If the subordinate fails or refuses to name any negative consequences of his/her action, the manager has to suggest them, still in the form of questions: 'Didn't that mean that . . . ?'
- Be specific. For instance, do not say 'You are always coming to committee meetings unprepared.' Instead say, 'At the committee meetings on 5th and 12th July you were supposed to table inspection reports but you did not have them ready.'
- Be positive. Praise good work. Reward is more effective than punishment. However, on the job it is sometimes necessary to point out to people specific errors or shortcomings and learning theorists usually agree that negative feedback can sometimes be helpful in 'unfreezing' self-satisfied people to new ideas. Mix any criticism with praise. Some people recommend a 'sandwich' approach – good things first, then any necessary criticism, then pleasant conclusion. This can be a useful formula so long as it does not become routine.
- Time your feedback carefully, usually as soon as possible after the given behaviour. However, people do not want or benefit from constant comment on their performance. Fortnightly feedback may be just as effective as weekly (Chhokar and Wallin, 1984).
- Direct your feedback towards behaviour that the receiver can control. It only increases someone's frustration to be told that they were not making themself clear, when their problem is a bad stammer.
- Check to make sure that the feedback has been understood.

*Source*: Chhokar, J. S. and J. A. Wallin (1984) 'A field study of the effect of feedback frequency on performance', *Journal of Applied Psychology*, vol. 19, no. 3, pp. 524–530.

to make sure that reports and other documents are available. Documentary evidence is often needed to establish fully and get agreement on the facts but it must not be used as a weapon to bludgeon the appraisees or expose them. It needs careful handling. Performance should be reviewed under a number of headings. Under each heading, the facts must be agreed, the reasons discussed and agreed (or at worst both points of view must be understood by both parties). Then the focus should switch to the future. An action plan should be worked out and written down. The training and opportunities to gain experience that may be required to carry out the agreed action plan should be discussed and also written down. The action plan should be directed at helping the person achieve a suitable pattern of career development. Both requirements asked of the individual and the training programme should be set in this context, so as to motivate and encourage. The manager's style in the performance review should be to avoid dominating the discussion, introducing unnecessary conflict, jumping to hasty conclusions or blaming others, particularly those who are not present to defend themselves.[60]

Reprimand interviewing is best regarded as a special case of giving performance feedback, so that many of the points made earlier in this section apply. In particular, managers' reluctance to give performance feedback generally is multiplied many times when it comes to reprimanding. And yet, as Fletcher[61] put it, 'A manager who cannot reprimand is as useless as one who cannot give orders.' It is most unlikely that people who are performing badly are doing so deliberately. The individual who says to himself or herself 'I am doing this job badly/ breaking company rules and I intend to go on doing so' is a rarity, and where it occurs there is usually some deeper-seated problem. Perhaps it indicates severe loss of morale in the organisation generally, or else that the individual has personal problems. In such cases the straightforward reprimand interview is not appropriate, and the points in Box 10.13 do not apply. This means that managers should be quite sure of the circumstances before embarking on a reprimand interview. Most poor performers, however, do not acknowledge this to themselves. Instead they are almost certainly either unaware of the required behaviour, or are making excuses to themselves – placing the blame elsewhere. The manager needs to establish early in the interview, or better still beforehand, which of these problems applies, as they naturally require different treatment.

## Customer relations

In business-to-business marketing, buyer–seller relationships rather than individual transactions are key. For suppliers of services, customers and clients judge service quality as much by the process, which of course includes interaction with suppliers' staff, as by the outcome. For other suppliers, the costs of attracting customers mean that it may be only on the second or third sale that a customer becomes profitable. Satisfaction with a buyer–seller relationship is related to trust, how far expectations are fulfilled and the salesperson's expertise, ethics and empathy.[62]

- In this context trust is defined as 'belief that a party is reliable and will fulfil their obligations in an exchange relationship'.[63] It results primarily from experience and therefore develops over time but also from, for instance, word of mouth. Seller traits that help create buyer trust are dependability, reliability, honesty, competence, customer orientation and friendliness.
- Where the perceived outcomes of interactions fail to meet expectations, dissatisfaction follows.

**Box 10.13**

### How to reprimand

Get agreement from the person being reprimanded on the facts, the causes and the remedies.

- Agree standards.
- Agree that there has been a gap.
- Agree the size of the gap.
- Agree who has responsibility for reducing the gap.
- Agree actions to reduce the gap.
- Agree measures and time for reducing the gap.

Set a time for a follow-up meeting (Stewart and Stewart, 1982).

- When agreeing standards, start by discussing work standards generally. Are results more important than procedures? How important is quality relative to output? How much value should be attached to completing undertakings on time? This general discussion leads into more specific topics related to the standards for the interviewee's job.
- When getting interviewees to admit the consequences of their failures and shortcomings for others, questions are more effective than statements. Do not ask the question and then answer it if they are slow to as this lets them evade the issue. Then, as described above for giving performance feedback, switch the theme to 'How you can improve', show that you have faith that they can, ask how you can help and plan a training programme.
- Make sure that the consequences of the poor performance, for colleagues, the individual and the organisation, are fully understood.
- Concentrate on the behaviour, not the personality of the offender.
- Make it as easy as possible for the offender to do what you want.
- Make it clear that you are sure of your facts, e.g. on how the job has been performed.
- Do not allow the interviewee to divert the discussion to excuses: 'Do you accept that you have left this customer's letter unanswered for five weeks?', 'Well, what can you expect with a ridiculous workload like mine? I was here until nine o'clock last night again, trying to sort out . . .'. Make it clear that you are not interested in excuses. You intend to establish what did and did not happen.

*Source*: Stewart, V. and A. Stewart (1982) *Managing the Poor Performer*. Aldershot: Gower Press.

- The expertise of the salesperson includes their ability to get answers from the supplying company.
- The salesperson's ethics are important, especially where the product is intangible or complex. Buyers use the seller's professional status as an indicator of ethics. Where this is not available, the relationship is vulnerable, especially if short-term goals drive the seller.
- Empathy has been called 'an affective response, more appropriate to someone else's situation than to one's own'.[64] For services that operate in unpredictable environments, such as airlines, 'an empathetic ability of service personnel to refashion the service offering in the most appropriate manner to meet client needs can be a very important attribute.'[65]

As this list clearly shows, the interactive behaviour of the interface personnel is critical to customer relations.

## Mediating

Mediation is a process whereby parties in conflict agree to accept the judgement of a third party. It may be formal, as in industrial tribunals, but this discussion deals only with informal mediation between colleagues or subordinates. Mediation can be better than arbitration in that decisions are owned by the parties. It is 'ordinarily quite effective in producing agreements that satisfy the disputants and to which they later comply'.[66] Mediators sometimes need to motivate the disputants to use conflict resolution procedures at all. People in conflicts often resist using these, as their motivation is to win, not to reach a fair settlement. Within organisations, pressure to reach a settlement can often be brought to bear. Timing can be important: mediators should try to 'catch' the parties when they think they may do better by using conflict resolution, not at other times. Most helpful, though, is a climate, built up over time, that supports the idea that intractable conflicts which are beyond the capabilities of the parties to resolve themselves should be resolved by mediation.

Mediators usually aim for either compromise or integration. Aiming for compromise means, in effect, setting up a negotiation between the parties. By openly dealing with it in this way the conflict can be resolved more quickly and rules and procedures can be adopted to ensure fair play. On the other hand, compromises generate lower commitment. Aiming for integration means trying to turn the conflict into a joint problem-solving exercise. Resolving the dispute is itself treated as a task in which the contenders, and other group members, collaborate. The best potential for integration is likely to be found in 'qualitative agenda items . . . rather than in those involving strictly economic values'.[67] For instance, instead of focusing on the size of the budget for a new proposal, discussion centres on the merits of the proposal itself; then, if it is accepted, the budget is seen as a means to an end and agreement is reached more easily. Aiming for integration does not guarantee agreement but the problem may be handled in a more positive spirit. Integration is most likely to succeed in work situations where, despite the current conflict, most members basically feel positive about their work and their colleagues.

Mediators should not place too great reliance on improving communication between the parties or on rational argument. When real conflicts of interest exist, hidden agendas and unclear communications may be all that prevent a complete breakdown of relationships.[68] Equally, rational arguments, if the listener is affected by a 'spirit of controversy', may produce only reactance – mental, if not verbal, counter-argument.[69] Precisely the same arguments or considerations will be used with opposite effect according to whether someone's feelings towards the other party are positive or negative. For instance, the argument that a certain course of action will create a precedent will be used to justify a refusal to co-operate with another party if relations are hostile or the most extensive collaboration if they are friendly. Conflict resolution is often undermined by the parties having unrealistic beliefs about their relative strengths or about their alternatives to a negotiated agreement. Mediators need to help parties reach realism on these points.[70] Listening and reframing are key mediator skills. A study of three different mediator listening styles found that empathetic listening facilitates more conflict resolution and dispute settlement and that empathetic mediators are seen as more fair and objective.[71] Some authors distinguish problem-solving from transformative mediation, where the former aims at resolving the immediate dispute and the latter at changing the parties so that they are better able to resolve conflict for themselves.[72] Table 10.5 summarises the differences.

Most of the above points on mediating make some claim to having universal validity. However, this is increasingly being challenged. In 1998 Kozan and Ergin,[73] for instance, pointed out that Western problem-solving approaches, which require the parties to confront the issues jointly and bring out into the open all concerns, may not be the best approach to conflict management in many collectivist cultures. Various studies have shown that in these cultures mediation is more intrusive than in individualist cultures. If a conflict is intercultural, expectations may vary as to how intrusive the mediations should be.

**Table 10.5 Problem-solving versus transformative mediation**

| | *Problem-solving mediation* | *Transformative mediation* |
|---|---|---|
| Assumptions about conflict | Conflict is a problem in need of a solution | Conflict is an opportunity for moral growth and transformation |
| | Conflict is a short-term situation | Conflict tends to be a long-term process |
| Ideal response to conflict | Take collaborative steps to solve identified problem; maximise joint gains | Facilitate parties' empowerment and recognition of others |
| Goal of mediation | Settlement of the dispute | Parties' empowerment and recognition of others |
| Mediator role – 1 | Mediators are experts, who direct problem-solving process | Secondary: parties are seen as experts, with motivation and capacity to solve own problems with minimum help |
| Mediator role – 2 | Mediators direct parties | Mediators are responsive to parties |
| Mediator actions – 1 | Mediators explain goal is settlement, design process to achieve settlement, set ground rules; may consult parties about these issues, but mediators take lead | Mediators explain concept of mediation, but let parties set goals, direct process, design ground rules; make it clear settlement is only one of a variety of possible outcomes |

**Table 10.5** ***continued***

| | *Problem-solving mediation* | *Transformative mediation* |
|---|---|---|
| Mediator actions – 2 | Mediators 'categorise' case, frame it for disputants | Mediators 'microfocus' on parties' statements, let them frame issues themselves |
| Mediator actions – 3 | Mediators direct the discussions, dropping issues which are not amenable to negotiation (for example, relational or identity issues) and focusing on areas 'ripe' for resolution (usually negotiable interests) | Mediators allow parties to take discussions where they want them to go, encouraging discussion of all issues that are of importance to the parties, regardless of whether or not they are easily negotiable |
| Mediator actions – 4 | | Mediators encourage mutual recognition of relational and identity issues as well as needs and interests |
| Mediator actions – 5 | Mediators discourage discussion of the past, as it tends to lead to blaming behaviours, focus instead is on the present and future – how to solve the current problem | Mediators encourage an examination of the past as a way to foster recognition of the other |
| | Emotions are seen as extraneous to issues: mediators try to avoid parties' emotional statements, or emotions are tightly controlled | Emotions are seen as an integral part of the conflict process; mediators encourage their expression |
| Mediator actions – 6 | Mediators use their knowledge to develop options for settlement; can be quite directive about settlement terms | Mediators encourage parties' deliberation of situation and analysis of options; parties' design settlement (if any) themselves and are free to pursue options at any time |
| Mediator focus | Mediators focus on parties' situation and interests, looking for opportunities for joint gains and mutually satisfactory agreements | Mediators focus on parties' interactions, looking for opportunities for empowerment and/or recognition of the other |
| Use of time | Mediators set time limits, encourages parties to move on or meet deadlines. Mediators move parties from 'stage' to 'stage' | Time is open-ended; parties spend as much time on each activity as they want to. No pre-set 'stages' as in problem-solving mediation |
| Mediation: definition of success | Mutually agreeable settlement | Any increase in parties' empowerment and/or recognition of the other – 'small steps count' |

**Box 10.14**

### How to mediate – key approaches

Get agreement on rules and procedures. So long as these appear neutral, that is, not prejudicial to the outcome, they can often be agreed upon when the parties are completely irreconcilable on the main issue. Eventually these rules and procedures may well provide a framework for determining the issue, but even if they do not, the fact of the agreement itself builds a bridge between the parties that can lead to compromise or reconciliation.

Help each side clarify its own goals. It may then emerge that one party is defending a position rather than its own interests, that the conflict is costing more than the potential gain. It may even show that the goal has in fact been lost or won or changed already and that the conflict is now purely expressive and lacks any functional purpose.

Use challenge. The objective is to get the parties to examine themselves, their motives, their behaviour and its consequences, such as its effect on others. There are five kinds of challenge:

1. Information challenge to clarify the parties' misperceptions or misinformation: 'What you two are saying is fully compatible – there's no real dispute between you – it's just that Bob is looking at it from the Personnel perspective and Jason is expressing the Marketing point of view.'
2. Experiential challenge, pointing out any discrepancy between one or both of the contenders' statements about themselves and the mediator's experience of them. 'Come on Bob, you know we tried that before and it didn't work.'
3. Strength challenge, pointing out the strengths of one or more contenders. 'Bob, with your sales record, you don't have to be sensitive on a point like this.'
4. Weakness challenge, pointing out the weaknesses of one or more contenders. 'Bob, are you sure your figures are right? Remember last year when we took a decision on the basis of figures produced by your department and it turned out they were wrong?'
5. Encouragement to action, pressing the contenders to take constructive action. 'Come on now, I'm sure this problem will sort itself out if we push on and try to get the outline plan filled in fully,' (Berenson *et al.*, 1968).

Research suggests that experiential and strength challenges are often more effective than weakness challenges (Kurtz and Jones, 1973).

*Sources*: Berenson, B. G., K. M. Mitchell and R. C. Laney (1968) 'Level of therapist functioning: types of confrontation and type of patient', *Journal of Clinical Psychology*, vol. 24, pp. 31–55.
Kurtz, R. R. and J. E. Jones (1973) 'Confrontation: types, conditions and outcomes', *The 1973 Annual Handbook for Group Facilitators*. San Diego, Calif.: University Associates.

## SUMMARY – WORK APPLICATIONS FOR RELATIONSHIP SKILLS

Giving feedback is one of the most important of a manager's responsibilities. Positive feedback should be given often. Feedback to help subordinates correct failings should be given when needed, though not so frequently that the recipient feels they are always being criticised. A key aim in giving 'negative' feedback is to get the other person genuinely to accept that there is a problem and that they need and intend to do something about it. To achieve this, while avoiding blaming, a questioning technique is used, which leads the subordinate to 'see' the problem and speak openly about it. Feedback should be two-way. Subordinates should be encouraged to express their views about the conditions in which they are working.

Formal performance reviews and reprimand interviewing are both best treated as special cases of giving feedback. Formal performance reviews should take place regularly. They are more comprehensive and use a more systematic procedure than informal feedback. Reprimand interviewers need to get agreement on values and on the existence of a fault; not allow the issue to be diverted to a discussion of work conditions or other employees' behaviour; concentrate on the behaviour, not the offender's personality; clarify the consequences of continuing with the behaviour; and be constructive about helping the offender to put things right.

Customer relations cover long-term relationships between sellers and buyers, advisers and clients. Five factors are linked to the perceived quality of these inter-organisational relations: trust, the degree to which expectations are fulfilled and the salesperson's expertise, ethics and empathy.

Mediators in work conflicts need to get agreement on procedures. Their function is also to help the parties reframe their goals and beliefs about their strengths, weaknesses and alternatives. They also help the parties examine themselves, their behaviour and its consequences, such as its effect on others. Empathetic listening has been shown to be the most effective kind. However, cultural expectations must be taken into account.

## CHAPTER OVERVIEW

Though task-based, work relationships have social and psychological aspects. In the interdependence model of relationships, the power constructs in interaction theory have been recast into a dependence form. Social orientations, a concept developed to overcome the limitations of these theories, which explain interaction behaviour solely in terms of outcomes, are durable solutions to recurring interaction 'problems'; they allow for the operation of factors such as trust and fear. Work relationships are also affected by communication, roles and norms.

Work relationships are often co-operative. Such relationships depend on and themselves help build trust. Many, though, are a mixture of co-operative, competitive and conflict behaviours, all of which can have positive effects on the work. However, damaging levels of conflict and counter-productive conflict-handling styles do occur and lead to the need for conflict resolution. Culture influences preferred conflict-handling styles and conflict resolution methods.

When prejudice, discrimination or harassment are marring work relationships, individuals may need to take action on their own behalf. Some suggestions are given.

Applications of work relationship skills include giving informal feedback, formal performance reviews, reprimand interviewing, customer relations and mediating. The interactive aspects of these are discussed.

## EXERCISES

1. This exercise reveals just how complex most jobs are and how many people we deal with daily. It shows how often we are internal customers ourselves and how often colleagues are internal customers of ours.

   (a) Take a sheet of paper and draw a circle in the centre. Enter your name in the circle. This is the centre of the star.
   (b) Add circles around your circle containing the people, departments or areas with whom you deal in doing your job. Many of these may be outside your department.
   (c) Draw an arrow between each of these circles and your circle.
   (d) If you receive things (instructions, materials, information, paperwork and so on) from this person or department, draw an arrow with the tip towards yourself.
   (e) If you give things (instructions, materials, information, paperwork and so on) to this person or department, draw an arrow with the tip towards that person. (Many lines will have arrow tips at both ends.)

   Select the two or three relationships that are most important to your job. Highlight these with bolder lines.

2. Reflect privately on two work relationships, one going well, the other badly. Note down factors, especially in your own behaviour, which have influenced the course of the relationship.

   In groups, pool your lists of factors, but not the details of the relationships, to produce lists of those factors that build and those that damage a relationship.

   In your groups, use the lists to produce 'do's' and 'don'ts' for developing and maintaining relationships.

   Draw up an action plan for dealing with a currently problematic relationship.

3. A female senior engineering consultant was concerned because the consultancy company she worked for was in danger of losing a client. The reason was that the two people, both men, who were supposed to be looking after this client were, in fact, failing to do it properly. She had no standing in the matter, and had heard of it through her women's network, where a woman staff member of the client had come up to her at the last meeting. The client was small, but so was the consultancy, 'We cannot afford to get a bad reputation', she said. Both the failing men were recognised problem cases: one was known

as difficult; disillusioned and moneyed, he was largely indifferent to his work, though he enjoyed a high reputation from past successes. The other was a brilliant newcomer, who had simply been asked to take on too much and was visibly under considerable stress; the woman consultant was afraid that any mention of the case to him might be the straw that broke the camel's back.

What should she do and how should she do it? You can handle this issue as a private study exercise or in group discussion or both.

4. Just over a year ago, a middle-sized international charity appointed a graduate of Oxford and Harvard Business School in his or her late twenties to the post of European Development Manager (EDM). S/he had also three years' experience with an investment bank. The charity was delighted to have attracted someone of this calibre. Now, however, a colleague, junior in status but considerably older, is seriously concerned because the EDM is hardly ever in the office, but almost always abroad visiting one of the three overseas units. Important projects that were in train when the EDM was appointed have lapsed through neglect, and no new ones have been started. The colleague is afraid that the charity's sponsors, who contribute its funds, may become disillusioned and withdraw support. S/he fears that the reason for the EDM's constant journeying is that s/he feels that the job represents a loss of status and the travel shores up his or her ego.

   *As a private study or group discussion exercise,* consider what the colleague should do. Nothing? Talk to the EDM? Talk to the EDM's boss, who was a major influence on his appointment and seems oblivious to what is going on? If so, what should she say? What factors might influence the response s/he gets in each case? Or should s/he write a memo? If so, what should s/he write?

   *As a role play,* enact the meeting with either the EDM or the boss or both.

5. Conduct a two-sided debate on a topic on which the two sides disagree. Each side is allowed to speak only when they have first summarised the previous speaker's points and got them to agree their version. Decide the first speaker with a toss of a coin.

6. A team, working for a university, is at loggerheads. The team leader, who is on the same professional level as the other members of the team, but has responsibility for the course on which they all teach, is regarded by the others as authoritarian, which is contrary to the ethos of the organisation, and rigid in her views. She is also a comparative newcomer, having been associated with the course for only three years, compared with more than ten for most of the others. She, in her turn, complains that the other team members refuse to do their share on the administrative side – 'I always have to chase them for every little thing, from marks to doing their share of the interviewing.'

Student recruitment has declined drastically. The line manager's view is that this is because of a decline in the market and increased competition. One team member's view, however, is that the responsibility lies with the slow processing of applications, because of the course leader's insistence on the time-consuming interviewing of every applicant.

*As a private study or group discussion exercise,* consider what might be the sources of conflict in this example.

7. Working in pairs of students/trainees from different cultures, answer the following for both cultures:
   (a) How do you define your group (race, ethnicity)?
   (b) Briefly describe your ethnic group.
   (c) How is it sub-divided?
   (d) What do you enjoy about your group (list 5 things)?
   (e) What do you dislike about your group (list 3 things)?
   (f) Has your group been the object of prejudice?
   (g) Describe your first experience with prejudice.
   (h) What are the kinds of stereotypes that are made about your ethnic group?
      (i) By others in general?
      (ii) By members of a dominant group?
      (iii) By members of a specific other minority group?
   (i) What is an appropriate response to someone who makes fun of ethnic groups or jokes or verbally attacks you personally with regard to ethnicity?
8. Describe three minority groups other than your own. The groups could be national, regional, ethnic, gender, gays, people with a specific disability, people of a given age group, social class, educational level or occupation.
9. Identify at least three goals for improving your intercultural relationships at work. Write several objectives you would like to accomplish by the end of this/next year.
10. Complete the rating scale given in Table 10.6. *See the Appendix to find out how to analyse your responses to this questionnaire.*
11. A woman senior Vice-President of a large Wall Street bank reports many problems because she does not know how to say 'No' to her bosses as they pile the work on thicker and deeper. It is not a problem of saying 'No' to sexual advances or anything of that sort. She very much wants to keep her job but is particularly concerned with what she senses are many 'female-bashing' practices she perceives herself to be receiving. She wants to know how to say 'No' and save both her face and the faces of those she is saying 'No' to.

    How would you advise her?
12. Give your teacher/instructor feedback on how the course is going so far.

**Table 10.6 Interaction rating scale**

Use this table to self-assess your performances in a range of intercultural work activities, including giving performance feedback.

| In the interaction (meeting/interview/negotiation) just completed, I feel I: | *Strongly Agree* — *Agree* — *Neither Agree Nor Disagree* — *Disagree* — *Strongly Disagree* |
|---|---|
| 1. was sensitive to differences in others' verbal language | X______X______X______X______X______X |
| 2. avoided assuming that others have the same values and attitudes as my own | X______X______X______X______X______X |
| 3. was sensitive to differences in others' non-verbal language | X______X______X______X______X______X |
| 4. was aware of my own stereotypes about other groups and tried not to be prejudiced by them | X______X______X______X______X______X |
| 5. treated the people in the interaction as individuals, rather than typical of their group | X______X______X______X______X______X |
| 6. avoided evaluating the other (sub)cultures represented as inferior | X______X______X______X______X______X |

13. The observers of any role play gain practice in giving feedback; this benefit can be increased by the observers themselves being observed as they give feedback and then given feedback on how they performed.

14. B is an Area Sales Manager for Kontrol, which makes and installs sophisticated boiler-control systems. S/he has arranged to see one of her sales representatives, P, at 10 o'clock to discuss targets for next year. P fails to arrive. At 10:15 B attempts to reach P by telephone at home and in his car, but there is no reply in either case. At 11:30 P knocks on B's door, all out of breath, and says 'I'm sorry I'm late, but I got stuck in traffic and then my car radiator boiled over. The public phone was out of order so I had to walk to the nearest garage to get them to come and get me on the road again.' B knows that this salesperson has failed to arrive for important meetings before – and that s/he always has a plausible excuse. S/he also feels that P should have telephoned from the garage.

    *As a private study or group exercise,* draft the next few dialogue units in the exchange between B and the sales representative. First assume that B acts in a skilled way in the exchange, then that s/he is unskilled about it. Think about how the sales representative might respond in each case.

    *As a role play,* conduct the succeeding dialogue between B and P.

For each of the cases in Exercises 15 to 17:

*As a private study or group discussion exercise,* plan the way you would conduct the interview as the manager of the subordinate. What points would you expect the subordinate to make? How should these points be dealt with?

*As a role play*, enact the feedback/reprimand interview.

15. The setting in this exercise is a department store where M is in charge of the Accessories Department. The previous day a complaint was received from a customer about being kept waiting at the scarf and gloves counter while the assistants chatted about holidays. M has asked one of the assistants to come and see him or her.

16. In this exercise a manager rightly suspects his/her subordinate of discrimination against a member of a 'minority' group; however, there is no firm evidence to prove it. Therefore, the manager has decided not to raise the matter openly, as this would probably lead the subordinate to deny it; instead, s/he decides to talk to the subordinate and attempt to get him/her to shift his/her attitude.

17. A male subordinate has reportedly been seen to 'inappropriately touch' a female colleague.

    (a) His manager gives him feedback.

    (b) This has happened before, and there have been complaints from female colleagues.

18. Complete the feedback rating scale in Table 10.7.

19. For each of the following cases:

    *As a private study or group exercise*, plan the way you would conduct a mediation between the representatives of the two groups and the questions

**Table 10.7 Feedback performance analysis questionnaire**

Rale your own or another person's feedback performance on the following scales:

| | | |
|---|---|---|
| I (s/he) used description more than evaluation | ×——×——×——×——×——× | I (s/he) was judging throughout |
| I (s/he) gave positive feedback as much or more than negative feedback | ×——×——×——×——×——× | I (s/he) gave entirely negative feedback |
| I (s/he) was specific about faults and errors | ×——×——×——×——×——× | I (s/he) gave nothing but generalisations |
| I (s/he) got agreement on standards of performance | ×——×——×——×——×——× | I (s/he) did not discuss the performance standards |
| My (his/her) feedback was well-timed | ×——×——×——×——×——× | My (his/her) feedback was too long after the event |
| I (s/he) checked that the feedback was understood and accepted | ×——×——×——×——×——× | I (s/he) just assumed that the feedback was understood and accepted |

you would ask of both sides. What points would you anticipate from each side? How should these points be dealt with?

*As a role play*, enact the mediation.

(a) In a Local Authority, smokers and non-smokers are ranged against one another. The non-smokers want a complete ban on smoking for all staff in the buildings and want staff who take 'smoking breaks' outside the buildings to be made to work extra time at the start of each day to make up. The smokers want rooms set aside for smoking in each of the buildings belonging to the institution and no time penalty.

(b) A round of promotion in a hospital has resulted in the promotion of five white nurses and none of the four black ones. The result has been a complete breakdown of communication between management and the black nurses, who are threatening to take their case to an industrial tribunal. The hospital has a contractual procedure that requires internal mediation before going to an industrial tribunal.

(c) In a small business that hires out a venue and caters 'events' for corporate clients, the Chief Executive has received several complaints about his/her new personal assistant (PA). They allege that s/he is uncooperative towards fellow staff, doing only the limited role in his/her precise job description, and sometimes rude to both them and clients. The PA counters that the existing staff are biased against him/her, because of his/her working class background/ethnicity/gender.

## FURTHER READING


Folger, J. P. and T. S. Jones (eds) (1994) *New Directions in Mediation: Communication, Research and Perspectives*. London: Sage.

*Harvard Business Review* (1994) *Negotiation and Conflict Resolution*. Cambridge, Mass.: Harvard Business Review Press.

Kelley, H. H. and J. W. Thibaut (1978) *Interpersonal Relations: A Theory of Interdependence*. New York: John Wiley & Sons.

Lussier, R. (1992) *Human Relations in Organizations: A Skill-building Approach*. Homewood, Ill.: Irwin.


## REFERENCES


1. Reis, H. T. (1996) 'Relationships' in A. S. R. Manstead and M. Hewstone (eds) *The Blackwell Encyclopaedia of Social Psychology*. Oxford: Blackwell, pp. 470–475.
2. Kelley, H. H. and J. W. Thibaut (1978) *Interpersonal Relations: A Theory of Interdependence*. New York: John Wiley & Sons.
3. Rusbult, C. E. (1983) 'A longitudinal test of the investment model: the development and deterioration of satisfaction and commitment in heterosexual involvement', *Journal of Personality and Social Psychology*, vol. 45, pp. 101–117.
4. Kelley, H. H. (1997) 'Expanding the analysis of social orientations by reference to the sequential–temporal structure of situations', *European Journal of Social Psychology*, vol. 27, pp. 373–404.

5. Gabarro, J. J. (1986) 'The development of working relationships' in J. W. Lorsch (ed.) *Handbook of Organisational Behaviour*. Englewood Cliffs, New Jersey: Prentice Hall.
6. Argyle, M. (1989) *The Social Psychology of Work*, 2nd edn. Harmondsworth, Middlesex: Penguin.
7. Argyle, M. and M. Henderson (1985) *The Anatomy of Relationships*. London: Heinemann and Penguin Books.
8. Jablin, F. M. (1979) 'Superior–subordinate communication: The state of the art', *Psychological Bulletin*, vol. 86, pp. 1201–1222.
9. Blau, P. M. (1955) *The Dynamics of Bureaucracy*. Chicago, Ill.: University of Chicago Press.
10. Sayles, L. R. and G. Strauss (1966) *Human Behavior in Organizations*. Englewood Cliffs, New Jersey: Prentice Hall.
11. Lindsley, S. L. (1999) 'Communication and "the Mexican way": Stability and trust as core symbols in Maquiladoras', *Western Journal of Communication*, vol. 63, no. 1, pp. 1–31.
12. Cohen, M. D. and J. G. March (1974) *Leadership and Ambiguity: The American College President*. New York: McGraw Hill.
13. Adams, J. (1965) 'Inequity in social exchange' in L. Berkowitz (ed.) *Advances in Experimental Social Psychology*, Vol. II. New York: Academic Press.
14. Deutsch, M. (1978) 'Equity, equality and need: What determines which value will be used as the basis of distributive justice?', *Journal of Social Issues*, vol. 31, pp. 137–149.
15. Schopler, J. and V. D. Thompson (1968) 'Role of attribution processes in mediating amount of reciprocity for a favour', *Journal of Personality and Social Psychology*, vol. 10, pp. 243–250.
16. Gouldner, A. M. (1960) 'The norm of reciprocity', *American Sociological Review*, vol. 25, no. 2, pp. 9161–9178.
17. Buunk, B. P. and W. B. Schaufeli (1999) 'Reciprocity in interpersonal relationships: an evolutionary perspective on its importance for health and well being' in W. Stroebe and M. Hewstone (eds) *European Review of Social Psychology*, vol. 10. Chichester: John Wiley, pp. 259–292.
18. Merton, R. K. (1957) *Social Theory and Social Structure*. Glencoe, Ill.: Free Press.
19. Kiesler, C. A. and S. B. Kiesler (1969) *Conformity*. Reading, Mass.: Addison-Wesley.
20. Lawler, E. E. III (1983) 'Reward systems in organizations' in J. Lorsch (ed.) *Handbook of Organisational Behavior*. Englewood Cliffs, New Jersey: Prentice Hall.
21. Argyle and Henderson, op. cit.
22. Holmes, J. G. (1991) 'Trust and the appraisal process in close relationships' in W. H. Jones and D. Perlman (eds) *Advances in Personal Relationships*, Vol. 2. London: Jessica Kingsley.
23. Leana, C. R. and H. J. Van Buren (1999) 'Organizational social capital and employment practices', *Academy of Management Review*, vol. 24, no. 3, pp. 538–555.
24. Gelfland, M. J. and A. Realo (1999) 'Individualism–collectivism and accountability in intergroup negotiations', *Journal of Applied Psychology*, vol. 84, no. 5, pp. 721–736.
25. Dirks, K. T. (1999) 'The effects of interpersonal trust on work group performance', *Journal of Applied Psychology*, vol. 84, no. 3, pp. 445–455.
26. Parks, C. D. and L. G. Hulbert (2000) 'High and low trusters' responses to fear in a payoff matrix', *Journal of Conflict Resolution*, vol. 39, no. 4, pp. 718–730.
27. Wicks, A. C., S. L. Berman and T. M. Jones (1999) 'The structure of optimal trust: Moral and strategic implications', *Academy of Management Review*, vol. 24, no. 1, pp. 99–116.
28. Handy, C. (1995) 'Trust and the virtual organization', *Harvard Business Review*, May–June, pp. 40–50.
29. Rubin, J. and B. Brown (1975) *The Social Psychology of Bargaining and Negotiation*. New York: Academic Press.

30. Raven, B. H. and A. W. Kruglanski (1970) 'Conflict and power' in P. Swingle (ed.) *The Structure of Conflict*. New York: Academic Press.
31. Hunt, J. (1982) *Managing People in Organisations*. New York: McGraw-Hill.
32. Blake, R. R. and J. S. Mouton (1964) *The Managerial Grid*. Houston, Tex.: Gulf.
33. Thomas, K. W. (1976) 'Conflict and conflict management' in M. D. Dunette (ed.) *Handbook of Industrial and Organisational Psychology*. Chicago, Ill.: Rand McNally.
34. Nicotera, A. M. (1994) 'The use of multiple approaches to conflict: A study of sequences', *Human Communication Research*, vol. 20, no. 4, pp. 592–621.
35. King, W. C. Jr and E. W. Miles (1990) 'What we know – and don't know – about measuring conflict: An examination of the ROCI-II and OCCI conflict instruments', *Management Communication Quarterly*, vol. 4, no. 2, pp. 222–243.
36. Knapp, M. L., L. L. Putnam and L. J. Davis (1988) 'Measuring interpersonal conflict in organizations: Where do we go from here?', *Management Communication Quarterly*, vol. 1, pp. 414–429.
37. Martin, G. E. and T. J. Bergmann (1996) 'The dynamics of behavioral response to conflict in the workplace', *Journal of Occupational and Organizational Psychology*, vol. 69, pp. 377–387.
38. Volkema, R. J., T. J. Bergmann and K. Farquhar (1997) 'Use and impact of informal third-party discussions in interpersonal conflicts at work', *Management Communication Quarterly*, vol. 11, pp. 185–216.
39. Gayle, B. M. and R. W. Preiss (1998) 'Assessing emotionality in organizational conflicts', *Management Communication Quarterly*, vol. 12, no. 2, pp. 280–302.
40. Cloven, D. H. and M. E. Roloff (1991) 'Sense-making activities and interpersonal conflict: Communicative cures for the mulling blues', *Western Journal of Speech Communication*, vol. 55, no. 2, pp. 134–158.
41. Franz, C. R. and K. G. Jin (1995) 'The structure of group conflict in a collaborative work group during information systems development', *Journal of Applied Communication*, vol. 23, no. 2, pp. 108–127.
42. Allport, G. W. (1954) *The Nature of Prejudice*. Cambridge/Reading Mass.: Addison-Wesley.
43. Pettigrew, T. F. (1971) *Racially Separate or Together?* New York: McGraw-Hill.
44. Amir, Y. (1969) 'Contact hypothesis in ethnic relations', *Psychological Bulletin*, vol. 71, pp. 319–342
45. Canary, D. J. and B. H. Spitzberg (1989) 'A model of the perceived competence of conflict strategies', *Human Communication Research*, vol. 15, pp. 638–649.
46. Waldron, V. R. and J. L. Applegate (1994) 'Interpersonal construct differentiation and conversational planning: An examination of two cognitive accounts for the production of competent verbal disagreement tactics', *Human Communication Research*, vol. 21, pp. 3–35.
47. Schein, E. (1981) 'SMR Forum: Improving face-to-face relationships', *Sloan Management Review*, Winter, pp. 43–53.
48. Haar, B. F. and B. Krahe (1999) 'Strategies for resolving interpersonal conflicts in adolescence: a German–Indonesian comparison', *Journal of Cross-Cultural Psychology*, vol. 30, pp. 667–683.
49. Ting-Toomey, S. (1988) 'Intercultural conflict styles: A face-negotiation theory' in Y. K. Young and W. B. Gudykunst (eds) *Theories in Intercultural Communication*. London: Sage.
50. Obuchi, K.- I. and Y. Takabashi (1994) 'Cultural styles of conflict management in Japanese and Americans: Passivity, covertness and effectiveness of strategies', *Journal of Applied Social Psychology*, vol. 24, pp. 1345–1366.

51. Oetzel, J. G. (1998) 'The effects of self-construals and ethnicity on self-reported conflict styles', *Communication Reports*, vol. 11, no. 2, pp. 133–144.
52. Ting-Toomey, op. cit.
53. Khoo, G. P. S. (1994) 'The role of assumptions in intercultural research and consulting: examining the interplay of culture and conflict at work', Paper given at the David See-Chai Lam Centre for International Communication Pacific Region Forum on Business and Managment Communication.
54. Augsberger, D. (1991) *Intercultural Mediation*, Philadelphia: Westminster Press.
55. Kozan, M. K. and C. Ergin (1998) 'Preference for third party help in conflict management in the United States and Turkey: An experimental study', *Journal of Cross-Cultural Psychology*, vol. 29, no. 4, pp. 525–539.
56. Cushman, D. and G. C. Whiting (1972) 'An approach to communication theory: Toward a consensus on rules', *Journal of Communication*, vol. 22, pp. 217–238.
57. Osgood, C. (1962) *An Alternative to War or Surrender*. Urbana, Ill.: University of Illinois Press.
58. Lawler, E. J., R. Ford and M. D. Large (1999) 'Unilateral initiatives as a conflict resolution strategy', *Social Psychology Quarterly*, vol. 62, no. 3, pp. 240–256.
59. Fey, C. J. and P. W. Beamish (1999) 'Strategies for managing Russian international joint venture conflict', *European Management Journal*, vol. 17, no. 1, pp. 99–106.
60. Rogers, C. (1951) *Client-centred Therapy*. London: Constable.
61. Adair, J. (1984) *The Skills of Leadership*. Aldershot: Gower Press.
62. Fletcher, J. (1973) *The Interview At Work*. London: Duckworth.
63. Dwyer, F. R., P. H. Schurr and S. Oh (1987) 'Developing buyer and seller relationships', *Journal of Marketing*, vol. 51, pp. 11–27.
64. Schurr, P. H. and J. L. Ozanne (1985) 'Influences on exchange processes: Buyers' preconceptions of a seller's trustworthiness and bargaining toughness', *Journal of Consumer Research*, vol. 11, pp. 939–953.
65. Hoffman, M. L. (1987) 'The contribution of empathy to justice and moral judgement' in N. Eisenberg and J. Strayer (eds) *Empathy and its Development*. Cambridge: Cambridge University Press.
66. Bitner, M. J. (1990) 'Evaluating service encounters: The effect of physical surroundings and employee responses', *Journal of Marketing*, vol. 54, pp. 69–78.
67. Kressel, K. and D. G. Pruitt & Associates (1989) *Mediation Research: The Process and Effectiveness of Third-party Intervention*. San Francisco: Jossey-Bass, p. 268.
68. Walton, R. E. and R. B. McKersie (1965) *A Behavioral Theory of Labor Negotiations*. New York: McGraw-Hill.
69. Kursh, C. O. (1971) 'The benefits of poor communication', *Psychoanalytic Review*, vol. 58, pp. 189–208.
70. Selznick, P. (1949) *TVA and the Grass Roots*. Berkeley: University of California Press.
71. Coser, L. (1961) 'The termination of conflict' in W. J. Gore and J. W. Dyson (eds) *The Making of Decisions*. New York: Free Press.
72. Kimsey, W. D., R. M. Fuller and B. C. McKinney (1993) 'Mediator listening, dispute reframing, and mediation outcome: A pilot study', *International Journal of Listening*, vol. 7, pp. 74–91.
73. Folger, J. P. and T. S. Jones (1994) *New Directions in Mediation: Communication Research and Perspectives*. Thousand Oaks, Calif.: Sage.
74. Kozan and Ergin, op. cit.

# 11 Working in groups and teams

## CHAPTER INTRODUCTION

Groups are defined as three or more people who are interacting. In this book we are concerned with task groups interacting either to make decisions or to solve problems, or as teams performing a function or carrying out a project. Certain conditions need to be met for a group to operate well. It must have a task that is suited to group handling, not, for instance, a problem requiring an instant decision. It must also operate within a culture that supports innovation, flexibility and trust. It must be composed of people with the right combination of abilities and knowledge to carry out the task, who have sufficient group skills and more co-operative than competitive motivations. On the surface, people working in groups are at their most co-operative. They are engaged in shared tasks, pooling their knowledge and abilities. However, it has been noted that, 'There is a tendency for people to talk as if collaborative behaviour were always better than competitive behaviour, but in practice to act competitively in situations that call for collaboration.'[1]

Many of the concepts that have helped us understand interactive behaviour in work relationships are also needed for understanding it in groups, including role behaviour, norms and co-operation, competition, conflict and conflict resolution. Most of what there is to understand about group work applies equally to both decision-making groups and teams but there are some further issues particular to the two different kinds of groups. There is, however, no suggestion that teams do not have to solve problems!

This chapter aims to help readers to understand how to work effectively in groups by explaining:

- how groups develop over time;
- the effects of group structure in terms of communication patterns, power and status differences and roles;
- cohesiveness and conformity pressures, including groupthink and risky or cautious shifts;
- the effects of conflict between work groups and methods of resolving it;
- applications of groupwork skills in decision-making groups and teams.

## HOW GROUPS DEVELOP

How do people who meet together to perform a task become an effective group? They do not fall instantly into working productively on that task. Because they are disparate individuals, with varying experiences, attitudes, hopes and expectations about the task and the group, a process of harmonisation is needed before a high and consistent level of productive work can occur. This process has been extensively researched and analysed, so that we now know that the process follows the same pattern in most developing groups.[2] Essentially there are four phases and three factors that affect the interaction to different degrees in the different phases. An early analysis of group development was provided by Tuckman (1965), who distinguished the group as a social entity and as a task entity.[3] Tuckman's stages of group development, set out in Table 11.1, have become known as forming, storming, norming and performing.

**Table 11.1 Tuckman's stages of group development**

| *Stages of group development* | *Group structure (the group as a social entity)* | *Task-activity development (the group as a task entity)* |
|---|---|---|
| 1. (Forming) | Testing and dependence – discovering what interpersonal behaviours are acceptable and behaving accordingly, what patterns of communication to use; will they collaborate or compete? | Group members exchange ideas and gather information about what they have to do – about the nature of the group task. What are they trying to or expected to achieve? In what time scale? With what resources? Is it feasible? How should they go about it? How often should they meet? |
| 2. (Storming) | Intra-group conflict – sometimes severe because of members' emotional response to the task demands and other group members, and prolonged, because they do not yet have a set of agreed norms to regulate these disagreements. | Trying to reach agreement on objectives and strategy. Emotional response to task demands – especially to discrepancy between the individual's orientation and the requirements of the task. |
| 3. (Norming) | Group cohesion develops. Members accept the group and the idiosyncracies of others; the group generates norms; harmony prevails – task conflicts are avoided. Figure 11.1 shows the process by which groups develop their norms. | Open exchange of relevant interpretations (opinions of information). Openness to other group members. |
| 4. (Performing) | Members are assigned particular functions or roles, so increasing effectiveness by clarifying relationships within the group and increasing efficiency through specialisation. The group's procedures are formalised. | Task solutions and ways of implementing them begin to emerge. |

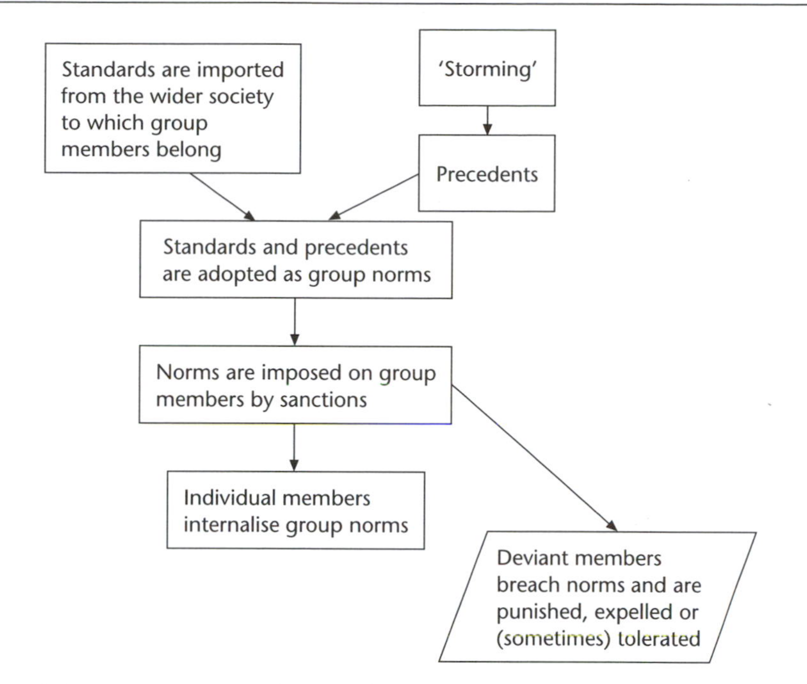


**Figure 11.1 The formation and operation of group norms.**

The three factors that influence group development in each of the four phases are individual needs, group needs and task needs:

1. When a group first meets, most members' predominating concerns are whether personal needs, such as the need to belong, are being met. How do they as individuals fit into the group and how are they received by it? (If a person behaves in ways that are important to that group, for instance, being willing to take on tasks such as keeping minutes, that individual will be socially attractive to other in-group members, regardless of interpersonal similarity.[4]) If these concerns are satisfied to an acceptable degree, they become of declining importance, though still present. If not, the group cannot reach the stage of functioning effectively and will remain liable to disruption.
2. At the start most group members are also concerned with how well this group they have joined is going to operate, what ground rules and procedures will apply and what kind of structure the group will have. This concern usually expands during the early phases of group development, as members confront the problem of making the group function well. In a successful group these problems are eventually largely resolved and concern with group needs diminishes.
3. Focusing on the task only becomes the dominant concern for most members when the issues of their own relationships within the group and those of the

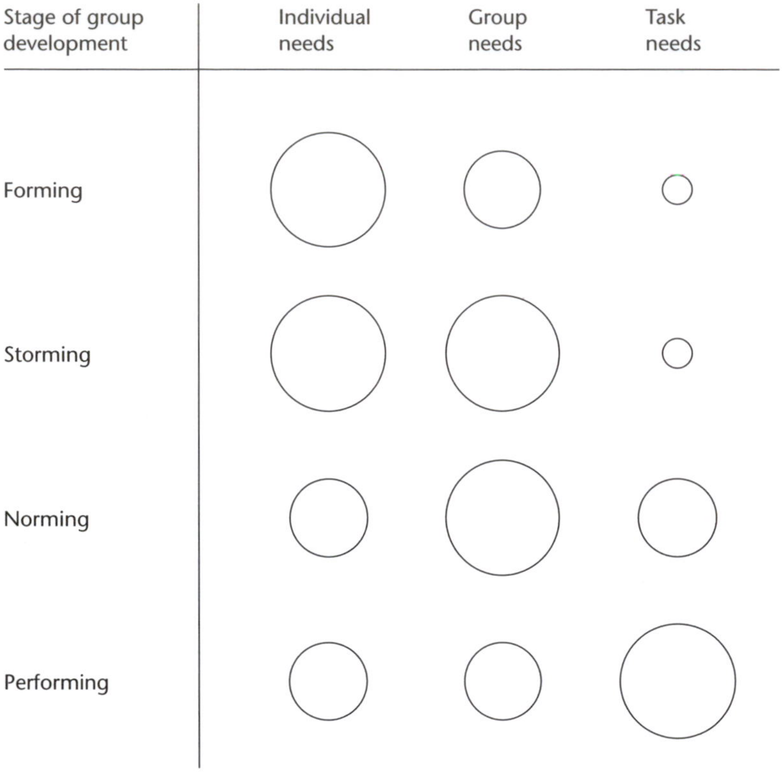

Stage of group development | Individual needs | Group needs | Task needs

Forming

Storming

Norming

Performing

The sizes of the circles indicate the influence of the different kinds of need at each stage of group development: a larger circle indicates a greater relative influence.

**Figure 11.2 Relative influence of individual, group and task needs on group members' behaviour at different stages of group development.**

group's operation are largely resolved. This is so even though at a superficial level the group is concentrating on task matters the entire time. The task-related discussions in the early stages of group development are often largely a vehicle for conducting the processes of resolving personal and group needs issues. This point can be confirmed by observing how often these opening discussions dry up inconclusively, get bogged down, provoke polarised positions or get diverted by irrelevant issues. Figure 11.2 shows the phases of group development and the relative impact of the three factors in each phase.

These are two additional points on group development:

4. The speed of the process, how cohesive the group is that emerges from it and even whether the group breaks up are influenced by how attractive the group is to its members. Group attractiveness can be analysed from two perspectives:

that of the outsider, which is the perspective of all its members during the forming stage and that of the insider while it is operating. Initially, groups are more attractive to members if they are prestigious, perceived by others as successful and co-operative, small and interactive, and if membership is voluntary or exclusive. Later, members can find the attractiveness of the group diminished if it makes unreasonable demands on them, if it is dominated by one or two members, if behaviour within the group is mainly competitive or if membership prevents individual members from getting other satisfactions.

5. Groups often move through the different phases of development in a non-linear fashion, repeating earlier phases in cycles. They might, for instance, revert to a norming phase from a performing one if a new task arose for which their existing norms provided insufficient guide. A change in group membership will commonly lead a group to revert to an earlier stage and have to rework its way through to performing effectively.

A more recent model of group development emphasises the identity concerns of members. Group interaction develops from early stages in which each person anxiously guards her or his own identity and seeks confirmatory links with similar others, through a stage in which group members join cliques based on similarity and engage in conflict with group members perceived as unlike them. If these stages are successfully negotiated, group members may reach an interdependency in which each person's perspective and contribution is valued.[5] However, more recently still, Reason[6] concluded from an observational study that what happens is a combination of group dynamics and personal development. Collaboration depends on group members developing the ability to suspend attachment to their own 'frames' that govern the way they see questions and issues and instead begin to peer into the frames of their colleagues.

## SUMMARY – HOW GROUPS DEVELOP

Effective groups emerge by a process of development, from a collection of individuals, to a cohesive body whose members are each performing functional roles and whose operation is controlled by a set of norms. This developmental process is often subdivided into stages known as forming, storming, norming and performing. For effective development, members' individual, group and task needs must be met. The relative importance of these needs changes as group development proceeds. Other processes suggested as influences on group development include identity negotiation and the cognitive development of individual members to the point where they can continually adjust their cognitive frames and learn afresh. All these developments depend on interaction within the group.

## GROUP STRUCTURE AND MEMBERS' INTERACTIVE BEHAVIOUR

In general, members of groups share important attitudes and are placed under normative pressure to do so. Individuals' behaviour varies, however, partly because of the influence of aspects of the group's structure, in particular its communication patterns, power and status differences within the group and group role differentiation.

### Communication patterns

In groups, communication and information exchange usually come to follow regular patterns. Five common patterns are illustrated in Figure 11.3. As the diagrams show, some patterns, such as the 'Y' and the star, are centralised and all communication is channelled through one person. Others, such as the chain, circle and web, are decentralised. Another difference is between open-channel patterns, such as the web, which has ten channels, and closed-channel systems such as the chain, with only four. There are several factors that affect which pattern a group adopts. These include whether or not there is an authority figure or nominated leader present, the characteristics of the task, such as time pressure, and the personalities and interpersonal dynamics of the group members. In face-to-face groups, chains and 'Y's are uncommon; stars, webs and circles, generally a little modified from the pure type, are the usual patterns.

The pattern of communication itself affects how accurately messages are transmitted and received, the level of task performance and the amount of satisfaction

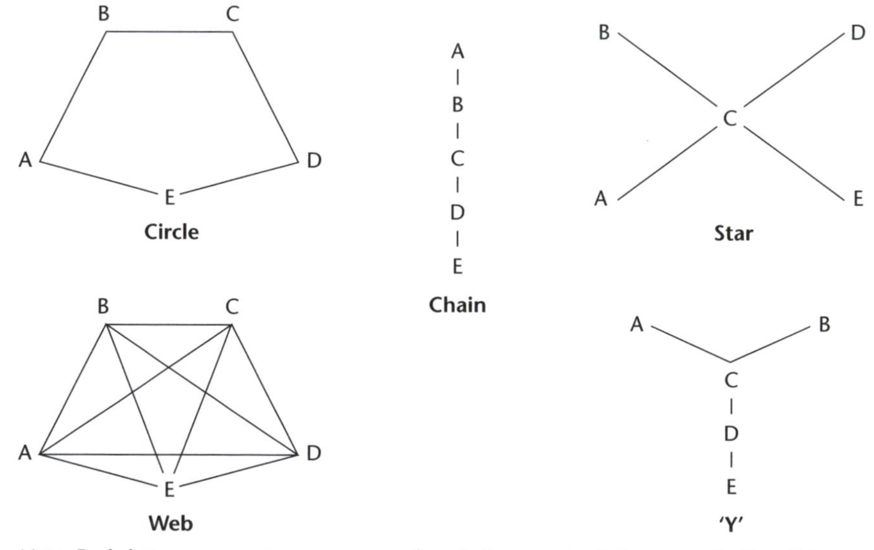


*Note*: Each letter represents a person, and each line a potential communication link.

**Figure 11.3 Five patterns of communication within groups.**

experienced by group members.[7] Messages are communicated more accurately when the message goes directly and through as few contacts as possible. Consider again the communication patterns shown in Figure 11.3. In the web it takes only ten contacts for every group member to communicate with every other and all these communications are directly between the sender and the receiver. On the other hand, for every member of the chain to communicate with every other takes 20 contacts, of which only 4 are direct. However, communication patterns have a further effect on task performance and member satisfaction. In three of the Figure 11.3 patterns, the star, the chain and the Y, one position is more central than the rest. This is position C. Centrality refers to the number of direct and indirect contacts that one position in a pattern potentially has with other positions. Direct contacts contribute more to centrality than indirect ones do. Position C is highest in relative centrality in the star, with four direct contacts, followed by in the Y, with three direct and one indirect contact, and then in the chain, with two direct and two indirect contacts. In the circle and the web no one position is more central than the others. Centrality helps determine the leadership role. In the star, C is in the best position to be leader. In the web, leadership is shared. Positions that are lower than the others in communication centrality lack much opportunity for action or influence, so that people in those positions may feel bored and excluded. Thus the positions 'A' and 'E' in the chain, and 'E' in the Y, are very likely to be occupied by people who feel alienated from the group.

Leader-centred groups, such as stars or Ys, are likely to perform specific tasks more rapidly than shared-leadership groups such as webs, but the latter appear to cope more easily with change and to sustain higher levels of member morale. Therefore, the effectiveness of the group will be influenced by the appropriateness of its communication pattern for the type of task to be accomplished. If the task requires swift action, centre-out direction and limited pooling of information and expertise, the star will be most effective. However, given a task for which all members' contributions are needed and group morale needs to be sustained over a long period, the web may well work best. From the perspective of this book, however, we are concerned less with how to structure a group than how to interact effectively as an individual within a group. From this perspective, the importance of group structure is its effect on the level of interpersonal skill required to 'get a hearing' and to cope with multiple simultaneous interpersonal interactions.

- In well-led groups with Y or star structures, the leader elicits members' contributions. There may be a signalling system by which members can indicate that they wish to speak. This system may be formal, 'through the chairperson', or informal, for example by raising the eyebrows or making a slight gesture. Other groups may include members who dominate the discussion by the loudness of their voice or a 'monologue' technique of speaking without breaks and over-talking others. (This behaviour is unskilled, and should be controlled by anyone who does it, but it undoubtedly occurs.) In such groups, members may need to use high levels of assertiveness to gain the group's attention.

- Groups require the members to handle very complex interactions. In webs and circles, which are the commonest face-to-face groups, each person is directing messages at more than one person at a time. Generally, group members will receive communication from a series of people. However, their outward communication will need to take into account the possible differences in how each member of the group reacts to what they say. The star, the other common face-to-face group pattern, simplifies interaction for most members but makes very great demands on the person in the central position. In all groups, however, even when speaking or listening to only one other person, each individual is attempting to interpret the reactions of others listening in. Each member is also repeatedly listening in on discussions even when s/he is not taking part in them.

## Power and status differences

Personal influence within a group is affected by power and prestige differences, which in turn result from either status or demeanour. Status characteristics theory says that when members of a group are ranked according to their standing on a status characteristic, they will tend to have the same rank in how often they initiate and receive communications, which is an accepted indicator of group power. A study of 224 research and development (R&D) teams of five members or more found that educational status, gender, seniority, company status, status as an expert in the group task and leadership status separately affect team status. It also found that membership interaction scores are positively related to team status. Figure 11.4 shows these relationships. The theory that demeanour is

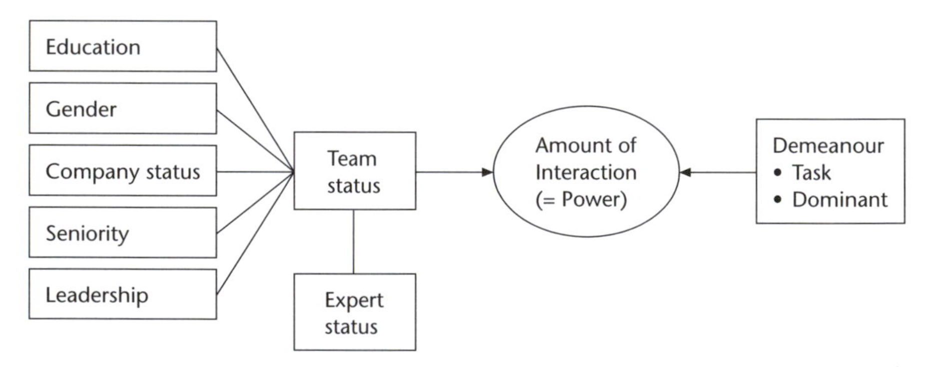


*Note*: expert means expert in the specific task of the team.

**Figure 11.4 Status and demeanour: claimed influence on individual power in a group as measured by amount of interaction.**

the important variable in determining who has power within a group contrasts 'dominant' against 'task' demeanour. A dominant demeanour involves threat – commanding, intrusive styles of interaction – while a task demeanour encompasses factual, confident, relaxed patterns that are not threatening. There is evidence that a task demeanour more effectively predicts and, by implication, produces influence than a dominant demeanour does. One recent study has brought together status characteristics and demeanour by asking what is the relative strength of a task demeanour against diffuse status characteristics, in this case race. The study has limitations of methodology, but suggests that task demeanour works in ways similar to status characteristics and can reduce the negative impact of low external status. Therefore, low-status members may be able to increase their influence by being confident in their ability at the group task.[9]

## Role differentiation

When people work together with two or more others, each usually takes on a role. They may, for instance, take on the role of group expert on a subject, or that of group moralist, clown, timekeeper, critic, sceptic or 'purse-strings holder'. Unlike the roles discussed in the previous chapter, which mainly adhere to an organisational position, these roles are informal and the titles unofficial. They refer to the tendency of individuals to behave in certain ways and have certain predominating concerns and to the tendency of other group members to accept and expect those behaviours and concerns from that individual. The roles listed above occur in some groups and not in others, but studies have found two kinds of roles that seem to arise in just about all work groups. These are the task leader and maintenance roles. The task leader is mainly motivated to get the group task done as effectively and efficiently as possible. This involves setting goals, establishing ways of working and chasing progress. The person in a maintenance role tries to keep the group functioning as a unit by providing support for others, seeking consensus and resolving conflicts. As well as personal inclination, it is group dynamics that determine who takes these roles. For instance, when a group includes a very strong task leader, i.e. is dominated by one person, it is likely that more people will take on a maintenance role than when no such dominant person is present.[10]

The fact that these roles emerge so frequently in work groups means that they can be used to help members gain their objectives and make the group function better. By recognising who is task-oriented and who is maintenance-oriented (following the guidance in Box 11.1), we can recruit them to our side, deploy them if they are in our 'team' and influence them in either case. In the following discussion a third type of behaviour is included which, though it is not really a role, is often found at meetings and requires careful handling: this is 'self-oriented' behaviour.

Box 11.1

### How to spot who is playing which role

**Task leader role**

This person is likely to take the initiative in proposing objectives, defining problems and suggesting procedures or ideas for solving problems. S/he may respond to another person's initiative with counter-proposals. Two task-oriented people in a meeting will often clash. They both have a preferred solution and they would both like to be the leader. During the meeting, task-oriented people seek more information, often of the 'hard-data' variety, and sometimes provide more than others do. They show concern for objectivity and probably act as if there is such a thing as the 'right' solution that can be found if everyone tries hard enough. They welcome a structured approach to decision-making. They like to get terms defined, though without semantic debates, to clear up confusion and to get the alternatives and criteria agreed. If the discussion wanders from the main issue, they try to get the group back on the track. They attempt to speed the group towards a conclusion by summarising, setting out the options and testing the group's view. They are more likely to propose a way of cutting short discussion of differences, for instance by a vote, than to encourage further exploration. They tend to be very conscious of time passing.

**Maintenance role**

These people offer encouragement and support in a sustained way to other people – both the task leaders and other group members. They are more likely to back up other people's suggestions rather than propose their own, though they may suggest ways out of interpersonal conflicts. They will try to reconcile disagreements, reduce tension and keep all members of the group involved and satisfied with the way the discussion is proceeding. If they do raise issues as problems, these are more likely to be about subjective considerations, such as whether a given solution fits in with group norms, than with external criteria or goals. If their own ideas or status are attacked, they will usually offer to compromise, admit an error or give in rather than endanger group cohesion.

**Self-oriented behaviour**

Some people in meetings may be feeling defensive, insecure or for other reasons more concerned with their own needs than either the task or the well-being of the group. Most people who feel they have been personally attacked will behave in a self-oriented way temporarily. Some people may be in a state of mind that leads to such behaviour more or less continuously. There is a range of ways in which these people may act. They may play the clown or be a wet blanket. They may repeatedly introduce irrelevancies or ride their hobby horse. They may insist on speaking at length when brevity is the norm. They may withdraw from the discussion, feign indifference and then when a group consensus appears likely, attempt to sabotage it by raising questions of 'fundamental principles' with a claim that these have been ignored up to this point.

## Cultural differences

Behaviour during groupwork is strongly influenced by the cultural values described in Chapter 2, as Table 11.2 shows. However, while individualists are likely to behave in the same competitive way in most groups, collectivists will behave co-operatively in groups composed of their in-group but in groups

**Table 11.2 Effects of culture on groupwork**

| *Effect of* | *High* | *Low* |
|---|---|---|
| Power distance | Difficulty in working in an unchaired or unsupervised group | Low deference to authority |
| Uncertainty avoidance | Preference for agendas and sticking to them, structured discussion, clear outcomes, minutes | Preference for informality |
| Masculine values | Task orientation predominates | Maintenance orientation predominates |
| Individualism | Competitive atmosphere | Co-operative atmosphere |
| Time orientation | Long: exploration of all issues before decision sought | Short: sense of urgency, pressure for closure |

composed of their out-groups may compete or, in the case of conflict arising, behave, 'uncharacteristically', with confrontation.

## SUMMARY – GROUP STRUCTURE AND MEMBERS' INTERACTIVE BEHAVIOUR

In groups, people who occupy or seize positions high in communication centrality are likely to be or become group leaders. People in positions low in centrality may become alienated. Group members concerned with cohesiveness should look to ways of preventing this. In leaderless groups, skill is needed to get a hearing and to cope with all the interactions that are going on simultaneously.

People who have external sources of status in a group, such as higher educational level, the right gender and company seniority are likely to find it easy to turn these into power bases. Those who lack these can gain power by showing themselves confident about their ability in the group's task, especially if they have real expertise in the area.

People working in groups often exhibit one of three types of role behaviour, task-, maintenance- or self-orientation. These roles can be recognised from behavioural cues. By behaving in ways that respond to the needs underlying those orientations, useful relationships can be established. Team effectiveness can be enhanced if the orientations of different members of the group are taken into account when team roles are allocated. Culture influences how co-operative or competitive group members are and towards whom.

## COHESIVENESS AND CONFORMITY PRESSURES

Why do some mature groups work together quite harmoniously while members of other groups are always fighting one another? Why, in other words, are some

Box 11.2

### How to use your understanding of different kinds of group role behaviour

One use of understanding the differences between the orientations is to guide your own choice of the most productive way of acting in different situations. Another use is to help build relationships with others within the wider group. In some cases you will want to 'recruit' them – that is to win them to your side or make them part of your team. In other cases you will be seeking a looser alliance on certain issues; at other times again you will be satisfied by merely ensuring their neutrality. Whichever is your objective, the appropriate behaviour on your part differs as between task-, maintenance- and self-oriented people. The reason for this is the underlying motivations that are driving the different ways of behaving.

**Task orientation**

This generally reveals a person who is high in needs for power and esteem and at the same time concerned for structure, a concern that originates in the safety need. With someone like this it is productive to show that you acknowledge any position of authority that they lay claim to, and to defer to them, especially on small points and side issues, making it clear that you are doing so: 'You're the expert on that point, John' or 'I think we should accept Sarah's judgement on this matter'. It helps to speak your agreement with them where you can. Showing concern for their concerns – for getting the task structured and progressing it – also attracts them to you. All this does not mean letting them dominate you. It is not your objective to let them recruit you.

**Maintenance orientation**

These people need to be liked, to belong. Non-verbal behaviour such as smiling, eye contact and nodding communicate your support to such people and they will feel a strong pressure to reciprocate by supporting you. You can then encourage them to bring that support out in the open by questioning them – 'Don't you agree, Caroline?', 'What do you think, Philip?', with reasonable confidence that whatever their views might be outside the meeting, inside it they will find it very difficult to disagree with you.

**Self-orientation**

Building relationships with people who are behaving in a self-oriented way is more difficult. In extreme cases there can be a danger of provoking a self- or group-destructive reaction from such a person. Sometimes, however, the problem lies not with the individual but with the dynamics of the group: self-oriented behaviour can be a person's response to being excluded from, or feeling themselves to be excluded from, task or maintenance roles. In fact, it never hurts to assume that that is the problem, and to give the self-oriented person a real job to do.

groups more cohesive than others? One explanation lies in the idea of the group's goals. People come together to achieve goals, whether material or social, that require joint action and/or interaction. Whether a group is cohesive or not depends on how successful it is in supplying rewards to its members, that is, in helping them achieve the goals that brought them into the group.[11] In work groups, even though membership may be involuntary, the same dynamic applies. If people do not get enough rewards from their group membership, though they may not be able to leave, they can be disputatious or unco-operative. The result may be a group that is low in cohesiveness. Another explanation is that the members of cohesive work groups, unlike those in non-cohesive groups, have high levels of attraction to one another. This attraction is based, not, as it would be in person-to-person relationships, on overall similarity, but on prototypical similarity, that is how similar they are in the respects which affect how well the group performs. Groups can work together cohesively even though members do not like each other personally.[12]

Members of groups who have not met previously and are not in one another's presence, a situation that arises frequently during computer-supported

**Box 11.3**

### How to support group cohesiveness

Groups that have difficulty in maintaining cohesiveness are usually low in attractiveness to their members. This may be because they are unsuccessful in competition with other groups (the football club that never wins a game), because membership is not prestigious (the football club at the bottom of the lowest league) or because they fail to meet members' expectations (the club tournament is badly organised and the pitch slopes) or needs (there is a lack of sociability). Therefore, to get a group of disaffected people to carry out a task, the best way is to increase their motivation for staying in the group and their loyalty towards it. This change may happen if the group is faced with an external threat, which, while it lasts, usually increases group cohesiveness. Equally, how leaders handle groups affects their cohesiveness. Encouraging group participation in decisions, integrating newcomers and isolated people, resolving conflicts, maximising interpersonal satisfactions and skilfully handling disruptive group members all increase group cohesion (Johnson and Johnson, 1987).

Even cohesive groups, however, can expect to include one or two 'deviant' members who break its norms from time to time. The more uncertainty (the less physical reality testing is available) and the more uniformity is seen to facilitate a desired outcome, the more pressure on deviants to conform (Turner, 1996). People who breach group norms all the time or too flagrantly are likely to be 'expelled' or isolated but most groups will tolerate some breaches. There are two kinds of people most likely to breach norms: relatively high-status and very low-status members. Those with high status have little to gain from conforming and can afford the luxury of not doing so. Often, in fact, a breach confirms their high status by demonstrating that they can get away with it. Very low-status people are getting few rewards from their membership of the group or organisation. Being excluded or isolated would not change their position much so they have little incentive to conform and may gain some satisfaction from defying the rules. For instance, in one series of meetings the author attended, it was always the person who had been passed over for promotion who expressed opinions that were clearly unacceptable to the others and who insisted on developing the theme despite the obvious impatience of the rest. Therefore, if you are trying to prevent the group being disrupted by breaches of its norms, keep an eye on its high- and low-status members.

*Sources*: Johnson, D. W. and R. T. Johnson (1987) *Joining Together: Group Theory and Group Skills*, 3rd edn. New York: Prentice Hall.
Turner, J. C. (1996) 'Social influence' in A. S. R. Manstead and M. Hewstone (eds) *The Blackwell Encyclopaedia of Social Psychology*. Oxford: Blackwell, pp. 562–567.

decision-making, appear to identify less with the group than is generally true for face-to-face groups. However, they contribute more total comments, although they make more comments anonymously, that is without expressions that would show their background or perspective.[13] These findings suggest that such groups may be less cohesive, but not necessarily less productive, than face-to-face groups.

Cohesiveness in part produces and in part is produced by the pressure members exert on one another to conform to the group beliefs and norms. This pressure can be tremendously powerful. In fact, people can be so induced to conform by group pressure that they will say that two lines of visibly different lengths are matches.[14] This happens even when underlying beliefs are not altered – they 'know' that the lines are of unequal length even while saying that they are the same. Findings such as these led to models which explained mob behaviour by the idea that being immersed in a group and feeling anonymous lead to a loss of 'self-hood' (de-individuation) and hence of control over behaviour. However, such models depend on a concept of the self as referring to a sense of individual uniqueness. As we saw in Chapter 3, it is now more accepted that the self may be defined at various levels including the collective self as well as the individual self. Evidence from a meta-analysis of research showed that being de-individuated increases the salience of social identity and so increases conformity to standards associated with the group. It also enhances the ability of group members to express their social identity in the face of out-group opposition. Thus, far from leading to uncontrolled behaviour, de-individuation maximises the opportunity of group members to give full voice to their collective identities.[15]

A further implication of the idea that we each have a number of collective selves as well as an individual self, is that our liking for other group members depends on how prototypical they are, that is, how closely they conform to the characteristics which for us define the group in comparison to other groups. In small interactive groups, where people know one another, personal and social patterns of liking coexist, with one or the other predominating, depending on what is going on. If the group is competing with another group, people will be more attracted to those group members who are most prototypical. If there is a dispute within the group, personal preferences may come to the fore.

The idea of norms has already been discussed. In groups, norms help reinforce group cohesiveness, regulate group processes, communicate values and enable members to know how to behave and predict what others will do. Most group norms are generated and accepted during the norming phase of group development. Both adhering to norms and deviating from them can be valuable: 'For a group to function effectively and smoothly there has to be a certain amount of agreement on how to do things; on the other hand, it is important for the group to adapt to changing conditions, and change is brought about by individuals deviating from the norms.'[16]

Conformity pressures can lead to two negative effects on group performance: groupthink and risky or cautious shifts.

### *Groupthink*

Groups that have worked together over a period of time and have been successful sometimes take conformity to an extreme, especially in crises. Such groups are quite likely to develop a conviction that the group is superior in knowledge and ability to almost everybody else and to mount conformity pressures so strong that any deviation from the group consensus is censored. Groups that do these things are victims of 'groupthink' and are liable to make catastrophically bad decisions. An example of a group vulnerable to groupthink might be an advertising agency team that has recently gained accounts against hot competition and is now up against a deadline in preparing a campaign for a client. Another might be a stockbroking team that has successfully launched several companies on the stock market but is now dealing with one where things are going wrong – adverse Press comment, qualification of accounts or other problems. Groupthink is

> a mode of thinking that people engage in when they are deeply involved in a cohesive in-group, when the members' strivings for unanimity override their motivation to realistically appraise alternative courses of action. . . . Groupthink refers to a deterioration of mental efficiency, reality testing and moral judgement that results from in-group pressures.[17]

Groupthink leads groups to avoid outside opinions and issues that are controversial within the group, to fail to question weak arguments, to discount warnings and to take decisions without enough consideration and rationalise them afterwards. Group members who have deviant views self-censor and any member who expresses deviant views is subjected to direct pressure to conform. All these behaviours impair decision-making.

### *Risky or cautious shifts*

Even in groups that are only recently formed or have no record of success to blur their judgements, conformity pressures can lead groups to make decisions that are either riskier or more cautious than the average of the decisions which the individual members would make on their own. For example, a group considering an investment proposal would be likely to take a more optimistic (or more pessimistic) view of the prospective return or to be more (or less) likely to discount uncertainties and unknowns than its members would be on average if they were considering the proposal on their own. The risky shift was the first to be discovered,[18] but later work revealed that sometimes a cautious shift occurs instead. The phenomenon is, in fact, polarisation. Knowing the views of other group members can result in a shift towards any original belief held by the

Box 11.4

## How to overcome groupthink

- Reform the group by introducing or, better, substituting for two or more members, people who are forceful, successful in their own right and powerful. It is no good substituting people whom the rest of the group can ignore, and a single substitute, even if quite powerful, will probably end up either espousing the shared beliefs or leaving the group (Janis and Mann, 1977).
- Supposing, however, that the person who becomes conscious of groupthink in a group is not well placed to initiate or promote membership changes. In most organisations there are strong pressures towards keeping successful teams together. If the groupthink ball is really rolling it will not be stopped easily by the counter-pressure of one person unless that person is extremely influential. Instead the member can attempt to alert the whole group to what is happening. Getting them to read *Victims of Groupthink*, a book by the originator of the idea (Janis, 1972), might be a first step. The concept of groupthink was developed by studying the events and decisions leading up to the disastrous Bay of Pigs expedition under US President Kennedy in 1962. It makes sobering reading for any 'gun-happy' group.
- Group members who are in the position of formal or informal leaders can do more. They can protect the right to be heard of members who express non-conforming views, and, by treating them seriously themselves, influence others to do likewise. They can bring in outsiders with valuable ideas or information to address the group. Finally, they can condense and re-present data so that it will not be ignored or distorted just because the members are suffering from information overload.
- To prevent groupthink arising, use structured controversy through advocacy subgroups (Hirschman, 1970). This technique involves the whole group first brainstorming to identify solutions to the problem at issue. Once options are agreed, each one is given to a subgroup for development and advocacy. The subgroups are given time to gather information about the options they are advocating and to prepare a justification for them. Then each subgroup in turn presents its option to the whole group and defends it against the criticisms of the rest of the group. The solution finally adopted may be one of the original options, perhaps modified by the advocacy process, but often it is a synthesis of the best features of more than one of the original ideas.

*Sources*: Hirschman, A. D. (1970) *Exit, Voice and Loyalty*. Cambridge, Mass.: Harvard University Press.
Janis, I. L. (1972) *Victims of Groupthink*. Boston, Mass.: Houghton-Mifflin.
Janis, I. L. and L. Mann (1977) *Decision-Making*. New York: Free Press.

group. Several studies have shown that when actual monetary costs or painful physical experiences are at issue the shifts still occur.[19,20] Houghton *et al.*[21] found that the law of small numbers bias (making a judgement by reliance on a too-small sample) and the illusion of control bias (overestimating the extent to which skill can increase the probability of success when chance, not skill, is an important factor) actually affects group decision-making even more than it affects individual decision-making.

Several explanations have been suggested for risky and cautious shifts. One is that groups are expected to have shared values about risk. Some favour conservativism, others 'courage'. In group discussion, members take a public stance which shows how far they share those values. They therefore tend to demonstrate their loyalty and 'fit' by supporting ideas that are more extreme than they are privately attracted to. Another explanation is that in groups people feel less personally responsible for mistakes, though this is a better explanation for risky shifts than for cautious ones. A third suggests that there is a kind of random element. Because during group discussion people are learning, gaining information and hearing arguments that they might not have known before, there will be a shift towards a more risky or more cautious decision according to whether the supporters of each happen to be more vocal, more persuasive or more numerous on this particular occasion.

Ideas for preventing risky and cautious shifts from doing damage are similar to those for countering groupthink – obtaining independent outside views before decisions are implemented, ensuring all relevant information is taken into account and using structured controversy.

## SUMMARY – COHESIVENESS AND CONFORMITY PRESSURES

The cohesiveness of a group is related to how attractive it is to its members, which in turn is a function of what rewards they get from membership. Enhancing the group's attractiveness, exposing it to external threat and increasing participative leadership are some ways of supporting cohesiveness. A group can exert great pressure on its members to adhere to its beliefs and norms. In extreme cases, these pressures produce groupthink or a polarisation of attitudes to risk that amounts to a distortion of judgement. Groupthink is best countered by reforming the group, protecting the right of deviant thinkers to be heard and structuring controversy. Risky and cautious shifts are less likely if a systematic decision-making process is followed, if independent views are obtained before decisions are implemented and again by using structured controversy.

## INTER-GROUP CONFLICT

Conflict within groups is just as dangerous as groupthink. The points made on conflict and conflict resolution in Chapter 10 should be read in the context of groups as well as person-to-person work relationships. Here I consider another problem – that of inter-group conflict. The following is a quotation from the response given by a Sales Manager, Sam Brown, to a question about how payment and credit were dealt with in his company:

> Well, basically we have a credit control department, and it's their job, and sometimes it seems to conflict with ours, because they're wanting paying, and, er, so are we, but it's not our job. I was being slightly jokey when I said that they to some extent conflict with

> us, but it's true, because they want to put the customer on stop list and not supply him with anything, and that sort of thing. The customer's a nuisance to some people. It's their job, and they only see the money side, and he hasn't paid for three months, and he should have paid within thirty days, and therefore he's a bad guy; and the customer hasn't told us why, and so he's a very bad guy. So then we have to act as mediators, because they've upset the customer – they might even have put it in the hands of solicitors – and the customer, the man we sell to, normally he's not involved in payment anyway, and he wants the goods, and it's the blasted accountants that are making a mess of everything.

Sam Brown has expressed here a set of attitudes not atypical of those to be found about relations between different groups in an organisation. He believes that the 'people in credit control' have different goals from the sales force, that the sales force's goals are the right ones, in the sense that the 'firm has to keep its customers happy or go under' and that the behaviour of the credit controllers is careless of the problems and realities faced by the salesmen, which are much more acute than those faced by the protected 'backroom boys' of credit control. No doubt the credit controllers' perspective is different – probably encompassing ideas such as that 'Sales personnel do not understand profit, to them it is "sales regardless", but what's the good of a sale if you can't get the money for it?', that the sales staff are dilatory about completing paperwork and that that is what leads to all these problems of putting customers on 'stop'. These kinds of differences between groups in how they perceive the common goal and each other can be quite damaging to the health of an organisation, leading to low levels of interdepartmental communication, poor co-ordination of efforts, and displacement of loyalty onto outside organisations.

This low-level lack of co-operation can easily turn into outright distrust and hostility when the two groups are in competition with each other – for example, for budgets, promotions or smarter offices. Thus, while the extensive use of groups in organisations is effective in many ways, it can have the negative consequence of giving rise to inter-group rivalries and conflicts, which are damaging to the overall effectiveness of the organisation. Research has shown that when two groups enter into win–lose competition, the behavioural dynamics themselves tend to increase rather than reduce the conflict. Within a group that is embattled against another, there is usually a sharp increase in cohesion, with members suppressing their differences from one another and identifying strongly with the position the group takes in the dispute. Conformity is demanded to a greater degree than normally, and the punishment for individuals who appear to breach group norms is increased. 'Maintenance' concerns are subordinated to those of the task. There is a shift towards a more autocratic style of leadership of the group, participatory decision-making is reduced or suspended and often the group adopts as leaders those who are most militant about the dispute. Members experience high levels of satisfaction with the group and feel greater loyalty towards it. Meanwhile, both groups come to regard the other as an enemy and to feel hostility towards its members. Instead of seeing the members of the other group as people with mixed qualities and characteristics, as non-embattled groups can, they use negative stereotypes, such as, 'They're a real bunch of little Hitlers' or 'Who do they think they are? Lord God Almighty?'[22] The other group's case is also misperceived and caricatured. Attempts to 'see it from their point of view' are generally failures and members proposing this approach attract suspicion. Any co-operative messages coming from the other side are ignored or distorted, any hostile ones attended to and resented. The other group's behaviour is attributed to personality rather than situation and every action by the other group is seen as an attempt to dominate. These assumptions about the other group's behaviour lead to actions that provoke that behaviour. Thus a self-fulfilling prophecy is set in operation.

The outcome, if the two groups are left to fight it out, is often a deadlock or, if one group is in a more powerful position (by virtue of information control, for instance, or access to non-impartial higher echelons), victory for that side and defeat for the other. Either outcome is damaging to the organisation as a whole. The stronger side may easily have the weaker case, while relations between the two groups can be permanently embittered. The problem is not necessarily solved by arbitration. When a full-blown conflict is resolved by arbitration which awards victory to one party, the winners will, predictably, regard the decision as just, but the losers, no matter how carefully the arguments leading to the decision are presented, are likely to consider the decision biased and unfair.

After the battle, the victors are satisfied with themselves, their leadership and their position. Winning 'proves' that they were right and the other group was wrong. There is little incentive, or tendency, to re-examine their perspective and little is learnt from the experience. They would do the same again in the same circumstances. The group relaxes, works on maintenance issues but not on tasks, even though important tasks may have been neglected during the fight, and confirms its leadership in its position. Meanwhile the losers are seeking a reason for their loss, blaming their leaders, the 'judge', foul tactics by the other party or their own weak or dissident members. Scapegoating is common. Members feel dissatisfied with their group, which loses cohesion and may replace its leaders. If the defeat seems to make future victory impossible or very remote, members become apathetic and the group may split up, if organisational constraints allow. If the group survives, perspectives on the issue and approaches to conflict are eventually re-examined and a lot of learning is achieved. The group throws itself into other tasks and may perform very effectively in the effort to retrieve self-respect, though maintenance issues are often neglected and can lead to future trouble.

The easy thing to say about win–lose inter-group competition is that it should never get started. A co-operative, problem-solving climate should prevail,

**Table 11.3 Inter-group conflict strategies**

| *Avoidance* | *Approach* |
|---|---|
| Resignation | Fighting |
| Withdrawal | Compromise |
| Isolation | Arbitration |
| Cover-up | Negotiation |

enlivened only by friendly win–win competition. But since in practice it occurs quite often, we need to consider the strategies open to a group in conflict with another. One way to conceptualise such strategies is in terms of an approach/avoidance continuum.[23] Avoidance means trying to avoid the issue or the people with whom there is conflict. Approach means trying to get closer to them and resolve the issue. Avoidance, except in collectivist cultures, is largely based on fear of conflict and is characterised by a tendency to deny, rationalise or avoid the problem. It is usually dysfunctional in European intra-cultural situations, both in terms of solving the problem and in its effect on those who practise it, who may suffer displaced anger and other negative feelings. Approach is more positive and less fear-based, but is not always functional, because some approach strategies can provoke win–lose fights and escalate conflict. The avoidance/approach continuum with the strategies associated with each is shown in Table 11.3.

Which of the four approach strategies two opposing groups are more likely to adopt depends on how they perceive one another. Fighting occurs when both groups perceive the other as not open to reason and as belligerently opposed to the interests of the other. Compromise tends to be adopted by groups that see their opponents as unreasonable but interested in peace. Arbitration by an outside party is preferred by groups that see their opponents as open to reason but belligerent. Negotiation is only likely to be adopted by groups that see their opponents as both open to reason and interested in peace. It is the best strategy because it is likely to produce a more pragmatic and accepted solution than an imposed one, it contributes to the development of the groups and is the only option that both resolves the conflict and avoids creating winners and losers. Arbitration postpones resolving the conflict and creates winners and losers, compromise does not resolve the conflict, and fighting may resolve the conflict but only by creating winners and losers. Unfortunately, groups' choice of strategy depends on perceptions that will probably be distorted during inter-group competition. The first step should be a careful examination of how realistic and fair the group's perceptions of the others are. An independent facilitator may help in this process.

## SUMMARY – INTER-GROUP CONFLICT

Conflict between groups within organisations easily escalates into full-blown hostilities, with significant and mainly damaging effects both during the battle and afterwards. Ways of dealing with competitive behaviour and conflict have been set out in Chapter 10. Groups' conflict-handling strategies can focus either on avoidance or on approach, with varying degrees of negative consequences. Negotiation is most likely to produce genuine conflict resolution and contribute to the groups' development but may be prevented by the distorted perceptions of the groups in disputes.

## WORK APPLICATIONS FOR GROUP SKILLS

Two types of group are especially important at work – groups whose main function is solving problems or making decisions and teams responsible for carrying out a project or function. In addition to the understanding and skills already described in this and previous chapters, effective group decision-making relies on understanding individual and minority influence and how to structure and improve group problem-solving. Good teamwork depends on knowing how to overcome competitive behaviour and low motivation in teams. In self-managed teams, the effects of distributed leadership need to be understood.

### Decision-making groups

Making decisions or solving problems jointly is different from doing it individually, as none of the participants know the 'answer' beforehand.[24] The task is not, therefore, to concentrate on accurately transferring a picture from one mind to another but rather to use an exchange of information to create a picture which is helpful to both parties but beyond the power of either to create single-handedly. That is, in true group problem-solving, it is as if each member has some pieces of a jigsaw, which cannot be completed until all members' pieces are brought together. This means that the mutual dependence of the participants is high.

What role do individuals play in determining a group's solution to a problem? One view has it that individuals retain their initial preferences throughout and one opinion prevails. Another (the persuasive arguments thesis), has it that individuals' views shift, but only in response to facts supporting other views. Hoffman and Kleinman[25] argue for the common-sense view and support their argument with research findings. All arguments that favour a solution, whether factual or not, contribute to the value of that solution for the group. Discussion is aimed at finding a single solution that gains the most support with the least opposition. Arguments may persuade by providing information to the group about the facts supporting a given solution, how many other members support it, other members' preferences and their strength of feeling about them, the willingness

**Box 11.5**

### European variations in group decision-making

In France, most internal company meetings are formal, chaired (a public occasion for the boss to show authority) and used for briefing not discussion. Contributions are rarely challenged because to do so questions the speaker's competence. Decisions are taken without consensus. These formal meetings may be preceded by informal meetings at which people come and go, interrupt and conduct side conversations, but the atmosphere tends to be adversarial and again consensus is not needed for decisions to be made.

In Germany, meetings between a manager and subordinates, as in France, are formal, more for handing down decisions than discussion. Divergent opinions and consensus are not expected. Informal meetings among peers are used for discussion and decision-making but only about topics already known beforehand; individuals are expected to contribute only when they are qualified to speak.

In Italy, formal meetings are a façade for the real action; informal meetings can seem chaotic and are used more for the decision-makers to assess support for various options than to decide. Multiple opinions may be expressed. Unless the 'face' of those who opposed the final decision is protected, they may work to undermine it.

In Spain, in traditional organisations, meetings, if held at all, are used to hand down instructions. In modernising companies, influenced by the United States, meetings where all are expected to contribute are on the increase, despite resistance from older managers who see them as unnecessarily time-wasting. Majority voting is not widely accepted.

In the Netherlands, groups are used for discussion and making decisions, ideas are discussed on their merits regardless of who makes them and all are expected to contribute, but their comments must be to the point.

In the United Kingdom, meetings are 'the most important management tool', used for formulating, discussing, approving, ratifying, communicating and implementing all major decisions. All participate, though status affects influence. Meetings normally over-run the time allowed, often by hours, because discussion of any issue tends to continue until some concrete outcome is agreed. People often attend and speak up at meetings without having read the papers first.

of opposing members to accede to the group and the position of the formal leader. As this list shows, the group's 'social reality' concerning the solutions to the problem are influential as well as more 'objective' facts about the issue.

A study by Gruendfeld *et al.*[26] looked at the effect of individuals' influence in groups when the individual had had a period of time working elsewhere and so, presumably, learning new things. They found that the individual's direct influence was reduced, i.e. that their ideas were significantly less likely to be used by the group. Returning group members were perceived as highly involved but argumentative. Their contributions were considered less valuable. On the other hand, all members produced more unique ideas after 'itinerant' members returned to their group of origin than before they left or while they were away. This suggests that the returners had indirect influence, that is they helped to change how rather than what people thought.

Another issue in group decision-making is the question of majority versus minority views. The majority might be expected to prevail, other things being equal. However, research has shown that if a problem is new and there are as yet no established views, a determined minority may succeed in crystallising the group around their views. Even if there is an established majority view, a minority that gives the impression of confidence and certainty and that refuses to yield can still affect the views of the majority. Studies have shown that a consistent minority of two persons responding 'incorrectly' (for instance, saying that slides are green when they are actually blue) over several trials can influence the majority. It seems the minority's confidence leads to tension with the majority perceivers' own initial position. Therefore the majority undergo a validation process of reassessing their own beliefs and more carefully attending to the minority position.[27] The effect is greater if there is a minority of at least two or three, and if their views appear to be objective rather than based on self-interest.[28] While majorities tend to produce more immediate, public and direct influence (i.e. compliance), minorities can change attitudes.[29] An extreme suggestion, in fact, is that only minorities can change attitudes, as the influence of the majority is always subject to the question (even in the mind of the person influenced) of whether it is compliance with power rather than attitude change that is occurring.

However, against the theory that majorities are converted by minorities because they process their arguments more centrally, evidence shows that strength of argument influences attitudes in the case of majority support but not in the case of minority support, indicating more systematic processing of the majority than the minority opinion.[30] Numerical support (especially majority support) is in itself motivating, leading people to engage in systematic processing, whereas minority messages are only processed systematically when it is difficult for the recipient to ignore the message.[31] According to this school of thought, in cases where the minority appears to convert the majority, systematic processing of the majority view leads to its rejection and the adoption of the alternative.

In studies of minority influence, targets more often embrace new approaches to problem-solving than the minority position,[32] or they examine the trade-offs among different perspectives.[33] These findings lead to a third view of minority influence – that it can be explained in terms of convergent versus divergent processing. Convergent information processing explicitly takes the source's position into account. Receivers view the issue from the perspective of the source's judgement. Divergent thinking takes multiple perspectives into account, of which the source's is one. Majority-supported arguments elicit convergent processing (because it is assumed to reveal the 'correct' thinking), leading to focal change accompanied by change on related issues. Minority-supported arguments, on the other hand, may elicit divergent processing (because it disrupts the presumed consensus and so is to be avoided), which at best leads to related change.[34] Figure 11.5 shows these differing opinions on minority influence.

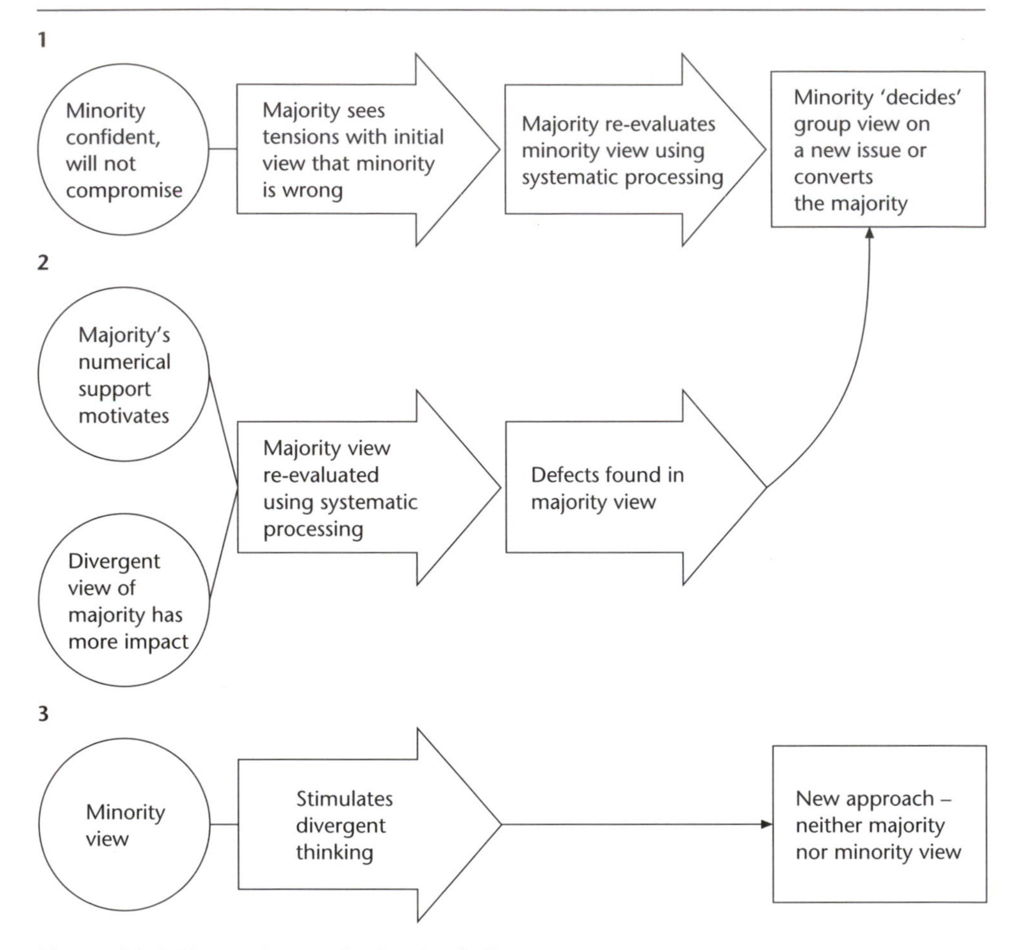


**Figure 11.5 Three views of minority influence.**

On the comparative quality of the decisions made by groups, the evidence is mixed. Writing in 1992, Watson *et al.* observed that most past studies found that group decision-making yielded no improvement over the best individuals.[35] However, these studies used groups that were given no time to develop and where there was no reward for improved performance. Watson *et al.* reported on the results of a study that corrected for these factors. Its findings were that the groups typically scored higher than their best member by approximately 70 per cent each time, and continued to improve over time. Also, the same individuals were rarely the best members on successive occasions. As the group's experience in problem-solving increased, the top scorer became less important to group success. Three possible reasons account for why group decision-making might be better than an individual's. These are that errors get corrected when suggestions are sifted by the group, that the group's social support helps members think clearly and that the competition among members for respect mobilises their energies for the task. Watson *et al.* suggest that these advantages take time to show benefits because newly formed groups are not likely to be efficient enough at processing information to take full advantage of the knowledge that members bring to the pool.

However, although groups can perform better than individuals at problem-solving and decision-making, they have a greater tendency to lead to people believing that erroneous conclusions are correct. Research by Clark and Stephenson[36] has recently shown that:

- the more people working on a problem (they call them available cognitive resources), the greater the number of accurate answers produced *but*
- the better the people concerned know one another, the more likely they are to be confident that errors are not wrong *and*
- the more professionally salient the task, the greater the risk of inaccurate answers being included at the expense of accurate answers, and the greater the confidence in answers which are just plain wrong.

Clark and Stephenson explain their findings in the following way:

> At the intellectual level, knowledge is shared and performance accordingly improved. At the interpersonal level, motivational processes lead to a greater confidence in generalisation and within the inter-group domain, the demands of social competition lead to illegitimate inference beyond the given evidence, with consequent impaired accuracy and, in addition, a denial of error in the form of increased confidence in wrong information.

Groups of senior executives in organisations may be less effective decision-makers than groups generally. Findings based on studying more than 265 live work meetings suggested that this can happen because organisational values inhibit good decision-making and their effects are amplified when senior executives work in groups.[37] Whereas 95 per cent of the executives in the study said that they preferred systems where innovation, risk-taking, flexibility and trust prevail, none of these characteristics was shown in the actual behaviour of the same executives in meetings. Instead, two patterns of behaviour occurred: either thoughtful, rational and mildly competitive behaviour or behaviour that was competitive first, thoughtful and rational second. Both were low on risk-taking. The likely reason for these behaviour patterns in meetings is that three values predominate in organisations. First, the significant human relationships are the ones which have to do with achieving the organisation's objectives and second, only the 'rational' is legitimate. These two values combine to mean that emotions are not significant and are not discussed even where they have clearly caused the meeting to 'bog down'. The third value that acts as a barrier to decision-making in meetings is that human relationships are most effectively

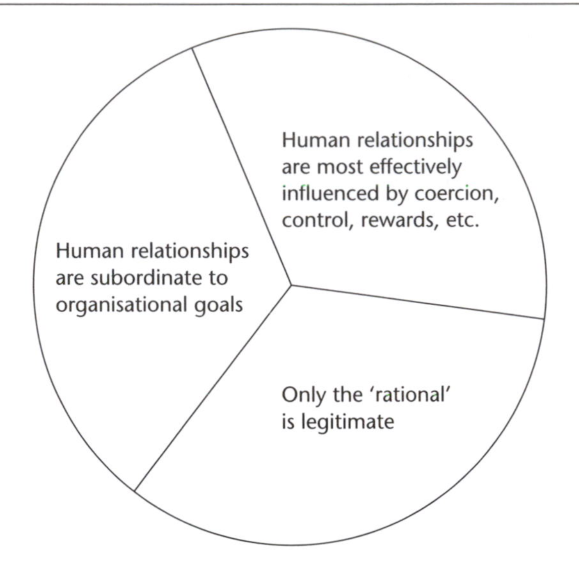


**Figure 11.6 Organisational values that are dysfunctional for decision-making in organisations.**

influenced through unilateral direction, coercion and control or by rewards and punishments. Figure 11.6 shows this view of dysfunctional organisational values.

These values are not really held by many of the executives as individuals; they are the ones 'imposed' by some organisational cultures. The gap between real 'human' values and organisational values means that senior executive are more commited to conforming than they are to solving organisational problems, that high levels of gamesmanship take place behind a screen of concern with tasks and that there is a lack of awareness of behavioural patterns and their effects. The greatest damage is done to important decision-making processes, not to minor ones.

## Improving the quality of group decisions

Ways of getting better decisions from groups include increasing participation, using productive controversy techniques, understanding decision-making processes, overcoming barriers to effective group problem-solving and being clear on certain dimensions of problems.

*Participation*: Vroom and Yetton identified three general criteria for good decision-making: the objective quality of the decision, the time taken to reach it and how acceptable the decision is to subordinates.[38] The third criterion draws attention to an important fact about decision-making at work. A decision or problem-solution is only as good as its implementation. No matter how brilliant, a decision is a poor one if it is carried out half-heartedly or if there is delay in implementing it because those responsible feel reluctant or indifferent about it. For this reason, good decisions are decisions to which those who will implement them feel commitment. People's commitment is higher for decisions that they have shared in making.

*Productive controversy*: groups out-perform solo individuals at the creative side of problem-solving, although nominal groups, composed of individuals who think about a problem alone then pool their ideas, produce significantly more ideas than interactive groups.[39,40] A variety of explanations have been given for this effect, ranging from the temptation to free-ride when people see their individual contributions as dispensable, to fear of criticism, but Diehl and Stroebe[41] found that 96 per cent of the effect was produced by 'production blocking' – the simple fact that in groups only one member can speak at any given time! A technique called 'productive controversy', described in Box 11.6, helps overcome limitations on group creativity.

**Box 11.6**

### How to handle group interaction to benefit from productive controversy

- Compose the group of as wide a range of people as possible, varying particularly in experience, attitudes, approaches and culture.
- Unite this heterogeneous group of people through giving them a 'co-operative goal structure'. That is to say, it should be made to their benefit as individuals to work together and co-operate, rather than compete.
- Set the group the task of finding information and ideas, not problem-solving.
- Let them first write down their ideas.
- Record all creative ideas, no matter how seemingly unsuitable, and thank their sponsors.
- Encourage lateral thinking. Brainstorming techniques may be used. To brainstorm, after a warm-up session, invite the group members to call out ideas relating to the problem as they occur. The group leader records all the ideas generated during the session on a flip-chart. The aim is to generate as many ideas as possible, the wilder the better. By being able to see other people's ideas recorded, individuals are able to find new combinations, 'hitch-hike' or 'free-wheel' on those ideas to produce new insights.
- Exclude all criticism and evaluation while ideas are being generated.
- Later, encourage and accept controversy among ideas, opinions, information, theories and perspectives.
- Develop a norm of persistence in the face of failure. Tell group members that they should expect to struggle and that discouragement is normal. Support and encourage them at these times of difficulty.
- Allow time for reflection after periods of intense work.

*Source*: Margerison, C. (1973) *Managing Effective Work Groups*. Maidenhead: McGraw-Hill.

*Structured decision-making*: there are a large number of 'stage' models available for structuring problem-solving, either by individuals or groups. One of the earliest was that of Dewey, who listed three stages of 'judgement'. First, there

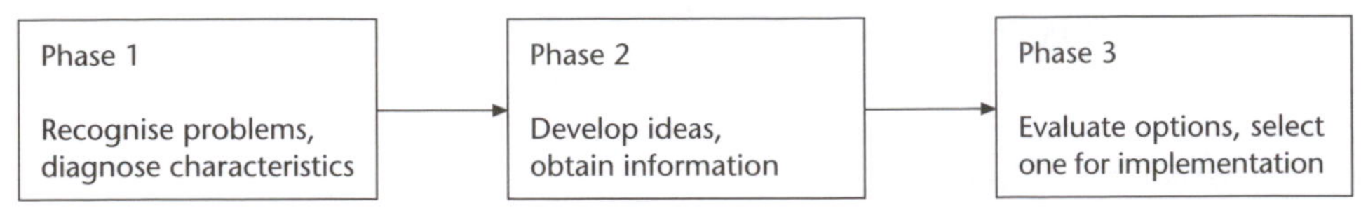


**Figure 11.7 A phase model of decision-making.**

must be a controversy consisting of opposite claims regarding the same objective situation, second, there must be a process of defining and elaborating these claims and finally a decision is made which closes the matter in dispute and serves as a rule or principle for the future.[42] Later models mostly switched away from Dewey's dialectical version to focus instead on information and choice. Simon also had three phases, but they are intelligence activity, design activity and choice activity.[43] Mintzberg used a decision-making model similar to Simon's for his study of live decision-making processes, covering 25 cases each lasting three to four months.[44] Figure 11.7 shows in diagram form an example of this kind of phase model.

Although the broad phases shown in Figure 11.7 are found in most group decision-making, in practice problem-solving does not follow orderly step-by-step sequences of activity even when a solo individual is involved, much less in the untidy interaction of a group. Back-tracking and leap-frogging are usual, while some individuals or groups will overlook one or more of the stages of decision-making altogether. Interruptions, delays and repeating arguments also crop up frequently in complex decision-making processes. Strategic decision-making is not a steady progression from one activity to the next but a dynamic process with periods of acceleration and delay, 'comprehension cycles' in which the persons involved gradually get a better grasp of a complicated question, and failure cycles in which they must return to previous phases if, for instance, conflicts stand in the way of an acceptable solution.[45] These irregularities have their value. Insisting too rigidly on procedure inhibits creative thinking and can prevent consensus developing. Indeed researchers have shown that groups actively structure their decision processes to adapt to various contingencies rather than using either a fixed or a random procedure.[46] All the same, there does seem to be a widespread belief among managers that a logical procedure should be followed in decision-making, which suggests that they have found some form of system to be helpful.

*Overcoming barriers*: progress through the stages of group problem-solving can be slowed up by barriers which mean that executives 'often come away from meetings tired and annoyed that objectives were not achieved'.[47] These barriers include failure to generate or develop relevant ideas, take decisions or follow up with effective action. Ways of overcoming these problems are given in Box 11.7.

**Box 11.7**

### How to overcome barriers to group problem-solving

- A shortage of good ideas points to the needs for recruiting better personnel to the group, for increasing the rewards for creativity or eliminating the penalties – especially the 'social' penalties for expressing ideas freely.
- Failure to develop ideas suggests the need to educate the group to look for the best available solution rather than the 'perfect' one and to encourage the search for strengths, not weaknesses, in ideas that are put forward.
- Where relevant ideas are developed but no decision is taken, the cause is often 'uncertainty avoidance' – not doing anything seems to leave the group in the known situation, whereas making a decision introduces the unknown. One possible solution here is to reduce the perceived risk attached to making mistakes – and perhaps increase, by punishment such as loss of status, the perceived risk attached to making no decision. Another method is to clarify what is often the case – that the two alternatives of action or inaction are not as asymmetrical as they seem. In practice, doing nothing is often more uncertain in its consequences because it hands control of the situation to outsiders.
- Decisions that result in no action point to a poor decision-making process, one in which those responsible for implementation were not fully consulted or involved and to which, therefore, they felt no commitment. Greater participation of all those affected by the decision is needed.
- Finally, action that does not produce the desired results indicates a poor decision; following a more systematic procedure as described above, or working for greater clarity in group discussion as suggested below, may be the remedy.

*Dimensional clarity*: Charles Margerison identified a number of dimensions on which clarity helps the progress of group discussions but on which they are in fact often confused. These dimensions are beliefs/facts, barriers/opportunities, symptoms/causes, evaluation/definition, means/ends and long term/short term.

Poor group-decision-making results when:

- beliefs, backed by too little evidence, are treated as if they were facts;
- avoiding risk leads to people being over-aware of the problems associated with any suggestion;
- analysis is superficial, so that symptoms instead of causes are diagnosed and treated;
- there is a lack of attention to what exactly the issues are – to definition – and an over-eagerness to rush to conclusions or evaluate;
- means become ends in themselves;
- there is a tendency to focus on plans for the distant future without thinking through their short-term implications.

Helpful group discussion is more likely to occur when it distinguishes facts from opinions, objectives from means and concentrates on opportunities, causes, definitions and the short to medium term. This programme really requires a collaborative effort from all the most influential of the group members, both to exercise self-discipline, even when the discussion becomes heated, and to take responsibility for tactfully steering the discussion in the 'right' paths when the other members stray.[48]

## Teamwork

Modern organisations, whether matrix, federation, network or adhocracy, make extensive use of teams. Even within traditional organisations, strategic business units, 'intrapreneurial' groups or internal consultancies require teamwork. More generally, many jobs require the collaborative efforts of specialists and knowledge from different sections or departments. Few people, whether they carry the label 'manager' or not, have any choice about whether they act as, and see themselves as, part of one or more teams.

**Box 11.8**

### European variations in teamwork

In France, a team is a group of specialists under an unequivocal leader. Germans regard teams similarly to the French but, in addition, teams are usually 'located' within the hierarchy and must be seen as explicit parts of the members' workload. In Italy, there is no concept of an equal sharing of power, so teams must have a respected leader. In the United Kingdom, the cultural preference for the security of group decision-making, plus a desire to contribute to a larger objective, make the British good team workers, though individual competitiveness and a blame culture can undermine this.

*Team building* begins by bringing together people with the right combinations of specialist knowledge, personal qualities and role orientations. Effective teams include at least one task-oriented and one maintenance-oriented person. The person in the task role ensures that momentum is maintained towards the completion of the task, and provides structure and leadership. The person in the maintenance role shields the task leader, handles conflict and interpersonal problems within the team, and assuages, placates and 'recruits' from other teams. This basic division of team roles into task and maintenance is helpful, but R. M. Belbin did research which showed that team performances are better if a more diverse set of roles is enacted.[49] The roles he identified in performance teams and the names he gave them are listed in Table 11.4. Belbin found that team members tended to adopt one or two of these roles fairly consistently, and that psychometric tests could predict which those roles would be.

Effective teams have the following characteristics. All members clearly understand and are committed to the team objectives. Mutual trust and support are high and communications are open and reliable, not guarded. Team members listen to one another, they understand and are understood. The team is self-controlling, conflicts are accepted and worked through. Members' abilities, knowledge and experience are fully used by the team.[50] Achieving all this takes skill.

**Table 11.4 Belbin's roles**

| *Role* | *Role name* |
|---|---|
| Co-ordinating | Chairman [sic] |
| Directing | Team leader |
| Creative thinking | Innovator |
| Critical thinking | Monitor-evaluator |
| Carrying out the task | Company worker |
| Looking after the personal relationships in the team | Team worker |
| Progress chasing | Completer |
| Keeping in touch with other teams | Resource investigator |

**Box 11.9**

Hirokawa and Keyton (1995) found that work team members believed that compatible work schedules, motivated group members, adequate informational resources, competent group leadership and organisational assistance made most difference to the effectiveness of volunteer-based work teams.

*Source*: Hirokawa, R. Y. and J. Keyton (1995) 'Perceived facilitators and inhibitors of effectiveness in organizational work teams', *Management Communication Quarterly*, vol. 8, no. 4, pp. 424–446.

The *problem of competitiveness*, already observed in the context of work relationships and decision-making groups, also arises in teamwork. Overcoming this problem is often achieved through having appropriate team goals. A team goal is a state of affairs that the members of a team want enough to work together towards bringing it about. For example, a team of marketing staff might have the goal of increasing sales by 3 per cent in the next period. A team of personnel staff might have the goal of ensuring that equal-opportunities practices are introduced in staff-selection procedures throughout the organisation. These superordinate goals need to be broken down into more immediate goals, so that each time the team meets, members have a specific and concrete target to aim for. In the examples given, these might be, for the marketing staff, one time to devise a pricing strategy, another to draft a briefing document for the sales force. For the personnel staff, they could be on one occasion to draw up a standard form of wording to cover the equal-opportunities issue in all recruitment advertisements and on another to plan a series of seminars for managers involved in selection. Both the examples given here illustrate co-operative goal structures, those in which team members can only obtain their goals if the other members of the team obtain their goal too. Goal structures can also be competitive or individualistic. They are competitive when for one or some members to attain their goal others must fail to attain theirs, as in a race. They are individualistic when there is no necessary relation between the goal attainment of one member and those of others – for instance in a group of students working on an assignment which will be submitted and marked individually.

Research into how different *types of goal* affect team behaviour has shown that co-operative goals lead to team members having greater acceptance, trust and liking for each other and more willingness to support each other. They also lead to team members exchanging more information, talking more things through, having more influence on each other and drawing more fully on the resources of the team. The other two types of goal affect teams differently. Competitive goals produce almost the opposite effects, while individualistic ones produce an intermediate pattern.[51]

**Box 11.10**

## Factors that help teams work well together

- Being a cohesive team. Cohesiveness 'develops if belonging to the group is rewarding in any of a variety of ways' (Argyle, 1981), for instance, if it has been successful in competition with other groups.
- Having members who are socially rewarding. Members of teams become popular mainly because of their ability and willingness to help others, but also through being socially rewarding, for instance friendly or cheerful. Neuman and Wright (1999) found that agreeableness and conscientiousness predicted peer ratings of team member performance better than measures of job-specific skills and general cognitive ability. (Similarly, at the group level of analysis, both agreeableness and conscientiousness predicted how supervisors rate work team performance, objective measures of work team accuracy and work completed.)
- Having powerful members who help others. Members become powerful in the informal hierarchy of a group if they can help others. For example, in a committee, the members with the greatest knowledge and whose ideas seem most useful will become informal leaders. In working groups, the leadership hierarchy can be seen in how often one person succeeds in influencing others and by which member is turned to when difficulties have to be dealt with. Status is also important, and is mainly based on level of skill or past achievements in relation to the work of the team.
- Ensuring that the goal structure is co-operative, not competitive or individualistic.
- Arguing can improve group outcomes, it has been shown (Infante *et al.*, 1994). Arguing is associated with constructive disagreements in organisational settings, whereas verbal aggressiveness is associated with destructive disagreements. (It was also found that participants perceived higher levels of verbal aggression in their discussion than observers did.) Meyers and Brashers (1998) showed that group outcomes could be predicted from the group's levels of reasoning activities and convergence-seeking activities.

*Sources*: Argyle M. (1989) *The Social Psychology of Work*, 2nd edn. Harmondsworth, Middlesex: Penguin, p. 114.
Infante, D. A., S. A. Myers and R. A. Buerkel (1994) 'Argument and verbal aggression in constructive and destructive family and organizational disagreements', *Western Journal of Communication*, vol. 58, no. 2, pp. 73–84.
Meyers, R. A. and D. E. Brashers (1998) 'Argument in group decision-making: Explicating a process model and investigating the argument–outcome link', *Communication Monographs*, vol. 65, no. 4, pp. 261–281.
Neuman, G. A. and J. Wright (1999) 'Team effectiveness: Beyond skills and cognitive ability', *Journal of Applied Psychology*, vol. 84, no. 3, pp. 376–389.

Keeping *team motivion* is another significant problem. Productivity loss occurs widely among individuals who are combining their efforts into a common pool. It can result from the low motivation of individuals who perceive no value to

**Box 11.11**

### How to motivate individual team members

J. A. Shepperd has suggested three broad categories of solutions, corresponding to each of the three types of perceptions which are sources of low productivity: providing incentives for contributing, making individuals' contributions seem indispensable and decreasing the cost of contributing.

1. Providing incentives for contributing.

   - Providing external reward for the individual by making individual contributions identifiable and able to be evaluated. This only works if comparison with the rewards gained by others is possible. However, when the external reward is social (e.g. social approval, liking, status), it need not be explicitly promised to be effective.
   - Providing internal reward for the individual. When individuals can personally evaluate their performance (either against an objective standard, a social standard or their own previous performances), they exert greater effort, even on boring tasks. This solution capitalises on the fact that, as well as being concerned that others evaluate them favourably, people are concerned to evaluate themselves favourably.
   - Providing intrinsic reward for the individual. When the task is seen to be intrinsically interesting or personally relevant, people exert more effort.
   - Providing external reward for the whole group. This can work if the incentive is very powerful.
   - Providing internal reward for the whole group. This can work if the individual identifies strongly with the group.

2. Making individual contributions seem indispensable. Shepperd acknowledges that this is a difficult task, but suggests that specialisation within the overall task to make individual contributions unique is one approach, while developing a climate that 'every little helps', is another.
3. Decreasing the costs of contributing. The costs of working hard on a group task include loss of time and energy diverted from more 'profitable' ventures, plus the psychological costs of perceived inequity if others are not pulling their weight. Ways of dealing with the latter include privatising, manipulating the feedback that individuals receive regarding the efforts of their co-workers (but there may be ethical and practical problems), or providing assurance that others' free-riding attempts will be punished (e.g. by ostracising them).

A different approach based on a similar diagnosis is to set the group size at four members. Group size is related to task motivation. It constitutes an inverted U-shaped curve peaking at four members, which is explained in terms of members' perceptions of their own indispensability. In large groups members perceive themselves as dispensable. Very small groups also may not motivate strongly because the perceived indispensability (efficacy) of the group as a whole may be low.

*Source*: Shepperd, J. A. (1993) 'Productivity loss in performance groups: A motivation analysis', *Psychological Bulletin*, vol. 113, no. 1, pp. 67–81.

contributing, who perceive no direct link from their contributions to getting something they want, or who perceive the costs of contributing to be excessive. Such perceptions result in social loafing, which includes free-riding, that is trying to gain the same outcome by less effort, and the sucker effect, trying to avoid the danger of contributing to the common effort when others do nothing or little. In effect, low productivity in teams can be viewed as a type of social dilemma, in that the behaviour that is in the best interests of the individual conflicts with the behaviour that is in the best interest of the group.

The role of leaders and managers in team building is described in Chapter 13. In 'new' organisations, and to some degree in traditional hierarchies, there has been a growth in the use of self-managed teams, which have no officially designated authority figure. However, to work well, self-managed should not mean 'leaderless', but having distributed leadership, where different people will assume different leadership roles. Figure 11.8 shows four types of leader who are needed in self-managed teams.[52] While these four kinds of leadership may read like another set of roles, there is an important difference. In self-managed teams, these individuals are needed not just to fulfil the role but also to lead the whole team in performing this function. Thus the spanning leader, for instance, is not someone who himself or herself acts as a link for the team, but someone who

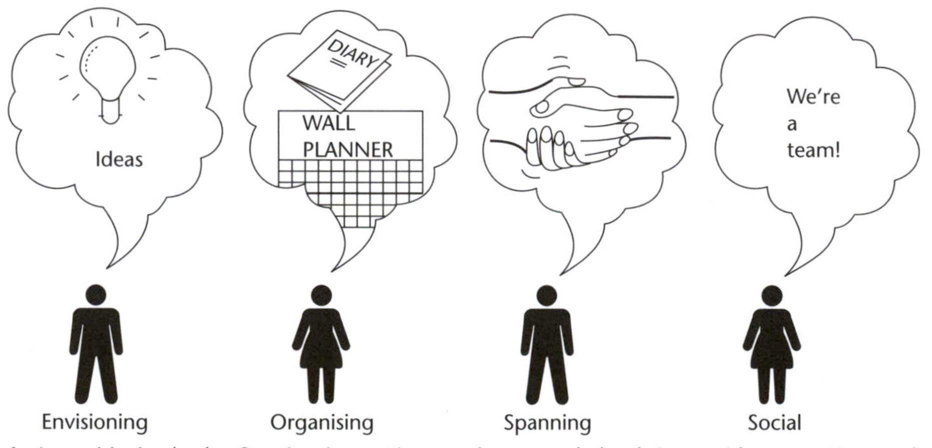


1. *An envisioning leader.* Creative, innovative people are needed to bring up ideas, question outdated ways of thinking, and define and champion overall goals. Such people, though needed, may not be good at team skills, so will need to be 'fostered' by other members of the team.
2. *An organising leader.* People who focus on details, deadlines, efficiency and structure are needed to ensure that the task gets done, though their form of leadership may impede the team when new directions are needed.
3. *A spanning leader.* The team needs a person to lead it in networking, developing and maintaining a strong image with outsiders, finding and obtaining resources, bargaining and political activity in the wider organisation and the world outside.
4. *A social leader.* People are needed who provide leadership in developing and maintaining team cohesiveness.

**Figure 11.8 Four types of leader needed by self-managing teams.**

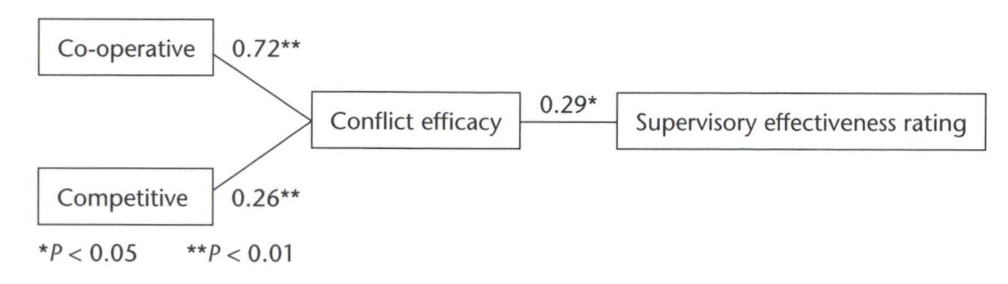


**Figure 11.9 Alper *et al.*'s model of conflict dynamics and outcomes.**

motivates, develops, and to some degree organises and directs the other team members in carrying out the team's 'external relations'.

There is evidence that team-based systems of control are more powerful and less obtrusive than their bureaucratic predecessors. Workers in self-managing teams, especially long-term workers, identify more strongly with their team than with their company, particularly in terms of loyalty.[53] Nevertheless, conflict does arise and must be dealt with. The team's own beliefs that it can so deal with issues as to manage the team's conflicts productively is correlated with how effective supervisors rate the team to be.[54] Belief in being able to deal with issues, as readers will recognise, is what Bandura's concept of efficacy means. Bandura himself considered that group efficacy exists and can have important effects on team performance.[55] Managing conflict for mutual benefit predicted a high level of conflict efficacy, which in turn predicted a high supervisory effectiveness rating.[56] Figure 11.9 shows a model of conflict efficacy.

## SUMMARY – WORK APPLICATIONS FOR GROUP SKILLS

Although controversy surrounds the question of the influence of individuals and minority opinions in group decision-making, the thinking of all of us is highly influenced by the thinking of those with whom we talk and otherwise interact. In principle, therefore, groups should be effective decision-makers, because they make use of the creativity released by interaction. In practice, however, there are significant barriers to effective group problem-solving. These include production blocking, competitiveness within groups and lack of clarity. Organisational cultures that elevate the 'rational' and support the view that human relationships at work must be strongly controlled and subordinated to organisational goals, leading to a lack of innovativeness, risk-taking, flexibility and trust. Composing problem-solving groups for effectiveness, increasing participation, better structuring of processes, increasing rewards for creativity, sub-optimising and working for greater clarity in group thinking are all methods that address recognised problems in group decision-making.

Effective teams are characterised by high commitment to team objectives, high mutual trust and support, open communication, working through of conflict and full use being made of members' actual and potential contributions. Most of the interpersonal interaction aspects of teams have been covered in earlier parts of this book, but two important and difficult areas are how to prevent competitiveness from destroying group cohesiveness and how to keep all members motivated and active over time. Solutions of both problems seem to revolve around rewards, including making membership rewarding, having goal structures that reward co-operation and careful adjustments to the rewards for and the costs of contributing. Many of these rewards and costs are social, not material, and depend on the interpersonal skills of leading group members.

In self-managed teams, leadership is distributed. Different individuals take on 'specialised' leadership roles. Overcoming conflict in self-managed teams is related to efficacy expectations and these in turn to co-operative behaviour patterns.

## CHAPTER OVERVIEW

Over and above those skills that have been described in previous chapters, the skills that group members need revolve mainly around facilitating the group's work by applying an understanding of group development, communication structures, power and status differences, role behaviour, conformity pressures, groupthink, risky or cautious shifts and inter-group conflict.

Compared with individuals, groups can make objectively better decisions to which people feel more commitment, while teams can perform functions and carry out projects better and more efficiently. This can only happen, however, if the people working in groups have the special skills and attitudes needed. If these skills are available it is likely that the group will be able to overcome the process barriers and achieve effective problem-solving and task performance.

## EXERCISES

1. Who is in your work team? We tend to think that our team members are those in the same department or all those who report to the same boss. Actually, most of us find that we work more with people from other departments than we do with people in our own. See if this is true for you.

2. To increase your awareness of the different types of group behaviour, and their impact on other group members, use the group behaviour coding form of Figure 11.10 to code the behaviour of other people you observe during any meeting, group discussion or other similar forum. Complete the forms as soon as possible after the meeting is over. Filling the forms requires you to code the behaviour of other group members along three dimensions – task-, maintenance- and self-oriented behaviours. Use one form for each type.

   Starting with task-oriented, fill each of the columns in each form:

| Form A. Task-oriented behaviour | | | |
|---|---|---|---|
| Name | Behaviour description | Impact on group | My feelings and responses |
| | | | |

| Form B. Maintenance-oriented behaviour | | | |
|---|---|---|---|
| Name | Behaviour description | Impact on group | My feelings and responses |
| | | | |

| Form C. Self-oriented behaviour | | | |
|---|---|---|---|
| Name | Behaviour description | Impact on group | My feelings and responses |
| | | | |

**Figure 11.10 Group behaviour coding forms.**

(a) List three, or in a small group, two, people in your group who have been most task-oriented.
(b) For each person, describe some behaviour that illustrates their task-orientation.
(c) Describe the impact on the group as you see it.
(d) Describe your reaction in terms of the impact of the behaviour on (i) your feelings; (ii) your action in response.

Repeat this for the maintenance-oriented and self-oriented forms. To code behaviours, use evidence; try not to use emotional overtones or general statements.

3. This role play consists of a meeting of a four-person team from the Human Resources Department of a hotel company. The team's task is to make

recommendations on the attributes required for both senior and junior posts in the following hotel units:

- housekeeping (cleaning and care of bedrooms and common areas);
- maintenance (electrical, plumbing, building);
- reception and customer service;
- catering (restaurants, bars and room service);
- general management and administration.

4. Four directors of a medium-sized private company that is experiencing financial difficulties meet to discuss ways of saving £500,000 per year. They have four proposals to consider, each of which would save about that amount:

   - Charge staff for use of the company car park.
   - Close the creche.
   - Close the fitness centre.
   - Remove the subsidy on the food in the company canteen.

   The role play consists of the meeting. Either each player is allocated a case to argue or it is left open as a genuine problem-solving discussion.

5. Work in a group to draw up a job description and person specification for a post in an overseas subsidiary of a company. The company could be in any field and the post could be in accounting, marketing, IT, production, Human Resources Management or any other business area according to the interests and experience of the group members. The country, too, can be chosen to suit the interests and knowledge of the participants. The post should be in middle management, with host nation personnel as subordinates, colleagues and superiors.

   The concern is both with the outcome of the discussion and the process, which should be observed by one or more observers. The group behaviour coding form may be used.

6. This is a role play of a meeting to discuss the discharge from hospital of an elderly patient who has been in hospital for six weeks following a fall and broken hip. The patient now has some mobility, but can neither walk nor stand without a frame; she is periodically confused. The patient lives alone in a home that has not been adapted for use by a person with disabilities; however, the accommodation is all on one level and the patient is very eager to go home. The purpose of the meeting is:

   - to decide if the home situation and the patient's condition are such as to allow the return home; and if so,
   - what adaptations to the home are required;
   - what home care arrangements are required; these might include to provide shopping, cooking, personal care, laundry, domestic cleaning and supervision of taking of medication;
   - what medical supervision and attendance are required.

*Roles*: hospital doctor, nurse, hospital social worker, home care supervisor, general practitioner, district nurse, patient, patient's next of kin.
The concern is both with the outcome of the discussion and the process, which should be observed by one or more observers. The group behaviour coding form may be used.

7. Two groups have been set the task of devising a system to improve communication among the ten members of a department, which is part of a commercial law practice. At the moment, communication among them is very limited; all are very busy, spending most of their working day in meetings with clients or representing them in negotiations. The problem is for them to keep one another informed of developments on client business. At present, if a client telephones when the solicitor who works on their account is with another client, or otherwise unavailable, there will probably be no one who knows what is going on or who can take any swift action. This angers clients and has led to some client losses.

   Procedure for the exercise:

   *Group A*: devise and note down as many different solutions as possible in the first 15 minutes. During this time, no solutions may be rejected and no criticism of any potential solution is to be considered. The group is to aim at maximum participation of all members. At the end of 15 minutes, no further solutions are to be generated. Make a note of the number of solutions generated. In the next 10 minutes, the available list is examined and assessed, using any system the group chooses, and the best selected. The best solution is then to be described and explained on at most half a side of A4 paper. The group also records its confidence in its solution, level of participation and satisfaction with the group. Each of these is measured by the average of the individual members scores from 1 to 5.

   *Group B*: in this group each solution is examined and assessed before the next is considered. Keep a tally of the number of solutions considered. After 25 minutes, write up the best solution on at most half a side of A4 paper. The group also records its confidence in its solution, level of participation and satisfaction with the group. Each of these is measured by the average of the individual members scores from 1 to 5.

   (a) Solutions are exchanged and assessed for quality by the 'opposing' groups.
   (b) The following items are recorded on a board so arranged as to allow comparison: each group's score on: number of solutions generated, quality of chosen solution (assessed by the opposing group), confidence in its solution, level of participation and satisfaction with the group (assessed by the group itself).

The class discusses which was the more creative group and why.

## FURTHER READING

*Harvard Business Review* (1996) *Decision Making*. Cambridge, Mass.: Harvard Business Review Press.
Hogg, M. A. (1992) *The Social Psychology of Group Cohesiveness: From Attraction to Social Identity*. London: Harvester Wheatsheaf.
Janis, I. L. (1972) *Victims of Groupthink*. Boston, Mass.: Houghton-Mifflin.
Levi, D. (2001) *Group Dynamics for Teams*. London: Sage.
Moreland, R. L. and J. M. Levine (1994) *Understanding Small Groups*. Boston, Mass.: Allyn & Bacon.
Wilson, G. (1995) *Self-managed Team Working*. London: FT Pitman.
Worchel, S. S., W. Wood and J. A. Simpson (1991) *Group Process and Productivity*. London: Sage.

## REFERENCES

1. Lau, J. B. and A. B. Shani (1988) *Behaviour in Organizations: An Experiential Approach*, 4th edn. Homewood, Ill.: Irwin.
2. Napier, R. W. and M. K. Gershenfeld (1981) *Groups: Theory and Experience*, 2nd edn. Boston, Mass.: Houghton Mifflin.
3. Tuckman, B. W. (1965) 'Developmental sequences in small groups', *Psychological Bulletin*, vol. 63, pp. 384–399.
4. Hogg, M. A. (1992) *The Social Psychology of Group Cohesiveness: From Attraction to Social Identity*. London: Harvester Wheatsheaf.
5. Srivastva, S., S. L. Obert and E. Neilson (1997) 'Organizational analysis through group processes: A theoretical perspective' in C. L. Cooper (ed.) *Organizational Development in the UK and USA*. London: Macmillan.
6. Reason, P. (1999) 'General medical and complementary practitioners working together: The epistemological demands of collaboration', *Journal of Applied Behavioural Science*, vol. 35, no. 1, pp. 71–86.
7. Moreland, R. L. and J. M. Levine (1994) *Understanding Small Groups*. Boston, Mass.: Allyn & Bacon.
8. Cohen, B. and X. Zhou (1991) 'Status processes in enduring work groups', *American Sociological Review*, vol. 56, pp. 179–188.
9. Aysan, S. (1989) 'Simultaneous effects of status and task cues: combining, eliminating or buffering', *Social Psychology Quarterly*, vol. 52, no. 4, pp. 327–335.
10. Rijsman, J. B. (1984) 'Group characteristics and individual behaviour' in P. J. D. Drenth, H. Thierry, P. J. Williams and C. J. de Wolff (eds) *Handbook of Work and Organisational Psychology*. New York: John Wiley and Sons.
11. Hogg, M. A., E. A. Hardie and K. J. Reynolds (1995) 'Prototypical similarity, self-categorization and depersonalized attraction; a perspective on group cohesiveness', *European Journal of Social Psychology*, vol. 25, pp. 159–177.
12. Hogg, M. A. and J. C. Turner (1985) 'Interpersonal attraction, social identification and psychological group formation', *European Journal of Social Psychology*, vol. 15, pp. 51–66.
13. Scott, C. R. (1999) 'The impact of physical and discursive anonymity on group members' multiple identifications during computer-supported decision making', *Western Journal of Communication*, vol. 63, no. 4, pp. 456–487.
14. Asch, S. E. (1956) 'Studies of independence and conformity', *Psychological Monographs*, vol. 70, no. 9.

15. Reicher, S. D., R. Spears and T. Postmes (1995) 'A social identity model of deindividuation phenomena' in W. Stroebe and M. Hewstone (eds) *European Review of Social Psychology*, vol. 6. Chichester: John Wiley, pp. 69–96.
16. Argyle, M. (1989) *The Social Psychology of Work*, 2nd edn. Harmondsworth, Middlesex: Penguin.
17. Janis, I. L. (1972) *Victims of Groupthink*. Boston, Mass.: Houghton-Mifflin.
18. Stoner, J. A. F. (1968) 'Risky and cautious shifts in group decisions: The influence of widely-held values', *Journal of Experimental Social Psychology*, vol. 4, pp. 442–459.
19. Wallach, M. A., N. Kogan and D. J. Bem (1964) 'Diffusion of responsibility and level of risk taking in groups', *Journal of Abnormal and Social Psychology*, vol. 68, pp. 263–274.
20. Bem, D. J., M. A. Wallach and N. Kogan (1965) 'Group decision-making under risk of aversive consequences', *Journal of Personality and Social Psychology*, vol. 1, pp. 453–460.
21. Houghton, S. M., M. Simon, K. Aquino and C. B. Goldberg (2000) 'No safety in numbers: Persistence of biases and their effects on team risk perception and team decision-making', *Group & Organization Management*, vol. 25, no. 4, pp. 325–353.
22. Stephan, W. G., C. W. Stephan, T. Stefanenko, V. Ageyev, M. Abalakina and L. Coates-Shrider (1993) 'Measuring stereotypes: A comparison of methods using Russian and American samples', *Social Psychology Quarterly*, vol. 56, no. 1, pp. 54–64.
23. Coser, L. (1961) 'The termination of conflict' in W. J. Gore and J. W. Dyson (eds) *The Making of Decisions*. New York: Free Press.
24. Torrington, D. (1982) *Face-to-Face in Management*. New York: Prentice-Hall International.
25. Hoffman, L. R. and G. B. Kleinman (1994) 'Individual and group in group problem-solving: the valence model redressed', *Human Communication Research*, vol. 21, pp. 36–59.
26. Gruendfeld, D. H., P. V. Martorana and E. T. Fan (2000) 'What do groups learn from their worldliest members? Direct and indirect influence in dynamic teams', *Organizational Behavior and Human Decision Processes*, vol. 82, no. 1, pp. 45–59.
27. Moscovici, S. (1980) 'Toward a theory of conversion behaviour' in L. Berkowitz (ed.) *Advances in Experimental Social Psychology*, Vol. 2. New York: Random House.
28. Maass, A and R. D. Clark III (1984) 'Hidden impact of minorities: Fifteen years of minority influence research', *Psychological Bulletin*, vol. 95, pp. 89–104.
29. Maass, A., S. G. West and R. B. Cialdini (1987) 'Minority influence and conversion' in C. Hendrick (ed.) *Review of Personality and Social Psychology*, Vol. 8. Beverly Hills, Calif.: Sage.
30. Mackie, D. M. (1987) 'Systematic and nonsystematic processing of majority and minority persuasive communications', *Journal of Personality and Social Psychology*, vol. 53, pp. 41–52.
31. De Vries, N. K., C. K. W. De Dreu, E. Gordjin and M. Schuurman (1996) 'Majority and minority influence; a dual role interpretation' in W. Stroebe and M. Hewstone (eds) *European Review of Social Psychology*, Vol. 7. Chichester: John Wiley, pp. 145–172.
32. Nemeth, C. J. (1992) 'Minority dissent as a stimulus to group performance' in S. Worchel, W. Wood and J. S. Simpson (eds) *Group Processes and Productivity*. Newbury Park: Sage, pp. 95–111.
33. Gruenfeld, D. H., M. C. Thomas-Hunt and P. H. Kim (1998) 'Cognitive flexibility, communication strategy and integrative complexity in groups' public and private reactions to majority and minority status', *Journal of Experimental Social Psychology*, vol. 3, pp. 202–226.
34. De Vries *et al.*, op. cit.
35. Watson, W., L. Michaelson and W. Sharp (1992) 'Member competence, group interaction and group decision-making: A longitudinal study', *Journal of Applied Psychology*, vol. 76, no. 6, pp. 803–809.

36. Clark, N. K. and G. M. Stephenson (1999) 'Social remembering: Individual and collaborative memory for social information' in W. Stroebe and M. Hewstone (eds) *European Review of Social Psychology*, Vol. 6. Chichester: John Wiley, pp. 127–160.
37. Argyris, C. (1960) *Understanding Organizational Behavior*. New York: Dorsey.
38. Vroom, V. H. and P. W. Yetton (1973) *Leadership and Decision-Making*. Pittsburgh: University of Pittsburgh Press.
39. Taylor, D. W., P. C. Berry and C. H. Block (1958) 'Does group participation when using brainstorming facilitate or inhibit creative thinking?', *Administrative Science Quarterly*, vol. 3, p. 23.
40. Mullen, B., C. Johnson and E. Salas (1991) 'Productivity loss in brainstorming groups: A meta-analytic integration', *Basic and Applied Social Psychology*, vol. 12, pp. 3–24.
41. Diehl, M. and W. Stroebe (1987) 'Productivity loss in brainstorming groups: Toward the solution of a riddle', *Journal of Personality and Social Psychology*, vol. 53, pp. 497–509.
42. Dewey, C. (1910) in H. Mintzberg, D. Raisinghani and A. Theoret (1976) 'The structure of "unstructured" decision processes', *Administrative Science Quarterly*, vol. 21, pp. 246–275.
43. Simon, H. (1947) *Administrative Behaviour*. New York: Free Press.
44. Mintzberg, H. (1973) *The Nature of Managerial Work*. New York: Harper and Row.
45. Poole, M. S. and J. Roth (1989) 'Decision development in small groups: IV. A typology of decision paths', *Human Communication Research*, vol. 15, pp. 323–356 and 'V. Tests of a contingency model', *Human Communication Research*, vol. 15, pp. 549–589.
46. Koopman, P. L., J. W. Brockhuysen and O. M. Meijn (1984) 'Complex decision-making at the organizational level' in P. J. D. Drenth, H. Thierry, P. J. Williams and C. J. de Wolff (eds) *Handbook of Work and Organisational Psychology*, Vol. 2. New York: Wiley.
47. Margerison, C. (1973) *Managing Effective Work Groups*. Maidenhead: McGraw-Hill.
48. Ibid.
49. Belbin, R. M. (1981) *Management Teams: Why They Succeed or Fail*. London: Heinemann.
50. Deutsch, M. (1949) 'The effects of co-operation and competition on group process', *Human Relations*, vol. 2, pp. 129–152, 199–231.
51. Worchel, S. S., W. Wood and J. A. Simpson (1991) *Group Process and Productivity*. London: Sage.
52. Barry, D. (1991) 'Managing the bossless team: lessons in distributed leadership', *Organizational Dynamics*, Summer, pp. 31–47.
53. Barker, J. R. and P. K. Tompkins (1994) 'Identification in the self-managing organization; characteristics of target and tenure', *Human Communication Research*, vol. 21, pp. 223–240.
54. Alper, S., D. Tjosvold and K. S. Law (2000) 'Conflict management, efficacy and performance in organizational teams', *Personnel Psychology*, vol. 53, no. 3, pp. 625–642.
55. Bandura, A. (1977) *Social Learning Theory*. Englewood Cliffs, New Jersey: Prentice-Hall, pp. 248–259.
56. Alper *et al.*, op. cit.

# 12 Working across cultures

## CHAPTER INTRODUCTION

The following extract, from a policy paper by policy group of the European Language Council, shows the importance and meaning of cross-cultural working across Europe:

> Social progress and the building of relations of peace and equality between people in Europe depends on the development of awareness of . . . cultural variety and difference. In the context of European integration, the national dimension is often perceived as the most salient, but it is not the only significant determinant of different cultural identities. Important determinants lie, for example, in class, gender, ethnicity, language, education, political or religious affiliation, and individual dispositions.

The European workforce of the early twenty-first century will be diverse – that is, it will consist of people from many different national and ethnic backgrounds and of women to nearly the same degree as men. More people with disabilities will be accepted into workforces. More people will claim acceptance at work of their differing sexual orientations, religious affiliations and family structures. Open labour and product markets will widen the already-wide diversity of the people met through work as customers, clients, suppliers, advisers, accountants, bankers, lawyers, patients, students, pupils and their parents. More people will experience a period of living and working in other European countries or further afield.

Chapter 2 of this book introduced the subject of cultural differences and how different national and cultural environments affect work and organisations, including organisational cultures. Chapter 3 showed how cultural differences affect work interactions. Chapter 7 began the process of learning how to communicate across cultures. Other chapters have touched on relevant aspects of culture. This chapter considers what it is like to work in relationships and groups alongside people from a different cultural background. It covers both working in a diverse organisation and working and living in a host country with a different culture from the sojourner's own. Finally, Chapter 13 will introduce some ideas on managing diversity face-to-face. This chapter aims to help readers gain an awareness and understanding of the following factors, traits and processes for working successfully in relationships and groups with people from diverse backgrounds:

- impediments to working with diverse others;
- processes that support intercultural work, including contact, communication and co-operative interdependence;
- traits that are needed to work cross-culturally;
- interpersonal skills for intercultural work;
- sojourning – culture shock and adjustment/adaptation;
- work activities applying intercultural skills: working in multicultural groups and intercultural/international negotiating.

## IMPEDIMENTS TO WORKING WELL ACROSS CULTURES

In Chapter 11, the effects of conflict between groups of people at work were discussed. Here the causes of such conflict and other problems in relations between groups are considered, especially as they arise in the workplace between members of different social categories such as ethnic groups, genders and so on. This is essential background for understanding how to work across cultures. Causes of inter-group friction at work include intrinsic inter-group biases, actual and perceived cultural differences, concerns about 'face', lack of predictability, diffuse anxiety, difficulty in sustaining self-conceptions and ethical issues. Figure 12.1 shows these causes and some of the behaviours they lead to.

In-group favouritism is well proven, even under 'minimal' social conditions, where research subjects are categorised randomly into groups.[1,2] These findings, however, relate to the distribution of positively valued items such as money. Where what is being distributed is unpleasant, such as a loud noise, no significant in-group favouritism is found in minimal groups. In-group favouritism does not extend to harming out-groups under minimal conditions.[3] However, in-group bias does occur in negative areas in the presence of aggravating variables, such as the out-group being a minority and/or 'inferior' group. Where people think that being associated with a particular out-group will threaten their positive social identity, they discriminate in both positive and negative inter-group evaluations and outcome allocations.

In real life, of course, there are often sharp power and status differences between groups and these can be perceived to be legitimate, stable and immutable.[4] Groups vary in size, demographic distribution, access to channels of mass communication and so on. These differences affect the form and content of inter-group behaviour. We are more likely to create stereotypes of people who are members of different groups from ourselves. Our stereotypes tend to favour our in-group. We tend to believe that out-group members are less attractive, capable, trustworthy, honest, co-operative and deserving than members of our in-group. As a result, we behave differently towards out-group members. Self-categorisation as a member or representative of a group, in the way described in Chapter 4, leads to inter-group differentiation and discrimination, in-group favouritism,

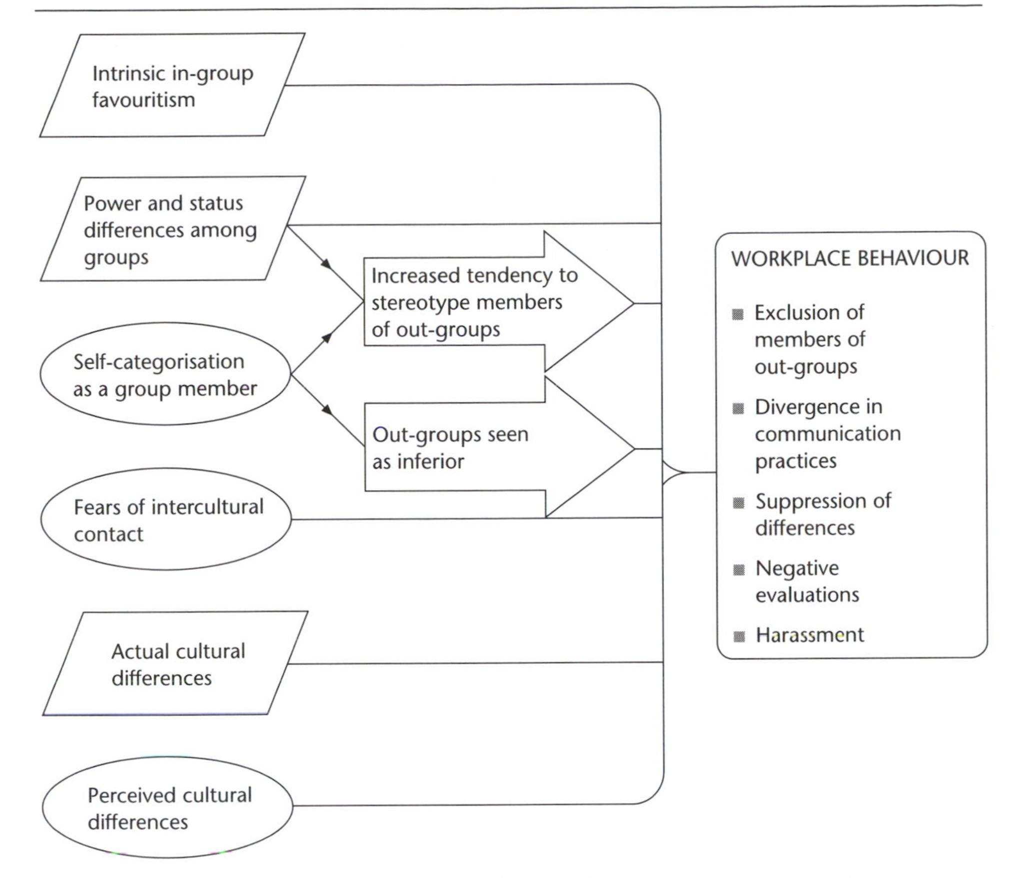


**Figure 12.1 Causes and consequences of intercultural problems at work.**

**Box 12.1**

A successful young English corporate lawyer, working for an American bank in London, said she was experiencing serious difficulties with the style of the Indian whose desk adjoined hers.

> He was recruited in Bangalore. He is a good mathematician and computer software designer. However, unlike previous Indians I've worked with, he's not been 'westernised' by going to business school or having similar experiences.
>
> He interrupts me all the time when I am in the middle of a complex drafting operation to ask me questions such as 'Is your hair naturally blonde?' and 'How do men and women in this country meet their partners?' I'm really upset by it, for several reasons. First, he distracts me from my work. Then, I resent his sexism. Other people in the office hear this going on, so unless I slap him down, I'm going to lose authority generally. On the other hand, I feel I should try to make allowances. Apart from the fact that he comes from a culture where women are rarely seen in positions equal or superior to his own, he is lonely and far from home. I think there's some sexism in management having placed him at my desk. There's little overlap in our work. I think they think I'll mother him.

*Source*: Interview, author's research.

perceptions of the superiority of the in-group over the out-group, stereotypic perceptions of in-group, out-group and self and conformity to group norms.[5] When asked about their fears in relating to people of a group different from their own, similar lists emerge from people of varied backgrounds. Fears usually include being judged, miscommunication, patronising or hurting others unintentionally,[6] face concerns, lack of predictability, diffuse anxiety, difficulty in sustaining self-conceptions and ethical issues such as the fear of being expected to offer bribes.

Actual and perceived cultural differences contribute to these fears about working cross-culturally. There are actual and perceived differences in the following:

- Communication styles, including language usage, the degree of importance given to non-verbal communication and norms regarding the appropriate degree of assertiveness.
- Attitudes toward conflict. Some cultures view it as a positive thing, others as something to be avoided. Some prefer to confront it in face-to-face meetings, others by working differences out quietly.
- Approaches to completing tasks, resulting from different judgements of the rewards associated with task completion and different ideas about time pressures.
- The importance attached to relationship-building generally in the work context and whether it should precede task-oriented work.
- Decision-making styles, for instance, whether to delegate or retain decision-making responsibilities, majority rule versus consensus. Individuals' expectations, about their own roles in shaping a decision, may be influenced by their cultural frame of reference.
- Attitudes toward disclosure, especially of emotions, personal information or the reasons behind a conflict or misunderstanding. In some cultures, it is not appropriate to self-disclose, or to ask questions that require the receiver to do so.

As a result of these cultural differences, plus stereotyping and prejudice, work environments in organisations with multicultural workforces are at risk of fostering behaviours that lead to poor work relationships. These behaviours include exclusion, divergence, suppression of deviation, misunderstanding and negative evaluations.

- Exclusion in the workplace is the practice of marginalising members of certain groups. Methods include limiting contact, excluding from conversations by avoidance or starting them only when selected individuals are present, and non-verbally or linguistically excluding outsiders who are present by using esoteric language. Other methods include changes in the content of information, especially to exclude individuals from job-related information. This may be deliberate or may result from assuming that they are not appropriate recipients.

- It is open to individuals in diverse work groups to diverge deliberately in their communication practices from members of other groups in order to increase social distance. Divergence includes adjusting ways of speaking (such as style, dialect, rules and primary language choice) to differ from those of a partner who is perceived as someone from whom disassociation is desirable.
- Suppression of divergent points of view and convergence towards 'average' views in decision-making is likely to lead to suppression of the views of minorities.
- Negative evaluations can lead to harassment, overt statements of negative stereotyping and stories with negative implications.[7]

## SUMMARY – IMPEDIMENTS TO WORKING WELL ACROSS CULTURES

In-group favouritism occurs as soon as people are divided into groups, no matter how artificial, but the bias is increased when there are differences of group size, status or power. Thinking of ourselves as a member of a group instead of as individuals, fear and actual or perceived cultural differences increase negative behaviour towards members of other groups. Negative intercultural work behaviours include exclusion of members of out-groups, divergence, suppression of deviation, misunderstanding and negative evaluations.

## PROCESSES OF INTERCULTURAL WORK

Contact, communication and co-operative interdependence have been proposed as helping to overcome impediments to intercultural working.

In Chapter 10 there was some discussion of the hypothesis of Allport (1954)[8] about the conditions in which contact reduces conflict. Later research focused on the idea that to be successful in changing the evaluation of an out-group, favourable contact with an out-group member must be defined as inter-group rather than interpersonal. That is, the contact must be seen as typical. However, Stephan and Stephan[9] pointed out a contrary thesis: that inter-group anxiety stems from expecting negative consequences for oneself *during contact*. This anxiety leads to information processing biases such as a narrowed focus of attention and simplified, expectation-confirming information processing, more stereotyping and less perceived out-group variability.

In many cases, poor intercultural relations are caused by fear of an out-group. In these cases, communication increases co-operation. It helps to create trust by reducing uncertainty and highlighting the benefits of mutual co-operation. Conflict is lowered and co-operation increases when contenders exchange an understanding of the situation, state to the other party that mutual co-operation is beneficial and mutual defection is harmful, explain their past actions,

**Box 12.2**

A field study of minority (Hindu) and majority (Muslim) subjects in a region of India investigated the effects of the amount of contact and its quality in terms of pleasantness and perceived equality (Islam and Hewstone, 1993). It found the following:

- The Hindu minority experienced more out-group contact than Muslims but reported higher inter-group anxiety and rated contact less pleasant and equal.
- The Hindu minority reported less positive out-group attitudes than Muslims. This finding is consistent with the theory that lower-status groups show stronger in-group bias (Mullen *et al.*, 1992).
- Generally, both the amount and quality of contact were associated with reduced inter-group anxiety. The effect was much stronger for quality of contact.
- When contact was perceived as inter-group, anxiety was higher, possibly because out-groups were perceived so negatively.
- The strongest predictor of perceived out-group variability was the amount of contact.
- Perceived out-group variability was a strong predictor of inter-group anxiety.
- Quality of contact was a strong predictor of out-group attitudes, especially for Hindus.
- There was a small negative effect of inter-group anxiety on out-group attitudes.

*Sources*: Islam, M. R. and M. Hewstone (1993) 'Dimensions of contact as predictors of inter-group anxiety, perceived out-group variability and out-group attitude: an integrative model', *Personality and Social Psychology Bulletin*, vol. 19. Figure 12.2 summarises these findings.
Mullen, B., R. Brown and C. Smith (1992) 'Inter-group bias as a function of salience, relevance and status: An integration', *European Journal of Social Psychology*, vol. 22, pp. 103–122.

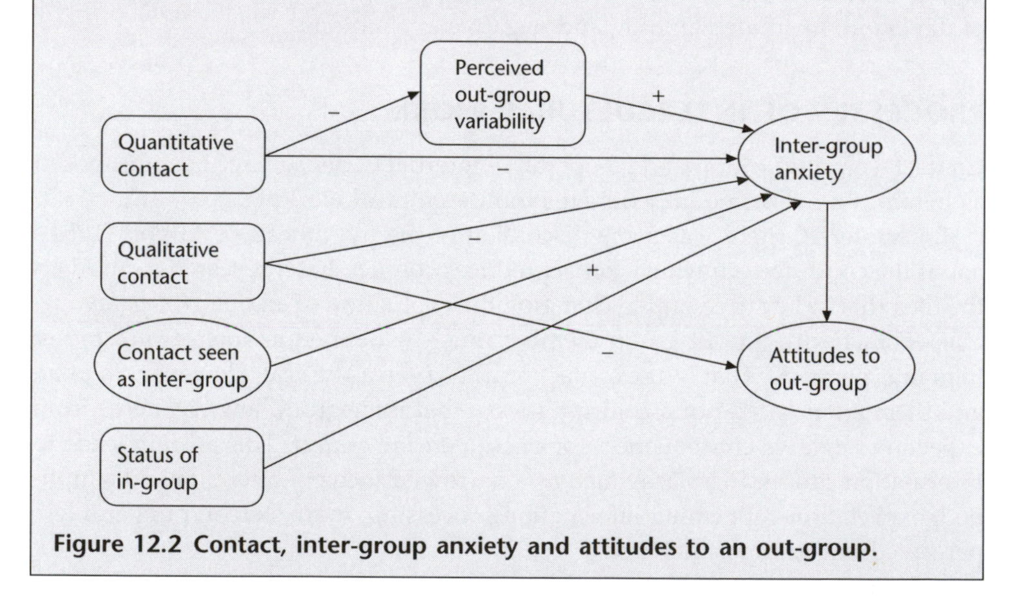


**Figure 12.2 Contact, inter-group anxiety and attitudes to an out-group.**

co-ordinate expectations, build trust through making sincere promises and try to develop norms. Thus, communication is a good way to alleviate fear. However, a small but significant number of groups are motivated by greed. In these cases, communication is not effective. In addition, behaviours that reduce trust, such as using promises or the language of the other group to 'set-up' opponents, are not available without communication.[10]

When groups have 'co-operative interdependence', that is 'share both the labour and the fruits of the labour', inter-group bias is lower.[11] It has been argued that in situations of co-operative interdependence, interaction is the main element that lowers bias. This is because it provides members with the opportunity to communicate, express values, argue, compromise, reach agreement and gain information about both in-group and out-group members. Other scholars, though, have argued that common fate and shared labour are together enough to reduce inter-group bias without interaction. There are practical consequences to these ideas: for instance, where it is difficult to get groups to interact or even communicate, the power of dispensing desirable resources might impose a common fate among the groups and so reduce their mutual bias.

**Box 12.3**

**Intercultural working from the perspective of an African-American executive**

The most difficult cultural fit has to do with nationality rather than race. . . . When I was a senior executive in France, my biggest challenge was that I wasn't French. I was perceived as a temporary American manager from headquarters. I therefore spent as much time as possible learning about French culture and spent 18 months in intensive French language courses. I also made efforts to work through local channels, formally and informally, and made every effort to represent the French position, balancing it with the global position. I learned that the best way for any foreigner to gain the credibility of local employees is to build relationships. That means adopting such simple and immediate practices as coaching those who need it, asking for help from those who can give it, and paying attention to informal matters like hanging out at the water fountain. For me, it meant having frank conversations with managers over what my appointment meant. The fact is, cultural biases must be identified clearly and then put in a proper perspective.

*Source*: Jim Kaiser, a senior vice president and general manager, *Harvard Business Review*, July/Aug. 1991.

## SUMMARY – PROCESSES OF INTERCULTURAL WORK

Contact, communication and co-operative interdependence have all been suggested as ways in which intercultural relationships can be fostered and conflict reduced. However, while they all appear to work in some circumstances, there are others in which they fail.

## BEHAVIOURS AND TRAITS FOR INTERCULTURAL WORK

This section describes behaviours and traits of individuals that help them work effectively across cultures. As Figure 12.3 shows, it covers having positive

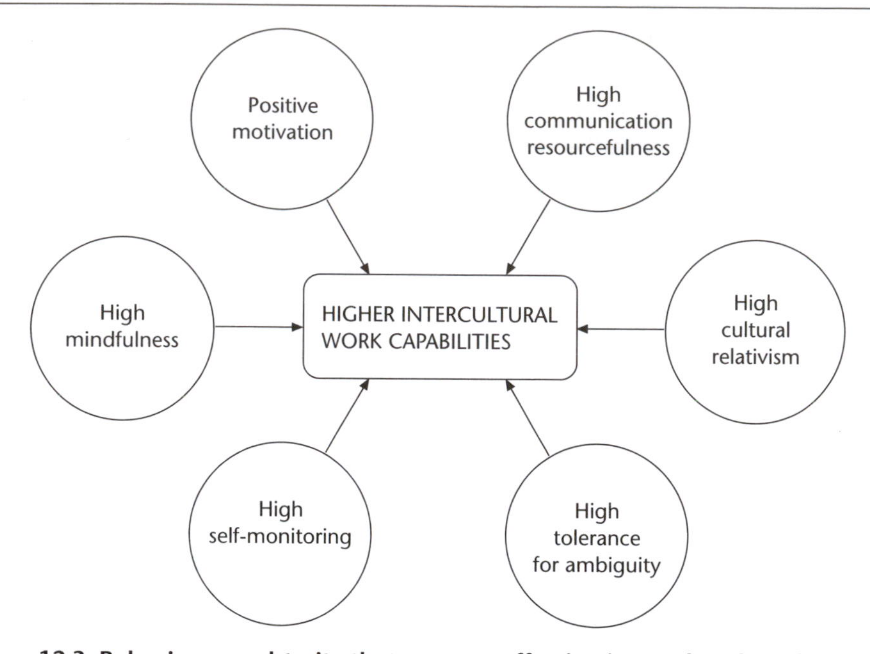


**Figure 12.3 Behaviours and traits that support effective intercultural working.**

motivations towards intercultural working, mindfulness, self-monitoring, tolerance of ambiguity, cultural relativity and communication resourcefulness.

*Positive motivations* towards cross-cultural working encourage people to engage with members of out-groups and so gain valuable experience. Just as fears about intercultural working occur in many cultures, so do hopes about it. These hopes are usually for dialogue, learning something new, self-development and understanding different points of view.[12]

*Being mindful* means being aware of both social perception and communication behaviour. Mindfulness depends on not being locked into habitual ways of categorising others, being open to new information (about members of out-groups) and being aware of more than one perspective.[13] Mindfulness both avoids caring too little about learning or improving and being over-concerned and thus defensive and closed to new ideas.

*Self-monitoring*, which was explained in Chapter 6, helps people to discover appropriate behaviour in new situations, modify their behaviour to changes in social situations and seek out information about others with whom they anticipate interacting.[14]

*Tolerance for ambiguity* means accepting situations where it is unclear what is happening, or why, or what the outcome is likely to be. People who are tolerant in this way are more inclined to seek out objective information. This means that their intercultural behaviour is more likely to be based on a realistic appreciation. People with lower tolerance for ambiguity tend to seek supportive rather than objective information, that is, to select and distort in such a way that they feel less psychological discomfort.

*Cultural relativism* means accepting that the norms, roles, values and behaviours of others are equally as valid as those into which we were socialised. Unfortunately, it is difficult to achieve. Following norms into which we were socialised is reflexive and requires little effort. Not following them, or following others, is non-reflexive and requires substantial effort. The key skill required is mindfulness, which, with practice, can become habitual. Cultural relativism involves trying to understand members of out-groups according to their own frame of reference. Bi-culturalism goes beyond this and involves accepting role-taking as part of the human condition, avoiding stylised verbal behaviour, being willing to accept the strain of adaptation, being well aware of conversational constraints and showing flexibility in conversational adaptation.[15] Cultural relativism has sometimes been criticised as if it implied moral relativism. However, the attempt to understand how people within a culture really perceive themselves, which is cultural relativism, need not imply adopting their ethical code.

**Box 12.4**

Huang (2000) of the National Chenchi University of Taiwan argues that the 'personal influence model' of business (*Gao Guanxi*) prevalent in Chinese societies is 'often performed in an unethical manner'. In particular, the author contends, there are problems of a neglect of social welfare in favour of the extended family; a lack of sense of social responsibility and the public interest; a tendency to secrecy and lack of openness and a low value placed on racial and gender equality.

*Source*: Huang, Y.-H. (2000) 'The personal influence model and Gao Guanxi in Taiwan Chinese public relations', *Public Relations Review*, vol. 26, no. 2, pp. 219–236.

*Communication resourcefulness* is the knowledge and ability to apply cognitive, affective (emotional) and behavioural resources appropriately, effectively and creatively in diverse interactive situations.[16] It is related to the degree to which novel situations are approached as learning experiences.

- Cognitive resourcefulness refers to whether we think of intercultural encounters as opportunities or as anxiety-ridden events. This influences how we approach interaction with members of out-groups.
- The emotions of an intercultural work relationship are ego-focused, other-focused, or some combination of the two. Culture plays a major role concerning which emotional meanings predominate. For individualists, ego-focused emotions are most common. These are concerned with 'justice', revolve around conflicting claims between the self and others, and look to resolve conflict by invoking impartial rules, principles or standards. Conversely, other-focused emotions, mainly experienced by collectivists, revolve around issues

of relationships and can be resolved through caring. Thus, emotional resourcefulness means achieving a good balance between relying on principles, rules and procedures for guiding and regulating work relationships, and relying on trust and caring. Highly individualistic, achievement-oriented people are often deficient in the 'other' dimension of affective resourcefulness and should attempt to shift in that direction. Other groups, including many women, may gain in emotional resourcefulness by more emphasis on their own needs and on principles rather than feelings.

- Behavioural resourcefulness means having a wide range of verbal and non-verbal ways of communicating in order to deal with different people in different situations. Being responsive to members of out-groups and open to learning from them, are other aspects of behavioural resourcefulness.

## SUMMARY – BEHAVIOURS AND TRAITS FOR INTERCULTURAL WORK

A wide range of behaviours and traits can contribute positively towards achieving effective intercultural working. They mainly depend on communication skills or emotional intelligence and are directed at reassuring members of out-groups of our good intentions and desire to establish good relations.

## INTERPERSONAL SKILLS FOR INTERCULTURAL WORK

Accurate social perception, managing anxiety and dealing with communication fear, communicating openness, using inclusive language, showing empathy and communicating a relationship as well as a task orientation are interactive processes needed for effective intercultural work.

In an intercultural context, *social perceptiveness* means having intercultural as well as interpersonal understanding. The main elements required for such understanding are self-awareness and awareness of cultural sensitivities, contexts, and impediments to intercultural communication.

- Without extended exposure to at least one other culture, most people remain unaware that their own behaviours, attitudes and beliefs are culture-specific. Therefore, a first step towards better intercultural understanding is to seek out such exposure at work or at leisure. Learning from such experiences then needs to be enhanced and speeded up by reflective observation, either alone or in discussion. The knowledge we seek is reflexive. We need to understand ourselves, our stereotypes, and our own prejudices, ethnocentrism, values and attitudes as much as, or more than, we understand those of others.
- It is easy for people who are ignorant of the sensitivities of another culture not only to set up barriers to good intercultural working, but even to cause serious

offence. Avoiding such situations comes from studying the culture of the people with whom we work. There is no substitute for experience in gaining knowledge of other cultures. For sojourners, this is the best alternative. However, realistically, many people in Europe now work alongside people from a very large range of countries and are unlikely to be able to visit all the countries represented. For them, the best source of information on a culture is the members of the culture with whom they interact in the course of work. Setting aside time to talk with as many of them as possible, about the sensitivities inculcated through their culture, is an excellent use of time. The following points should, though, be kept in mind. First-hand experience is necessary to understand the many subtleties of any culture. What is logical and important in a particular culture may seem irrational and unimportant to an outsider. In describing another culture, we tend to stress the differences and overlook the similarities. In interacting with people from another culture, however, we tend to assume more similarity than actually exists. Stereotyping may be inevitable among those who lack frequent contact with another culture but an understanding of the limited truth of stereotypes is essential. Personal observations of others about another culture should not be taken as objective evidence. Many subcultures often exist within a single ethnic group, language group, religion or nationality, differentiated by education, age, gender, socio-economic status, education and exposure to other cultures. Highly educated people of a given cultural group are less likely to reveal indigenous language and communication patterns than less educated people. Cultures are continually evolving; therefore, understanding another culture is a continuous process. To best understand a culture, we need to understand the language of that culture.[17]

- All interaction takes place within a context.[18] The context of interaction can magnify or reduce how aware the participants are of their cultural differences. For instance, task-related talk among technicians has a context where nobody may be thinking about cultural differences. Another contextual factor is how well people know one another. Consciousness of cultural differences will be lower among long-term work colleagues (though background knowledge of details of difference will be greater) than between new acquaintances. However, there has often been an over-reliance on this factor, resulting in poor work relations between people from different cultures.
- Being aware of the sorts of impediments described earlier in this chapter can also help in avoiding them.

The effects of *anxiety* and *uncertainty* on intercultural work communication were described in Chapter 7, where ways of overcoming them were set out in Box 7.6. Some further ideas are given in Box 12.5.

*Communicating openness* to others' perspectives generally leads to openness from them. Box 12.6 suggests how.

**Box 12.5**

### How to overcome fear of communicating in intercultural work relations

- Identify situations that give rise to communication fear.
- Notice when your fearful expectations are proved wrong.
- Notice and analyse your successes as well as your failures.
- Check that when a situation requiring communication gives rise to apprehensiveness in future, the problem is not caused by over-generalising from instances that do not apply this time.

*Source*: McCroskey, J. C. (1984) 'The communication apprehension perspective' in J. A. Daly and J. C. McCroskey (eds) *Avoiding Communication: Shyness, Reticence and Communication Apprehension*. Beverley Hills, Calif.: Sage, pp. 13–38.

**Box 12.6**

### How to present yourself as open to others' values and views

- Listen openly and actively (see Box 5.6), without interrupting or criticising.
- Ask rather than tell.
- Frame questions openly: 'What do you think?', 'What do you mean by . . . ?', 'Can you give me an example of . . . ?'
- Where culturally acceptable, solicit feelings specifically: 'How do you feel about . . . ?'
- Withhold preconceived opinions.
- When expressing views, make it clear that you understand that they are only opinions which may be disagreed with.
- Acknowledge different values, beliefs and perceptions as valid: 'I see what you mean'.
- Provide reassurance: 'Don't worry – this won't go any further'.
- Avoid calling a view that you disagree with bad or wrong.
- Make statements in a form which acknowledges one's own subjectivity, such as 'I feel uneasy when Mr Ling does not appear to react to what I am saying', rather than generalising or laying claim to objectivity, as in 'Chinese are inscrutable'.

*Inclusive language* aims to respect the preferences of the person or group to whom, or about whom, we are communicating. Using non-inclusive language not only creates barriers but also adversely affects the self-concept and self-confidence of members of the excluded or negatively portrayed group. For instance, women in business are undermined by the routine use of expressions such as 'businessman', 'chairman' or referring to any manager as 'he'. Inclusive language avoids using generic masculine words or titles to refer to all persons. In English, this is always possible with a little ingenuity. If the expression sometimes becomes a little awkward, that is a price worth paying. Inclusive language also avoids using terms that reinforce demeaning attitudes based on age (geriatric), disability (spastic), ethnicity (wog), gender (doll), national origin (frog, hun), religion (infidel) or sexual orientation (pansy). The examples given are so offensive as to be rarely heard now, but many others are still in use.

Being *empathetic* means accurately understanding the thoughts and motivations of another person in an interaction and putting oneself in another's shoes when making a judgement about them. It does not necessarily mean agreeing with them or sympathising with them, only really trying to understand them. Total empathy with another person is probably impossible, even when both come from the same culture and sub-culture. However, most people's communication with others would be more successful if they could increase their ability to empathise and, equally importantly, if they could convey an intention to empathise. Chapter 5 explained how to listen empathetically. To convey empathy involves asking open-ended questions, such as 'What was the experience like for you when . . . ?', openly listening empathetically and paraphrasing the other person's words (e.g. by 'What I think I hear you saying is . . .', 'Is this what you mean?') to check for understanding and to show a sincere attempt to understand. It also involves checking out verbal and non-verbal cues to find out what another is feeling: 'I sense you are feeling . . . angry . . . sad . . . glad . . . afraid. Am I reading you correctly?', paying attention to any of one's own non-verbal messages that may make another person uncomfortable and mirroring elements of the other person's body language, tone and pace, as appropriate.

People from individualist cultures are at risk of provoking a culture clash if they act with people from collectivist cultures according to what may be their usual priority of getting on with the task 'regardless'. It is well known that Arabs and other Middle-Easterners prefer to do business by *building a relationship* before proceeding to the negotiation. The same applies to people of many other nationalities and ethnicities. Equally, men often impose a communicative style that alienates their women colleagues, clients or patients. They should try instead to increase the amount of 'relationship' orientation they communicate at work. Box 12.7 gives suggestions on how.

**Box 12.7**

**How to communicate a relationship as well as a task orientation**

- Remember people's names and small details about them learnt unobtrusively or by asking.
- Use people's names according to their culture (e.g. patronym first).
- Initiate conversations on non-work topics.
- Be sensitive to nuances.
- Reciprocate acts of consideration.
- Take care not to use humour inappropriately.
- Find common ground with counterparts.
- Support others' communication.
- Bring others into discussions.
- Thank others for their work or contribution.
- Praise above-standard work (in public or private according to the other person's culture).
- Where appropriate give candid feedback (in private).

## SUMMARY – INTERPERSONAL SKILLS FOR INTERCULTURAL WORK

Accuracy in intercultural social perception is increased by face-to-face exposure to people from other cultures. This increases our awareness of our own cultural biases as well as helping us learn about others' different values, beliefs and motivations. Overcoming anxiety in intercultural communication and self-presenting as open to intercultural experience facilitate work with people from diverse backgrounds. Using inclusive language, conveying empathy and communicating a relationship orientation are important communication skills for intercultural working.

## SOJOURNING

Sojourners are people who live and (in this book) work abroad for a period of months or years but are not permanent emigrants. Sojourners face the need to adapt in a far more radical way than people who only work in diverse organisations in their own country.

> Sojourners and expatriates at the beginning of their stay will be in an environment where all cultural cues are ambiguous, if not intimidating, their language skills may not be adequate to meet their . . . needs and they will be deprived of the ordinary reinforcement routinely received in the home culture.[19]

In Europe, mobility of labour across national and cultural boundaries grew exponentially in the late twentieth and early twenty-first centuries. Corporate transfers of personnel accounted for some of this growth, as businesses internationalised. Some of it, however, was brought about by people taking advantage of the common labour market to seek work and career opportunities with foreign companies in foreign lands. Despite lack of organisational support, such sojourners usually have one considerable advantage in making the necessary adjustments: they wanted to go. Positive motivation has been shown to be a major factor in successful adaptation.

The difficulties of sojourner adaptation should not, however, be underestimated. For example, about 80 per cent of expatriate assignments made by a French multinational of younger, 'high-potential' managers in its European network, all of whom had had the benefit of an eight day international management programme, were cancelled as failures.[20] A major cause of expatriate failure is culture shock, brought on by a number of things including the language barrier, loneliness, difficulty in penetrating the host society, not knowing how to react in a series of difficult situations and always being the centre of attention. The symptoms range from mild to severe homesickness, feeling frustrated, alienated, isolated, irritable, lonely, depressed and rigid. One author goes so far as to compare culture shock to temporary schizophrenia, because sufferers experience the sensation that 'things are coming in too fast, they lose their grip and get lost.'[21] One influential, but less extreme, view of what causes culture shock is based on the idea that much of what we call culture operates on the unconscious level. Sojourning creates an 'experience of separation' from the home culture and group that leads to greatly heightened awareness of culture. In this way, culture shock eventually allows the individual to 'move beyond culture' in a way that is not available to non-sojourners.[22,23] This interpretation is to some extent confirmed by a research finding: Canadian expatriates who were more effective at the task of transferring skills to members of the host culture, admitted to having experienced higher levels of culture shock than less effective executives. Further support comes from the finding that adjustment is highly salient to sojourners – while it is going on the problems and solutions associated with it are often central in the sojourner's consciousness.[24]

Not surprisingly, in view of the significance of the problem, a large amount of research has been undertaken into sojourner adjustment and adaptation. The findings fall into two categories: factors and processes.

Motivation to adapt is perhaps the most important *factor* determining whether, and how fast, sojourners overcome culture shock. Motivation to adapt depends in part on expected length of stay – the longer, the higher the motivation.[25] Personal variables are very important, implying that selection of suitable individuals may outweigh training and social support. For example, one study found that, of two individuals, one experienced a given sojourning situation as constraining, while the other found the same situation liberating. How an individual interprets the situation may be an intervening variable between personality and expatriate effectiveness. In terms of personality, one study found that 'caringness' is negatively correlated with expatriate effectiveness, whereas self-centredness, self-monitoring, adroitness and low security-consciousness are positively correlated.[26] Other authors have suggested that having a drive to communicate, broad-based sociability, cultural flexibility, a cosmopolitan orientation and collaborative negotiation style are positive factors for success as expatriates, and should be used by businesses as selection criteria.[27]

There are several models of the *processes* of sojourner adjustment, going back to Lysgaard (1955), who found that sojourners go through three stages of adaptation: initial adjustment, crisis and regained adjustment.[28] A more pessimistic, 'inverted U-shaped curve' model hypothesises that after an initial stage in which sojourners adapt rapidly, they often become frustrated with day-to-day living and retreat to the stability and comfort of home-culture friendships. Whereas other models focus on psychological factors, especially emotions, a more recent model focuses on the role of communication in the adaptation process. The sojourner adapts by communicating extensively with the people of the other culture. In interactions with people of the new culture, the sojourner gradually learns the ways of the new culture. The sojourner 'grows into a new kind of person at a higher level of integration'.[29]

Intercultural sojourning is a process of stress, adaptation and growth. In new environments, people have difficulty in coping. They suffer from information overload, uncertainty about others' expectations, difficulty in interpreting others' communication behaviours and so on. These experiences are stressful. An initial response to stress, for many individuals, is to resort to defence mechanisms such as selective attention, self-deception, denial, avoidance, withdrawal, hostility, cynicism and/or compulsively altruistic behaviour. Luckily, these responses, which are not helpful to adapting, are usually temporary. The 'natural' response to stress is to adapt.[30] Positive responses to the new environment include assimilation (acting on the environment so that aspects of it may be incorporated into the internal mind-set) and accommodation (adjusting the internal mind-set to the external realities). Elements of the new culture are learnt and elements of the old 'unlearnt'. These responses lead to growth, in particular to an increased ability to adapt to further environmental changes. As they gain experience at making the transition to a new host environment, people get better at it. As they begin to adapt successfully, sojourners can perform more effectively, both at work and in living. They start to feel more cheerful, which is directly related to an increased ability to communicate. They gain an expanded and more flexible sense of themselves as a person. They begin to have an 'intercultural identity'. Figure 12.4 shows these processes in a flowchart.

**Box 12.8**

> **European Language Council policy paper on working and living abroad – extract**
>
> At this level, the focus is on communication between speakers, speaking or writing in diverse concrete socio-cultural relationships and situations, especially in the contexts of work and the practical experiences of everyday life. Participants in such communication must be able to understand that their own and others' words and actions produce meanings which are mutually dependent on the specific context and relationship. Effective intercultural communication takes account of relevant customs, practices and attitudes, whether shared or not, and incorporates a recognition and negotiation of the specificity of the intercultural situation.

## SUMMARY – SOJOURNING

Living and working in a foreign country make high demands on individuals' ability to cope. Many international assignees actually 'fail' and return home. Nearly all sojourners experience culture shock but it can be overcome. Successful adaptation comes from understanding that culture shock is normal, and by avoiding negative responses such as the following: selective attention,

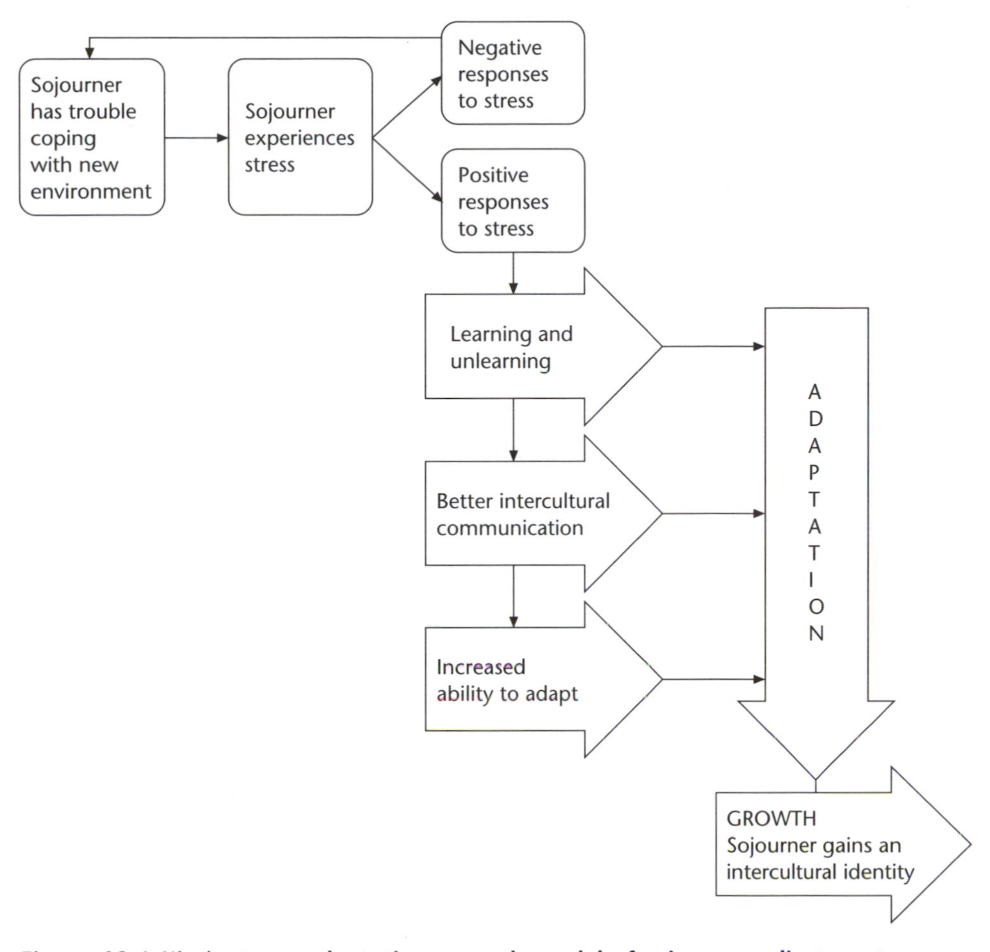


**Figure 12.4 Kim's stress–adaptation–growth model of sojourner adjustment.**

*Source*: Based on Kim, Y. Y. (1988) *Communication and Cross-Cultural Adaptation: An Integrative Theory*. Clevedon: Multicultural Matters.

self-deception, denial, avoidance, withdrawal, hostility, cynicism or compulsively altruistic behaviour. These can be counteracted by developing positive responses such as assimilation and accommodation.

## WORK APPLICATIONS FOR INTERCULTURAL SKILLS

All the work activities described earlier in this book have significant cultural and intercultural aspects. In most cases these aspects are referred to in the sections describing them. Two activities are included here, partly because they have attracted most attention in the literature and partly because they illustrate two different aspects of this chapter. The first is working in culturally diverse groups and the second is intercultural/international negotiating.

**Table 12.1 Advantages of diverse groups – task activities**

| *Problem-solving stage* | *Advantages of diverse groups over homogeneous groups* |
|---|---|
| Problem exploration and identification | More sources of information and ideas on causes of the problem; more complete survey of goals |
| Generating ideas for alternatives | More diverse ideas, more inventive alternatives, higher-quality solutions to problems |
| Evaluating alternatives | Less bias in information processing<br>Less groupthink (see Chapter 11) |
| Implementation planning | Greater tendency to work out contingency plans |
| Overall | Less groupthink; less deference to group leadership |

## Working in culturally diverse groups

There are benefits of cultural diversity in group problem-solving, as shown in Table 12.1. However, these can be lost because the social problems of group development – forming, storming and norming – are more severe for heterogeneous groups. Stress and tension levels in culturally diverse groups often exceed those in homogeneous groups due to a lack of trust and communication inaccuracies.[31] Group members from different cultures often disagree over important meanings, such as the causes of events, what counts as admissible evidence, the relevance of specific information and the possible conclusions that can be drawn.[32] The more routine the task, the less good a diverse group will be at it. The more innovative, one-off or unusual the task, the more it is suited to intercultural groupwork: 'The more senior the team members, the more likely they are to be working on projects that can benefit from diversity. Diversity is therefore extremely valuable to senior executive teams, both within and across companies.'[32] Box 12.9 gives guidance on making intercultural group work effective.

## Intercultural/international negotiating

This section builds particularly on the material on negotiating in Chapter 9, highlighting aspects that are different in intercultural negotiations. There has been a general tendency for theories about negotiation to ignore culture and be assumed to apply universally. However, this idea is beginning to be challenged. For example, Weiss and Curhan (1999) suggest that international business negotiations are characterised by two levels of differences beyond those found in domestic business negotiations. First, there are individual-level differences in negotiator priorities, preferences, perspectives and scripts; second, there are societal-level differences in national endowments, preferences (tastes), legal, economic and political systems, and government involvement.[33]

**Box 12.9**

### How to overcome problems with intercultural group work

- Select the group's members for the contribution they can make to the task and for having the traits, skills and attitudes described earlier in this chapter, not for their ethnicity or gender.
- At first, focus on members' equivalent professional qualifications and experience.
- Later, acknowledge cultural differences and emphasise their potential benefits for completing the group task. Members should become aware of their own stereotypes and strive to speed up the process of seeing each member of the group as an individual.
- Search for a co-operative goal until it is found.
- Emphasise equality and participation.
- Ensure that all communication is in terms of mutual respect (Adler, 1991).
- Use an appropriate process, such as the following 5-step method of problem-solving across cultures, to overcome the process barriers created by diversity (Harris and Moran, 1991).
  - Describe the problem as understood in both (all) cultures.
  - Analyse the problem from both (all) cultural perspectives.
  - Identify the basis for the problem from both (all) perspectives.
  - Solve the problem through synergistic strategies.
  - Determine if the solution is working multiculturally.

*Sources*: Adler, N. (1991) *International Dimensions of Organizational Behaviour*, 2nd edn. Belmont, Calif.: Wadsworth.
Harris, P. R. and R. T. Moran (1991) *Managing Cultural Differences*. New York: Gulf Publishing.

**Box 12.10**

### Cultural variations in negotiation

- People from the former Soviet Union have a 'heritage of suspicion toward negotiation' but are learning to overcome this (Kremenyuk, 1996). In the pre-Soviet and Soviet periods, the negotiating perceptions of Russians included positive views of struggle and power but negative views of compromise and rhetoric. Their negotiating behaviour displayed a lack of initiatives, openness and constancy. While evidence is not yet available to confirm whether these traits persist, there is a presumption of continuity that requires verification (Kimura, 1996).
- A study found many similarities in the bargaining behaviour of Russians and Americans. Despite this, the outcomes of the process, in terms of both profit and satisfaction, were quite different in the two cultures (Roemer and Neu, 1999).
- Norms and customary expectations determine what is considered fair when there is no standardised measure of value. For instance,

  > Indonesian business relationships involve looking out for one another's interests. Looking out for the interests of a traditional Indonesian may involve areas that Westerners are uncomfortable with. Topics of conversation may eventually come around to what you can do to help the Bapak. Advice on foreign schools and corporate internships for the Bapak's children would certainly be appreciated. (Whitfield, 1999)

*Sources*: Kimura, H. (1996) 'The Russian way of negotiating', *International Negotiation Journal*, vol. 1, no. 3.
Kremenyuk, V. A. (1996) 'Negotiations in the former Soviet Union: new structure, new dimensions', *International Negotiation Journal*, vol. 1, no. 3.
Roemer, C. and Neu, J. (1999) 'A comparison of American and Russian patterns of behavior in buyer–seller negotiations using observational measures', *International Negotiation Journal*, vol. 4, no. 1.
Whitfield, George B. III (1999) *Bapakism II – The View Across Cultures*, www.expat.or.id/business/bapakism2.html.

In cross-cultural negotiations, there may be competing principles and values. For instance, justice (fairness) goals may be more important in individualist than in collectivist cultures. When Americans (individualists) and Japanese (collectivists) were asked to rate their conflict experiences in terms of goal orientation, the Americans were strongly oriented towards achieving justice, but the Japanese were more motivated by a concern for relationships with others. Although Americans and Japanese had common expectations about the efficacy of tactics, Americans preferred assertive tactics, whereas Japanese preferred avoidance tactics.[34] Another study found that Americans consider non-personal factors, such as technical expertise and financing terms, as more important than personal factors in successful negotiations with the Saudis. Yet, from a Saudi viewpoint, personal relationships may be important in generating pre-negotiation contacts. Equally, to Saudis, cultural factors, linked to patience, language and social customs, may help to prevent breakdowns in the negotiation process.[35]

**Box 12.11**

During the 1994 GATT talks between the Americans and the Japanese Prime Minister over rice tariffs an observer commented: 'Their discussion went on parallel lines. This was obvious to both sides before they even started. In fact, it wasn't even really a discussion. It was like exchanging jabs in the first stage of a boxing match. I guess the second round will have to take place in Geneva'. (An eleventh-hour agreement was eventually reached.)

Two studies demonstrated that the higher negotiators' collectivism, the higher their co-operativeness. However, this applied where negotiation partners were from the same ethnic or national group. We still do not know whether negotiation by collectivists with out-group members would produce competition. In conditions where negotiators would not be held accountable for the outcome, high collectivism produced less co-operative intentions and behaviour and achieved lower outcomes than low collectivism. Co-operative responses among collectivists may be sustained by mutual monitoring and sanctioning but might not apply in situations where monitoring is not possible.[36]

**Box 12.12**

There can be a dilemma over how far to accommodate to another culture when issues of principle are involved. For instance, although Japanese women are often highly educated, they are not accepted in the higher echelons of the corporate world. To send a woman, however senior, to negotiate in Japan, is likely to prejudice the outcome. Yet for some European organisations, it is unthinkable to deny a woman such an assignment just on the grounds of her gender.

Reynolds[37] argued that national culture, organisational culture and personality dimensions affect cross-national buyer–seller negotiations through their impact both on the product utilities desired and emphasised and on preferred interaction styles. Product utilities affected by cultural differences include preferences for novelty, curiosity and pleasure, functional versus non-functional features, level of emotional utility, security utility and social interaction. Interaction style preferences which are similarly affected include degree of task-, self- and people-orientation, preference for traditional interaction and level of formality. How compatible the buyer and seller are along these dimensions, determines whether a sale is made, satisfaction with the sales interaction and the degree of relationship building.[38]

In most European countries, complex negotiations are split up into separate issues that are attacked sequentially and settled one at a time. The final agreement is the sum of the several concessions made on individual issues; progress can easily be measured. Negotiators used to a sequential approach often experience difficulties when negotiating with people who discuss all issues with a holistic approach. In such an approach, issues are dealt with independently, not in any predetermined sequence, concessions may come only at the end of a negotiation and nothing is settled until the end.[39,40] Box 12.13 gives guidance on negotiation with holistic negotiators.

**Box 12.13**

### How to negotiate with holistic negotiators

- Set explicit limits or ranges for the negotiation process.
- Seek to establish general 'principles' early in the negotiation.
- Focus on potential areas of agreement and seek to expand them.
- Avoid taking the negotiation issues in sequence.
- Avoid hostility, confrontation or emotion.
- Give the other party something to 'take home'.
- Prepare to negotiate as a team.
- Above all, respect your holistic counterparts (Kirkbride and Tang). For instance, remember that 'the Chinese may be further behind in technology and industrial organisation than we are, but for centuries they have known few peers in the subtle art of negotiating. When measured against the effort and skill the Chinese bring to the bargaining table, American executives fall short' (Pye, 1986).

*Sources*: Kirkbride, P. S. and S. F. Y. Tang (1990) 'Negotiation: lessons from behind the Bamboo Curtain', *Journal of General Management*, vol. 16, no. 1, pp. 1–13.
Pye, L. W. (1986) 'The China Trade: Making the deal', *Harvard Business Review*, July/Aug., p. 74.

'Parallel' negotiation training (i.e. training taking place concurrently with the negotiation itself) can contribute to a successful intercultural negotiation. It can help the parties to deal with obstacles to negotiation. These include how they define or 'frame' the conflict and negotiations (as a win–win or win–lose process), build the parties' confidence and sense of empowerment, and improve the design, structure and implementation of the negotiation process itself.[41]

## SUMMARY – WORK APPLICATIONS FOR INTERCULTURAL SKILLS

Diversity of any kind, but especially intercultural diversity, makes groupwork processes more problematic because high levels of adaptation and accommodation to different others are required. To compensate, diverse groups are potentially more productive because of the wider range of ideas, information and perspectives that the members can contribute.

International negotiators also experience difficulty, because of both fundamental value differences and differences in preferred and expected ways of negotiating. Respect for the negotiating skills of counterparts is essential.

## CHAPTER OVERVIEW

Exclusion of members of out-groups, divergence, suppression of deviation, misunderstanding and negative evaluations can result from intrinsic inter-group biases, actual and perceived cultural differences, concerns over loss of face, lack of predictability and ethical issues. These are often added to by diffuse anxiety and difficulty in sustaining self-conceptions. Behaviours, traits and processes that support intercultural working, are mainly directed at reassuring members of out-groups of good intentions and a desire to establish good relations. They mainly depend on interpersonal skills such as accurate and unbiased social perception, communication or emotional intelligence. Although a case can be made for the beneficial effects of impersonal processes such as intercultural contact and co-operative interdependence, conscious efforts to develop these interpersonal skills are more effective. This means that to overcome culture shock and to adapt to living and working in a new environment, sojourners need to apply techniques and understanding that lead through stress to adaptation and growth.

A high level of adaptation and accommodation to different others is required for success in intercultural work activities, such as working in culturally diverse groups and international negotiating.

## EXERCISES

1. Prepare and submit a typed research report entitled 'The five best and five worst aspects of my culture.' The purpose of this report is to think deeply about one's own culture, in order to develop the same process when thinking about the culture of colleagues or members of external organisations.

Understanding how your own culture operates helps develop the skills to understand how other cultures work.

The aspects may be formal or informal rules (norms), ways of behaving, customs, beliefs, expectations or prejudices associated with your culture. The ten aspects will each be identified with a short paragraph describing the aspect and its impact on any of the following that apply: majority and minority population groups, the economy, politics, international relations and/or personal relationships. In separate paragraphs describe any changes or pressures for change and current attitudes towards the particular aspect chosen.

*Adapted from an activity in:* Foster, D. A. (1992) *Bargaining Across Borders.* New York: McGraw-Hill Publishing Company.

2. Give inclusive alternatives to the following non-inclusive terms: businessman, chairman, clergyman, fellow worker, fireman, forefathers, foreman, freshman, layman, mankind, manpower, man-made, postman, poetess, spokesman, stewardess, suffragette, workman, gentleman's agreement, man on the street, straw man and right-hand man.

3. Using a passage in which the masculine pronoun is repeatedly used to represent both genders, find the least clumsy way you can to re-express it.

4. Using any of the role plays given in other chapters, individualists act like collectivists, high 'achievers' like people with high relationship orientations, and so on. An observer gives feedback on the success/failure of the role shifts; the players on how it felt.

5. Topics for discussion in mixed-culture groups.

   (a) What is culture?
   (b) Culture shock.
   (c) Differences among European cultures in:

   - communication rules;
   - attitudes to gender and age;
   - language used to refer to people of different genders, ages, types of disability, other countries, other ethnicities, etc.;
   - gift-giving customs;
   - proverbs.

*Based on*: Kresovich, B. M. 'More discussion activities to develop skills in intercultural communication for Japanese university students in EFL.', ericae.net/edu/ED333713.HTM.

6. Nearly all the role plays in the exercises of other chapters can be given an intercultural emphasis, by allocating each role player one or more of the following cultural orientations:

   (a) You have an active orientation – that is you come from a society in which change is generally seen as progressive and beneficial. Also, people are expected to try actively to meet their desires. People are believed to make their own luck. You consider that when things go wrong, people should accept personal responsibility, but you are an optimist – you think that anyone can do almost anything if they try hard enough. You believe that it is right for people to attempt to control nature and that technology is capable of solving all major human problems eventually, including the ones created by technology itself.
   (b) You have a passive orientation – that is, you come from a society in which change is generally seen as threatening and it is believed that it is best to 'let sleeping dogs lie'. There is a degree of fatalism in your make-up – you believe that most of what happens to people results from forces outside their control and that their best course is to adapt and co-exist with those forces. People should accept their fates. People should also try to co-exist with nature, not to dominate it. You point to environmental degradation, global warming and the risk of terrorist attacks with weapons of mass destruction as some of the negative consequences of so-called technological advance.
   (c) You are an individualist. This means that you do not allow your behaviours to be strongly influenced and defined by others: you prefer self-sufficiency. For you, societies are loosely-knit social frameworks in which people primarily operate as individuals. For you, the task prevails over the personal relationship.
   (d) You are a collectivist. Your behaviours are strongly influenced, even defined, by others: you give full recognition to your interdependent roles and obligations to your in-group. For you, societies are composed of tight networks in which people operate as members of in-groups and out-groups, expect to look after other members of their in-group in need, and expect their group to look after them. For you the personal relationship prevails over the task.
   (e) You are high in power distance, which is defined by the degree of separation between people of various social statuses. To put this another way, in your society the less powerful members expect and accept that power is distributed unequally. This means that you endorse hierarchies. In your culture, relations between unequals are formal, often patron–client in format, information flow is formalised and restricted, and companies are organised in rigid vertical hierarchies.

(f) You are low in power distance, which is defined by the degree of separation between people of various social statuses. To put this another way, in your society most people believe that power should be distributed about equally. This means that you endorse egalitarianism. In your society, relations are open and informal, information flows are functional and unrestricted, and companies tend to have flat hierarchies and matrix organisations.

(g) You are high in uncertainty avoidance, which refers to the extent to which a culture prefers to avoid ambiguity. You prefer explicit rules and set procedures to contain uncertainty. In your society, families, groups and organisations tend to be closed to outsiders. Your society puts stress on compliance and obedience, punishes error and non-conformity, and rewards conformity, loyalty and attention to detail.

(h) You are low in uncertainty avoidance, which refers to the extent to which a culture prefers to avoid ambiguity and the way in which it resolves uncertainty. This means that you tolerate ambiguity and prefer flexibility in responses. You tend to find rules and procedures irksome or see them as obstacles to be circumvented. In your society, people tend to accept outsiders at all levels, stress personal choice and decision-making, reward initiative, team-play and risk-taking, and stress development of analytical skills.

(i) You are high in achievement values, which define quality of life issues. This means that you endorse assertiveness, competition and aggressive success. In your society, people tend to believe that matters of material comfort, social privilege, access to power and influence, status and prestige, and the wherewithal to consume are related to ability. There is also the belief that with enough opportunity any individual who really wants these benefits of society can acquire them. The corollary of this, is that those who do not have the ability, or the character, cannot and should not have them, since they are essentially a reward for hard work and success. Your culture rewards financial and material achievements with preferential social prestige and status, and attributes strong character and spiritual values to such high achievers.

(j) You are high in relationship values, which define quality of life issues. This means that you value modesty, compromise and co-operative success. In your society, living well in material comfort and having other high standard of living factors are believed to be matters of birth, luck, or destiny. *or*

(j) You are high in relationship values, which define quality of life issues. This means that you value modesty, compromise and co-operative success. In your society, material comfort and lifestyle are considered less an indication of a person's character and value than their religious devotion, their social conscience, their intellectual or artistic abilities, their stature as a wise elder, or their rights as a fellow member of a caring society.

(k) You tend to think in universalistic terms – that is, you prefer to draw on general principles rather than to explain things through anecdotes or lists of examples.

(l) You tend to think in particularistic terms – that is, you prefer to explain things through anecdotes or lists of examples rather than by drawing on general principles.

(m) You believe it appropriate to limit the display of feeling in interaction, especially at work. However strongly emotions are felt, you consider, they should be controlled. You are embarrassed when others display strong emotions and consider displays of anger, delight or intensity in the workplace as 'unprofessional'.

(n) In your society, the display of feeling is an accepted part of life, including working life. You believe that if people have strong emotions, they should show them, not bottle them up. You find people who do not show their feelings cold and heartless; they frighten you somewhat and you do not trust them.

(o) Your sense of how life should be lived is a specific one. In your society, people keep their public and private lives separate – they do not, for instance, readily invite business acquaintances to their homes. They live their lives in a series of overlapping but separate compartments. To be expected to do business with members of your own or your business equivalent's family present, for instance, would make you very uncomfortable.

(p) Your sense of how life should be lived is a diffuse one. In your society, people's public and private lives intermingle – for instance, they readily invite business acquaintances to their homes. To you, it is natural to have members of your family present when you do business.

(q) You are a meritocrat – you believe that what matters is what people have achieved through their own efforts, rather than from their position resulting from external factors. You believe that status is something people should receive for their achievements rather than from birth or fortune. Naturally, you expect others to acknowledge their appreciation for what you yourself have achieved.

(r) You give people their due according to their age and experience, education, professional qualifications and position in society, based on birth and fortune. That is how status is ascribed in your society and you support that approach, believing that the alternative can make for instability and discontent. Naturally, you expect to receive the deference due to someone in your own societal position.

(s) Your concept of time is a linear one – you hate wasting time, are usually conscious of the passage of time, have fairly short time horizons. You like to see projects brought to fruition within a year or so at most, but believe in doing one thing at a time. Planning for the future is a major concern of yours.

(t) Your concept of time is that it is a cycle – your preoccupations are with the seasons coming round, the life cycle; you are always interested in the history of any project you are involved with – often more than the future. '*Plus ça change, plus c'est la même chose*' to some extent sums up your attitude to change. You are rarely in a rush, believe in 'more haste, less speed' and have long time horizons – it is not when projects are completed that matters, so much as that they are really fruitful. On the other hand, you are quite happy to have a large number of different balls in the air at once.

7. This exercise is a role play based on the following true incident: 'In a Russian factory, where a UK manager with extended international experience was production manager in the late 1980s, he found that three-quarters of the width of an important supply road was blocked by rubbish, waste materials, etc. These slowed everything down because vehicles could not pass. He asked to get it cleared.' The local manager's role briefing includes the points that the road had been used to store unwanted materials ever since s/he came to work there ten years before, that the so-called 'blockage' did not directly affect the operation of the factory and that there would be resistance from the workforce at being asked to do this work.

   The nationalities of the participants can be changed as required, but should be chosen to be compatible with the culture of the international manager being an active orientation (Cultural briefing a, Exercise 6) and that of the local manager being a passive orientation (Cultural briefing b, Exercise 6).

   *Role A* is the production manager, *Role B* the local manager.

8. Role play the meeting described in the following two role descriptions:

   *Role A*: In your work as a computer trainer, you often encounter people who doubt your authority and expertise. Sometimes they ask to 'speak to the boss'. You are the boss. You believe their attitude is strongly influenced by *your skin colour and your age – you are in your twenties**. Introduce yourself to a prospective client and discuss their requirements.

   *Role B*: You have the responsibility for contracting out the computer training for the 20 staff in the regional office of your organisation. The representative of one company, which will be competing for the work, is about to call on you to introduce himself/herself and discuss your requirements. Your understanding is that this person will be leading the training team.

When this person enters, you will find that they are *young and from an ethnic minority**. While you would always deny that you are prejudiced, this particular combination of attributes does give rise to some doubts in your mind about whether this person would be a competent trainer or team leader.

* Adapt as required – gender, disability, social class (accent), apparent sexual orientation, etc.

9. In this role play there are two parties, who can be either individuals or teams.

   *Role A*: Your job involves negotiating for a major utility (electricity) based in one region of the country (one country) with big customers in another region (another country). Sometimes the people you deal with are quite upset at the idea of getting their power from a company based outside their region (country) – it offends their regional (national) sympathies. They never mention it, but it affects their overall attitudes. Introduce yourself to a prospective customer.

   *Role B*: In this role play you represent a major regional (national) customer for an electricity supplier based in another region (country). Although you would never mention it, you are quite upset at the idea of getting your power from a company based outside your region (country) – it offends your regional (national) sympathies. A representative of the prospective supplier is about to call on you to introduce himself/herself.

10. The author observed a detailed negotiation over a leasing arrangement for a catering space in a unique London venue, a ship moored on the Thames. An agreement in principle had been reached at a previous meeting. The rental of the space for the period was to be £10,000. The participants were the Chief Executive of the catering business, an American, a successful Malaysian woman restaurateur (R), and her husband, an English accountant. The following was known from the outset:

    - the lease could only be guaranteed for a total of six months, because the ship was for sale;
    - that to get round the delays in obtaining a licence for the new restaurant the woman restaurateur would initially have to operate as a manager within the existing business, with financial adjustments;
    - that the kitchen for the space was small and might not pass a health inspection. Despite these obstacles, R was excited by the prospect of a restaurant in a unique location with river views.

    Early in the negotiation, two 'facts' emerged:

    - The kitchen had, two days before, been ripped out because of the health concerns; to reinstate it would cost £1500 of which the Chief Executive was asking R to pay half.

- The Chief Executive's main subordinate seemed to blow hot and cold on the idea, while another senior colleague was actively opposed; this mattered to R, who needed a 'happy' atmosphere in which to work enthusiastically.

The discussion ranged to and fro over these 'hard' and 'soft' issues, with R or her husband taking the lead for their side accordingly. The delays to an early opening date and over the loss of the kitchen were a major stumbling block, both because of the short guaranteed period to cover costs and because R, self-described as 'head-on – a typical Malaysian' wanted to get started 'now'. Both husband and wife made what seemed to the author a disproportionate obstacle of the unexpected £750 needed for the kitchen; at this point it started to appear that their hidden agenda was to get out of the agreement in principle made previously. The Chief Executive made no concessions but worked hard to present matters in a different light, acceptable to R and her husband – for instance, to explain away the attitudes of his subordinates.

After three hours, a further fact emerged: to get a new licence for the space, it would first have to be delicensed, which would create the risk that the authorities would not relicense it. On this, which would be unacceptable to the Chief Executive's Board, the negotiations foundered; it was agreed to make contact again if an opportunity opened up through the sale of the ship to a purchaser who wanted to continue the existing business.

Identify the cultural and non-cultural obstacles to the negotiation in this example.

11. Complete the rating scale in Table 12.2 to assess your overall intercultural communication performance in a recent interaction.

**Table 12.2 Rating scale for intercultural interactions**

| | *Strongly Agree* | *Agree* | *Neither Agree Nor Disagree* | *Disagree* | *Strongly Disagree* |
|---|---|---|---|---|---|
| In the interaction (meeting/interview/ negotiation) just completed, I feel I was consistently able to: | | | | | |
| 1. make accurate predictions | X______X______X______X______X______X | | | | |
| 2. be mindful | X______X______X______X______X______X | | | | |
| 3. tolerate ambiguity | X______X______X______X______X______X | | | | |
| 4. manage anxiety | X______X______X______X______X______X | | | | |
| 5. empathise | X______X______X______X______X______X | | | | |
| 6. adapt my behaviour through cultural relativism | X______X______X______X______X______X | | | | |

*Since this scale is transparent, no scoring guide is needed.*

**Table 12.3 Intercultural performance questionnaire**

| When I interact at work with people from backgrounds different to my own, I tend to: | *Strongly Agree* | | | | *Strongly Disagree* |
|---|---|---|---|---|---|
| 1. use similar phrasing and vocabulary, formality level and non-verbal behaviour as my interlocutor | X | X | X | X | X |
| 2. share topic selection and turn taking | X | X | X | X | X |
| 3. maintain my interlocutor's face | X | X | X | X | X |
| 4. minimise interruptions, corrections and evaluations | X | X | X | X | X |
| 5. adjust my speech-rate, loudness, framing and focusing moves in order to maximise ease of understanding for my interlocutor | X | X | X | X | X |
| 6. recognise whether the interaction was status-marked | X | X | X | X | X |
| 7. recognise people who are highly dependent on their group and whose sense of group solidarity is high | X | X | X | X | X |
| 8. appropriately adjust my behaviour for people who are highly dependent on their group and whose sense of group solidarity is high | X | X | X | X | X |
| 9. recognise people who feel that they or their group is disadvantaged | X | X | X | X | X |
| 10. appropriately adjust my behaviour for people who feel that they or their group is disadvantaged | X | X | X | X | X |
| 11. distinguish members of dominant and subordinate groups and remember how that status is likely to affect their initial orientations | X | X | X | X | X |
| 12. pay attention to others' needs, motivations and behaviours | X | X | X | X | X |
| 13. monitor other interactors' communication strategies to identify them as convergence, divergence or maintenance | X | X | X | X | X |
| 14. use a wider range of communication strategies than normal | X | X | X | X | X |
| 15. select and use an appropriate communication strategy | X | X | X | X | X |
| 16. be sensitive to the other interactors' evaluations of my own behaviour as accommodative or not | X | X | X | X | X |
| 17. be sensitive to the other interactors' attributions of my own behaviour as due to myself, my situation or my group | X | X | X | X | X |
| 18. monitor my own attributions of other interactors' behaviour as due to themself, their situation or their group | X | X | X | X | X |
| 19. be aware of the implications of attuning behaviour by my interlocutor | X | X | X | X | X |
| 20. be aware of the implications of counter-attuning behaviour by my interlocutor | X | X | X | X | X |

12. Complete the questionnaire in Table 12.3. *See the Appendix to find out how to analyse your responses to this questionnaire.*

13. Complete the questionnaire in Table 12.4 to assess how hard you will have to work to adjust in another country. *See the Appendix to find out how to analyse your responses to this questionnaire.*

**Table 12.4 Questionnaire for prospective sojourners**

Rate your answers to the questions below. Use a scale of 1 to 5, 1 being low, a firm 'no', and 5 being high, a firm 'yes'. All family members going should rate themselves.

i. Do I look forward to meeting and getting to know some of the people in a foreign country?
ii. Am I willing to learn about the history, geography, arts, sports and politics of the foreign country? Will I learn their language?
iii. Am I willing to leave behind friends and family and to reach out to make new relationships?
iv. Am I willing to leave behind the identity I have established in my community or job to go where no one knows my accomplishments, interests, talents or foibles?
v. Do I feel good about myself? Am I emotionally strong?
vi. Am I in good health and physically able to live overseas?
vii. (if applicable) Are the children well adjusted, self-confident and performing satisfactorily in school?
viii. (if applicable) Am I capable of giving up my job or my role as spouse/parent without great resentment or stress?
ix. (if applicable) Is my marriage, strong, stable, mutually supportive?
x. Do I truly want to go on this assignment?

This was posted on the Internet:
URL=http://www.adm.uwaterloo.ca/infoiso/dest/settle/culture.html

## FURTHER READING

Adler, N. J. (1991) *International Dimensions of Organizational Behavior*, 2nd edn. Belmont, Calif.: Wadsworth.

Gudykunst, W. B. and Y. Y. Kim (1992) *Communicating with Strangers: An Approach to Intercultural communication*, 2nd edn. New York: McGraw-Hill.

Guirdham, M. (1999) *Communicating Across Cultures*. Basingstoke: Macmillan. Also relevant to Chapter 7 of this book.

Kim, Y. Y. (1988) *Communication and Cross-cultural Adaptation: An Integrative Theory*. Clevedon: Multicultural Matters.

## REFERENCES

1. Rabbie, J. M. and M. Horwitz (1969) 'Arousal of ingroup–outgroup bias by a chance win or loss', *Journal of Personality and Social Psychology*, vol. 13, no. 3, pp. 269–277.
2. Tajfel, H., M. G. Billig, R. P. Bundy and C. Flament (1971) 'Social categorization and intergroup behaviour', *European Journal of Social Psychology*, vol. 1, pp. 149–178.
3. Blanz, M., A. Mummendey and S. Otten (1995) 'Perception of relative group size and group status: effects on intergroup discrimination in negative evaluations', *European Journal of Social Psychology*, vol. 5, pp. 231–247.
4. Hogg, M. A. and D. Abrams (1988) *Social Identifications*. London: Routledge.
5. Ibid.
6. DuPraw, M. E. and M. Axner (1997) *Fears and Hopes for Intercultural Communication*. Washington, DC: National Institute of Dispute Resolution.
7. Larkey, L. K. (1996) 'The development and validation of the workforce diversity questionnaire', *Management Communication Quarterly*, vol. 9, no. 3, pp. 296–337.

8. Allport, G. W. (1979) *The Nature of Prejudice*. Reading, Mass.: Addison-Wesley (original work published 1954).
9. Stephan, W. G. and C. W. Stephan (1985) 'Inter-group anxiety', *Journal of Social Issues*, vol. 41, pp. 157–175.
10. Majeski, S. J. (1995) 'Conflict and co-operation in international relations', *Journal of Conflict Resolution*, vol. 39, no. 4, pp. 622–646.
11. Gaertner, S. L., J. F. Dovidio, M. C. Rust, J. L. Nier, B. S. Banker, C. M. Ward, G. R. Mottola and M. Houlette (1999) 'Reducing intergroup bias: Elements of intergroup cooperation', *Journal of Personality and Social Psychology*, vol. 76, no. 3, pp. 388–402.
12. Du Praw and Axner, op. cit.
13. Langer, E. (1989) *Mindfulness*. Reading, Mass.: Addison-Wesley.
14. Snyder, M. (1974) 'Self-monitoring of expressive behavior', *Journal of Personality and Social Psychology*, vol. 30, pp. 526–537.
15. Kim, M.-S., J. E. Hunter, A. Miyahara, A. Horvath, M. Bresnahan and H. Yoon (1996) 'Individual-vs. culture-level dimensions of individualism and collectivism: Effects on preferred conversational styles', *Communication Monographs*, vol. 63, pp. 29–49.
16. Ting-Toomey, S. (1989) 'Communicative resourcefulness: An identity negotiation perspective' in M. K. Asante, W. B. Gudykunst and E. Newmark (eds) *Handbook of International and Intercultural Communication*. Newbury Park, Calif.: Sage.
17. Gudykunst, W. B. and Y. Y. Kim (1992) *Communicating with Strangers: An Approach to Intercultural Communication*, 2nd edn. New York: McGraw-Hill.
18. Katriel, T. (1989) 'From "context" to "contexts" in intercultural communication research' in S. Ting-Toomey and F. Korzenny (eds) *Language, Communication and Culture: Current Directions*. Newbury Park, Calif.: Sage.
19. Bennett, J. M. (1986) 'Modes of cross-cultural training: conceptualising cross-cultural training as education', *International Journal of Intercultural Relations*, vol. 10, pp. 117–134.
20. Segalla, M., L. Fischer and K. Sandner (2000) 'Making cross-cultural research relevant to European corporate integration: Old problem, new approach', *European Management Journal*, vol. 18, no. 1, pp. 38–51.
21. Maher, B. A. (1994) 'The shattered language of schizophrenia' in G. R. Weaver (ed.) *Communication, Culture and Conflict: Readings in Intercultural Relations*. Needham Heights, Mass.: Ginn Press, pp. 199–206.
22. Hall, E. T. (1959) *The Silent Language*. New York: Doubleday.
23. Hall, E. T. (1976) *Beyond Culture*. New York: Doubleday.
24. Kim, Y. Y. (1988) *Communication and Cross-cultural Adaptation: An Integrative Theory*. Clevedon: Multicultural Matters.
25. Ibid.
26. Kealey, D. J. (1989) 'A study of cross-cultural effectiveness: theoretical issues, practical applications', *International Journal of Intercultural Relations*, vol. 13, pp. 387–428.
27. Black, J. S. and H. B. Gregersen (1999) 'The right way to manage expats', *Harvard Business Review*, March/April, pp. 52–64.
28. Lysgaard, S. (1955) 'Adjustment in a foreign society: Norwegian Fulbright grantees visiting the United States', *International Social Science Bulletin*, vol. 7, pp. 45–51.
29. Kim, Y. Y. (1994) 'Intercultural personhood' in W. B. Gudykunst and Y. Y. Kim (1997) *Communicating with Strangers: An Approach to Intercultural Communication*. New York: McGraw-Hill.

30. Triandis, H. C., E. R. Hall and R. B. Ewen (1965) 'Some cognitive factors affecting group creativity', *Human Relations*, vol. 18, no. 1, pp. 33–35.
31. Hayles, R. (1982) 'Costs and benefits of integrating persons from diverse cultures into organisations', Paper presented at the 21st International Congress of Applied Psychology, Edinburgh, Scotland.
32. Adler, N. (1991) *International Dimensions of Organizational Behaviour*, 2nd edn. Belmont, Calif.: Wadsworth.
33. Weiss, S. E. and J. J. Curhan (1999) 'Adopting a dual lens approach for examining the dilemma of differences in international business negotiations', *International Negotiation Journal*, vol. 4, no. 1, pp. 2–13.
34. Ohbuchi, K.-I., O. Fukushima and J. T. Tedeschi (1999) 'Cultural values in conflict management: goal orientation, goal attainment and tactical decision', *Journal of Cross-Cultural Psychology*, vol. 30, no. 1, pp. 51–71.
35. Al-Ghamdi, S. M. (1999) 'Success and failure factors in Saudi-American negotiations: American views', *International Negotiation Journal*, vol. 4, no. 1, pp. 14–20.
36. Gelfland, M. J. and A. Realo (1999) 'Individualism–collectivism and accountability in intergroup negotiations', *Journal of Applied Psychology*, vol. 84, no. 5, pp. 721–736.
37. Reynolds, P. D. (1986) 'Organizational culture as related to industry, position and performance: A preliminary report', *Journal of Management Studies*, vol. 23, no. 3, pp. 333–345.
38. Kale, S. H. and J. W. Barnes (1992) 'Understanding the domain of cross-national buyer–seller interactions', *Journal of International Business Studies*, 1st quarter, pp. 101–132.
39. Rackham, N. and J. Carlisle (1978) 'The effective negotiator', *Journal of European Industrial Training*, vol. 2, no. 6, pp. 6–11.
40. Graham, J. L. and R. A. Herberger (1983) 'Negotiators abroad – Don't shoot from the hip', *Harvard Business Review*, July/Aug., pp. 160–168.
41. Chigas, D. V. (1997) 'Unofficial interventions with official actors: Parallel negotiation training in violent intrastate conflicts', *International Negotiation Journal*, vol. 2, no. 3, pp. 23–31.

# 13 Leadership

## CHAPTER INTRODUCTION

Leadership can be defined as 'the ability of an individual to influence, motivate and enable others to contribute towards the effectiveness and success of the organisation of which they are members'. This definition has been shown by a cross-cultural research project called GLOBE (Global Leadership and Organisational Behaviour Effectiveness) to be acceptable to representatives from a wide range of cultures.[1] The increasing concern with 'capturing individual capabilities and motivating the entire organisation to respond to the demands of the environment' means that there is an emphasis on leadership as the key to successful strategy implementation.[2] Growth, development and prosperity are seen to depend on developing a creative, consultative culture in which individuals can contribute fully. Human capital will be the 'strategic resource of the future'.[3] The role of managers must change from directing to facilitating, coaching and counselling.[4]

This chapter aims to help readers to understand how to enact leadership face-to-face by explaining the following:

- trait, style and contingency theories of what is required in successful leaders;
- transformational versus transactional leadership;
- how to gain acceptance as a leader, by meeting followers' expectations of their leader's knowledge, competence, status, group identification, motivation, action and communication skill;
- communication, impression management and framing for effective leadership;
- how to influence subordinates and improve their performance by encouraging participation;
- leaders as team builders: goal setting and managing conflict within the team;
- cultural and gender differences in leadership;
- face-to-face leadership in diverse organisations;
- how to apply face-to-face leadership skills to chair meetings and delegate.

## THE NATURE OF LEADERSHIP

Essentially, leaders are people who are followed. Being followed is not automatic, even for appointed leaders. In the words of Goffee and Jones in 2001: 'Now that we are in the age of empowerment, followers are hard to find.'[5] Appointed leaders who fail to influence their followers are leaders in name only. True leaders influence their followers because they have some power over them and know how to mobilise that power, or because they persuade their followers to act or think in a certain way. Therefore, the earlier chapters on the face-to-face skills of using power and persuasiveness give much of the material on leadership; so does Chapter 11, on group processes, because we often consider leadership of a group rather than an individual. Further issues concerning the social skills of leadership are covered in this chapter, beginning with trait, style, situation and transformational theories.

**Box 13.1**

Spanish Telecom's CEO Juan Villalonga resigned on 26 July 2000. *The Economist* reported that a string of high-risk deals propelled Telefonica into the big league of global firms in mobile communications and television.

> 'Shareholders were delighted; Mr Villalonga became wealthy and increasingly convinced of his own genius. Then it all went wrong. First, in May, Telefonica's board opposed Villalonga's plan to merge with a Dutch rival. Then, last month, Spain's stockmarket regulator reopened an old investigation into share dealings by Mr Villalonga in 1998. Having initially dismissed speculation that he was under pressure to quit, he now seems to have bowed to just that.
>
> Although telecoms firms need deal-driven, high achieving bosses if they are to compete in the industry's rapid restructuring, they also need leaders who can keep their feet on the ground. Mr Villalonga became more autocratic and heavy-handed the more Telefonica expanded. In the end, he lost the support not just of the team around him but also of his political patrons' (*The Economist*, 2000).
>
> 'Leadership is inherent in the relations among individuals, not in the individuals themselves' (Fernanda, 1991).

*Sources*: Fernanda, R. M. (1991) 'Structural bases of leadership in intra-organization networks', *Social Psychology Quarterly*, vol. 54, no. 1, pp. 36–53.
*The Economist*, 22 July 2000, p. 76.

Early studies of leadership were based on the assumption that there are identifiable *traits* or styles of behaviour that distinguish leaders from followers and successful from unsuccessful leaders. The purpose of the studies was to find the traits or styles that correlate best with effective leadership. One review article showed that researchers had found positive correlations, albeit often weak ones, with the following traits: intelligence, self-confidence, awareness of the motives of others, habitual responsibility, initiative, persistence, task orientation, goal orientation, entrepreneurialism, originality in problem-solving, influencing skill, the capacity to structure social systems according to the purpose in hand and willingness to absorb uncertainty, frustration, delay and stress on behalf of others.[6] The article concluded, however, that successful leaders combine many of these traits – no one characteristic distinguishes between more and less successful leaders.

*Style theories* develop the theme that it is combinations of a number of traits that determine leadership. They identify different types of style that subsume bundles of traits. Style is the 'consistent pattern of behaviour that you exhibit when you attempt to influence other people'.[7] A common leadership typology identifies three styles: autocratic, democratic and laissez-faire. Autocratic leaders dictate to their followers without consultation; democratic leaders involve their followers in decision-making; laissez-faire 'leaders' abdicate their leadership role, participating in decision-making on the same level as their followers. It seems reasonable to suppose, as style theories do, that such fundamental differences in leadership style affect how well a group works, the quality of its decisions and the satisfaction levels of the members of the group. Goleman[8] reported in the *Harvard Business Review* that research by Hay/McBer consultants, drawing on a random sample of 3871 executives from a 20,000 database, concluded that there are six leadership styles: coercive, authoritative, affiliative, democratic, pace-setting and coaching. They also found that different styles affect performance and results, flexible use of different styles is effective, and each style springs from a different component of emotional intelligence.

A review of leadership style research concluded that there is a single style of leadership that contributes positively to group productivity, cohesion and satisfaction. It is a style that clearly defines roles, tasks and expectations for group

**Box 13.2**

### European variations in leadership styles

French managers are expected to show a high degree of analysis and technical knowledge and to answer questions precisely. Participative leadership is generally not understood or accepted.

In Germany, the manager's authority is rarely questioned, on the basis that they know what they are talking about. In contrast in Sweden, managers adopt a coaching style. Subordinates are given suggestions, not instructions, because the person doing the job is considered the most expert. The manager's role is to listen, persuade and reconcile contradictory positions.

In Italy, authority is personal, vested in the owner or chairperson of the business or someone who has their confidence. This may or may not be a person with an official leadership role. Personal qualities, such as being charismatic and creative, are as important as being technically competent. This contrasts with Germany, where leaders are expected to be strong, decisive, competent and hard working – personality is less important.

In the Netherlands, with its low power distance culture, authority is often derived from deep experience within the company. In Spain, implementation of plans and decisions depends on personal negotiation with the people who have to carry them out. Responsibility rests with the leader, who is expected to show courage and decisiveness. The manager's authority in Spain depends on how the subordinate regards him (or, rarely, her) rather than position. In the United Kingdom, the nature of the authority system is in flux and more disputed than in most other European countries.

members but also shows concern for the well-being and contributions of group members – i.e. it is a style that combines the positive aspects of autocratic and democratic leadership, while avoiding their negative aspects. This is a helpful conclusion. However, research also shows that style theories need a serious caveat: the best style varies according to the situation. If a decision is needed urgently, the autocratic style is most effective. If implementing the decision will demand the energies of numbers of unsupervised workers, the democratic style is best. Among professionals, a laissez-faire style may be the right one.

Dissatisfaction with style theorising turned leadership research in a different direction: *situational theories* of leadership. Situational theorists have generally subdivided approaches to group work into task and relationship (maintenance) orientations (as discussed in Chapter 11). Some leaders are 'high-task' in their approach to work with a group of followers, others are 'high-relationship'. The studies ask in which situations high-task, or conversely high-relationship, leaders are more effective. A series of studies, in which leadership effectiveness was defined in terms of a group's performance in achieving its goals, found no consistent relationship between task- or maintenance-oriented leadership behaviour and group effectiveness. One was more effective in some situations and the other in others, thus confirming the basic situational theory.[9]

Situations can be classified on three dimensions relevant to leadership effectiveness. These are: the clarity of the group's task, the quality of the relationship between leader and followers and the amount of power held by the leader. When all three are high – the task is clear, the relationship is good and the leader is powerful – or when all three are low, task-orientation is more effective. Intermediate situations are ones in which a maintenance-oriented leader will empower the group more than a task-oriented one will. Research has provided some confirmation of this theory. As a guide to how to behave as a leader, though, situational leadership theory has significant drawbacks, since most situations have been shown to be mixed. For instance, they might combine ambiguous tasks, good relationships and moderately powerful leaders. In mixed situations, the theory is an unclear guide. In addition, other factors in the situation, for instance, the size of the work group or the overall culture of the organisation, affect what style of leadership is most effective.

More recent developments of situational leadership theories have introduced another factor into the descriptions of situations – the maturity of the followers or group members. Maturity is defined in terms of the particular task that the group is confronting. That is, a mature group is one that is experienced in carrying out this type of task, is able to set high but realistic goals and can accept responsibility for outcomes. Task and relationship orientations are conceptualised as two separate dimensions, instead of one as in earlier situational studies. This means that task- and relationship-oriented behaviours can be combined. The possibilities can be presented as a matrix as shown in Figure 13.1. The

| High relationship/low task | High relationship/high task |
|---|---|
| Low relationship/low task | Low relationship/high task |

**Figure 13.1 Task- and relationship-oriented behaviour matrix.**

leader behaviour, shown in each quadrant of the matrix, is appropriate or not according to the task maturity of the group. Low-relationship with high-task leadership is needed by very immature groups to enable them to get on with the task at all. As such groups mature, however, they progress through a need for high-task with high-relationship leadership, then high-relationship with low-task leadership, to a state of high maturity where the need for leadership of any kind is minimal. At this point, a low-relationship with low-task approach by the nominal leader works best. Figure 13.2 shows this model, in which a curve suggests the most appropriate leadership style, labelled 'telling', 'selling', 'participating' and 'delegating', for the job-related development of the subordinates.[10]

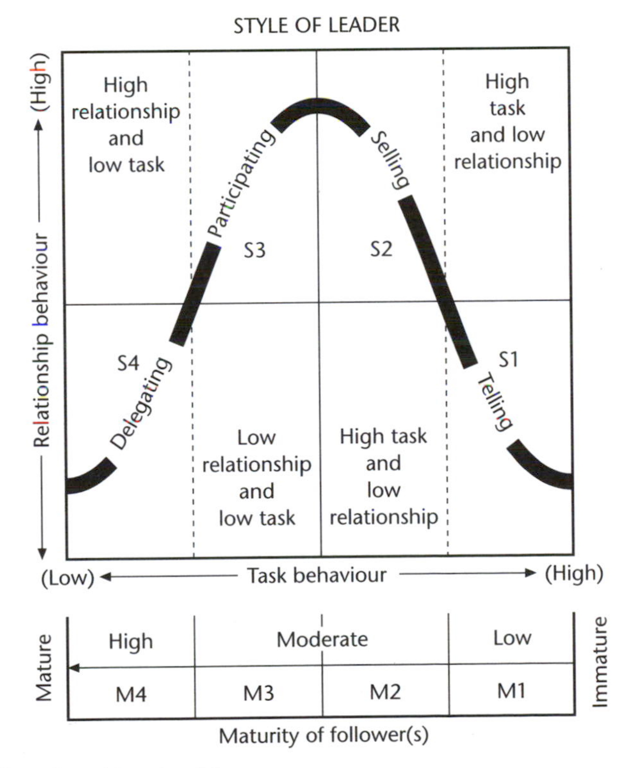

**Figure 13.2 Situational leadership.**

*Source*: Reprinted by permission of the publisher from Hersey, P. and K. Blanchard (1982) *Management of Organization Behaviour: Utilizing Human Resources*, 3rd edn. Englewood Cliffs, New Jersey: Prentice Hall, p. 152.

Culture researcher F. Trompenaars has criticised these situation (or contingency) theories as 'still searching for the "one best way".'[11] A later interpretation of situational leadership theory, which may take into account this criticism, advocates identifying the salient face wants of the followers and adapting leadership style accordingly. In 1991, communication-oriented research by Zorn and Leichty[12] showed that leaders' messages allow followers to have more independence and that followers also demand more as those followers gain experience. This research suggests that, in practice, leaders often implement the model of adapting to the maturity of their followers.

Later, leadership study turned from trait and situation analysis to a concern with the elements of 'strategic vision' that can be found in successful leaders and organisations.[13] Charisma became the practical focus of leadership studies.[14] Charisma, though, means something other than mere outstanding personal attractiveness. It means '*transformational leadership*'. This is a 'quality of leadership that moves organisations in radically new and better directions and transforms their culture, often substituting concern for service, total quality, long-termism and optimism for preoccupations with products and production, output and costs, bottom lines and gloom' (which are sometimes referred to as transactional leadership). Transactional leadership, in contrast, involves exchanging rewards and punishment for performance, using power that comes from organisational position and closely guarding information.

Transformational leadership encourages participation and sharing of power and information. It also seeks criticism. It has resulted in staff who show the highest effort, performance and job satisfaction; it is also related strongly to organisational morale, team cohesion and commitment. Both team and organisational measures of success show that transformational leadership increases performance.[15] Transactional and transformational leadership are compared in Table 13.1. Several approaches distinguish leadership from management, which

**Table 13.1 A comparison of transactional and transformational leadership**

| | *Transactional leadership* | *Transformational leadership* |
|---|---|---|
| Concerns | Products, output, costs, bottom line | Service, quality, long-termism, optimism |
| Promotes performance by | Rewards and punishments | Vision and charisma |
| Approach to power | Guarded by leader | Participative |
| Approach to information | Guarded by leader | Shared |
| Outcomes | Can be negative, gloom | High staff effort, performance, job satisfaction<br>High organisational morale<br>High team commitment<br>High organisational success |

is defined as concerned with the routine, but the concept of transformational versus transactional leadership does so particularly strongly.

**Box 13.3**

### Critique of leadership theories

- Trait research has found only complex combinations of characteristics that correlate with effective leadership.
- Style theories, and most situational theories, seek to over-simplify the complexity of leadership.
- Transformational leadership in business often means only that senior managers allocate more power to themselves, while excluding others from decision-making. This happens despite evidence that more participative methods of management are required to ensure business success. To succeed, organisations 'need a review of previous over-reliance on the transformational impact of visionary leaders and its associated emphasis on the importance of monolithic organisational cultures' (Tourish, 1998).

*Source*: Tourish, D. (1998) 'The God that failed: replacing false messiahs with open communication', *Australian Journal of Communication*, vol. 25, no. 2, pp. 99–114.

## SUMMARY – THE NATURE OF LEADERSHIP

Trait, style and situational leadership theories provide ideas to help gear mental orientations towards leadership roles. However, they are limited in their guidance on how to enact those roles face-to-face. Transformational leadership, in contrast to transactional, supposedly encourages participation, shares power and information and seeks criticism. However, it is linked to a strategic vision which may, in practice, mean disempowering followers.

## GAINING ACCEPTANCE AS A LEADER

Successful leaders enable groups to achieve their goals, but also act like and have the attributes of leaders in the perceptions of their followers. A 1991 article in *Social Psychology Quarterly* commented, 'The important thing is not that the leader possess superior qualities, but that his [sic] followers believe that he possesses these qualities.'[16] There are particular attributes and behaviours that followers look for in leaders. These vary with the situation and with who the members of the following group are. However, the attributes mostly fall under the seven headings shown in Figure 13.3. They are: knowledge, competence, status, identification with the group, motivation, action to promote the group's goals and communication skills.

1. The higher managers rank within a hierarchy, the higher the expectations that they will be well informed and embody implicit institutional knowledge.[17]

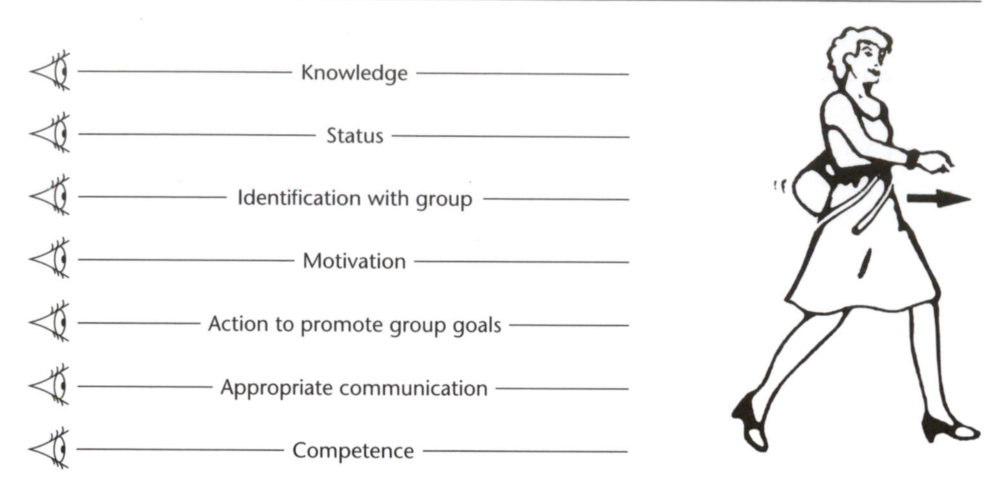


**Figure 13.3 Dimensions of followers' perceptions of leaders.**

2. The competence required of their leaders by followers relates, not only to tasks in which the group is engaged, such as formulating the theme of an advertising campaign or deciding budgetary allocations, but also to their ability to keep the group operating smoothly and progressing towards its goals. Research shows that perceived influence in a group is related to 'air time' – to how much of the time a person participates and contributes to discussion. Actual influence, on the other hand, is more closely related to expertise than to air time.[18] Leaders need to have both perceived and actual influence. Groups where the same people who contribute most are also the most expert take better decisions, because it is clearer whose contributions to accept.
3. Leaders' status is particularly linked to the status their followers perceive them to have outside the group. Departmental heads, for instance, negotiate at a higher level for resources for their department. They also act as spokespersons for their department, defend its interests and reputation and promote its contribution to the overall company welfare. Their successes in these activities, and the respect that they appear to receive from colleagues outside the department, affect their status in the eyes of the staff within it.
4. People more readily accept influence attempts, especially from change agents, from others who are seen both as loyal to the group, and as identifying with its interests.[19] Since successful leaders by definition must be successful influencers, it is clear that their followers must perceive them to be closely involved with the group.
5. Leaders' motivations must be seen as 'high and sincere where group concerns are at stake'.[20] A so-called leader whose actions seem to be motivated by self-aggrandisement is likely to lose influence, whereas one who is attributed motives of sustaining and promoting the group gains acceptance.

6. Leaders must also be seen to be active in pursuing the group's goals. They must be seen to recruit and deploy people, set targets, and direct, co-ordinate and control group activities. Followers expect their leaders to be going somewhere and to know the way. 'Fair' leaders receive more positive endorsements from followers, except in inter-group competition, when favouring the in-group gets more endorsements.[21]
7. Finally, gaining acceptance as a leader depends on communicating appropriately. Research showed that in a situation of conflict over leadership and authority, leadership was legitimised by using certain linguistic strategies, whereas using other strategies placed some contenders for leadership at a disadvantage.[22]

Gaining acceptance as a leader is made more difficult for the victims of sexual, racial and disability prejudice. One study showed that subordinates have differing expectations and perceptions of a supervisor based on biological sex, that female managers are given less power than equivalent males and that subjects prefer masculine sex-typed managers regardless of biological sex.[23] Studies in which actual performance indicators are equalised between men and women, generally find an overall slight tendency to favour male leaders. This tendency is increased under the following conditions:

- where the woman leader's style corresponds to male stereotypes (i.e. is autocratic, not interpersonal and participative);
- for roles usually occupied by men as against those occupied equally by both sexes or where the sex distribution is unknown;
- in some organisational contexts, such as sports and athletics coaches, business and manufacturing, there is generally a slightly more favourable evaluation of male business managers than female business managers;
- men are more likely to devalue women than women are; women are largely neutral.

There is, however, no evidence of increased bias against either competent, successful women leaders or those in higher positions in an organisation.[24]

Jackson and Hirsch[25] found that British men and women perform similarly in managerial positions and have similar degrees of managerial potential. Knott and Natalle[26] assessed superiors' perceptions of their male and female managers in middle and upper levels of the organisation. They discovered that female managers are rated higher at putting people at ease. They argued that sex differences do not make a difference in perceptions of leadership ability, once the manager has gained organisational experience. Despite this, there is not only a low representation of females in managerial positions, but women executives, by and large, are under-utilised, undervalued and limited in their career prospects.

The evidence on prejudice and discrimination against women leaders is particularly unfortunate. The reason for this is that their leadership styles may be the ones most suited to the current needs of organisations, where team behaviours are seen as increasingly important for management. (See the section on gender differences in managerial style later in this chapter.) The manager of the future may need to be concerned less with giving instructions and controlling subordinates and more with maintaining a network of relationships across the organisation and with 'outsiders' such as customers.

Petty and Bruning[27] surveyed 2432 US men and women and found that, overall, 'consideration' and 'initiating structure' appeared to be effective for both male and female leaders. These behaviours also correlated positively with male and female subordinates' satisfaction with supervision. Thus, the criteria used to assess managers may discriminate against women, but may also be based on a model of management that is no longer appropriate for the work that managers do. Appointment and promotion panels tend to emphasise the dominant, assertive, decisive aspects of behaviour and downplay the team building behaviour. Despite the barriers to success for women, however, many are in fact succeeding. As Davidson and Cooper reported, 'if a female manager is able to relay her success and confidence to her subordinates, any doubts they have about working for her disappear.'[28]

## SUMMARY – GAINING ACCEPTANCE AS A LEADER

Becoming accepted as a leader calls for the following: creating and fostering belief in the leader's knowledge, competence, high status, involvement with the group, motivation to place its interests before his or her own and activity in pursuit of its goals. To do this, leaders use the skills of understanding others' behaviour, impression management and communication. Women and members of ethnic or other minorities face engrained prejudice in gaining acceptance as leaders. However, the evidence available, which deals with women as leaders, suggests that these groups may have leadership styles better suited to the new types of organisation than other groups.

## COMMUNICATING LEADERSHIP

Leaders need to be highly competent communicators. Sypher[29] argued that leadership is essentially a communication activity. Leadership is seen not as created through the structures of a group, organisation or society, but as constructed through members' interactions. In making interventions to 'provide leadership', individuals need to be aware of how their colleagues will perceive the intervention. As Grunig[30] pointed out, many Chief Executive Officers (CEOs) operate symbolically, giving inspiration more than actually telling people exactly what to do. People who suffer from high levels of communication apprehension (CA) may provoke negative responses from their followers in regard to their leadership qualities. Hawkins and Stewart[31] found that people who self-reported high levels of CA were also those who received lower ratings in emerged leadership, social attraction and task attraction. Those self-reporting as low in CA scored higher overall on these ratings and their scores improved over time.

**Box 13.4**

In some countries managers feel they can relax more as they climb the ranks. In France and Germany, the opposite tends to happen. Bosses rarely spice up their presentations with anecdotes or jokes, put their feet up on desks or slouch. Executive behaviour is restrained because authority is not something to be taken lightly. The phrase, '*Ce n'est pas serieux*' springs easily to French executive lips to admonish unprofessional behaviour. Contrast such Franco-German sobriety with a certain exhibitionism in the British character. . . . For them, management is about wheeling and dealing, holding it together and making it work: 'You want to watch? You won't get bored.' This is not France, where proving managerial worth means whipping out a Grande Ecole diploma, nor is it Germany, with its emphasis on professional and relevant knowledge – both too cerebral to lend themselves to excited observation.

*Source*: Barsoux, J.-L. (1992) 'Follow the leaders', *International Management*, July/Aug., pp. 40–41.

Effective conversational forms by leaders are positive, coherent, facilitate work-related and personal goals, increase members' identification with the group and decrease their need for legitimation.[32] Directive leader communication can influence group decision-making behaviour. When groups are assigned a leader who uses a directive style and argues for a specific decision, the groups' decisions are influenced. Also affected are the decisions made by individual group members after the discussions and their perceptions of conflict, confidence in the group decision and compliance with the leader.[33] Other research has shown that leadership involves using cognitive and social processes to interpret events for other people. Communication with followers has a central role in transformational leadership but communication research to some extent shifts the usual understanding of charisma. The leadership literature emphasises the dramatic, energetic and confident aspects of style, but Holladay and Coombs[34] found that friendly, attentive, dominant and open communicator styles predict charisma. Followers' perceptions of leaders' charisma are unaffected by whether charismatic messages are delivered using weak or strong delivery techniques. Communicator style is important, but this is not a function of delivery, rather of content and language. To explain these unexpected findings the researchers pointed out that friendliness and attentiveness correlate with social attractiveness. Charismatic leaders, they conclude, are attractive to followers, who identify with them.

Gardner and Cleavenger[35] investigated impression management strategies associated in people's minds with transformational leadership, using the five-strategy model proposed by Jones and Pittman (1982; see Chapter 6). Of the five strategies, exemplification and ingratiation correlated positively with perceptions, not only of transformational leadership, but also of leader effectiveness and follower satisfaction. Self-promotion and intimidation were negatively related, while supplication had no correlation. All leaders frame leadership for their followers. For example, one manager might choose to frame leadership as 'leading troops into battle', while another might frame it as 'supporting subordinates and facilitating their work'. While the effectiveness of different frames varies according to the organisation or unit's composition or situation, leaders are also influenced by deeply held internal images of how the world works.[36] To frame successfully, leaders must enable other people to see the world they see. Frames are communicated through language, metaphors, specification, personalisation and the other devices given in Table 6.5 and the related text. A framing perspective on leadership sees it as realised in 'the everyday and routine aspects of the job – in a succession of moments rather than in landmark decisions'. Leadership is seen as learned, exercised daily and inclusive. To achieve this, leaders must use forethought and must lead themselves through critical analyses of themselves, the organisation and the context.[37]

## SUMMARY – COMMUNICATING LEADERSHIP

Perceptions of leader effectiveness and transformational ability, as well as follower satisfaction, are strongly influenced by how the leader communicates. High levels of communication apprehension create difficulties for leaders. Positive, coherent and directive styles of leader communication are influential. Exemplification and ingratiation are more effective leadership impression management strategies than intimidation or self-promotion. Leaders use communication to frame leadership in accord with their own vision.

## INFLUENCING SUBORDINATES

Gaining acceptance, communicating and framing leadership are, though vital, not enough. If individual subordinates, groups and meetings are to function well, they must be led in the right direction and they must be influenced effectively. Leaders use influence to encourage participation, build teams, resolve conflicts and set goals. In practice, the level of trust a manager feels towards a subordinate affects their choice of influence mode. Managers prefer coercive measures rather than reward or persuasion when trying to influence distrusted workers. Persuasion is preferred when workers are highly trusted. In intermediate situations, managers prefer the use of reward as an influence mode.[38] These

**Box 13.5**

A recent study of 1,500 employees found that the most powerful motivator for people is genuine, on-the-spot recognition from managers. Despite this fact, 53 per cent of employees in the study report that they seldom if ever have been personally thanked by their managers for a job well done, and 75 per cent have seldom if ever received a positive note, a public acknowledgement or group recognition from their managers. Is it any wonder, then, that 70 per cent of employees and managers are afraid to speak up at work – due to mistrust and fear of embarrassment, ridicule, demotion or job loss?

*Source*: Jill Dann, Course Tutor of the Chartered Institute of Personnel and Development course on Emotional Intelligence, quoted in G. Davies (2001) 'Make use of your emotions', *Ambassador*, April, p. 22.

choices are affected by the motives that managers attribute to their subordinates – external motives (e.g. fear of punishment) to workers who are not trusted and internal motives (wanting to do one's best) to highly trusted workers.

Effective leadership of small groups and meetings involves encouraging participation:

- Participation increases the range of inputs, knowledge and skills brought to bear on problems.
- Participation can enable leaders to opt for solutions that they might otherwise have rejected because of doubt about their acceptability. After a discussion in which a wide range of ideas has been explored and opinions expressed, leaders have a clearer idea of the limits that will be accepted by their followers. These may be wider than they realised.
- Participation increases substitutability. Where all are kept informed through participation, the members are often better able and more willing to take over each other's work if needed.
- By training the members to see what needs doing, participation can reduce the leader's workload in the long run.
- Participation can lead to more commitment, more mutual encouragement and higher morale of group members.
- Participation develops members as judges of others' contributions.[39] In participating, 'members gain first-hand insight into the possible solutions of the problem that faces the group. . . . As members are getting trained in the performance of tasks, they will gain insight into the competence of other members of the group.'[40]
- Participation relieves the problem of control. Where members share information and a frame of reference, the statement of a problem in itself implies to the members that certain solutions are possible and others are unacceptable. In these circumstances, the adopted solution is more likely to be one to which the members are committed, so that their performance in the tasks entailed by the solution do not need to be monitored in the way they do when the solution is seen by them as imposed.

**Box 13.6**

A woman had risen to Head of Children's Books at a lively young publishing house, when the company was taken over by what she termed 'men in grey suits'. She kept her job, because her department was outstandingly successful. She decided to leave, though, after a senior management meeting, when she was asked, 'Why is your department so successful?' 'I told them that I trusted my staff, gave them lots of discretion and involved them as much as possible in what was going on. They didn't want to know; worse, they were antipathetic to the whole idea. I couldn't work in a company like that.'

*Source*: Interview, author's research.

There is some evidence that participatory leadership is more valued and more effectively implemented in 'alternative' organisations.[41] There is also evidence that the very meaning of participation varies cross-culturally, for instance within Europe. Stohl[42] examined the cultural variability of the meanings of worker participation with a sample of managers from five European Union nations. Meanings for participation varied by culture in terms of Hofstede's dimensions of power distance and uncertainty avoidance.

**Box 13.7**

### How to implement participation face-to-face

- Do not present the group with a problem. Instead help the group to decide whether they have a problem and what, precisely, the problem is.
- Make a list of all suggestions so that all types of considerations are included.
- Protect individuals from the criticism of other group members by interpreting all remarks in a favourable light.
- Good suggestions may be kept in the discussion by asking 'How would that work out?'
- Do not hasten the solution by capitalising on the first good idea or in any other way reflect your preferences.
- When the list of solutions is fairly complete, ask probing questions, e.g. 'How can we change things so as to combine some of these features?' (Maier and Solem, 1952).
- Implementing participation face-to-face depends on an increased emphasis on two-way communication. 'Properly crafted communication strategies' are essential and can perform an integrative function for managers and staff, building a new partnership identity in the workplace (Tourish, 1998).

*Sources*: Maier, N. R. F. and A. R. Solem (1952) 'The contribution of a discussion leader to the quality of group thinking: the effective use of minority opinions' in D. Cartwright and A. Zander (eds) *Group Dynamics*. New York: Row, Peterson.
Tourish, D. (1998) 'The God that failed: replacing false messiahs with open communication', *Australian Journal of Communication*, vol. 25, no. 2, pp. 99–114.

To build more effective teams, and so get better results at work, the leader's own behaviours and competencies are important. A comparison of high- and average-performance teams found significant differences in the extent to which their leaders obtained outside support, tolerated uncertainty, showed personal qualities, such as courage, and confronted inadequate performance.[43] Beyond this, team effectiveness depends on mutual trust. Leaders build trust in two ways, by openness in communication and by allowing subordinates to have more discretion.

- Rules of thumb as given in some management books, such as 'Ask subordinates to express their feelings openly', do not work to create trust, because unless a high level of trust already exists, who but a fool would express negative feelings openly to a boss? Openness in communication must start with the power or authority figure. Managers must entrust themselves to their subordinates before the reverse process occurs. This means telling subordinates things which, if they chose to, they could use to the manager's cost. Usually these are things that would be regarded as indiscreet or slightly inappropriate to tell subordinates within the prevailing organisational culture, though not things which genuinely do need to be kept secret. Managers need good judgement in these matters.
- Giving people high discretion equally amounts to an offer of trust by management. This is usually reciprocated, and can lead to an increasing spiral of trust. Closely limiting subordinates' discretion implies a lack of trust by management. This, too, is usually reciprocated and leads to increasing distrust. However, a manager will rarely get away with pretending to trust subordinates, while really hedging around their discretion or closely monitoring their actions. A manager has to take a risk and to back his or her judgement of the subordinates, reinforced, as it should be, by better judgement of people learnt from applying the lessons of Chapter 5.

Conflict within teams, due to differences between individuals, is inevitable. Work teams consist of individuals who differ from one another, not only in experience, abilities and knowledge, but in perceptions, emotions, beliefs and attitudes. On the one hand, these differences are of vital importance in innovation and problem-solving. On the other hand, these same differences are the source of inevitable disagreements that may cause inefficiency, delay, frustration and highly unsatisfactory compromises. Leaders have a range of strategies available to them for managing team conflicts. These include a divide-and-rule strategy, suppressing differences and working through them.

- Dealing separately with the conflicting individuals or subgroups, or 'divide and rule', discourages communication between the disagreeing parties. It results in a complex star communication network. It also stimulates competition for the leader's favour, leading to rivalry and secrecy. This strategy will not help build a strong team.
- Leaders can, and often do, suppress differences, ignore emotional undertones and demand objectivity and rationality. 'We will stick to the facts in this

Box 13.8

### How to build trust and develop teams by incremental steps

1. Have individual discussions with team members.
2. When you are reasonably sure that most members of the team trust you personally, call a meeting of the whole team to discuss team-building issues. These include what the personal objectives of the team members are, and how team membership fits in with that; what your strengths and weaknesses are as a team (but not those of individuals at this stage); and what the chief tasks of the team are. These must be discussed with a genuine openness. You must be determined not to impose your own preconceptions, but to reach a real agreement, no matter how long it takes. Be prepared for the outcome to be a conception of the team's chief task that resembles neither the formal organisation chart nor the job descriptions.
3. Allow team members considerable freedom in deciding the organisation of work within the team.
4. Later, when the team has been in existence for some time and is showing signs of 'gelling', analyse the current state of the team to attempt to agree on those characteristics that require improvement – and those that are strengths. Use a rating scale, such as the one given in Exercise 8, to be completed by each team member anonymously. Use this analysis as a basis for discussion. If all goes well, each member begins to recognise the impact of their behaviour on others. More often than not, members discover that the reactions of others to their own words and actions are not the same as they thought they were. Thus the feedback provides them with an opportunity to test their perceptions against reality and to modify their future behaviour if they choose to do so. However, if the feedback takes the form of a critical attack that puts members on the defensive, it is highly unlikely that they will either understand or accept it. The guideline is that the feedback should tell the other member: 'This is how your behaviour affected me.' Sincere feedback is one of the foundations on which mutual trust is built.
5. Generalise from the feedback. It is not enough that a particular problem may have been solved. Will the analysis of this single experience help the team to recognise the problem in other forms and deal with it? The probability is that it will not, unless the team has answered the question 'What have we learned from this experience?'
6. Kidder (1981) argued that 'Soul' is the Real Secret of team success – expressed through a symbolic framework including initiation rites, diversity, example rather than command, specialised language, stories that carry history and values that reinforce team identity, humour and play (which reduce tensions and encourage creativity), ritual, and ceremony to renew the spirit. Concrete examples include giving teams names (Hardy Boys, Eagle Group), awards, such as the 'All-nighter' award, and progress charts.
7. Remember that the process cannot be rushed.

*Source*: Kidder, T. (1981) *The Soul of a New Machine*. New York: Little, Brown and Co.

meeting.' They may demand conformity or decide in favour of one alternative after hearing the arguments for each. Suppressing differences leads group members to passive compliance, instead of active support, and to engaging in protective behaviour. Examples include: getting decisions from the leader without bringing them up for group discussion, wrangling over unimportant details or lining up support in advance of a meeting. Suppressing differences is counter-productive for team building.

- Working through differences means setting in motion processes that will lead to greater self-awareness on the part of the contending parties. One method is for the leader deliberately to engineer a 'challenge' of the type described in Box 13.9. By separating out individuals from the warring groups, the destructive dynamics of the inter-group conflict are disrupted. By working jointly and face-to-face on a task, the contenders are more likely to be forced to abandon their unrealistic and unfair stereotypes. The subgroups themselves meet some of the needs otherwise served by the groups in contention, and so weaken the motivation to support and fight for them.

**Box 13.9**

### How to deal with subordinates in conflict by 'challenge'

1. Call both parties to a meeting, allowing at least a day for the purpose.
2. At the meeting, treat the conflicting parties as if they were one large group.
3. Get the participants to clarify the issues and propose alternatives in a plenary session.
4. Deploy 'working subgroups', each composed of roughly equal numbers of each of the conflicting parties to research and advocate each alternative.
5. Get the working subgroups to report back, possibly on another occasion, to a plenary session, carefully chaired by the leader. All the other subgroups criticise and explore the implications of the proposed solution, until one gains acceptance from members of both the warring parties.

Weider-Hatfield and Hatfield[44] researched the effects on subordinates of managers who used different conflict management styles. They characterised the styles as collaborating, forcing and accommodating. The effects on subordinates were measured in terms of four rewards. These were: system rewards, such as pay and promotion; job rewards, such as having responsibility; performance rewards, such as achievement confidence; and interpersonal rewards, such as recognition. Results showed significant positive relationships between a manager's collaborating strategies and subordinates experiencing interpersonal and performance rewards but significant negative relationships between a manager's forcing strategies and those same outcomes. No relationship was found between a manager's accommodating strategies and subordinates' perceived rewards or between any of the strategies and system rewards.

While, as Chapter 10 showed, the culture of the manager makes a significant difference to the choice of conflict management strategy, the gender of the manager may not. Gayle[45] researched how managers of different genders use conflict management strategies. A survey of 302 managers and employees from 11 organisations found little or no difference in management style between the genders. This applied regardless of the gender of the person responding, the other person in the conflict, or the supervisor.

As well as helping resolve conflict and control competition, leaders can reduce the tendency for conflict and competition to arise in the first place, by the way they help to structure the team's goals. It was pointed out, in Chapter 11, how co-operative team goals help overcome competitiveness. Therefore, a leader who wants his or her team to have high productivity, morale and effectiveness, will aim to get them to adopt co-operative goals, rather than competitive or individualistic ones.

## SUMMARY – INFLUENCING SUBORDINATES

The level of trust managers feel in their subordinates affects their choice of influence mode. However, there are substantial benefits, in terms of the unit's performance, the subordinates' development and the leader's work load, when leaders encourage participation. Face-to-face, they do this mainly by their communication style.

To build better teams, leaders need to create mutual trust, through openness in communication and through giving people scope to use their own discretion. To manage differences within teams, leaders should aim to work through them, rather than adopt a 'divide-and-rule' strategy or one of suppressing differences. By setting, or helping to set, co-operative goals for teams, leaders can lend structural support to their efforts to get the team to have high productivity, morale and effectiveness.

## CULTURAL AND GENDER DIFFERENCES IN LEADERSHIP STYLES

### Culture

Writing of Europe, Stohl[46] commented that, 'Cultural diversity exists and it influences the processes of organising in recognisable and systematic ways' (p. 97), that 'Cultural differences among nations do indeed make a difference – often a substantial difference – in the way managers and workers behave in organisational settings' (p. 98) and that 'Limited and limiting cultural interpretations are widely perceived as problematic for the new Euro/international manager' (p. 99).

A large number of studies point to how national/cultural differences affect leadership methods within Europe. Some of these are now discussed.

The GLOBE research project found two broad clusters of culture values – North/West and South/East Europe. Within these clusters, differences in leadership prototypes tend to mirror differences in culture. The authors commented, 'On the basis of these results it is hardly possible to speak of a single typically

European culture or one distinct European management style', although on some dimensions European scores are different from at least some other regions in the world. More specifically, the research found the following:

- both within and outside Europe, values such as charismatic/value-based leadership and team-oriented leadership are universally endorsed;
- within Europe, there is a range of views on the benefits of narcissistic, participative, humane and autonomous leadership;
- in relative terms, middle managers in the countries of South/East Europe show high scores for the value they place on managers being administratively competent, autocratic, conflict inducing, diplomatic, face saving, non-participative, procedural, self-centred and status conscious.

The researchers pointed out that the history and environment of the South/East European cluster of countries is different from those of the North and West of the continent, supporting the findings of culture difference in attitudes to leadership. These differences include language (Anglo-German versus Latin/Slavic), proximity, religion, economic systems (capitalism versus recent socialism), economic development, technological development, industrial versus agricultural economies and climate.[47]

Another study based on interviews with 12 managers from each of five European countries (the Netherlands, Germany, France, England and Denmark) found support for Hofstede's dimensions, despite using a different methodology. For instance, Denmark measured low on Hofstede's uncertainty avoidance and power distance; Danish managers stressed informal actions and suggested that participation cannot be mandated, but rather evolves from the daily interactions between managers and workers. Over 40 per cent of their responses reflected an interpretation of participation in terms of rights of individuals as part of collectivities – i.e. concerns of direct democracy (percentages in other country clusters ranged from 10 per cent to 20 per cent). French managers, in contrast, emphasised formal/structural rather than informal/interpersonal interpretations of participation; France measured high on uncertainty avoidance and power distance. Hofstede himself commented that over two-thirds of French managers view a business organisation as a system of authority. They need to know what is required of them and to whom they are accountable. However, they regard intervention as not merely interference but also a questioning of their professional integrity, which is an important part of their moral profile.[48] French managers have been shown to have a far more difficult time accepting subordination than English managers, even though both cultural groups perceive hierarchy as necessary and appropriate under the same conditions.[49]

The findings of a research project reported in 2000 by Segalla *et al.*[50] include the following:

- Italian, English and French respondents usually use market logic to hire new managers. They often choose to hire foreign, multilingual employees with an elite generalist educational background. German and Spanish managers, on the other hand, hire local managers with more technical training.
- Germans alone promote managers based on objective performance criteria. The French are at the other extreme in basing promotion criteria on seniority or group loyalty.
- Germans base remuneration on objective performance criteria where the French believe it should be based on group, not individual performance.
- The choice of whom to 'lose' when staff reductions are needed, also brought out core differences. The English said that they would base the choice on the ratio of performance to salary cost. More than 70 per cent would dismiss a middle-aged, high-salary manager with average performance. However, less than 10 per cent of Germans would dismiss the same manager. The French appear less concerned with ratio of performance to salary than the Italians or Spanish. French managers would lose average-quality employees, but younger more likely than older ones.
- The Germans combine logics. To give security, they use group logic for hiring and firing. To give incentives, they use market logic for promotion and pay.

Although these findings point to significant cultural differences in leadership approaches, the researchers suggested that managerial actions are as much influenced by the context of the problems as the managers' underlying value systems.

In a comparison of management in six nations – British, French, German, American (USA), Japanese and Arab – Torrington[51] highlighted a number of differences in manager–subordinate relations. These can be understood in terms of cultural dimensions:

- The British are willing to 'listen' to subordinates (being low in uncertainty avoidance) and are 'addicted to old boy networks' (they are high in masculinity).
- The French are high in power distance (preserved through formality) and individualism (expressed through 'intellectualism').
- Americans are high on individualism and achievement, leading them to embrace a 'tough', results-oriented approach to manager–subordinate relations.
- Japanese, though high on achievement, are strongly collectivist, which produces the 'nurturing father' type of manager.
- Germans are high on uncertainty avoidance, shown in adherence to routines and procedures, and in close control of subordinates, who are seen as apprentices.
- Arab managers are intermediate on all dimensions except power distance, where they are high. The distance between manager and subordinate is maintained through the high value placed on loyalty and the avoidance of interpersonal conflict.

Looking beyond Europe, Evans *et al.*[52] concluded the following from their research:

- Manager–subordinate relationships are generally less flexible in an Asian enterprise. Asian managers are more likely to insist on the 'how' of work than be results oriented.
- Whereas, in the West, workers sell their time to the organisation and have no obligation outside that time, for Asian workers the relationship is more general and long term. There is less pressure for results within a limited time frame.
- The paternalistic values of Asian culture, which are respect and obedience towards one's parent, extend to obeying one's boss. Managers act as father [sic] figures. Japanese management is often described as consultative paternalism.
- Luck is often used in Asian explanations of business success/failure.
- Top managers in Asia spend most time building social relationships and on ceremonial engagements. Thus more operational decisions are left to middle management.
- Management in the West is more overtly aggressive than in Asian companies.

## Gender

A previous section noted that there is no evidence of a gender difference in leadership abilities, despite prejudice to the contrary. There is, though, evidence for a difference in style.

1. A review of published research concluded:

> When social behavior is regulated by other, less diffuse social roles, as it is in organisational settings, behavior should primarily reflect the influence of these other roles and therefore lose much of its gender-stereotypical character. . . . Nevertheless, women's leadership styles were more democratic than men's even in organisational settings. This sex difference may reflect underlying differences in female and male personality or skills (e.g. women's superior social skills) or subtle differences in the status of women and men who occupy the same organisational role.[53]

2. Another review of 370 comparison studies of men's and women's leadership styles included 289 in natural organisational settings, 56 in assessment situations and 25 in laboratory studies. Some were self-reports, some ratings by managers, supervisors, subordinates, peers or independent judges; the average age was late thirties and their positions ranged from first-line supervision to top management. The review concluded as follows:

- 'The strongest evidence . . . for a sex difference in leadership style occurred on the tendency for women to adopt a more democratic or participative style and for men to adopt a more autocratic or directive style . . . 92 per cent of the available comparisons went in the direction of more democratic behaviour from women than men.' This difference, which occurred in all three situations, was attributed to womens' greater interpersonal skills and complexity.

- In assessment and laboratory settings, male managers were more task- and less interpersonally-oriented than female, but in natural organisation settings these differences disappeared.[54]

3. A study that focused on time off for family concerns, found gender differences in how assertively managers exert influence over their subordinates:

- Two categories of female managers (female managers of males and females) were among the three most assertive groups (male managers of females being less assertive).
- Female managers used more assertive tactics when their employees were male than when they were female. This could be to compensate for a perceived power differential based on biological sex or because the managers anticipated difficulties in gaining their position and so adopted unilateral strategies to get their way without their partner's co-operation.
- Females seemed less likely to appeal upwards than males, probably because of a lack of self-confidence in their leadership ability.[55]

4. By 1990, Ferrario[56] found UK women managers adopting a combination of people- and task-oriented styles of management. He compared the leadership styles of 104 female and 95 male managers and found that a higher proportion of women, rather than assuming more people-oriented styles, tended to be both task- and people-oriented. These are generally considered to be the appropriate managerial styles for team leadership. More of the men were found to have laissez-faire leadership styles.

5. Successful women team leaders in public relations (PR) have been found to emphasise two-way communication and the use of compromise in dealing with conflict resolution. Assertiveness, empathy for staff and logical arguments are typical of women PR leaders.[57]

6. Rosener asserted, but without any clear evidence, that women's style of leadership is transformational, men's transactional.[58]

## SUMMARY – CULTURAL AND GENDER DIFFERENCES IN LEADERSHIP STYLES

There is substantial evidence of differences in management styles among European countries and between Europe and other regions such as Asia. The differences seem to correspond to cultural differences such as those identified by Hofstede. However, some researchers, while acknowledging national differences, suggest that managerial actions are as much influenced by the context of the problems as the managers' underlying value systems.

Differences in participativeness are found between male and female managers, with women showing a greater tendency to be democratic; beyond this, the evidence is contradictory.

## FACE-TO-FACE LEADERSHIP IN DIVERSE AND INTERNATIONAL ORGANISATIONS

There is a difference between equal opportunity initiatives, which 'relate to groups of people who are under-represented in the workforce', and managing diversity, which 'is a means to foster organisational change by valuing the individual'. Diversity is connected to positioning the organisation so that it is able to 'take commercial advantage' of social and demographic changes. Thomas R. Roosevelt Jr[59] illustrated, in a case study of Avon, the cosmetics company, how having a workforce representative of all potential customers is a key to many companies' success as global competition continues to increase. Women and members of minorities represent the customer base whose expendable income will be most likely to increase, while there are clear relations between diversity, creativity and competitive advantage. However, there are also downsides to diversity management. It can allow some line managers to avoid the realities of discrimination, prejudice and unfair treatment.[60]

**Box 13.10**

**How to take practical steps to value diversity**

1. Enhance awareness.
2. Get people to realise that we should not want individuals to be assimilated into a corporate culture at the expense of their own identity and uniqueness.
3. Launch a programme of activities designed to foster an understanding of how men and women, or people in different ethnic groups, differ in values, attitudes, behavioural styles, ways of thinking and cultural background.
4. Change the core culture. 'Valuing diversity' requires very fundamental changes in individual values, social relationships and management processes. It is likely to require significant long-term approaches, as well as changes to incentive systems if different behaviour is to persist beyond short-term 'drives'.

*Source*: Roosevelt, T. R. Jr (1991) *Beyond Peace and Gender: Unleashing the Power of Your Total Work Force By Managing Diversity*. New York: AMACOM.

Like leadership in diverse organisations, international leadership demands a rethink of what may be entrenched ideas and practices.

Western management theories and practices may not work well in other cultures. Leaders should consider the nature of the host culture and its relationship to management style. For example:

- Performance appraisal systems assume that employees' performance will be improved if they receive direct feedback about what their superior thinks of them. However, while this may well be the case in individualistic cultures, in some Southern European countries which are more collectivist, direct feedback can destroy the interpersonal relationship between manager and subordinate. In such cultures, feedback should rather be given indirectly. Performance appraisal systems also generally fail to take into account differences in the responses of women and men.[61] Women's self-evaluations are more likely to mirror the feedback they receive than are men's. (See Box 10.11.)
- Under Management by Objectives (MBO), subordinates have to negotiate about their objectives with their superiors. The system therefore assumes a cultural environment in which issues can be settled by negotiation rather than rules; this means a medium to low power distance and a not too high uncertainty avoidance. In the German environment, it had to be adapted to the more structured culture of a stronger uncertainty avoidance – and so had to be made much more formal than the US model.
- Strategic management assumes an environment of weak uncertainty avoidance, in which deviant strategic ideas are encouraged. Although it is taught in countries with stronger uncertainty avoidance cultures, such as Germany or France, its recommendations are rarely followed there, because in these cultures it is seen as the top managers' role to remain involved in daily operations.
- Programmes for the humanisation of work require adaptation for the culture. In the United States, the prevailing form is 'job enrichment', which means giving individual tasks more intrinsic content. In Sweden, a more feminine, less individualistic country, the development of semi-autonomous work groups in which members exchange tasks and help each other has been more successful.[62]
- When change management practices are not adapted for cultural differences, change outcomes differ from what was intended. Surviving rapid change depends on increased flexibility and commitment of the workforce, because all the following must be overcome: resistance to change, inability to cope with the effects of change and lack of skills to manage change. Increased flexibility and commitment of the workforce are correlated with successful diversity management.[63]
- Performance-related pay can run up against the barriers that, in more collectivist cultures than the Anglo-Saxon, employees may not accept that individual members of the group should excel in a way that reveals the shortcomings of others. Their definition of an 'outstanding individual' is one who benefits those closest to him or her.
- Customers in more collectivist cultures also take offence at the selling techniques of some salespeople: they prefer to build up relationships carefully and maintain them.[64]

In effect, these problems with the cross-cultural transfer of Western, especially US, management techniques originate in the cultural preferences of subordinates. Some of these include the following:

- In countries such as Austria, Israel, Denmark and New Zealand, where employees are not seen as afraid, and bosses are not often autocratic or paternalistic, employees express a preference for a consultative style of decision-making. They like a boss who 'usually consults with his/her subordinates before reaching a decision'. In countries on the opposite end of the power distance scale, such as Malaysia, Guatemala and Panama, employees are less likely to prefer a consultative boss. Instead, many among them express a preference for a boss who decides autocratically or paternalistically. However, some switch to the other extreme, preferring a boss who governs by majority vote.[65]
- People with strongly individualistic values will expect their bosses or managers to be aware of them as individuals, take their personal views into account in decision-making and reward them according to their performance. People with collectivistic values may have similar expectations in regard to the group of which they are a member, but for themselves, as individuals, they will expect to be treated more like a child is by its parent. For example, they will not expect to be fired for poor performance; as Hofstede put it, you do not sack your child.
- People with more feminine work values, including women, semi-skilled and unskilled workers in many countries as well as most inhabitants of countries such as Sweden, Norway and the Netherlands, expect their leaders to be resourceful, identify with the interests of the group they lead and represent it effectively in the wider organisation or world. However, they do not judge their leader according to the level of aggressiveness or even decisiveness they display. Like people with low power distance values, they will expect a participative management style. Masculine values are the ones that lead followers to support autocratic, highly assertive and decisive leaders.

## SUMMARY – FACE-TO-FACE LEADERSHIP IN DIVERSE AND INTERNATIONAL ORGANISATIONS

Imposing management practices rooted in Western cultures can have negative effects in diverse and international organisations. An understanding of the different expectations of subordinates from different cultures is needed, to allow management practices and styles to be adapted. Appreciating the special contributions of women and members of minorities, and providing support so that those special contributions can be realised, are first steps to valuing diversity. Ultimately, however, embedding diversity may require a change in the core culture of the organisation.

## WORK APPLICATIONS FOR FACE-TO-FACE LEADERSHIP

Interactive leadership skills are especially needed when chairing meetings, particularly large ones, or delegating.

### Chairing meetings

This discussion of chairing skills assumes a large meeting of more than ten persons and a degree of formality in the proceedings. Chairpersons have important duties, such as drawing up an agenda and ensuring that it is covered, making clear the terms of reference, knowing and communicating to the meeting the rules and procedures governing its deliberations, ensuring that minutes are taken and circulated and so on. In keeping with the rest of this book, these will not receive much attention here, concentrating instead on the behavioural skills of chairing meetings.

Interpersonal skills begin with awareness. For a chairperson, this means 'being aware of the main processes of behaviour in groups and able to prevent these processes interfering with the effective working of the committee'.[66] More than this, chairpersons should be able to use their understanding of group and individual behaviour to advance the meeting in its task. Chairing skills can be analysed under five headings: the basics, sources and uses of the chairperson's own power, chairpersons' roles, handling individuals in meetings and controlling group processes in meetings.

#### *Basic chairing skills*

Basic chairing skills include being well prepared, anticipating which agenda items will cause problems, and allocating time and the agenda order accordingly. Ways of introducing agenda items should be thought through beforehand, to make sure that the issues will be described carefully before they are evaluated. As far as possible, the meeting should discuss first what processes need to be gone through to reach a decision, or decision criteria. The time when different parties start advocating their preferred solutions should be delayed, because this can polarise the meeting into opposed camps. It is essential for the chairperson to know, or have a reliable aide who knows, any rules and regulations governing issues to be decided, and any precedents that will advance the discussion. Otherwise a great deal of time can be wasted discussing possibilities that in the end turn out not to be feasible. More than this, precedents, and even regulations, often embody a surprising amount of wisdom and save each new meeting the trouble and waste of time of re-inventing the wheel.

Chairpersons must know how to handle issues on which the meeting is getting seriously 'bogged down'. They must be able to recognise which of these can be settled to majority satisfaction by a 'guillotining' procedure, such as a vote, which should be deferred to the next meeting to give members time to think about them and which should be referred to a subcommittee or working group. Getting this right is largely a matter of experience, but carefully analysing events and performances can increase the value of even a little experience. Chairpersons must be skilled in calling speakers, silencing ramblers, interrupters, and people conducting 'private' side conversations, summarising, testing for consensus, and in performing all these functions in such a way that the meeting will seem to most participants to be fair and to be making progress.

**Box 13.11**

### How to use 'lubricating' expressions to progress the business of the meeting

- 'Does the meeting see any objection to the proposal?' This is a strong 'steer', because it implies that if there are no objections there must be assent to the proposal. 'Steers' have their uses but should not be over-used if you want to seem fair.
- 'In the absence of a sparkling discussion, I will pick out an item that concerns me.' This is used to raise an issue when there are initially no comments on an agenda item. The chairperson's request for discussion of an issue is given more force by the reminder to the meeting that probably others were not well prepared – thus the chair gains power from the fact that s/he was. Ironic humour is used to soften the 'reprimand'.
- 'A year ago, this committee agreed . . .'. Referring to past decisions and drawing out the implications of past precedents is a good way for chairpersons to steer debate without appearing over-directive. Usually the collective memory of past decisions is very poor and a reading of old minutes will yield gems for use in this way. This technique is open, naturally, to members other than chairpersons.
- 'We must move on to the next item.' 'I will take two more points on this issue.' 'We must reach a decision on this one now; will someone propose a motion?' Simply moving the meeting forward in a direct way is often necessary. Once you have committed yourself to progressing, you must insist, despite some people's desperate attempts to prolong the debate, or you will appear weak.
- 'Do you wish to push your argument to a proposal?' Challenging a member to put their proposal to a vote can show them that no matter how strongly they feel, they are not carrying their colleagues with them. The chairperson is usually in a better position to observe the reactions of others than the speaker is. This is one way of deploying this advantage. On other occasions the chairperson may wish to avoid a vote, which can be destructive when it reveals the lack of agreement within a meeting. By noticing the support round the table for the speaker and saying 'You're getting some nods around the table – we'll note that' or 'You're not getting much support for this one', the vote can be avoided.
- 'I would like to guide the meeting . . .'. The chairperson often has relevant information that other members lack. Bringing it forward in this way is legitimate and useful. It is often more acceptable to acknowledge what you are doing openly than to attempt to exert influence covertly. This can lead to loss of trust as others come to think that is what you are always doing, even when you are not.

### Power

The chairperson has several sources of power. These include general acceptance (legitimacy) of their role of controlling discussion and helping the meeting make decisions; authority, based on position, which should be used to achieve the meeting's purposes, not to get their own way; and being better placed to use body language than anyone else at the meeting. There is no reason for chairpersons to feel inhibited about using their power. Research has shown that both the satisfaction participants get from meetings, and the eventual output of the meeting, are positively related to how firmly the chairperson controls the meeting. Dissatisfaction and poor performance, however, result from abuse of chairpersons' power. Abuses include: the chairperson talking too much, inhibiting free discussion by keeping the meeting going too fast, failing to provide enough time for the meeting to develop its own solutions or over-steering by too much use of leading questions and offering suggestions.[67]

### Roles

A good chairperson appropriately combines the roles of a facilitator and a leader, and places emphasis according to the needs of the group and the meeting. The differences between the two roles are as follows: whereas leaders take responsibility for the work of the group, take initiatives and, where necessary, take control and make decisions, facilitators act as the group's neutral servant and refrain from evaluating or contributing ideas. There are, however, many similarities between the functions of leaders and facilitators. For instance, both should focus group energy on common tasks and protect individuals and their ideas from attack. Table 13.2 sets out the similarities and differences between the two roles. Chairpersons must always take responsibility for activities which both

**Table 13.2 Leading and facilitating**

| *Facilitators and leaders both* | *Facilitators do and leaders do not* | *Leaders do and Facilitators do not* |
|---|---|---|
| Focus group energy on common tasks | Act as neutral servants of the group | Take responsibility for the work of the group |
| Suggest other methods and procedures | Refrain from evaluating or contributing ideas | Take initiatives |
| Protect individuals and their ideas from attack | | Where necessary, take charge |
| Encourage participation | | |
| Help the group find the best solution | | |
| Co-ordinate pre- and post-meeting logistics | | |

leaders and facilitators perform. However, whether they do or do not take initiatives, evaluate contributions and make decisions, depends on the meeting they are chairing, and especially on the maturity of the members of the group at handling the type of task with which the meeting is dealing.

### *Handling individuals*

An individual at a meeting is the same person as outside the meeting but the situation does, undoubtedly, lead to some, perhaps most, people behaving somewhat differently from 'normal'. The tendency to adopt a task-, maintenance- or self-oriented stance has already been discussed. The chairperson, who should, of course, be practising a mix of task and maintenance behaviours, will find that being aware of who is taking which role helps to decide whom to call as the next speaker, to speed progress with the meeting's tasks, or to pour oil on troubled waters, according to the need at that juncture. Other aspects which need to be thought about are individuals' rights in meetings, the emotions which may be fuelling individuals' self-oriented behaviours and the tendency to compete rather than collaborate.

**Box 13.12**

**Individuals' rights in meetings**

Individuals are entitled

- to be kept informed of what is going on – especially not to be misled into basing his or her contributions on premises that are known to be false;
- to have their perspectives receive attention (but not repeatedly, contrary to the wishes of the others present);
- not to be subjected to uncontrolled attacks from others;
- not to waste their time;
- not to be affected by prejudice or discrimination. Women, for instance, often feel under differential pressures in meetings – to speak up, even when they have nothing to say, or to keep strictly to the point, even though men feel free to meander. They can often be ignored, even to the point where the chairperson will introduce the meeting by saying, 'Good morning, gentlemen.' Men interrupt women more than they do other men and more than women interrupt anyone. It can be a continual struggle for women to have their say. The women who cope best with this make their presence felt early in the meeting and have armed themselves against the implicit pressure coming from male colleagues that being vocal is unfeminine. Other women need to be protected by the chairperson.

In large meetings a great deal of behaviour is affected by emotions. Because their direct expression is 'illegitimate' there, these can gain in force as the meeting continues. This often results in people adopting polarised and intransigent attitudes. In seasoned performers, these emotions will usually be disguised by a highly 'rationalistic' verbal content and a poker-player's manner: steady voice and impassive features. It is, however, important for the chairperson to identify the primary emotion affecting the behaviour. S/hewill have to try to reduce the frustration of those people at the meeting who feel that others are suppressing or failing to understand their position. Fortunately, such meetings often last long enough to let the primary emotions of the main participants become obvious. Patterns of responses quickly emerge which can be easily analysed, with a little practice, by listening for the emotional underlay as well as the argument.

- Defensiveness is one emotion that is common in meetings. People can feel under attack by what is being said, or by the mere fact that discussion on a particular subject is taking place. They may read criticism of their past conduct into the situation – criticism that they almost certainly see as unfair. They are frustrated by the lack of opportunity to explain or defend themselves openly. To handle defensiveness, a skilled chairperson can bring the issue into the open, especially if the emotion is, as often, based on a false perception of other people's attitudes: 'I think John and Peter may feel that raising this issue in this way amounts to an attack on their work. I certainly don't see it as a criticism, but I think we should discuss it and give them the opportunity to explain how the problem arose.' However, when clearing the air in this way would be inadvisable, perhaps because some participants *are* very critical of John and Peter, eye contact, attentive listening to and stroking the defensive persons can give some reassurance.
- A feeling of insecurity is another common emotion in meetings. Some people feel that their contribution is not worth making, that they will not be listened to and that they are, in sum, thoroughly marginal as far as others in the meeting are concerned. This can often be a particular problem in organisations that purport to be democratic, so that 'staff assemblies' or similar gatherings are called, but where status hierarchies in fact prevail, so that low-status members are inhibited from speaking. Not only will these persons' contributions, which may be valuable, not be made, but these individuals are likely to leave the meeting with a diminished sense of self-worth and a resentment of the way they have been treated. In handling insecurity, the chairperson should promote a supportive climate. S/he should also call for comment from those who are feeling insecure, and if they protest that they have nothing to say, insist gently but firmly that s/he wants to hear their views. Those at the meeting who may be inclined to ride roughshod over low-status participants, or exploit and exacerbate their sense of weakness, should be kept under control.
- A great deal of what is said in meetings serves a self-expressive rather than a functional purpose. Some people really do seem to love the sound of their own voice, or think themselves so clever that anything they say will be worth others listening to. They have very little regard for how much of what they say is really contributing to the purpose of the meeting. Often these behaviours

do emanate from people who are genuinely quite clever, but their behaviour in meetings is not. To deal with these people, the chairperson must be prepared to silence them as often as it takes for them to get the message that s/he is allocating the air time and is not a member of their fan club. The temptation to attack them should be resisted. If they are clever, their continued contributions are wanted but under, not out of, control.

- Sources of aggressive behaviour have been described in Chapter 6. In meetings, aggressive behaviour is like pride and self-love, and unlike defensiveness and insecurity, in that the chairperson's concern is to contain and control the behaviour rather than placate the emotion that caused it. Behaviour in meetings can be inappropriately competitive. The real solutions are long term and call for leadership of a high order. Chairpersons handling large meetings should treat inappropriate competitiveness in the same way as inappropriate self-love or aggressiveness: not indulge it, but move on.

### *Controlling group processes*

Controlling group processes in meetings involves dealing with conformity pressures, risky shifts, breaches of norms and conflict. Conformity pressures can lead to the meeting accepting the first solution offered. The chairperson can prevent this by asking the meeting to consider a second opinion. Dreaming up a reasonable alternative may call for some quick thinking, but even a poor alternative is better than none – it may provoke thought. Committees are in danger of adopting over-risky or over-cautious solutions to problems because of the 'risky-shift' phenomenon. An alert chairperson will notice if this is happening and point out the dangers, or exceptionally even veto the decision. Flagrant or persistent breach of norms by 'deviants' will upset many and reduce the productivity of the time spent in the meeting. While not all non-conformity should be suppressed, beyond a certain point a chairperson must be prepared to slap down those who breach norms. Conflict in large meetings must be controlled, even minimised. At the very least the meeting must be kept focused on issues, not personalities.

## Delegation interviewing

In Anglo-Saxon cultures, delegating is considered a central function of management. It allows managers to carry out the range of work for which they have responsibility, concentrate on key aspects of their job, develop subordinates, widen their experience and train successors. A strict separation of manager and subordinate roles sends the message to workers that they are only responsible for what they are specifically told to do. Managers who neglect to, or cannot, delegate are failing to develop the human resources for which they have responsibility. They also are often forced into a 'firefighting', crisis-ridden style of management, because work overload means that problems become critical before they are dealt with. Sometimes an organisation has a policy or approach that places obstacles in the way of managers who want to delegate. For instance, managers are expected to know the details of what is going on in their section, and even small mistakes are held against them. In this kind of case, managers need to sort out with their bosses some arrangement that will allow them to delegate, which is an important part of their job. More often, however, the obstacles are in the manager's own mind. They include fear of unpopularity resulting from handing out tough assignments, distrust of subordinates' ability to do the job to the manager's perfectionist standards or, conversely, their fear that subordinates will be seen to be able to do the job better than the manager him- or herself.

**Box 13.13**

**European variations in delegatees' expectations**

In France, delegatees expect detailed lists of tasks and close supervision of their performance; in Germany, clear, written instructions, but not close supervision. In Italy people will be surprised to have responsibilities delegated unless a close, trusting relationship is in place. Delegation is not applied systematically. In the United Kingdom, instructions are generally expressed as polite requests.

Delegation is primarily about entrusting authority to others. This means that they can act and initiate independently; and that they assume responsibility for certain tasks. If something goes wrong, the manager remains responsible. The trick is to delegate in such a way that things get done but do not go (badly) wrong. With delegation, subordinates have the authority to react to situations without referring back to their manager.

As Box 13.14 shows, delegating demands careful planning, to decide what work is to be done, what can and should be delegated and to identify and match abilities, development needs and potential of subordinates with the delegatable tasks. Not all tasks are suitable for delegation. For instance, if a finely balanced decision is needed, that would have serious consequences for the entire operation if the wrong choice were made, a manager would be evading his or her responsibilities to delegate it. Similarly, time pressure can make delegation an inappropriate solution. Equally, the type of work group made up from the manager's subordinates needs to be taken into account. If the entire team is young and inexperienced, no matter how enthusiastic, it may not be wise to delegate responsibilities that could well be delegated if a more experienced subordinate were available. Current work loads, performance, preferences for type of work and direction of development, also need to be considered during the preparation stage.

**Box 13.14**

### How to enable someone else to do work for you

- Ensure that they know what you want, including your priorities and time constraints, have the authority to achieve it and know how to do it. Do not attempt to delegate authority you do not have yourself!
- Do not create confusion and resentment by appearing to be delegating when you are really not, e.g. if you are getting a subordinate's views on a decision that you will make yourself, make that clear.
- Ensure that the subordinate feels free to tell you if your assignment is unrealistic.
- Establish a system to ensure a flow of information. Include regular exchanges between your staff so that each is aware of what the others are doing. Also include briefings on the information that you have received in your role as manager.
- Train your staff to apply the same criteria as you would yourself, by example and full explanations.
- Avoid asking for progress reports without notice. Instead, agree beforehand how often and when you actually need information; decide and agree the reporting schedule at the onset in writing.
- Once you have delegated, avoid making decisions that subordinates can make. Check the decisions, tell the subordinates when they are wrong and explain very carefully why. If the subordinates are nearly right – congratulate them and suggest possible modifications, but leave them to decide.
- Avoid subordinates getting frustrated by finding that their decisions are not implemented.
- Give praise when subordinates spot and deal with their own errors.

The delegation interview with the subordinate is 'the heart of the delegation process. It determines, more than anything else, the outcome of a delegated function. The face-to-face discussion of and assignment of work are central to the process.'[68] There are three aspects to the delegation interview:

1. To communicate clearly what the task or project is and involves, what outcomes are looked for, what standards are expected, what resources are available, and what benefits to the subordinate are likely to flow from successfully undertaking this additional or new responsibility. It is also to receive from the subordinate what their reactions to the proposal are and how they see themselves developing within this role.
2. To agree with the subordinate that they have accepted the work. Some writers refer to this as contracting, to emphasise the type of commitment that is needed. It is also to agree on the method of work, its nature, the means and timing of reporting, standards of performance and the degree of delegated authority, accountability and responsibility.
3. To discuss the subordinate's hopes and fears, establishing communication channels through openness, showing respect, reinforcing positive behaviour and high performance and establishing trust.

It is bad practice to conduct the delegation interview and then assume that what was agreed will be implemented without further effort from the manager. Follow-through is necessary, in case the subordinate has misunderstood any part of the new role s/he is expected to play. The manager needs to ensure that the subordinate has the resources and authority required for the job. This means, for instance, that others are informed of the delegated responsibility s/he has undertaken, and are alerted to the need to supply information, equipment, staff or other necessaries. The manager needs to be readily available to the subordinate, especially in the early days after the delegation comes into effect, to supply needed information, help resolve problems, provide support for initiatives, and to encourage and show interest in the subordinate's progress. Gradually, the delegatee should be weaned towards greater independence. Like coaching, delegation is a process that moves a learner from dependence to relative independence. Results must be assessed. Mistakes should not be made too much of unless they persist. Initially they should be treated as inevitable and simply corrected. The precise plan of the delegation may need to be modified with experience. The subordinate may need to take on more to make sense of the role, or less to have a tolerable workload, or some other modification may be needed. Good performance should, as always, be acknowledged.

## SUMMARY – WORK APPLICATIONS FOR FACE-TO-FACE LEADERSHIP

Good chairing involves command of a range of basic chairing skills, such as calling speakers and ensuring an appropriate pace of movement through the agenda. Skilled chairpersons use their power, derived from legitimacy, authority or body language, to progress the purpose of the meeting. They do not abuse their power to get their own way. Ideally, also, chairpersons act to guarantee individuals' rights, defuse emotions that may be producing behaviour counter-productive to the work of the meeting, encourage co-operative and control competitive behaviour. Chairpersons can act either as facilitators or as leaders, according to the situation. Their responsibilities include understanding and controlling group processes.

At the heart of successful delegation lies interaction between managers and their subordinates. In the delegation interview three tasks must be accomplished: exchange of information, agreement on the scope and nature of the delegation, and establishment of an effective working relationship.

## CHAPTER OVERVIEW

A successful approach to leadership can be underpinned by a knowledge of leadership traits and styles and an understanding of how to vary approaches according to the work motivations and task maturity of subordinates. Leaders who aim to transform organisations, by getting their followers to pursue a strategic vision, need to encourage participation and share power and information. They should also seek criticism. Enacting leadership in face-to-face meetings involves matching subordinates' expectations of their leaders and communicating, self-presenting and framing their leadership effectively. There are cultural and gender differences in leadership which affect the expectations of subordinates. Influencing subordinates, acting as team builders and improving their performance require taking responsibility for setting goals that reward co-operative efforts and avoiding goals that reward competitiveness. Leaders also initiate, structure and control discussions, inform and support group members, evaluate outcomes and deal with intra-team competitiveness and conflict. In diverse and international organisations, leaders need to create a climate in which the contributions of women and members of minorities can be fully realised and rewarded.

Chairpersons need a range of basic chairing skills, plus an ability to use the power of the chair to achieve the meeting's goals. They also need to sustain individuals' rights and handle their emotions and to regulate group processes in meetings. Successful delegating depends on providing effective leadership face-to-face, in order to clarify responsibilities and build working relationships.

## EXERCISES

1. In your group projects for other subjects, pay attention to how tasks are delegated.

2. Think of the best and worst managers you have known. Why were they the best and worst respectively?

3. Think of the best and worst team you have been in. Why were they the best and worst respectively?

4. Think of the most charismatic leader you have known. What made him or her charismatic?

5. Pinpoint leadership aspects and issues described in the text of this chapter which might be illustrated by the following examples:

   (a) Three co-equal managers are in a meeting with a group of all their secretaries. The managers have agreed beforehand to re-allocate both tasks and offices among the secretaries. The meeting has been called to tell the secretaries about the proposed changes. All the managers are aware that their proposals may be ill-received. There is an awkward pause, then one starts to explain the position and the proposals.

(b) A college has experienced a period when there have been few new initiatives taken, and those few have been minor and seemed to lead in different directions. The college has obtained no new endowments, established no new centres of excellence, attracted no new academics of high reputation. The trouble, say the staff, lies with the Directorate: 'We've got no leadership' is the way they express it. Do you agree?

(c) A chaired meeting began at 2 p.m. and at 5 p.m. was still on the third of seven agenda items. Impatience and tension among some of those present was becoming palpable; others were enjoying the opportunity to ride their hobby horses. One of the impatient ones turned to her neighbour and whispered: 'He's a useless chairperson; he's got no idea of how to lead a meeting.'

(d) A group of colleagues is discussing a knotty problem. There are six in the group, but one person is mainly silent, listening. After an hour, the discussion gets 'bogged down', and one person says, 'We don't seem to be getting very far, do we?' Then, addressing the silent member, 'Come on, Steven, you haven't said much, but you're the only one who knows what top management is up to. Give us a lead, can't you?'

6. Role play deciding the chairperson and secretary of a meeting.

7. This exercise concerns a meeting between the general manager of a small organisation (20 staff), which can be in any sector, and a subordinate to whom the responsibilities of office manager are being delegated. These are in addition to his or her current responsibilities (which could be marketing or IT). The new responsibilities are: the internal and external mail; reception and telephones; secretarial/typing/filing; the recruitment, induction, supervision and evaluation of the four full-time and three part-time staff engaged in this work.

   *As a private study or group discussion exercise,* plan the delegator's (the general manager's) approach to the delegation interview. What questions or objections should s/he anticipate from the delegatee? *As a role play,* enact the delegation interview.

8. Complete the team effectiveness rating scale given in Table 13.3.

9. For practising chairing skills, a six-role meeting is required. The agendas can include the following items:

   (a) A sub-committee has recommended that the organisation (which might be a national NGO similar to the National Trust) adopt a strictly representational policy on membership of the Committee – members of all significant 'minorities' are to be represented in strict accordance with their proportionate membership of the organisation. This will require

**Table 13.3 Rating scale for team effectiveness**

The following questions ask about the performance of a team. Choose a position on a scale by circling the number which is closest to your feelings.

|  | | | | | | | |
|---|---|---|---|---|---|---|---|
| 1. How well does the team define its tasks? | min. | 1 | 2 | 3 | 4 | 5 | max. |
| 2. How well are roles allocated within the team? | min. | 1 | 2 | 3 | 4 | 5 | max. |
| 3. How well are information and ideas communicated within the team? | min. | 1 | 2 | 3 | 4 | 5 | max. |
| 4. How often do decisions reflect a consensus of all members' views? | min. | 1 | 2 | 3 | 4 | 5 | max. |
| 5. How well are differences between members accommodated? | min. | 1 | 2 | 3 | 4 | 5 | max. |
| 6. How much openness is there within the team? | min. | 1 | 2 | 3 | 4 | 5 | max. |
| 7. How much trust is there within the team? | min. | 1 | 2 | 3 | 4 | 5 | max. |

either a big expansion of the committee or a major shift in its composition with most existing members losing their 'seat' – probably both.

(b) In an international oil company, a proposal to set a target of having an increase in the number of senior managers who are female from 4 to 20 per cent by 2002.

*Role A* is the chairperson; *Roles B to F* (or more) the other participants.

10. You are the owner and manager of a restaurant with ten staff – two chefs, six waiters, two cleaners and bottle washers. You have a problem – the restaurant needs redecorating, which will take two weeks. You would like to close the restaurant and get all the staff to take their holidays at that time. This is the opposite of the usual arrangement, whereby a holiday rota is drawn up and staff are required to take their holidays at different times, to allow the restaurant to remain open.

    *As a private study or group discussion exercise*, consider how you will handle the problem of getting your staff to agree to this change.

    *As a role play*, enact the meeting between the owner and the ten staff.

11. Receive feedback on your 'leadership in interaction' performance from observers or other interactors, who may use the rating scale given in Table 13.4 to guide their feedback.

## FURTHER READING

Bodd, D. and D. Buchanan (1992) *Take the Lead: Interpersonal skills for Project Managers*. Hemel Hempstead: Prentice Hall.

Brotherton, C. (1999) *Social Psychology and Management: Issues for a Changing Society*. Buckingham: Open University Press.

Davidson, M. J. and R. J. Burke, (2000) *Women in Management*. London: Sage.

**Table 13.4 Leadership in interaction feedback rating scale**

1. To what extent did the leader appear competent at keeping the group operating smoothly?

   Extremely competent x—x—x—x—x—x Not at all competent

2. To what extent did the leader appear to keep the group steering towards its goals?

   Extremely competent x—x—x—x—x—x Not at all competent

3. To what extent did the leader come across as identifying with the interests of the group?

   Extremely high identification x—x—x—x—x—x Extremely low identification

4. To what extent did the leader initiate (problem-solving) ideas?

   To a large extent x—x—x—x—x—x Not at all

5. How far did the leader set targets for group activity?

   To a large extent x—x—x—x—x—x Not at all

6. How well did the leader brief the group on the meeting – its background and purpose?

   Extremely well x—x—x—x—x—x Not at all well

7. Did the leader:

| | Yes | No |
|---|---|---|
| Express acceptance of others' contributions? | | |
| Encourage others? | | |
| Discipline others when necessary? | | |
| Relieve tension with humour? | | |
| Get others to explore disagreements? | | |
| Summarise progress? | | |
| Evaluate the feasibility of ideas that were proposed? | | |
| Test the consequences of proposed solutions? | | |

Kotter, J. P. (1998) *What Leaders Really Do*. Cambridge, Mass.: Harvard Business School Press.
McMahon, T. (1990) *Big Meeting, Big Results*. Lincolnwood, Ill.: NTC Business Books.
Northouse, P. T. (2000) *Leadership: Theory and Practice*, 2nd edn. London: Sage.
Schwartz, A. E. (1995) *Delegating Authority*. London: Cassell.

## REFERENCES

1. Javidan, M. (1997) *Global Leadership and Organizational Behavior Effectiveness Project*. Calgary: University of Calgary.
2. Bartlett, C. A. and S. Ghoshal (1989) *Managing Across Borders, The Transnation Solution*. Boston, Mass.: Harvard Business School Press.
3. Naisbitt, J. and P. Aburdene (1985) *Re-inventing The Corporation*. New York: Warner Books.
4. Chalofsky, N. E. and C. Reinhart (1988) *Effective Human Resource Development*. San Francisco: Jossey–Bass.
5. Goffee, R. and G. Jones (2001) 'Why should anyone be led by you?', *London Business School Alumni News*, June–August.
6. Stogdill, R. (1974) *Handbook of Leadership*. New York: Free Press.
7. Ibid.

8. Goleman, D. (2000) 'Leadership that gets results,' *Harvard Business Review*, March/April, pp. 78–90.
9. Fiedler, F. (1967) 'Style or circumstance: The leadership dilemma', *Psychology Today*, vol. 2, no. 10, pp. 38–46.
10. Hersey, P. and K. Blanchard (1977) *Management of Organisational Behaviour: Utilising Human Resources*, 3rd edn. Englewood-Cliffs, New Jersey: Prentice-Hall.
11. Trompenaars, F. (1993) *Riding the Waves of Culture: Understanding Cultural Diversity in Business*. London: Nicholas Brealey.
12. Zorn, T. E. and G. B. Leichty (1991) 'Leadership and identity: A reinterpretation of situational leadership theory', *Southern Communication Journal*, vol. 57, no. 1, pp. 11–24.
13. Peters, T. J. and R. Waterman (1993) *In Search of Excellence*. New York: Warner Books.
14. Bryman, A. (1992) *Charisma and Leadership in Organisations*. London: Sage.
15. Colwill, N. (1995) 'Sex differences' in S. Vinnicombe and N. L. Colwill (eds) *The Essence of Women in Management*, Hemel Hempstead: Prentice Hall.
16. Fernanda, R. M. (1991) 'Structural bases of leadership in intraorganisation networks', *Social Psychology Quarterly*, vol. 54, no. 1, pp. 36–53.
17. Iedema, Rick A. M. (1998) 'Institutional responsibility and hidden meanings', *Discourse & Society*, vol. 9, no. 4, pp. 481–500.
18. Bottger, P. A. (1984) 'Expertise and air time as bases of actual and perceived influence in problem-solving groups', *Journal of Applied Psychology*, vol. 69, no. 2, pp. 214–221.
19. Cartwright, D. (1951) 'Achieving change in people: some applications of group dynamics theory', *Human Relations*, vol. 4, pp. 381–393.
20. Argyle, M. (1978) *The Social Psychology of Work*, 2nd edn. Harmondsworth, Middlesex: Penguin Books.
21. Platow, M. J., S. Hoar, S. Reid, K. Harley and D. Morrison (1997) 'Endorsement of distributively fair and unfair leaders in interpersonal and inter-group situations', *European Journal of Social Psychology*, vol. 27, pp. 465–494.
22. Brenton, A. L. (1993) 'Demystifying the magic of language: A critical linguistic case analysis of legitimation of authority', *Journal of Applied Communication*, vol. 21, no. 3, pp. 227–244.
23. Turner, L. H. and S. A. Henzl (1987) 'Influence attempts in organizational conflict: The effects of biological sex, psychological gender and power position', *Management Communication Quarterly*, vol. 1, no. 1, pp. 32–57.
24. Eagly, A. H., S. J. Karau and M. G. Makhijani (1995) 'Gender and the evaluation of leaders: A meta-analysis', *Psychological Bulletin*, vol. 117, no. 1, pp. 3–22.
25. Jackson, C. and W. Hirsh (1991) 'Women managers and career progress: the British experience', *Women in Management – Review and Abstracts*, vol. 6, no. 2, pp. 10–16.
26. Knott, K. B. and E. J. Natalle (1997) 'Sex differences, organizational level, and superiors' evaluation of managerial leadership', *Management Communication Quarterly*, vol. 10, no. 4, pp. 523–540.
27. Petty, M. M. and N. S. Bruning (1980) 'A comparison of the relationships between supervisory behaviour and measures of subordinates' job satisfaction for male and female leaders', *Academy of Management Journal*, vol. 23, no. 4, pp. 717–725.
28. Davidson, M. and C. Cooper (1992) *Shattering the Glass Ceiling: The Woman Manager*. London: Paul Chapman.
29. Sypher, B. D. (1991) 'A message-centered approach to leadership', *Communication Yearbook*, vol. 14, pp. 547–559.

30. Grunig, L. (1993) 'Image and symbolic leadership: Using focus group research to bridge the gaps', *Journal of Public Relations Research*, vol. 5, no. 2, pp. 95–125.
31. Hawkins, K. and R. A. Stewart (1991) 'Effects of communication apprehension on perceptions of leadership and intragroup attraction in small task-oriented groups', *Southern Communication Journal*, vol. 57, no. 1, pp. 1–10.
32. Barge, J. K., C. W. Downs and K. M. Johnson (1989) 'An analysis of effective and ineffective leader conversation', *Management Communication Quarterly*, vol. 2, no. 3, pp. 357–386.
33. Cruz, M. G., D. D. Henningsen and B. A. Smith (1999) 'The impact of directive leadership on group information sampling, decisions, and perceptions of the leader', *Communication Research*, vol. 26, no. 3, pp. 349–369.
34. Holladay, S. J. and W. T. Coombs (1993) 'Communicating visions; an exploration of the role of delivery in the creation of leader charisma', *Management Communication Quarterly*, vol. 6, pp. 405–427.
35. Gardner, W. L. and D. Cleavenger (1998) 'The impression management strategies associated with transformational leadership at the world-class level: A psychohistorical assessment', *Management Communication Quarterly*, vol. 12, no. 1, pp. 3–41.
36. Fairhurst, G. T. and R. A. Sarr (1996) *The Art of Framing: Managing the Language of Leadership*. San Francisco: Jossey-Bass.
37. Ibid.
38. Riccillo, S. C. and S. Trenholm (1983) 'Predicting managers' choice of influence mode: The effects of interpersonal trust and worker attributions on managerial tactics in a simulated organizational setting', *The Western Journal of Speech Communication*, vol. 47, pp. 323–339.
39. Torrance, E. P. (1956) 'Group decision-making and disagreement', *Social Forces*, vol. 35, pp. 121–142.
40. Klein, J. (1961) *Working with Groups*. London: Hutchinson.
41. Buzzanell, P., L. Ellingson, C. Silvio, V. Pasch, B. Dale, G. Mauro, E. Smith, N. Weir and C. Martin (1997) 'Leadership processes in alternative organizations: Invitational and dramaturgical leadership', *Communication Studies*, vol. 48, no. 4, pp. 285–310.
42. Stohl, C. (1993) 'European managers' interpretations of participation: A semantic network analysis', *Human Communication Research*, vol. 20, no. 1, pp. 97–117.
43. Kolb, J. (1996) 'A comparison of leadership behaviors and competencies in high- and average-performance teams', *Communication Reports*, vol. 9, no. 2, pp. 173–184.
44. Weider-Hatfield, D. and J. D. Hatfield (1996) 'Superiors' conflict management strategies and subordinate outcomes', *Management Communication Quarterly*, vol. 10, pp. 189–208.
45. Gayle, B. M. (1991) 'Sex equity in workplace conflict management', *Journal of Applied Communication*, vol. 19, no. 3, pp. 152–169.
46. Stohl, op. cit.
47. Javidan, op. cit.
48. Gordon, C. (1996) *The Business Culture in France*. Oxford: Butterworth.
49. Stohl, op. cit.
50. Segalla, M., L. Fischer and K. Sandner (2000) 'Making cross-cultural research relevant to European corporate integration: Old problem, new approach', *European Management Journal*, vol. 8, no. 1, pp. 38–51.
51. Torrington, D. (1994) *International Human Resource Management*. Hemel Hempstead: Prentice Hall.
52. Evans, W. A., K. C. Hau and D. Scully (1989) 'A cross-cultural comparison of managerial styles', *Journal of Management Development*, vol. 8, no. 3, pp. 5–13.

53. Wanous, J. P. (1977) 'Organizational entry: Newcomers moving from outside to inside', *Psychological Bulletin*, vol. 84, pp. 601–618.
54. Eagly, A. H. and B. T. Johnson (1990) 'Gender and leadership style: A meta-analysis', *Psychological Bulletin*, vol. 108, no. 2, pp. 233–256.
55. Turner and Henzl, op. cit.
56. Ferrario, M. (1990) Leadership styles of British men and women managers (unpublished MSc dissertation, UMIST), quoted in M. J. Davidson and C. L. Cooper (1992) *Shattering the Glass Ceiling: The Woman Manager*. London: Paul Chapman.
57. Aldoory, L. (1998) 'The language of leadership for female public relations professionals', *Journal of Public Relations Research*, vol. 10, no. 2, pp. 73–101.
58. Rosener, J. (1990) 'Ways women lead', *Harvard Business Review*, Nov.–Dec., pp. 119–125.
59. Roosevelt, T. R. Jr (1991) *Beyond Peace and Gender: Unleashing the Power of Your Total Work Force By Managing Diversity*. New York: AMACOM.
60. Ford, V. (1996) 'Partnership is the secret of progress', *People Management*, Feb., pp. 34–36.
61. Roberts, T.-A. (1991) 'Gender and the influence of evaluations on self-assessments in achievement settings', *Psychological Bulletin*, vol. 109, no. 2, pp. 297–308.
62. Hofstede, G. (1980) 'The business of international business is culture', *International Business Review*, vol. 3, no. 1, pp. 1–14.
63. Dibella, A. J. (1993) 'The role of assumptions in implementing management practices across cultural boundaries', *Journal of Applied Behavioural Science*, vol. 29, no. 3.
64. Trompenaars, op. cit.
65. Hofstede, G. (1994) *Cultures and organizations: Software of the mind*, London: Harper Collins.
66. Argyle, op. cit.
67. Maude, B. (1975) *Managing Meetings*. New York: National Industrial Conference Board.
68. Lowy, A. and P. Finebone (1986) 'Delegation: a process as well as a strategy' in J. W. Pfeiffer and L. G. Goodstein (eds) *Developing Human Resources, 1986 Annual*. Princeton, N. J.: University Associates.

# Appendix

## CHAPTER 1

### Exercise 3: Table 1.2 Difficult situations questionnaire

When you have completed your questionnaire you can analyse it to show which of five common types of situation are more or less stressful for you personally, according, that is, to the 'self-report' you have made in the questionnaire. The five types of situation are:

1. Situations requiring assertiveness, measured by Questions 1, 3, 5, 11, 15, 16, 19, 23.
2. Situations involving being conspicuous or being assessed for a 'live' performance, measured by 10, 12, 17, 18, 19.
3. Dealing with people face to face: 'superiors', measured by 2, 4, 5, 13, 22, 23, 24.
4. Dealing with people face to face: subordinates, measured by 4, 8, 14, 20, 21.
5. Dealing with people: equals and mixed groups, measured by 4, 6, 7, 9, 15, 22.

Note that some questions are scored more than once. By calculating your mean scores for the five types of situation and comparing them, you can identify which type seems to cause you most difficulty.

In this book, ways to act assertively are suggested and discussed in Chapter 6, on impression management; this same material and the rest of Chapter 6 are also helpful in improving your ability to handle situations which involve being conspicuous or being assessed. Most advice for dealing with bosses or 'superiors' will be found in Chapter 8, on influencing by persuasion and in Chapter 9, especially the section on handling other people's power assertions. For dealing with subordinates, Chapter 12, on leadership, is especially relevant. For dealing with the generality of people at work Chapter 7, on communicating, and Chapter 8, on influencing, are most immediately helpful. It is important to stress, however, that interpersonal skills are interactive, so that, for example, gaining in ability to assess other people's motives and attitudes, covered in Chapter 3, will improve your ability to influence others and to communicate and so help you deal more effectively with the generality of people at work. For this reason it is better not to attempt 'short-cut' approaches to improving by reading specific chapters in isolation, but to treat the book as a course and work through it from start to finish.

## CHAPTER 4

### Exercise 3: Table 4.3 Self-awareness questionnaire

This questionnaire helps you to assess whether you have an independent or interdependent self-concept.

*Scoring*: Strongly agree 5, Agree 4, Neither agree nor disagree 3, Disagree 2, Strongly disagree 1.

Items 1, 4 and 9 are reverse scored.

Add your scores and divide by 10.

Scores of 3.6 or above suggest an independent self-construal; 2.5 or below an interdependent self-construal; 2.6 to 3.5 mixed.

## Exercise 7: Goals Scale

Although this measure is labelled the Goals Scale, it is designed to assess how optimistic or hopeful the individual is. Hope is defined as a cognitive set comprising agency (belief in one's capacity to initiate and sustain actions) and pathways (belief in one's capacity to generate routes) to reach goals.

For an overall measure, add your scores for all six items and divide by 6.

For a measure of 'agency' (how effective you rate yourself generally), add your scores on items b, d and f and divide by 3.

For a measure of 'pathways' (how clearly you see the routes to meeting your goals), add your scores on items a, c and e and divide by 3.

Scores of 6 and over may reveal an optimistic or hopeful bias; scores of 3 and below a pessimistic bias; scores of 4 or 5 a realistic attitude.

Based on Snyder, C. R., S. C. Sympson, F. C. Ybasco, T. F. Borders, M. A. Babyak and R. L. Higgins (1996) 'Development and validation of the State Hope Scale', *Journal of Personality and Social Psychology*, vol. 70, pp. 321–335.

# CHAPTER 5

## Exercise 6: Table 5.8 Attribution errors questionnaire

**Scoring**: Strongly agree 5, Agree 4, Neither agree nor disagree 3, Disagree 2, Strongly disagree 1. Calculate your scores on the scales as grouped below.

Scales 1 to 3 score the fundamental attribution error; scores above 9 over-attribute others' behaviour to dispositions.

Scale 4 (reverse scored); scores above 3 point to the actor–observer error.

Scales 5 to 7; scores above 11 indicate the false consensus effect.

Scales 8 and 9; high scores suggest the false uniqueness effect.

Scales 10 and 11; scores above 6 point to the actor–observer error.

An overall mean score above 3.5 points to a high tendency to make attribution errors.

# CHAPTER 6

## Exercise 5: Table 6.8 How assertive was your behaviour?

**Scoring**: Strongly agree 5, Agree 4, Neither agree nor disagree 3, Disagree 2, Strongly disagree 1

10 items. 1, 2, 3, 4, 5 and 10 are all scored positively. Items 6, 7, 8 and 9 and are reverse scored. Calculate mean (divide by 10); if item 3 is omitted, divide by 9.

Scores: 1.0 to 2.9 – low appropriate assertiveness
3.0 to 3.9 – medium appropriate assertiveness
4.0 to 5 – high appropriate assertiveness

## CHAPTER 7

This scale scores how clearly you communicated.

### Exercise 14: Table 7.6 Communicating clearly scale

Scoring: 13 items, all scored positively.
Strongly agree 5, Agree 4, Neither agree nor disagree 3, Disagree 2, Strongly disagree 1
Calculate mean (divide by 13)
Scores: 1.0 to 2.9 – low clarity
3.0 to 3.9 – medium clarity
4.0 to 5 – high clarity

### Exercise 23: Table 7.8 Inter-group interaction scale

This scale scores your awareness of barriers to intercultural understanding.
Scoring: 11 items, all scored positively
Strongly agree 5, Agree 4, Neither agree nor disagree 3, Disagree 2, Strongly disagree 1
Calculate mean (divide by 11)
Scores: 1.0 to 2.9 – low awareness of barriers
3.0 to 3.9 – medium awareness of barriers
4.0 to 5.0 – high awareness of barriers

## CHAPTER 9

### Exercise 9: Table 9.4 How well did you negotiate?

Total your score and work out the mean by dividing the number of items (usually ten, but nine if the answer to Item 9 was 'Not applicable') for comparison against your score on each item. Those items scoring below average may be the ones to pay attention to in future negotiations.

## CHAPTER 10

### Exercise 10: Table 10.6 Interaction rating scale

This scale measures cultural sensitivity.
**Scoring**: 6 items, all scored positively.
Strongly agree 5, Agree 4, Neither agree nor disagree 3, Disagree 2, Strongly disagree 1
Calculate mean (divide by 6)
Scores: 1.0 to 2.5 – low cultural sensitivity
2.6 to 3.5 – medium cultural sensitivity
3.6 to 5.0 – high cultural sensitivity

# CHAPTER 12

## Exercise 11: Table 12.3: Intercultural performance questionnaire

This questionnaire is designed to help you measure your intercultural performance, either by self-assessment or by feedback from a supportive but objective colleague.
Scoring: 20 items, all scored positively.
Strongly agree 5, Agree 4, Neither agree nor disagree 3, Disagree 2, Strongly disagree 1

To find your overall self-reported intercultural performance score, add your scores on all the items and calculate the mean (divide by 20).
Scores of 3.6 to 5.0 – high self-assessed intercultural performance rating
Scores of 2.6 to 3.5 – medium self-assessed intercultural performance rating
Scores of 1.0 to 2.5 – low self-assessed intercultural performance rating
More significant, possibly, are your scores on individual items as these may reveal areas where you believe yourself to have weaknesses.

## Exercise 12: Table 12.4 Questionnaire for prospective sojourners

How to score: Total your answers.
If your score is 40 or above, you should be able to adapt readily in the new environment.
If your score is less than 30, you will experience difficulties. Look again at the questions where you scored low, and think about how you could work to raise the scores, or reconsider the assignment.

# Index